THE
INTERNET
FOR
SCIENTISTS
AND
ENGINEERS

1996 EDITION

THE
INTERNET
FOR
SCIENTISTS
AND
ENGINEERS

1996 EDITION

Online Tools and Resources

Brian J. Thomas

SPIE Optical Engineering Press

A Publication of SPIE—The International Society for Optical Engineering
Bellingham, Washington USA

Library of Congress Cataloging-in-Publication Data

Thomas, Brian J.
    The Internet for scientists and engineers: online tools and resources /
Brian J. Thomas. — 1996 ed.
        p. cm.
    Includes bibliographical references and index.
    ISBN 0-8194-2148-0 (softcover)
    1. Internet (Computer network)   I. Title.
TK5150.875.I57T48   1996
004.6'7—dc20   96-3204
                                                                               CIP

Published by
SPIE—The International Society for Optical Engineering
P.O. Box 10
Bellingham, Washington 98227-0010
Telephone 360/676-3290
Fax 360/647-1445
E-mail spie@spie.org
WWW http://www.spie.org/

Printed in the United States of America.

10 9 8 7 6 5 4 3 2 1

For my mother

CONTENTS

PART II: SCIENCE RESOURCES ON THE INTERNET

PREFACE TO THE SECOND EDITION

History will remember 1995 as the Year of the Net. Unlike preceding information technologies—print, radio, telephone, television, telefax—the Internet didn't seep into our daily lives gradually. Rather, it exploded onto the scene with all the subtlety of a fission reaction.

Now, this doesn't mean that the net has actually become part of everyone's daily life. The truth is, a relatively small number of people actually use e-mail on a regular basis, and far fewer still have access to a web browser. Nevertheless, it would be difficult to find someone who hasn't at least heard of the Internet or World Wide Web today. More than anything else, the net has become a well-advertised promise.

In the world of science and engineering, things are a little different. Because virtually all research and academic institutions have been on the Internet for years, most individuals working in these communities have easy access to e-mail, the web, and other Internet elements. That being said, there are still many institutions and individuals who do not have access to the Internet, as least as a daily work-tool. However, if e-mail's ubiquity is any kind of indicator, the scientific and engineering communities as a whole will quickly jump into the Internet jetstream very soon, whether they plan to or not. The pressure to be "on the web" will be compelling and even overpowering.

The big news is, of course, the World Wide Web. In less than a year, the web has completely overshadowed every other aspect of the Internet. In fact, for most of the world, the web is or will be the Internet. Web browser tools are now providing the front end to access virtually all the things you can do on the Internet, including e-mail, FTP, Usenet news, gopher, and WAIS. In fact, practically every feature and tool discussed in this book can now be accessed using one of the more sophisticated web browsers. As a result, for the millions of people just now getting online, many of the "traditional" Internet elements disappear behind the user-friendly interface of the web browser. Of course, these browsers are generally not yet as sophisticated or full-featured as some of the more traditional software interfaces used to access Internet services, but they are improving quickly. In short, this aspect of the web phenomena is a good thing: it marks the beginning of the Internet as a tool that is just as accessible as a word processor or spreadsheet.

So what does this all mean for scientists and engineers? First and foremost, it means instant access to incredible quantities of information hitherto unavailable. It is beyond description, really, to convey how much data—both raw and processed—is online today, and by the end of 1996, it will no doubt grow exponentially once again. And the next wave is going to vastly improve the usability of that data as well. The big movement right now is toward providing fully searchable databases accessible from the web, something that has been either missing or rudimentary until now. However, soon you will be able to search for and purchase products, publications, services, software—anything imaginable—and in many cases, you'll be able to receive what you purchase via the Internet as well. For the professional scientist or engineer, this will mean access to published materials as quickly as they are released, and interactive collaboration with colleagues anywhere in the world as easily as if they were just down the hall.

These sweeping changes in the online world have made a second edition of this book not only a possibility, but a necessity. While many of the concepts here will remain valid in 1996 and beyond, the focus of the Internet has clearly moved to the World Wide Web, and therefore this second edition concentrates on the new tools, capabilities, and resources that have surfaced in the past twelve months in that realm.

Of particular import are the tools for searching the Internet, which have developed and matured into highly valuable starting points for net exploration. Free online search services such as Yahoo, Lycos, and WebCrawler have made the Internet's intricate web more navigable for even the most demanding explorer. However, it's also true to say that these search tools are useful only as starting points. Most are semi-automated scanners of what's on the net, and as such they also serve up a lot of interference with their signals. This book's Resources section attempts to take off where automated search tools end, giving the practicing scientist or engineer a comprehensive and prescreened slice of the best the web has to offer in the disciplines covered. The number of *web* resources listed here has doubled over what appeared in the first edition of this book. And as the web continues to expand, so will the need for accurate, reliable resources that filter the noise and chart a clear path to useful information.

Brian Thomas
January 1996

PREFACE

This book was written to serve three basic purposes: first, to introduce readers to the process of getting online; second, to provide a basic tutorial to primary Internet software "tools"; and last, to point to a variety of resources compiled specifically for the professional scientist or engineer.

The original idea for this book was that it would be a sort of Occam's razor approach in that it would forgo all the extraneous aspects of the Internet that most books provide, and would instead give only enough information to get the job done. No filler.

Well, even without the filler, the final product is embarrassingly larger than was originally intended, a tribute mostly to the Internet going supernova this past year. In the end, it was everything I could do to stop writing and go to press. The target is virtually untrackable.

Why the Internet?

The underlying assumption made in offering a book such as this is that the Internet is an important tool for many professionals working in the sciences. Why is it important? I think there are a number of arguments:

- Electronic mail, not long ago considered only an internal mechanism, is quickly becoming the telephone of the future. The ability to communicate with someone in an unobtrusive but effective and comprehensive way has tremendous advantages for both the sender and receiver. It is also an excellent way to communicate with a number of people simultaneously, and to route or forward information to others.

- The ability to exchange visual information in readable and reusable formats—such as charts, figures, tables, images, databases, software code—

opens up possibilities for collaboration at the global as well as local levels. With the sciences' reputation for specialization, the ability not only to communicate but also to actually work with colleagues in the same field scattered all over the world makes long-distance collaboration feasible.

- The resources for online research are multiplying at an astounding rate. Searchable databases, library holdings, alerting services, preprints, and other information systems are all changing the way research is done. And it isn't only the research community that is pushing this. Library shelves are overflowing with journals and proceedings, and with acquisitions budgets receiving deep cuts, a likely scenario for the future is one in which libraries archive electronically, share holdings, and become information clearinghouses instead of closets.

- Finally, the speed at which advancements in research and applications will only increase as use of electronic communications grows. Those who do not have access to this information freight-train may one day find themselves left at the station.

Is this Book for You?

The fact that you're reading a book with a title like this lets me assume a number of things. The first is that you're at least interested in the sciences, and chances are you're either in a science-related educational program, or are a professional in some science-related field.

The second assumption throughout this book is that you will want full access to the Internet. What is "full access"? It means having an online account that gives you access to at least the four basic Internet activities: electronic mail, telnet, FTP, and the Usenet. Having full access will allow you to get the most out of the Internet as an R&D tool.

Now I'm going to contradict what I just said. In writing this book, I also recognize that many people—even after reading about all the vast stores of information you can find on the Internet—are still not sure "learning" the Internet is worth their time, and therefore this book also recognizes the needs of those of you who plan to perhaps start out with an e-mail account and see how it goes. This is certainly a reasonable approach, since the Internet is like any other resource: invaluable for some, and a waste of time for others.

The final assumption I want to make is that you're not reading this for fun (although you'll certainly end up having some), and that you want to make the most out of your time on the Internet.

How to Read this Book

Learning the Internet means learning new terminology, and computers are second only to aviation in the abundance of arcane jargon. Therefore, a glossary is included here, as well as a bibliography for further reading recommendations.

Formatting and Typesetting Conventions

Because not everyone will read this book in a linear fashion, words that appear in the glossary appear in italic type throughout the book. My intent is that this will go a long way to alleviate the guilty feeling I get every time I use one of the Internet's abundant acronyms or a term that sounds like technical doublespeak.

Boldface text is used to show a command that you would enter (type) on your computer.

Courier typeface, indented as show below, is used in two ways to help you follow the online examples used throughout this book:

```
Bold typeface indicates a command you would enter or
type, almost always followed by the Return or Enter key.

Regular Courier represents what you should see on your
computer screen during a particular example.
```

Note that some examples use full "windows" to represent what you see on the computer, and others show only the text you would see. Both serve the same purpose; it's just that sometimes getting a "real" picture of what your computer might look like was easier to get from window "screen shot" instead of a text representation.

Internet Addressing Conventions

A standard syntax is evolving for Internet resource addresses. The format is called a Uniform Resource Locator, or URL. Gopher, telnet, FTP, and World Wide Web sites are usually referred to in written communication using this format:

type of service://address/path

type of service://login information

Some examples:

```
ftp://rtfm.mit.edu/pub/usenet/compression-faq

telnet://spie.org
```

```
gopher://rtfm.mit.edu/pub/usenet/compression-faq

http://www.apple.com
```

Internet addresses are discussed in detail in the chapter on electronic mail.

References and Resources

At the end of each chapter is a section called "Just the FAQs." This is where I list places to get more information on the topics covered in that chapter. In most cases, the first and best way to get information is to retrieve documents on the Internet called FAQs, short for Frequently Asked Questions. These are documents created by Internet users all over the world who are often experts in the particular topic area. These FAQs are usually associated with an Internet newsgroup (a topical interest group using the Internet's Usenet bulletin board feature). More on newsgroups later.

Since some readers of this book may only have access to e-mail at this time, I've provided instructions on how to retrieve each FAQ document listed through the use of a mail server. This means all you need to do is send a message to the address provided to receive the complete FAQ document via e-mail. Of course, all of these FAQs are available via FTP from the archive site provided as well.

Acknowledgments

No book is an island, and without all the people who helped me, I would have been left stranded and adrift. My sincere gratitude and respect rings out for all those who rescued me at various (and often crucial) junctures.

My first thanks are to Rick Hermann, who held the book's rudder throughout the journey, and whose editorial skills are exceeded only by his patience; Dixie Cheek, for editing the entire Resources section; and to Eric Pepper, who talked me into this, and who has my eternal respect for his dedication to serving the scientific community through publishing.

Next are the people whose technical skills and expertise were invaluable. My thanks to: Dave Denton, for the cover design and the hours he spent salvaging the mess I'd made of the figures; Kenn Herman and Alex Peachey, for their help with the Windows sections; Khan Klatt, for the perspectives on Unix; Pete Slisz, for design ideas and specs that made the Resources readable; Kevin Tripp, who helped manipulate the resources sections; and Kate Weisel, for the conversion work in Adobe PageMaker.

This book was reviewed by a group of individuals chosen for their knowledge of and respect within the professional scientific, engineering, and Internet communities. Their comments, corrections, and insights vastly improved its content. My respect and thanks to: Henri H. Arsenault, Université Laval; James A.

Harrington, Rutgers University; Kevin N. Montgomery, NASA Ames Research Center (Sterling Software); James R. Sheats, Hewlett-Packard Co.; and Scott Yanoff, University of Wisconsin–Milwaukee.

For all my friends and colleagues who endured me this past year, my indebtedness to all of you, especially: Janice Gaines, for the island farm retreats; Marybeth Manning, for mental health counseling; and Andria Pierson, for friendship.

Finally, to my online mentor, friend, and fellow aviator, Robert Dorsett, who wrote, collected, researched, critiqued, and edited significant portions of this book, and from whom I've learned more about the net and computers than I could ever quantify, I rock my wings in salute.

Part I

INTERNET ACCESS, TOOLS, AND NAVIGATION

Chapter 1

INTRODUCTION

What Is the Internet?

Physically, the Internet is a lot of computers connected to each other, using only telephone lines, each talking a common language, or protocol, known as *TCP/IP* (Transmission Control Protocol/Internet Protocol).

In essence, this setup is really no different from any other computer network, whether it be the Unix network at the local university, or two personal computers connected to each other. As long as two computers speak a common protocol, they can exchange information. And that is what the Internet is all about—information exchange.

Metaphysically, the Internet is an international community connected by computers of every size, shape, and form. It is a cooperative effort on the grandest scale, and it would grind to an ignominious halt without the voluntary support of thousands of people all over the world.

The primary mission of the Internet is communication—of ideas, work, play—you name it. Everything else is a means toward that end.

What Can I Do on It?

The first thing to remember is that being "connected to the Internet" can mean a whole range of possibilities—anything from sending a simple e-mail message to a colleague across the state, to logging into another computer halfway around the world to search and retrieve sounds, graphics, and even movies.

There are basically four things you can do on the Internet:

1. Communication
2. Document or file transfer
3. Interactive browsing
4. Reading and posting to topic-specific bulletin boards.

Corresponding directly to these activities are four basic tools:

1. E-mail—electronic message exchange
2. FTP (File Transfer Protocol)—moving electronic documents, images, sounds, etc.
3. Telnet—accessing another computer system's database or archives
4. Usenet—global bulletin board messaging system.

In addition, in recent years some new tools have emerged that expand upon these four basic activities. These don't really fall into any one category, but rather they integrate many Internet processes in ways that can simplify and enhance the activity:

1. World Wide Web (WWW)—a hypertext interface to information on the Internet
2. Gopher—an information browser that lets you retrieve what you find
3. Veronica—an enhancement to gopher that searches many gopher databases
4. WAIS—a powerful tool for searching some large databases
5. Archie—a simple but effective mechanism for searching FTP archives.

This book concentrates on all of these services and ignores many others, such as IRC (Internet Relay Chat) and MUDs (Multi-User Domains), that are not (yet, at least) considered part of the researcher's toolbox. I've also ignored things like UUCP (Unix-to-Unix Copy) and Hytelnet (Hyper-Telnet) because they only add noise to what's already becoming a bewildering array of options. I've stuck to what I consider the mainstream.

What's in the Internet Toolbox?

Before we move ahead, some short definitions of many of the services you'll read about here should help cut through all of the jargon that you'll encounter when learning about the Internet.

The Basic Services

E-mail

Electronic mail, or e-mail, is the cornerstone of all that happens on the Internet. It is a simple service that allows two people to send messages to each other in a near-real-time manner. All you need to send an e-mail message is a computer with some kind of connection to the Internet, and software on your computer that is designed for this purpose. There is a wide array of *e-mail software* packages available today, and many of the best of them are shareware or freeware.

E-mail has many similarities with the paper mail system we're all familiar with. Everyone on the Internet has an *e-mail address*, just like your own post office address. All you need is someone's address and you can send them all sorts of things—documents, pictures, audio or videotapes. You can also send these kinds of things using e-mail, as long as what you're sending is *digitized*, that is, converted to a computer-readable format.

Of course, with e-mail you're not limited to sending a message to just one person. You can send the same message to lots of people. You can also attach a document or image to your message, or you can retrieve documents from other computers on the Internet by sending a command (such as "send filename.txt") to a particular address. E-mail can also be used to retrieve documents from *FTP servers* and for taking part in special interest group discussions such as listservs and Usenet newsgroups.

FTP
File Transfer Protocol, or "FTP," refers to an Internet tool that allows you to move a file from one place to another. The word "file" is used to include any type of digital entity — documents, images, artwork, movies, sounds, and software. Anything you can store on a computer can be moved with FTP. Many computers on the Internet have *anonymous FTP archives* containing public-access files that you can download to your computer.

The word "FTP" is used both as a noun and a verb; hence, you can "use FTP to get the file" or you can "FTP the file."

Telnet
Telnet, a term used to mean *remote login*, is the ability to access and control another computer somewhere on the Internet. You can *log in* to the other computer and can then use the software on that computer. Often this service is used to search an information archive such as a public database or library resource. You can also use telnet to log into your own Internet computer from another computer somewhere on the Internet. For example, if you were at a conference in another city and had access to a computer on the Internet, you could telnet to your own *Internet account* and read your e-mail.

Usenet News
Usenet is a global *bulletin board* service that uses the Internet as an access point. It is composed of thousands of topical groupings that you can read to keep current on the discussions (i.e., the "news") in those groups. A message posted to a *newsgroup* can be read, forwarded (via e-mail), or *followed up* by posting a public response. A series of messages on the same topic is called a *thread*. Over the years, many newsgroups have become extremely well-organized and moderated and include living documents as part of their purpose. These documents, called *FAQs* (Frequently Asked Questions), try to answer many of the questions

that someone new to the group would have, so as to keep the discussions in the group from covering the same ground over and over. Usenet is an excellent tool for science professionals. Because the Usenet's origins are in that community, these groups are often frequented by world experts in many fields, and therefore are a great place to ask questions or catch up on the timely topics in disciplines ranging from archaeology to zoology and everything in between.

The Extended Services

Archie
Archie is a simple function that searches FTP archives on the Internet. It is accessible through both telnet and e-mail, as well as through freely available client software that you can obtain and install on the computer you use to access the Internet. Archie is a great tool for finding files when you know part or all of the file's name.

Gopher
Gopher is a software tool that connects a variety of computers and information archives on the Internet and displays them as a series of menu items. It was originally developed at the University of Minnesota as a campus-wide information system, but it quickly caught on as a way for anyone on the Internet to publish information and organize network resources. There are over 5,000 active gopher servers now, with more being added daily.

Veronica
Veronica is the companion tool to gopher. Veronica lets the user perform keyword searches of *gopherspace*. The results of the search are presented as a menu with items leading to more specific information. You access veronica through a gopher server, just like gopher itself.

Online Databases
There are a growing number of computers on the Internet that provide free or for-fee access to information archives. These are most often accessed using the telnet function (see above). Depending on their purpose and format, online databases can be broadly grouped into a variety of categories: Wide-Area Information Servers (WAIS), Campus-Wide Information Services (CWIS), Online Public Access Catalogs (OPAC), and commercial online services.

World Wide Web (WWW)
The World Wide Web is the newest and fastest growing Internet function. It is an ingenious front end to much of the information already on the Internet using the concept of hypertext to link information. Hypertext refers to a system of "point-and-click" connections between information that allow the user to jump from one information source to another on the Internet without even thinking about it. All of the technical aspects of moving from computer to computer are hidden, leaving the researcher free to explore without interference.

Chapter 2

GETTING ONLINE

This chapter explains the fundamental options you have for getting online, what each option offers in terms of what you can expect and do, and how the options relate to the concept of the *Internet* as a worldwide communications network.

The Business of Internet

Who Provides Internet Access?

While there are a growing number of organizations who provide Internet access, they can be divided into three basic categories.

Internet Service Provider (ISP): Regional or national organizations that sell various degrees of access to the Internet, primarily for individual users. You can either log into and use their computer system and software to access the Internet, or gain access using your own software. If you want faster or nonmodem access, you can also purchase a *dedicated* phone line connection with special hardware. Internet service providers are sometimes called *public-access Internet hosts.*

Commercial Online Services: Large, self-contained online environments where users have access to services provided and maintained by the vendor, as well as (more recently) access to the Internet. These services usually require that you install and use software that they have developed to connect with and navigate their computer system. The major commercial online services we'll mention here are CompuServe, America Online, GEnie, and Delphi. There are more, but such a discussion could quickly get out of control. Note also that a few of the large Internet service providers such as PSINet and Netcom also offer software interfaces for their systems that let you cruise the web.

A note of caution here about commercial online services. Yes, they offer access to the Internet as part of their services. However, this access is not quite the same as the kind of access you have with an ISP. Again—remember that you are on their computer system when you log in, as opposed to the "direct" type of connection we talk about later in this chapter. This means that the commercial online service will require that you use their proprietary software as an interface to the Internet as well. The limitations imposed by this type of connection vary from service to service, but in general they are not as full-featured as a direct connection, and are often slower.

Bulletin Boards (BBS): Usually locally sponsored computer systems that offer e-mail, file exchange, and areas for electronic discussions, as well as varying degrees of access to the Internet. These are usually pay or partially free services.

Are You Already Online?

If you can already exchange e-mail messages with someone who is not at your location, or *site,* chances are you are already on the Internet. If you have an e-mail address with an "@" symbol in it, you are probably on the Internet at least for e-mail.

If you have an *account* on a commercial online service such as CompuServe or America Online, then you are on the Internet to the degree of service provided by them. All of the major providers offer Internet access today, albeit through their own proprietary software interfaces.

Even if you don't currently have e-mail, your workplace or local university may have a connection that you can access. There's only one way to find out— ask someone who knows, such as your network administrator or a colleague who's already "on the net."

If you find you have or could get net access, the next thing to do is see just how extensive your access is. Again, finding someone who knows is really the best way to go.

Hardware and Software

This topic is by far the most difficult one to address adequately. The number and variety of computer systems in use today far exceeds the scope of this book. In fact, it far exceeds the scope of *any* book.

Basic Hardware

Regardless, you know you need a computer, and unless your location already has a dedicated Internet connection and some kind of network that gives your computer access to it, you'll also need a modem.

The assumption of this book is that you have these two hardware elements, as well as telecommunications software, and that you have already tested everything to make sure it works properly. If you haven't gotten that far, I suggest you read the rest of this chapter in order to see what your online options are.

Basic Software

In addition to telecommunications software, which gives you a basic conduit between your computer and your Internet access computer, you will also use software to do things on the Internet, such as sending messages (e-mail), browsing libraries (telnet), and retrieving documents (FTP). It's important to remember that these basic Internet functions all operate on the same principles, regardless of which software interface you happen to be using.

The Internet and Unix

While the past year has seen a marked increase in Internet access solutions that don't directly involve Unix, it's still probable that your first experience with the Internet will be through a computer operating system called Unix. This is because much of the work done in developing the Internet was done on Unix-based computers. Unix also has a variety of *flavors*, but for most Internet functions it is relatively generic.

Because the Internet's founding work was done on Unix computers, the vast majority of computers on the Internet today are Unix-based. And as a corollary, nearly all the Internet service providers today use Unix computers as Internet servers.

So, regardless of what kind of computer and software *you* have, the majority of computers you'll encounter and explore on the Internet use some flavor of Unix, and therefore this book presents examples that use basic Unix operating system commands, along with some popular Unix utilities for accessing the Internet.

The Internet and Personal Computers

That being said, this book does recognize (and support!) the increasing popularity and availability of direct Internet access by personal computers, either through a direct connection through a business or school's computer system, or through a dial-up SLIP or PPP connection. Therefore, at the end of each chapter I have included sections on my favorite Windows and Macintosh tools for navigating the Internet and how to get started with them. These sections are not meant to be comprehensive, but should serve adequately as a starting point, as well as provide pointers to further resources.

Further, as background for these sections on Windows and Macintosh software, I have also included an appendix on setting up TCP/IP networking software on these computer platforms, including SLIP and PPP software, as well as many pointers to resources for these computers.

Basic Connection Options

There are a four basic ways to connect to the Internet:

- **Direct**
- **Remote Dial-up**
- **SLIP/PPP**
- **Commercial Online Service**

Each of these options varies in terms of what you can and cannot do, how much they cost, and what equipment and software you need. More confusing, perhaps, within each of these categories you can find providers who offer bits, pieces, or the whole pie. So at this point in our research what's important is understanding the *connectivity* differences.

Direct Connection

Most large organizations with an internal computer network (colleges, universities, research institutions, etc.) are directly connected to the Internet via a *dedicated* phone line. This direct line means they are a final destination, or *domain*, on the Internet, such as **nasa.gov** or **aip.org,** and that they can then supply people within their organization with a connection to the Internet through a personal computer or workstation. This kind of connection is sometimes called a *gateway.*

Depending on the setup, individual computer workstations with this kind of direct connection may have an Internet address(the electronic equivalent of a street address) and maintain its own software tools for communicating with the Internet. If you have this kind of connection available at your organization, your e-mail may be stored on the larger computer (which is always running, unlike yours that you probably turn off at the end of the day), but your access to other Internet computers is direct. This means that if you transfer a file from another computer on the Internet, that file will be downloaded directly to your workstation's hard drive, where you can immediately access it.

The other possible setup here is that your connection to the Internet is through a dummy or remote terminal that gives you access to a central computer elsewhere in your organization. In this situation, the central computer (or another connected computer) has the direct connection, and you may be given some degree of access to Internet services through your interface with the main computer.

Summary

This kind of setup is the ultimate in Internet connections — but because of the significant expenses involved—often over US$10,000 annually—it's usually only an option when provided by your employer or school. The next closest thing to a personal direct connection is the emergence of *ISDN* (Integrated Digital Services Network) lines offered by some telephone companies. While availability of and support for ISDN will continue to be uneven in 1996, the technology has definitely established a foothold in the online community.

Fees

Direct connections are often yearly contracts that can include a leased telephone line, routing equipment, and server software. Pricing is usually based on a number of factors, including *bandwidth,* volume, number of users, and business purpose (for-profit, nonprofit, educational, etc.).

Access

Current lists of organizations that provide Internet access for multi-user facilities can be obtained from the following center, as well as your local telephone directory listings:

```
NSF Network Service Center (NNSC)
BBN Laboratories Inc.
10 Moulton St.
Cambridge MA 02138 USA
Voice: 617/873-3361
E-mail: nnsc@nnsc.nsf.net
```

Remote Dial-up Connection

Remote dial-up connections mean that you use your personal computer and a modem to connect to a larger computer somewhere (usually in your town, maybe even your workplace) and *log in* to that computer in order to use its connection to the Internet. The larger computer is sometimes called a *host* or *server,* and your computer would be called a *client* or *remote.*

Remote dial-up connections are popular because just about anyone can go out and get an account from an Internet service provider for a reasonable monthly fee, and it can provide nearly complete access to all aspects of the Internet. All you need is a computer, a modem, and some basic telecommunications software. The rest of the software is on the host computer.

Of course, this means you're limited to the host computer's operating system as well, so if it's Unix (as most are), then you're going to have to learn a few Unix commands in order to navigate your way around the Internet.

Typically, with this kind of connection you have an e-mail name, or *address,* that you pick or are assigned, such as **janice@netcom.com.** You dial up the host computer using your computer and modem, then log in using your e-mail name and password. Once you're in, you use the host computer's software to read and answer your e-mail, read Usenet news, and telnet to other computers on the Internet.

If you've gone somewhere and downloaded documents or software using FTP, you'll then need to download it to your personal computer using your tele-communications software. With a remote dial-up connection, anything you upload or download has to go first through the host computer. Think of the host computer as a transfer station. This is not the case with a SLIP/PPP connection, and is one of the primary differences between the two kinds of connections. Often you will find that ISPs offer SLIP/PPP as an add-on service to their standard remote-access accounts.

Summary
Remote dial-ups can be an excellent way to get services such as e-mail, FTP, telnet, Usenet news, gopher, and even some World Wide Web browsing, although this latter feature may be available as text-only (no graphics). Services often include some disk space on the host computer for storing files that you've downloaded from another location.

Fees
Usually $10–$40 a month, plus some setup fees, depending on the kinds of services offered. Make sure you determine that the access telephone number is a local call. Those fees don't include any long distance charges.

Access
Check your local telephone directory (often under "Computers–Networking"), or use the online resources provided at the end of this chapter.

SLIP/PPP Connection

A *SLIP/PPP* connection is really a cross between a direct connection and a remote dial-up connection. SLIP (Serial Line Internet Protocol) and PPP (Point to Point Protocol) are essentially the same thing, so it's easiest to discuss them as if they were. SLIP and PPP are software that allows you connect via modem to another computer, and once you connect, you really become an actual *domain* on the Internet, at least until you sever your modem connection. You do not use any computing resources *per se* on the host computer, and therefore all of the Internet software tools you use are ones that you put on and run from your hard drive. In other words, your personal computer is running all the software that interfaces with the Internet.

This may all sound like smoke and mirrors, but there are some not-so-subtle differences. The biggest one that a SLIP/PPP connection makes possible is full access to the World Wide Web (WWW) using a graphical user interface such as Netscape. The WWW is a hypertext-based network of computers on the Internet that is growing at an astronomical rate, due mostly to ease of use and a graphical user interface capable of displaying pictures, sounds, and movies. The difference here is that you need a *direct* connection (via SLIP/PPP in this case) to the Internet to access the World Wide Web with full graphics capability. Therefore, a computer with a remote dial-up connection cannot access the WWW except as a text-based connection. (There are, I should note, a few service providers who offer software interfaces to the web from a simple Unix shell account, but they are not the norm.)

Most often, service providers who offer remote dial-up connections also offer SLIP/PPP connections. The difference on your end is software. First, you cannot use the same telecommunications software that you use for a remote dial-up account. Instead, you need either SLIP or PPP software. Service providers ask you to specify which of these two methods you wish to use, and they should be able to provide you with software for either (in most cases this is freeware or shareware). The differences between SLIP and PPP are subtle, but the general opinion is that PPP is newer, better implemented, and replacing SLIP in the long run. If you have the option, go with PPP.

Another piece of the software puzzle for SLIP/PPP connections is *TCP/IP* software, which also must be installed on your computer. The software is available in fully supported commercial packages, as well as shareware and public domain versions. The big advantage of buying commercial software is technical support. If you opt for using public domain software (which is often quite good), you rely on friends and people on the Internet for help if you need it.

The above information holds true for your Internet access tools as well. You can buy a package from a commercial vendor, or collect various tools from sources on the Internet.

See Appendix for a list of software vendors and locations for specific computer types.

Summary

SLIP/PPP connections are becoming more popular as the software gets better and more Internet service providers offer this option. The major advantage SLIP/PPP has over remote dial-up is that you access the Internet directly with your own computer, and therefore the Internet becomes in many ways just an extension of your own computer.

For Windows PC and Macintosh owners there are numerous software tools for doing normal Internet activities such as e-mail, telnet, FTP, and browsing the World Wide Web. Software browsers for the WWW have recently taken a quantum leap forward in terms of sophistication and stability, and the number of WWW sites out there to explore continues to grow daily.

The major disadvantage still with the direct connection is the complexity of setting up the TCP/IP software on your computer. However, this too is quickly being remedied with solutions such as Internet in a Box, The Internet Access, Microsoft's Windows95, and Apple Computers' current operating system.

Fees

Most often, SLIP/PPP is just an add-on option to a remote dial-up account, and therefore expect to pay the $10–$40 a month for the remote access, plus an additional $10–$20. Again, make sure you determine that the access telephone number is a local call. Increasingly, ISPs are offering PPP-only accounts, where there is no access to a shell account available.

Access

Check your local telephone directory (often under "Computers–Networking"), or use the online resources provided at the end of this chapter.

Commercial Online Services

Commercial online services usually refers to a handful of national or international online services that offer a complete online environment, and more recently, access to some or all of the Internet's features.

The major U.S.-based commercial services are generally agreed to be the following. There are a few others that fall loosely into this category, but this is a good start:

CompuServe (CIS)	800/524-3388
America Online (AOL)	800/827-6364
GEnie	800/638-9636
Delphi	800/695-4005

These online services are different in many ways from the previous three Internet access options outlined above. Whether these differences are advantages or disadvantages is up to you and what you want from an online service.

All of these services offer local phone access to most areas of the country. They do this by using phone service providers such as Tymnet, SprintNet, Datapac, or their own proprietary network to connect your local call to the commercial provider's host computer. This also means if you travel with a laptop, you can usually access your online account from different cities with only a local call.

With most of these services, you are sent (via floppy disk) all the software you need to access the service, including the telecommunications software, which is built in. All you need is a computer and a modem. You enter the phone number they give you, click a few buttons, and bingo—you're online. And once you're there, everything is displayed through a graphical user interface designed for your computer type. You navigate by pointing-and-clicking. You see something you want to read, you just click on it. If you want to download it to your own computer, just click again.

Some services utilize the same concepts, but offer instead a *command-line interface* (CLI, also called *text-based* or *character-based*). You must have and configure telecommunications software on your computer to access this type of service.

With all commercial services, you become part of a separate online world that they have created for you. You can upload and download files, send e-mail to other users on the system or anyone on the Internet, or read messages posted in forums created on the online service. In the past year or so, these commercial services have started to add access to many of the Internet's offerings such as the Usenet bulletin board system, FTP file transfer, and even remote login via the telnet function. However, as I noted in Chapter 1, the level and quality of Internet access from commercial providers continues to be limited. Don't expect to be able to use Netscape or Mosaic from one of these services.

Summary

The major advantage of using a commercial online service is that a "canned" online environment becomes a virtual extension of your personal computer system. They supply the interface and telecommunications software to run on your computer.

If all you want is an e-mail address, a commercial service is an option to consider. Commercial accounts are also a good introduction to online services in general, since they are in many ways a more user-friendly microcosm of the Internet.

Finally, for anyone who travels with a computer, commercial services can be a cost-effective way of communicating via e-mail while on the road. Many of these services are also making connections to telephone carriers outside of the U.S., which will greatly expand the utility of these services.

Fees

Each commercial online service seems to have gone out of their way to invent their own unique fee structure. For example, while America Online and GEnie have fixed hourly rates, CompuServe and Delphi have multilayered plans that can include a monthly base rate for different connection speeds or *baud rates*, peak-hour surcharges, and add-on charges for using different online forums or areas.

Access

Use the 800 numbers listed above to obtain the most current access information.

What Next?

We've just covered a lot of ground. The guidelines below should help you put it all together and make some decisions about what to do next.

1. Think carefully about what you want to do online. The rest of this book should give you a good idea of the kinds of activities available, what kind of online service you'll need to access them, and what being "online" generally is about.

2. If you can, find out first what's already available from your employer or school. For many professionals this is an excellent option, especially for those in large organizations, since they're likely to already be an Internet *node*. Many organizations with a direct connection even offer some kind of dial-up access so you can get on the Internet from home via modem.

3. If you're on your own and want basic e-mail and nothing else, get an account with a commercial online service like CompuServe, America Online, GEnie, or Delphi.

4. If you want a "full connection" to the Internet and don't mind a text-only interface with a few Unix commands to learn, start shopping for a local Internet service provider that offers remote dial-up accounts.

5. If you want a "full connection" to the Internet and are willing to pay a little more for a pretty interface and more advanced navigation software, start shopping for a local Internet service provider that offers SLIP or PPP accounts.

    Remember, though—for this type of connection you'll have to install TCP/IP software on your computer, as well as all the software tools you'll use to work on the Internet. This is by no means a deterrent, as some of these software tools can make life on the Net much easier, but it is a factor. Setting up your system will take more time and learning on your part than if you were to go with the remote dial-up account discussed above.

    For a list of where to get Windows and Macintosh software for this kind of connection, see the Appendix.

6. If you don't feel like you're ready to decide—read on!

Where to Find Internet Access Providers

There are, of course, other connectivity options we did not include in this discussion, such as local bulletin boards (BBSs), *UUCP*, *FidoNet*, and mail-only gateways such as *MCI Mail*. Many of these are perfectly fine ways to get online. There are also some new and very innovative software solutions such as The Internet Adapter that allow you to log into a standard Unix shell account and basically emulate a SLIP/PPP type of account.

However, for various reasons I've avoided discussing these here. One reason is because some of these services offer only e-mail and maybe Usenet news. In other cases, the sheer newness of the option defies approaching it with any authority on my part. Finally, space—or lack thereof—was a deciding factor in many instances. I just had to draw the line somewhere, and trying to list all the ways you can get online is at best a line drawn in sand.

The first place to look for an Internet service srovider is your local phone book, probably listed under "Internet" or "Computers–Networking." ISPs have sprung up everywhere, and most towns have at least one available.

In addition, below are a couple of online resources that may be helpful. Both are obtainable via e-mail.

Another great option, if available, is to ask friends or colleagues who might already be online. Also, the Usenet newsgroups in the **comp.infosystems** hierarchy is another good source.

Lists of Providers Available Online

There are two primary resources for finding Internet service providers online.

PDIAL—Public Dialup Internet Access List

The PDIAL is maintained by Peter Kaminski and lists major access points. You can get the PDIAL by sending an e-mail message to

```
info-deli-server@netcom.com
```

with the following text in the message body (not the "subject" line):

```
send pdial
```

NIXPUB

The NIXPUB is a public document that lists a wide variety of Internet access points. You can get the nixpub list by sending an e-mail message to

```
mail-server@bts.com
```

with the following text in the message body:

```
get PUB nixpub.long
```

If you don't have an e-mail account yet, try to find someone who does and have them retrieve and print these lists for you.

Just the FAQs

To get the FAQ listed below, send the command shown to

```
mail-server@rtfm.mit.edu
```

This is an e-mail server that will automatically send you the file you've requested. Send this command in the body of your e-mail message. *Remember that this server is Unix-based: Use upper- and lower-case letters exactly as shown.* You may also retrieve the files noted using FTP.

Introduction to Internet Services

Send this command:

```
send pub/usenet/news.answers/news-newusers-intro
```

Chapter 3

YOUR FIRST LOGON

This chapter discusses the basics of "logging in" to your online account, as well as some navigation and housekeeping processes, using a typical Unix Internet "shell" account. Other terms for logging in include *log on* and *sign on*.

Logging in requires either making a direct connection through a network you're on at work or school, or through a modem connection to a phone number that connects you to the host computer. As every situation will be slightly different, so you'll have to get and use instructions from somebody there who knows.

Username and Password

When you first sign up for an online account, you'll either be asked to choose a unique (to their system) *username,* or they will assign one for you. Your username is the name you'll use to log in to an online computer system. You'll also be assigned a temporary password and (hopefully) instructions on how to change it once you get online.

Your username will also be the front half of your Internet e-mail address, so if you are given the option to pick one yourself, skip down to the section on Your E-mail Address in Chapter 4.

Your First "Session"

The Unix operating system has programs called "shells" that interpret your commands. The most common shells are the "C" shell and the "Bourne" shell.

You usually have your choice of which you want to use; others are often available as well. The shell you use will dictate to some extent what you see on your screen and the commands you use. The term "shell" is simply Unix jargon for what kind of software you are using to command the computer. Again, you'll need to consult whatever support documentation is available for your system.

The first screen you see when you start the login process will look something like this:

```
ULTRIX V4.3 (Rev. 44) (henson - %t)

login:
```

You now type in your username and a password, which is case-sensitive just like everything else in Unix. If this is your very first login, the password you have will be a temporary one assigned by the system administrator. As I mentioned, you'll want to change this right away. Do it sometime during the first session. (If you need help, try typing **man passwd** at the command prompt to bring up the online help manual on changing passwords.)

If all goes well with entering your username and password, the next thing you'll see is something like this:

```
ULTRIX V4.3 (Rev. 44) (henson - %t)

login: briant
Password:
Last login: Sun Aug 21 09:36:58 from rws21.xpr.cs.wwu
ULTRIX V4.3 (Rev. 44) System #23: Tue Jun 14 12:05:33
PDT 1994
UWS V4.3 (Rev. 10)
>>>>>>>>>>>>>>>>>>>>>>>>>>>>>>>>>>>>>>>>>>>>>>>>>>>>>>>>>
The Annex modem system will be out of service on Thurs-
day, August 18th,
from 8 a.m. until 5 p.m.
<<<<<<<<<<<<<<<<<<<<<<<<<<<<<<<<<<<<<<<<<<<<<<<<<<<<<<


Type vt220 unknown
TERM = (vt100)
%
```

Note the "Type vt220 unknown" message above. It showed up during the login process, followed by the next line "TERM = (VT100)". This was the computer telling me that it recognized I was using VT220 terminal emulation, and that I couldn't use that here, and so did I want to switch to the default, VT100? I pressed the Return key to accept the default.

A quick note about terminal emulation. Regardless of what kind of computer you actually have, when you are on a network and connected to another computer, the other computer needs to know what kind of computer you are emulating. That is, it needs to know how your keyboard is mapped so when, for example, you type Control-H on your keyboard, the other computer knows you typed Control-H and therefore can respond the way you wanted. The standard terminal to emulate in the Internet world is VT100, which is an option on almost all modem (terminal emulation) software today. When on the Internet, you should try to "look like" a VT100 (or a higher VT number, like VT240) terminal if at all possible.

Now, back to our logon. The last line on the login screen above (the lone % symbol) is the *command prompt* on this particular system. The command prompt is where you type instructions (commands) for the computer to execute. Unix can dish out a number of different-looking command prompts depending on how the computer is configured and which shell you are using. On your system, you might instead see the $ symbol (for a Bourne shell), or the % symbol (for a C shell), or maybe even a custom prompt like [**henson1**]: or **/directoryname/username/>**

Admittedly, this is all background noise. I include it to make a point that everyone's situation will be slightly different. Just know what your command prompt looks like and go from there.

Exploring the Host Computer

The first thing we should do now that we're logged on is to see where we are, as well as what's here. In this section we will spend quite a bit of time exploring many of the standard Unix commands, as well as discussing the concepts behind the functions they perform.

By the way, if the Delete key only creates more characters on your screen, use the key combination Control-H to delete what you've typed if you need to while in Unix (that is, press the Control key and the "h" key at the same time). Another arcane Unix convention. It's not the only option, of course, but it works.

I'm going to be redundant, because it's really important: to delete what you've typed, press the Control and h keys.

Where Am I?

Let's see what your directory is called. Type the following command at the command prompt and press Return (or Enter):

```
% pwd
```

You have just invoked the **print working directory** command, and the system responds by printing out the name of your directory, like this:

```
/user10/briant
```

This tells me that my home directory—where my files are stored by default — is named **briant** (same as my username—what a surprise), and that it resides in a subdirectory named *user10,* which is accessible from the computer's *root directory.*

Navigating Directories

This is important information. Now, if you ever get lost while roaming around the directories on your Internet host computer, just type

```
% cd
```

and you'll be transported back to your *home directory.* The **cd** command is short for *change directory.* If you don't add anything further to it, it will assume you want to go "home."

Everyone who has an account on your host computer also has a home directory, but you can't access what's in theirs, and they can't access what's in yours. (Unless of course you or they change the *access privileges,* which we'll leave alone for now.)

We know *cd* means *change directory,* so let's really change directories. Type **cd,** then a space, then two periods (with no spaces between them), like this:

```
% cd ..
```

You just told the computer to go "up" one directory, which here would mean we should now be in the *user10* directory, which we can easily verify by typing pwd again:

```
% pwd
/user10
```

Looking Inside Directories

We know where we are, so now let's see what's here. Go ahead and type the ls command, which is short for "list files":

```
% ls

!user10     n8846822      n9142279    n9241127
aiya        n8847459      n9142328    n9241181
briant      n8940799.tar  n9142917    n9245910
cjp         n8941067      n9143165    n9241328
glenng      n8943766      n9143634    n9241943
gregg       n8943872      n9143642    n9242039
iain        n8944130      n9143937    n9242057
johnnyf     n8944139      n9143968    n9242101
larry       n8944385      n9144071    n9242141
lisac       n8944413      n9144087    n9242314
lost+found  n8945300      n9144357    n9242519
```

I can see that I'm not the only person with a home directory in the *user10* directory. But I can at least see how my directory (*briant*) looks to everyone else in *user10*.

Now I have two options for getting back to my home directory. I could type **cd,** as we learned. Or, I could type **cd** plus the directory I want to move *down* to, which in my case is *briant.*

```
% cd briant
```

and I'm back in my home directory. Now obviously typing just plain **cd** would have been easier, but we wanted to see how to navigate directories, both **up** and **down.**

So, what's in my home directory? Use the **ls** command again:

```
% ls

img_sept94.hqx    bin       mail      protections
News      log      pdial.txt         usenet_faq.txt
```

Doesn't tell me much. To find more information about what's in here, I can add an *option* to my **ls** command. An option is something you add to a command to modify how it performs or displays the results. In this case, if I instead type **ls -l**, I'll get a listing with more information:

```
% ls -l
total 134
-rw——    1 briant   7996 Aug 18 15:36 img_sept94.hqx
drwx——    3 briant    512 Jan  2  1994 News
drwxr-x—x 2 briant    512 Feb 10  1993 bin
-rw——    1 briant 11366 Oct 19  1993 log
drwx——    2 briant    512 Aug 17 23:01 mail
-rw——    1 briant 70134 Aug 17 19:08 pdial.txt
-rw——    1 briant  1621 Nov  4  1993 protections
-rw——    1 briant 40731 Aug 17 22:50 usenet_faq.txt
```

Notice this time the contents were displayed in a nice itemized list (the **-l** option stands for *long,* as in "long format"). As for the information on the far left, the letter *d* tells me what's a directory, that is, a subdirectory in my own home directory. The rest of the information (rwxr-x—x) has to do with *privileges,* that is, who can read, write, or execute files, or otherwise search, if a directory.

Next to the privileges information is a number that tells me how many documents or other directories are in each directory.

If I wanted to see what's in the *News* subdirectory, for example, I would type

```
% cd News
```

Then do another **ls -l** to see what's in there. Typing **cd ..** moves me back up to my home directory. And so on.

Now if you wanted to see *all* the files in this directory, we would use the **ls** command again and this time add the **-a** option (for "all"). Like this:

```
% ls -l -a
total 264
drwxr-x-x    6 briant     1024 Aug 21 12:40 .
drwxr-xr-x 242 root       8704 Jul 15 02:16 ..
-rwxr-x-x    1 briant       29 Feb 10  1993 .Xdefaults
-rw——        briant     8563 Jul  8 06:49 .addressbook
-rwxr-x-x    1 briant       30 Feb 10  1993 .cshrc
-rw——      1 briant       20 Dec 30  1993 .gopher
-rw——      1 briant        0 Jul 25  1993 .gopherrc
-rwxr-x-x    1 briant       30 Feb 10  1993 .logout
-rw——      1 briant       30 Feb 10  1993 .mailrc
-rw——      1 briant        4 Jul 27 09:53 .msgsrc
-rw——      1 briant    15994 Feb 10  1993 .neon_expert
-rw——      1 briant    39404 Jun 30 07:03 .newsrc
-rw——      1 briant    39422 Jun 30 07:03 .newsrc.bak
drwx——     2 briant      512 Jun 30 07:03 .nn
-rw——      1 briant     3383 Sep 16  1993 .pine-debug1
-rw——      1 briant      617 Aug 21 12:40 .pinerc
-rw-r—r—     1 briant       28 Nov 21  1993 .plan
-rwxr-x-x    1 briant       31 May 20  1993 .profile
-rw——      1 briant       42 Mar 17  1993 .rhosts
-rw——      1 briant     7996 Aug 18 15:36 img_sept94.hqx
drwx——     3 briant      512 Jan  2  1994 News
drwxr-x-x    2 briant      512 Feb 10  1993 bin
-rw——      1 briant    11366 Oct 19  1993 log
drwx——     2 briant      512 Aug 17 23:01 mail
-rw——      1 briant    70134 Aug 17 19:08 pdial.txt
-rw——      1 briant     1621 Nov  4  1993 protections
-rw——      1 briant    40731 Aug 17 22:50 usenet_faq.txt
```

Quite a mess, but that's what you get when you ask for everything.

Reading Files

Let's take a look inside one of these files. The filenames starting with a period (.) are files that Unix uses, and we can modify some of them (they're sometimes called "dot files" for obvious reasons).

The *.plan* file listed here is a small file many users create that displays when someone uses an Internet command called **finger,** which brings up information about a person, or a list of users on a particular computer on the Internet.

To look at what my *.plan* file says, we can use the **more** command, which reads text files one screen at a time (convenient for large files):

```
% more .plan
```

```
Hey! Quit reading my plan!
```

If the document is longer than what would fit on your screen, you'll see something like − More − (38%) at the bottom of your screen, indicating that you have already displayed 38% of the file's contents. If you press Return, you'll advance one line at a time; if you press the space bar, you'll advance one screen at a time. Pressing the **q** key will stop everything and return you to the command prompt.

To read my *.plan* file I could have also used the **cat** command, which displays the whole file in one big scroll, so if it's long, the rest of it just scrolls up into the screen, where (depending on your computer) you might not be able to scroll it back down to see it.

The *finger* Command

While we're here, we might as well try out the **finger** command too. To see information about a specific user, type **finger username.** If the person is not on your computer system, you would have to type the complete e-mail address, so it would be

```
finger briant@henson.cc.wwu.edu
```

Let's try it:

```
% finger briant
```

```
Login name: briant               In real life: Brian Thomas
Directory: /user10/briant                    Shell: /bin/csh
On since Aug 21 16:47:06 on ttyp2 from rws21.xpr.cs.wwu
Plan:
```

```
Hey! Quit reading my plan!
```

Logging Out

That's enough Unix practice to get the idea, so let's "log out" or quit our session for now. To log out, just type **logout** at the prompt:

```
% logout
logged out - Sun Aug 21 14:19:11 PDT 1994
```

If for some reason (maybe not this time, but during another session) the server responds to your logout command with something other than a nice clean logout, don't panic. Just issue the **logout** command again. If you were connected to the host computer via modem, it's a good idea to issue the "hang-up" command from your terminal emulation software, just to be sure you're completely disconnected from the host computer.

By the way, if you ever get *really* stuck and can't get the host computer to log you off, even after trying all the commands you can think of (**logoff, bye, quit, exit, Control-S, Control-Q,** etc.), you can always use the "hang-up" command from your telecommunications software. The host computer will sense that it's no longer connected to you and will log you out automatically. Nothing is damaged by this kind of disconnection, although it is a last resort.

In the chapters ahead we'll be using some new commands to invoke software programs such as **telnet** and **ftp** to explore the Internet.

More Unix Commands

There are a few more basic Unix commands that you might need to know sometime.

Accessing Online Help

Typing **man** (short for *manual*) , followed by a Unix command, will bring up the horrible Unix online help. Use the **man** command as a last resort if you cannot find any printed Help documentation from your Internet service provider or network administrator. If you do have to use **man** and don't know the name of the command you're looking for, type **man -k** followed by a keyword (such as "copy," "delete," etc.) to bring up a list of commands for that keyword. It's ugly, but you'll probably find what you want. If you get really desperate, try typing **man ls** to see all options listed.

Copying Files

There are times when you may wish to either copy a file to another directory on your Unix host (for example, if you wanted to put it in a public directory for someone else to copy). Use the **cp** command to copy a file, using the following format:

```
% cp  filename  new_filename
```

Note that you specify the new filename, which is logical, since it makes no sense to copy a file as the same filename.

So this is what we could do:

```
% cp gate.uu gate2.uu
```

This would create a new file in the same directory with the name *gate2.uu*. If you wanted to copy the file into a different directory, you would add the directory path to your filename, like this:

```
% cp gate.uu storage/gate2.uu
```

This would make a copy of *gate.uu* called *gate2.uu* and put it in the directory named *storage*. In this case you could also leave out the new filename and it would create a file called *gate.uu* in the new directory.

Moving or Renaming Files

To move a file or rename it, use the **mv** command. The syntax is identical what you used for the **cp** command discussed above.

Note that the **mv** command is very useful when dealing with long filenames that are sometimes found on the Internet, especially if your personal computer is limited to short filenames. Files created and stored on Unix, VMS, or Macintosh computers can have relatively long filenames, like *This_is_ a_great_scan_of_a_carbon_molecule.gif*, or the filename has spaces or other weird characters. Filenames like this are often problematic for some computers and telecommunications software. Sometimes you'll even get a file that you can't do anything with. It's best to rename the file to a shorter name, like this:

```
% mv really_long_filename.gif cool.gif
```

If for some reason the filename is so wacky that even your Unix host refuses to recognize it, try using the wildcard asterisk (*) character and use only enough of the filename to distinguish it from others in your directory, like this:

```
% mv really* cool.gif
```

Be careful with this technique, however, since really could match multiple files in your directory.

Transferring Files via Modem

Most Unix computers can send files via a modem connection to your home or work computer (if that is how you connect to your Internet host computer). To send a file, your modem and the Unix computer need to agree on a command language or protocol to use for the transfer. The most common protocols are ZMODEM, XMODEM, YMODEM, and Kermit. ZMODEM is definitely the preferred option, so try it first. Most telecommunications software today supports ZMODEM; however, you also need to determine if your Unix host supports it.

The best way to find out what kinds of transfer protocol your Unix host supports is by asking someone who would know—a system administrator or knowledgeable colleague. If support is hard to find, you can try to invoke various possibilities by typing commands at your command prompt. First, to see if you have ZMODEM available, try typing **sz**. If you get something that looks like this, then you're on the right track:

```
% sz

Send file(s) with ZMODEM/YMODEM/XMODEM Protocol
        (Y) = Option applies to YMODEM only
        (Z) = Option applies to ZMODEM only
Usage:  sz [-12+abdefkLlNnquvwYy] [-] file ...
        sz [-12Ceqv] -c COMMAND
        sb [-12adfkquv] [-] file ...
        sx [-12akquv] [-] file
        1 Use stdout for modem input
        + Append to existing destination file (Z)
        a (ASCII) change NL to CR/LF
        b Binary file transfer override
        c send COMMAND (Z)
        d Change '.' to '/' in pathnames (Y/Z)
        e Escape all control characters (Z)
        f send Full pathname (Y/Z)
        i send COMMAND, ack Immediately (Z)
        k Send 1024 byte packets (Y)
        L N Limit subpacket length to N bytes (Z)
        l N Limit frame length to N bytes (l>=L) (Z)
        n send file if source newer (Z)
        N send file if source newer or longer (Z)
        o Use 16 bit CRC instead of 32 bit CRC (Z)
        p Protect existing destination file (Z)
        r Resume/Recover interrupted file transfer (Z)
        q Quiet (no progress reports)
        u Unlink file after transmission
        v Verbose - provide debugging information
        w N Window is N bytes (Z)
      y Yes, overwrite existing file (Z)
- as pathname sends standard input as sPID.sz or envi-
ronment ONAME sz 1.36 08-31-87 for V7/BSD by Chuck
Forsberg
%
```

What happened here is that I typed only **sz** without any other *modifiers*, and therefore Unix displayed information telling not only how to use **sz**, but also commands for YMODEM and XMODEM. From here, as we've learned, we can probably get more help by typing **man sz** to bring up Unix's basic help utility.

ZMODEM is nice for a number of reasons, the best of which is that you probably won't have to send commands on both your computer and the host computer to initiate a transfer. This is true whether you are *uploading* a file from your computer to your Unix host, or *downloading* a file to your own computer from the Unix host computer. Whichever one is storing the file you want to move, you just invoke the ZMODEM command from that computer, and the receiving computer will accept the transfer.

Another reason ZMODEM is the protocol of choice is because it has more advanced error-correcting processes that help transfer your file in spite of telephone line noise or other problems.

For our ZMODEM example, to transfer the file called *pdial.txt* from my Unix account to my home computer, I would type the following at the Unix command prompt:

```
% sz pdial.txt

sz: 1 file requested:
pdial.txt

Sending in Batch Mode

Transfer completed.
%
```

The file then appears on my hard drive after the transfer process is complete. Remember that your telecommunications software on your computer will determine where the file will be placed. This software will also determine how you *upload* files to your Unix host computer, since the command to send the file will be part of the telecommunications software.

What if you don't have ZMODEM on your Unix host computer? Chances are very good that you'll have some other program such as XMODEM or Kermit. The two major differences between these programs and ZMODEM is they are generally slower, and they require that you initiate commands on both computers to initiate a transfer (i.e., they are not "smart" enough to detect an incoming file; they must be "told" there's a file coming before the process starts). Note also that some ZMODEM packages also require a command at the receiving end before accepting a file. On the Unix side of things this command is probably **rz** for "receive ZMODEM."

In any case, the procedure is simple. We'll use Kermit as an example, since it's an old standby on many Unix computers. To transfer a file from your Unix host to your own computer, type **kermit** at the command prompt just to see what happens:

```
% kermit
C-Kermit, 4E(072) 24 Jan 89, VAX/Ultrix
Type ? for help
C-Kermit>
```

Okay, this is typical. We've entered Kermit's command mode, since our prompt has just changed to **C-Kermit>** , and we can now type a question mark for help if we want some. For now, we'll skip that part and go straight to a file transfer.

First, we have to prepare our own computer for a Kermit transfer. How you do this will vary according to what telecommunications software you are using, but usually it's a command labeled something simple like "Receive Kermit." Then, on the Unix host, you type **send** and then the filename:

```
C-Kermit>send pdial.txt
```

When the file is finished transferring, you'll be returned back to the Kermit command prompt, and from there you can type **exit** to return to your Unix command prompt.

If you wanted to use Kermit to send a file from your own computer to your Unix account, the process is reversed. First, on the Unix host, you would type receive to get Kermit ready to **receive** your file, then on your computer you would initiate a send command along with designating a file to be transferred.

There are, of course, many variations to this procedure, such as placing the Unix host in "server mode" and then initiating all commands from your personal computer.

Deleting Files

The **rm** command removes a file from your directory. If you type **rm myfile.txt**, the file named *myfile.txt* will be deleted—permanently. You can also delete multiple files with similar names by using the asterisk (*) symbol as a "wildcard." For example, if you type **rm myfile.***, all filenames beginning with *myfile* will be deleted, so if you also had files named *myfile.wfw* and *myfile.wp*, both will be deleted. Be careful with the **rm** command—there is no Unix command for "undelete."

Stopping a Process

If you started something on your Unix host that you want to stop or *kill,* as it's sometimes called, the usual command is either Control-Z, Control-C, or Control-Q.

Just the FAQs

To get any of the FAQs listed below, send the commands shown to

```
mail-server@rtfm.mit.edu
```

This is an e-mail server that will automatically send you the file you've requested. Send these commands in the body of your e-mail message. *Remember that this server is Unix-based: Use upper- and lower-case letters exactly as shown.*

If you wish to retrieve more than one FAQ, just enter each command on a separate line in your message. You may also retrieve the files noted using FTP.

Introduction to Unix

Send this command:

```
send pub/usenet/news.answers/unix-faq/*
```

Modems and Telecommunications

Send this command:

```
send pub/usenet/news.answers/modems/*
```

Chapter 4

ELECTRONIC MAIL

What is E-mail?

Electronic mail, or *e-mail*, is the foundation of all that happens on the Internet. The basic function of e-mail is the same as with regular postal service mail: to send and receive information. But e-mail is much more powerful than paper mail (or "snail-mail," as many online folks deride it). With e-mail you can send and receive just about anything you use or create on your computer—words, formatted documents, programs, photos, images, and sounds. It's all a matter of making sure that you *encode* the contents correctly, and that the receiver of such information has the proper software to *decode* it.

E-mail Software

Whether you get online through your employer's direct Internet connection, a remote account on someone else's computer, or a personal SLIP or PPP account, you'll be using some kind of e-mail software package.

On a Unix or VAX computer it might be called something like *Elm* or *Pine* or just plain old *mail*, and often on large internal computer systems there will be a custom menu on your screen that lists something like *Mail*, which is probably the mail system your company or university has chosen for you.

On a PC or Macintosh computer, you might have something like Eudora, Microsoft Mail, QuickMail, FirstClass, or cc:Mail. You may even have a choice. And if you have an account with a major commercial service like CompuServe, you have—you guessed it—CompuServe mail. The point is that there are many e-mail interfaces in use today, and they all look and act slightly different and have different bells and whistles.

However, they all have some basic, common features as well, and because it would be impossible to describe every e-mail interface available, our discussion will concentrate on the basics, using Pine, a free e-mail and newsreader package developed at the University of Washington that is quickly becoming a standard interface option on most computer systems that offer Internet access.

The reason I've chosen Pine instead of the standard Unix **mail** program is that **mail** has a clunky command-line interface that is somewhat anomalous among today's e-mail software. Pine, on the other hand, is representative of many e-mail interfaces available today for Unix, VMS, Macintosh, and Windows computers, and is therefore a more suitable exemplar.

Finally, because direct and SLIP/PPP connections are becoming increasingly common, later in this chapter we'll also take a look at the undisputed champion of freeware Windows and Macintosh e-mail interfaces, Eudora, from QUALCOMM.

Addressing and Sending E-mail

Let's start with the basics of addressing and sending e-mail. As with paper mail, you need to know the address of the intended recipient of your letter.

See the section on Finding Someone's E-mail Address at the end of this chapter for tips on this topic.

Electronic mail has its own addressing system, called *domain name addressing*. This is the electronic equivalent of postal addresses. Like postal addresses, e-mail addresses go from specific to general, in order to route the message to the right computer and person. Generally, e-mail addresses have a *username* (also called a *user ID*, often the person's account name on their computer system), one or more *location identifiers*, and a *domain*. There is also an @ ("at") symbol that separates the user ID from the locations and domain, and sometimes additional characters like % and ! symbols. My e-mail address is typical:

```
brian@mom.spie.org
```

brian	is my user ID
mom	is a computer mailserver name
spie	is our location identifier
org	is a domain (non-profit organization)

Here are some other examples:

    jbreck@huey.jpl.nasa.gov

    arseno@phy.ulaval.ca

    sab@media-lab.media.mit.edu

The portion of the address to the right of the @ symbol is referred to as the *domain name*. The domain name moves from most specific information at the left (often the computer's "name") to the most general (the type of site).

Let's break down that last one into its individual parts:

sab	is the user name (in this case, the owner's initials)
media-lab	is a computer name at MIT
media	is a subdomain at MIT
mit	is a location identifier
edu	is a domain (educational institution)

In the examples above, the address owners have used some portion of their name or a cognate for their user or account name. Some organizations require that names follow specific conventions. For example, some services combine the first three letters of your first and last name to create your account name. Others require the use of an account number rather than a name.

Your E-mail Address

When you subscribe to an online service, you are usually given some degree of choice in choosing your user ID or username, which in most cases is also part of your e-mail address. The part you can't choose is everything after the @ symbol, that is, all the domain information, since that belongs to the service provider. Notice I said "some degree of choice." In other words, you can't always get what you want.

Some service providers give you more options than others. Whether this is good or bad is personal opinion. For example, everyone at CompuServe has a numerical user ID assigned by CompuServe. You don't have a say in the matter—you're just 77482.333, or whatever, and that's the end of it. On the Internet you become **77482.333@compuserve.com,** because that's their addressing scheme (see the later section on converting addresses for commercial online services).

At the other end of the spectrum, there are service providers who let you pick a user ID of your design, provided it's not already taken elsewhere on their service, and that it meets certain computer-designated criteria. So, for example, if I just got an account at service provider called CTSNet, I could request the username brian, and if there were not already a user named brian at CTSNet, then they might say okay, and I would become

```
brian@ctsnet.com
```

There are, of course, some technical restrictions on e-mail names on the Internet, and these don't always match what is permitted or restricted on a commercial service provider. For example, on America Online, you can have a username that contains a space. This is because AOL's online environment allows spaces. So if I pick *brian thomas* as my AOL username, everyone else with an AOL account addresses messages to me at exactly that address.

However, if someone outside of the America Online environment tries to send a message to **brian thomas@aol.com,** most likely their message will be returned as an error, because spaces are not permitted anywhere in an Internet e-mail address. The moral of the story is, wherever you get your online access, think globally when picking your username.

Choosing a Username (and E-mail Address)

If you're given any degree of choice, I suggest picking a username that somehow relates to your real name so that others can better identify you by your address, and remember your address more easily. Common practice is to use a combination of your first name, middle initial, and last name.

Some examples, using my name:

- bjt
- bthomas
- b_thomas
- bjthomas
- thomasb
- thomasbj
- bthom

Things to avoid:

- spaces
- periods or any other punctuation marks
- long names or text strings
- special characters (!, %, *, #, etc.—most of these would be rejected by the service provider anyway)
- cute family names (trust me—I've had **baba3@aol.com** haunting me since 1989)

More about Domains

Every address has a domain that helps identify the type of organization it was sent from, or the geographical location of the organization. Typical domain types:

.com	commercial venture, such as **compuserve.com**
.edu	educational institution, such as **dartmouth.edu**
.org	a private or non-profit organization, such as **spie.org**
.gov	government institution, such as **nasa.gov**
.mil	military site, such as **navy.mil**
.net	gateways or administrative hosts on the Internet, such as **nwnet.net**

Sites not in the U.S. end with a two-letter country code. For example:

.ca	Canada
.cn	China
.dk	Denmark
.de	Germany
.jp	Japan
.ch	Switzerland
.uk	United Kingdom
.se	Sweden

The United States actually has a country code (.us), but you won't see it very often. A function of our renowned ethnocentricity, perhaps.

Sending Messages to Commercial Online Services

As I've mentioned, most commercial online services have both an internal e-mail system, where subscribers send and receive messages to each other, as well as an Internet *gateway*, where mail from the Internet is converted so that it can be read on the commercial service.

In other words, if you have an account on America Online with the username *jimb* and your friend has an account on CompuServe with the username *76543,3324*, the only way you can exchange e-mail is to use the two services' gateways for exchanging e-mail.

What this means is, while your AOL or CompuServe addresses might work for other subscribers at those services, they will not work with each other or on the Internet unless they conform to the Internet's domain name addressing system.

The solution is, thankfully, simple: in order to e-mail someone with an account on a commercial online service, you use the service's Internet equivalent. Often this is as simple as adding the commercial service's domain name to your friend's e-mail address. For example, *jimb* becomes **jimb@aol.com**. Other services might require a bit more modification, such as the CompuServe address, which needs to have the comma in the username changed to a period, so *76543,3324* becomes **76543.3324@compu-serve.com**.

The whole gateway situation is easiest if the other person sends you a message first, since you get to see how their e-mail address was converted by the online services' gateways, and just mail to that address (or even easier, use your e-mail software's Reply feature).

Following is a table showing some common commercial services and their e-mail conversions. See the "Just the FAQs" section of this chapter for further resources.

Online Service	Send mail to:
ALAnet	user%ALANET@intermail.isi.edu
Alternex	user@ax.apc.org
America Online (AOL)	user@aol.com
ATTmail	user@attmail.com
Applelink	user@applelink.apple.com
BITNET	user@site.bitnet
	If the above doesn't work, try using one of the gateways below:
	userid%host.bitnet@a.gateway.address
	where a.gateway.address is one of the following:
	cornellc.cit.cornell.edu
	cunyvm.cuny.edu
	mitvma.mit.edu
	vm1.nodak.edu
BIX	user@bix.com
Comlink	user@oln.comlink.apc.org
CompuServe	7xxxx.yyy@compuserve.com
	(make sure you change the comma to a period!)
Delphi	user@delphi.com
EASYnet/DECNET	user@host.enet.dec.com
eWorld	user@eworld.com
FidoNet	firstname.lastname@p4.f3.n2.z1.fidonet.org
GEnie	user@genie.com
GeoNet	user@geo1.geonet.de (for recipients in Europe)
	user@geo2.geonet.de (for recipients in the UK)
	user@geo4.geonet.de (for recipients in North America)
Glasnet	user@glas.apc.org

JANET	user@address.domain.janet.a
	(example: vax.ox.ac.uk)
MCI	1234567@mcimail.com
Peacenet	user@igc.apc.org
Prodigy	user@prodigy.com
Sprintmail	/G=firstname/S=lastname/O=organization/
	ADMD=TELEMAIL/C=US/@sprint.com
THEnet	userid%host.decnet@utadnx.cc.utexas.edu

Common E-mail Elements

One of the first things you might like to do on your new online account is explore your e-mail software. In this example we'll use a popular e-mail program for Unix called Pine. Pine is one of many relatively simple e-mail interfaces available for Unix computers, along with others such as Elm, Mush, and Metamail. Most modern e-mail software interfaces are similar in functionality to pine, and therefore while your specific mailer's commands and interface may be a little different, the basic concepts are the same.

There is, I feel obligated to note, a standard Unix mail utility called (you guessed it) **mail**, but it's so unbelievably obtuse and limited that any Unix manager who doesn't install something better for users should be questioned. Pine is freely available from the University of Washington at

```
ftp.cac.washington.edu/mail
```

If the Unix computer you are going to read mail on has only Unix **mail**, I encourage you to talk to your provider about getting Pine or something equally user-friendly.

At the Unix command prompt, you would type

```
% pine
```

to invoke the Pine e-mail software. If you get a message like "pine: Command not found," then you don't have Pine software available and you'll need to find another program on the computer to read your mail.

If you don't seem to have Pine, type the following command at the prompt:

```
% man -k mail
```

This should bring up a list of all available commands related to e-mail.

If this still doesn't help you, ask your system administrator for a list of what is available, how to access it, and how to access the online help for it.

Back to our example:

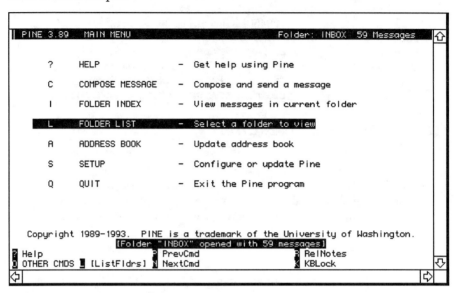

Notice all the command options are listed at the bottom of the screen. At the top it tells me I have one message in the folder named "inbox." Most e-mail software interfaces give you all of the functions shown here, such as creating mail folders, an electronic address book (so you don't have to remember everyone's e-mail address), and an index command to show all the files in your current e-mail directory. Note that your e-mail directories are probably stored in your personal Unix directory.

Regardless of what computer and software you use, every mail message consists of the same basic elements. Each message is divided into two sections: the *message header*, and the *message body*.

Message Header

The outgoing message header contains all of the address information for both the sender and recipient, as well as other information such as who else was "copied" on the message, and often a "Subject" line to help identify messages from only their headers.

Headers also pick up information as your message is sent to its recipient. Your e-mail software adds hidden text that itemizes the message size, origination location, and other miscellaneous information. By the time the message arrives at its destination, it may have a whole paragraph of cryptic text that recounts all the routers the message passed through, the message's unique ID number, and so on. See "Return Message Headers" below if you're interested.

Here is an example of a typical outgoing message header as you might see it:

```
-----------------------------------------------------------
To:   Peter Kaminski <kaminski@netcom.com>
CC:   Patricia Cutts <patricia@pacificrim.net>
Attachment:
Subject:  Permission to republish the PDIAL resource
-----------------------------------------------------------
```

Note that with most e-mail software you don't see your own name in a From field. The software automatically inserts it for you.

In addition to the To and Subject fields, message headers may also contain any or all of these fields as well:

CC: Short for "Carbon Copy." This line shows who was also copied on the message.

BCC: Short for "Blind Carbon Copy." Same as CC, but names on this line are not seen by any of the message's recipients. It's somewhat sneaky. It's also a great way to send a message to a large list of people and protect everyone's identity, for example, on a subscription mailing list. This is a handy feature, but if you use it, make sure the people you blind copy understand what it's all about. If you just BCC someone out of the blue, they're often confused by why they received a message that does not show their e-mail address anywhere on it.

Reply to: If you want replies to be sent to a different e-mail address, that address goes in this field.

Keywords: Words that the sender adds to help recipients sort and classify the message for archival or searching purposes. You will rarely see this line in a message.

Attachment: The name of an attached electronic file, plus other information about the file that will help the receiver's mailer software decide how to handle it.

Sometimes it is sufficient to write a message in plain ASCII text, no special fonts, formatting, or page layout required. When appearance is important, or if exchanging documents in their original word-processed form is key, the attached document feature is handy. The e-mail program allows the user to specify the location of the file and transfers the attached file piggyback to the e-mail message.

The important thing to remember is that a Unix mailer's attach feature will literally insert the file into the message area of the e-mail message. This assumes the person on the receiving end has a similar mail utility that can recognize the attached file and let them "save" it as a discrete file on their computer. Such software may also encode the document so that binary characters are not lost during transmission, and again this assumes the software on the receiving end can recognize and convert such encoding (more on encoding later). Conversely, commercial online services' "attach" features currently only support attaching a document to be sent to another user on that service, not to someone outside "on the Internet." In short, you'll have to make sure you know what your recipient has on their end before sending an attached document.

Message Body

The message body is the area where you type your message. It appears below the header. To finish off the example above, here's what the whole message might look like:

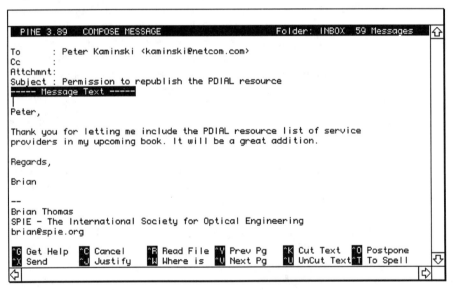

Signatures

The last three lines in the example above are called a *signature*, or "sig." As a courtesy to the recipients of your e-mail messages, you should "sign" your message with at least your full name and e-mail address at the end of the message. Most e-mail programs allow you to set up a signature that gets appended automatically to all your outgoing e-mail messages. The automated signature can be either a feature of the e-mail software or the computer operating system itself.

Some individuals choose to include extensive contact information in their signatures, such as phone, fax and street address. Others choose to add disclaimers emphasizing that the opinions they express in their e-mail are not necessarily the opinion of their Internet provider (often, the sender's employer). The general rule is to keep your signature useful and unobtrusive. Long quotations from Hesiod's *Theogony* are not often appreciated in the spirit with which they are offered.

Managing E-mail

As mentioned, most e-mail utilities have functions to help manage your e-mail. For example, you can view a list of your most recent e-mail, as well as save and view e-mail into other e-mail directories that you can define as you wish. For example, you could create a mail directory (or folder) called *work* in which you put all your work-related correspondence. This helps you organize your e-mail, since you'll often want to save messages for further reference. Usually you will have a single folder that all mail first gets put into when it arrives. This is usually called something like *newmail* or *inbox*. Below is a listing of my inbox folder right now in Pine. I've displayed it like this using the **i** (for "index") command.

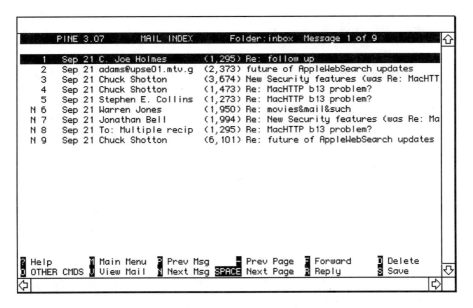

This shows that I have nine messages here, and that I've already read the first four, since there is no **N** in front of them. To read one of these messages, use the arrow keys to highlight (or "blacklight" in this case) the message you want to read an press Return. I'll read the first one on the list:

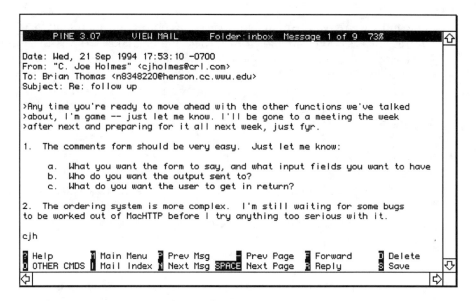

At this point I could save this message in a different folder (I could also do this from the index) by using the **save** command (**s**) listed among all the other commands at the bottom of the screen.

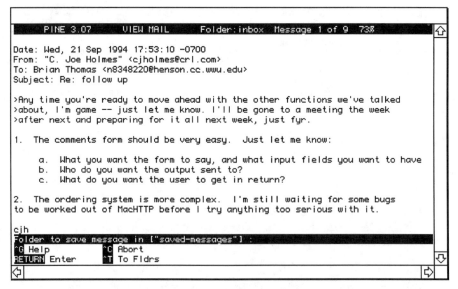

Here Pine is smart enough to offer to put the message in a default folder named *saved-messages,* or I could name a new folder, or I could use the **^T** command (which means press the Control and T keys simultaneously) to choose among all the folders I have previously created. Pressing Return would save my message in the default folder.

Another must-have feature for any e-mail software package is the ability to create nicknames (or *aliases*, as they are sometimes called). This feature lets you create shorthand designations for e-mail addresses, so instead of having to type **peter@cosy-.sbg.ac.at** every time I want to send a message to my friend Peter at the University of Salzburg, I just type "Peter" and it goes to him. Here's what a Pine address book looks like:

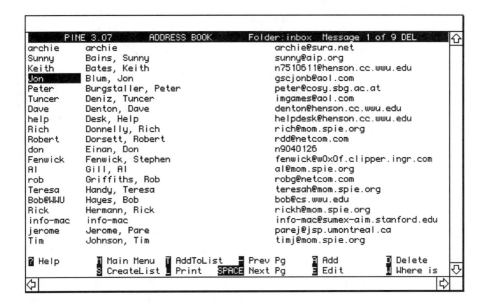

```
      PINE 3.07        ADDRESS BOOK       Folder:inbox  Message 1 of 9 DEL
archie      archie                  archie@sura.net
Sunny       Bains, Sunny            sunny@aip.org
Keith       Bates, Keith            n7510611@henson.cc.wwu.edu
Jon         Blum, Jon               gscjonb@aol.com
Peter       Burgstaller, Peter      peter@cosy.sbg.ac.at
Tuncer      Deniz, Tuncer           imgames@aol.com
Dave        Denton, Dave            denton@henson.cc.wwu.edu
help        Desk, Help              helpdesk@henson.cc.wwu.edu
Rich        Donnelly, Rich          rich@mom.spie.org
Robert      Dorsett, Robert         rdd@netcom.com
don         Einan, Don              n9040126
Fenwick     Fenwick, Stephen        fenwick@w0x0f.clipper.ingr.com
Al          Gill, Al                al@mom.spie.org
rob         Griffiths, Rob          robg@netcom.com
Teresa      Handy, Teresa           teresah@mom.spie.org
Bob@WWU     Hayes, Bob              bob@cs.wwu.edu
Rick        Hermann, Rick           rickh@mom.spie.org
info-mac    info-mac                info-mac@sumex-aim.stanford.edu
jerome      Jerome, Pare            parej@jsp.umontreal.ca
Tim         Johnson, Tim            timj@mom.spie.org

? Help         M Main Menu   T AddToList   - Prev Pg    A Add       D Delete
               S CreateList  Y Print    SPACE Next Pg   E Edit      W Where is
```

These are some of the nicknames I've created so I don't have to type in their full address every time. Even better, Pine let's you include the person's real name as part of the nickname, so when I type **Jon** in the **To:** field of a mail message, it shows up like this to both me and Jon:

```
     Jon Blum <gscjonb@aol.com>
```

The Internet's e-mail protocol lets you type addresses like this without sending back an error (it just ignores everything in front of the first < character). This nickname feature is also valuable in that you can create lists of people attached to single nickname, so if you have a group of people you send mail to regularly, you can make up a name like "my-friends" and then list all their e-mail addresses in the nickname. This is one way to make your own mail server. I have a friend right now who publishes an online baseball magazine using Pine's address book this way.

These and many other features are standard on modern e-mail software, and can make your life a lot easier.

Return Message Headers

When you receive a message, you many notice that it not only contains the standard Date:, To:, From:, and Subject: lines, but also a whole bunch of other unsightly text strings. Like this:

```
----------------------------------------------------------
Received: from munnari.OZ.AU by henson.cc.wwu.edu
(5.65/WWU-H1.2/UW-NDC Revision: 2.26 ) id AA02435;
Sun, 8 May 1994 19:30:54 -0700
Received: from bbs.ausom.oz (via sol) with SunIII
(5.83—+1.3.1+0.50)id AA20446;
Mon, 9 May 1994 12:31:19 +1000 (from
jimb@bbs.ausom.oz.au)
Received: by bbs.ausom.oz.au (5.64)
        id AA12738; Sun, 8 May 94 15:10:06 EST
From: jimb@bbs.ausom.oz.au (Jim Brandi)
Message-Id: <9405080510.AA12738@bbs.ausom.oz.au>
Subject: Re: IMG re-send requests
To: briant@henson.cc.wwu.edu (Brian Thomas)
Date: Sun, 8 May 94 15:10:04 EST
In-Reply-To: <9405060108.AA00808@henson.cc.wwu.edu>;
from "Brian Thomas" at May 5, 94 6:15 pm
X-Mailer: ELM [version 2.3 PL11]
----------------------------------------------------------
```

This is the return message header, and it contains routing and other information essential and unique to this e-mail message. Depending on what your e-mail software does with it, you may see it at the top or bottom of an incoming message, you may not see it at all, or you may even be able to display or hide it on the fly (Eudora, for example, does this).

For the most part, while it can be valuable in tracing e-mail transmission problems, you should be able to get by in life without ever having to use it.

"Bounced" or Undeliverable Mail

If you send a paper letter to a friend but write down the address incorrectly, your letter comes back from the Post Office with big "ADDRESS UNKNOWN" stamped across it. E-mail has a similar mechanism, and it's quite common.

Suppose you (**you@your.mail.address**) send an e-mail message to me at **bryan@spie.org** (misspelling my first name as *bryan* instead of *brian*). A few minutes or hours later you will get a "daemon" message that looks something like this:

```
Date: Tue, 10 May 1994 06:42:00 -0700
From: Mail Delivery Subsystem <MAILER-DAEMON@spie.org>
Subject: Returned mail: User unknown
To: you@your.mail.address

    — Transcript of session follows —
While talking to spie.org:
```

```
>>> RCPT To:<bryan@spie.org>
<<< 550 <bryan@spie.org>... User unknown
550 bryan@spie.org ... User unknown

    — Unsent message follows —
Received: by your.mail.address
AA10322; Tue, 10 May 1994 06:42:00 -0700
Date: Tue, 10 May 1994 06:41:00 -0700 (PDT)
From: You <you@your.mail.address>
Subject: Just thought I'd misspell your name!
To: bryan@spie.org
Message-Id: <Pine.3.07.9405100600.E10100-
k101000@your.mail.address>
Mime-Version: 1.0
Content-Type: MULTIPART/MIXED; BOUNDARY="0-158475305-
768577310:#10100"
```

And so on. A mail *daemon* (see the second line in the example above) is a software program, in this case running on the mail server-computer at **spie.org**, that processed the incoming message and determined that there was no user named **bryan** there.

Daemons also reside at "higher levels" on the Internet to deal with message problems on those levels, such as invalid domain names. For example, an e-mail message sent to **brian@spie.com** will be intercepted by a daemon and returned as "site unknown," since **spie.com** does not exist (it's **spie.org**).

Composing E-mail Messages

While I'll be the last person to tell you *what* to write, I will offer some things to consider when composing your e-mail messages.

Structural Rules

Reading messages on a computer screen can be at best tolerable, and at worst, an utter nightmare. Consider these rules of the road when composing your e-mail to make your e-mail easier to read:

- Keep line lengths to 60 columns (or characters) or less.
- Use a monospace typeface such as Courier to display your e-mail.
- Use both upper and lower case, and only use ALL CAPS IF YOU REALLY MEAN TO SHOUT.
- Keep paragraphs short, and use two <returns> between them to create a space between.
- Don't use tabs—they don't translate. Use spaces to indent instead.
- If responding to a previous message, clearly mark and quote the other message succinctly, if possible.
- Keep your signature short and useful. No cute sayings or "ASCII art."
- Send the message to yourself first (and save a copy) if you think formatting might be a problem.

Netiquette

Writing e-mail can quickly become so commonplace that we forget its power to be misinterpreted or even to wound. E-mail is probably closer to spoken communication than written, despite its text-bound façade. Like verbal communications, e-mail runs the entire spectrum of tone and purpose, from sending a close friend a quick note on the latest *Star Trek* episode you saw to submitting a manuscript to a professional journal.

With that in mind, the best advice is to write for the occasion. For communications to close colleagues and friends, write as you would speak. For formal business correspondence, write as you would write a letter.

There is, I should note, a tendency toward the casual side with e-mail in business correspondence. This is partly because of the immediacy of e-mail, and partly because, as the *New Yorker* cartoon aptly pointed out, "On the Internet, no one knows you're a dog." In many ways the Internet is a classless society, where annual income and titles have no tangible value, and are generally frowned upon if stated overtly.

Propriety

- Always remember you are writing to another person. Treat people with respect.
- Always remember that the other person *might* forward your message to someone else (it happens).
- Use smileys judiciously and *special* characters (like asterisks) to clarify tone of voice.
- Don't use shorthand acronyms unless you know the reader will understand them.
- Sign with a short, informative signature block
- Review your message before sending it. It's easy to think you'll come back to check something and then forget.
- Read all the messages in your inbox before replying to any them. Sometimes messages received later preclude you from having to respond. This is especially true when you're on an e-mail *listserv*.
- Be concise.

And finally, my personal rule of thumb: Wait 24 hours before sending any message you write in distress or anger. Chances are you won't send it after reading it again the next day. E-mail's "instant gratification" is a dangerous and seductive blade.

Common Conventions

Since the nuances of a face-to-face conversation are lost in e-mail messages, most veterans of the Internet use *emoticons*, or *smileys*, as they are more commonly called. These can be used to convey some of the emotional nuance of a message.

While these may seem a little cute upon first encounter, after a while you may begin to see how important they are to avoid misunderstandings and convey tone of voice, which we often take for granted in face-to-face and phone conversations. And because e-mail can be so much less formal than a paper letter, it's important to make your message as clear as possible.

Generally, smileys are used as a kind of punctuation, most often at the end of a sentence. For example, if I sent this message to a friend,

```
The Mariners lost again last night. I'm quite upset.
```

I could be joking or serious. There are no clues given.

However, if I change it to

```
The Mariners lost again last night. I'm quite upset ;-)
```

then it's clear that I'm being sarcastic, and that I'm not really upset at all. In fact, I might be happy about it.

Some Common Emoticons (emotional icons):

:-)	smile
:-(	frown
;-)	smile and wink
:-o	oh oh!
:-D	big grin
:-|	neutral or disinterested
:-/	disconcerted

Another communication oddity unique to the Internet is a kind of Internet shorthand, using acronyms of phrases people say all time. These are very casual in tone, and are best used between friends or people you know will understand them.

On the extreme side, people make up new ones all the time. You just have to tolerate it, I guess.

Some Common Shorthand Acronyms

BTW	by the way
FYI	for your info
TIA	thanks in advance
TTFN	ta ta for now
ROTFL	rolling on the floor laughing
IMHO	in my humble/honest opinion
TFS	thanks for sharing (used sarcastically)
RTFM	read the @#$%! manual!

L8R	later (as in, goodbye)
TTYL	talk to you later (or TTYS for "soon")

Another common e-mail (and Usenet) practice is the use of some character, usually the > symbol, to show a direct and quoted reference to some previous message. For example, let's look at the message shown previously:

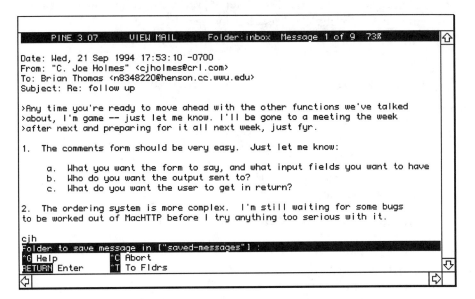

```
   PINE 3.07      VIEW MAIL     Folder:inbox  Message 1 of 9  73%

Date: Wed, 21 Sep 1994 17:53:10 -0700
From: "C. Joe Holmes" <cjholmes@crl.com>
To: Brian Thomas <n8348220@henson.cc.wwu.edu>
Subject: Re: follow up

>Any time you're ready to move ahead with the other functions we've talked
>about, I'm game -- just let me know. I'll be gone to a meeting the week
>after next and preparing for it all next week, just fyr.

1.  The comments form should be very easy.  Just let me know:

    a.  What you want the form to say, and what input fields you want to have
    b.  Who do you want the output sent to?
    c.  What do you want the user to get in return?

2.  The ordering system is more complex.  I'm still waiting for some bugs
to be worked out of MacHTTP before I try anything too serious with it.

cjh
Folder to save message in ["saved-messages"] :
^G Help           ^C Abort
RETURN Enter      ^T To Fldrs
```

The first three lines preceded with the > character are from my previous message to Joe, and he's quoted them so I could remember what I asked him. Note that he didn't quote all of my message to him, just a specific piece and only enough to give me the context. Most e-mail software will automatically insert (or give you the option to insert) the > character in a message when you choose the Reply or Forward feature. Then you can delete what parts of the message are not appropriate for quoting (like the header!) and respond point by point if appropriate. This makes for highly effective communication. On the Usenet, which we'll discuss later, you'll see such quoting used extensively in message *threads* since there are often many messages posted every day, and you'll want to show what exactly you're referring to when you post your own messages to a newsgroup.

Finding Someone's E-mail Address

The most efficient way to find a person's e-mail address is to call them on the telephone. There are tools and methods to finding e-mail addresses; however, there is no one central directory of everyone's e-mail address and no guarantee that your colleague is listed. Hours and hours can be spent searching for e-mail addresses in an attempt to surprise a long lost buddy. Save yourself the time and energy and just call him (or at least someone who knows his address). If you're determined to use a more "modern" method, get the FAQ on how to find someone's e-mail address (see the end of this chapter).

Macintosh E-mail Software

If your Macintosh is connected to the Internet either directly or via a SLIP/PPP connection, and if your network or service provider has set up a POP mailbox for your e-mail address, then you can use an e-mail package directly on your Macintosh.

Eudora is the undisputed leader for reading e-mail on the Macintosh. The Eudora version we'll look at here is freeware from QUALCOMM. There is also a commercial version that adds a variety of handy features.

Eudora comes with an excellent *Readme* file that explains setting up Eudora, as well as all of Eudora's features. Read this file! Eudora is incredibly powerful. We'll look at the basics here; more information is available at the QUALCOMM FTP site cited at the end of this section.

When you first launch Eudora, you'll need to enter some address information into the window that comes up when you select Settings... from the Special menu:

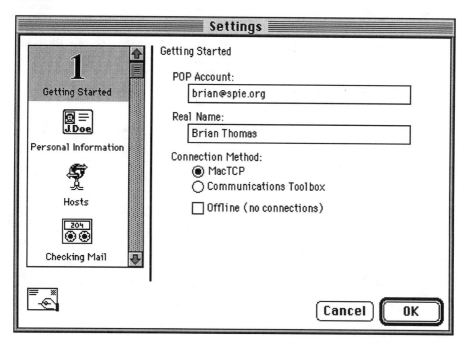

Enter in the address of your POP mailbox and your name as you wish it to appear on outgoing messages. Also select MacTCP. Next click the Hosts setting in the left-hand window and you'll notice that Eudora entered the name of your POP mailbox address in the right field. In this settings window all you need to type in is the name of your SMTP server, which like your POP mailbox is assigned to you by your administrator or service provider.

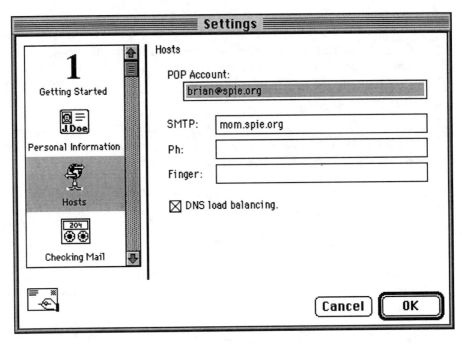

While there are a few more setup items in Eudora to explore, those are the basics. After saving your Settings, you can check your mail by selecting Check Mail from the File menu. Here's what the main "In" box looks like in Eudora after receiving incoming mail:

R	Jane E. Lybecker, SPIE	12:00 PM 11/9/94	2	Database Standards Update!
R	SUED%MOM@MOM.SPIE.ORG	1:51 PM 11/9/94	2	CESSE reports/updates
F	Janice Gaines, SPIE	2:27 PM 11/9/94	2	Out of the office
	Kevin Tripp, SPIE	3:44 PM 11/9/94	2	web suggestions
	Robert Dorsett	9:24 AM 11/9/94	7	Humor
	Eric Pepper	8:58 PM 11/9/94	3	fyi
	brian@MOM.SPIE.ORG	7:00 AM 11/11/94	3	fyr
D	Eric Pepper	5:21 PM 11/11/94	11	fyi
•	Eric Pepper	5:28 PM 11/11/94	4	Marybeth and I visited with these people
D	John Arthur December	8:14 PM 11/11/94	2	http://www.spie.org
D	Kevin Tripp, SPIE	2:35 PM 11/15/94	3	an interesting view of the role/future of
D	TERRY%MOM@MOM.SPIE.ORG	5:47 PM 11/17/94	1	"The Syposia Profile System" suggested by
D	SUED%MOM@MOM.SPIE.ORG	12:53 PM 11/27/9	2	CESSE upcoming meeting agenda
	brian@MOM.SPIE.ORG	7:21 AM 11/28/94	2	Windows TCP/IP stuff
	Dorothomas@aol.com	12:09 AM 11/29/9	1	RE: a good deal on a printer
	rdd@netcom.com	7:24 PM 11/29/94	3	RE: Marathon, the Demo
	Kevin Tripp, SPIE	12:32 PM 12/3/94	1	wanda
	archana@hkusub.hku.hk	3:32 PM 12/3/94	2	WWW PAge
R	AL@MOM.SPIE.ORG	5:28 PM 12/3/94	2	net problems
R	jim@MOM.SPIE.ORG	2:04 PM 12/4/94	1	PPP dial-in
	Brooks Seymore	5:51 PM 12/4/94	3	RE: hiya
R	Scott Walker, SPIE	Monday	2	
F	denton@henson.cc.wwu.e	Monday	2	RE: references?
	Janice Gaines, SPIE	Monday	3	fyi
	Janice Gaines, SPIE	Monday	4	fyi
	Janice Gaines, SPIE	Monday	3	in case you haven't heard of this stuff
R	m3047@halcyon.com	Tuesday	2	arns -- appletalk through IP tunneling
	Marybeth Manning	Wednesday	1	things went as planned :-) I need to touc
	Marybeth Manning	Wednesday	1	RE: fyi - the extracted item below from A
	Eric Pepper	Wednesday	3	internet tutorial
	Janice Gaines, SPIE	Thursday	2	give me a call about this
	Brian Thomas	Thursday	8	net providers a la Apple listserv
	Public-Access Computer	Thursday	4	PACS Review Gopher Menu Changed

260/807K/285K

Double-clicking on any of the messages here displays that message in a window, and you can choose to reply to, forward, redirect, or save the message in a Eudora folder you've already created, or a new one.

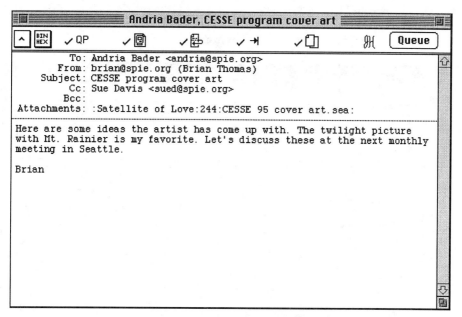

Of course, I've only scraped the surface of Eudora's features here. You can get the latest version of Eudora directly from the QUALCOMM FTP archive listed below, or from many *Info-Mac* mirror sites (see Appendix):

ftp.qualcomm.com

For more information on setting up your Macintosh computer on the Internet, see Appendix.

Windows E-mail Software

If your Windows PC is connected to the Internet either directly or via a SLIP/ PPP connection, and if your network or service provider has set up a POP *mailbox* for your e-mail address, then you can use an e-mail package directly on your PC.

Eudora is the undisputed leader for reading e-mail in Windows. The Eudora version we'll look at here is freeware from QUALCOMM. There is also a commercial version that adds a variety of handy features.

Eudora comes bundled with excellent instructions that explain how to set it up, as well as details on all of Eudora's many features. Read this file! Eudora is incredibly powerful. We'll look at the basics here; more information is available at the QUALCOMM FTP site cited at the end of this section.

Setting up Eudora is easy. Open the Configuration window and type in your POP mailbox account name (usually your e-mail address), your name as you want it to appear in outgoing messages, and the numerical address or domain name of your SMTP server computer. If for some reason you want your return address to be different than your e-mail address, you can fill in this field as well. The rest of the options are environmental controls.

```
┌───────────────────────────────────────────────────────────────┐
│                        Configuration                            │
│  ┌─ Network Configuration ────────────────────────────────────┐│
│  │  POP Account:      │brian@spie.org                    │     ││
│  │                                                             ││
│  │  Real Name:        │Brian Thomas                      │     ││
│  │                                                             ││
│  │  SMTP Server:      │192.149.147.1                     │     ││
│  │                                                             ││
│  │  Return Address:   │                                  │     ││
│  │                                                             ││
│  │  Check For Mail Every   │10 │   Minute(s)                   ││
│  │                                                             ││
│  │  Ph Server:        │                                  │     ││
│  └─────────────────────────────────────────────────────────────┘│
│  ┌─ Message Configuration ────────────────────────────────────┐│
│  │  Message Width: │80│   Message Lines: │20│   Tab Stop: │8│  ││
│  │                                                             ││
│  │  Screen Font:  │Courier New      ▼│   Size: │9 │           ││
│  │                                                             ││
│  │  Printer Font: │Courier New      ▼│   Size: │12│           ││
│  │                                                             ││
│  │  ⊠ Auto Receive Attachment Directory: │C:\SLIP\MAIL\EUDORA│││
│  └─────────────────────────────────────────────────────────────┘│
│  ⊟                                          [Cancel]    [OK]     │
└───────────────────────────────────────────────────────────────┘
```

Here's what an "In" box looks like in Eudora:

```
┌──────────────────────────────────────── In ──────────────────────────────┐
│ [ 14/17K/0K ]  [🏠]  [ ][ ][ ][ ]  [🖨]                                    │
├───────────────────────────────────────────────────────────────────────────┤
│ • │ Peter Burgstalle │11:29 AM 12/12/9│ 2│ Hellcats                        │
│ • │ AMY@MOM.SPIE.ORG  │11:56 AM 12/12/9│ 2│ RE: new editor                  │
│ • │ MARILYN@MOM.SPIE  │12:26 PM 12/12/9│ 2│ New Meeting to add to Conf. Code│
│ • │ JULIE%MOM@MOM.SP  │12:30 PM 12/12/9│ 2│ SECTION 125 FORM                │
│ • │ Laurel S. Kirkma  │12:46 PM 12/12/9│ 2│ Christmas message               │
│ • │ BABS@MOM.SPIE.OR  │01:40 PM 12/12/9│ 1│ Virtual Reality/IEEE            │
│ • │ Lani Middleton,   │03:08 PM 12/12/9│ 1│ Jim's MacTCP                    │
│ • │ ANDRIA%MOM@MOM.S  │04:13 PM 12/12/9│ 2│ SD94                            │
│ • │ Einan Don         │04:29 PM 12/12/9│ 2│ CESSE brochure                  │
│ • │ HELEN%MOM@MOM.SP  │04:31 PM 12/12/9│ 1│ LABORATORY COMPUTER SPECIALISTS,│
│ • │ Einan Don         │04:32 PM 12/12/9│ 2│ CESSE Brochure                  │
│ • │ Eric Pepper       │05:07 PM 12/12/9│ 2│ RE: Ahh. Must be nice to have a │
│ • │ Eric Pepper       │05:08 PM 12/12/9│ 2│ fyi                             │
│ • │ Eric Pepper       │05:09 PM 12/12/9│ 3│ html                            │
└───────────────────────────────────────────────────────────────────────────┘
```

Double-clicking on any of the messages here displays that message in a window, and you can choose to reply to, forward, redirect, or save the message in a Eudora folder you've already created, or a new one.

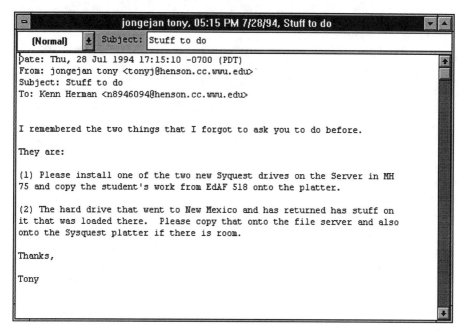

```
                 jongejan tony, 05:15 PM 7/28/94, Stuff to do

[Normal]    Subject: Stuff to do

Date: Thu, 28 Jul 1994 17:15:10 -0700 (PDT)
From: jongejan tony <tonyj@henson.cc.wwu.edu>
Subject: Stuff to do
To: Kenn Herman <n8946094@henson.cc.wwu.edu>


I remembered the two things that I forgot to ask you to do before.

They are:

(1) Please install one of the two new Syquest drives on the Server in MH
75 and copy the student's work from EdAF 518 onto the platter.

(2) The hard drive that went to New Mexico and has returned has stuff on
it that was loaded there.  Please copy that onto the file server and also
onto the Sysquest platter if there is room.

Thanks,

Tony
```

I've just scraped the surface of Eudora's features here. You can get the latest version of Eudora directly from the QUALCOMM FTP archive listed below, or from most Windows FTP archives (see Appendix):

ftp.qualcomm.com

For more information about setting up your Windows PC on the Internet, see Appendix.

Just the FAQs

To get any of the FAQs listed below, send the commands shown to

mail-server@rtfm.mit.edu

This is an e-mail server that will automatically send you the file you've requested. Send these commands in the body of your e-mail message. *Remember that this server is Unix-based: Use upper- and lower-case letters exactly as shown.*

If you wish to retrieve more than one FAQ, just enter each command on a separate line in your message. You may also retrieve the files noted using FTP.

Country Codes
Send this command:
```
send pub/usenet/news.answers/mail/country-codes
```

Sending E-Mail to Commercial Online Services
Send this command:
```
send pub/usenet/news.answers/mail/inter-network-guide
```

FAQs:Finding Someone's E-mail Address
Send this command:
```
send pub/usenet/news.answers/finding-addresses
```

Chapter 5

ELECTRONIC MAIL SERVERS

Using E-mail to Retrieve Documents

Mail servers, or *file servers,* as they are sometimes called, let you retrieve documents from other computer archives using only e-mail. You send a text-string "command" such as "send filename.txt" to another e-mail address, and the computer at that address processes your command and automatically sends the document "filename.txt" back to your e-mail address. You can either use it in e-mail form or open it using a word-processing application on your computer.

Why Would I Want to Use a Mail Server?

There are many large computer archives of information that include documents, images, and programs all available for public use. Quite often the files available are the same ones you can access via FTP.

However, if you don't have FTP capabilities yet you do have an e-mail account, you can retrieve files through a mail server. Granted, it's not quite as straightforward as FTP access, but if you can't FTP, a mail server is your only option.

Some Examples

In the previous chapter, the section on finding someone's e-mail address ended with typical instructions on how to retrieve a file named *finding-addresses* at a mail server with the address **mail-server@rtfm.mit.edu**.

Of course, for the example above, I provided the filename for you to retrieve.

So what if you don't know what files are available at a particular location? Easy—just send the word "help" to the server address. Like this:

```
------------------------------------------------------------
To       : mail-server@rtfm.mit.edu
CC       :
Subject  :
------------------------------------------------------------
help
```

Most mail servers will respond to a *help* request by returning to you a set of instructions on how to use their server, as well as an index of available files, or at least further instructions on how to retrieve an index.

Like the files on your personal computer, the files available from a mail server are arranged in *directories*. Since a mail server could be any one of a number of computer types, not all mail servers use the same set of commands. Mostly these differences show up in the way you designate a file's location.

For example, if the mail server is using the Unix operating system, you might send the following command to retrieve a file named *blue_laser.txt* that is located in the "optics" subdirectory:

```
send optics/blue_laser.txt
```

However, if the mail server is using the VMS operating system, you would send this command instead:

```
send [.optics]blue_laser.txt
```

Either way, the only way you'll ever know what files are available and how to retrieve them from a particular mail server is to first send the *help* command to the server.

The point here is not to make this sound complicated. But like most Internet endeavors, you have to read the instructions. You'll see the acronym *RTFM* over and over on the Internet, because reading the manual is a fundamental rule of the road.

Where to Find E-mail Servers

In Part II of this book, Science Resources on the Internet, you will find, organized by technology, a listing of relevant mail servers.

For further information on finding mail servers, get Jonathan Kamens' document on "How To Find Sources" by sending e-mail to

mail-server@pit-manager.mit.edu

with the following message on one line exactly as it's written but without the line-breaks shown here:

```
send usenet/comp.sources.wanted/How_to_findsources_(READ
_THIS_BEFORE_POSTING)
```

or get the file via FTP from

```
ftp://pit-manager.mit.edu/pub/usenet/
comp.sources.wanted/
How_to_find_sources_(READ_THIS_BEFORE_POSTING)
```

FTPMail

Mail servers only provide access to files in their computer archives. A different and relatively new service called *FTPMail*, however, provides access to most FTP archives. The FTPMail service involves sending specific FTP commands in an e-mail message in order to get the FTP site's computer to send you the files you want—via e-mail.

The FTPMail service is available from a few major computers on the Internet. They have been set up for public access as a service to the Internet community.

Again, FTPMail server commands vary slightly from one service to the next. It is best to send a "help" message before making assumptions.

To retrieve a file, send an e-mail message to one of the addresses below and specify the FTP site address, the file directory path, and the filename. If the file is not a text file set the transfer type to **binary** and **uuencode**. If the file is large specify **compress**. Remember that you are communicating with a computer, not a human. Only correctly spelled and meaningfully ordered commands will be recognized.

Here are addresses to three primary FTPMail servers. The BITFTP server was created especially for *BITNET* users, but may be accessed by Internet users, too.

```
Internet:    ftpmail@decwrl.dec.com

             ftpmail@sunsite.unc.edu

BITNET:      bitftp@pucc
```

Getting Help from the FTPMail Server

Send the message shown on the next page to receive the Help file that lists commands and useful information.

FTPMail Help message:

```
------------------------------------------------------------
To       : ftpmail@decwrl.dec.com
CC       :
Subject  :
_____

help
```

Here is a list of common FTPMail commands received from the Help request above.

Command	Description
ascii	Sets file type transfer to ASCII
binary	Sets file type transfer to binary (use for binary or compressed files)
btoa	Sends file using "binary to ascii" encoding
chrid <directory name>	Changes to directory named (only allowed one chdir per FTPMail session)
chunksize <size>	Splits reply into specified size-byte (default=64K)
compact	Compacts file to be transferred (using Huffman encoding)
compress	Compresses file to be transferred (using Lempel-Ziv encoding)
connect	Specify which FTP site to connect to. Defaults to gatekeeper.dec.com, anonymous.
dir	Long directory listing (filename, size, date)
get <file>	Get file specified (maximum 10 get requests per FTPMail session)
help	Sends document listing commands and helpful hints
index <keyword>	Search for the keyword in FTP server's index
ls	Short directory listing (just filenames)
quit	Ends requests and signals FTPMail server to ignore the rest of the email message (useful if you have an automatic signature file)
reply <mail address>	Set the reply address (since headers can be wrong)
uuencode	sends the file using "uuencode" process

A Sample FTPMail Session

The sample session below connects to the default FTP site **decwrl.dec.com**, specifies an ASCII file transfer from the FTP site **spie.org**, navigates to the *meetings* directory, and then downloads the file *exhibit_schedule.txt*. It then quits the "script" and ignores the automatic signature at the bottom of the message.

Notice that the subject line was left blank. Some FTPMail servers use the contents of the subject line in subsequent correspondence about the request. In

that case, entering a meaningful and attention-getting phrase would be helpful
in monitoring the progress of your request.

```
------------------------------------------------------------
To: ftpmail@sunsite.unc.edu
From: briant@henson.cc.wwu.edu (Brian Thomas)
------------------------------------------------------------
connect spie.org
ascii
uuencode
chdir [.meetings]
get exhibit_schedule.txt
quit

Brian Thomas
brian@spie.org
------------------------------------------------------------
```

Here is the status response I received a few moments later:

```
------------------------------------------------------------
From: File Transfer by Mail <ftpmail@SunSITE.Unc.EDU>
Date: Sat, 20 Aug 1994 18:35:09 -0400
To: briant@henson.cc.wwu.edu
Subject: <FTP EMAIL> response

<FTP EMAIL> response
ftpmail has received the following job from you:
      reply-to briant@henson.cc.wwu.edu
      open spie.org anonymous briant@henson.cc.wwu.edu
      mode ascii
      uuencode
      cd [.meetings]
      get exhibit_schedule.txt

ftpmail has queued your job as: 922108.7249
Your priority is 9 (0 = highest, 9 = lowest)
Requests to sunsite.unc.edu will be done before other
jobs.
There are 4 jobs ahead of this one in the queue.
2 ftpmail handlers available.

To remove send a message to ftpmail@sunsite.unc.edu
containing just:
delete 922108.7249
------------------------------------------------------------
```

Following this message was the file I requested from **spie.org**, as well as another message from the FTPMail server telling me my "job" was processed successfully. Seems a little overkill, but it's only a machine.

Just the FAQs

To get the FAQ listed below, send the command shown to

`mail-server@rtfm.mit.edu`

This is an e-mail server that will automatically send you the file you've re-quested. Send this command in the body of your e-mail message. *Remember that this server is Unix-based: Use upper- and lower-case letters exactly as shown.* You may also retrieve the files noted using FTP.

Mail Servers

Send the command:
`send pub/usenet/news.answers/mail/archive-servers/faq`

Note: The first portion of this FAQ lists software for running your own mail server; the second portion lists some public server addresses.

Chapter 6

DISCUSSION LISTS

Discussion lists, often called "listservs" (for software it's named after) or "mailing lists," are an essential communication tool on the Internet. Using only e-mail, discussion lists connect colleagues from around the world to discuss issues related to specific topics. The only requirement is that you have an Internet-accessible e-mail address. Discussion lists are especially useful in the sciences, since there are so many specialized interests that finding someone whose interests are similar is often difficult.

For the purpose of this chapter, I will use the term *discussion list* to refer to any e-mail type of list, including listservs and mailing lists. Later in this chapter I describe the different types of discussion lists.

When you join a discussion list, you are joining a group of people who also "subscribe" to the group. Basically, there's a "group e-mail address" that everyone sends messages to, and from there the message "explodes" to the entire group list. You and everyone else on the list receive messages sent to this e-mail address. You can choose to read, delete, or respond to any message you receive. You can also leave or "sign off" the list at any time.

Some people join a discussion list and never actually "talk," but rather just read the ongoing discussions. This is sometimes called "lurking," and is perfectly acceptable. In fact, it's a good idea to lurk on a new list for a while to see what the topics are, get the "tone" of the conversation, and watch for an FAQ posting. (Most discussion lists with an active Frequently Asked Questions document have it posted to the list on a regular basis.) On the other hand, you can jump into a conversation or "thread" on a list at any time. In many ways, discussion lists are like bulletin boards, except that you don't have to go somewhere to read them. They come to you instead.

Moderated v. Unmoderated Lists

The content and quality of the messages in a listserv are dependent on the people participating. In some cases, a list will be *moderated* by one person knowledgeable in the subject area and will filter out unwanted or inappropriate messages. The moderator then forwards the messages to the subscribers.

Finding Discussion Lists

There are easily tens of thousands of discussion lists active today, and more are added or changed all the time.

The first place to look for discussion lists is right here in the Resources portion of this book. Within each of the technology areas covered here, there are a number of discussion lists shown, along with some further information where available.

In addition, listservs through the BITNET network are indexed and can be queried by e-mail. To find a listserv of interest send e-mail to:

    listserv@bitnic.bitnet

with the message

    list global/keyword

where the keyword is a topic you are interested in. For example:

    list global/sensors

In response you will receive a roster of all the lists that use your keyword to describe their topical focus.

Listservs v. Mailing Lists

As I've noted earlier, the terms "listserv" and "mailing list" are both used to describe an e-mail discussion list. Note, however, that the term "listserv" itself describes a specific and common set of software commands for using the **listserv** software on the BITNET computer network (see below). However, you will also see "mailing list" or "listserver" used to describe listserv-like discussion groups that don't use the BITNET's listserv software. In some cases, the mailing lists are handled manually by a list manager.

Despite the fact that they serve the same purpose, the difference between listservs and mailing lists in the way they operate is significant enough that we'll discuss them separately here.

Listservs

When I first encountered listserv addresses on the Internet, I thought they were very confusing. Thus, I am motivated to explain them clearly here. Compounding my confusion was the fact that few books I've read tackle this issue with any breadth, yet for the science professional, listservs and discussion lists in general are one of the best tools for meeting colleagues with like interests in a useful forum. If you are interested in joining any of the thousands of listserv discussion lists active today in the scientific community, this section is here to save you a lot of time and confusion.

The term "listserv" refers to software developed for IBM/VM computers running on BITNET ("Because It's Time NETwork"), which for many years was a network unto itself, but which now is virtually indistinguishable from the Internet. The listserv software automates the process of managing a discussion list. This is why some Internet purists will squirm whenever the word *listserv* is used to describe a mailing list system that does not actually use the listserv software. However, for most of us the distinction is only a matter of knowing how to join (subscribe), participate in, and quit (unsubscribe) the list.

The other distinction is addressing. The key thing to remember about listserv discussion lists is that they're still somehow associated with BITNET, and therefore the Internet addresses you use to connect with the lists are not standard for everyone.

Understanding Listservs

Listservs usually have two addresses associated with each list. The *listserv address* begins with the word **listserv** and is used to subscribe and unsubscribe to the list. All other administrative type requests are also sent to the listserv address. The *list address* begins with the name of the list and is used when participating in discussions on the list. The thing to remember here is to send your subscription requests to the listserv address, *not* the list address. If you send your subscription request to the actual group address, your message may be sent erroneously to all the people in the group. Not a great way to introduce yourself.

Again—send your "subscribe" message to the **listserv@** address, not the list address itself. **This is very important.**

Here's an example. In the Resources section of this book you've found the following discussion list:

astro
astro@gitvm1
Astronomy Discussion List

The first line is the actual name of the discussion list—what they call themselves. The last line is obviously the list's discussion topic.

The second line is the important one—the *listserv address*. This is *not* the list address. If you send a message to this address, you are sending it to the entire list, therefore if you want to subscribe to the list, you would need to send your message to the *listserv address*, which would be **listserv@gitvm1**. I know I'm beating this topic into the ground, but it's important.

Now here's the other important part. Notice the Internet address for this list. There's something wrong. We learned in Chapter 4 that all Internet addresses have a domain suffix such as **.edu** or **.org**. The addresses above do not have domains, so unless you're actually on BITNET yourself, you'll probably need to add something to this address to make it a valid Internet address. I say *probably* because it's not true in all cases. This is where discussion lists get a little murky.

Understanding Listserv Gateways

Here's what you need to know. In most books and lists on discussion lists (including this one), you'll find that they list addresses such as the one above. I suspect this is a legacy issue from when the BITNET was more of a closed system (there are still a lot of people who are on the BITNET system in some manner). Regardless, to subscribe to one of these lists (that is, one you find without a domain suffix), you'll need to add something to get your message over to the BITNET computer that controls the listserv.

There are two ways to do this. First, try adding **.bitnet** to the listserv address. For example:

listserv@gitvm1.bitnet

If this works—great. If it doesn't, it's because your particular location on the Internet doesn't quite mesh with BITNET. The alternative in this case is to try sending your message through one of the BITNET *gateways*, which are computers on the Internet that will (if you use the proper syntax) redirect your message to the BITNET computer that controls the listserv you're looking for. Here's the syntax using the example above and a gateway computer at City University of New York (CUNY):

listserv%gitvm1@cunyvm.cuny.edu

All you're doing now is changing **listserv@gitvm1** to **listserve%gitvm1**, and then sending the whole message to a standard Internet address (**cunyvm.cuny.edu**).

Here are some other listserv gateways that you can use:

> **cornellc.cit.cornell.edu**
> **cunyvm.cuny.edu**
> **mitvma.mit.edu**
> **vm1.nodak.edu**

Finally, I should note again that use of these gateways and the "trick" of adding **.bitnet** to the listserv address do not apply to anyone already on BITNET. In that case, you would simply send your message to the listserv address listed without the domain suffix (e.g., **listserv@gitvm1**).

Subscribing to Listservs

Subscribing to listservs is easy once you get the addressing issue out of the way. Continuing with our example above, you would send your subscription message to the listserv address, **listserv@gitvm1**, modified as necessary as noted above. Most listservs require only the word "subscribe," the *list name*, and a first and last name (or an e-mail address, if you prefer; however, some require *two* words). All of these go in the message body. The Subject line is ignored.

For example, if Al Gore wanted to join the **astro** listserv, his subscription message would look like this:

```
------------------------------------------------------------
To       : listserv@gitvm1.bitnet
CC       :
Subject  :
------------------------------------------------------------
subscribe astro al gore
```

The listserv computer would then automatically send Gore a notification that it had received his subscription request.

There are a few different types of subscription processes. Some listservs will add you to their distribution immediately. Others will ask that you confirm your address by responding to their notification (within a specified amount of time). And others will refer your request to a person, moderator, or manager who will then add you to the list. I've even encountered some that send you a message that says something like, "Your subscription request has been received. To confirm, please enter a password in the space shown and forward this message back to xyz@some_address." This kind of procedure usually means the list is moderated and that the moderator wishes to control who subscribes, usually for the benefit of the legitimate listserv members.

Most likely, in addition to a subscription confirmation, you'll also receive an automated "Welcome" message. It will describe how to participate in discussions, list reference material if appropriate, and describe some of the listserv features. *Keep this message.* Save it in a e-mail folder or on your hard drive. Later on, if you decide you want to unsubscribe to the list, you'll need the information in this message.

Unsubscribing to a Listserv, and Other Commands

If you join a listserv and decide later to leave or *unsubscribe,* you need to send a **signoff** command to the listserv address (the same address you used to subscribe). Don't forget to tell the listserv computer the name of the list you wish to signoff from:

signoff astro

Listservs have many other services available through the e-mail system, such as file retrieval (e-mail servers). To learn more about these, send the word help to any **listserv@** address and you will receive more information.

Mailing Lists

As I mentioned earlier, there are also listserv-like mailing lists managed either automatically or manually. These mailing lists also have at least two addresses, a subscription address (similar to the **listserv@** address) and the actual discussion list address. Many use the form

listname-request@an.internet.address

for the subscription address. In this case the list is most likely managed manually (the subscription requests sent to the **-request** address are manually added to the distribution list).

There are also other software programs that use listserv-like addresses in the form of

majordomo@an.internet.address

and

listproc@an.internet.address

Though these are run by a software program, some elements are run manually. In either case, a concise, syntactically correct subscription request is the most efficient means to join a list.

The differences between listservs and mailing lists appear in the other features of the software. For example, to leave a list some mailing lists respond to the command **unsubscribe** or **unsub**. Others will only respond to the command **signoff**.

Most mailing lists will respond to the command **help** when sent to the subscription address, and will return to you a list of commands you can use for that list. Useful information about commands is also usually included in the "Welcome" message you receive after subscribing. Some welcome messages go so far as listing the name and e-mail address of the moderator or manager of the list.

Subscribing to Mailing Lists

Subscribing to a mailing list is not much different from subscribing to a listserv, except that there is no single standard. In most cases the addressing system is exactly the same; however, make sure you know what the proper address for subscribing is for every list you join. It may be completely different from anything you've seen before.

Usually, if your "subscribe" message is missing a phrase or is not listed in the correct order, the mailing list will simply send you an error message with more complete instructions. Remember to use the listserv-like address, not the discussion list address. Here is a sample subscription request to **gps@tws4.si.com**, a mailing list for anyone interested in global positioning systems. Note that we send it to **gps-request**, not the list name itself.

```
-----------------------------------------------------------
To: gps-request@tws4.si.com
CC:
Subject :
-----------------------------------------------------------
subscribe gps bill clinton
```

Discussion List Netiquette

The same guidelines discussed for e-mail and Usenet *netiquette* ("net etiquette") apply here as well. Here are some additional guidelines to help you avoid the usual mistakes:

- Make sure you post your administrative requests (subscribe, help, etc.) to the correct e-mail address. There's nothing more annoying than seeing someone send a Help message to the actual discussion list address.

- Before ever posting to the discussion list, find out if there's an FAQ (Frequently Asked Questions) document for the group, and if there is, read it.

- Post only appropriate messages to the group. Keep personal messages between you and the person. Sometimes you or someone else will start a valid discussion on the list that then becomes too specific or personal, at which point you should take the conversation "off line," which means "stop posting to the list and continue your discussion with the other person via e-mail directly." This is especially true if a more emotional discussion on the topic develops. Keep *flame wars* off line.

- Be careful when using the "Reply" feature of your e-mail software when reading a message posted to the group so that you don't accidentally send a personal message to the entire group. Make sure your message is going where you want it to.

- When you see someone else make one of the mistakes listed above, try to direct the person in the right direction. Don't ridicule them for their errors. It doesn't do anyone any good. If the list is moderated well, you'll never see inappropriate or misplaced messages. If the list is unmoderated, do your best to play "benevolent guide."

- Keep blatant commercial messages out of the group unless you know the information is of interest to the group, or the information is in response to a request from someone else on the list. And even so, in the latter case, it's often best to send the information directly to the requester instead of to the whole group.

Electronic Journals and Newsletters

In addition to discussion lists, there are a variety of online journals and newsletters that use e-mail as the distribution mechanism. These publications are sometimes electronic-only, or they can also be a subset of a paper publication. Many are refereed, or at least moderated. They usually have an established frequency, and can sometimes be accessed through an FTP site or gopher server as well. Some even charge a fee for subscribing, in which case you would send your check to a postal address, along with your e-mail address, and then be subscribed to the publication by the list manager, editor, or moderator.

As with listservs and mailing lists, to subscribe to an "e-journal" or newsletter, you must first find the electronic publication's address and the commands used. In any list of such publications, this information should be provided. The Science Resources portion of this book lists numerous online publications and provides information on how to subscribe.

Just the FAQs

To get the FAQ listed below, send the command shown to

```
mail-server@rtfm.mit.edu
```

This is an e-mail server that will automatically send you the file you've re-quested. Send this command in the body of your e-mail message. *Remember that this server is Unix-based: Use upper- and lower-case letters exactly as shown.* You may also retrieve the files noted using FTP.

Finding Mailing Lists

Send the command

```
send pub/usenet/news.answers/mail/mailing-lists/*
```

(Warning: the above command will result in delivery of a master list of mailing lists that is very long and will arrive in multiple mail messages.)

Chapter 7

FILES AND FORMATS

This chapter explains a variety of file types you'll find on the Internet, and how to identify and use them.

ASCII v. Binary

This is background information for the sections that follow. This topic seems somewhat esoteric at first glance, but it's extremely important for anyone who wishes to use much of the scientific and engineering reference material available on the Internet.

ASCII (American Standard Code for Information Interchange) is the accepted standard for information exchange. The elemental unit in computer communications is the *byte,* which can represent 256 values, so correspondingly there are 256 ASCII characters (also known as "8-bit ASCII"). ASCII is used to map a value to a character. So, for example, letter A is 65, and therefore the letter Z is 90 (25 letters after A).

While different computers never seem to agree on anything, one thing they do generally agree on is what is represented in the first 128 values of ASCII. The first 33 values are control codes, which are used by terminals and interfaces in consistent manners. For example, ASCII character 7 is a "bell," and therefore to make a computer terminal beep, all a program has to do is output an ASCII value of 7. The remaining 95 values of the 128 are used to represent printable characters such as letters of the alphabet, numerals, and basic punctuation marks.

On the other side of the fence, there are still the 128 *additional* ASCII characters that signify different things to different computers, so that an umlaut over the letter *u* on one computer might translate to a little rabbit symbol on another. Typographers have a field day with this last 128.

This is where the binary part comes in. Messaging systems intended for use on multiple computer types (e.g., e-mail) use the first 128 characters of ASCII. These are the *lingua franca* of computers. Programs and non-text images are represented with ASCII as well, but these use all 256 possible characters, and therefore if viewed as "raw" text they would look like garbage. These files are normally called *binary* files to distinguish themselves from human-readable, or ASCII, files. (Minor point: this refers to the *elemental* relationship: a binary file, when parsed through a suitable word processor, may be entirely readable.)

Binary files don't read well, and usually don't propagate well through messaging systems such as Internet e-mail. As we'll discuss in this chapter, this is the reason standards exist for further encrypting raw binary data. The process of *encoding* is used to convert this raw binary data to the 95 human-readable ASCII values, thereby allowing the user to incorporate, transfer, and edit such messages with very simple text editors and messaging systems.

What's the Point?

To use e-mail to send or receive any file with binary characters, you will have to *encode* (on sending) or *decode* (on receiving) the file. The Internet's e-mail protocol does not recognize binary characters; it sees only the human-readable ASCII characters and everything else discarded during transmission. Read on.

Document and File Types

Throughout this book and on the Internet, you'll hear the words *document* and *file* used generically and interchangeably to describe just about anything you can store in computer memory. This includes, but is not limited to:

- simple ASCII text documents,
- complex documents stored in a proprietary format such as WordPerfect, Excel, and PageMaker,
- digital images stored in either proprietary formats such as Photoshop or Illustrator, or in one of many standard compression formats such as GIF, TIFF, EPS, and JPEG,
- digital sound files stored in a variety of compression formats,
- digital movies stored as *QuickTime* files or a similar format,
- *executable* files that are part of, or complete, software programs.

On the Internet you will find literally millions of files to *download* (transfer to your computer), and it helps to know a little bit about these files before wasting your time downloading something that you can't read or use.

Formatted Text

We've already talked about ASCII text and binary files. A formatted text file is any file saved in a format that uses anything more than just the ASCII letters, numbers, and punctuation. This means any file that isn't specifically saved as "text only" in your word processing software, and it definitely means any spreadsheet, desktop publishing, drawing, painting, or presentation software. Basically, you have to go out of your way nowadays to save something that doesn't use some kind of formatting.

Images and Graphics

There are hundreds of software programs that will create some kind of picture—black-and-white drawings or illustrations, color pictures, digital photographs, and so on. Therefore there are also hundreds of *formats* in which to save image files (I use the terms *image* and *graphics* inter-changeably).

Image files are almost always binary, and they take up huge amounts of space. A full-screen (640 × 480 pixel resolution), photographic quality (24 bits per pixel), uncompressed photograph will occupy more than one megabyte (1 MB) of your hard drive. Compressed, its size drops to 100 K (your mileage may vary).

The other reason to compress is, of course, speed. A 1-MB file will take ten times longer than a 100-K file to get from point A to B. And since a lot of us pay by the hour for our online endeavors, compression can translate directly into money saved.

So, on the Internet, compression is king, and the vast majority of images you'll find will be in one of three common image types: GIF, JPEG, and TIFF. All of these have become file format and compression *standards,* and as such are also used extensively outside of the Internet, especially in the desktop publishing and digital imaging industries. Some, such as GIF, are always compressed, whereas others, such as TIFF, have uncompressed formats as well.

GIF Images

GIF stands for Graphic Interchange Format and is a standard format for images that was developed by CompuServe to be a device-independent method of storing pictures. It includes Lempel-Ziv-Welch (LZW) compression, which makes the files fairly small. GIF is a *lossless* compression, meaning that the act of compressing/decompressing does not degrade the image quality in any way. The GIF format is by far the most prevalent for displaying graphics on the World Wide Web. GIF files are usually recognizable by a *.GIF* or *.gif* filename extension.

JPEG Images

JPEG stands for Joint Photographic Experts Group (the original name of the committee that wrote the standard). Its increasing popularity is based on its high (actually, variable) compression ratio, and it appears that it will replace the GIF format altogether within a few years. Unlike GIF, however, JPEG files are usually *lossy,* meaning that they sacrifice some of their resolution during the compression process, due to dithering or averaging of individual pixel groupings in an image. This makes JPEG most effective for images with a pixel depth of at least four bits (16 grays or colors). JPEG files usually have *.JPG* or *.jpg* as filename extensions.

TIFF Images

TIFF stands for Tagged Image File Format. It is widely used in the desktop publishing field because of its flexibility and compatibility with a variety of software programs. However, for a number of reasons it has not become a common format for image files on the Internet, at least not to the degree JPEG has reached. TIFF files usually have *.TIF* or *.tif* file extensions.

Here is a sample of file format types and their extensions (so you can recognize them when you see them on the Internet):

.arc	ARCed file (archive file that contains many other files)
.arq	DOS compression format (competes with ARC and ZIP)
.bin	Binary file, used in many situations
.doc	Document file (ambiguous, often ASCII text or MS Word)
.exe	Executable program file (either system specific or self-extracting
.gif	Image file (Graphics Interchange Format)
.gz	GNU compress (popular Unix format)
.hlp	Help file (sometimes ASCII)
.hqx	BinHex file (binary data coded to ASCII—typically Macintosh)
.lzh	For files archived with LHA.EXE
.me	Not really a format, but usually stands for text, as in "read.me"
.ps	PostScript file
.pkg	Applelink Package file
.sea	Self expanding archive file (unstuffs itself)
.sit	Stuffit file(s) from Aladdin
.tar	Compressed with Unix tar (tape archive) utility
.tex	T_eX source file
.tif	Tagged Image File Format (TIFF)
.txt	Text file (generic ASCII)
.uue	uuencoded (binary data coded to ASCII) file
.Z	Compressed using Unix *compress* software
.zip	Zipped file(s) compressed with PKZip or similar
.zoo	Zoo file(s) compressed

PostScript

PostScript is a remarkable *page description language* developed by Adobe Systems to describe pages of text and images with ASCII-based coding. It is perhaps the most versatile and universal language for communicating with printers. It is capable of drawing to computer screens and any kind of drawing device.

Many documents available on the Internet are available in both ASCII text and

PostScript versions. PostScript is also the format of choice for saving figures and images for journal submissions, as well as other publications. PostScript files usually have a *.ps* filename extension.

If you download a PostScript file, you'll need to send it to a PostScript-compatible printer, which will have the necessary software to "decode" and print it.

While there are some PostScript *previewing* programs available, most are in the "pioneering" stages and should be left to the People Who Care.

Although some PostScript files are supposed to be 7-bit ASCII, don't count on it. Always transfer using methods appropriate for binary files.

Like any good universal standard, there's more than one version. In fact, with PostScript, there are not only multiple versions (PostScript1, PostScript2, etc.), but different *flavors* of those versions. So, if your document doesn't print correctly, it's probably because the file is formatted in a version of PostScript that your printer doesn't speak, or because there are fonts encoded in the PostScript document that your printer does not have. Sometimes missing fonts will be converted to a similar available font, and other times they'll be converted to something really hideous, like Apple's Monaco typeface.

Encapsulated PostScript
Finally, there's *EPS,* or Encapsulated PostScript. This is a separate standard for importing and exporting PostScript language files in all environments. It is usually a single-page PostScript language program that describes an illustration. The purpose of the EPS file is to be included as an illustration in other PostScript language page descriptions. You probably won't run into too many of these on the Internet, but if you ever want to convert a manuscript or other publication to the PostScript format, you might use the EPS format to save your figures and images. EPS files usually have an *.eps* or *.EPS* filename extension.

T_eX and Derivatives

T_eX (pronounced "tek") is a software system used to typeset text, especially text containing mathematics. It is quickly becoming the de facto standard format for submitting manuscripts for most scientific journals and reference publications.

Over the years the original T_eX standard has been converted to numerous sets of *macros* with names like LaT$_e$X, RevT$_e$X, VorT$_e$X, and BibT$_e$X, all designed to make it easier for the writer to format a paper or other typeset documents in T_eX.

There are also style sheets distributed by publishers that can be used to format a paper for a particular publication. For example, the American Mathematical

Society publishes and distributes style sheets for submitting to the AMS's journals. For the truly determined, there is even a program called METAFONT that allows users to design their own fonts.

Emerging Formats

In the last few years a number of new document formats have hit the street, all designed to be the next "killer app" on our way to the elusive "paperless office." The most notable of these is a category loosely called *portable documents*.

One of the biggest hassles with computers is there are so many of them, and so any document you create with your software requires that someone else have either the same software or some other software that will translate it. Portable documents are supposed to change all that by letting you convert your WordPerfect or Photoshop or Mathematica documents as a generic "cross-platform" document that can be read on any computer. And not only can you create multipage archives, but you can add hypertext links, electronic sticky notes, and all sorts of other features. Needless to say, the technical obstacles here are not negligible.

Nevertheless, the concept is alluring, so much so that large software companies like Adobe and WordPerfect, as well as smaller ones like No Hands Software, have started their own standards, and the race is on.

Adobe's product, called *Acrobat,* draws on that company's already pervasive PostScript language, and requires that you have a *reader* or *viewer module* on your computer in order to use a file formatted in Acrobat's *PDF* (Portable Document Format). The PDF documents can be read on any computer with a reader module installed. Adobe distributes free reader software modules for many types of computer operating systems, and it's also being integrated into some World Wide Web browsers such as Netscape as an *inline viewer* module.

Other products, such as No Hands Software's Common Ground, focus on the opposite approach: they build a reader module into every document created, with surprisingly little overhead added to the document, thanks to some built-in compression. What you end up with is virtually a software program that will "run" your document on a variety of computers.

I mention these examples here and now because, despite their early quirkiness and lack of standardization, they do have some tremendous promise for resolving perhaps the toughest obstacle in scientific publishing today, specifically, how to distribute electronic documents in a universally readable format, in a way that maintains the integrity of all the text, figures, equations, and images. Already on the Internet there are files with *.pdf* and *.cgi* extensions.

Encoding

When to Use Encoding

One of the nice things about e-mail is that just about any computer can read it, because e-mail is nothing but letters and numbers and maybe some punctuation here and there. And in order to make the Internet's e-mail system accessible to many different computers, the language, or *protocol*, used to transfer e-mail between them only allows those first 128 ASCII characters. Anything else is not seen and is therefore lost during transmission.

So now what happens when you want to send your WordPerfect for Windows document or Lotus spreadsheet to a friend also on the Internet? Or maybe you want to send a nifty *Star Trek* trivia game you found, or a picture of your latest home-built particle accelerator? Well, one option, if you can arrange it, is to use FTP (file transfer protocol), since FTP will allow files to be sent in binary format without modification. (We talk about FTP at length in Chapter 9.)

But what if FTP is not an option? The solution is to *encode* the document using one of the many software utilities (programs) designed specifically to make an 8-bit binary file look like a 7-bit ASCII file, for the purpose of transmitting it as part of an e-mail message. When the other person receives the message with the encoded file, they in turn must *decode* the message with a similar utility.

Standard Encoding Methods

There are two common encoding methods you'll find used on the Internet, plus a new, more integrated scheme gaining rapid acceptance.

UUEncode

The most common Internet encoding scheme is called *uuencoding* (pronounced "you you encoding"), originally developed for computers running the Unix operating system (UUCP—Unix-to-Unix CoPy) was the precursor to today's Unix *sendmail* program, and it used uuencoding. Metaphorically speaking, uuencoding puts a protective shell around the file so that it may travel as an e-mail message. This "shell" adds approximately 35% more to the total size of the file. Once decoded, it is recognizable in its original format. Files converted to the uuencoded format generally have a file extension of *.uu* or sometimes *.uue* — it's up to the person or software doing the encoding.

One sure way to identify how a file is encoded is to open it up in a text editor and look at it. A uuencoded file starts out something like this—usually with the statement "Begin 644" at the top of the file:

```
------------------------------------------------------------
begin 644 Picture_of_My_Cat

M3W1H97((@4G5S<VEA;B!796)S97)V97)S(%1H92!C;VYN96T:6]N<R!T:.&%T
S_0?EZQ\':#!!%%B5HHHAR:DER:DTE1MHT60>GEYGZGVW$N<)JBD9K0,0IX+$Q$H
\.G=FY<<Z&GE59#(4<))8_X:%M^XGXQH(34S"K$T6'QO**(516B)?6_EW\Y_06%
NW'VC@IZ8B4;J8TT.VOM0DEOY1VOY_+1]>)9PJB;3>01:#&64(NFS[>VX_7?U+
\)>"1%02JL#H(M$^W3(E2[+&TBB2IATN'#]?\A8?#!W[<%TU0CR2A54($UF[ESK
._ZA1WM_'?NEOB4E(T@6&(M&B&)Y.GS#0@_3^NW?B0*>*)C3R[&R,YC31(UKD
=?UVM_P![^8<>4ZQ1_#T@:E,<8U45*(6D=XS*7*I()+3???87]+VM_7B3AU!A=;
M)'18DZ1P26I9I3#K6W>^CU]Y.GS#0@_3^NW?B0*>*)
```

(and so on...)
```
------------------------------------------------------------
```

(A word of warning: if you ever open an encoded file like this to see what it is, don't modify the file in any way or you'll corrupt it. Just close the file without saving. If you use the "save" feature in your word processor, chances are it will add formatting to the file that will also corrupt it.)

BinHex

The second common encoding format, known as *binhex*, is used specifically for Macintosh files. Macintosh files are unique in the computer world because they contain (often, but not always) two *forks*—a *data fork*, and a *resource fork*. The former contains text characters only, while the latter contains all the other stuff, such as binary computer code, formatting, etc. I'm not going to delve any further into this explanation, but suffice it to say that nearly all Macintosh files you find on the Internet are encoded as binhex files. This doesn't mean if you have a Macintosh you can't read uuencoded files. There are plenty of utilities out there to handle that conversion. It just means if you have a Macintosh and you want to send or receive other Macintosh files, you can choose either binhex or uuencode. Both will do the job.

Like uuencoded files, you can identify a binhex file by looking at it in a word processor. They always start out like this:

```
------------------------------------------------------------
(This file must be converted with BinHex 4.0)

:S_0?EZQ\':#!!%B5HHHARGDETR:DTE1MHT60>GEYGZGVW$N<)JBD9K0,0IX+$Q$
H\.G=FY<<Z&GE59#(4<))8_X:%M^XGXQH(34S"K$T6'QO*(516B)?6_EW\Y_06
%NW'VC@IZ8B4;J8TT.VOM0DEOY1VOY_+1]>)9PJB;3>01:#&64(NFS[>VX_7?U
+\)>"1%02JL#H(M$^W3(E2[+&TBB2IATN'#]?\A8?#!W[<%TU0CR2A54($UF[ES
K._ZA1WM_'?NEOB4E#(T@6&(M&B&)Y.GS#0@_3^NW?B0*>*)C3R[&R,YC31(UK
D=?UVM_P![^8<>4ZQ1_#T@:E,<8U45*(6D=XS*7*I()+3  (and so
on...)
```

```
------------------------------------------------------------
```

The actual content of the file starts and ends with a colon (:), so if you look at a file this way and don't see colons on both ends, the file is corrupt and you should try downloading it again. It could also be just a bad file, in which case the originator will need to binhex the original file again.

By the way, the warning stated above for uuencoded files is true for binhex files as well. If you look, don't save it unless you know what you're doing.

MIME

The new kid on the block is something called MIME (Multipurpose Internet Mailing Extension). Instead of using a separate utility for encoding/ decoding, the MIME standard is being built into e-mail software to both encode outgoing messages and decode incoming ones. MIME relies on the use of standardized filename extensions (see table earlier in this chapter) to accomplish the task. As more mail software incorporates the standard, manual encoding/decoding of binary files will become an automated process.

UUEncoding Files

More frequently, e-mail software on Internet host computers is or has the ability to be linked to Unix's **uuencode** and **uudecode** commands. If this is the case with your Internet connection, you'll probably never have to think about encoding or decoding. It will happen automatically.

But, if you need to know how to uuencode a file, here's how it's done.

You'll use the following format:

```
uuencode your_filename temp_filename > new_filename.uu
```

Here's a real-life example: I have a file in my directory called *russian_gateways.wp* that is saved in a WordPerfect format. I want to send it to a colleague in Salzburg, but I need to send it to her using e-mail as she does not have FTP access. If I attach it without encoding it, the file will arrive with all the WordPerfect attributes removed, and it will be virtually unreadable.

Here's a look at the file in my directory:

```
% ls -l

total 176
drwx——   3 n8348220    512 Jan  2  1994 News
drwxr-x—x 2 n8348220    512 Feb 10  1993 bin
-rw-r-r-  1 n8348220 86528 Sep 21 11:14 course_rev1
-rw——    1 n8348220  2859 Aug 25 19:56 inbox
-rw——    1 n8348220 11366 Oct 19  1993 log
drwx——   2 n8348220    512 Sep 23 21:17 mail
-rw——    1 n8348220  1621 Nov  4  1993 protections
-rw-r-r-  1 n8348220    985 Sep 21 11:11 russian_gateways.wp
```

Now, to encode it, I would type:

```
% uuencode russian_gateways.wp gateways.wp > gate.uu
```

What I've done here is told Unix to take a file named *russian_gateways.wp* and, using a new (temporary) filename of *gateways.wp*, create the encoded file *gate.uu*. In other words, you save it under another name before encoding it, in order to leave your original file unchanged.

Let's list the file directory again to see if it worked:

```
% ls -l
total 178
drwx——   3 n8348220     512 Jan  2  1994 News
drwxr-x–x 2 n8348220     512 Feb 10  1993 bin
-rw-r–r–  1 n8348220     586 Sep 21 11:12 cessna.gif.hqx
-rw-r–r–  1 n8348220 86528 Sep 21 11:14 course_rev1
-rw——    1 n8348220   1385 Sep 28 05:41 gate.uu
-rw——    1 n8348220     859 Aug 25 19:56 inbox
-rw——    1 n8348220 11366 Oct 19  1993 log
drwx——   2 n8348220     512 Sep 23 21:17 mail
-rw-r–r–  1 n8348220 70134 Sep 21 11:17 pdial.txt
-rw——    1 n8348220   1621 Nov  4  1993 protections
-rw-r–r–  1 n8348220     985 Sep 21 11:11 russian_gateways.wp
%
```

Note that the new encoded file, *gate.uu*, is about a third larger than the original (1385 bytes v. 985 bytes). This is because the uuencoding process adds about that much as part of the encoding algorithm.

Again, the reason we assign a new filename (*gateways.wp*) is to protect our original file before encoding it. Note that this is also the filename that the file will become when someone *decodes* the file.

If for some reason we wanted to see what the encoded file looks like, we could look at it using the **more** command, like this:

```
% more gate.uu

begin 644 gateways.wfw
M3W1H97((@4G5S<VEA;B!796)S97)V97)S(%1H92!!C;VN96T;6]N<R!R:&%T
M(&%R92!M;;W)E(')E;;&%E8FQE(&%R92!S:&]W;B!I;B!B;B!V;D.B!296QC;VT@
M3VYL:6YE("A`A-;W=C;W<I(&%M+3TDM."!F;VT<R!R960@;i;U5E;F1E9%T`36]S
M8V]]W($QQ88F5R=75R&;75;M($yA~;W=C;W<;W<I&(%M+3TEM."!F;VO<R!R96-O;6UE
M;;'1S>6X@Q@25S>YS;&ET71%71E(&R]F($YU8VV8F5O87($`4A%.E8S8Y]S8]S&V]N=5
M;W-C;;;W<;V<;W<2@8VN@86RY9&ET69N2]F($;9E69]597%F($5F($`$]0@?E8R5
M;FEE;=R)S:&]W;B!I;B!I;B!B:&]W;&%E(&%R92!C;VUM(&F]N(&M]O&;]O&@;VU
M;;FF%E7;>66]R)S:&]W.'!5.E8R8]S8]S&]W?!N@U-@;U5E;F1E&9@!?\`@35D
```

end

The file has a *begin* and an *end* statement. This is what the decoding software will use to know when to start and stop decoding the file as it's inserted into the e-mail message I'll send my colleague in Salzburg. At this point all I would have to do is attach this file to an e-mail message using my e-mail software's Attach File feature. Note that while this function will vary slightly with various e-mail software interfaces, the basic purpose is the same: you will take the entire contents of this *gate.uu* file and insert it into the body of your e-mail message. Since the file is now simple ASCII text, it will arrive at its destination intact, where the recipient can decode it into its original WordPerfect format.

Decoding Files

Decoding files is even easier. If you receive an e-mail message with an attached uuencoded file, first save the e-mail message as a text file. Note that many e-mail software interfaces will recognize the incoming message as having an attached file and will then ask you if you want to save the file. Either way, after your file is saved in your Unix directory, just type uudecode and then the filename:

```
% uudecode gate.uu
```

After a few seconds (depending on how big the file is), you'll again see your command prompt, at which time you can list your directory and see the new file:

```
% ls -l
total 179
drwx------    3 n8348220      512 Jan  2  1994 News
drwxr-x-x    2 n8348220      512 Feb 10  1993 bin
-rw-r--r--   1 n8348220      586 Sep 21 11:12 cessna.gif.hqx
-rw-r--r--   1 n8348220    86528 Sep 21 11:14 course_rev1
-rw------    1 n8348220     1385 Sep 28 05:41 gate.uu
-rw------    1 n8348220     2859 Aug 25 19:56 inbox
-rw------    1 n8348220    11366 Oct 19  1993 log
drwx------    2 n8348220      512 Sep 23 21:17 mail
-rw-r--r--   1 n8348220    70134 Sep 21 11:17 pdial.txt
-rw------    1 n8348220     1621 Nov  4  1993 protections
-rw-r--r--   1 n8348220      985 Sep 28 06:05 gateways.wp
%
```

Note that the original file, *gate.uu*, is still there, along with the new file, *gateways.wp*.

At this point you're ready to use the WordPerfect file, which will contain all the formatting from the original (fonts, tables, styles, equations, etc.). If you still need to move the file to another computer (for example, your computer at home, which has the WordPerfect software you'll need to view the file), you can download it via modem or FTP. Note that when you use your modem to download the file, you do not need to encode/decode it. This is because the software used to transfer files via modem does in fact recognize all characters, not just the 7-bit ASCII text characters. And of course with FTP, just make sure you transfer it as a binary file (see the chapter on FTP for more information).

Of course, you could have also downloaded the encoded file directly to another computer first and then decoded on that computer, providing you had software to decode it. Even though uuencoding is a Unix feature, there are free- and shareware utilities for most personal computers that will allow you to uuencode and uudecode files. But it's probably faster and easier to do on your Unix Internet host computer.

Compression

Chances are you already use or at have at least encountered some form of file compression. DOS/Windows users have PKZip and PackIt, Macintosh users have Stuffit or Compact Pro, and Unix users have **compress** or **tar**. And that's just naming a few. On top of all this we have compression methods for image files, such as GIF, JPEG, and even MPEG for movie files.

Just about everything you'll see on the Internet is compressed in some way, since disk space is a precious commodity, and online time costs money. Downloading a huge uncompressed file will cost you more online time than a smaller compressed version of the same file.

Once again, the name of the game here is variety. Fortunately we have a couple things in our favor. The first is standardized file extensions, so common in the DOS world, which serve well to tell us what someone has done to a file so that we can attempt to undo it. The second is that there are a number of utilities for each computer platform that will convert files into their original precompressed format, even files compressed on a different computer type.

Compression Methods

Because compression methods are (or least were originally) specific to different computer types and operating systems, I'm not going to talk about them too much here, except to give my usual Unix examples for those of you with Internet access through a Unix computer.

I tend to divide the use of compression on the Internet into two categories:

1. Compression of files that can (eventually) be used on any computer, such as plain text files, images, and formats such as WordPerfect or Excel, which are often readily translated by similar software on a different computer (e.g., you can import a Word for Windows file into WordPerfect for the Macintosh).

2. Compression of files that are specifically designed to work on only one kind of computer, such as computer programs, often called *applications* or *executables*.

Generally compression isn't a problem, since there are many tools out there for each computer system to compress and decompress files in the "standards" established for those computers. Note, however, that there are numerous "standards" for each computer type, just as there are different word processors and spreadsheets for your computer.

However, the Internet is a homogeneous network, connecting computers of all types. The only thing they all have in common is the way they talk to each other. This means you can transfer a file to your computer with great ease, only to find out you can't translate it. Right?

Well, kind of. First, if you have a PC running Windows, chances are you're not interested in downloading any shareware programs designed to run on Unix computers. Second, as we've already discussed, image files are generally one of three formats—JPEG, TIFF, and GIF, which are not only already compressed (usually), but also viewable using common utilities available for most computers.

However, there are times when you may want to view a file or maybe a group of files created by someone on their Unix word processor, and you have a Macintosh or Windows PC. Fear not, as for most computers there are also some smart utilities that let you decompress files from different kinds of computers. For more information about utilities for Macintosh or Windows utilities, see the "Just the FAQs" section at the end of this chapter.

Unix File Compression

Now for our Unix examples. Most Unix computers have a number of programs available for compressing files. There are also utilities for grouping files together in an archive that allow you to compress only one file that contains many other files within it.

We'll show some examples of some of the more common Unix compression and archiving utilities.

Using Unix *compress* and *uncompress*

Unix's compress and uncompress program is widely available and used. You can usually spot one by the .Z filename extension.

Here's a directory listing with three files of the same size.

```
% ls -l
total 9
-rw-r--r--  1 root    root          0 Sep 27 22:40 compress
-rw-r--r--  1 root    root       2167 Sep 27 22:39 lasers1.txt
-rw-r--r--  1 root    root       2167 Sep 27 22:40 lasers2.txt
-rw-r--r--  1 root    root       2167 Sep 27 22:39 lasers3.txt
```

The three files are identical. Let's compress the first one, using Unix compress.

```
% compress lasers1.txt
```

Now let's see what happened:

```
% ls -l
total 7
-rw-r--r--   1 root   root        0 Sep 27 22:40 compress
-rw-r--r--   1 root   root      525 Sep 27 22:39 lasers1.txt.Z
-rw-r--r--   1 root   root     2167 Sep 27 22:40 lasers2.txt
-rw-r--r--   1 root   root     2167 Sep 27 22:39 lasers3.txt
```

Notice that the size of the file we compressed is about 4 times smaller, and that it now has a .Z extension to show it's been compressed.

To decompress a file, just type **uncompress** followed by the filename:

```
% uncompress lasers1.txt.Z
```

There are other compression utilities you might find on your Unix host, such as **gzip** ("Gnu zip"). Ask your system administrator for more information on what's on your host computer.

Creating Archives Using *tar*

The **tar** program (short for "tape archive"—the old way of archiving) lets you bundle files together as a single file, much like you would create a StuffIt file on your Macintosh, or a PKZip file on your PC.

Using tar is easy, but note that it does not compress the files, it only bundles them. If you want to compress them, use **compress** or another utility after you create the *.tar* archive.

Let's archive the three files shown in the previous example and call the new file *laser_files.tar*:

```
% tar   laser_files.tar laser*
```

The wildcard (*) tells the Unix computer to create an archive called *laser_files.tar* and put in it all files that start with the text *laser*.

To extract files from a *.tar* archive, just add **-x** to the tar command, followed by the name of the archive:

```
% tar -x laser_files.tar
```

What's Next?

1. Find out what kind of encoding and compression utilities you have available on your computer, or on a host computer you use for your Internet connection. Get the FAQs listed below for your specific computer type for information and pointers on some of these utilities and where to find them.

2. As usual with the Internet, the easiest way to find some answers might be to ask someone who knows—a net-savvy colleague, a system administrator, or your online service's representative. Ask them for instructions on encoding and compression utilities for your computer type.

3. If you want to send or receive a binary file and FTP is an option, take it! See the Chapter 9, FTP, for more information.

Regardless of how you go about it, it's inevitable that you'll have to learn to use some new software, even if it's only for attaching a file using your e-mail software.

Try not to get discouraged by all the options and new terminology, which tend to just add noise to the situation. The reality is, unless you get into some serious file transferring, chances are your e-mail software will handle most situations just fine.

Just the FAQs

To get the FAQs listed below, send the commands shown to

```
mail-server@rtfm.mit.edu
```

This is an e-mail server that will automatically send you the file you've requested. Send these commands in the body of your e-mail message. *Remember that this server is Unix-based: Use upper- and lower-case letters exactly as shown.*

If you wish to retrieve more than one FAQ, just enter each command on a separate line in your message. You may also retrieve the files noted using FTP.

Introduction to Internet Services
Send this command:

```
send pub/usenet/news.answers/news-newusers-intro
```

Introduction to Binary File Formats (Images)
Send this command:

```
send pub/usenet/news.answers/pictures-faq/part2
```

Introduction to Binary Imaging Utilities
Send this command:

```
send pub/usenet/news.answers/pictures-faq/part3
```

JPEG FAQ
Send this command:

```
send pub/usenet/news.answers/jpeg-faq
```

T$_e$X FAQ
Send this command:

```
send pub/usenet/news.answers/tex-faq
```

PostScript FAQ
Send this command:

```
send pub/usenet/news.answers/postscript/faq/part1-4
```

Compression FAQ
Send this command:

```
send pub/usenet/news.answers/compression-faq/*
```

Introduction to Unix *compress*
Send this command:

```
send pub/usenet/news.answers/z-faq
```

Chapter 8

TELNET

Telnet is a powerful Internet tool that lets you use other computers on the Internet. This action is also called "remote login," and it means you can browse library card catalogs, search for papers or journals of interest, establish an account for commercial (pay) services, or any number of things. You can even telnet to another computer to perform Internet activities that you might not be able to access from your computer, such as the World Wide Web.

One key thing to remember about telnet is that it's only a way to connect your computer to another computer. Once you are logged in to that other computer, everything you type and see on your screen will be an interaction between the two computers. As the marketing slogan goes, "It's the next best thing to being there."

This ability to remotely log into another computer also means that you will need to play by their rules. For the most part, this isn't a problem, since you'll soon find that most of the people who offer public access telnet sites have created special user interfaces to help you use their system. Generally these systems, while not adhering to any standard, are easy to learn by using the online help system.

What Can I Do with Telnet?

As you read or browse this book, you'll find a variety of services accessible through telnet. The first and most common usage is access to online databases, including:

- Wide-Area Information Servers (WAIS)
- Online Public Access Catalogs (OPACs)
- Campus-Wide Information Systems (CWIS)
- Commercial databases such as Dialog, CARL/UnCover, and Inspec.

All of these services are explained in the Online Databases chapter of this book.

Another useful feature of telnet is the ability to use a computer's software to do things on the Internet that you perhaps can't do from your computer. For example, in order to use gopher or veronica (discussed later), your computer needs to have gopher *client* software installed and must have a direct connection to the Internet. Many people don't have this software or type of connection; however, to use gopher or veronica, they just telnet to a public computer that does have the gopher software, and do their gophering (or veronicking?) from there.

Most recently, some public telnet sites have also installed software clients or browsers for accessing information on the World Wide Web.

Remote Login via Telnet

The procedure for logging into a publicly accessible telnet host is reasonably straightforward, but there are a couple of quirks I'll mention, too.

First, you need to know where to go. This book is full of places to go, and once you start your own Internet explorations, you will undoubtedly find more. A telnet "address" is, like all Internet addresses, either a number separated by dots, such as **192.149.147.1**, or two or more words separated by dots, such as **spie.org**. Both of these examples are actually the same address as far as the Internet is concerned. Remember that all Internet addresses are really four numbers separated by dots. Some, but by no means all, of these addresses have *domain name addresses* to make them easier to remember. It's up to the people who own the computer whether they "name" their computer or not.

Most public telnet sites ask you enter a login name or user ID and (rarely) a password to access the computer, much as you would your own online account. Most of the time you'll know in advance what the login name is, because most references to telnet sites in this book and elsewhere will include this information with the telnet address.

Many publicly accessible computers prompt you with the appropriate commands to enter their service as a guest.

So, a typical reference to a telnet site might be something like your colleague telling you to "telnet over to pac.carl.org and get that paper by Heisenberg." Well, in this case that's all the information you need, since CARL (Colorado Alliance of Research Libraries) doesn't even require a login name. And your colleague gave you CARL's Internet address, so you're all set.

Other times you'll see a telnet address list both the Internet address along with the login name. For example, to access NASA's SpaceLink database, you telnet to **spacelink.msfc.nasa.gov** and log in as "guest".

Increasingly, popular telnet sites, especially commercial databases, will require you to open an "account" the first time you want to log on. This is usually because the organization running the telnet computer wants to both limit access in some ways and keep track of who is logging on. Or, in the case of a commercial database service, your account will be used to bill you for whatever services you use while logged into that computer.

Telnet Command Mode

When you type **telnet** at the Unix command prompt without entering an address to telnet to, you enter into telnet's command mode, and your command prompt changes to **telnet>**, waiting for commands. Once you're in telnet command mode, you can type a question mark (?) to display all the commands you can use:

```
         Q - Delete Print Job           Z - CONTRL                        ⇧

                        Enter command here : x
Connection closed by foreign host.P-1994 16:59:10.30
/user10/n8348220%telnet
telnet> ?
Commands may be abbreviated.  Commands are:

close           close current connection
display         display operating parameters
mode            try to enter line or character mode ('mode ?' for more)
open            connect to a site
quit            exit telnet
send            transmit special characters ('send ?' for more)
set             set operating parameters ('set ?' for more)
unset           unset operating parameters ('unset ?' for more)
status          print status information
toggle          toggle operating parameters ('toggle ?' for more)
slc             change state of special charaters ('slc ?' for more)
z               suspend telnet
!               invoke a subshell
environ         change environment variables ('environ ?' for more)
?               print help information        .
telnet>                                                                   ⇩
```

The most important thing to note here is that from the telnet command prompt, you use the commands **open** and **close** to initiate and terminate connections to computers you want to telnet to:

```
telnet> open jsc.nasa.gov
```

Two more important points. First, you'll rarely need to use the **close** command because the remote computer usually offers a special command to sign off. Second, remember that if you do use the **close** command, you'll still need to use the **quit** command to exit telnet and get back to your Unix command prompt.

A Typical Telnet Session

I think it would be fair to say that there's no such thing as a "typical" telnet session. Every host computer is slightly different. Most publicly accessible telnet computers have some sort of customer user interface or "shell" designed to make your visit easier. Usually it is easy to get around a new site by just looking for the commands, usually at the bottom of your screen, or by reading the online help, also usually noted somewhere.

For a practice telnet session, we'll remotely log into NASA's SpaceLink, since we've already mentioned it. The Unix command for telnet is, well, "telnet":

    % telnet **spacelink.msfc.nasa.gov**

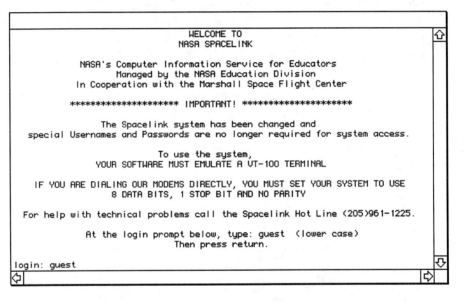

```
                            WELCOME TO
                          NASA SPACELINK

             NASA's Computer Information Service for Educators
                   Managed by the NASA Education Division
             In Cooperation with the Marshall Space Flight Center

        ********************* IMPORTANT! *********************

                  The Spacelink system has been changed and
        special Usernames and Passwords are no longer required for system access.

                          To use the system,
             YOUR SOFTWARE MUST EMULATE A VT-100 TERMINAL

        IF YOU ARE DIALING OUR MODEMS DIRECTLY, YOU MUST SET YOUR SYSTEM TO USE
                    8 DATA BITS, 1 STOP BIT AND NO PARITY

        For help with technical problems call the Spacelink Hot Line (205)961-1225.

                 At the login prompt below, type: guest  (lower case)
                          Then press return.

login: guest
```

This is typical: as soon as you connect to the other computer, you are told how to log in. In this case, we're instructed to type **guest** (lower case) and then press Return, which displayed the message shown on the facing page.

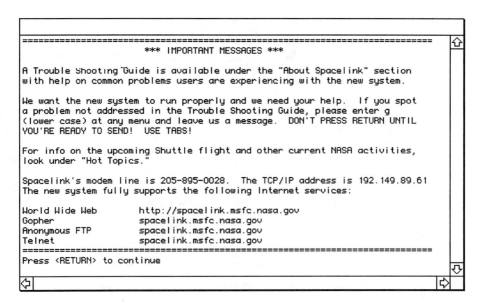

Again, typically the host computer will display some important information, such as where to report questions or problems, and other ways to access the same information we'll be looking at in our telnet session. Why is this important? Well, for one thing, telnet is limited to looking at information only; you can't get, or download, anything. Yet in my explorations at SpaceLink I found a number of images of the Shoemaker-Levy comet impact that I would like to look at. In order to get those images back to my computer to view, I would need to download them through some other kind of access to SpaceLink that offered file transfer capabilities, such as FTP, gopher, or World Wide Web.

Moving on, here's SpaceLink's main menu:

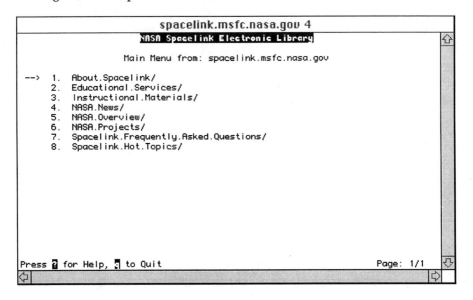

Now that we're successfully logged in, all commands to navigate the computer are determined by the remote computer. Watch for menu items that lead you to Help screens and the key commands used if you get stuck and need to get out. In this case, all you have to do is type a question mark to bring up an online Help menu:

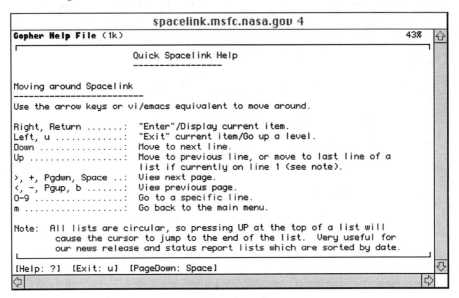

At this point we're ready to explore the directories. Navigating is simple—in this case, NASA has emulated its gopher site and so getting around is the same as if you used a gopher to log in (more on gophers in a later chapter). All you really need are the arrow keys to point to menu items, and then the Return key to move to a selected item.

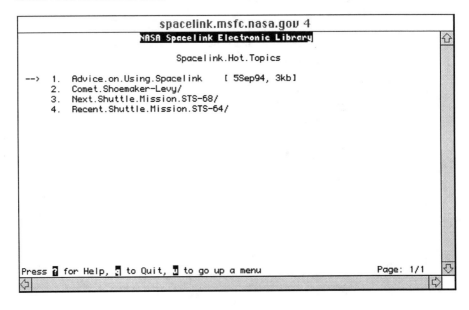

From here I cheated and skipped ahead a few menus to look at the countdown and payload information about the next shuttle mission:

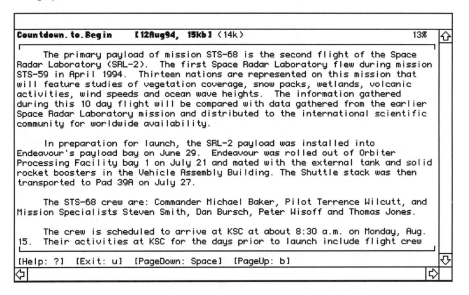

That's all there is to it, most of the time. From here we could type **u** to exit and then be back at our familiar Unix command prompt. There are, of course, countless variations to what we just did, and we'll outline a few of those below, but in general telnet is a simple tool.

Telnet to a Specific Port

One of the quirks with telnet I mentioned is that you'll sometimes see, in addition to an Internet address, a number called a "port" that you will need to add to the Internet address to initiate the telnet session. Ports are just like different doors into the same computer. In fact, when you telnet to a computer without using a port, you're really logging into the default port for the telnet command, which is 23.

An example using port 601 on a computer called **interesting.place.com**:

```
% telnet interesting.place.com 601
```

Terminal Emulation

Most computers you log into will ask you for "Terminal Type" or something similar. Basically, there are many different computer terminals out there, and the remote computer needs to know what keys you're pressing during your session. You should know (or if you don't, find out) what kind of terminal you have or are "emulating" in order to work on the Internet. If you are on a computer at work or school, ask the system administrator or someone else who knows. If you're connected via a modem, your telecommunications software settings determine what kind of computer terminal you are emulating.

Usually, the remote computer will either ask you if VT100 is okay (default), or give you a list of terminal types to choose from.

What Is "tn3270"?

Yet another computer quirk, this time from a specific computer type that you may encounter on the Internet, so I'll just mention it. IBM mainframe computers have a markedly different interface to most other "command line" computers you'll use in that they use a "full screen" mode of displaying and navigating. This means that other terminal emulations (outside of 3270 emulation) won't work with these computers.

In many cases, the IBM computer you connect to will take care of the situation itself by taking the terminal you tell it you're using and converting most of the elements for you. However, you will need to know about some special keys used on these 3270 computers.

If, however, the IBM computer you're logging into does not provide you with its own version of 3270 emulation, you will need to log in instead with a different telnet tool called *tn3270*. In other words, instead of typing

```
telnet jsc.nasa.gov
```

you would type

```
tn3270 jsc.nasa.gov
```

This of course presupposes that the tn3270 software is installed on your host computer. If it is not (i.e., if you get "command unknown" when you try using tn3270), then you'll need to talk to your system administrator, who can help you by setting you up with a compatible keyboard mapping.

Troubleshooting

Although there's not much that can go wrong during a telnet session, there are a few error messages you might see on your screen:

- "Unknown host" usually means you've either typed the host address incorrectly, or the telnet address has been changed or perhaps no longer exists. It happens.

- "Foreign host not responding," or something similar, usually means that something is not working between you and the other computer. Most likely it's that the other computer is not online at that particular moment (due to maintenance, changes, etc.). You might try connecting at a later time.

- "Max users exceeded" or a similar clue let's you know that the computer you're trying to access is too busy with other users to let you in. Most computers on the Internet will only allow a pre-determined number of guests at any one time, so as to not affect the performance for people who work at that site.

Macintosh Telnet Software

If your Macintosh computer is connected to the Internet either directly or via a SLIP/PPP connection, you can use telnet software directly from it.

NCSA Telnet, developed and distributed as freeware by the National Center for Supercomputing Applications, is probably the least complicated of all the Internet software tools. No setup windows, no numbers to plug in. Just select Open from the File menu, and then type in the address of where you want to telnet to:

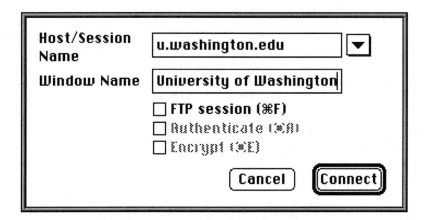

Once the connection is established, NCSA Telnet will bring up a terminal window with the login screen or prompt, just as if you were on a character-based Unix terminal.

Where to Find NCSA Telnet

You can get the latest version of NCSA Telnet via FTP from the following archive, or from any *Info-Mac* mirror site (see Appendix):

`ftp.ncsa.uiuc.edu`

For more information on connecting your Macintosh computer to the Internet, see Appendix.

Windows Telnet Software

If your Windows PC is connected to the Internet either directly or via a SLIP/PPP connection, you can use telnet software directly from it.

Of the many telnet shareware programs available for Windows, QVTNet is one of the finest. The program can also be used for FTP, and the commercial version of QVTNet can do a variety of Internet functions.

There is virtually no setup for QVTNet. Similar to the Macintosh example shown above, all you do is click on the Terminal button to display a window that requests a telnet site address. Here you can specify an IP address or domain name, as well as a port number, if required. QVTNet does allow some customization for each telnet window. You can select the terminal emulation type that you prefer, which key acts as the backspace key, and several other personal preferences.

Where to Find QVTNet

You can download the latest version of QVTNet from any of the following FTP sites, or from most major Windows FTP archives (see Appendix):

    sunsite.unc.edu/pub/micro/pc-stuff/ms-windows/
    wuarchive.wustl.edu/systems/ibmpc/win3/winsock/

For more information on connecting your Windows PC to the Internet, see the Appendix.

Just the FAQs

There are no known FAQs specifically for telnet at this time. This is no doubt a reflection of the fact that telnet *per se* is really a function of the computer you are connecting with. The telnet connection function itself is simple and relatively specific to the software you are using.

Chapter 9

FTP

File Transfer Protocol

FTP, short for *file transfer protocol*, is a simple tool for transferring files between computers. It's one of the easiest things you can do on the Internet.

With FTP, you can transfer your own files to a colleague's site, or tap into the millions of files available in the public domain. The most attractive characteristic about FTP is that it enables file transfer between dissimilar computers. It doesn't matter that you are working on a PC and the file is stored on a larger computer using Unix.

Anonymous FTP

Many people on the Internet use FTP to retrieve publicly accessible files. Many FTP sites allow users to log in as an *anonymous* user and retrieve files that have been stored expressly for the purpose of sharing. Software programs, instructions and guides to Internet resources, images and sound files, and miscellaneous materials are all stored on FTP sites around the world.

For the purpose of this book, we use *FTP* to mean *anonymous FTP*.

The vast majority of FTP sites are computers at commercial, nonprofit, government, and educational organizations who support information exchange both to and from their location through a public access via the Internet. This philosophy of free exchange is a fundamental element of the Internet's existence. Any site that allows such public access using FTP is referred to as an "anonymous FTP site."

What Is a "Mirror Site"?

As a way of helping distribute the load away from some of the major FTP sites on the net, hundreds of smaller sites cooperate as *mirrors* for many of these main repositories. A *mirror site* usually contains exactly the same files and directories as the site it's mirroring and is usually updated nightly. Try FTPing to a mirror site if you are not permitted access to the original site. Particular mirror site addresses (especially for high-traffic sites) are sometimes displayed in the "Welcome" message of a site that has mirrors.

For more information and a listing of popular mirrors, see Appendix.

What Is an "FTP Address"?

FTP sites use the same addressing scheme as the rest of the Internet. What this means is that each location has a discrete address that looks a lot like an e-mail address, except without the username prefix and @ symbol.

Here are some examples of typical FTP addresses:

```
ftp.uu.net
rtfm.mit.edu
sunsite.unc.edu
spie.org
ftp.intercon.com
```

Notice that some of them use "FTP" as part of their address, while others do not. There's no standard way of naming an FTP site. In fact, you will occasionally see an FTP site name that's just a string of numbers separated with periods, like this:

```
192.149.147.1
```

This is the FTP site's IP *address* on the Internet. Every Internet address is in fact made up of four numbers, each separated by a period. If the site has not registered a *domain name* for their computer's IP address, then the site is known to everyone as (in the case above), "192, dot 149, dot 147, dot 1"—that's how you would say it, instead of saying "spie dot org," which is in fact the address given above. In other words, the IP address **192.149.147.1** is the same as the domain name **spie.org**, and FTPing to either one of them will get you to the same place.

Where Do I Find FTP Sites?

You can find addresses for FTP sites in a number of ways. A book like this is good place to start, especially since the sites listed in the Resources section of this book often have short descriptions of what you'll find at a given site.

After you've been to a few places on the Internet, either through FTP or one of the other methods such as telnet, you'll begin to naturally collect your own list of valuable resources.

Connecting to an FTP Site

When you use FTP to retrieve (or "get," as it's usually called) files anonymously, the other computer should let you log in with a username of *anonymous*, and then your password is your personal e-mail address, which will not be shown on screen when you type (but for the purpose of the example below, it's shown). For example, at the login prompt, I would type the following to log into an anonymous FTP site, or *server*:

```
ULTRIX V4.3 (Rev. 44) (henson - %t)

login: anonymous
Password: brian@spie.org
```

Note than in most cases you can use a login name of *ftp* instead of *anonymous* and get the same results (easier to type), but this doesn't always work.

There are very few commands you'll need to use FTP, and most of them are nearly universal Unix commands, so you've already learned most of them. It helps to remember that once you successfully connect with an FTP host, the commands you type are now being input to that computer, not your or your host computer.

Essential FTP Commands

Here are some essential commands. Note that many are standard Unix commands you've already learned (see the chapter on Your First Logon).

You type:	What happens:
ftp	starts an FTP session (on a Unix host)
open *hostname*	attempts to make a connection to the host computer address you type
close *hostname*	closes your current connection, if any
cd ..	move up one directory
cd *directoryname*	move to a specified subdirectory
dir	display the current directory's content
ls	display the current directory's content (similar to **dir**, but less information is displayed about each file and directory)
pwd	display the name of the directory you are in
ascii	prepare to transfer ASCII text files only
binary	prepare to transfer files with binary characters

get *filename*	transfer (download) a file **from** the FTP archive
put *filename*	transfer (upload) a file **to** the FTP archive
mget *filenames*	transfer (download) multiple files **from** the FTP archive
mput *filenames*	transfer (upload) multiple files **to** the FTP archive
prompt	turn on/off the prompting mode for mget or mput
quit	end an FTP session (other commands might be **bye**, **exit**, **logout**)

Logging In

Using the address for the University of North Carolina shown above (**sunsite.unc.edu**), we'll walk through a typical FTP "session."

In most cases, FTP sites regulate the number of simultaneous anonymous logins to their FTP archives. If there are too many users at a particular time, you will get a message to that effect, and you'll have to try again later.

From the command prompt on my host computer, I first type the **ftp** command to start the FTP software, then I use the **open** command followed by the FTP site's address. Once connected, I logged in as "anonymous" and typed my e-mail address at the Password prompt:

```
% ftp

ftp> open sunsite.unc.edu

Connected to sunsite.unc.edu.
220 calypso-2 FTP server (Version wu-2.4(1) Mon May 9
18:03:22 EDT 1994) ready.

Name (sunsite.unc.edu): anonymous

331 Guest login ok, send your complete e-mail address as
password.

Password: my_e-mail_adress
```

Now, at this point, the UNC computer sent a whole bunch of text onto my screen:

```
      WELCOME to UNC and SUN's anonymous FTP server
          Office for Information Technology
                SunSITE.unc.edu

250 An OpenLook FTPtool can be found in
250 /pub/X11/Openlook/Ftptool4.3.unc.1.tar.Z

250 For information on submitting software to this archive,
250 retrieve /how.to.submit.

250 We archive most of the SUN related Usenet news groups
```

```
250 here as well as distributing SUN related announcements.
250 Pub/wais contains a Sparc binary for a simple wais
250 client that you can run in your terminal window.

250 We suggest that you download it and follow the
250 installation instructions (they're simple) so that
250 you may begin to use WAIS for your searching and
250 retrieval.

250 If you e-mail to info@sunsite.unc.edu you will be sent
250 help information about how to use the differenct services
250 sunsite provides.

250 We are experimenting with description based searches and
250 downloads from this archive with WAIS. If you would like
250 to try this, get and read the file
250 /pub/wais/FTP-wais.readme.

250 We use the Wuarchive experimental ftpd. if you "get"
250 <directory>.tar.Z or <file>.Z it will compress and/or tar
250 it on the fly. Using ".gz"  instead of ".Z" will use the
250 GNU zip (/pub/gnu/gzip*) instead, a superior compression
250 method.

250 Mail suggestions and questions to
250 ftpkeeper@sunsite.unc.edu.

250 Guest login ok, access restrictions apply.

FTP>
```

At first glance this "Welcome" message might seem a little excessive, but actually it serves a good purpose by telling us about other resources UNC offers and how to access them. Notice it also tells us where to get more information about "submitting software" to the archive. FTP works both ways, after all.

Just ignore all the "250" numerals preceding each line. This is a typical Unix convention when displaying a system message such as this.

Displaying and Navigating Directories

Before moving deeper, I want to add an encouraging note by saying that although everything we're doing here may seem a bit convoluted at first, after a few tries on your own it quickly becomes as commonplace as working on your own computer at work or home.

Okay, now that you're logged in, you'll be at the "top" level directory of the computer's FTP archives. Let's use the **dir** command to list the contents of the directory we're in:

```
ftp> dir
```

```
200 PORT command successful.
150 Opening ASCII mode data connection for /bin/ls.
total 8379
-rw-r—r—    1 root  wheel     2001 Aug  2 1993 DISCLAIMER.readme
-rwxr-r—    1 FTP   wheel 8537512 Aug 23 06:52 IAFA-LISTINGS
-rw-r-r—    1 root  wheel     1116 Aug 20 1992 IAFA-SITEINFO
-rw-r-r—    1 root  wheel      263 Feb  4 1994 README
-rw-r-r—    1 root  daemon     534 Aug 18 1993 US-Legal-Regs-ITAR
-rw-r-r—    1 root  wheel     1559 Nov 19 1993 WELCOME
drwxr-xr-x 2 root  daemon     512 Feb  3 1994 bin
drwxr-xr-x 2 root  wheel      512 Aug 13 1992 dev
drwxr-xr-x 3 root  daemon     512 Aug 20 1993 etc
-rw-r-r—    1 root  daemon    8868 Sep  5 1992 how.to.submit
lrwxrwxrwx 1 root  daemon      13 Oct 15 1993 ls-lR
drwxr-xr-x 7 root  wheel     1024 Aug 23 08:12 pub
drwxrwx-wx 5 root  FTP-admi 2560 Aug 23 17:51 uploads
drwxr-xr-x 3 root  wheel      512 Mar 11 1992 usr
226 Transfer complete.
1008 bytes received in 0.05 seconds (20 Kbytes/s)
ftp>
```

Here you might want to look for a file that contains a current directory listing, with some details about what each file in the directory contains. This directory or "readme" file is usually named something like *ls-lR.txt* or *00readme.txt* or *INDEX.txt*. Again, there is no standard, but it should be obvious if there is one available.

At this point you might want to download this index file to your own host computer and read it there as reference for this FTP archive. Remember that FTP is only a file transfer tool. Technically you cannot "read" a text file using FTP. However, there might be another option that lets you read the index without having to close your FTP connection. At many FTP sites you can use the **get** command (normally used to download files) to display the contents of a file instead. The command, as you would type it at the FTP prompt, is

```
ftp> get filename -
```

where the filename is the name of the index or readme file you want to look at. The hyphen after the filename tells the host computer to display the file's contents instead of actually downloading the file (the **get** command). More about these commands in the examples below. A final word of caution here: avoid using the **get filename** - command on any file you think might be large, especially a binary file. The whole file will start scrolling onto your screen and you'll need to use the Unix abort command (**Control - c**) to stop it.

No matter what you do, keep in mind that an FTP archive is a resource that many other users are trying to access, so it's considered a poor online practice to spend a lot of time browsing files aimlessly when instead you could read the index, find what you want, get it, and log off.

Another common convention for anonymous FTP sites is the use of a *pub* ("public") directory. When you first log in, look for a directory named *pub* and then change to that directory (type **cd pub**). If there is a public directory like this, that's where you'll probably find everything available for public download. Everything "above" this directory most likely requires a registered username and password to access. (This is usually for people who actually work for the organization that owns this computer.)

Be aware that some sites organize their files in a logical and hierarchical manner. Others provide cross-references to files and are more circular in structure.

Now let's move to the *pub* directory and list the files there:

```
ftp> cd pub
250 CWD command successful.

ftp> dir
200 PORT command successful.
150 Opening ASCII mode data connection for /bin/ls.
total 36
-rwxr-xr-x    1 root    daemon    1989 Mar  2 18:17 .cache
drwxr-xr-x    2 root    daemon     512 Jul  6  1993 .cap
-rw-r-r—     1 root    daemon     929 Jun 24 15:31 INDEX
drwxr-xr-x   18 ewt     FTP-admi  1024 Aug 27 04:05 Linux
drwxr-xr-x    7 root    daemon     512 Apr  6  1993 UNC-info
drwxr-xr-x   33 root    wheel     1024 Jul 22 16:04 academic
drwxr-xr-x    8 root    daemon     512 Mar 25 00:02 archives
drwxr-xr-x   24 root    wheel     1024 Mar 25 00:04 docs
drwxr-xr-x   29 root    wheel     9728 Jun 24 16:26 gnu
drwxr-xr-x   12 root    daemon     512 Feb 18  1994 languages
drwxr-xr-x   11 root    daemon     512 Aug 17 19:02 multimedia
drwxr-xr-x   19 root    daemon     512 Jul 21 22:04 sun-info
226 Transfer complete.
1540 bytes received in 0.28 seconds (5.4 Kbytes/s)
ftp>
```

For the purpose of further exploration, I'm interested in the "academic" directory listed here, so I'll go "down" one more directory and then list the contents.

```
ftp> cd academic
250 CWD command successful.

ftp> dir
200 PORT command successful.
250-/pub/academic software for academic purposes;
250 broken by area of 250-knowledge
250-
250-check INDEX for a list of contents and descriptions
250-
250 CWD command successful.
```

```
150 Opening ASCII mode data connection for /bin/ls.
total 40
-rwxr-xr-x  1 23     wheel    2877 Aug 27 11:15  .cache
drwxr-xr-x  2 root   daemon    512 Aug  9  1993  .cap
-rw-r—r—    1 root   daemon    843 May  6  1993  INDEX
-rw-r—r—    1 root   daemon    129 Oct  6  1992  README
drwxr-xr-x  6 root   daemon    512 Jun 14 15:49  agriculture
drwxr-xr-x  6 hock   FTP-admi  512 Feb 14  1994  astronomy
drwxr-xr-x  6 root   daemon    512 Jun  3  1993  biology
drwxr-xr-x  4 root   daemon    512 Jun  3  1993  chemistry
drwxr-xr-x  8 root   daemon    512 Jun  9  1993  comp_science
drwxr-xr-x  4 root   daemon    512 Dec  2  1993  data_analysis
drwxr-xr-x  7 root   daemon    512 Jan  5  1994  economics
drwxr-xr-x  3 root   daemon    512 May 14  1993  education
drwxr-xr-x  4 root   daemon    512 May 14  1993  engineering
drwxr-xr-x  5 root   daemon    512 Apr  8 19:49  environment
drwxr-xr-x  5 root   daemon    512 Jun  1 17:52  geography
drwxr-xr-x  3 root   daemon    512 Jun  3  1993  geology
drwxr-xr-x  4 root   daemon    512 Jul 23 11:14  literature
drwxr-xr-x  5 root   daemon    512 Jun  3  1993  mathematics
drwxr-xr-x  7 root   daemon    512 Nov  2  1993  medicine
drwxr-xr-x  2 root   daemon    512 Jul 15 18:42  pharmacy
drwxr-xr-x  5 root   daemon    512 Jan  5  1994  physics
drwxr-xr-x  3 root   daemon    512 Aug 23  1993  psychology
226 Transfer complete.
2268 bytes received in 0.17 seconds (13 Kbytes/s)
ftp>
```

Clearly a lot of stuff here. Physics? Okay:

```
ftp> cd physics
250 CWD command successful.
ftp> dir
200 PORT command successful.
150 Opening ASCII mode data connection for /bin/ls.
total 15
-rwxr-xr-x   1 root   daemon   146 Mar 10  1993  .cache
drwxr-xr-x   2 root   daemon   512 Jan  5  1994  .cap
drwxrwxr-x  11 cfh    fusion  1024 Jul 13 14:12  Cold-fusion
drwxr-xr-x   6 root   daemon  1024 May 25 07:33  Electro-mag
-rw-r—r—     1 root   daemon   214 Jan  4  1994  INDEX
-rw-r—r—     1 root   daemon   517 Jan  4  1994  wratten.iafa
-rw-r—r—     1 root   daemon  8691 Oct 25  1993  wratten.zip
226 Transfer complete.
469 bytes received in 0.21 seconds (2.2 Kbytes/s)
FTP>
```

Now let's use the special **get** command mentioned above to view the *INDEX* file listed here. Note that I type **INDEX** in all capital letters, since Unix is case sensitive:

```
ftp> get INDEX -
200 PORT command successful.
150 Opening ASCII mode data connection for INDEX (214 bytes).
150 /pub/academic/physics

Cold-fusion/    information and papers about low tempera-
                ture fusion
Electro-mag/    mirror of the MIT electro-magnetics
                archive
wratten.zip     Wratten color filter transmittance/
                absorbance data
226 Transfer complete.
remote: INDEX
219 bytes received in 0.08 seconds (2.7 Kbytes/s)
```

Now, this is good information. We can tell the file named *wratten.zip* contains some data we might want to look at, so let's download, or "get," it.

Downloading Files

Before using the **get** command to transfer a file to our host computer, we need to first determine if the file is an ASCII file or a binary file. Unlike e-mail, which does not recognize binary characters, FTP does let you transfer binary files intact, but you have to make sure you're set up for binary by typing **binary** at the FTP> prompt before transferring the file, like this:

```
ftp> binary
200 Type set to I.
```

(The "I" above refers to the word "image." Originally it was used to mean "transfer the *binary image* of a file, as opposed to converting the file to ASCII before transfer.)

So, how do we know if a file is binary or ASCII text? Actually, the larger question here is what format they're saved in, be it compressed, encoded, or just plain text. A file's *extension* is usually the best clue as to its formatting. The table in the earlier chapter on Files and Formats can help you determine a file's format from its extension, and then whether to download it as a binary or an ASCII text file. The rule of thumb is, when in doubt, use binary. It can't hurt.

In this example, the file we want is a *.zip* file, a common compression method on DOS-based PCs. You should always assume a compressed file is binary. Since we've already set our transfer preference to binary, all we have to do now is use the **get** command:

```
ftp> get wratten.zip
150 Opening BINARY mode data connection for wratten.zip
150 (8691 bytes).
226 Transfer complete.
local: wratten.zip remote: wratten.zip
8720 bytes received in 0.41 seconds (21 Kbytes/s)
ftp>
```

That's it. Note the line about *local:* and *remote:*, which tells you that the local machine (UNC's FTP server) sent a file called *wratten.zip*, and the remote site (your host computer) received a file of the same name. You could have, if you wanted to, renamed the file as part of the transfer process. Let's say we wanted to rename it something we would remember better, like (in this case) *color_data.zip* (it's usually a good idea to keep the same extension). Our download procedure would go like this:

```
ftp> get wratten.zip color_data.zip
200 PORT command successful.
150 Opening BINARY mode data connection for wratten.zip
(8691 bytes).
226 Transfer complete.
local: color_data.zip remote: wratten.zip
8691 bytes received in 0.34 seconds (25 Kbytes/s)
ftp>
```

Now we've changed the filename. By the way, another good reason to change a filename is that even though the Unix computer you're downloading from supports long filenames, computers such as DOS PCs are more limited. You'll see some horrid filenames on the Internet. Like this:

```
Sci.Physics_Frequently_Asked_Questions_(3_4)_General_Physics
```

When you eventually download this file to your PC, you'll probably end up with something like *sciphys.ics*, since DOS will truncate the name, providing it even recognizes it as valid in the first place (the extra period will probably throw it off right away). And that's assuming that your telecommunications program doesn't choke on it first. I know that if I try to download a big filename like this using the ZMODEM transfer protocol, it aborts immediately. So, I have to rename the file first (see next section for more information).

Where Is the File I Transferred?

Where your downloaded files end up after "FTPing" them depends on your particular setup and connection. Normally files are transferred to whatever computer you are sending the **ftp** command from. More specifically:

- If you have a remote dial-up or "shell" account with an Internet service provider, any files you download will probably end up in your personal directory on your provider's host computer. If the file is a plain ASCII text file and you want to read it, you can use the Unix **more** or **cat** commands to read the file.

In this case, if you wish to move the file to your personal computer, then you will need to *download* it from the host, using a *transfer protocol* such as ZMODEM, XMODEM, or Kermit.

- If you have a direct connection to the Internet through a local area network (probably through your employer or university), the files you transfer could end up on your personal computer workstation, or on the main computer system at your location.

- If you have a SLIP or PPP connection to an Internet service provider (or your employer or university), any file you transfer via FTP is downloaded directly to your computer's hard drive. The FTP software you use on your computer (such as Fetch, NetManage FTP, or WS FTP) gives you some control over where your files end up on your hard drive.

Ending Your FTP Session

When you're finished with your browsing or downloading, you can either type **quit** or **bye** at the FTP> prompt to disconnect from the other computer and return to your own host environment. When you "quit" this way you should be back at your host's normal command prompt.

But note that if you end your FTP session by typing **close** instead, you will disconnect from the other computer (known as "closing your session"), but you'll still be in your host computer's FTP command mode (and your command prompt will still be FTP>). At this point your host computer will interpret all commands as FTP-related, so if you start typing commands and you get a message like "Not connected", it means you still need to type **quit** or **bye** to get back to the Unix command prompt.

Uploading Files

Obviously, the laws of physics (but not necessarily software engineering) demand that since we can download files from a distant computer to our computer, we should also be able to upload files from our computer to a distant computer. The command for uploading using FTP is yet another tribute to brevity of Unix: **put**.

The **put** command has a number of uses. While you probably won't do as much *putting* as *getting*, it's still a necessary tool. Perhaps you've created a data profile of a project you're working on, and decide to upload it to the Internet for others to look at. Or maybe you're presenting a journal or proceedings paper—written in T_eX with a bunch of PostScript figures that go with it—and the publisher has an FTP server where you can post your paper to them in a more secure manner than e-mail.

For the most part, uploading files via FTP is the same as downloading them. You log in to the other computer using FTP and then upload the file using **put**. If it's a binary file, type **binary** at the prompt first. Then look for a directory called *incoming* or *uploads*. This is probably where you're expected to upload any files, unless someone at that site has specifically told you another directory name to upload to. Chances are if you try to upload files while in any directory except the right one, your upload will not be accepted. This is for security reasons. Systems administrators want to check any files being uploaded to their computers for viruses, propriety, and possible duplication.

Transferring Multiple Files

The **get** and **put** commands let you move one file at a time. If you go to an archive and find more than one file to download (or want to upload more than one), use the **mget** and **mput** commands. For example, referring back to the *pub/academic/physics* directory we were in just a while ago, this is what it would look like to download both the *wratten.zip* and *wratten.iafa* files listed there.

```
FTP> mget wratten.zip wratten.iafa
```

Notice that when you use **mget** or **mput**, you can't rename the file on the fly, since you have to list the files you want transferred separated by a space.

Another option for **mget** and **mput** is using a wildcard, usually an asterisk (*), to download or upload a group of files, or even a whole directory (be careful with this command though). For example, above I could have just typed:

```
FTP> mget wra*
```

Since both files I wanted started with "wra", I could use the asterisk (*) symbol to get every file starting with those three letters. The **mget** and **mput** commands will prompt me, however, to confirm each filename before transferring, just in case I really didn't want all of the files. If you're sure you want all of them, type the word **prompt** at the FTP> prompt before making your transfer. This turns off the prompting feature.

Using the **mput** command is the same as **mget**. Just remember that everything you type after you type **mput** at the FTP> prompt will be interpreted as a filename to be transferred. You can't change the filename during the transfer like you can with the simple **get** command.

Non-Anonymous FTP

Of course, FTP is also used for more secure operations. In such cases you need a valid username and password to access a particular computer. This is common, for example, for organizations who wish to let only certain people access their computer.

If you ever try to log into an FTP site and get a message that says something like "Access Privileges Denied," it probably means the computer is for employee or student use only, and requires a registered username and password to log on.

Macintosh FTP Software

If your Macintosh computer is connected to the Internet either directly or via a SLIP/PPP connection, you can use FTP software directly from it. This means that software you download will be transferred directly to your computer's hard drive.

When moving files around the Internet you will need software that can speak FTP. The hands-down best program for the Macintosh is called Fetch.

Fetch gives you a Macintosh-like interface to FTP servers that makes FTP quite simple. It even displays FTP servers' menus with the files-and-folders icons so familiar to Macintosh users.

Setting up Fetch is a breeze. The online help feature is context-sensitive and complete. Refer to it for a complete explanation of all setup options. We'll take a look at the basics here.

When you first launch Fetch, you'll see the Open Connection window (it opens by default, but you can change this setting):

```
╔═══════════════ Open Connection... ═══════════════╗
║                                                   ║
║   Enter host name, user name, and password        ║
║   (or choose from the shortcut menu):             ║
║                                                   ║
║   Host:        ┌─────────────────────────────┐    ║
║                │ rtfm.mit.edu                │    ║
║                └─────────────────────────────┘    ║
║   User ID:     ┌─────────────────────────────┐    ║
║                │                             │    ║
║                └─────────────────────────────┘    ║
║   Password:    ┌─────────────────────────────┐    ║
║                │                             │    ║
║                └─────────────────────────────┘    ║
║   Directory:   ┌─────────────────────────────┐    ║
║                │                             │    ║
║                └─────────────────────────────┘    ║
║   Shortcuts:  ┌──┐      ┌──────────┐  ┌────────┐   ║
║               │▼ │      │ Cancel   │  │   OK   │   ║
║               └──┘      └──────────┘  └────────┘   ║
╚═══════════════════════════════════════════════════╝
```

Here is where you type the Internet address, or *URL* (Uniform Resource Locator), of the FTP server you wish to log into. In the figure above, note that I have only the FTP site address listed (**rtfm.mit.edu**). No user ID or password. Fetch is smart enough to take the e-mail address you've entered in the Preferences window and use it to log into anonymous FTP sites. Unlike the Unix way of doing FTP, here you need only enter the address of the site you want to visit, and Fetch enters the word *anonymous* when it's supposed to, then your e-mail address as the password.

From this menu you can also choose to open a Shortcut, which is just a listing of places you've been before that you've saved as a Shortcut under the Customize menu. You could also choose Open Bookmark, which is similar to a Shortcut in many ways, except that a Bookmark is actually a small file created when you choose the Save Bookmark option from the File menu (handy if you wish to send a colleague the exact location of a file or archive you've discovered—just e-mail them the bookmark file you've created). Fetch comes preloaded with a few Shortcuts to popular places, as well as nearly forty Bookmarks that will take you directly to many important Macintosh places on the Internet, such as Apple, Northwestern University (home of John Norstad's *Disinfectant*), and a long list of Info-Mac mirror archives.

Here's what the top level directory of MIT's **rtfm.mit.edu** archive looks like:

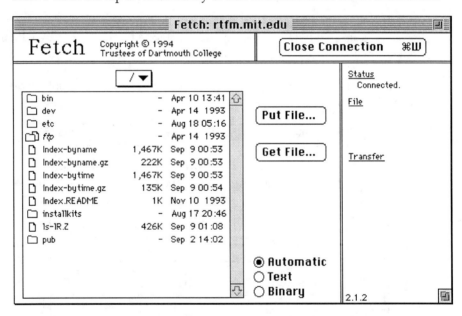

From here Fetch is true to the Macintosh interface. Double-clicking on a folder icon changes to that directory (provided it's publicly accessible). To download a file, you can either highlight it and click the Get File... button, or just double-click the filename. If you think the file is binary and don't want to trust Fetch's auto-sensing option, click the Binary button before downloading. Most of the time the Automatic setting works correctly, but occasionally it misreads the file as ASCII. Uploading files is the reverse of this procedure.

Where to Find Fetch

You can find the latest version of Fetch via FTP from the following site, or from any Info-Mac mirror site (see Appendix).

```
ftp.dartmouth.edu/pub/software/mac
```

For more information on connecting your Macintosh computer to the Internet, see Appendix.

Windows FTP Software

If your Windows PC is connected to the Internet either directly or via a SLIP/PPP connection, you can use FTP software directly from it. This means that software you download will be transferred directly to your computer's hard drive.

There are a variety of shareware FTP utilities on the Internet. Since WS-FTP is one of the most popular, I will use it to demonstrate how FTP works in the Windows environment.

When you first launch WS-FTP it will prompt you for your e-mail address. This is so WS-FTP can automatically enter *anonymous* and your e-mail address (as a password) whenever you log into an anonymous FTP server. This means all you have to do is enter the site's address; WS-FTP takes care of the rest of the login chores. You can change this option later if you wish.

Now let's look at the Connect window, the first half of WS-FTP:

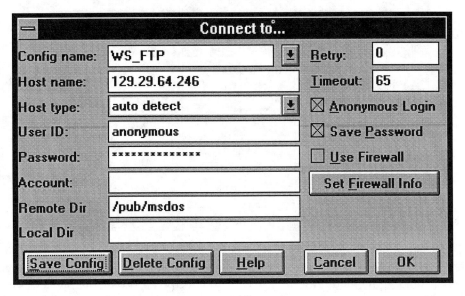

The Host Name field is where you enter the FTP address you wish to connect to. If you know the directory path to the directory you want to move to, you can enter it now in the Remote Dir field. There is also a Save option to permanently add the information in this window to a pop-up window of addresses, which you can later enable for convenient access to a place you've already been. To add sites to this list, fill in the information you wish to save, including a name you wish to call the site, and select the Save button. The site will automatically be added to the list for future use. If the site you add requires a special login name and password, then you must remember to disable the Anonymous Login check box and fill in the relevant fields.

Once connected to an FTP site, you'll then see two sets of list views in the window. On the left is your local directory structure, and on the right is the remote listing:

Let's look at WS-FTP in action. In the Host Name window I typed **ftp.cica.indiana.edu** and logged into the FTP archive there, then found the latest version of PKZip (here *pkz204g.exe*) and started downloading it.

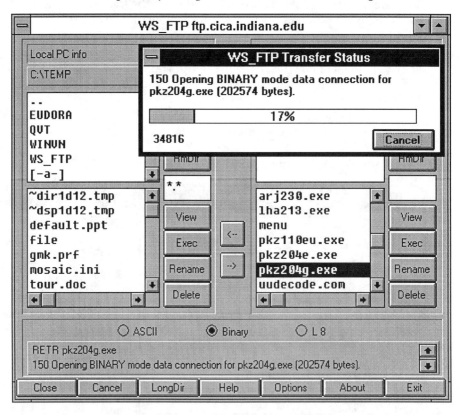

This window works much like the Windows File Manager. The upper box of each list displays directory names, and the lower box lists the files in the current (highlighted) directory. To change directories you can double-click on the directory name or select the ChgDir button and manually enter the path and directory name. To view a file at the FTP archive (without actually downloading it), select the filename and click the View button. The default viewer will be used to display the file.

Before downloading a file, first make sure the Local System list view shows the directory in which you want the file to be placed on your computer. Next, if the file is *binary*, select the Binary button (if you're not sure, select Binary anyway, just to be safe). Next, select the filename in the Remote System's file listing and click the left-pointing arrow between the two list view boxes. To upload a file, click the right-pointing arrow.

Where to Find WS-FTP

You can get the latest version of WS-FTP from the location listed below, or from most Windows FTP archives (see Appendix):

```
ftp.cica.indiana.edu/pub/pc/
```

For more information on connecting your Windows PC to the Internet, see Appendix.

Just the FAQs

To get the FAQ listed below, send the command shown to

```
mail-server@rtfm.mit.edu
```

This is an e-mail server that will automatically send you the file you've requested. Send this command in the body of your e-mail message. You may also retrieve the files noted using FTP. *Remember that this server is Unix-based: Use upper- and lower-case letters exactly as shown.*

Introduction to FTP

Send this command:

```
send pub/usenet/news.answers/FTP-lists/faq
```

Chapter 10

USENET NEWS

What is Usenet?

Usenet, conceptually, is a huge bulletin board system. People send e-mail style messages, formatted in a special manner, which are processed and interpreted as *posts* by computers running appropriate software. These posts are collected into *newsgroups,* or topical associations of like interests, which anyone on a site can then read.

Usenet is not a "thing," it's a state of mind. It is what most people mistakenly call "the Internet," but it isn't a physical object or organization. It's not *really* a network, although it uses physical networks to propagate itself. Nobody runs it, nobody owns it, nobody really sets any rules on how it works. One writer has called it a "logical network," but a better description is *controlled anarchy.*

Usenet has one major advantage over mailing lists: when you send out a message to a newsgroup, you're mainly sending one copy to each of the machines that subscribe to Usenet. This one copy is archived, and users can reference that one copy. In a certain amount of time (ranging from one day to one month), the machine automatically deletes the file, to make room for new files.

This is much more efficient than mailing lists, which could conceivably send a hundred copies of a post to each of a computer's one hundred users. This is horribly wasteful, in terms of disk storage.

There are two types of newsgroups: moderated and nonmoderated. Moderated groups are effectively edited by one or more people, who scan and process submissions before posting: this way, the quality of a newsgroup can be ensured.

Nonmoderated groups, which include most groups, are just like bulletin board systems, gab-fests in which anyone can speak their mind on absolutely anything. Want to talk about aerospace engineering in **sci.bio**? Go for it! But just be prepared for the flame mail when you do.

Conduct on Usenet is complex, mainly because you don't know who you're dealing with. To address these issues, the notion of "netiquette" has arisen, with individuals listing recommended rules of contact, most intended to reduce the phenomenon of *flaming*. These rules are listed in the newsgroup **news.announce.newusers**.

Lastly, it's important to remember that what few rules that exist on Usenet are purely artificial and arbitrary. There's an anarchistic "consensus" on certain things, but the bottom line is, the written rules are written by people who just felt like sitting down and writing rules. Some important rules, such as those pertaining to newsgroup creation, are similarly arbitrary, but are tolerated solely because nobody else has offered better solutions. Nobody owns anything, and nobody has enforcement power (although whoever provides your access to the Internet can control what you see). It's not even clear whether the usual laws of libel apply, since anyone can forge a Usenet message, usually pretty easily.

What Usenet Is Not

Usenet is not a reference resource. It is simply a collection of people with interests that may or may not coincide. People like to interact, and some people go to great lengths to help others out.

A recent phenomena is that of people abusing the net: high schools telling students to find a Ph.D. on the net to help out with some arcane physics problem, for instance, or students not bothering to utilize a reference library, instead preferring to get others to do their legwork for them. The line here between viable resource and oracle for the perpetually lazy is a fine one.

More and more moderators are pushing back on this type of behavior, rejecting messages that contribute nothing to others' awareness of an issue. There's nothing wrong with asking a question, just as long as it somehow benefits the net as a whole: often the difference is one between "gimme this" and "gimme this *because* I'm doing this." Explaining what one is all about often also means the difference between individuals either ignoring or actually reacting in a helpful manner to an inquiry.

Newsgroup Naming Conventions

Each newsgroup has a name. For example,

```
sci.aeronautics.airliners
```

refers to all current posts that refer to that subject matter.

Newsgroups often refer to hierarchies. In this case, the levels of the hierarchy are separated by periods. So **airliners** is a group in the **aeronautics** hierarchy, which is in the **sci** hierarchy.

The hierarchy is used to clearly delineate a group. So, for example, in this case, the **aeronautics** hierarchy might only contain the one group, **airliners**—but it just as easily could contain a hundred newsgroups.

Any site administrator can create a newsgroup. Many sites have "local" newsgroups, which are intended for use within the company or university. So, for example, the University of Texas at Austin has groups such as **utexas.general**, **utexas.forum**, and so forth.

Groups that are genuinely local to a machine usually have names without hierarchies, such as **general** or **forum** or **gripe**.

A site administrator can offer to "export" his newsgroups to other machines. So if University A wants to be aware of University B's activities, they can be made available to University A's users. Usually, groups without hierarchies won't be exported, but it's no problem at all for a completely foreign machine, like **netcom.com**, to read all of the **utexas.*** hierarchies [an asterisk (*) is a Unix meta-character meaning "all possibilities"; since Usenet was born on Unix machines, it tends to use a lot of such jargon].

The Usenet universe is generally defined by a select set of hierarchies. These are:

alt	Alternative groups (not at all sites)
comp	Computer-related topics, the heart of the Net
misc	Anything that doesn't fit elsewhere
news	Usenet administration
rec	Recreational topics
sci	Science and technology (non-computer)
soc	Social chatter, sociology, cultural issues
talk	Miscellaneous politics and rhetoric, mostly.

It's important to note that other newsgroup hierarchies can and do exist (Netcom, a large national service provider, lists over 300 unit root-level hierarchies), which use the Usenet software (as described above), but they aren't really "Usenet" per se. This might include the **bit.*** groups, which are gatewayed from BITNET, the **clari.*** groups, which are part of the Clarinet wire news service, and others.

In effect, when we refer to "Usenet," we're referring to the two thousand or so distinct discussion groups in the canonical hierarchy.

Basic Software — The **rn** Newsreader

There are a few news packages commonly found on Unix Internet hosts nowadays. The most common are **readnews**, **nn**, and **rn**. **Readnews** is mostly obsolete, but it's simple, and gets the job done. Of the latter two, **nn** is gaining in popularity but is still relatively new and therefore less common than **rn**, which is widely available in many flavors, such as **rn**, **trn**, **rrn**, **xrn**, and many others. It's a fairly sophisticated newsreader. We'll use **rn** for our sample session.

With the vast diversity of machines capable of reading news, which can include Unix machines, Macintosh and DOS computers, and even IBM mainframes, it's impossible to cover all the possibilities. If **readnews** or **rn** (**rrn**, **trn**, **xrn**) are not installed on your system, contact your system administrator for assistance. Remember that Usenet access is not a given; your service provider must be specifically set up to receive a *newsfeed* from somewhere on the Internet.

In **rn**, many commands are "hot keys." You type them, and something happens. You may or may not see what you type. In many modes, however, you must type and then press the Return key on your keyboard. It will take some practice to figure out which method goes where.

At any point in **rn**, you can press **h** for a quick list of options available.

For a concise list of options, if you're on a Unix machine, try typing:

```
% man rn
```

This will invoke the Unix **man** page for rn, and give you a 40-odd page summary of its feature set.

Starting Up **rn**

To start up the **rn** newsreader on your system, type

```
% rn
```

and press the Return key at your command prompt. If that doesn't work, try typing **readnews**. If that also isn't available, try variations of **rn**, such as **trn**, **rrn**, or **nn**—or even **man -k news**.

Once **rn** starts up, it will most likely ask you to subscribe to every single group. This is a long and tedious process; on some machines, there will be more than

10,000 newsgroups to process. To avoid this process, type

```
% rn -q
```

(-q is a flag standing for "quick."). The newsreader prompt will just start up and wait for you to do something. Note that you are no longer at the Unix prompt, but in the **rn** newsreader environment.

Once you start up, the first thing to do is start subscribing to newsgroups. For a start, type

```
g sci.aeronautics
```

to subscribe to the **sci.aeronautics** newsgroup. Next you'll see

```
Newsgroup sci.aeronautics is currently unsubscribed
to - resubscribe? [yn]
```

To which you would type **y** or press the space bar.

To unsubscribe from a newsgroup, simply go to that newsgroup and then press the **u** key. The system will ask for verification before unsubscribing you from that group.

To list groups that match a certain keyword, for example, if you want to list all groups containing the word "aviation," you would type

```
l aviation
```

and press the Return key: all such groups would then be displayed.

To start up **rn** and read only a specified group, type

```
rn rec.aviation.simulators
```

This will start up **rn** and show you only **rec.aviation.simulators**.

If you wish, you can also edit your list of subscribed-to newsgroups: this is kept in a file in your home directory, called *.newsrc*. Each line contains the newsgroup name and a listing of articles you've read:

```
sci.aeronautics.airliners: 1-1826
rec.aviation.simulators: 1-6617
comp.sys.mac.games: 1-73779
```

As you become more familiar with **rn**, editing this file directly, then running **rn**, may be easier than using the interface. A small *.newsrc* file is a key in keeping **rn** running efficiently, so "pruning" the *.newsrc* file for unsubscribed newsgroups occasionally is a good idea. Unsubscribed newsgroups would be identified with an exclamation point:

```
misc.forsale.computers.mac! 1-40463
```

Note that all command-level options (**-q**, **-c**, newsgroup names) can be combined. For convenience, they can also be kept in a *.trnrc* file in the home directory. For example:

```
-q
-hexp
-hmessage
-hreply
-hdist
-horg
-href
-hkey
-hdate
-hlin
-hsender
-hfol
-hnews
-hin-rep
-hsum
-hx
-i=-1
```

tells **rn** to ignore all recently-created groups (so you won't be asked to subscribe/unsubscribe to the known universe every time you log on), ignores various headers in every message, and will display one line of the content of a message before prompting you to hit the spacebar.

To quit **rn**, press **q** and you will be returned to your shell environment.

Reading Articles

It's important to note that news is a very fleeting phenomenon. When you start out, you're just jumping onto a freight train—the entire system of messages is constantly moving. Nothing's kept forever. Some machines keep news for a month, and some keep news for an hour. The point is to check news frequently, especially on a high-volume group (some groups can go through 300 or more messages a day).

Also, be sure to save copies of messages in your personal directory if there's something you wish to keep: it may not be there if you want to go back later.

If you just want to see if there is news, without reading news, just type

```
% rn -c
```

This will display a list of newsgroups and a count of the unread articles in each group.

If you find the length of headers tiresome (and some posting software can add 50 or more), you can use an -h header, as in

```
% rn -h Message-ID
```

to stop the newsreader from displaying the **Message-ID**: line in every post.

If you are using a slow terminal, then typing something like

```
% rn -i=20
```

can be useful: this causes rn to only display 20 lines before presenting a "more" prompt. Use whatever number you like.

Once you are in rn, it will display a list of subscribed-to newsgroups, such as:

```
Unread news in rec.aviation.simulators        3 articles
Unread news in comp.sys.mac.games            22 articles
Unread news in clari.biz.industry.aviation    1 articles
Unread news in rec.travel.air                23 articles
Unread news in rec.aviation.military         18 articles

3 unread articles in rec.aviation.simulators—read now?
[ynq]
```

Once you get to this point, just hit the spacebar: the system will then display new messages, starting with **rec.aviation.simulators**.

The **rn** program has two operational modes: there's a *message-reading* mode, when you're "in" a newsgroup, and a *navigation* mode, "outside" the newsgroup. When you first start up **rn**, you're in the navigation mode; when you press the spacebar, you're in the message-reading mode.

When reading a message, if you wish to skip it and go to the next one, hit the **n** key (upper- or lowercase).

If you wish to reply to the person who sent a message, press the **r** key. To reply and include the full text of his message in that reply, press the **R** key (remember, **rn** is case-sensitive).

To read a specific message number again, just note the number, and type it in again.

Here are some other important commands:

s	Save current message
q	Quit the active newsgroup (and return to navigation mode)
P	Go to previous newsgroup
- (hyphen)	Go to previous group (one you've already quit)
N	Go to next newsgroup
g *newsgroup*	Go to named newsgroup

To save a message and instantly mail it to someone else, type

```
s | mail -s "Lookee here!" friend@anothermachine.com
```

Posting Your Own Articles

Before posting an article, be sure to check the current netiquette guidelines in **news.announce.newusers**. Again, these are simply a set of common-sense rules on how to conduct oneself on the net: failure to take them seriously usually reflects pretty poorly on new .

When posting, be sure to keep your line length less than or equal to 72 columns. This gives people who may reply to your messages enough room to annotate them.

When posting new messages or follow-ups to multiple groups, *always* list all groups when your newsreader gives you the opportunity. This is called cross-posting. This will usually be presented in a prompt such as:

```
Newsgroups:
```

So to post to **sci.aeronautics** and **sci.aeronautics.simulation**, type:

```
Newsgroups: sci.aeronautics,sci.aeronautics.simulation
```

(Note that there are no spaces between the newsgroup names.) This allows messages to be stored more efficiently on host sites, and also allows readers to only read your message on one group, rather than every single copy on all the groups you posted to. This is all a way of advising you not to post a message ten times if you want to send it to ten groups: instead, just post once, to ten groups. There *is* a major, functional difference.

If you wish to post a follow-up message to a message you're reading, type **f** to follow up to the message without including a copy, or **F** to follow up while including a complete copy of the message.

When posting a follow-up message, feel free to edit the original message. There's nothing worse than wading through a 10,000-line message only to see a one-line contribution of "Me too!" or "I agree!"

When you post to a moderated newsgroup, the message will actually be mailed to the moderator of the group, who may take several days to process it. You may, therefore, have to wait awhile before seeing it appear in the appropriate newsgroup.

When you post to a nonmoderated group, the message will generally appear on your local machine in a period from five minutes to a few hours, depending on how the site administrators have the software configured.

Command Summary for **rn**

Software

rn	a popular, general-purpose newsreader
trn	a version of **rn** that uses **nntp** (the newsgroup protocol) to find its messages
readnews	another, older, general-purpose newsreader
nn	another popular newsreader
Pnews	posting software **rn** uses
postnews	an older posting package

Command-Line Options

-c	see if there is any new news
-q	start **rn** without being offered newly created newsgroups
-i=n	display **n** lines of a message before displaying the "n" prompt
-h *name*	don't display a header line with *name* in it

Navigation Options

g *name*	go to newsgroup *name*
q	quit **rn**
u	unsubscribe from current newsgroup
N	go to next newsgroup
P, -	go to previous newsgroup
\<spacebar\>	start reading messages in next newsgroup
l *identifier*	list all groups whose name contains *identifier*
s	save message
h	help

Message-reading Options

q	quit message mode and return to navigation mode
P	read previous message
N	skip to next message
#	read message with article number of #
f	follow up to message without including message
F	follow up to message while including message

r	send personal reply to poster of message without including message
R	send personal reply to poster of message while including message
h	help

Macintosh Usenet Software

If your Macintosh computer is connected to the Internet either directly or via a SLIP/PPP connection, you can use newsreader software directly from it. This gives you many more options for sorting through the vast quantities of information posted every day on the Usenet.

John Norstad's NewsWatcher is one of many good freeware packages for reading Usenet newsgroups on the Macintosh. Others I could recommend would be Nuntius and InterNews. I just happen to like NewsWatcher, mostly because of the way it creates and displays custom groupings, and the interface design.

In the Appendix I discuss the *TCP/IP* connections involved in setting up your Macintosh on the Internet. This includes a discussion of something called the *NNTP news server.* See Appendix for more background on this topic.

The first thing you need to do after launching NewsWatcher is enter the NNTP news server address provided by your network administrator or service provider. Sometimes this a separate (not always, but often) address from your mail server. Sometimes it's the same. Enter this address in the Server Addresses section under the Preferences menu, as shown below:

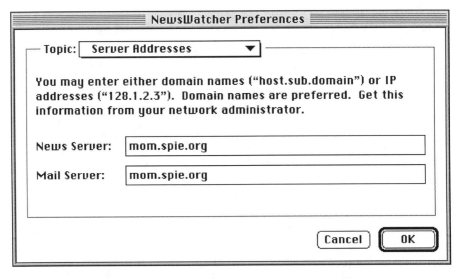

In the case above, my mail server just happens to be on the same computer as my news server. So why does NewsWatcher need to know my mail server's address? Because there are times when you are reading news that you may wish to respond via e-mail instead of a public posting to the group. NewsWatcher will use this information to let you send e-mail through its software. It just makes everything that much easier.

That's about the only setup item you need to worry about to get started. After you launch NewsWatcher for the first time, select Rebuild Full Group List from the Special menu, and then wait for NewsWatcher to find your news server and then "build" a full list of newsgroups available at your site. This may take a while, but you only need to do it once (and then update occasionally). From the full group list, which may have thousands of newsgroups listed, you can make personalized sets of newsgroups, such as the ones shown below.

The process of creating customized groupings is a simple drag-and-drop from the full group list to either an existing group window or a new group. Just drag the newsgroup name from the full group list onto the other group window and it will be copied there. When you open one of these customized groups, all the newsgroups you've added show up in a list showing the number of unread messages in each. From there you can pick the groups you want to display, and then read them in a variety of ways.

```
╔═════════════════════ Science ═══════════════════╗
║ 28 groups                                        ║
╟──────────────────────────────────────────────────╢
║    253     news.announce.conferenc...          ⬆ ║
║     98     sci.answers                           ║
║   2308     sci.astro                             ║
║     22     sci.astro.planetarium                 ║
║     14     sci.bio.technology                    ║
║    191     sci.cognitive                         ║
║     31     sci.cryonics                          ║
║     30     sci.data.formats                      ║
║   3615     sci.electronics                       ║
║    306     sci.engr                              ║
║     13     sci.engr.biomed                       ║
║    279     sci.engr.chem                         ║
║    554     sci.engr.mech                         ║
║    119     sci.geo.meteorology                   ║
║    472     sci.image.processing                  ║
║     71     sci.med.physics                       ║
║     38     sci.med.psychobiology                 ║
║     23     sci.med.radiology                     ║
║      7     sci.nanotech                          ║
║     31     sci.nonlinear                         ║
║   2584     sci.physics                           ║
║      2     sci.physics.accelerators              ║
║     29     sci.psychology.research               ║
║     19     sci.research                          ║
║     38     sci.research.careers                  ║
║     36     sci.research.postdoc                  ║
║     45     sci.op-research                       ║
║    302     sci.optics                          ⬇ ║
╚══════════════════════════════════════════════════╝
```

Once you've found a group you're interested in, just double-click on the group name to bring up the individual message list:

```
┌──────────────────────── sci.image.processing ───────────────────────┐
│ 72 articles, 72 unread                                               │
├──────────────────────────────────────────────────────────────────────┤
│  -       David Bourgin (The ...   Color space FAQ                     │
│  ▷  2    Rob Ekkers              Re: Is there a cheap image analysis package? │
│  -       Craig Reinhart         Re: 2D edge detection code wanted     │
│  -       Ron Natalie            Re: YPF/DCW Geographical Data Formats--- Code? │
│  ▷  3    Alan A. Rakes          Re: 2dfft in C ?                      │
│  ▷  2    sei@netcom.com         Used Equipment                       │
│  ▷  5    Patrick Moran          Re: Shrinkwrapping binary blobs       │
│  -       Reynolds               [Q]: Text Recognition methods...      │
│  -       S Venkateswaran        Industrial Applications of Machine Vision ? │
│  -       Mark Burge             Re: Snakes and Active Contours        │
│  ▷  2    Nick Mein              Re: Watershed algorithm shortcut?     │
│  -       Chris Dodge            Help w/ BrookTree Parts               │
│  -       Kevin Wang             IPOT 95 Exhibition Contact Address?   │
│  -       paggio@sssup1.sssup... metacarpal joint shape               │
│  ▽  3    Mathieu Pilard         White noise to gaussian noise         │
│          Wilhelm Meier          Re: White noise to gaussian noise     │
│          Sergio Servetto        Re: White noise to gaussian noise     │
│  -       Stephane PERRIN        Help: Snap shot on MSDOS              │
│  ▽  2    Amy Caplan             K-L transform, PCA questions          │
│          Tat Jen Cham           Re: K-L transform, PCA questions      │
│  -       Jacob Sparre Andersen  Re: BMP file format (FAQ!)           │
│  -       Rajiv Malhotra         Wigner Transforms.                    │
│  -       Larry Cornell          Re: HELP: Need to scan microfilm!     │
│  ▷  2    Tian van Heerden       3D model from stereo image pairs?     │
│  -       hdkbahs1               libtiff CIELab?                       │
│  ▷  2    stubbsc@jeflin.tju.edu How to read and view IMB-PC *.EPS files │
│  -       John Hunt              Graduate Program in Optical Communications and Signal Processing │
│  -       Michelle O'Connell     Petaflops Frontier Workshop February 6, 1995 │
│  -       Michael C. Burns       ANNOUNCE: pnmsmooth.c Version 2.0     │
│  -       Chih-hung Tan          Book for sale: Computer Imaging Recipes in C │
│  -       Md. Shoaib Bhuiyan     [Q]Canny edge detection-- useful for ramp intensity images? │
│  -       Burkhard Schillinger   Looking for SNARK-users (CT software) │
│  -       Jim Vaughan            Re: Digitised MRI/CT Scan Body Sections │
│  -       Sharon Ensbury         Postscript printer descriptions - help │
│  -       Matt Roughan           Re: Watershed program is needed       │
│  ▷  2    Alber, Thomas          Reducing the resolution of raster maps preserving thin objects │
│  -       El-Khairy Amer         WANTED: Frame Grabber.                │
│  -       ANDROUTSOS Dimit...    *** Color Calibration References? *** │
│  -       mph432                 HELP Hough transform                  │
│  ▷  2    Jeffrey Cohen          NIH Image Macros for Cardiac Function Measurements │
│  -       Ojars - Balcers        Re: HELP: Need to scan microfilm! - sci.image.processing #11444 │
└──────────────────────────────────────────────────────────────────────┘
```

Note the small triangles on the left, along with some numbers. The triangles denote a message thread with two or more messages. Click on the triangle to see the responses to the original posting (as shown with two of the topics above), which drop down much like folders do in a standard Macintosh (System 7) directory listing. This makes scanning for topics really easy, since you only have to look at the topic title once. NewsWatcher makes Unix's **rn** look rather archaic at this point. Once you've read news this way, it's painful to go back.

Where to Find Newswatcher

You can get the latest version of NewsWatcher via FTP at the site listed below, or at any Info-Mac mirror archive (see Appendix):

```
ftp.acns.nwu.edu/pub/newswatcher
```

For more information on connecting your Macintosh to the Internet, see Appendix.

Windows Usenet Software

If your Windows PC is connected to the Internet either directly or via a SLIP/ PPP connection, you can use newsreader software directly from it.

One of the most popular Windows newsreaders is WinVN, so I will use it to illustrate access from your Windows PC. Like most good news software, WinVN is a *threaded* newsreader, which makes sifting through the Usenet's massive structure relatively painless.

In the Appendix I discuss the *TCP/IP* connections involved in setting up your PC on the Internet. This includes a discussion of something called the *NNTP news server.* See Appendix for more background on this topic.

The first thing you need to do after starting WinVN for the first time is enter the NNTP news server address provided by your network administrator or service provider. Sometimes this a separate (not always, but often) address from your mail server. Sometimes it's the same. First, select the Configure Com menu option, then type in the address or domain name of your NNTP news server in the NNTP (News) field. Enter your account's SMTP address in the SMTP (Mail) Server field. If it's the same as your NNTP news server computer, then you can leave this blank as shown below. After configuring the communication parameters, you may want to select the Configure Personal option. The information you provide here will be used when you post messages to Usenet.

News Server Configuration

NNTP (News)	mom.spie.org
TCP port	119
SMTP (Mail) Server	

Mail Transport
- ○ Disabled
- ○ Use MAPI
- ○ Use SMTP
- ⦿ Auto Select

☒ Demand Logon

Optional news server authorization information:

Username	brian@spie.org|
Password	******

[OK]   [Cancel]

Like most newsreaders, WinVN lets you pick out the groups you want to read regularly and lets you "subscribe" to them for easier sorting and retrieving. Once you find a group you like, you can highlight it and then subscribe to it under the Group menu. The subscribed group will automatically be moved to the top of the group list. And since new newsgroups are created all the time, every once in a while you should rebuild your master newsgroup list.

After you've selected a newsgroup to view, you can double-click on the group name, which will retrieve a listing and display the titles in a new window. By double-clicking on a title, you can bring up another window containing the actually message body, as shown here:

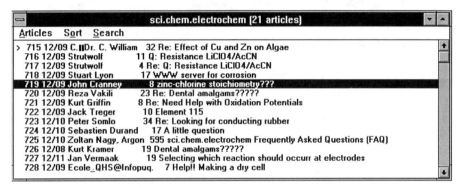

After reading the message you can choose to post a follow-up article to the newsgroup, forward the message to yourself or a colleague via e-mail, or reply directly to the author of the posting. You also have the option of saving the article as a text file under the File menu.

In order to move quickly through new, unread articles, you can press the spacebar to page down through them. When the end of the article is reached, the program will automatically bring up the next unread article when the spacebar is again pressed.

Where to Find WinVN
You can get the latest version of WinVN from any location listed below, and from most Windows FTP archives (see Appendix):

```
titan.ksc.nasa.gov/pub/win3/winvn/
scss3.cl.msu.edu:/pub/pc/win/winvn/titan.ksc.nasa.gov/
olymp.wu-wien.ac.at/pub/pc/windows/
coli.uni-sb.de/pub/pc/
```

For more information on connecting your Windows computer to the Internet, see Appendix.

Just the FAQs

To get any of the FAQs listed below, send the commands shown to

      `mail-server@rtfm.mit.edu`

This is an e-mail server that will automatically send you the file you've requested. Send these commands in the body of your e-mail message. Remember that this server is Unix-based: Use upper- and lower-case letters exactly as shown.

If you wish to retrieve more than one FAQ, just enter each command on a separate line in your message. You may also retrieve the files noted using FTP.

Usenet Guidelines and Submission Instructions
Send this command:

      `send pub/usenet/news.answers/news-answers/*`

General Questions (and Answers) Collected from Usenet
Send this command:

      `send pub/usenet/news.answers/usenet-faq/*`

Overview of Newsreader Software for Many Computer Types
Send this command:

      `send pub/usenet/news.answers/usenet/software/part1`

***nn* Newsreader FAQ**
Send this command:

      `send pub/usenet/news.answers/usenet/software/nn/faq/*`

*Note that many of these requests will result in multiple files being sent to your e-mail address (the * character means you'll get all files in the specified directory).*

Chapter 11

TOOLS FOR SEARCHING

Often when describing the Internet to someone not familiar with it, I'll get asked a question that goes something like this:

"Can we do a search on _____ ?"

This is a perfectly reasonable question. This person has probably heard me raving about what a great resource the Internet is; and really—what good is a resource if you can't find something in it?

Well, to be brutally honest, the Internet isn't exactly a giant database that you can readily search using familiar research tools such as keyword or Boolean searches. Rather, it's more like a trying to find how to spell a word by using the dictionary: You have to have a pretty good idea of the spelling in order to find the word.

Likewise, on the Internet, you need to know where to look to make searching effective. Unfortunately, for the professional doing research for a project, the tools available for searching the *entire* Internet are crude and often ill-suited for real research. This is not really a shortcoming in the tools, it's just that the structure and size of the Internet makes it virtually impossible to "search" it the way one would a database.

That being said, the tools that have been developed—archie, gopher, and veronica—can do some useful tasks, and when combined with a little experience, they can be worth the effort. In this chapter we'll outline what you can do with each of these tools, as well as point out their limitations. Tools for searching the World Wide Web are discussed in Chapter 13.

Archie

Archie is the companion software tool to FTP (file transfer protocol). The archie program searches a constantly updated index of FTP sites, filenames, and descriptions. Users can "ask" archie where to find a specific file, what file performs a specific function, and what FTP sites are available given a specific geographic area, and what files do they archive.

By now you may have guessed archie's fundamental limitation, especially for research work: you have to know, or at least be able to guess, all or part of the filename you're looking for. This makes archie a great tool for finding a piece of software that someone tells you about, or perhaps a picture of something, where you could search for "hologram" and get a reasonably informative reply.

What and How Archie Searches

Archie is really a database of the contents of thousands of anonymous FTP sites around the world. Each month, the archie program samples all the registered sites and compiles a master file directory listing for each site, which is then compiled into one big database that you can query.

Archie is simple and performs a few basic functions:

- A "name search" will query the listing of files for all FTP sites and reply with a listing of FTP site addresses, pathnames, and filenames that contain the indicated keyword.

- A "Whatis" search will reply with a listing of files with titles or descriptions matching the keyword indicated.

Archie will also do things like list all FTP hosts currently monitored, or list all files known at a particular site. I wouldn't recommend using the latter option unless you're sure it's a small FTP site.

Finding Archie

There are a few different ways to query archie:

- Send an e-mail message to an archie server, to which you'll receive a response as an e-mail message.

- Use an archie "client" installed on your local Internet host computer.

- Use an archie "client" on another computer that you access via telnet remote login.

- Query through a gopher server installed either on your or another computer you access through telnet (see the next section on gopher).

Each of these access methods does the same thing: it queries a master archie database and returns to you the results of your search.

Searching Archie

In each case above, the general principles are the same. You tell archie to search for something by typing **prog keyword** where *keyword* is a filename or part of a filename you're looking for. (I've always thought the use of **prog** was a bit obtuse, but that's computers for you.)

For example, to use archie with e-mail, just send a message to an archie server such as **archie.sura.net** (in which case you would address your message to **archie@archie.sura.net**), and then put your command in the message body, like this:

```
prog holography
```

The results of your search will be automatically e-mailed back to you when ready.

If instead you were accessing archie from your Unix shell account that had an archie client installed, you would (probably) type **archie** at the command prompt, and then at the archie prompt type your search commands, like this:

```
archie> prog holography
```

If you don't have an archie client installed on your host computer, you can try telneting to a public archie server, such as **archie.sura.net**. At the login prompt type **archie** and away you go.

Customizing Your Archie Search

There are a few commands you can use to modify your archie search. Depending on how you access archie, you might also be able to modify other parameters as well, but for now we'll just outline the search options.

Before you start an archie search, you can "set" the archie server to search in a particular way. Again, you just type the command, press Return, and then type your search parameters.

For example, let's say that instead of searching for all files with the word "holography" in them, we instead knew the exact filename we were looking for, *holographic.gif*. For this search we could use the "set search exact" option:

```
archie> set search exact
archie> holographic.gif
```

Here are all the search options and what they are used for:

Command	Description
set search exact	precise search for keyword
set search subcase	case sensitive substring search
set search sub	case insensitive substring search
set search regex	sophisticated "regular expression" search (for more information use **help regex**)

Some Public Archie Servers

archie.ans.ne	147.225.1.10	(ANS NY USA)
archie.au	139.130.4.6	(Australia)
archie.doc.ic.ac.uk	146.169.11.3	(United Kingdom)
archie.edvz.uni-linz.ac.at	140.78.3.8	(Australia)
archie.funet.fi	128.214.6.102	(Finland)
archie.internic.net	198.49.45.10	(AT&T NY USA)
archie.kr	128.134.1.1	(Korea)
archie.kuis.kyoto-u.ac.jp	130.54.20.1	(Japan)
archie.luth.se	130.240.18.4	(Sweden)
archie.ncu.edu.tw	140.115.19.24	(Taiwan)
archie.nz	130.195.9.4	(New Zealand)
archie.rediris.es	130.206.1.2	(Spain)
archie.rutgers.edu	128.6.18.15	(Rutgers USA)
archie.sogang.ac.kr	163.239.1.11	(Korea)
archie.sura.net	128.167.254.195	(SURAnet MD)
archie.sura.net(1526)	128.167.254.195	(SURAnet MD)
archie.switch.ch	130.59.1.40	(Switzerland)
archie.th-darmstadt.de	130.83.22.60	(Germany)
archie.unipi.it	131.114.21.10	(Italy)
archie.univie.ac.at	131.130.1.23	(Austria)
archie.unl.edu	129.93.1.14	(Nebraska, USA)
archie.uqam.ca	132.208.250.10	(Canada)
archie.wide.ad.jp	133.4.3.6	(Japan)

Macintosh Archie Software

If your Macintosh computer is connected to the Internet either directly or via a SLIP/PPP connection, you can use Archie search software directly from it.

By far the most innovative archie client for the Macintosh is Peter Lewis's **Anarchie** (pronounced "anarchy"). It does a stellar job of sampling FTP servers and bringing back search results.

When you first launch Anarchie, you'll see a window like the one shown on the next page.

```
┌─────────────────────────────────────────────────────┐
│ ▤▣▤▤▤▤▤▤▤▤▤▤▤▤▤▤▤▤ Archie ▤▤▤▤▤▤▤▤▤▤▤▤▤▤▤▤▤▤▤ │
│                                                       │
│  Server: │archie.internic.net  ·            │  ▼     │
│                                                       │
│  Find:   ▐hologram                          ▌        │
│                                                       │
│  ◉ Sub-string (dehqx)        ☐ Case sensitiue        │
│  ○ Pattern (dehqx*.hqx)                               │
│  ○ Regular Expr (dehqx.*\.hqx)   Matches: │ 20   │   │
│                                                       │
│  ( Cancel )           ( Saue )        (( Find ))     │
└─────────────────────────────────────────────────────┘
```

The pop-up menu at right (the downward facing triangle) brings up a list of over 20 preset archie servers all over the world from which you can choose to point your search. The default server, shown above, is InterNIC's archie site.

All you do is enter the term you want to search for, decide if you want to make it a sub-string, pattern, or regular expression search, whether you want the search to be case sensitive, and how many matches you want archie to find before stopping. In the example above, I've entered the term "hologram" and then entered "20" for the number of matches I wanted to limited the search to. Then I clicked the Find button, which brings up the search-in-progress window:

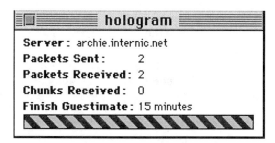

Don't let the "15 minutes" estimate fool you. For some reason, Anarchie seems to always start off with that number there. After a while, if you see that no numbers are appearing in the "Packets Received" line, it's probably best to click the window closed (to stop the search) and either enter a more specific term or quit searching altogether.

Perhaps the best thing about Anarchie is that after it goes out and finds possible "hits" for your search, it then brings up a list of those hits, which are complete site/directory/file listings, as shown below in the results from my "hologram" search:

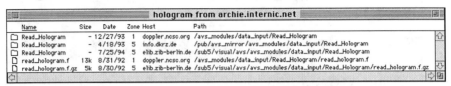

If I now double-clicked on any of the folders or files shown in this list, Anarchie would then go out and try to get the file (or enter the directory) shown via common FTP. There's no need to fire up Fetch to go get it.

Where to Find Anarchie
You can get the latest version of Anarchie via FTP from the site listed below, or from any Info-Mac mirror archive (see Appendix):

```
redback.cs.uwa.edu.au/Others/PeterLewis
```

For more information on connecting your Macintosh to the Internet, see Appendix.

Windows Archie Software

If your Windows PC is connected to the Internet either directly or via a SLIP/ PPP connection, you can use Archie search software directly from it.

WinSock Archie is an excellent Archie client for Windows, and also makes a nice complement to WS-FTP. I'll use it here for the purpose of illustration. When first launched, WinSock Archie asks for your e-mail address, and once you supply it you are ready to use the search program.

If you have both WS-FTP and WinSock Archie on your computer, you can select FTP Setup from the Options menu and designate WS-FTP as your FTP program. This will make it easy for you to directly download (using WS-FTP) any files you find.

To search for a file, first enter the search parameters, select the type of search you want, choose a server to use (from the preloaded list, or type in your own), and then click the Search button. If you find the server you chose is slow or unavailable due to heavy use you can abort the search with the Abort button.

Here I did a simple substring search for "pkunzip" using the archie database at InterNIC, which found many places where PKUnzip was archived.

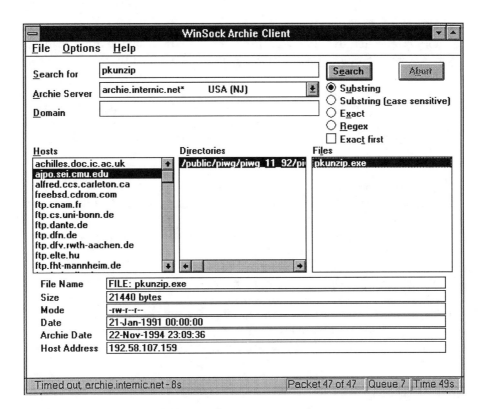

When a search is finished the results are presented in the fields in the middle of the window. Here I highlighted a site close to my location (the farther the site, the slower the download), and then I double-clicked on the filename. Since I'd told WinSock Archie that WS-FTP was my preferred FTP program, WinSock Archie then called up WS-FTP to start downloading the file.

Where to Find WinSock Archie

You can get the latest version of WS-Archie from one of the locations listed below, or from most Windows FTP archives (see Appendix):

```
ucselx.sdsu.edu/pub/ibm/winsock/
ftp.uga.edu/pub/msdos/mirror/winsock/
ftp.cc.utexas.edu/microlib/win/tcpip/
```

For more information on connecting your Windows computer to the Internet, see Appendix.

Gopher

Gopher is a software tool that connects a variety of computers and information archives on the Internet and displays them as a series of menu items. From these menus you can select and display the information without having to type in IP addresses or remotely log in to the other computer. Gopher does all this in the background. It's a lot like being on one big computer system. Even better, gopher is a "stateless" connection—it logs on, gets the menu or information on your screen, and then logs off. This helps keep traffic on the Internet to a minimum while providing a more simple interface for the user.

Originally developed at the University of Minnesota (Home of the Golden Gophers!) as a *campus-wide information system* (CWIS), it quickly caught on as a way for anyone on the Internet to publish information and organize network resources. There are over 5,000 active gopher servers now, with more being added daily.

Gopher is a just another way to find resources on the Internet. There are no materials out there in a format that only gopher can see. And therein actually lies one of gopher's limitations as a research tool: gopher menus are generally not developed by trained librarians, and therefore the organizational structure of "gopherspace" is somewhat erratic.

When using gopher, each menu item connects to another menu that branches off to yet another series of menus until you reach the document, image, sound file, etc. Some menu items point to other Internet resources. While exploring gopher menus, you'll often find that you end up a long way from where you started, and you really don't know how you got there. This is both a blessing and a curse.

Why Use Gopher?

Gopher is useful when you are faced with the question "Is there anything out there on the Internet that is useful for me?" Gopher allows you to see resources on the Internet as if they were all sitting in your own computer.

Connecting to Gopher

Like archie, gopher is a client-server arrangement. You need client software on a computer you're using, and you need to connect to a server somewhere. You can access gopher in three basic ways: a software client running on your Internet host computer; through a campus-wide information server (CWIS) or the World Wide Web (WWW); or by telneting to a public gopher client. We discuss access through CWIS and WWW in later chapters on those topics.

As with most Internet functions, gopher client software is available for most personal or workstation computers, as well as mainframes. If you don't have client software on your computer, you can try telneting to one of the hosts listed below.

Again, the type of connection to the Internet will determine the method in which you navigate the series of menus. Remote connections will require the user to enter words or letters from the command line, and any files you retrieve will require further downloading to your personal computer.

A direct connection will provide simple point-and-click capability if your computer has this kind of interface. If not, the chart below is useful for those connecting remotely and relying on a command-line interface.

Gopher menus can be customized. When you have reached a resource that is useful to you, you can issue the **bookmark** command and the menu item will be added to your own personalized menu.

Gopher Menu Items

Before we run through a sample gopher session, it might help to know some of the common abbreviations and symbols. These will help you identify each item in a gopher menu:

.	text file
/	a directory
?	a searchable index
<tel>	a telnet session to the indicated source
<CSO>	a searchable phonebook
<Bin>	a file in binary code
<)	a digitized sound file (the symbol is meant to look like a speaker)

Gopher Menu Commands

Here are some common commands for getting around in a gopher session. When in doubt, you're almost always given a command for **help**, usually just a question mark (?). In most cases, some of the more common commands are shown at the bottom of your computer screen.

The primary keys for gopher are the arrow keys, which are used to move from one menu choice to the next, and the Return key, which displays whatever menu item or document you have marked.

Basic Commands

up	move to previous line
down	move to next line
right	display menu item
>	view next page
+	view next page
pagedown	view next page
space	view next page
<	view previous page
-	view previous page
pageup	view previous page
b	view previous page

0-9	go to specific line number
m	go to main menu

Bookmark Commands

a	add current item to bookmark list
A	add current directory/search to bookmark list
v	view bookmark list
d	delete bookmark/directory entry

Other Commands

s	save current item to a file
D	download a file
q	quit with a prompt to confirm action
Q	quit unconditionally
=	displays technical information about item
O	change options
/	search for item in menu
n	find next search item
o	open a new gopher server
!	shell escape

Some Gopher Sites Accessible via Telnet

IP Address	Log in as:	Location
consultant.micro.umn.edu	gopher	US (MN)
gopher.uiuc.edu	gopher	US (IL)
gopher.uwp.edu	gopher	US (WI)
panda.uiowa.edu	panda	US (IA)
gopher.unc.edu	gopher	US (NC)
info.anu.edu.au	info	Australia
gdunix.gd.chalmers.se	gopher	Sweden
tolten.puc.cl	gopher	Chile
ecnet.ec	gopher	Ecuador

Gophering Around

Now we're ready to gopher. Since I don't have gopher software on my computer, I'm going to telnet to one of the public gopher sites listed above. If you already have gopher client software on your host computer, you just get to skip the telnet part and point yourself immediately to a gopher server of your choice. As part of this session we'll visit a menu that lists "All the Gopher Servers in the World," which isn't really true but it's probably close enough.

First we'll telnet to **consultant.micro.umn.edu** and log in as "gopher" for our username:

```
% telnet consultant.micro.umn.edu
```

```
* * *  University of Minnesota * * *
   * * Public Gopher Access * *

Type 'gopher' at the login prompt
AIX Version 3
(C) Copyrights by IBM and by others 1982, 1993.
login: gopher
---------------------------------------------------------
This machine is a public gopher client.

You are sharing this machine with many other people from
all around the internet.

To get better performance we recommend that you install a
gopher client on your own machine.  Gopher clients are
available for Unix, Macintosh, DOS, OS/2, VMS, CMS, MVS,
Amiga, and many others

You can get these clients via anonymous FTP from
boombox.micro.umn.edu in the directory /pub/gopher

The Gopher Team thanks you!
---------------------------------------------------------

Last unsuccessful login: Mon Aug 15 17:42:30 CDT 1994 on
pts/0 from arcwelder.mi
cro.umn.edu
Last login: Thu Sep  8 19:21:57 CDT 1994 on pts/11 from
books.viterbo.edu
TERM = (vt100)
Erase is Ctrl-H
Kill is Ctrl-U
Interrupt is Ctrl-C
I think you're on a vt100 terminal
Welcome to the wonderful world of Gopher!

Gopher has limitations on its use and comes without
a warranty.  Please refer to the file 'Copyright' in-
cluded
in the distribution.

Internet Gopher Information Client 2.1 patch-1
Copyright 1991,92,93,94 by the Regents of the University
of Minnesota

Press RETURN to continue
```

A typically lengthy telnet Welcome screen. But again, good information. They not only encourage us to use our own gopher client if we can (instead of freeloading on theirs), but they also tell us where to get clients for all sorts of computers. If you have a direct or SLIP/PPP connection to the Internet, take their advice and get a client on your own computer.

Note also that this screen tells us some very important key combinations: Control-H backspaces and erases, Control-U will "kill" the command you just typed, and Control-C will interrupt your session and release control back to your host computer.

From here we press the Return key and see the main gopher menu:

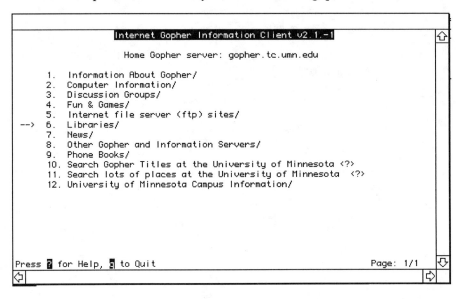

The arrow on the left is controlled by the up or down arrow. I've moved it down to Item 6—Libraries. I could have also typed the number 6 for the same result. Either way, now I can press Return to move "down" to the Libraries menu.

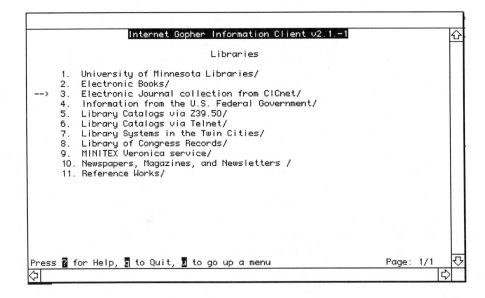

We have just connected to the CICnet gopher server, somewhere in the midwestern United States, and are no longer looking at computer resources at the University of Minnesota. This is what gopher is all about—seamless navigation among thousands of computers on the Internet.

So again we'll arrow down, this time to Item 4 to get a list of subject headings. Note that every menu here has a slash (/) after it. This means it's a directory, not a file.

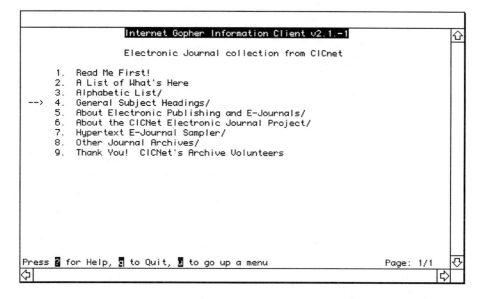

The next menu is too long to fit in a single screen, as noted by the "Page: 2/2" in the lower right-hand corner. I moved to this second page by pressing the spacebar once.

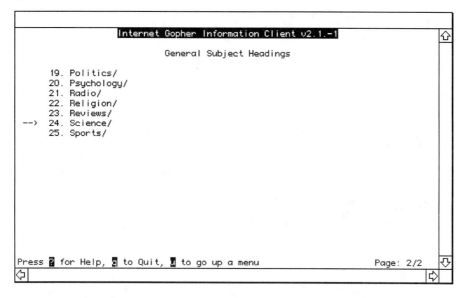

From Science we'll go down yet another level to display this menu:

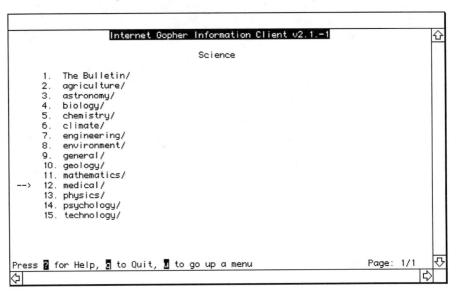

And from here to the Medical directory:

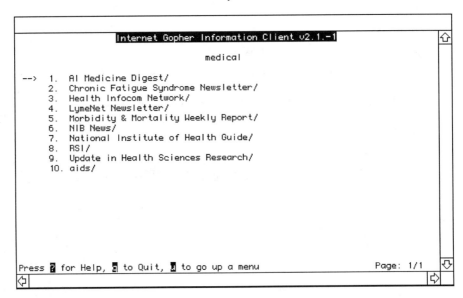

Note that we still haven't seen any files to look at or retrieve, only directories. Granted, this is a large archive, but it also exemplifies the limits of gopher for certain purposes. Thankfully, you'll see that tools like veronica add a needed layer of flexibility to gopher.

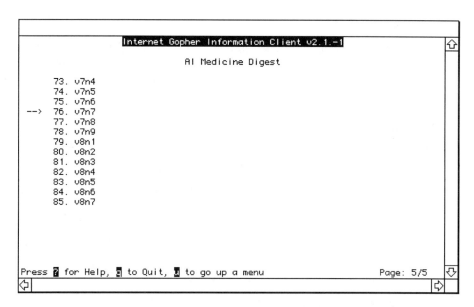

Documents at last. Notice that I'm five screens deep in this list of documents. Again, the organizational structure here assumed that I wanted to go from the oldest to the newest editions of the AI Medicine Digest, and therefore I had to navigate a bit to get to the current editions. Pressing Return now brings up the actual digest, as shown below. From here I can read it or save it as text. Typing ? would show me what my options were.

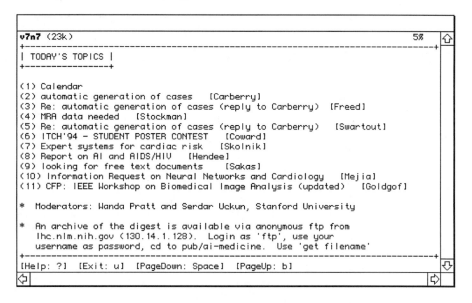

More on Navigation

The exercise above left me about eight levels deep into a directory structure. To log off, you have to back your way out of those directories the same way you came in. This is relatively easy. Just use the **u** key to keep moving up until you get to a menu that lets you quit, in this case, the UMN main menu.

But before we quit, let's explore one more menu item:

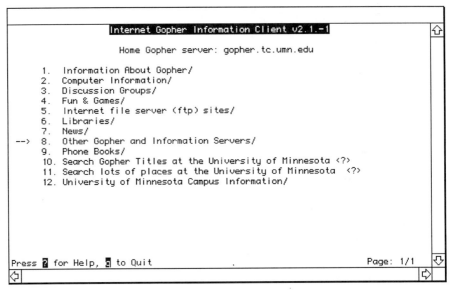

```
          Internet Gopher Information Client v2.1.-1              ⇧

                 Home Gopher server: gopher.tc.umn.edu

        1.   Information About Gopher/
        2.   Computer Information/
        3.   Discussion Groups/
        4.   Fun & Games/
        5.   Internet file server (ftp) sites/
        6.   Libraries/
        7.   News/
  -->   8.   Other Gopher and Information Servers/
        9.   Phone Books/
        10.  Search Gopher Titles at the University of Minnesota <?>
        11.  Search lots of places at the University of Minnesota  <?>
        12.  University of Minnesota Campus Information/




Press ? for Help, ? to Quit                    .           Page: 1/1  ⇩
⇦                                                                      ⇨
```

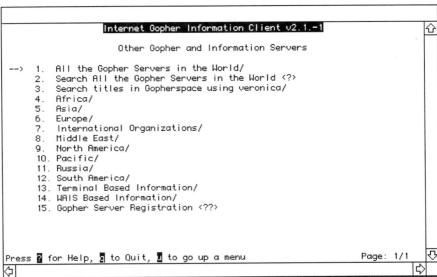

```
          Internet Gopher Information Client v2.1.-1              ⇧

                 Other Gopher and Information Servers

  -->   1.   All the Gopher Servers in the World/
        2.   Search All the Gopher Servers in the World <?>
        3.   Search titles in Gopherspace using veronica/
        4.   Africa/
        5.   Asia/
        6.   Europe/
        7.   International Organizations/
        8.   Middle East/
        9.   North America/
        10.  Pacific/
        11.  Russia/
        12.  South America/
        13.  Terminal Based Information/
        14.  WAIS Based Information/
        15.  Gopher Server Registration <??>


Press ? for Help, ? to Quit, ? to go up a menu        Page: 1/1  ⇩
⇦                                                                  ⇨
```

As I mentioned earlier, you can usually find a listing of gopher servers from a gopher main menu under the "Other Gopher and Information Servers" menu, as shown on the next page:

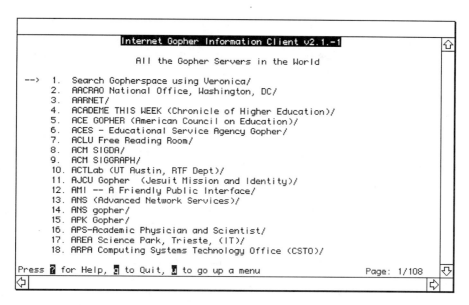

```
┌──────────────────────────────────────────────────────────────────┐
│              Internet Gopher Information Client v2.1.-1          △ │
│                                                                   │
│              All the Gopher Servers in the World                  │
│                                                                   │
│  -->  1.  Search Gopherspace using Veronica/                      │
│       2.  AACRAO National Office, Washington, DC/                 │
│       3.  AARNET/                                                 │
│       4.  ACADEME THIS WEEK (Chronicle of Higher Education)/      │
│       5.  ACE GOPHER (American Council on Education)/             │
│       6.  ACES - Educational Service Agency Gopher/              │
│       7.  ACLU Free Reading Room/                                │
│       8.  ACM SIGDA/                                             │
│       9.  ACM SIGGRAPH/                                          │
│      10.  ACTLab (UT Austin, RTF Dept)/                         │
│      11.  AJCU Gopher  (Jesuit Mission and Identity)/           │
│      12.  AMI -- A Friendly Public Interface/                   │
│      13.  ANS (Advanced Network Services)/                      │
│      14.  ANS gopher/                                           │
│      15.  APK Gopher/                                           │
│      16.  APS-Academic Physician and Scientist/                │
│      17.  AREA Science Park, Trieste, (IT)/                    │
│      18.  ARPA Computing Systems Technology Office (CSTO)/      │
│                                                                   │
│ Press ? for Help, q to Quit, u to go up a menu     Page: 1/108  ▽ │
│ ◁                                                              ▷  │
└──────────────────────────────────────────────────────────────────┘
```

Note that there are 108 screens that compose this listing, so while this is certainly an impressive list, it's perhaps not the most efficient way to find gopher servers on a particular topic. The science resources section of this book is probably a better place to start (see Appendix).

Macintosh Gopher Software

If your Macintosh computer is connected to the Internet either directly or via a SLIP/PPP connection, you can use gopher software directly from it.

TurboGopher, from the home of gopher—the University of Minnesota—is probably the most popular Macintosh gopher client. It usually comes preconfigured to log directly into the UMN gopher server, but you can change that setting to have it log into your favorite server or none at all.

```
┌────────────────────────────────────────────────────┐
│ ▦            Preferences                            │
│                                                      │
│  Home Server:  │gopher.tc.umn.edu               │   │
│                                                      │
│  Port:         │70        │                          │
│                                                      │
│  Character Set Filtering  ◉ None ○ ISO Latin 1 ○ Japanese │
│                                                      │
│  ┌ Change ┐ Default Font: Geneva 12                 │
│  ┌ Change ┐ Gopher+ Helper Applications             │
│  ┌ Change ┐ Download Folder: (None selected)        │
│                                                      │
│  Miscellaneous   ☐ Large Windows   ☐ Extended Views │
│                                                      │
│                                     ┌ Done ┐        │
└────────────────────────────────────────────────────┘
```

Unless you change the default gopher home (above), there's really nothing to set up with TurboGopher. Just type in the name or IP address of the server you want to go to, along with a port number if given (leave the default 70 there if not), and TurboGopher takes you there and then displays the gopher menu in a Macintosh window that looks similar to the Fetch FTP interface. Beyond this simple interface, there are a few basics to getting around in TurboGopher that I'll discuss here.

One nice option shown in the Preferences menu above is the ability to assign helper applications to incoming files. This option uses the Macintosh's ability to recognize file types and assign applications to open those files whenever they are downloaded with or viewed in TurboGopher. For example, you can configure TurboGopher so that any *RTF* (Rich Text Format) document you encounter will be opened (and converted) automatically in your favorite word processing program. If this option weren't set, the RTF file would show up on your Macintosh in a generic format and you would have to convert it yourself.

Using TurboGopher on the Internet is easy. If you know the address of a gopher server you want to explore (e.g., if you find a site in the Resources section of this book), select Another Gopher from the Gopher menu, then type in the address as shown below. Note that this example also has a nonstandard port number that I have also entered:

In a few seconds you should see the top-level directory of the gopher server, in this case, the University of California at Santa Barbara, as shown on the next page:

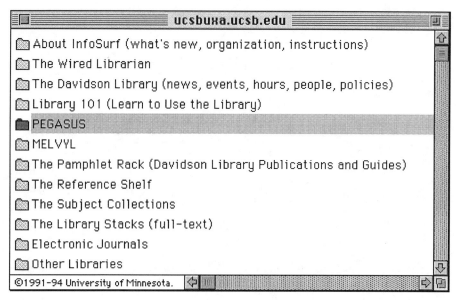

Double-clicking on any of the menu items here (all directory folders in this example) open that directory. Actual files show up as document icons in the menu, and double-clicking on one of them will display them on your Macintosh. That's really all there is to it. Other options are explained in TurboGopher's excellent online Help menu.

Where to Find TurboGopher

You can find the latest version of TurboGopher via FTP from the following site, or from any Info-Mac mirror site (see Appendix).

boombox.micro.umn.edu/pub/gopher/Macintosh-TurboGopher/

For information on connecting your Macintosh computer to the Internet, see Appendix.

Windows Gopher Software

If your Windows PC is connected to the Internet either directly or via a SLIP/ PPP connection, you can use gopher software directly from it.

There are a few programs available that provide a nice front-end for the Internet's gopher services. One of the most popular Windows gopher clients is WSGopher.

Like most gopher clients, WSGopher is virtually plug-and-play. As with any Windows program, you must first create a program item for WSGopher after unzipping the archive. Then make sure you fill in the "Working Directory" with the directory where *wsgopher.exe* and *wsgopher.ini* reside. Then go ahead and launch WSGopher.

The first time you launch WSGopher it will probably log in to some major go-

pher server like the University of Minnesota or the University of Indiana. You
can change this later if you want.

To go to a gopher server of your choosing, just bring up the Open Gopher
option and type in the address and port number (if given) in the fields as shown
here:

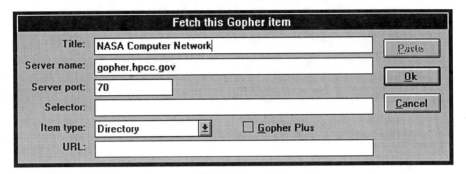

Once you're connected you'll see the site's (in this case, NASA's) main menu:

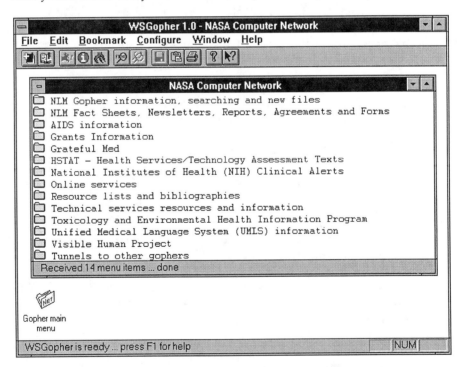

Now you're ready to double-click your way down through the site's archives.
It's that simple.

Among WSGopher's many options is the ability to set up a wide range of viewer programs for text, graphic, and audio files. Since gopher can also utilize FTP and telnet protocols, you can also set up default programs that will be launched when a file is requested or a telnet session is initiated.

If you know the address of a particular gopher (as we did above) and wish to add the gopher to a permanent menu, this can be done from the Bookmarks menu with the Add Bookmark option. Just fill in the address and the name you wish to appear on the menu. Most gophers use the default port 70, but some gophers are set up on different ports. You should make sure you enter the correct port where the gopher can be found when creating a Bookmark.

Finally, a small set of icons at the bottom of the window can also be used to navigate *gopherspace*, as it's sometimes called. You can use the items to go backward, forward, and home, as well as several other navigational options.

Where to Find WSGopher

You can find the latest version of WSGopher via FTP from the following site, or from most Windows FTP archives (see Appendix):

boombox.micro.umn.edu/pub/gopher/Windows/

For more information on connecting your Windows computer to the Internet, see Appendix.

Veronica

Veronica ("very easy rodent-oriented network index to computerized archives") is the companion tool to gopher. Veronica lets the user perform keyword searches of gopherspace. The results of the search are presented as menu items leading to more specific information.

With all these tools and funny names, I try to think in analogies so I can remember what something does. For me, veronica is to gopher what archie is to FTP. Why? Remember that archie is just a searchable database of what is located on a lot of FTP sites. Similarly, veronica is just a searchable database of what is listed in gopher menus.

Where do we find veronica? Usually access to veronica is through the "All the Gophers in the World" or "Other Gopher and Information Servers" on most main gopher menus.

Searching with Veronica

Veronica is a relatively simple searching tool. Here are some options and hints to remember when constructing searches:

- searches are not case sensitive;
- you can use logical operators **and** and **or**;

- any space between keywords is interpreted as the logical operator **and**;
- interpretation of the query begins from the right;
- if in doubt of the interpretation, use parentheses to enclose the words you want searched first.

For more detailed instructions, retrieve the "How to Compose Veronica Searches" document from the veronica menu.

Now, to get at veronica, we go back to our gopher connection and dig down through the menus:

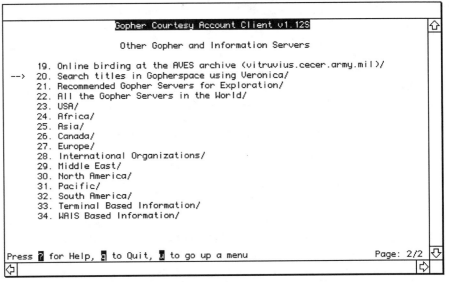

Now we have to pick the kind of search and the server to search:

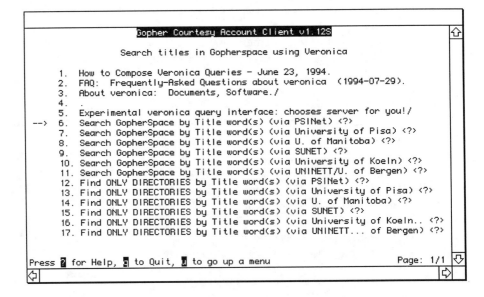

I've chosen to search on title words (that is, filenames) through the PSINet (a large commercial Internet site) server:

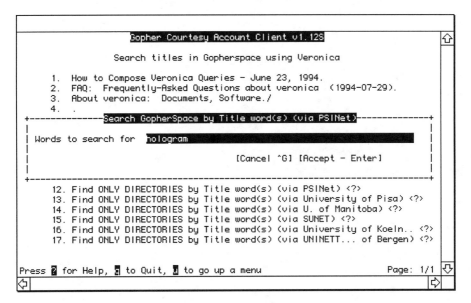

```
            Gopher Courtesy Account Client v1.12S                    ⇧

            Search titles in Gopherspace using Veronica

     1.   How to Compose Veronica Queries - June 23, 1994.
     2.   FAQ:  Frequently-Asked Questions about veronica  (1994-07-29).
     3.   About veronica:  Documents, Software./
     4.   .
   +---------------Search GopherSpace by Title word(s) (via PSINet)---------------+
   |                                                                               |
   | Words to search for  hologram                                                 |
   |                                                                               |
   |                             [Cancel ^G] [Accept - Enter]                      |
   |                                                                               |
   +-------------------------------------------------------------------------------+
     12. Find ONLY DIRECTORIES by Title word(s) (via PSINet) <?>
     13. Find ONLY DIRECTORIES by Title word(s) (via University of Pisa) <?>
     14. Find ONLY DIRECTORIES by Title word(s) (via U. of Manitoba) <?>
     15. Find ONLY DIRECTORIES by Title word(s) (via SUNET) <?>
     16. Find ONLY DIRECTORIES by Title word(s) (via University of Koeln.. <?>
     17. Find ONLY DIRECTORIES by Title word(s) (via UNINETT... of Bergen) <?>


Press ? for Help, q to Quit, u to go up a menu              Page: 1/1  ⇩
◁                                                                     ▷
```

In the search "window" that displays, you enter your search term(s) and press Enter or Return (same thing on most keyboards).

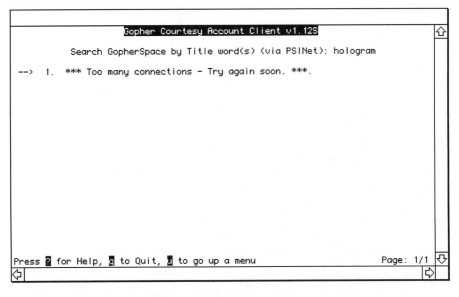

```
            Gopher Courtesy Account Client v1.12S                    ⇧

        Search GopherSpace by Title word(s) (via PSINet): hologram

  -->  1.  *** Too many connections - Try again soon. ***.












Press ? for Help, q to Quit, u to go up a menu              Page: 1/1  ⇩
◁                                                                     ▷
```

Here is one of the first limitations of veronica. While the concepts are great, the reality is that there are a lot of people trying to use a few resources, and that means lots of traffic jams. At this point you would have to go back up a menu using the **u** command and choose a different site to search with veronica. I've done this enough to know that it's not efficient research.

I went back and found another server to search for "hologram," and after a long wait, I received these results:

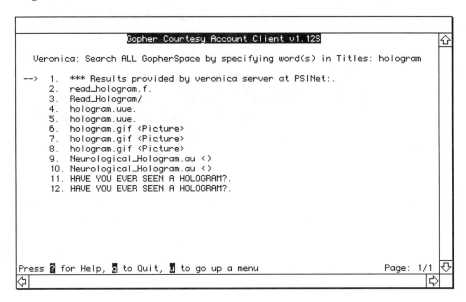

Not exactly impressive. By arrowing down and using the = key, you can often see the source of each of these files. This one looked good, so I selected it and here's what happened:

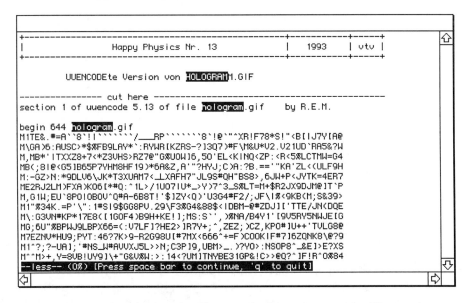

What happened here is that the file I was looking at was a GIF file—an image. The image is uuencoded. This is of absolutely no use to me, since as a encoded binary file it's probably hundreds of pages of text like this. This is the kind of file for which you would need to use FTP to retrieve. There are a few gopher clients out there that are actually smart enough to switch to an FTP session to retrieve a file like this, but in this situation it still wouldn't work, since we are telneting to another computer and using its gopher client. If we could download a file via FTP, it would be transferred to the computer we were remotely logged into, not our own Internet computer. The only way you can successfully transfer a file from one computer to another is if your computer is running the actual transfer software, such as FTP.

Just the FAQs

To get the FAQ listed below, send the command shown to

    `mail-server@rtfm.mit.edu`

This is an e-mail server that will automatically send you the file you've requested. Send these commands in the body of your e-mail message. You may also get these files via FTP from this location. *Remember that this server is Unix-based: Use upper- and lower-case letters exactly as shown.*

Gopher and Veronica FAQ

Send this command:

    `send pub/usenet/news.answers/gopher-faq`

Chapter 12

ONLINE DATABASES

WAIS—Wide-Area Information Servers

Wide-Area Information Servers are standardized databases with hypertext features. They allow natural language searches, meaning you can type whole sentences like "find all papers on polymers and aircraft composite materials" and the software will interpret your query as a Boolean construction.

Like the WWW and gopher, WAIS is a client-server arrangement, so you need access to client software, either on your Internet host computer, or via telnet to a public WAIS client. Because WAIS is still relatively new, client software is still in its infancy. However, support for WAIS is growing quickly, as are new clients under development.

WAIS clients are able to retrieve text or multimedia documents stored on the servers. From your client software, you first request documents using keywords. The WAIS server then searches a full-text index for the documents and return a list of documents containing the keyword. You can then request the server to send a copy of any of the documents found.

Although the term "Wide Area" implies the use of large networks such as the Internet to connect clients to servers distributed around the network, WAIS can be used between a client and server on the same machine or a client and server on the same LAN. Some large organizations use the WAIS client-server arrangement to provide staff members with access to a database or series of databases.

WAIS uses the Z39.50 query protocol to communicate between clients and servers. You'll often see this obtuse designation used to reference a WAIS database. Unfortunately, it's not exactly mnemonic.

At the time of this writing there are over 500 known WAIS databases. Topics range from recipes and movies to bibliographies, technical documents, and newsgroup archives.

What Kinds of Resources Are on WAIS Servers?

WAIS resources are databases of information; however, they are exceptionally good at handling complex textual information, so in many ways they are much more than a typical database. The ability to search on a full-text index is a powerful tool.

The kinds of information resources you'll find in WAIS databases are typically bibliographies, books, archie databases (FTP files), library catalogs, and many Internet-related databases such as archives of Usenet group messages and discussion lists.

What's So Great about WAIS?

WAIS was originally developed as a joint effort by Thinking Machines, Apple Computer, Dow Jones, and KPMG Peat Marwick. As such, it has its roots in the concept of archiving large amounts of varying types of information for easy retrieval. The original project was to create something corporate executives could rely upon for retrieving information without having to learn all sorts of query language nuances.

WAIS queries are not Boolean constructions such as, "Search for MEDICAL and IMAGING but not CAMERA." Instead, WAIS searches sources that you specify using natural language queries, such as, "Find information on medical imaging." Notice I didn't say "but not cameras." This is because, at least for now, WAIS does not recognize this exception operator.

By now you might be thinking this is a limited system. Not true. What WAIS does bring back from your search is a list of documents that is *ranked* by which documents have the most occurrences of the words you were searching on. This is sometimes called *relevance ranking*, because you can also refine your search by identifying one or more documents in your search results that are close to what you're looking for, and then WAIS will go out and find other documents that have similar content.

Let's make up an example of this *relevance feedback* concept in action. Say you search on the word *conductor*. The WAIS search results included documents on superconductors, heat conductors, semiconductors, and trains. By selecting one of the documents on semiconductors as input for relevance feedback, words like *detectors, solid state,* and *photomasks* will become keywords in subsequent searches, and therefore you shouldn't get any documents returned on train conductors; they will be weeded out by the relevance feedback mechanism.

Accessing WAIS

The easiest way to get started with WAIS is to telnet to a public access WAIS site using the **swais** (Screen, or Simple, WAIS) interface. This is a command-line interface to WAIS that is similar in function to using a WAIS client on your own computer, which is definitely the way to go if you can and if you plan to do a lot of WAIS searching.

Below are three sites you could telnet to and log in with the username *wais* and your e-mail address as the password:

```
sunsite.unc.edu
wais.wais.com
quake.think.com
```

Let's try one:

```
% telnet wais.wais.com
```

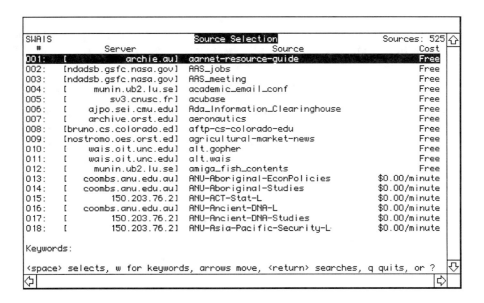

This is the "Directory of Servers" that lists nearly all of the WAIS databases you can connect to on the Internet. Note that there are 525 server sources listed here (see upper right-hand corner of screen). Since I don't want to have to scroll through all of them one by one, the first thing I'll do is look at the Help menu by typing a question mark (**?**):

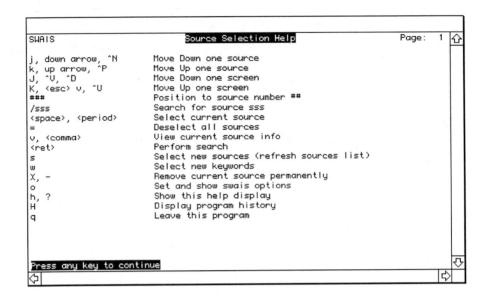

Because of the number of sources to choose from, this Source Selection Help menu will come in handy. To scroll more quickly, we'll use the capital J and K keys (note that the ^ next to a letter means "press the Control key and that letter simultaneously"; for example, ^V means "Control-V"). We can come back to this menu at any time for reference.

Now, we press any key to get back to our menu. Here's what this screen is all about. There are 525 WAIS databases listed here that you can choose to search. This screen is only a way to tell the WAIS client we're using at **wais.wais.com** which sources we want to look at. Why? Because there's no sense searching a database called "cisco-packet" when you're looking for weather information.

For now, since we're just exploring, I happen know that *The Scientist* newspaper is archived by the InterNIC, so I'll look for that source by typing a slash (/) to bring up the Search for Source option, and then type **the** (which is enough of the publication's title to get me to the line item) followed by a Return to go there (see facing page):

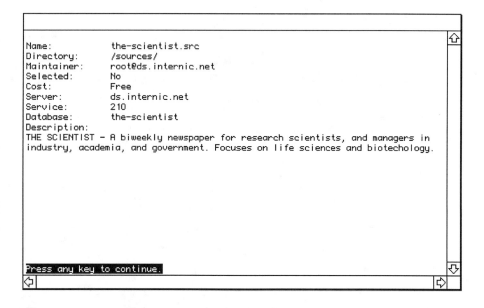

From here I can find more information about the source by typing the **v** key:

Simple and to the point.

Back at the source selection menu, we'll mark **The Scientist** source as the database we want to search by pressing the spacebar while it's highlighted. You can select multiple sources to search this way as well. To deselect a source, just press the spacebar again. At this point we can also enter our keywords. Let's try to find information about semiconductors. Note that I'm going to search on both *semiconductor* and *semiconductors*. WAIS searches the actual text of the documents, and I want to make sure I get both occurrences, singular and plural.

There are no wildcards in WAIS, as there are with other kinds of database searches.

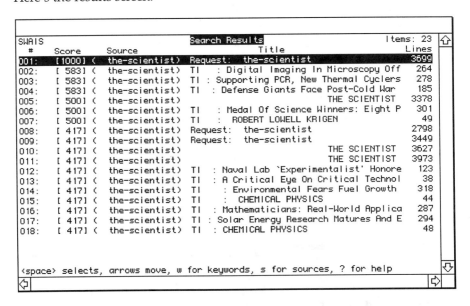

Here's the results screen:

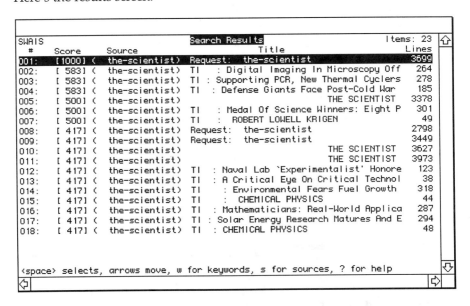

Excellent. There are 23 documents (in this case, articles) that matched my search. Note the "Score" numbers to the left of each entry. This is a WAIS trademark. The results of the search are ranked according to ratio of hits per words in the document. The number 1000 is always the most relevant document, and all others are scored in order of decreasing relevance from there.

So in the case above, the difference between our first ranking document and our second, at a score of 583, is significant. It could mean that the first article is in fact extremely relevant and the rest are not, or it could also mean that the first article is much smaller yet contains the search terms in a much higher ratio than the other documents. This is one of the peculiarities of relevance-ranked searches. Note, however, the Lines column at the far right. This tells you how many lines are in each article. Clearly this first article is large, so perhaps it is not the case that the search-term-occurrences-to-file-size ratio is a factor here. But be careful. An article that's 3000 lines long is going to take a while to sort through. My guess is this is a whole issue of *The Scientist* magazine, whereas some of the other ones listed here are single articles and are probably more useful as such. Let's look at the second one on the list. Just arrow down to it (or type the number 002) and then press the spacebar:

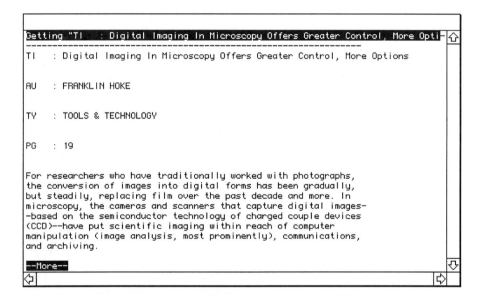

At this point you may wish to save the article. Here's where having your own WAIS client is handy. Whenever you telnet to another computer and use its software, you can no longer access the functions on your own Internet host computer. The only thing your own computer knows is that you're off somewhere doing a telnet session, and it just waits there patiently for you to come back.

This particular server (**wais.wais.com**) does have a command (press m while the article is selected in the list) to e-mail yourself an article, but when I tried it it didn't work, so perhaps it's again limited to a client accessing the WAIS database directly, instead of through another computer.

So, the only way to save this article is to—if you can—capture the screen buffer while reading the article. On a Unix computer, you can try using the script command to save what's on the screen as text. On a computer with a windowing interface, it might be easy to capture text from the screen buffer using either a command in your telnet software (such as **Save as Text**), or a Capture Log function, or even just copying text from the window using the Clipboard.

To end our WAIS session, we need to get back to the sources list, and then type **q** and we're back at our host computer.

Macintosh and Windows WAIS Software

If your Macintosh or Windows PC is connected to the Internet either directly or via a SLIP/PPP connection, you can use WAIS software directly from it. This software is generally more powerful than the simple WAIS command-line interface demonstrated above. However, it's also very new, and therefore I am choosing not to illustrate its use here. New software clients have a predictable tendency to change radically during the early stages, and therefore demonstrating them tends to prematurely age books such as this.

But don't let my trepidation stop you from trying out some of these new personal computer WAIS clients. One of the best places to find a number of them is the University of North Carolina's FTP server at

```
sunsite.unc.edu/pub/packages/infosystems/wais/clients/
```

Most of the major FTP sites are also starting to archive these new clients.

OPACs—Online Public Access Catalogs

Over the past few years, many libraries have converted their traditional card catalog systems to online databases, and many now provide online access to them. Many also offer gateways to commercial systems such as Dialog, MEDLINE, and Inspec. However, these are sometimes limited to registered patrons of a given library. For example, if you were a faculty member of a university, you would probably have access to most if not all of your university library's OPAC, including these proprietary databases, whereas members of the community might be limited to only searching the author, title, and subject database for the institution's own holdings.

What Can I Do with an OPAC

OPACs are useful for compiling bibliographies, especially as they often contain more information than the traditional card catalogs did due to their limitations, as well as offering a more interactive searching environment. This can save you a lot of time.

A good place to start exploring with OPACs is a large library system. Following is a session on MELVYL, the University of California's vast archive of their statewide library system. Later I'll provide some other site addresses to explore. Each OPAC is unique in terms of commands and navigation; however, most are easy to learn and navigate.

We start by telneting to MELVYL's Internet address, **melvyl.ucop.edu**. Once we're there, we see the following screen:

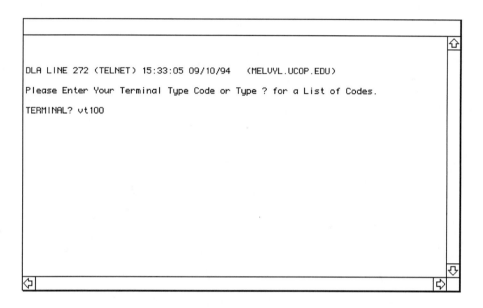

```
DLA LINE 272 (TELNET) 15:33:05 09/10/94   (MELVYL.UCOP.EDU)

Please Enter Your Terminal Type Code or Type ? for a List of Codes.

TERMINAL? vt100
```

We've learned this is typical for a telnet login—the MELVYL computer wants to know what terminal type we are emulating, and VT100 is the default, so we press Return and get the Welcome screen.

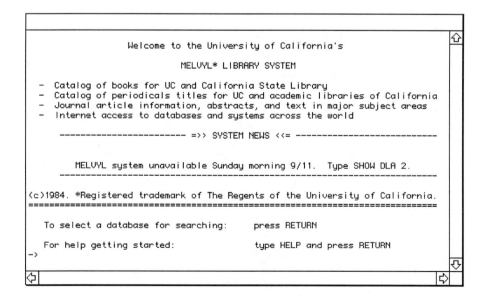

```
                    Welcome to the University of California's

                         MELVYL* LIBRARY SYSTEM

     -  Catalog of books for UC and California State Library
     -  Catalog of periodicals titles for UC and academic libraries of California
     -  Journal article information, abstracts, and text in major subject areas
     -  Internet access to databases and systems across the world

          ----------------------- =>> SYSTEM NEWS <<= ----------------------------


          MELVYL system unavailable Sunday morning 9/11.  Type SHOW DLA 2.
     -----------------------------------------------------------------------------
(c)1984. *Registered trademark of The Regents of the University of California.
=================================================================================
     To select a database for searching:     press RETURN

     For help getting started:               type HELP and press RETURN
->
```

From here we'll press Return again to get to a list of databases we can search. MELVYL is so large that it contains a number of specialized databases, plus access (often for UC students and staff only) to many commercial (pay-as-you-go) databases.

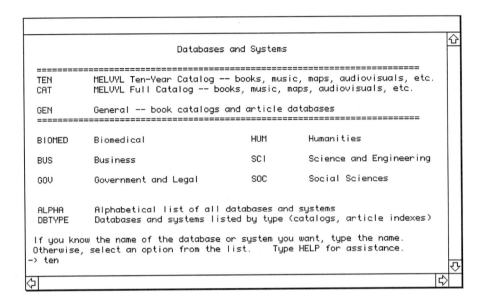

From here I'll type **ten** to move to the Ten-Year Catalog Database.

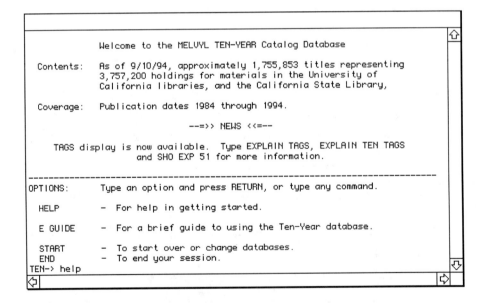

Time to invoke the online Help, which is often the only way we'll ever get to see all the possible commands.

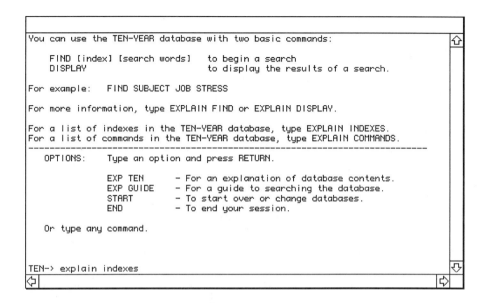

```
You can use the TEN-YEAR database with two basic commands:

    FIND [index] [search words]    to begin a search
    DISPLAY                        to display the results of a search.

For example:   FIND SUBJECT JOB STRESS

For more information, type EXPLAIN FIND or EXPLAIN DISPLAY.

For a list of indexes in the TEN-YEAR database, type EXPLAIN INDEXES.
For a list of commands in the TEN-YEAR database, type EXPLAIN COMMANDS.
-------------------------------------------------------------------
   OPTIONS:    Type an option and press RETURN.

               EXP TEN    - For an explanation of database contents.
               EXP GUIDE  - For a guide to searching the database.
               START      - To start over or change databases.
               END        - To end your session.

   Or type any command.


TEN-> explain indexes
```

Now we'll ask MELVYL to "explain indexes" to learn more about the commands we'll need to explore the online indexes.

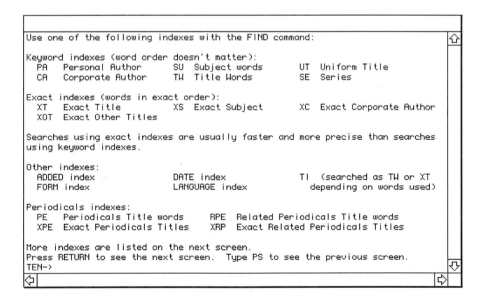

```
Use one of the following indexes with the FIND command:

Keyword indexes (word order doesn't matter):
  PA   Personal Author      SU  Subject words      UT  Uniform Title
  CA   Corporate Author     TW  Title Words        SE  Series

Exact indexes (words in exact order):
  XT   Exact Title          XS  Exact Subject      XC  Exact Corporate Author
  XOT  Exact Other Titles

Searches using exact indexes are usually faster and more precise than searches
using keyword indexes.

Other indexes:
  ADDED index              DATE index            TI  (searched as TW or XT
  FORM index               LANGUAGE index            depending on words used)

Periodicals indexes:
  PE    Periodicals Title words     RPE  Related Periodicals Title words
  XPE   Exact Periodicals Titles    XRP  Exact Related Periodicals Titles

More indexes are listed on the next screen.
Press RETURN to see the next screen.  Type PS to see the previous screen.
TEN->
```

After this I used the **ps** command to go back to my search screen [which wasn't necessary, since the **TEN—>** prompt (lower left corner) appears here too and tells me I can search the Ten-Year Database from here].

To start my search, I'll pick a wide topical area, such as semiconductors. So I typed **find subject semiconductor** and this is what I got:

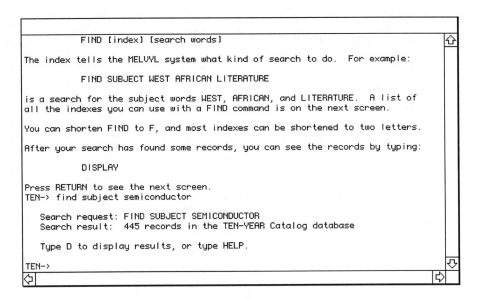

Perhaps 445 records is a little excessive. I now know I should search on a narrower term, so I try **find subject semiconductor physics**:

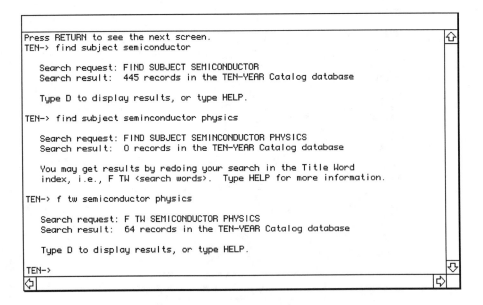

Okay, I admit I cheated and really did two steps above. My subject search on semiconductor physics turned up zero hits, but then I noticed the line there that said "You may get results by redoing your search in the Title Word index, i.e., F TW <search words>." So that's what I did. I typed **f tw semiconductor physics** and got 64 records. Then I typed **d** to display the results:

```
Search request: F TW SEMICONDUCTOR PHYSICS                          ⇧
Search result:  64 records in the TEN-YEAR Catalog database

Type HELP for other display options.

18. Conference on the Physics and Technology of Semiconductor Devices and
       Integrated Circuits (1992 : Indian Institute of Technology, Madras, India)
         Conference on the Physics and Technology of Semiconductor Devices and
       Integrated Circuits : proceedings, 5-7 February 1992, Indian Institute of
       Technology, Madras, India / B.S.V. Gopalam, editor ; J. Majhi,...  New
       Delhi : Tata McGraw-Hill Publishing in cooperation with SPIE, c1992.
         Series title:  Proceedings of SPIE--the International Society for Optical
       Engineering ; v. 1523.
            UCB    Engin      TK7871.85 .C7485 1992
            UCD    Phys Sci   TS510.S63 v.1523
            UCI    Main Lib   TS510 .P632 v.1523
            UCLA   Engr/Math  QC 610.9 C637 1992
            UCSD   S & E      TK7871.85 .C7485 1992




Press RETURN to see next screen. Type PS to see previous screen.
TEN->                                                               ⇩
⇦                                                                   ⇨
```

Here's the 18th entry, which I scrolled down to using the Return key. Not too many surprises here—a typical bibliographic citation, including the locations of every copy in the UC library system.

Now, to see what other options I have here, I typed **help**:

```
   You have just seen one of several screens of the                ⇧
      short display of your search result.

   Your search
      FIND TW SEMICONDUCTOR PHYSICS
   retrieved 64 records for items at all libraries.

Type NS to see the Next Screen of display.  You can also use any of the
following display options.  Type EXPLAIN DISPLAY for more information.

   To display a record number or group of records      D 3 6 8-10
   To display using another option (REVIEW, SHORT, LONG)  D LONG
   To display every nth record                         D BY 3
   To display certain fields in the record             D TI SU
   To display a combination of the above               D 10- REV

You can also:
   Type SHOW SEARCH to see other current results available for display.
   Type SHOW HISTORY to see your search history.
   Type EXPLAIN ADD ON to find out how to broaden or narrow your search result.
   Type EXPLAIN COMMANDS to find out what other commands you can use.
   Type END to end your session.
TEN->                                                               ⇩
⇦                                                                   ⇨
```

There are a lot of options for refining things. Since 64 citations is still too broad, I typed **explain add on** to see how to narrow my search:

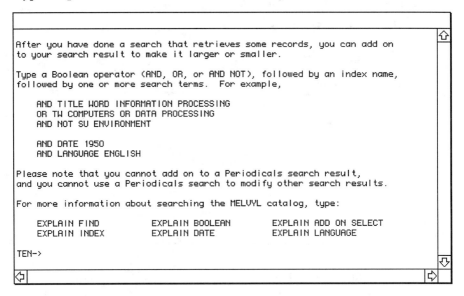

```
After you have done a search that retrieves some records, you can add on
to your search result to make it larger or smaller.

Type a Boolean operator (AND, OR, or AND NOT), followed by an index name,
followed by one or more search terms.  For example,

    AND TITLE WORD INFORMATION PROCESSING
    OR TW COMPUTERS OR DATA PROCESSING
    AND NOT SU ENVIRONMENT

    AND DATE 1950
    AND LANGUAGE ENGLISH

Please note that you cannot add on to a Periodicals search result,
and you cannot use a Periodicals search to modify other search results.

For more information about searching the MELVYL catalog, type:

    EXPLAIN FIND          EXPLAIN BOOLEAN        EXPLAIN ADD ON SELECT
    EXPLAIN INDEX         EXPLAIN DATE           EXPLAIN LANGUAGE

TEN->
```

Turns out I can add a Boolean phrase to my original search, so I'll try adding the word **laser** to my search by typing **and tw laser**:

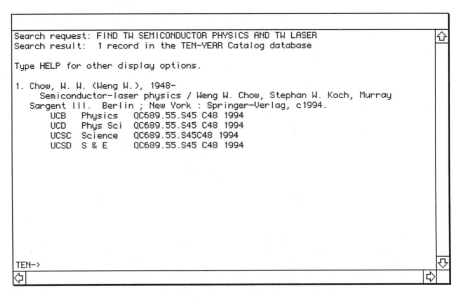

```
Search request: FIND TW SEMICONDUCTOR PHYSICS AND TW LASER
Search result:  1 record in the TEN-YEAR Catalog database

Type HELP for other display options.

1. Chow, W. W. (Weng W.), 1948-
       Semiconductor-laser physics / Weng W. Chow, Stephan W. Koch, Murray
   Sargent III.  Berlin ; New York : Springer-Verlag, c1994.
       UCB   Physics    QC689.55.S45 C48 1994
       UCD   Phys Sci   QC689.55.S45 C48 1994
       UCSC  Science    QC689.55.S45C48 1994
       UCSD  S & E      QC689.55.S45 C48 1994

TEN->
```

That certainly narrowed it down. Only one book on semiconductor laser physics. But remember—I specified a *title search*. There are certainly many more books that deal with this topic, but the search is only as smart as the searcher. Depending on what I was really looking for, I might have chosen some other index, such as a keyword or subject index.

That's enough screen-hopping to get the idea. There are a huge number of options here to explore.

To quit our session, we can either type **start** to take us back to the main MELVYL menu, or **end** will quit our telnet session completely.

Remember that every computer you telnet to may have different commands to navigate and perform actions. Whenever you telnet to a new computer, find out where the online help is and read it.

How to Find OPACs

There are an astounding number of OPACs on the Internet today. Below are a few to get you started, but for a more comprehensive source, see the Just the FAQs section at the end of this chapter.

Institution	Internet Address	Login Name
Australian National University	library.anu.edu.au	library
California PolyTechnic State University	library.calpoly.edu	none
Carnegie-Mellon University	library.cmu.edu	none
Colorado Alliance of Research Libraries	pac.carl.org	none
University of California	melvyl.ucop.edu	none
University of Washington	uwin.u.washington.edu	none

Commercial Databases

There are a number of companies that offer document delivery services from large archival databases they own. Usually these organizations purchase or procure abstracts, citations, and full-text manuscripts from a number of publishers in an attempt to offer searches of the world literature base in one or more scientific disciplines.

Below is some information about a few of the larger commercial databases. For further information, see the Just the FAQs section at the end of this chapter.

MELVYL

MELVYL is a major online content provider offering access to the University of California library system and to the California State Library catalog. While it's not commercial per se, it does offer access to commercial services such as MEDLINE, INSPEC, Current Contents, PsycINFO, and others. Searchable library catalog access is unrestricted, while many of the other databases require a password and/or University of California student or staff ID number. MELVYL can be accessed through the NETLIB library gateway at most Internet telnet sites. See the table in the previous section on OPACs for telnet access information.

CARL/UnCover

UnCover is an article access and delivery service available through the CARL System and requiring no fees or special logon privileges for searching the database. More than 4,000 current citations are added daily to UnCover, which offers fax copies of articles from the database for a fee. For information, contact CARL at **database@carl.org**, or for UnCover help, call 303/758-3030.

The British Library Document Supply Center (BLDSC) (article delivery) is also available through CARL. 54,000 currently received titles, 170,000 out-of-print journals. The BLDSC is the most complete document delivery service in the world. Base fee is $19/article copyright-cleared.

CARL—Colorado Alliance of Research Libraries
Marketed and supported by CARL Systems, Inc.
3801 East Florida St., Suite 300
Denver, CO 80210
303/7580-3030
Fax 303/758-0606
Internet **help@carl.org**

Dialog

The databases on the Dialog system contain more than 260 million records across a wide range of disciplines and scientific/engineering technologies. Dialog's holdings include CompendexPlus, one of the largest engineering databases in the world. Dialog fulfills requests through Dialog SourceOne:Engineering, and also offers delivery of documents from the collections of Delft University of Technology and the Royal Academy of Arts and Sciences.

Contact:
Dialog Information Services
3460 Hillview Ave.
Palo Alto, CA 94304
800/334-2564
415/858-3785
fax 415/858-7069

FAXON

A subscription-based acquisition and management service, including document delivery. For an account, call 800/766-0039.

The FAXON Company
15 Southwest Park
Westwood MA 02090
800/766-0039
617/329-3350
617/329-9875
Internet **help@faxon.com**

INSPEC

INSPEC is the leading English-language abstracting and indexing service providing abstracts and source information from the world's published literature in physics, electronics, and computing. Offers online access, tape services, and paper abstract journals.

INSPEC
U.S. orders and information:
INSPEC Department
IEEE Service Center
445 Hoes Lane
P.O. Box 1331
Piscataway, NJ 08855-1331
201/562-5549
Fax 201/981-0027

UK and overseas:
INSPEC Publication Sales
Institution of Electrical Engineers (IEE)
P.O. Box 96
Stevenage
Herts SG12SD
United Kingdom
44 438 313311
Fax 44 438 742792

MEDLINE

MEDLINE is one of the National Library of Medicine's bibliographic databases, containing references to over 3700 journals.

MEDLINE covers all aspects of biomedicine, including the allied health fields as well as the biological and physical sciences, humanities, and information sciences as they relate to medicine and health care.

MEDLINE is accessible from numerous campus-wide information systems. The best way to find access to MEDLINE is often through a local university library's online services. Many university systems restrict access to local residents or affiliates only. For example, the University of Washington's CWIS, known as UWIN, grants access to local users who use the same Internet service provider (NorthWestNet) as the university. If you try to access MEDLINE through UWIN from a location outside of the local area (domain), you see a different set of UWIN menus and MEDLINE is no longer an option.

Here are some libraries that offer limited access to MEDLINE via telnet:

melvyl.ucop.edu
lib.dartmouth.edu

library.umdnj.edu (log in as LIBRARY)
utmem1.utmem.edu (log in as HARVEY)

OCLC

OCLC is the producer of the Online Union Catalog, available on both its FirstSearch and EPIC services. For full-line product descriptions and membership information, contact an OCLC-affiliated regional network.

Access FirstSearch via telnet to **epic.prod.oclc.org** (132.174.100.2)

OCLC (Online Computer Library Center, Inc.)
6565 Frantz Rd.
Dublin, Ohio 43017-3395
614/764-6000

Springer-Verlag Science Journals Project

Offers tables of contents and BiblioAbstracts of many important scientific journals via e-mail before print publication.

Springer-Verlag GmbH & Co. KG, New Technologies/Product Development
PO Box 10 52 80
W-6900 Heidelberg, Germany
fax +49 622 487 648

Professional Societies

Many professional societies in the sciences operate online services, both for a fee and free. These often include useful features such as world event calendars, technology FAQs, journal submission information, online publications, searchable databases, and even abstracts and other online technical resources.

There are thousands of professional societies, and their online capabilities are growing daily. If you have access to the World Wide Web (see Ch. 13), here is a great place to start:

```
http://www.lib.uwaterloo.ca/society/overview.html
```

Another way to find a society online is to guess at their Internet address based on either their name or, more commonly, an acronym associated with their name. Most societies will also have a **.org** domain suffix, since most are non-profits and do not fit under the **.com** category.

For example, if you wanted to find out if the American Institute of Physics was online, you could try to connect via FTP to either **ftp.aip.org** or just **aip.org**. Chances are, if the organization is out there, one or even both of these addresses will work. In the same way, you can test for telnet, gopher, and WWW access. Examples:

> **http://www.aip.org or http://aip.org**
> **gopher://gopher.aip.org or gopher://aip.org**
> **telnet://aip.org**

Just the FAQs

To get any of the FAQs listed below, send the command shown to

> `mail-server@rtfm.mit.edu`

This is an e-mail server that will automatically send you the file you've requested. Send these commands in the body of your e-mail message. *Remember that this server is Unix-based: Use upper- and lower-case letters exactly as shown.*

WAIS Resources

WAIS FAQ
Send this command:

> `send /pub/usenet/news.answers/wais-faq/getting-started`

WAIS Current Sites List
A list of current WAIS sites is available via FTP at

> `quake.think.com/wais/wais-sources.tar.Z`

WAIS Mailing Lists

wais-interest
  Subscribe to: **wais-interest-request@think.com**
  This is a moderated list used to announce new releases for the Internet environment.
wais-discussion
  Subscribe to: **wais-discussion-request@think.com**
  The WAIS-discussion is a digested, moderated list on electronic publishing issues in general and Wide-Area Information Servers in particular. There are postings every week or two.
wais-talk
  Subscribe to: **wais-talk-request@think.com**
  The WAIS-talk is an open list (interactive, not moderated) for implementors and developers. This is a technical list that is not meant to be used as a support list.

OPAC Resources

Current list of OPACs

Retrieve via FTP from:

```
ftp.unt.edu/pub/library
```

Or via gopher from any of these following sites:

```
yaleinfo.yale.edu:7000
gopher.utdallas.edu
gopher.sunet.se
```

Chapter 13

WORLD WIDE WEB

The World Wide Web, or simply the "web," is an ingenious front-end to much of the information already on the Internet, although that information is best if it's modified specifically for access on the WWW. Like gopher, the web provides an entry point to the Internet that expands outward in an exploratory way using many of the basic Internet tools such as FTP, telnet, Usenet, and even gopher. This chapter explains the two primary methods of accessing the web, first through what's known as a line browser, where only text is displayed with only rudimentary formatting, and second—increasingly common—through a *graphical browser*, which takes full advantage of the web's capabilities.

The web was originally developed at CERN, the European Laboratory for Particle Physics. Its first stated purpose (from the original proposal) was to "provide a common (simple) protocol for requesting human readable information stored at a remote system, using networks." The overlying objective was simple: give scientists a way to exchange many kinds of data (text, graphics, figures, databases) using a concept known as *hypertext* for the purpose of advancing their research. From this test-bed, the implementation and response from the online community has exploded into the most promising Internet access method ever.

What is Hypertext?

The key to the WWW is the use of hypertext, an idea that goes all the way back to Vannevar Bush in 1945. Twenty years later, Ted Nelson coined the term *hypertext*, but it's only been recently that the term and the implementation has made its way into the mainstream.

The web is a radical departure from the hierarchical world you've read about or explored on the Internet so far, where drilling down through directory trees is the normal way to navigate. The fundamental concept behind hypertext is that information can be stored and retrieved in a nonhierarchical structure. So instead of moving through directories of information, such as you would during an FTP or telnet session, you can instead "jump" from one place to the next through a series of "links" created by someone.

The concept of a "link" is important here. A link can literally connect a single word in an online journal on a computer in Tokyo to a proceedings paper on a computer in Brussels. And by "connect" we mean that you simply select the word (using a mouse or key command) and you are immediately transported to the other document halfway around the world. And it doesn't even have to be a document. It can be a graphic, a sound, a movie—practically anything that can be saved in a computer-readable format.

Here's a real example. Suppose you were reading the paragraph above on your computer screen, and the first portion looked like this:

The concept of a **link** is important here. A link can literally connect a single word in an online **journal** on a computer in **Tokyo** to a proceedings **paper** on a computer in **Brussels**.

Now, suppose your computer had a mouse connected to it, and you used the mouse to click on the word **journal** above. What would happen? Chances are you would find yourself connected to the computer in Tokyo and on your computer screen would be the very journal being discussed. Or, click on the words **Tokyo** or **Brussels**, and you would probably end up on the computers referenced in those cities.

Behind the Smoke and Mirrors

Much of what happens on the World Wide Web goes on behind the scenes using an Internet protocol called HTTP, or HyperText Transport Protocol. HTTP is extremely efficient at what it does because it does not have any "search" functions to slow it down. You simply click **here** and you go **there**. Not much to get in the way. This is not to say that WWW servers cannot be searched for information; they can be, but they don't use the HTTP protocol to do the work; rather, the work is done by software either on your computer or the server computer you're connected to, or through an FTP or telnet connection. HTTP works together with many other Internet tools.

The language that HTTP "speaks" best is called HTML (HyperText Markup Language). HTML is a subset of SGML (Standard Generalized Markup Language), which is a powerful language for "tagging" documents for electronic format and structural uses. Many journals today are tagging their text and figures in SGML to make for easier electronic access and manipulation of the publications. As a much simpler subset, HTML is becoming increasingly popular for similar applications that don't require the breadth of SGML.

Clients and Servers on the Web

The WWW uses the client-server model of computer interaction. Any computer on the Internet that "speaks" HTTP is said to be a "web server," and any computer that can access that server is a "client." This concept allows multiple kinds of computers to talk to each other. The client and server software, while designed to be used specifically on either a VAX or Unix or Windows or Macintosh computer, must still transmit and receive information in the HTTP protocol, and then display the information on your computer (which has the client software on it) according to the established standards. More about clients later.

Uniform Resource Locators (URLs)

An URL (pronounced "earl") is basically a way of specifying the location of something on the Internet. That location can be as general as a computer name, or as specific as a single letter on a document on a server anywhere in the world. An URL is what's used in HTML to make hypertext links.

Let's look at an example. Right now I'm typing on a computer that is connected directly to the Internet. My computer's Internet *domain name* is **cozumel.spie.org**. In other words, if I were running my own anonymous FTP *server* from here, you could log in from a Unix prompt or other FTP software by typing

```
% ftp cozumel.spie.org
```

I could also be running a WWW server from here, or a telnet server, or a gopher server. So what if I were running a WWW server? How would you log in? You would use the URL for my computer. It would look like this:

```
http://cozumel.spie.org
```

This is a standard URL address. Note that the kind of connection is shown by the *http* at the beginning, telling you and the Internet that this is a WWW server you're looking for. If someone wanted to tell you my FTP address, they might write

```
ftp://cozumel.spie.org
```

Of course, they could also have told you to "FTP to **cozumel.spie.org**", but the emerging standard for writing this kind of information is the URL standard. URLs can really be used to describe just about any kind of connection on the Internet, including FTP, telnet, gopher, Usenet, and e-mail, as show in these examples:

```
telnet://cozumel.spie.org
gopher://cozumel.spie.org
news://cozumel.spie.org
mail://cozumel.spie.org
```

Let's take this a step further. On my computer right now I'm typing in a document called *web_chapter.html*, which is stored in a directory called *book* directly on my hard drive. If I were running a web server from this computer, you could directly access this specific document by typing the following address in your WWW browser's **Open URL** command:

```
http://cozumel.spie.org/book/web_chapter.html
```

I could even go so far as to point you to a particular word on this page by marking the word with the HTML language, so you might type an URL something like this, where you would be taken directly to the word on the page:

```
http://cozumel.spie.org/book/web_chapter.html#word23
```

This is really the key to the World Wide Web's ability to use all of the protocols in conjunction with HTML. By embedding addresses such as those above into hypertext links, the WWW is an environment that draws on all kinds of connections from a single user interface—your World Wide Web browser.

Web Browsers

As with all Internet resources, getting on the World Wide Web requires a software tool. In the case of the Web, this tool is often called a *client* or *browser*. The terms are used interchangeably.

There are basically two ways to access a browser. The first and preferred way is to have one installed on the computer you use to access the Internet. The second way is to telnet to another computer on the Internet that offers public access to its WWW browser.

There are also different kinds of browsers. If your Internet computer is text-based (also known as a *command-line interface*), such as a Unix host you are connected to, then a web browser on that computer would be called a *line browser*.

If your Internet computer has graphics capabilities, such as a Windows, Macintosh, or XWindows workstation, and if it's connected directly to the Internet through either a LAN or dial-up SLIP/PPP type connection, then you could choose one of the many new graphical browsers that are being developed and distributed on the Internet today.

There is also a third and new category of browser, which can best be described as "service-specific." If you have an account with one of the major commercial online services such as America Online or CompuServe, or major online service provider such as Netcom, you may be able to (or forced to) use their customized software for browsing the web.

While the Web can certainly be accessed using a line browser, it's really designed to work best with the graphical browsers that take full advantage of the web's ability to bring you all kinds of digital media such as pictures and sounds, as well as more readable formats and interactive features such as online forms. The graphical browsers also rely heavily on the mouse for navigating and selecting information, whereas line browsers have you enter a selection number or skip from link to link using the arrow keys.

As a departure from the earlier chapters of this book, where I have used a Unix command-line (or "shell") account for most examples, in this chapter we'll look at both command-line and graphical browsers, because it's really the graphical browsers that the web was designed for, and the comparison is valuable. Chances are if you use the Internet long enough, you'll find yourself using a graphical interface to the World Wide Web. It is quickly replacing line browsers in all but the most limited circumstances.

Surfing the Web

The process of navigating and exploring the World Wide Web is often called "surfing." I've always wondered why this term (instead of others such as searching, browsing, etc.) has stuck in the net community. A colleague made the following suggestion:

> *From an old surfer: You're trying to harness a force that's really uncontrollable and can at times be really scary but really fun, too. You're always looking for the killer wave (read "site"). The lifestyle (literally and figuratively) is semi-nomadic. Finally—it's addicting.*

That said, let's look at some net surfing tools, conventions, and techniques.

Line Browsers

There are two kinds of line browsers common on the WWW. The only real difference between the two is that one uses numbers in brackets like this [1] to denote a link, and the other uses boldface type like **this**. This last type is known as the *Lynx* browser and seems to be the most common line browser in use today, so we'll use it for our example. I should also note here, however, that some of the larger Internet service providers like Netcom have recently developed their own custom line browsers for WWW access.

To use a Lynx browser, you either need to have it installed on your Internet host or telnet to another computer that lets you use their browser. Like all the Internet tools you might use from your Internet host computer, you have to know what you have first. The best way is to ask someone who knows (like your service provider). You can also try typing **lynx** at your command prompt. Chances are if it's installed, this will be the access command.

For our demonstration, we'll telnet to a public access site. There are numerous sites that offer this service, and we've listed a few at the end of this section. The University of Kansas offers a public Lynx browser at **ukanaix.cc.ukans.edu**, so we'll go there. (The U of K just happens to also be the place where Lynx was developed.) The login name we use for this site is **www.**

```
% telnet ukanaix.cc.ukans.edu


The University of Kansas
IBM AIX Version 3 for RISC System/6000
(C) Copyrights by IBM and by others 1982, 1990.


For assistance call 864-0110 or to report network prob-
lems call 864-0200


Login as 'kufacts' for  access to the Campus Wide Infor-
mation System.
               'history' for history network resources
               'ex-ussr' for former Soviet Union info


login: www


Your Terminal type is unknown!


Enter a terminal type: [vt100]
```

Pressing Return now tells the remote computer that we'll accept the default VT100 terminal type, resulting in the following text display:

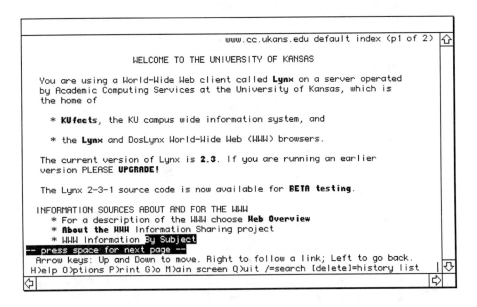

Note the use of boldface type here. Every word or phrase that is bold is actually a hypertext link. The commands at the bottom of the screen tell us that we can use the up and down arrow keys to skip to the next hypertext link (shown here by the black box over the words **By Subject**), and we can use the right and left arrow keys to either select a link (and therefore take you to wherever it leads), or move backward to a previous link. Pressing Return initiates the link indicated by the highlighted text. I'll use the right-arrow key to jump to the **By Subject** index:

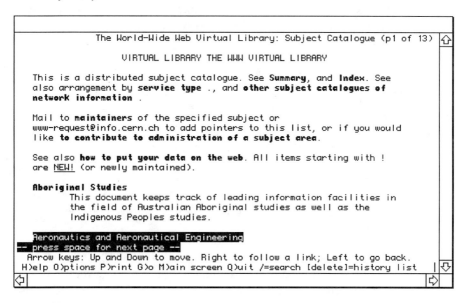

Now, as it turns out, we're at the web server at the CERN high energy physics lab in Switzerland, home of the WWW. We're at the top of the WWW Virtual Library page, which is a master index of jump points to many areas of interest. From here I can go to many different WWW servers by just arrowing to the topic of interest and pressing Return. For one final example, I'll select the Aeronautics and Aeronautical Engineering link above:

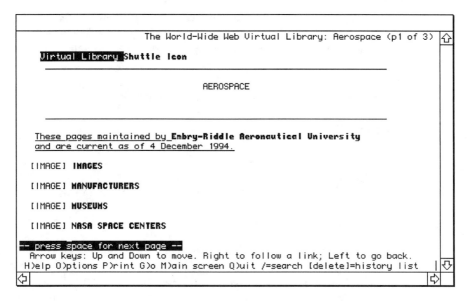

Now although it may look like we're still at CERN, we're actually at Embry-Riddle Aeronautical University, a major hub for accessing web servers in aeronautics. You could continue on indefinitely, moving from site to site, or selecting actual files or directories of interest at a given web location. Line browsers may not be as visually spectacular as graphical browsers, but they are a powerful Internet tool, offering the full hypertext capability that makes the web a valuable resource.

We'll end our tour of line browsing the WWW here with a list of public access sites you can try if you don't have access to WWW client software on your own computer.

Line Browsers Available via Telnet

Following is a list of some WWW public-access sites available via telnet:

info.cern.ch
> No password is required. This is in Switzerland, so continental U.S. users might be better off using a closer browser (faster connection).

ukanaix.cc.ukans.edu
> A full-screen browser "Lynx" that requires a VT100 terminal. Log in as **www**. Lynx is still the best plain-text browser, so move mountains if necessary to get your own copy!

www.njit.edu
> (or **128.235.163.2**) Log in as **www**. A full-screen browser at the New Jersey Institute of Technology.

vms.huji.ac.il
> (or **128.139.4.3**). A dual-language Hebrew/English database, with links to the rest of the world. The line-mode browser, plus extra features. Log in as **www**. Hebrew University of Jerusalem, Israel.

sun.uakom.cs
> Slovakia. Has a slow link, so use only from nearby.

info.funet.fi
> (or telnet **128.214.6.102**). Log in as **www**.

fserv.kfki.hu
> Hungary. Has slow link, so use only from nearby. Log in is as **www**.

Graphical Browsers

Graphical browsers for the World Wide Web are really what it's all about. You can literally point and click your way around the world to some of the most amazing archives of information you could ever imagine. The recent past has seen an explosion of Web sites that serve up everything from real-time satellite radar mappings to personal travel journals sprinkled with full-color photographs. More recently, online databases with sophisticated searching and purchasing capabilities are appearing online as well.

Browser Wars

In the beginning, there was Mosaic, the graphical browser developed at the National Center for Supercomputing Applications (NCSA) and distributed freely on the Internet. However, by the end of 1995, Mosaic was virtually overrun by an influx of new browsers, led by the enormously successful Netscape from the new company of the same name. Thus began *Browser Wars*.

There are now at least a dozen different web browsers available for a given computer platform, including software distributed by America Online, Prodigy, Spyglass, PSINet, Netcom, Microsoft, and others. All of these browsers have their own specific sets of capabilities and features. Most of them will display web pages designed to conform to the HTML 2.0 standard, and therefore have a certain level of consistency. However, each browser developer is trying to establish its own standard features *beyond* HTML 2.0, and therefore chaos abounds.

At present, Netscape continues to push the development envelope by creating feature-sets far beyond the current HTML standard, and while the elements of the HTML 3.0 standard are still being discussed, Netscape is pushing past and capturing a very large segment of the browser market, which forces other browser developers to either adopt Netscape's own standards or remain in the minority.

This all may sound like an irrelevant discussion in a book like this, but I believe it's not. The browser you choose to access the World Wide Web will dictate what you can do and see on the web. For example, if you choose to use a browser that does not support *tables*, a feature that allows tabular data to be displayed in an organized manner, you may visit a site that has information you wish to read, but all the text appears as a jumbled mess on your computer screen. Taken to the extreme, your choice of browser can dictate whether you'll have features such as online purchasing or perhaps the ability to view certain images or figures. There are also significant differences in performance between browsers, again with Netscape being recognized as one of the fastest browsers around. As with any industry, commerialization of the Internet has brought forth increased capabilities, as well as confusion.

Exploring the Web with Netscape

As I write this, Netscape accounts for almost 75% of the browsers in use on the Internet, and as such, is an obvious choice for demonstration purposes. However, beyond sheer market share, Netscape also offers some of the most innovative "extensions" to the current standard, and demonstrating these features is a good way to show the potential and the future of the Web. It will also go a long way toward not making this book obsolete the month after it's published.

The Windows, Macintosh, and XWindows versions of Netscape all undergo continual facelifts, but they all look and act basically the same, and support the same features. The differences are mostly in menu titles and other interface aspects that are more a function of what is "normal" for each of these computer types, and in fact even those standards have changed along the way, so that no two versions of Netscape are the same, regardless of computer type.

The first thing you can do when you get Netscape is go somewhere with it. You really don't need to configure anything before using Netscape (providing your computer is already set up to access the Internet). There are certainly things you may want to customize, but you don't have to.

Netscape comes with a "Directory" menu that provides instant access to a few important sites built directly into the program, including places to seach the web from. By selecting one of these, your Netscape browser would go out and find the site selected and log into its web server and home page. It's a nice way to get started.

But since you're holding a book full of places to go, we'll use one of them for a starting example instead. With the Lynx browser example in the previous section, we telnetted to the University of Kansas, and then found a link there that took us to CERN and then Embry-Riddle. But what if the University of Kansas didn't have a link set up for us to use? Like everything on the Internet, we can use an URL to go where we want on the WWW, although one of the major advantages of the WWW is that you often do not need an address, since everywhere you go can be a jumping off point to other locations using hypertext links.

NASA's homepage is an excellent example of a central information hub for the many different NASA sites on the web. Opening Netscape's "Open Location" menu item, we'll just type in the NASA URL to get there:

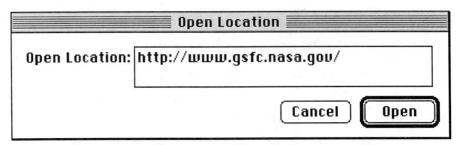

All I've done here is direct Netscape to access NASA's homepage at the address **http://www.gsfc.nasa.gov**. Note that I added a slash (/) mark after the address as well. This is a convention that helps some WWW browsers find the home page if one is not specifically given, as in this case. It's not essential; just a habit of mine that sometimes helps.

Colors, Backgrounds, and Imagemaps

Shown below is NASA's home page. The large graphic at the top of the page is called an *imagemap*, which means that, if your browser supports the imagemap feature (most do), you can simply click on various locations of the image to take you to other locations. The web server (in this case, NASA's) interprets the location of your mouse-click on the image, and translates it into an URL location. So, really, it's the same as clicking on a hypertext link.

Note again that, as with the Lynx text browser, links to other places or documents are usually underlined. If you have a color display on your computer, these links will also show as different colors. In the not-so-distant past, you could count on a blue link to signify someplace you had not yet visited, and a red link to show a place you visited recently. All that has changed, however. With most web browsers today you can customize the colors of the links, or let the web sites you visit control the colors. This is also true for the background of your browser window. Again, you can often dictate a color of your choice; however, most people allow the web sites they visit to control the background colors, since many sites are designed to take advantage of this feature. Many of the more sophisticated sites will try to change the background color and link colors of your browser when you visit them, and some even change the background to a custom texture or graphic. The difference on a visual level can be quite dramatic, much like the difference between a black-and-white newspaper and a full-color glossy magazine.

Saving Text and Printing

One of the best things about browsing the web with Netscape or most other graphical browsers is the ability to do so many functions from just one interface. For example, if you arrive at a web site that has lots of interesting documents you want to read later, you have a number of options. First, you could save the document as a text file on your hard drive. Some more advanced browsers let you save as formatted text as well, and you'll want to use this option if available, because even when stripped of their HTML tags, documents on the WWW are often long strings of text that run together without breaks. The formatted text option can be a real eye saver.

As an alternative, if you prefer the look of a document as viewed in your Netscape browser, you can usually save the document on your computer as an HTML-encoded file, which means you can come back later and view it with your Netscape browser software with all the nice formatting and readable text still intact. The process of viewing HTML-formatted files directly from your own computer is usually a menu option called something like Open Local or Open File, meaning "open a file that's already on a local hard drive, not on the Internet."

Still another option is to print a WWW document you're viewing directly to your printer. Some browsers even let you save a web page as a PostScript file so that you can then send it to a PostScript-compatible printer, where even the graphics will be faithfully reproduced.

Customizing Your Web Browser

For the more serious web surfer, most of the current browsers support some truly innovative ways to allow you to personalize your online environment, and to make exploring even easier.

Viewing Text and Graphics

Netscape and most other browsers allow you to select your favorite typeface (font) and size for your browser's display. Be careful about what you choose, however. There are usually two choices to be made: *proportional font* and *fixed font*. Remember that it's your browser that determines the typeface style; however, it's the web *server* that tells the browser the *relative* size and style of the typeface. What happens is, you tell your browser to use Times Roman to display proportional text at 12 points. This is your default text size, which is scaled up and down in your browser, depending on what the server you are visiting tells your browser to do.

For example, there are six relative sizes of headlines in the HTML standard (H1, H2, H3, etc.). When you access a page on a web server, the HTML *tags* your browser "reads" may tell the browser to display a particular headline as an "H1". This means whatever font you've chosen as your proportional font will be scaled up to display as a large headline, probably two or three times the size of the 12-point default you've designated. This is how web browsers work with the HTML tags to create a semi-customized viewing environment. You choose the typeface and basic text size, and the browser scales it up and down, or adds bold or italics for emphasis.

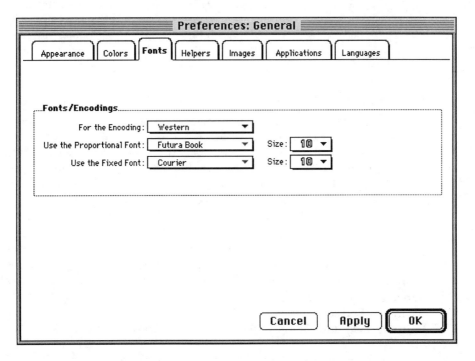

Choice of a *fixed font* is just as important. Fixed fonts are used by web browsers to display text that needs to maintain the formatting of the original document. For example, if you wanted to serve up a document that had four separate columns of numbers, and you wanted those numbers to stay in well-defined columns to make the document easy to read, you would choose this approach. Choosing a monospace typeface such as Courier will display information correctly when it is designated by the server as *fixed* (the HTML tag is actually called *preformatted*). Of course, the increased use of the *tables* feature (see Tables and Frames, below) is replacing the need for preformatted text in many situations.

Finally, you'll need to make some choices about how images are handled when encountered on the web. The main point here is, if you're connected to the Internet via a modem, you'll probably want your browser to not automatically load graphics; instead, you would choose which individual graphics should load by clicking on them with your mouse. Many new web surfers opt to load every graphic as it's encountered, and then wonder why the web is so slow.

The truth is, many of today's web sites are filled with graphics. From a modem connection, or when connecting to a web site far away, this can make for very slow browsing. Turning off your browser's auto-load feature may not be the prettiest way to view the web, but it's certainly the most efficient. In the worst-case scenario, choosing to load all the graphics can even mean that you can't access a certain site, because the download time will exceed the server's *timeout* limit and will abort the transfer in midstream. This can be very frustrating.

Most good web sites also offer a "text-only" version of their pages from a link on their homepage, which makes it even easier for all of us with modem connections.

Bookmarks and Hotlists

One of the first things you can do when you find a new web browser is open a personal list of favorite places to go. Such lists are called by a variety of names—bookmarks, hotlists, hotlinks, etc. They are nothing more than a way of saving an URL address for future retrieval—the equivalent of a personalized online phone book. Web browsers continue to get more sophisticated in the ways they let you create, edit, and display bookmarks. Most let you create any number of separate lists and load them on the fly, or create lists that have sublists attached.

The first time you go somewhere on the web you think you'll want to come back to at some other time, just find the menu option that lets you "Add Bookmark" (under the Bookmarks menu in Netscape), and it will be appended to the default list in your web browser. When you want to see what's in your bookmarks, find something similar to Netscape's "View Bookmarks" command to display a window listing all the addresses you have saved.

From here you can add, edit, or delete links as you wish. You can even give it a name with an easier mnemonic hook than the plain URL address would provide. For long URLs, bookmarks are an especially handy feature. One tip that I'll add from hard-learned experience: as with any other important digital information that would be hard to recreate, back up your bookmark files regularly to some other location.

When your web exploring gets out of hand and your bookmarks list starts

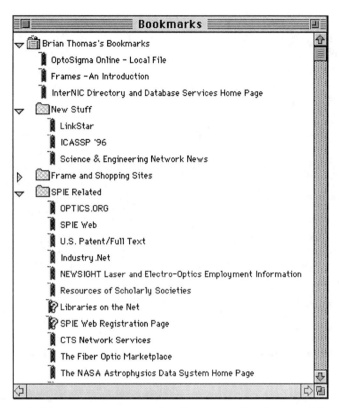

getting unwieldy, you can start using the customized menu features of your browser to organize the information into smaller groups of bookmarks, as shown above in what's called a *hierarchical* or *cascading menu*.

Another browser feature that I find especially helpful is one that allows you to click on a hypertext link in a document and, if you continue to hold down the mouse button for a second or two, a *pop-up menu* displays. This menu gives you options not only to connect to the link in the normal way, but also to retrieve the entire document it links to and save it on your computer's hard drive. For anyone interested in the HTML tagging language or starting their own web server, this is useful information. It may also les you add the link as a bookmark without actually loading the link location, as well as save an image or graphic directly to your computer. Finally, it lets you copy an URL address to your computer's clipboard and then paste it into a document directly.

Helper Applications

Helper Applications are applications on your computer that you tell your web browser to launch when you run across something in your web surfing that your browser cannot handle. For example, if you were visiting a music archive and clicked on a *AIF* or *WAV* file (both are audio formats used with computers), the audio-clip file would automatically be transferred to your computer's hard drive. However, your browser's work is then done, because it can't play audio clips. But as a shortcut, you can tell your browser to launch a certain application (in this case, one that can play audio files) whenever it sees a certain type of file or filename extension (in this example, .aif or .wav). This same concept is used to launch external graphics viewers, video players, and other applications that work with your browser to create a seamless working environment while you're on the web.

Here is what Netscape's Helper Applications window looks like:

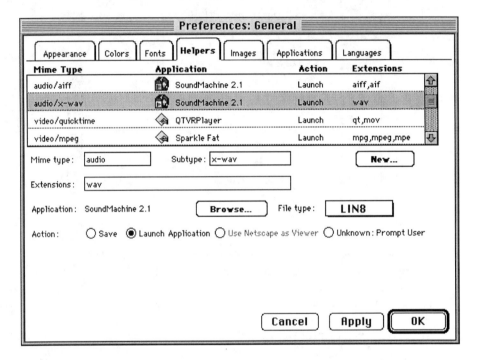

Enhanced Web Features

Some of the most important innovations in web browsers recently have been those that attempt to organize and display information more efficiently, as well as make it easier to navigate. Following is a look at some of the most important ones.

Tables and Frames

The *tables* feature is one that most browsers now support. It is a simple solution to organizing information that is best suited for tabular display—such as numerical tables or spreadsheet information. Prior to the tables feature, there was no way to display information in columns *and* rows. Another more recent development from Netscape is the *frames* feature, which gives web authors more control over the web window by allowing the creation of "windows within windows," each with their own specific attributes. Below is an example of a site that combines both frames and tables. Here the frames feature allows the user to scroll a long list of tabular data formatted as a table, while the table's column heads remain stationary, so the reader never has to scroll back up to see what the header elements are. Note also that on the left-hand side of the browser's main window is a full-length vertical window that contains a scrolling list of navigation links that remain constant.

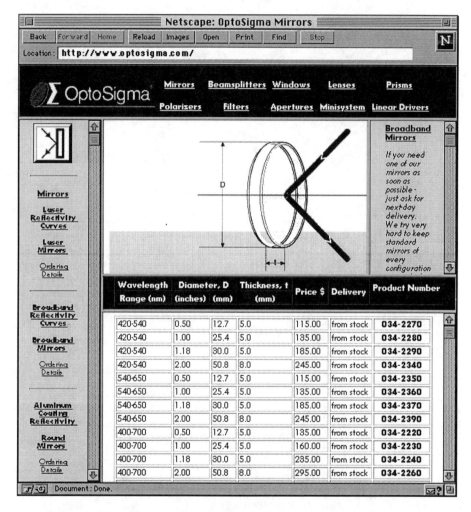

The frames feature is a significant change in the way web browsers work, not only for the reasons noted above, but also because it changes some of the standard browser features, such as navigation and formatting tools.

Online Forms

The use of *online forms* is commonplace on the web today. The *forms* feature allows users to type in information in database-style fields, and then when all the information is entered, a button is usually activitated to send the information to the web server, where it is processed. Typical uses for online forms include querying a database, registering for a service, or purchasing goods.

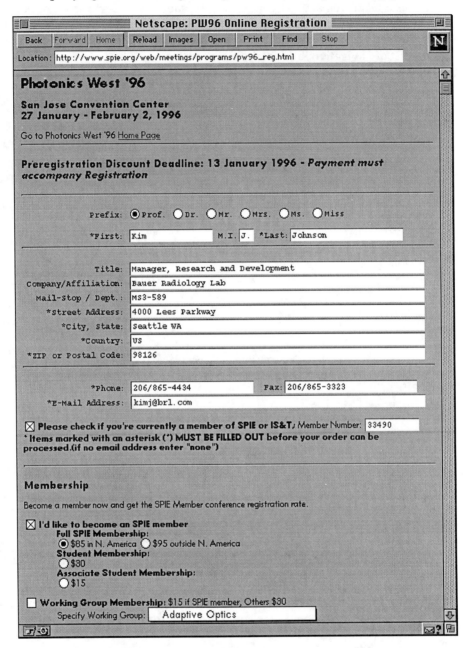

Above is an example of a registration form using the form feature in Netscape. The information was entered by clicking the mouse in the first field, and then using the tab key to jump to successive fields. The user then clicks the SEND button (not shown here), and then receives a reply back from the server saying that the information has been captured successfully. Increasingly common, the service may also send the user an additional confirmation via e-mail, provided the user supplied a valid e-mail address on the form.

Multimedia on the Web

The promise of true multimedia functionality on the web is well-advertised in the popular literature. In reality, the word *multimedia* is often stretched to include just about anything new or not "straight HTML." Below are a few of the most promising technologies being implemented on the web today. Note that nearly all of these nascent technologies depend on the ability to make the browser (client) take on as much work as possible, in an effort to resolve performance issues caused by limited bandwidth.

Java

Java is Sun Microsystems' hybrid of C and C++ languages optimized for handling client/server actions on the web. All this really means is that with a *HotJava* player linked to your browser, you can download small *applets* of computer code that will automatically launch a custom application on your computer, which is then continually fed by the web server. Some common examples of what this technology can do include continuously updated stocks and mutual funds data that can automatically update a client's portfolio, or real-time animations played directly inside your browser's window. Obviously, this is sophisticated technology and has as many obstacles as it does potential uses. But there is tremendous movement and financial support behind this technology, and it seems clear it will find the applications necessary to make it successful.

Inline Viewers

The term *inline viewer* usually refers to the ability to embed applications inside a web browser's window, thereby eliminating the need for *helper applications*. The best example of this so far is Netscape's ability to display documents formatted for Adobe Systems' *Acrobat* format. Acrobat uses a proprietary file format called *PDF* (Portable Document Format) that Netscape can now read directly instead of requiring that the user launch the Acrobat application separately. In other words, the two software applications are effectively merged into one application—the web browser. Other up-and-coming inline viewer modules includes multimedia presentations created with and for Macromedia's *Director* program.

VRML and QuickTime VR

Virtual Reality Modeling Language (VRML), from Silicon Graphics and InterVista Software, is now touted as a standard for transmitting navigable 3D models over the web. The challenge here, as with most other web innovations, is to keep the playback speed acceptable. The VRML environment works by transmitting dimensions and texture commands to the web browser, which handles the actual rendering and manipulation. So all the server is really doing is sending mathematical descriptions of objects and their locations, and the browser fills everything in, thereby reducing the amount of bandwidth needed. Combined with Apple Computer's well-established QuickTime VR technology, also slated for integration into Netscape, the two technologies promise to bring 3D animations over the web.

Audio and Video Online

Progressive Networks' RealAudio technology has been widely embraced by the browser development community, and promises to deliver near-real-time audio over the web using a technique called *streaming*. Like Java, this technique again involves establishing a somewhat direct connection with a browser and then feeding the highly compressed audio data to the browser, where it is decompressed and played on the fly. Very heady stuff if they can pull it off.

In the video world, technologies such as Xing Technologies' StreamWorks are aiming to deliver FM-quality audio and lower-quality video to web browsers, but admittedly the bandwidth requirements here still look relatively upscale. An ISDN connection will probably be the entry level for anything in video for quite some time.

Where to Find Netscape Software

You can get the latest version of Netscape from the following online archives:

```
FTP
    ftp1.netscape.com
    ftp.pu-toyama.ac.jp/pub/net/WWW/netscape   (Japan mirror)
WWW
    http://www.netscape.com/comprod/mirror/index.html
    http://mistral.enst.fr/netscape/ (Europe mirror)
```

Or contact Netscape Communications via telephone:

```
    From Europe: +33 1/46.92.27.25
    From everywhere else: +1 415/528-2555
```

Searching the WWW

It was not so long ago that searching the World Wide Web was nearly impossible, and custom indexes maintained by individuals were really the only way to find information in an organized manner. However, there are now a number of fast and innovative public search sites to help point to Internet resources using anything from simple keywords to full-fledged Boolean search queries. Most of these search engines work by preindexing and updating pointers to a huge number of URLs on the web, so when you enter a search term, you're only searching a database somewhere on the web, not the actual Internet itself, which would be impossibly slow.

Below are some primary web sites that offer a public search interface. Note that some (AltaVista and DejaNews, for example) even allow you to search archives of Usenet newsgroup messages.

AltaVista
    http://www.altavista.digital.com/
CUSI (searches many search sites)
    http://Web.nexor.co.uk/susi/cusi.html
DejaNews (searches Usenet postings)
    http://www.dejanews.com/
ExCite
    http://www.excite.com/
InfoSeek
    http://www2.infoseek.com
Lycos
    http://www.lycos.com
OpenText
    http://www.opentext.com/
WebCrawler
    http://webcrawler.com/
W3 Search Engines
    http://cuiwww.unige.ch/meta-index.html
Yahoo
    http://www.yahoo.com

Just the FAQs

To get the FAQs listed below, send the commands shown to

mail-server@rtfm.mit.edu

This is an e-mail server that will automatically send you the file you've requested. Send these commands in the body of your e-mail message. If you wish to retrieve more than one FAQ, just enter each command on a separate line in your message. You may also get these files via FTP from this location as well.

WWW FAQs

Send the following commands:

```
send pub/usenet/news.answers/finding-sources
send pub/usenet/news.answers/www/*
```

Part II

SCIENCE RESOURCES ON THE INTERNET

Resource Listings Index

INTRODUCTION

The information sources in this section offer a variety of starting points for exploration. They are by no means an attempt to be comprehensive. No book about the Internet could possibly be that. But there are many important information points listed here, and they in turn often point to further resources.

Any omissions the reader may discover are by no means intentional. This is true for the topics chosen as well. In both cases, a line had to be drawn somewhere, lest this book go unpublished due to exceeding the binding's physical capabilities. I was also told that exceeding 500 pages would bring certain punishments that only a publisher could devise.

By far the most often-listed resources in this book are on the World Wide Web. This is both an encouragement and a reality. The WWW is the easiest way to use the Internet, and people have figured this out, to the point where it's not only overtaking all other information sources on the net—it's replacing them.

However, even if you don't have access to a WWW browser yet, don't forget that many of the WWW resources listed here overlap with FTP and gopher counterparts. For example, an FTP site named **ftp.science-resources.com** may also have a WWW mirror named something like **http://www.science-resources.com**. Sometimes just trying a likely address will get you somewhere you didn't even know existed. I've found more than a few places on the net this way.

Using the Science Resources Guide

Usenet Listings

The Usenet sections here are listings of the primary newsgroups for the fields covered, and include some background information where available, such as when the group was founded, who the moderator is (if applicable), and the group's charter, if available. In most cases the newsgroup charters have been truncated to provide only a basic description of the group. Many charters are pages long.

Frequently Asked Questions

These sections list the appropriate FAQs for the field and where to find them on the Internet.

Discussion Lists

There are thousands of discussion lists active on the Internet today. I've tried to list some of the primary ones in each field. If you are not familiar with discussion lists and how to subscribe to them, refer to Chapter 6, Discussion Lists. Note that among the site listings there are gopher and WWW sites that offer current sources of discussion lists in specific topical areas. This is becoming increasingly common.

FTP Resources

Writing this book really made me realize how difficult it is to find FTP resources in a systematic manner. Many sites that I already knew about were ones I'd learned of through chance or word-of-mouth. Except for the major software archives and their mirrors (see Appendix), FTP archives are scattered, but there are a few out there, and I've included some of the significant ones when I found them. The industrious reader looking for FTP archives would do well to search among the WWW listings here, since many WWW servers also house FTP archives, no doubt because they started out with FTP services long before the web even existed.

Gopher Resources

You can access the gopher sites listed here by either telneting to a public gopher server, or by using a gopher client on your personal computer workstation. See the chapter on Tools for Searching earlier in this book.

Remember that the gopher addresses here will bring you to the "top" of the gopher server you're accessing. From there you might find exactly the resource you're looking for. However, other times you will arrive at a large archive covering many topical areas, and therefore you will need to "gopher down" through the site's directories to find the specific resource or topic you seek. While there are new gopher browsers arriving that "parse" WWW-like URLs for specific gopher locations, the URLs themselves are so convoluted and unfriendly that most users will find them unusable. Imagine typing something like **gaia.ucs.orst.edu/11/osu-i%2bs/osu-d%2bo/caec** when instead you could just type **gaia.ucs.orst.edu** and start looking around. I've opted for this latter type of entry point wherever possible.

So, if you arrive at a gopher site and don't see any file or directory that's obviously what you're looking for (or what's listed here in this book), first see if the site offers some method of searching the server; for example, a "search this gopher server," "browse this site," or "use veronica to search" menu option. If so, select the search option and type in a keyword, perhaps even from the description of a resource listed in this book.

If there is no search option, look for obvious directory names. For example, if you're looking for an electronic anthropology journal called "World Heritage Jrnl." and see a directory named "Electronic Serials," open that directory and chances are you'll find what you seek. And remember that using a gopher is much like using a library: the possibility of serendipitous discovery is always present—and distracting.

World Wide Web Resources

As mentioned, the vast majority of resources offered here are on the web. During the compilation of this *1996 Edition*, it was remarkable to see just how much the web had grown in only 12 months, not only in size, but in the quality of the resources available. As a result, more than ever, the resources listed here were chosen as those that best represented the disciplines covered. Interestingly enough, the best resources are not always where one might expect to find them. Often instead they are found in the "personal home page" of one or more individuals who are intensely involved in a given technology, and as a result have compiled truly impressive collections of links that cover the spectrum far better than the often-neglected "departmental" or "corporate" home pages. In this way the Internet has not changed during its growth spurt: it's still the individuals out there who continue to keep it fresh and useful.

About the URL Listings

I have tried to format all the addresses in this book as they would normally be used within a browser program or command line interface. To avoid possible confusion caused by long addresses, the Internet addresses here are not hyphenated—they wrap around to the next line with no hyphenation. This may look a little odd at first, but at least you know that when you see a hyphen, it's actually part of the address (many Internet addresses do have hyphens, unfortunately).

Also, WWW resources are listed as full URLs that include the *http://* prefix, which many of the newer web browsers no longer require you to enter. I've included them here, however, because some older browsers require this prefix information. All other addresses in this section do not use the URL form recommended as a standard in the preface of this book. Again, this was to avoid confusion, since with most Internet software today you don't actually type *gopher://* when entering a gopher address.

Aeronautics & Aerospace

See also Astronomy & Astrophysics, Engineering, Medicine, Optics, Physics

Usenet Newsgroups

misc.transport.air-industry (Moderated)
Created by: Helen Rose <hrose@kei.com>
Moderated by: Helen Rose <air-industry-request@kei.com>
Submissions go to: air-industry@kei.com
Call for Votes Date: March 7, 1995
Newsgroup-based Mailing List: No
Charter (from Call for Votes):
This would be a moderated newsgroup providing a forum for the discussion of all aspects of the airline industry. These discussions would include, but are not limited to
- Airline deregulation in Europe, effect on member states, and passengers.
- The financial health (or lack thereof) of airlines.
- Airliner models as related to airline routes, resource allocation, capacity, etc.
- Comments about the industry from insiders (most US airlines have one or more employees who read/post to the net, we hope to attract serious comments from these posters to this group).
- Discussion of all aspects of airline management.
- Announcement of fare changes and discussion of their effects on airline yields.

rec.aviation
Created by: geoff@peck.com (Geoff Peck)
Call for Votes date: August 28, 1992
Newsgroup-based Mailing List: No.
Charter: The rec.aviation re-organization created thirteen sub-groups in the rec.aviation hierarchy. A recent vote created a fourteenth group, rec.aviation.questions. Four of the fourteen groups are moderated, all by the same person.

rec.aviation.announce (Moderated)
Information and events considered of general interest to all readers of rec.aviation.
Moderated by: Geoff Peck (aviation-announce-request@peck.com)
Submissions go to: aviation-announce@peck.com

rec.aviation.answers (Moderated)
The rec.aviation "FAQ" group.
Moderated by: Geoff Peck (aviation-announce-request@peck.com)
Submissions go to: aviation-answers@peck.com

rec.aviation.hang-gliding
Created by: Dennis R. Owen <paintman@svpal.org>
Call for Votes Date: April 14, 1995
Newsgroup-based Mailing List: No.
Charter (from Call for Votes):
The newsgroup will be open to the discussion of all topics relating to hang gliding such as: operation and mainte-nance of hang gliders, paragliders and other foot-launchable non-powered aircraft; related equipment and accesso-ries; groups and associations; flying events; and flying sites.

rec.aviation.homebuilt
Experimental aircraft: design and con-struction.

rec.aviation.ifr
For IFR pilots and students.

rec.aviation.marketplace
Created by: W. R. Mercier <wrmercier@delphi.com>
Call for Votes Date: April 7, 1995
Newsgroup-based Mailing List: No.
Charter (from Call for Votes):
rec.aviation.marketplace will be an open forum for parties wanting or selling

aircraft, parts, components, service and related items. No off-topic advertising, either commercial or otherwise will be encouraged.

rec.aviation.military
Military aspects of aviation.

rec.aviation.misc
Anything which doesn't fit elsewhere.

rec.aviation.owning
Ownership.

rec.aviation.piloting
Piloting issues in general.

rec.aviation.products
Products of general interest.

rec.aviation.rotorcraft
Created by: Paul Andrew Papasavas
<paul@mars.superlink.net>
Call for Votes Date: April 24, 1995
Newsgroup-based Mailing List: No.
Charter (from Call for Votes):
Rec.aviation.rotorcraft will be a forum for discussion of all types of rotary wing aircraft such as but not limited to: helicopters (piston, turbine, etc...), autogyros, gyrocopters, and Osprey's.

In addition, it will provide a forum for the discussion of topics specifically related to rotary wing aircraft such as: airworthiness directives, regulatory mandates, helicopter industry news, and flight training centers

rec.aviation.simulators
PC simulators, for "armchair pilots."

rec.aviation.soaring
Gliders.

rec.aviation.stories (Moderated)
Hangar-flying.
Moderated by: Geoff Peck
(aviation-announce-request@peck.com)
Submissions go to: aviation-stories@peck.com

rec.aviation.student
Student pilot issues.

rec.aviation.questions (Moderated)
An oracle of knowledge, answered by

pilots hand-selected by Peck. This group was created March 9, 1994, by Geoff Peck.
Moderated by: Geoff Peck
(rec-aviation-questions-request@peck.com)
Submissions go to: rec-aviation-questions@peck.com

rec.aviation.ultralight
Created by: Ralph K. Williamson
<ralphw@bangate.compaq.com>
Call for Votes Date: August 30, 1994
Newsgroup-based Mailing List: No.
Charter (from Call for Votes):
The rec.aviation.ultralight newsgroup will be open to the discussion of all topics relating to the operation, construction and maintainance of ultralight aircraft, microlight aircraft and light aircraft in general.

rec.models.rc
Newsgroup-based Mailing List: No.
Charter: Radio controlled models, with an emphasis on radio-controlled aircraft.

rec.models.rockets
Newsgroup-based Mailing List: No.
Charter: Model rockets.

sci.aeronautics (Moderated)
Created by: rdd@wilbur.pr.erau.edu
(Robert Dorsett)
Moderated by: Mary Shafer
(shafer@spdcc.com)
Submissions go to:
aeronautics@wilbur.pr.erau.edu
Call for Votes date: February 23, 1993
(original group: Fall 1989)
Newsgroup-based Mailing List: No.
Charter (from Call for Votes):
A moderated discussion-group dealing with atmospheric flight, specifically: aerodynamics, flying qualities, simulation, structures, systems, propulsion, and design human factors.

sci.aeronautics.airliners (Moderated)
Created by: rdd@wilbur.pr.erau.edu
(Robert Dorsett)
Moderated by: Karl Swartz
(kls@ditka.chicago.com)
Submissions go to: airliners@chicago.com
Call for Votes date: September 29, 1992
Newsgroup-based Mailing List: No.
Charter (from Call for Votes):

A moderated discussion group on airliner technology: the design, construction, performance, human factors, operation, and histories of transport-category airplanes.

sci.aeronautics.simulation (Moderated)

Created by: rdd@wilbur.pr.erau.edu (Robert Dorsett)
Moderated by: Robert Dorsett (rdd@wilbur.pr.erau.edu)
Submissions go to: aero-simulation@wilbur.pr.erau.edu
Call for Votes date: June 8, 1994
Newsgroup-based Mailing List: No.
Charter (from Call for Votes):
A moderated discussion group dealing with the implementation of flight and systems models on computers. This includes, but is not restricted to:

- the definition of such models
- acquisition and modeling of flight parameters
- design and implementation of onboard systems models
- design and implementation of powerplant models
- standardization of commonly required data, such as flight parameter databases, navaid databases, etc.
- design of cab-based implementations of flight simulators.

sci.space

Sci.space was one of the original net.* newsgroups.
Newsgroup-based Mailing List: Yes (space@uga.cc.uga.edu).
Charter: Space technology.

sci.space.news (Moderated)

Moderated by: Peter Yee (yee@atlas.arc.nasa.gov)
Submissions go to: sci-space-news@news.arc.nasa.gov
Newsgroup-based Mailing List: No.
Charter: All forms of space announcements: NASA press releases, satellite tracks, etc.

sci.space.policy

Created by: gwh@soda.berkeley.edu (George William Herbert)
Call for Votes date: November 10, 1993

Newsgroup-based Mailing List: No.
Charter (from Call for Votes):
Policy issues not directly related to technical issues in any space field, including government policies, budget priorities, mission type priorities, goals of space programs, the role of governments and space agencies in developing space, etc. Any discussions on technical issues where person feels the moderated groups are not giving full range of expression are also appropriate.

sci.space.science (Moderated)

Created by: gwh@soda.berkeley.edu (George William Herbert)
Moderated by: George William Herbert and Steve Willner (sci-space-science-request@isu.isunet.edu)
Submissions go to: sci-space-science@isu.isunet.edu
Call for Votes date: November 10, 1993
Newsgroup-based Mailing List: No.
Charter (from Call for Votes):
For discussing planetary and non-planetary space science; including technical issues in planetary science, planetary science space missions, techniques, goals, and information about the planets themselves, space astronomy, physics, space science in general, stellar science (ours and others), etc. Questions about space science, the planets, etc. The primary emphasis is on doing science in or about space; sci.astro remains the appropriate group for astronomy per se.

sci.space.shuttle

Newsgroup-based Mailing List: No.
Charter: Discussions on orbiter technology.

sci.space.technology (Moderated)

Created by: gwh@soda.berkeley.edu (George William Herbert)
Moderated by: George William Herbert (sci-space-tech-request@isu.isunet.edu)
Submissions go to: sci-space-science@isu.isunet.edu
Call for Votes date: November 10, 1993
Newsgroup-based Mailing List: No.
Charter (from Call for Votes):
Technical issues and directly related policy issues on all aspects of space flight; space launch vehicles present, past, proposed,

and propulsion (including poorly or undeveloped methods such as ion, solar sail, laser-sail, antimatter, etc); space station design, engineering, operations, and goals; and any other types of space-craft technology, engineering, operations, and related topics. Technical issues involved in developing space resources, colonization of space, etc. Technical, costing, and directly related policy decisions will also be appropriate. Questions about space technology, operations, engineering, etc. are all appropriate, at any level.

Frequently Asked Questions

Astro/Space Frequently Seen Acronyms

mark@ncar.ucar.edu (Mark Bradford)
sci.answers.

R/C Flying

Maintainer: shamim@howland.isu.edu (Shamim Mohammed)
Where on Usenet: rec.models.rc
Where it's archived:
rtfm.mit.edu:pub/usenet/rec.models.rc/ R_C_Flying:_Part_1_of_2_rec.models.rc_FAQ
rtfm.mit.edu:pub/usenet/rec.models.rc/ R_C_Flying:_Part_2_of_2_rec.models.rc_FAQ
What it's for: Issues of interest to people who fly remote controlled aircraft.

rec.aviation FAQ

Maintainer: geoff@peck.com (Geoff Peck)
Where on Usenet: rec.aviation.answers
Where it's archived:
rtfm.mit.edu:pub/usenet/ rec.aviation.answers/aviation/faq
What it's for: Commonly asked questions pertaining to general aviation: training, technology, etc.

rec.aviation.simulators FAQ

Maintainer: john@jg.cso.uiuc.edu (John Mechalas)
Where on Usenet: rec.aviation.simulators
Where it's archived:
rtfm.mit.edu:pub/usenet/

rec.aviation.answers/aviation/simulators
What it's for: Issues pertaining to the use of PC-based simulators.

Space FAQ

Maintainer: leech@cs.unc.edu (Jon Leech)
Where on Usenet: sci.space.tech
Where it's archived:
rtfm.mit.edu:pub/usenet/sci.space
What it's for: Exhaustive treatment of the commonly asked questions regarding space and space technology.

Discussion Lists

aerosp-l
aerosp-l@sivm
Aeronautics & Aerospace History

aiaa
aiaa@arizvm1
AIAA Listserv

aircraft
aircraft@iubvm
The Aircraft

airplane-clubs
airplane-clubs-request@dg-rtp.dg.com (Matthew Waugh)
Mgmt. of group-ownership of aircraft.

aviation
aviation@brufpb
General Aviation List

aviation-theory
aviation-theory@mc.lcs.mit.edu
Aerospace engineering

elements
elements-request@alsys.com (Gary Morris KK6YB)
Orbital elements, timely.

fea-l
sysop@mecheng.fullfeed.com
Finite Element Analysis.

hang-gliding
hang-gliding-request@virginia.edu (Galen Hekhuis)
For enthusiasts of all forms of non-powered flight.

gps digest
gps-request@tws4.si.com
Global Positioning Systems.

grumman-gang

owner-grumman-gang@xmission.com
(Mark A. Matthews)
Owners of Grumman aircraft.

sedsnews
sedsnews@tamvm1.tamu.edu
News about Space from SEDS

sifr-l
sifr-l@ubvm
IFR/SIFR Task Force

simula
simula@bitnic
(Peered) The SIMULA Language List

skunk-works
skunk-works-
request@harbor.ecn.purdue.edu
For discussion of airplanes produced by
the Lockheed Skunk Works

space
space@ubvm
(Peered) SPACE Digest

space-l
space-l@wvnvm
SPACESTAT User's Group

space-sh
space-sh@uga
sci.space.shuttle Digest

spacenws
spacenws@uga
sci.space.news digest

spacepol
spacepol@uga
sci.space.policy digest

spacesci
spacesci@uga
sci.space.science digest

tss-list
tss-list@mitvma
Transportation Science Section List

ultralight-flight
ultralight-flight-request@ms.uky.edu
Ultralight aircraft.
ftp: ftp.ms.uky.edu, pub/mailing.lists/
ultralight-flight

Aeronautics & Aerospace Resources

FTP Resources

Advisory Circulars
ftp://hawk.flight.com/pub/ACirculars/

Air and Space Photos (GIF format)
photo1.si.edu/images/gif89a/air-space

Airline, country and airport codes
ftp://exxilon.xx.rmit.edu.au/pub/air/

Airman's Information Manual
gopher://venus.hyperk.com:2101/1/

Ansett Airlines
gopher://cis.anu.edu.au:3000/7?Ansett

Aviation Archives
ftp://wilbur.pr.erau.edu/

CENA, Center for Aerial Navigation
Studies
ada.cenaath.cena.dgac.fr

Center for Advanced Aviation System
Development
ftp://fwux.fedworld.gov/pub/faa/faa.htm

FAA archive
ftp://fwux.fedworld.gov/pub/faa/faa.htm

FAA databases for airports, VORs, and
airways.
seas.smu.edu/flight

FARS
ftp://ftp.flight.com/pub/FARS/

Federal Aviation Regulations (FARs)
archive.
ftp.hyphen.com/Fly

JSC aviation archive
ftp://aviation.jsc.nasa.gov/pub/fly/data/

Military aircraft information
ftp://byrd.mu.wvnet.edu/pub/history/military/
airforce

Northwestern University aviation
ftp://eecs.nwu.edu/pub/aviation

Skydiving archive
ftp://ftp.eng.ufl.edu/skydive

Univ. of Texas, Science of Aeronautics
Archive
rascal.ics.utexas.edu/

Gopher Resources

Aeronautics at the Florida Institute of
Technology
gaia.sci-ed.fit.edu

Airman's Information Manual
gopher://venus.hyperk.com:2101/1/

American Institute of Aeronautics and
Astronautics
isumvs.iastate.edu

Ansett Airlines
gopher://cis.anu.edu.au:3000/7?Ansett

Federal Aviation Regulations (FARs)
organized through gopher.
mchip00.med.nyu.edu

Indiana Univ. Aeronautical engineering.
lib-gopher.lib.indiana.edu:3050

Lancaster Univ. England
micros.hensa.ac.uk

Marine Data BBS/Aeronautical Charts/
Aerial Photographs
esdim1.esdim.noaa.gov

MIT Aeronautics and Astronautics
gopher.mit.edu:3714

NASA Aeronautics Network (AERONet)
Computer Network
gopher.hpcc.gov

NASA National Aeronautics and Space
Administration
lib-gopher.lib.indiana.edu:3050

rec.aviation newsgroup gopher at NWU
av.eecs.nwu.edu

Roy Smith's Aviation Gopher
gopher://mchip00.med.nyu.edu/11/aviation

Univ. of Kassel, Future ATC, New Systems
and Technologies Implementation in the
Cockpit.
gopher.hrz.uni-kassel.de

Univ. of Michigan
ott22.engin.umich.edu

Univ. of Western Australia
uniwa.uwa.edu.au

US Navy
ra.nrl.navy.mil

WWW Resources

Advanced Air Transportation Technologies
http://www.nas.nasa.gov/AATT/

Aerodynamic Facilities and Simulation
http://ccf.arc.nasa.gov/ao/index.html

Aeronautical Radio, Inc. (ARINC)
http://www.arinc.com/

Aeronautical Simulation Facilities
http://scott.arc.nasa.gov/code_a/code_ao/

Airborne Science & Flight Research
Division
http://airsci-www.arc.nasa.gov/

Airmen Knowledge Test Information
http://acro.harvard.edu/GA/
airmen_test_links.html

Ames Research Center
http://www.arc.nasa.gov/

AMR
http://www.amrcorp.com

Andrews Univ.
http://www.andrews.edu/AVIA/

ARPA - Advanced Research Projects
Agency
http://ftp.arpa.mil/

Aviation Airworthiness Alerts
http://acro.harvard.edu/GA/aaa_links.html

Aviation Image Archives
http://acro.harvard.edu/GA/
image_archives.html

Aviation Museum Locator
http://www.brooklyn.cuny.edu/rec/air/
museums/museums.html

Aviation Publications
http://acro.harvard.edu/GA/av_publ.html

Aviation Week Group
http://www.datapro.mgh.com/

College of Aeronautics, Laguardia Airport,
NY.
http://www.mordor.com/coa/links.html

Computational Human Engineering
Research Office
http://ccf.arc.nasa.gov/af/aff/midas

Cranfield Univ., College of Aeronautics (United Kingdom)
http://www.cranfield.ac.uk/aero/aero_menu.html

Daimler-Benz Aerospace
http://www.daimler-benz.com/dasa/dasa_e.html

DLR German Aerospace Research Establishment
http://www.dlr.de/

Douglas Aircraft Company
http://www.dac.mdc.com/

Dryden Flight Research Ctr.
http://mosaic.dfrf.nasa.gov/dryden.html

Dryden Research Aircraft Photo Archive
http://www.dfrf.nasa.gov/PhotoServer/photoServer.html

Embry-Riddle Aeronautical Univ.
http://macwww.db.erau.edu/

European WWW Aviation Server
http://www.math.ethz.ch/~zari/zari.html

FAA Center for Aviation Systems Reliability
http://www.cnde.iastate.edu/faa.html

FAA Education
http://web.fie.com:80/web/fed/faa/

FAA Human Factors Home Page
http://www.faa.gov/aar/human-factors/welcome.htm

FAA Library at FEDWORLD
http://www.caasd.org/

FAA Mike Monroney Aeronautical Center
http://www.mmac.jccbi.gov/

FAA Office of Commercial Space Transportation
http://www.dot.gov/dotinfo/faa/cst/ocst.html

FAA Program Analysis and Operations Research Lab
http://www.orlab.faa.gov

FAA Technical Center
http://www.tc.faa.gov/

Federal Aviation Administration
http://www.faa.gov/

Federal Aviation Regulations
http://acro.harvard.edu/GA/fars.html

Florida Institute of Technology
http://www.fit.edu/soa/soa.html

French Research Ctr. on Air Traffic Control
http://www.cenatls.cena.dgac.fr/English/index.html

General Aviation WWW Server
http://adswww.harvard.edu/MITSA/ga_info.html

General Electric
http://www.ge.com

Goddard Space Flight Ctr.
http://hypatia.gsfc.nasa.gov/GSFC_homepage.html/

GPS Overview
http://wwwhost.cc.utexas.edu/ftp/pub/grg/gcraft/notes/gps/gps.html

GPS/MET Program
http://pocc.gpsmet.ucar.edu/

Graduate Aeronautical Labs.
http://www.galcit.caltech.edu/

Hang Gliding/Para Gliding and other foot launch aircraft.
http://cougar.stanford.edu:7878/HGMPSHomePage.html

High Powered Rocketry
http://seds.lpl.arizona.edu/ROCKET/rocket.html

IEEE Aerospace and Electronic Systems Society
http://rsd1000.gatech.edu/public_html/bobt/AESS_Home_Page.html

IEEE Control Systems Society
http://eewww.eng.ohio-state.edu/~yurkovic/css.html

International Aviation Events Calendar
http://acro.harvard.edu/IAC/int_airshows.html

Jet Propulsion Laboratory
http://www.jpl.nasa.gov/

Johnson Space Ctr.
http://www.jsc.nasa.gov/jsc/JSC_homepage.html

Kennedy Space Ctr.
http://www.ksc.nasa.gov/ksc.html

Langley Research Ctr.
http://mosaic.larc.nasa.gov/larc.html

Lewis Research Center
http://www.lerc.nasa.gov/
LeRC_homepage.html

Lockheed Martin Corporation
http://www.lockheed.com/TRW

Marshall Space Flight Ctr.
http://hypatia.gsfc.nasa.gov/
MSFC_homepage.html

McDonnell Douglas Aerospace - Houston
http://pat.mdc.com/

Meteorology Index
http://www.met.fu-berlin.de/DataSources/
MetIndex.html

Mig-29 tours (commercial)
http://www.interedu.com/mig29/mig29/

MIT Rocket Society
http://www.mit.edu:8001/activities/mitrs/
home.html

MIT Soaring Association, a WWW server
dedicated to soaring.
http://adswww.harvard.edu/MITSA/
mitsa_homepg.html

MIT Weather Radar Lab.
http://graupel.mit.edu/Radar_Lab.html

More Aviation Images
http://www.flight.com/images.html

NASA Ames Aviation Operations Branch
http://olias.arc.nasa.gov/

NASA Dryden
http://www.dfrf.nasa.gov/

NASA Engineering
http://epims1.gsfc.nasa.gov/engineering/
engineering.html

NASA Langley Technical Report Server
http://techreports.larc.nasa.gov/ltrs/ltrs.html

NASA National Aeronautics and Space
Administration
http://hypatia.gsfc.nasa.gov/
NASA_homepage.html

NASA Scientific and Technical Information Program
http://nova.sti.nasa.gov/STI-homepage.html/

NASA Technical Report Server
http://techreports.larc.nasa.gov/cgi-bin/NTRS/

National Oceanics and Atmospheric
Administration
http://www.noaa.gov/

Northwest Mountain Region
http://www.tc.faa.gov/NM/anm-hp.html

Numerical Aerodynamic Simulation
http://www.nas.nasa.gov

Parks College, St. Louis Univ..
http://www.slu.edu/PARKS/parks_home.html

Part-Task Simulation Laboratory
http://olias.arc.nasa.gov/facilities/part-task/
part-task.html

Penn State Univ., Aerospace Engineering
http://www.psu.edu/aero/aero.html

Purdue Univ.
http://roger.ecn.purdue.edu

Raytheon and E-Systems
http:www.raytheon.com

rec.aviation newsgroup.
http://adswww.harvard.edu/MITSA/
news_groups.html

Rockwell International
http://www.rockwell.com/

SAIC Science Applications Intl. Corporation
http://www.itl.saic.com/

sci.aeronautics.airliners archive
http://www.chicago.com/airliners/
archives.html

Service Difficulty Reports
http://acro.harvard.edu/GA/sdr_links.html

Skydiving at the Univ. of Florida.
http://www.cis.ufl.edu/skydive/

Southern Illinois Univ. at Carbondale
http://www.siu.edu/departments/ctc/aviation

Space Activism Home Page
http://muon.qrc.com/space/start.html

Space Colonies
http://www.nas.nasa.gov/RNR/Visualization/
AlGlobus/SpaceColonies/spaceColonies.html

Space Studies Institute
http://www.astro.nwu.edu/lentz/space/ssi/
home-ssi.html

SPACEHAB, McDonnell Douglas in
Huntsville.
http://hvsun4.mdc.com:1025/SPACEHAB/
SPACEHAB.html

St Cloud State Univ. Aviation
http://condor.stcloud.msus.edu/aviation/

Stanford Univ.
http://aero.stanford.edu/aeroastro.html

Students for the Exploration and Development of Space (SEDS)
http://seds.lpl.arizona.edu/

United States Air Force
http://www.af.mil/

United Technologies
http://www.utc.com/

Univ. of Illinois-Willard Airport, Institute of Aviation
http://www.aviation.uiuc.edu/institute/contents.html

Univ. of Notre Dame
http://www.nd.edu/Departments/EN/AME/HomePage.html

Unofficial L-1011 Home Page
http://users.aol.com/tristar500/l1011/

Weather, Weather maps, and other weather related must see items
http://rs560.cl.msu.edu/weather/

Western Michigan Univ.
http://www.wmich.edu/aviation

WWW.Flight.Com
http://www.flight.com/enter.html

Airlines

Aer Lingus
http://www.hursley.ibm.com:80/aer/

Aeroflot
http://www.seanet.com/Bazar/Aeroflot/Aeroflot.html

Air Canada
http://www.aircanada.ca/

Air Cruise America
http://www.webcom.com/~aca/

American Trans Air
http://www.xmission.com/~aoi/fata.html

Austrian Airlines
http://www.aua.co.at/aua/

Big Island Air
http://www.ilhawaii.net:80/pt/bigair.html

Canada 3000 Airlines

http://vanbc.wimsey.com/~gordona/cmm.html

Canadian Airlines International
http://www.CdnAir.CA/

Cathay Pacific
http://www.cathay-usa.com/

China Northwest Airlines
http://www.demon.co.uk/virtual/China-Northwest.html

Comair, Delta Connection
http://www.iac.net/~flypba/oh.home.html

Delta Airlines
http://www.delta-air.com

Eagle Canyon Airlines
http://cybermart.com/eagle/

Federal Express
http://www.fedex.com/about_fedex.html

Frontier Airlines
http://www.cuug.ab.ca:8001/~busew/frontier.html

KLM
http://www.ib.com:8080/business/klm/klm.html

Lauda Air
http://www.laudaair.com/engl/indexe.htm

Lufthansa
http://www.tkz.fh-rpl.de/tii/lh/lhflug-e.html

Mexicana Airlines
http://www.mexicana.com/index.html

Northwest Airlines
http://www.winternet.com/~tela/nwa-info.html

Õslandsflug
http://www.mmedia.is/eng/loccomp/icebird.html

Qantas Airways
http://www.anzac.com/qantas/qantas.htm

Singapore Airlines
http://www.technet.sg/InfoWEB/communications/industry.html

Southwest Airlines
http://www.iflyswa.com/

TWA
http://www.inlink.com/~jack/twa.html

United Airlines Flight Center
http://www.ualfltctr.com/

Virgin Atlantic
http://www.fly.virgin.com/atlantic/

Agriculture

See also Biology & Biotechnology

Usenet Newsgroups

sci.agriculture
Created by: cactus@clinton.com (L. Todd Masco)
Call for Votes date: November 27, 1993
Newsgroup-based Mailing List: No.
Charter (from Call for Votes):
This newsgroup is intended for the discussion of any topics related to farming and agriculture. Topics for discussion include, but are not limited to:
- Land management
- Water management
- Soils
- Erosion (prevention of)
- Forestry
- Hydroponics
- Aeroponics
- Aquaculture
- Permaculture
- Economic aspects
- Advice and assistance including personal experience
- Announcement of forthcoming courses and conferences
- Discussion and criticism of literature.

sci.agriculture.beekeeping
Created by: Adam Finkelstein
<adamf@hopper.itc.virginia.edu>
Call for Votes date: March 22, 1994
Newsgroup-based Mailing List: No.
Charter (from Call for Votes):
Discussion on all aspects of beekeeping, bee-culture, and products of the hive.

Sci.agriculture.beekeeping will provide beekeepers, bee scientists, farmers, and the general public one place for apicultural information. An FAQ is needed for bee-culture and beekeeping from African bees, to bee venom therapy. The curious are invited to discuss bee lore or ask questions, and the experienced beekeepers will be able to advise and help with the anecdotal information so necessary to beekeeping.

sci.bio.ethology
Created by: Unknown
Call for Votes date: Unknown
Newsgroup-based Mailing List: No.
Charter : Animal behaviour and behavioral ecology.

sci.bio.evolution
Created by: Unknown
Call for Votes date: Unknown
Newsgroup-based Mailing List: No.
Charter : Discussion of all matters pertaining to evolutionary biology.

sci.bio.herp
Created by: Unknown
Call for Votes date: Unknown
Newsgroup-based Mailing List: No.
Charter : Discussion of scientific issues related to herpetology.

Discussion Lists

aaae
aaae@purccvm
American Assoc. for Agricultural Education (numerous other sublists available)

Agmodels-l
jp@unl.edu (Jerome Pier)
Agricultural simulation.

agric-l
agric-l@uga
Agriculture Discussion

camase-l
camase-l@hearn
Quantitative Methods of Research on Agriculture

csanr-l
csanr-l@wsuvm1
Ctr. for Sustainable Agriculture and
Nature Research

dairy-l
dairy-l@umdd
Dairy

fao-bull
fao-bull@irmfao01
Food and Agriculture Organization, AFCO
Tec

fao-doc
fao-doc@irmfao01
Food and Agriculture Organization

fao-info
fao-info@irmfao01
The Food and Agriculture Organization
INFO LIST

faolist
faolist@irmfao01
Food and Agriculture Organization Open
Discussion forum

farm-mgt
farm-mgt@ndsuvm1
Farm Mgmt.

fish-ecology
fish-eco@searn
Academic forum on fisheries ecology and
related issues

fish-junior
fish-jun@searn
Academic forum on fisheries ecology and
related issues

fishfolk
fishfolk@mitvma
Fisheries Social Science Network

food-law
food-law@uminn1
Laws Dealing with Food Science

foodlink
foodlink@wsuvm1
Food Safety Issues

goats
goats@wsuvm1
For Goat Lovers and Managers

hih-l
hih-l@vtvm1
Human Issues in Horticulture

hort-l
hort-l@vtvm1
Va Tech Horticulture Dept. - Monthly
Releases

hortpgm
hortpgm@vtvm1
Va Tech Horticulture Dept.

imagrs-l
imagrs-l@csearn
Digital Image Processing

pasa-l
pasa-l@psuvm
PASA-L Pennsylvania Assoc. of Sustainable Agriculture

pltrynws
pltrynws@sdsuvm
PLTRYNWS Poultry Health, Production
and Mgmt.

pnwmarkt
pnwmarkt@wsuvm1
Agricultural Market News for WA and OR

rusag-l
rusag-l@umdd
Russian Agriculture

savvy-l
savvy-l@vtvm1
Virginia Sustainable Agriculture thru
Virginia

soils-l
jp@unl.edu (Jerome Pier)
Soil science.

sustag-l
sustag-l@wsuvm1
Discussions about Sustainable Agriculture

wcdrt-l
wcdrt-l@ualtavm
Western Canadian Dairy Research and
Technology

wdamage
wdamage@ndsuvm1
Wildlife Damage Mgmt.

Agriculture Resources

Gopher Resources

AgResearch Wallaceville, Upper Hutt,
  New Zealand
  weka.warc.cri.nz

Alabama Cooperative Extension Service
gopher.acenet.auburn.edu

Aquaculture
snymorva.cs.snymor.edu

AquaNIC (aquaculture)
thorplus.lib.purdue.edu

Auburn Univ, College of Agriculture
Gopher
eli.ag.auburn.edu

Bees and Beekeeping - Ohio State Univ.
sun1.oardc.ohio-state.edu

Cornell Univ, CENET
empire.cce.cornell.edu

CYFER-net USDA ES Gopher Server.
cyfer.esusda.gov/

Extension Service USDA Information
zeus.esusda.gov/

Flood Gopher
cesgopher.ag.uiuc.edu

Library of Congress (LC MARVEL)
marvel.loc.gov

Master Gardener - Texas A&M Univ.
leviathan.tamu.edu

Michigan State Univ., Outreach/Extension/Community Affairs
burrow.cl.msu.edu

N.Z. Pastoral Agricultural Research Inst.,
Invermay
gopher.invermay.cri.nz

National Agricultural Library (NAL)
gopher.nalusda.gov

National Institute of Agrobiological
Resources - Japan
gopher.dna.affrc.go.jp

NetVet Veterinary Resource Line
netvet.wustl.edu/

North Carolina Cooperative Extension
Service
twosocks.ces.ncsu.edu

North Carolina State Univ. Library
dewey.lib.ncsu.edu

Not Just Cows: A Guide to Internet/Bitnet
Resources in Agriculture and Related
Sciences
una.hh.lib.umich.edu

Oregon State Univ, Oregon Extension
Service Gopher
gopher.oes.orst.edu

PENpages (Penn State Univ.)
penpages.psu.edu

Poultry Science Gopher - Texas A&M
Univ.
poultry-gopher.tamu.edu

RiceInfo (Rice Univ. CWIS)
riceinfo.rice.edu

Sustainable Agriculture Information - Via
Sunsite
calypso.oit.unc.edu

Swedish Univ. of Agricultural Sciences
pinus.slu.se

Texas A&M
gopher.tamu.edu

Texas A&M (Texas Agricultural Extension
Service Linux Gopher)
leviathan.tamu.edu

United States Dept. of Agriculture,
Economics and Statistics Gopher
usda.mannlib.cornell.edu

Univ. of California - Santa Barbara Library
ucsbuxa.ucsb.edu:3001

Univ. of Florida - Institute of Food and
Agricultural Sciences
gnv.ifas.ufl.edu

Univ. of Nebraska-Lincoln - Agriculture &
Natural Resources Database
unlvm.unl.edu

Univ. of Nevada (Agriculture Collection)
gopher.unr.edu

USDA agricultural and economic research
services (searchable)
calypso.oit.unc.edu

USDA Economics and Statistics
usda.mannlib.cornell.edu

Virginia Cooperative Extension Gopher
gopher.ext.vt.edu

WWW Resources

Aberdeen Univ.
http://www.abdn.ac.uk/~agr342/

Ag-Links
http://www.gennis.com/aglinks.html

Agricultural Biotechnology Ctr., Hungary
http://www.abc.hu/

Agricultural Biotechnology International
Conference
http://www.lights.com/abic/

Agricultural Genome WWW Server
http://probe.nalusda.gov:8000/index.html

Agriculture Hotlist
http://www.bae.ncsu.edu:/bae/people/faculty/
walker/hotlist.html#AgriEnv

Agriculture Online
http://www.agriculture.com/

Agriculture Virtual Librarian
http://galaxy.einet.net/galaxy/Engineering-
and-Technology/Agriculture.html

Alaron Products Limited
http://nz.com/NZ/Commerce/alaron/

American Society of Agricultural Engineers
http://asae.org/

Asia Regional Agribusiness Project
http://www.milcom.com/rap/

Biofuels Information Network (U.S. Dept.
of Energy)
http://www.esd.ornl.gov/BFDP/
BFDPMOSAIC/binmenu.html

CENET, the Cornell Extension NETwork
http://galaxy.einet.net/hytelnet/OTH085.html

Cereal Rust Lab
http://www.umn.edu/rustlab/

Chickadee Creek Cattle Services
http://www.teleport.com/~chick/

City Farmer's Urban Agriculture Notes
http://unixg.ubc.ca:780/~cityfarm/
urbagnotes1.html

Clemson Univ.
http://agweb.clemson.edu/

Crop Production Science
http://ekolserv.vo.slu.se/

Department of Plant Breeding WAU
http://www.spg.wau.nl/pv/

European Bank of Glomales - (BEG)
http://www.ukc.ac.uk/biolab/beg/index.html

farm wholesale greenhouses
http://www.teleport.com/~plastec/

Florentine CNR Institutes - Agriculture
and Forest
http://www.area.fi.cnr.it/agris.htm

Florida Agricultural Information Retrieval
System
http://hammock.ifas.ufl.edu/

Florida State Univ. Agriculture Index
http://www.cs.fsu.edu/projects/group3/
agri.html

Frescargot Farms Snail Farming Ventures
http://www.paccon.com/snails/

Genome & Genetics - Agricultural
Genome
http://probe.nalusda.gov:8000/index.html

Hillside Farm
ftp://users.aol.com/mszaller/farm.htm

IFA Nurseries, Inc.
http://www.ifainc.com/~ifainc/

Iowa Farmer Today
http://www.infi.net/fyiowa/ift/index.htm

Maize Genome Database
http://teosinte.agron.missouri.edu/top.html

Meat Animal Research Ctr.
http://sol.marc.usda.gov/

Missouri Univ.
http://ssu.agri.missouri.edu

Munich Univ. of Technology
http://www.edv.agrar.tu-muenchen.de/
hello.html

National Agricultural Library
http://www.nalusda.gov/

National Dairy Database
http://www.inform.umd.edu:8080/EdRes/
Topic/AgrEnv/ndd/

National Farmers Organization
http://www.agriculture.com/agworld/nfo/
nfoindex.html

National Institute of Animal Health, Japan
http://ss.niah.affrc.go.jp/index.html

National Taiwan Univ.
http://flood.hy.ntu.edu.tw/ntuae/home.html

NCSU Soil Sciences
http://www.soil.ncsu.edu/

NetVet Veterinary Resource Line

http://netvet.wustl.edu/

NewCROP
http://newcrop.hort.purdue.edu

North Carolina Agricultural & Technical
State Univ.
http://rhema.ncat.edu/

North Carolina State Univ. Cooperative
Extension Service
http://gopher.ces.ncsu.edu/

Norwegian Implement Company Store
http://athos.phoenixat.com/power/store.html

NSF SUCCEED Agricultural Engineering
Visual Database
http://succeed.edtech.vt.edu/Indexes/
Agricultural%20and%20Env.html

NYSAES WWW Server
http://aruba.nysaes.cornell.edu:8000/
geneva.htm

Oklahoma State Univ. Agronomy
http://clay.agr.okstate.edu/agrover.htm

Ostriches On Line
http://www.achiever.com/ostintro.html

OSU Agricultural Sciences
http://www.orst.edu/mc/coldep/agrsci.htm

Oxford Univ. Plant Sciences
http://ifs.plants.ox.ac.uk/

SAC (The Scottish Agricultural College)
http://www.sac.ac.uk/

Salmon Select Distributors Home Page
http://rampages.onramp.net/~salmon/
index.html

Science of Food and Agriculture Index
http://www.netins.net/showcase/cast/
sfae_ndx.htm

Sea Urchin Harvesters Association -
California
http://seaurchin.org/

Southwest Agricultural Weather Service
Center
http://swami.tamu.edu/

Strategic Management in Agribusiness
http://128.146.140.187/ae601/

Technical Univ. of Nova Scotia Agricultural Engineering
http://www.tuns.ca:80/ae/

Texas A&M Univ.
http://ageninfo.tamu.edu/

Texas A&M's AGropolis
http://agcomwww.tamu.edu/agcom/agrotext/
agcommap.html

UCR - Biological, Agricultural and
Medical Resources
http://lib-www.ucr.edu/bioag/

Univ. of Arizona College of Agriculture
http://ag.arizona.edu/aginfo.html

Univ. of Calif. Coop. Ext. Livestock/
Natural Resources
http://www.ucop.edu/anrhome/coop-ext/
Uccelr/uccelr.html

Univ. of Florida Institute of Food
http://gnv.ifas.ufl.edu/

Univ. of Tennessee at Martin
http://unix1.utm.edu/

Univ. of Tennessee Institute of Agriculture
http://solar.rtd.utk.edu/campuses/utia.html

USDA-ARS National Soil Erosion Lab
http://purgatory.ecn.purdue.edu:20002/
NSERL/nserl.html

USDA GrainGenes Database
http://wheat.pw.usda.gov/graingenes.html

USDA Research Database
http://medoc.gdb.org/best/stc/usda-best.html

USDA Soil Conservation Service - Missouri
http://www.mo.scs.ag.gov/

Virginia Tech
http://www.cals.vt.edu/

WAIS Resources

Agriculture Mailing List Info
wais.cic.net:210

Grain Seed (WAIS, U. North Carolina)
sunsite.unc.edu:210

Anthropology

See also Archaeology

Usenet Newsgroups

sci.anthropology
Created by: claird@NeoSoft.com (Cameron Laird)
Call for Votes date: April 24, 1992
Newsgroup-based Mailing List: No.
Charter (from Call for Votes):
sci.anthropology is a worldwide forum for the comprehensive interests of professionals in and students of the science of anthropology. This includes the four conventional categories of archaeologic, biologic, linguistic, and socio-cultural anthropology, along with the wealth of more specialized sub-disciplines, and all professional concerns.

The subject matter of anthropology certainly overlaps that discussed in sci.econ, sci.archaeology, sci.bio, and a variety of other newsgroups. The aim of sci.anthropology is to enrich these discussions, not compete with them. The particular role of sci.anthropology is to synthesize, bringing together

a. biologic and psychologic domains,
b. scientific and humanistic modes,
c. neophyte and experienced participants, and
d. data from diverse cultures and species,

for example. Always, the unifying perspective and tone of sci.anthropology will be that of contemporary academic anthropology.

sci.anthropology specifically invites contributions in all languages, from those with all levels of formal education.

sci.anthropology.paleo
Created by: danny@orthanc.cs.su.oz.au (Danny Yee)
Call for Votes date: November 24, 1993
Newsgroup-based Mailing List: No.
Charter (from Call for Votes):
sci.anthropology.paleo is for the discussion of the evolution of the genus Homo, and more generally of the primates. Some of the topics likely to be covered include:

- primatology (primate social interactions, comparative morphology, ape languages, etc.)
- paleoanthropology "proper" (discussion of new fossil finds, etc.)
- the origins of human language and cognition
- the origins of distinctive human morphological features (bipedalism, big brain, hairlessness, etc.)
- biological and genetic variation in Homo sapiens relevant to our evolution (e.g. mitochondrial DNA studies)
- sociobiological arguments that rely on evolutionary considerations.

soc.genealogy.african
Created by: Michael Emery <MEmery@aol.com>
Call for Votes Date: 10 Oct 1995
Newsgroup-based Mailing List: No.

soc.genealogy.australia+nz
Created by: Andrew Billinghurst <billinghurst@slim.agvic.gov.au>
Call for Votes Date: August 14, 1995
Newsgroup-based Mailing List: No.

soc.genealogy.benelux
Created by: Johan Berteloot <svjohan@alpha.ufsia.ac.be>
Call for Votes Date: May 8, 1995

Newsgroup-based Mailing List: No.

soc.genealogy.computing
Created by: Kaleb Keithley <kaleb@x.org>
Call for Votes Date: October 11, 1994
Mailing list: gencmp-l@mail.eworld.com
Charter (from Call for Votes):
Discussion of computer-based
genealogical tools/resources of any type.

soc.genealogy.french
Created by: Kaleb Keithley <kaleb@x.org>
Call for Votes Date: October 11, 1994
Mailing list: gen-fr-l@mail.eworld.com

soc.genealogy.german
Created by: Kaleb Keithley <kaleb@x.org>
(part of the soc.roots re-org)
Call for Votes Date: October 11, 1994
Newsgroup-based Mailing List: No.

soc.genealogy.jewish (moderated)
Created by: Kaleb Keithley <kaleb@x.org>
Call for Votes Date: October 11, 1994
Moderated by: Susan King <sgjewish-req@trace.cgsg.com>
Mailing list: jewgen@mail.eworld.com
Submissions go to:
sgjewish@trace.cgsg.com

soc.genealogy.medieval
Created by: Don Stone
<stone@rowan.edu>
Call for Votes Date: May 3, 1995
Newsgroup-based Mailing List: No.

soc.genealogy.methods (Moderated)
Created by: Kaleb Keithley <kaleb@x.org>
Call for Votes Date: October 11, 1994
Moderated by: Brian Leverich et al <soc-genealogy-methods-request@rand.org>
Mailing list: genmtd-l@mail.eworld.com
Submissions go to: soc-genealogy-methods@rand.org

soc.genealogy.misc
Created by: Kaleb Keithley <kaleb@x.org>
Call for Votes Date: October 11, 1994
Mailing list: genmsc-l@mail.eworld.com

soc.genealogy.surnames (Moderated)
Created by: Kaleb Keithley <kaleb@x.org>
Call for Votes Date: October 11, 1994
Moderated by: Bill Mills et al <soc-

genealogy-surnames-request@mail.eworld.com>
Mailing list: gennam-l@mail.eworld.com
Submissions go to: soc-genealogy-surnames@mail.eworld.com
Charter (from Call for Votes):
Group for queries about relatives or
ancestors.

Frequently Asked Questions

Anthropology FAQ
Maintainer: Allen H. Lutins
Where on Usenet: sci.anthropology,
sci.archaeology
Where it's archived: FTP://
ftp.neosoft.com/pub/users/claird/
sci.anthropology/
Anthropology_network_FAQ
What it's for: Anthropology endeavors.

Discussion Lists

anthro-l
anthro-l@ubvm.cc.buffalo.edu
General Anthropology Topics

jwa
jwa@ubvm
The Jrnl. of World Anthropology

mapc
mapc@utoronto
MAPC - Materialist Anthropology & the
Product

nativenet
gst@gnosys.svle.ma.us (Gary S. Trujillo)
Indigenous issues.

pan
pan@gwuvm
Physical Anthropology News List

Anthropology Resources

FTP Resources

Fourth World Documentation Project
ftp.halcyon.com/pub/FWDP/WWW/fwdp.html

INQUA repository at Wisconsin Geology
geology.wisc.edu/pub/inqua/

Native American information
ftp.cit.cornell.edu/pub/special/Native Profs/
usenet/

Oriental Institute
oi.uchicago.edu/

World Data Centre-A for Paleoclimatology
ngdc1.ngdc.noaa.gov/paleo/

Gopher Resources

Anthropology and Culture
riceinfo.rice.edu

ANU-Radiocarbon-Abstracts
cheops.anu.edu.au

Applied Anthropology Computer Network
gopher.acs.oakland.edu

Bishop Museum
bishop.bishop.hawaii.org

Bryn Mawr Classical Review
gopher.lib.virginia.edu:70/11/alpha/bmcr

Ecolab Gopher
julian.dac.uga.edu

Environmental sciences
life.anu.edu.au/11/landscape_ecology

FAQ: Internet Resources in Anthropology
spirit.lib.uconn.edu

Heritage Conservation, Historic Preservation and Archaeology Resource Guide
spirit.lib.uconn.edu

Jrnl. of World Anthropology (JWA)
wings.buffalo.edu

Pacific, Prehistory & Archaeology
cheops.anu.edu.au

Peabody Museum of Natural History at Yale Univ.
gopher.peabody.yale.edu

UWA Anthropology Information
uniwa.uwa.edu.au

World Email Directory of Anthropologists (WEDA)
wings.buffalo.edu

World Heritage Newsletter
gopher.cic.net

Telnet Sites

National Archaeological Database
inadb@cast.uark.edu:23

WWW Resources

American Journal of Physical Anthropology
http://sunsite.nus.sg/wiley-text/lif/lif187.html

American Journal of Primatology
http://sunsite.nus.sg/wiley-text/lif/lif188.html

American Univ.
http://www.american.edu:70/0/
academic.depts/cas/anthro/antmain.html

Anthap—Applied Anthropology Computer Network
http://www.acs.oakland.edu/~dow/
anthap.html

Anthropoetics: The Electronic Journal of Generative Anthropology
http://www.humnet.ucla.edu/humnet/
anthropoetics/home.html

Anthropology WWW Virtual Library
http://elab-server.usc.edu/anthropology.html

ANU Bioinformatics
http://life.anu.edu.au/

Archaeological Dialogues
http://archweb.LeidenUniv.nl/ad/
home_ad.html

Archaeological Fieldwork Server
http://durendal.cit.cornell.edu/TestPit.html

Archaeological Museum of Cagliari, Italy
http://www.crs4.it/HTML/RUGGIERO/
MUSEO/mus_ind.html

Archaeology at UCONN
http://spirit.lib.uconn.edu/archaeology.html

Archives for the USENET newsgroup sci.anthropology.paleo and anthro-l discussion list
http://www.anatomy.su.oz.au/danny/
anthropology/index.html

ArchNet - Univ. of Connecticut Dept. of Anthropology
http://spirit.lib.uconn.edu/HTML/archnet.html

Arctic Circle
http://www.lib.uconn.edu/ArcticCircle/

Asian Studies
http://coombs.anu.edu.au/WWWVL-AsianStudies.html

Berkeley Museum of Paleontology
http://128.32.146.30/welcome.html

California Regional Primate Research Ctr.
http://www.crprc.ucdavis.edu/crprc/homepage.html

California State Univ. at Northridge
http://www.csun.edu/~hfant005/anthhome.htm

Citizen Band Potawatomi Tribe
http://www.qns.com/~barrettj/homepage.htm

Classics and Mediterranean Archaeology
http://rome.classics.lsa.umich.edu/welcome.html

Colby College
http://www.colby.edu/rel/Archaeology.html

CSAC Ethnographics Gallery
http://lucy.ukc.ac.uk/

Ctr. for Advanced Studies, Research and Development in Sardinia
http://www.crs4.it/HTML/homecrs4.html

Ctr. for Anthropology Communications
http://pegasus.acs.ttu.edu/~wurlr/index.html

Cultural Studies and Critical Theory
http://english-server.hss.cmu.edu/Theory.html

Culture and Society of Mexico
http://www.public.iastate.edu/~rjsalvad/scmfaq/scmfaq.html

Deutsche Datenquellen
http://www.rz.uni-karlsruhe.de/Outerspace/VirtualLibrary/index.html

Electronic Zoo / NetVet - Primates
http://netvet.wustl.edu/primates.htm

Ethnographics Laboratory at the Univ. of Southern California
http://www.usc.edu/dept/elab/welcome

Ethnology Resources
http://sosig.ac.uk/Subjects/ethno.html

Evolution
http://golgi.harvard.edu/biopages/evolution.html

Fossil Hominids
http://rumba.ics.uci.edu:8080/faqs/fossil-hominids.html

Gorilla Home Page
http://larch.ukc.ac.uk:2001/gorillas/index.html

Great Sioux Nation
http://www.state.sd.us/state/executive/tourism/sioux/sioux.htm

HADDON: An Online Catalogue of Archival Ethnographic Film
http://www.rsl.ox.ac.uk/isca/haddon/HADD_home.html

Hamline Univ.
http://www.hamline.edu/depts/anthropology/index.html

Heritage Conservation, Historic Preservation and Archaeology Resource Guide
http://hpb.hwc.ca:7002/Internet_Resource_Guide.html

Human-Languages Page
http://www.willamette.edu/~tjones/Language-Page.html

Institute of Egyptian Art and Archaeology
http://www.memst.edu/egypt/main.html

Institute of Social and Cultural Anthropology, Univ. of Oxford
http://www.rsl.ox.ac.uk/isca/index.html

Intl. Council on Monuments and Sites (ICOMOS)
http://hpb.hwc.ca:7002/ICOMOS_description.html

Journal of Field Archaeology
http://jfa-www.bu.edu

Journal of Material Culture
http://www.sageltd.co.uk/journals/details/mco.html

Journal of World Anthropology
http://wings.buffalo.edu/academic/department/anthropology/jwa/

Kinship and Social Organization: An Interactive Tutorial
http://www.umanitoba.ca/anthropology/kintitle.html

Library of Congress
http://lcweb.loc.gov/homepage/lchp.html

Linkages School of Social Sciences at the Univ. of California at Irvine
http://eclectic.ss.uci.edu/linkages/linkages.html

LMBM - Lexeme - Morpheme Base
Morphology
http://www.bucknell.edu/~rbeard

Ojibwe Language and Culture
http://www.willamette.edu/~tjones/languages/
ojibwe-main.html

Oneida Indian Nation
http://nysernet.org:80/oneida/

Oregon State Univ.
http://www.mc.maricopa.edu/anthropology

Oxford Univ. Institute of Social and
Cultural Anthropology
http://www.rsl.ox.ac.uk/isca/index.html

Population Studies Ctr.
http://www.psc.lsa.umich.edu/

Primate Info Net
http://night.primate.wisc.edu/pin/

Pueblo Cultural Ctr.
http://hanksville.phast.umass.edu/defs/
independant/PCC/PCC.html

Queen's Univ.
http://jupiter.qub.ac.uk/stephen/arch.html

Radiocarbon journal WWW Server
http://packrat.aml.arizona.edu/

Robot Archaeologist
http://www.usc.edu/dept/raiders/story/
index.html

Russian and East European Studies
http://www.pitt.edu/~cjp/rees.html

Skull Module
http://www.csuchico.edu/anth/Module/
skull.html

Social Science Information Gateway
http://sosig.esrc.bris.ac.uk/

Southwest, Cultural, Historical, Geological
and Anthropological Pointers
http://www.frontier.net/southwest.html

Stanford Univ.
http://www-leland.stanford.edu/group/anthro/

Theoretical Anthropology
http://www.univie.ac.at/voelkerkunde/
theoretical-anthropology/

UC-Berkeley Museum of Paleontology
http://ucmp1.berkeley.edu:80/welcome.html

United Keetoowah Band of Cherokee
Indians
http://www.uark.edu/depts/comminfo/UKB/
welcome.html

Univ. of Auckland
http://www.auckland.ac.nz/ant/anthro.htm

Univ. of Bradford, Archaeological Sciences
http://www.brad.ac.uk/acad/archsci/
homepage.html

Univ. of California at Irvine
http://www.socsci.uci.edu/anthro/index.html

Univ. of California at Santa Barbara
http://www.sscf.ucsb.edu/anth/index.html

Univ. of Montana
http://150.131.101.200/anthro/

Univ. of Nebraska at Lincoln
http://www.unl.edu/anthro/Homepage.html

Univ. of New England
http://mutz.une.edu.au/server_data/Arch/
ArchBrochure.html

Univ. of Oklahoma
http://www.uoknor.edu/anthropology/

Univ. of South Dakota
http://sunbird.usd.edu/anth/

Univ. of Southampton
http://avebury.arch.soton.ac.uk/

Univ. of Texas at Austin
http://www.dla.utexas.edu/depts/anthro/
main.html

Univ. of Virginia
http://minerva.acc.virginia.edu/~anthro/

Univ. of Waterloo
http://arts.uwaterloo.ca/ANTHRO/rwpark/
anthro.html

Univ. of Western Australia
http://www.arts.uwa.edu.au/AnthropWWW/
OVERVIEW.HTM

Univ. of Western Ontario
http://yoda.sscl.uwo.ca/anthropology/

Washington State Univ.
http://www.wsu.edu:8080/~anthro/
anthhome.html

Web Languages Resources Site
http://babel.uoregon.edu/yamada/guides.html

Archaeology

See also Anthropology

Usenet Newsgroups

sci.archaeology
Created by: vgibbs@nmsu.edu
Newsgroup-based Mailing List: No.
Charter (from Call for Votes):
1. To exchange information on various corcerns in ARCHAEOLOGY, including method and theory, pot hunting, egyptology, typology, dating, and other related topics.

2. To facilitate ongoing debates and comments on ideas or research that may not necessarily be in a publishable form.

3. To query other interested earth scientists about resources which could be made generally available. (e.g. programs, images, data, references)

4. To keep each other informed on upcoming events of interest to social science researchers and computing in the field of archaeology.

sci.archaeology.mesoamerican
Created by: edanien@sas.upenn.edu (Elin Danien)
Call for Votes date: March 31, 1994
Newsgroup-based Mailing List: No.
Charter (from Call for Votes):
The aim of sci.archaeology.mesoamerican is to provide an open discussion forum for the mesoamerican archaeology community on the internet. This newsgroup would allow rapid, timely and focussed discussions of opinions and information that would take months or years (or not at all) on conventional paper journals.

Topics for discussion would include:

Announcements of new excavations/ discoveries/interpretation. Cultures covered include, but are not limited to: Maya, Aztec, Toltec, Zapotec, Mixtec, Olmec, Teotihuacan, Gulf Coast.

Also North American and South American Cultures Inca, etc.
Software
Databases
Hardware/Equipment - specs, opinions,
Applications
Techniques
Announcements/reviews of papers/ conferences.
General Discussion /opinions/ questions.
Positions vacant.

Archaeology Resources

FTP Resources
American Schools of Oriental Research Newsletter
ftp://oi.uchicago.edu/pub/asor/

CONTENTS - Religious Studies Publications Journal
ftp://panda1.uottawa.ca/pub/religion/contents-project-overview.txt

Fourth World Documentation Project
ftp.halcyon.com/pub/FWDP/

Newsletter for Anatolian Studies
ftp://oi.uchicago.edu/pub/research/nas/

Oriental Institute Research Archives Acquisitions List
ftp://oi.uchicago.edu/pub/oi/resarch/

Pirradazish: Bulletin Of Achaemenian
Studies
ftp://oi.uchicago.edu/pub/research/
achaemenid/

TOCS-IN: Tables of Contents of Journals
of Interest to Classicists
ftp://ftp.epas.utoronto.ca/pub/tocs-in/

Gopher Resources

Aboriginal History Jrnl.
cis.anu.edu.au

Ancient History Bulletin
tornade.ERE.UMontreal.CA:7071/11/english/
prepub/ahb

Anthropology and Archaeology Corner,
Univ. of Oxford
rsl.ox.ac.uk

Anthropology and Archaeology Journals
marvel.loc.gov

Anthropology and Culture
riceinfo.rice.edu

Applied Anthropology Computer Network
gopher.acs.oakland.edu

Asian Studies Facility — COOMBSQUEST,
Australian National University
cheops.anu.edu.au:70/11/ResearchFacilities/
ASIAN

Brown Univ., Ctr. for Old World Archaeology and Art
gopher.brown.edu

Bryn Mawr Classical Review
gopher.lib.virginia.edu:70/11/alpha/bmcr

Center for Non-Western Studies, Leiden
University - Newsletter
oasis.leidenuniv.nl:70/11/.cnws/.newsletter

Chicano/LatinoNet Gopher — UCLA
latino.sscnet.ucla.edu:70/11/

Cultural Theory (from CMU)
english-server.hss.cmu.edu

Ecolab Gopher: Archaeology of the
Southeastern United States
julian.dac.uga.edu

Electronic Antiquity: Communicating The
Classics (U. Tasmania)
info.utas.edu.au

Ethnomusicology Research Digest
gopher.cic.net

FAQ: Internet Resources in Anthropology
spirit.lib.uconn.edu

General Resources in Area Studies
marvel.loc.gov

Indigenous Peoples — Library of Congress
marvel.loc.gov:70/11/global/socsci/area/
native

Indigenous/Native BBSs
gopher.tamu.edu:70/00/.data/ethnic/bbs.list

Inter-Tribal Network
cscns.com:70/11/
News%20and%20Information/itn

Jerusalem One Network
jerusalem1.datasrv.co.il:70/1

Jewish Studies — Library of Congress
marvel.loc.gov:70/11/global/socsci/area/
jewish

Journal of World Archaeology from SUNY
Buffalo.
wings.buffalo.edu/11/academic/department/
anthropology/jwa

Jrnl. of World Anthropology
wings.buffalo.edu

Latin American Network Information
Center — Univ. of Texas
emx.cc.utexas.edu:70/11/ilasut

Latin American Studies — Library of
Congress
marvel.loc.gov:70/11/global/socsci/area/latino

Listservs in Anthropology
ucsbuxa.ucsb.edu:3001

Middle East Studies — Library of Congress
marvel.loc.gov/11/global/socsci/area/mideast

New Guinea Research Project — The Field
Museum, Chicago
fmppr.fmnh.org:70/00/.fmnh/.acad/.ant/
.newguinea

NY - Israel Project of Nysernet
Israel.nysernet.org:71/1

Omni-Cultural-Academic-Resource
gopher.stolaf.edu

Peabody Museum of Natural History
gopher.peabody.yale.edu

Race and Ethnic Studies Institute, Texas A&M Univ.
gopher.tamu.edu

Scholia Reviews
ccat.sas.upenn.edu:5070/11/scholia

Texas A&M Univ.
tamuts.tamu.edu

Univ. of Georgia
julian.dac.uga.edu

Univ. of Glasgow
govan.cent.gla.ac.uk

Univ. of Montana
wilcox.umt.edu

Univ. of Washington
huxley.anthro.washington.edu

Welsh Language and Culture Archive
calypso.oit.unc.edu:70/11/sunsite.d/welsh.d

Women's Studies
marvel.loc.gov

World Heritage Newsletter
gopher.cic.net

Worldwide Anthropology Email Directory
wings.buffalo.edu

WWW Resources

A.S.S.O. Net — Underwater Archaeology & Speleology
http://www.mclink.it/assoc/assonet/assonet.htm

Aboriginal Studies — WWW Virtual Library, Australian National Univ.
http://coombs.anu.edu.au/WWWVL-Aboriginal.html

African Studies — Univ. of Pennsylvania
http://www.sas.upenn.edu/African_Studies/Home_Page/Ab_AFSTD.html

Al Mashriq - The Levant Cultural MultiMedia Servers
http://www.hiof.no/ludvigsen/webdoc/levant_servers.html#Archaeology

Ancient Civilizations of the Andes
http://www.rain.org/~pjenkin/civiliza.html

Ancient Near East resources
http://spirit.lib.uconn.edu/archnet/near_east.html

Ancient Palestine Gallery, Univ. Museum — Univ. of Pennsylvania
http://philae.sas.upenn.edu/ANEP/ANEP.html

Annual Egyptological Bibliography
http://www.leidenuniv.nl/nino/aeb.html

Anthropology and Ecology Institute at Geneva
http://anthropologie.unige.ch/DAE/AboutTheDAE.html

ARACHNION. A Journal of Ancient Literature and History on the Web
http://www.cisi.unito.it/arachne/arachne.html

Archaeological Museum of Cagliari, Italy
http://www.crs4.it/HTML/RUGGIERO/MUSEO/mus_ind.html

Archaeological Regions
http://spirit.lib.uconn.edu/ArchNet/Regions/Regions.html

Archaeological Research at Oslonki, Poland — Princeton Univ.
http://www.princeton.edu/~bogucki/oslonki.html

Archaeological Research in the Arctic — Univ. of Waterloo
http://watarts.uwaterloo.ca/ANTHRO/rwpark/ArcticArchStuff/ArcticIntro.html

Archaeological Society of British Columbia
http://mindlink.net/glen_chan/asbc.html

Archaeological Survey in the Eastern Desert of Egypt — Univ. of Michigan
http://rome.classics.lsa.umich.edu/projects/coptos/desert.html

ArchNet - Europe
http://www.bham.ac.uk/BUFAU/Projects/EAW/index.html

ArchWeb: Nederlandse Archeologie — Leiden Univ., NL
http://archweb.leidenuniv.nl/archweb_gb.html

Arctic Circle: Univ. of Connecticut
http://spirit.lib.uconn.edu/ArcticCircle/index.htmll

Arkansas Archaeological Survey
http://www.uark.edu/campus-resources/archinfo

ArtServ at Australian National Univ.
http://rubens.anu.edu.au/

Austrian Archaeology — An evolving
resource on selected Austrian sites
http://home.telecom.at/~ufischer/archat1.html

Barges, Lake Tahoe
http://www.indiana.edu/~scuba/
EB.htmlEmerald Bay Historic

Base d'Anthropology Physique du Niger
— Institut de Recherche en Sciences
Humaines de l'Universite de Niamey
http://www.orstom.fr/bani/welcome.html

Biblical Archaeologist: Perspectives on the
Ancient World from Mesopotamia to the
Mediterranean
http://scholar.cc.emory.edu/scripts/ASOR/BA/
ASOR-BA.html

British Archaeology from The Council for
British Archaeology
http://britac3.britac.ac.uk/cba/ba/ba.html

Bulletin of the Society for American
Archaeology from UC Santa Barbara.
http://www.sscf.ucsb.edu/SAA

Cahokia Mounds State Historic Site,
Illinois
http://medicine.wustl.edu/~kellerk/
cahokia.html

Canadian Heritage Information Network
http://www.chin.gc.ca/

Canadian Museum of Civilization -
Mystery of the Maya
http://www.cmcc.muse.digital.ca/cmc/
cmceng/mminteng.html

CEIPAC: The study of ancient economy in
the Roman Empire — Univ. of Barcelona
http://aliga.cesca.es:1025/~zopcgp01/
historia/ceipac/ceipac.htm

Center for Advanced Studies, Research
and Development in Sardinia
http://www.crs4.it/HTML/homecrs4.html

Center for Archaeological Research at the
Univ. of Auckland
http://www.auckland.ac.nz/ant/car.html

Center for World Indigenous Studies/
Fourth World Documentation Project
http://www.halcyon.com/FWDP/fwdp.html

Centre National de la Prehistoire — France
http://dufy.aquarel.fr:8001/html/cnp.html

Centre Pierre Paris — Universitè de
Bordeaux
http://silicon.montaigne.u-bordeaux.fr:8001/

Ceramic Traditions of Mali — Mission
Archèologique et Ethnoarchèologique
Suisse en Afrique de l'Ouest
http://anthropologie.unige.ch/expo/maesao/
intro.html

Chicago House Bulletin
http://www-oi.uchicago.edu/OI/PROJ/EPI/
Epigraphic.html

CIDOC Newsletter
http://www.natmus.min.dk/cidoc/
volume6e.html

CIESIN: Consortium for International
Earth Science Information Network
http://www.ciesin.org

Classics and Mediterranean Archaeology
— Univ. of Michigan
http://rome.classics.lsa.umich.edu/
welcome.html

Colby College
http://www.colby.edu/rel/Archaeology.html

Connecticut State Museum of Natural
History
http://spirit.lib.uconn.edu/ArchNet/Museums/
Museums.html

Conservation OnLine (CoOL)
http://palimpsest.stanford.edu/

Cornell Univ.
http://spirit.lib.uconn.edu/ArchNet/Depts/
Univ./cornell/cornell.html

Council for British Archaeology
http://britac3.britac.ac.uk/cba/

Cultures — Pomona College
http://arcturus.pomona.claremont.edu/Ancient

Dead Sea Scrolls Exhibit — UNC Expo
http://sunsite.unc.edu/expo/
deadsea.scrolls.exhibit/intro.html

Departamento de Prehistoria y
Arqueologia — Universidad de Sevilla
http://polifemo.us.es:8080/

Djoser Complex — Univ. of Pennsylvania
http://ccat.sas.upenn.edu/arth/zoser/
zoser.html

Dutch State Service for Archaeological Investigations and Center of Expertise ARCHIS.
http://www.archis.nl

Early Ceramic Periods of Moquegua: A Reappraisal
http://demog.berkeley.edu/~bandy/SAAPaper.html

Earth Science Information Network
http://www.ciesin.org

Edinburgh Ras Shamra Project: Cuneiform Texts from Ugarit
http://www-ersp.div.ed.ac.uk

Egyptology at Cambridge Univ.
http://www.newton.cam.ac.uk/egypt/

Field Archaeology Unit — Univ. of Birmingham
http://www.bham.ac.uk/BUFAU

Functional Analysis of Flake Tools from Chiripa, Bolivia
http://demog.berkeley.edu/~bandy/tapdoc1/doc1.html

GIS and Remote Sensing for Archaeology: Burgandy, France — Rutgers Univ.
http://deathstar.rutgers.edu/projects/france/france.html

Great Zimbabwe
http://wn.apc.org/mediatech/VRZ10011.HTM

Greek and Roman Civilization, Univ. College Dublin
http://www.ucd.ie/~sspence/classics.html

Greg Reeder's Egypt Page
http://www.sirius.com/~reeder/egypt.html

Historical and Archaeological CD-ROMS — Multimedia Management
http://www.demon.co.uk/history/cdroms.html

Institute of Egyptian Art and Archaeology — Univ. of Memphis
http://www.memst.edu/egypt/main.html

International Association of Computing in Archaeology, AIACE
http://www.cineca.it/visclab/aiace/aiace.htm

Internet Archaeology
http://intarch.york.ac.uk

Ioudaios Reviews
http://www.lehigh.edu/lists/ioudaios-review/

Iowa Office of the State Archaeologist
http://www.uiowa.edu/s/osa/index.html

Japanese Art
http://nearnet.gnn.com/gnn/wic/visart.11.html

JASON Project Voyage V: Expedition to Belize
http://seawifs.gsfc.nasa.gov/JASON/HTML/JASON_V_EXPEDITION.html

Jewish Studies Judaica eJournal
http://shamash.nysernet.org/~ajhyman/jsjej.html

Journal for Semitics - Tydskrif vir Semitistiek
http://www.unisa.ac.za/0/unisa/uit/semit.html

Journal of Field Archaeology
http://jfa-www.bu.edu/

Journal of Hebrew Scriptures
http://www.ualberta.ca/ARTS/jhs.html

Journal of Northwest Semitic Languages
http://www.sun.ac.za/local/academic/onos/jnsl/jnslhome.html

Journal of Roman Archaeology
http://www-personal.umich.edu/~pfoss/jra/JRA_Home.html

Journal of the Assyrian Academic Society
http://www.garlic.com/~agabrial/jaas.htm

Journey Through Time: Manitoba Archaeology
http://www.umanitoba.ca/anthropology/Manitoba/index.html

Judaism and Jewish Resources
http://shamash.nysernet.org/trb/judaism.html

KMT: A Modern Journal of Ancient Egypt
http://www.sirius.com/~reeder/kmt.html

Krannert Art Museum
http://www.ncsa.uiuc.edu/General/UIUC/KrannertArtMuseum/KrannertArtHome.html

L'archeologie sous les mers, Ministere de la culture et de la francophonie.
http://www.culture.fr/culture/archeosm.htm

La Maison de l'Orient Mediterranean — Universite de Lyon
http://auguste.univ-lyon2.fr/mom/texte/mom.html

Lab. for Archaeological Chemistry
http://spirit.lib.uconn.edu/ArchNet/Museums/wisconsin/wisclab.html

Learning to Read Rome's Ruins
http://sunsite.unc.edu/expo/vatican.exhibit/
exhibit/b-archeology/Archaeology.html

Leptiminus Archaeological Project, Tunisia
— Univ. of Michigan
http://rome.classics.lsa.umich.edu/projects/
lepti/lepti.html

Material Culture of the Ancient
Canaanites, Israelites and Related
Peoples
http://philae.sas.upenn.edu/ANEP/ANEP.html

Maxwell Museum of Anthropology —
Univ. of New Mexico.
http://www.unm.edu/~mtsnmc/Maxwell/
MMhp.html

MayaQuest. Join an expedition in search
of Mayan culture
http://mayaquest.mecc.com/

Megaliths of Morbihan
http://www.ingress.com/~mkzdk/carnac/
morbihan.html

Melbourne North Eastern Turkey Project
— Univ. of Melbourne
http://adhocalypse.arts.unimelb.edu.au/Dept/
Arch/NETurkey/home.html

Mesoamerican WWW Page
http://copan.bioz.unibas.ch/meso.html

Middle East Studies Association Bulletin
http://www.cua.edu/www/mesabul

Museo Chileno De Arte Precolombio
http://www.conicyt.cl/otros/museo/inicio.html

Museums and Research Facilities
http://spirit.lib.uconn.edu/ArchNet/Museums/
Museums.html

National Air & Space Museum
http://ceps.nasm.edu:2020

NativeWeb — Univ. of Kansas
http://kuhttp.cc.ukans.edu/~marc/
native_main.html

Netherlands Institute for Near East —
Univ. of Leiden
http://www.leidenuniv.nl/nino/nino.html

New England Classical Journal
http://www.circe.unh.edu/classics/necn&j.html

Newsletter for Targumic and Cognate
Studies
http://www.uwyo.edu/a&s/relstds/ts/ntcs.htm

Newsletter of the American Oriental
Society
http://www-personal.umich.edu/~jrodgers/
news19a.htm

Newstead Project: A Roman fort in
Scotland — Univ. of Bradford
http://www.brad.ac.uk/acad/archsci/field_proj/
newstead/newstead.html

o de Prehistoria y Arqueologia —
Universidad Autonoma de Madrid
http://www.uam.es/Facultades/FiloyLetras/pa/
paginas/homepage.html

Offline: Columns from Religious Studies
News, Council on the Study of Religion
Bulletin, and CSSR Bulletin
http://www.ccer.ggl.ruu.nl/ccer/names.html

Old Bulawayo
http://www.bham.ac.uk/BUFAU/Projects/OB/
bulawayo.html

Old World Archaeology Newsletter
http://www.wesleyan.edu/classics/OWAN.html

Oneida Indian Nation
http://nysernet.org/oneida/

Online Archaeology.
http://avebury.arch.soton.ac.uk/Journal/
journal.html

Oriental Institute — Univ. of Chicago
http://www-oi.uchicago.edu/OI/default.html

Origins of Celtic Art — An electronic
dissertation proposal — Univ. of
Virginia
http://faraday.clas.virginia.edu/~umw8f/Cze/
HomePage.html

Oxford Radiocarbon Accelerator Unit
http://sable.ox.ac.uk/departments/rlaha/

Pluto Press Books in Anthropology
http://www.demon.co.uk/bookshop/

Pomona College
http://arcturus.pomona.claremont.edu/

Pre-Columbian Art
http://www.ncsa.uiuc.edu/General/UIUC/
KrannertArtMuseum/Guide/PreColumb/
PreColumb.html

Quebec Archaeological Association
http://www.gouv.qc.ca/gouv/francais/minorg/
mccq/dpm/organis/aaq/aaq.htm

Queen's Univ.
http://jupiter.qub.ac.uk/stephen/arch.html

Roman Archaeology
http://www.umich.edu/~pfoss/
ROMARCH.html

Royal Palace at Caserta
http://www.mimesys.iunet.it/Reggia/
reggiaing.html

Ruins at Rione Terra in Pozzuoli
http://www.mimesys.iunet.it/RioneTerra/
rioneterraing.html

Scriptorium: Center for Christian Antiquities
http://www.scriptorium.org/scriptorium

Seventh Nordic Conference on the Application of Scientific Methods in Archaeology. Conference information from the Univ. of Helsinki.
http://www.helsinki.fi/~arla_www/
viinordic.html

Smithsonian Institution
http://www.si.edu/

Social Science Information Gateway
http://sosig.esrc.bris.ac.uk/new.html

Society for American Archaeology Bulletin
http://www.sscf.ucsb.edu:80/SAABulletin/

South Carolina Institute of Archaeology and Anthropology
http://www.cla.sc.edu/sciaa/sciaa.html

South Dakota Archaeology, Univ. of South Dakota
http://www.usd.edu/anth

Southwestern Archaeology
http://seamonkey.ed.asu.edu/swa

State Archives of Assyria Newsletter
http://www.helsinki.fi/science/saa/
news15.html

Sudan Archaeological Society of Berlin
http://www.v-connect.com:5430/SAG/
welcome.html

TC: A Journal of Biblical Textual Criticism.
http://scholar.cc.emory.edu/scripts/TC/
TC.html

TELA: The Electronically Linked Academy: Scholars Press
http://scholar.cc.emory.edu/

Thai Heritage Page
http://www.cs.ait.ac.th/~wutt/wutt.html

Trent & Peak Archaeological Trust — Univ. of Nottingham
http://www.ccc.nottingham.ac.uk/~aczkdc/
tpat.html

UC Museum of Paleontology
http://ucmp1.berkeley.edu/

United States Geological Survey
http://info.er.usgs.gov/USGSHome.html

United States Holocaust Museum
http://www.ushmm.org/

Univ. of Bradford, Dept. Archaeological Sciences
http://www.brad.ac.uk/acad/archsci/
homepage.html

Univ. of Calgary, Current Research
http://www.ucalgary.ca/UofC/faculties/SS/
ARKY/research.html

Univ. of Kentucky Classics
http://www.uky.edu/ArtsSciences/Classics/

Univ. of New England
http://mutz.une.edu.au/server_data/Arch/
ArchBrochure.html

Univ. of Oxford, Institute of Social and Cultural Anthropology
http://www.rsl.ox.ac.uk/isca/index.html

Univ. of Southampton
http://avebury.arch.soton.ac.uk

Univ. of York
http://www.york.ac.uk/depts/arch/
welcome.htm

West Virginia Archaeology
http://www.wvlc.wvnet.edu/wvarl/archp.html

Yale Univ. Art Gallery
http://www.cis.yale.edu/yuag/yuag.html

Zagarell's Archaeology Page — Current Research in India and Iran
http://www2.wmich.edu/~zagarell

Artificial Intelligence

See also Computer Science, Virtual Reality

Usenet Newsgroups

comp.ai (moderated)
Moderated by: John Grohol, George Briggs, and Al Black (psy-research-request@psy.psych.nova.edu)
Submissions go to: psy-research@psy.psych.nova.edu
Newsgroup-based Mailing List: No.
Charter: Artificial intelligence discussions.

comp.ai.alife
Created by: C. Titus Brown <brown@reed.edu>
Call for Votes Date: June 29, 1994
Charter (from Call for Votes):
Artificial Life is the study of artificial living systems and their constituent entities.

comp.ai.doc-analysis.ocr
Created by: Christopher Vance <cvance@cfar.umd.edu>
Call for Votes Date: May 8, 1995
Newsgroup-based Mailing List: No.
Charter (from Call for Votes):
The comp.ai.doc-analysis.ocr newsgroup will be open to discussion of algorithms for solving Optical Character Recognition (OCR) and related tasks, the development of commercial and public domain OCR software, document image understanding topics directly related to OCR, and discussion of currently available OCR software and hardware tools.

comp.ai.doc-analysis.misc
comp.ai.doc-analysis.misc would be appropriate for more general document understanding topics.

comp.ai.jair.announce (Moderated)
Created by: Matthew L. Ginsberg <ginsberg@CS.Stanford.edu>
Moderated by: Steven Minton (jair-announce-request@ptolemy.arc.nasa.gov)
Submissions go to: jair-announce@ptolemy.arc.nasa.gov
Call for Votes date: June 23, 1993
Newsgroup-based Mailing List: Yes.
Charter (from Call for Votes):
The purpose of the proposed group is to facilitate the distribution of the new Jrnl. of AI Research.

Announcements and abstracts. This group will primarily be used to announce the publication of new papers; when a paper has been accepted to the journal, the abstract will be posted here.

comp.ai.games
Created by: Dan Thies <rtfm@cyberspace.com>
Call for Votes Date: January 22, 1995
Newsgroup-based Mailing List: No.
Charter (from Call for Votes):
The newsgroup comp.ai.games will provide a forum for the discussion of artificial intelligence in games and game-playing. The group will explore practical and theoretical aspects of applying artificial intelligence concepts to the domain of game-playing.

This newsgroup is not an appropriate place for the discussion of machine specific coding problems, nor is it the proper place to discuss strategies for defeating computer opponents in existing games. There are other newsgroups already in existence to answer these questions.

comp.ai.jair.papers (Moderated)
Created by: Matthew L. Ginsberg
<ginsberg@CS.Stanford.EDU>
Moderated by: Steven Minton
(jair-papers-
request@ptolemy.arc.nasa.gov)
Submissions go to: jair-
papers@ptolemy.arc.nasa.gov
Call for Votes date: June 23, 1993
Newsgroup-based Mailing List: Yes.
Charter (from Call for Votes):
The purpose of the proposed group is to
facilitate the distribution of the new Jrnl.
of AI Research.

Accepted papers: postscript, LaTeX or
other source suitable for text search,
supporting code or other data that would
not normally be included in articles due to
size limitations.

Discussion of issues arising out of
accepted papers will presumably take
place on comp.ai.

comp.ai.neural.nets (moderated)
Moderated by: John Grohol, George
Briggs, and Al Black
(psy-research-
request@psy.psych.nova.edu)
Submissions go to: psy-
research@psy.psych.nova.edu
Newsgroup-based Mailing List: No.
Charter: All aspects of neural networks.

comp.ai.nlang-know-rep (moderated)
Moderated by: John Grohol, George
Briggs, and Al Black
(psy-research-
request@psy.psych.nova.edu)
Submissions go to: psy-
research@psy.psych.nova.edu
Newsgroup-based Mailing List: No.
Charter: Natural languages.

comp.ai.philosophy (moderated)
Moderated by: John Grohol, George
Briggs, and Al Black
(psy-research-
request@psy.psych.nova.edu)
Submissions go to: psy-
research@psy.psych.nova.edu
Newsgroup-based Mailing List: No.
Charter: The philosophy of artificial
intelligence.

comp.ai.shells (moderated)
Moderated by: John Grohol, George
Briggs, and Al Black
(psy-research-
request@psy.psych.nova.edu)
Submissions go to: psy-
research@psy.psych.nova.edu
Newsgroup-based Mailing List: No.
Charter: Shell programming.

comp.cog-eng (moderated)
Moderated by: John Grohol, George
Briggs, and Al Black
(psy-research-
request@psy.psych.nova.edu)
Submissions go to: psy-
research@psy.psych.nova.edu
Newsgroup-based Mailing List: No.
Charter: Cognitive engineering.

comp.human-factors (moderated)
Moderated by: John Grohol, George
Briggs, and Al Black
(psy-research-
request@psy.psych.nova.edu)
Submissions go to: psy-
research@psy.psych.nova.edu
Newsgroup-based Mailing List: No.
Charter: Issues related to human-com-
puter interaction.

sci.cognitive
Created by: Donald Peterson
<D.M.Peterson@computer-
science.birmingham.ac.uk>
Call for Votes date: May 11, 1992
Newsgroup-based Mailing List: No.
Charter (from Call for Votes):
Cognitive science is an inter-disciplinary
investigation of cognition, involving
cognitive psychology, artificial intelligence, computer science, human-computer interaction, philosophy of mind,
philosophy of science, linguistics, neuroscience, cognitive anthropology and other
disciplines. The 'mind's new science' has
been around since the mid-50's, and has
entered an institutional phase with
textbooks, journals, centres of research and
teaching etc. However, due to its inter-
disciplinary and international character,
channels of communication devoted
specifically to cognitive science are still
needed, and the group sci.cognitive is

intended to serve this end.

The group should serve as an open forum for discussion of all aspects of cognitive science: empirical work, cognitive modelling, theory, methodology, foundational, historical and social issues etc.

The group should also facilitate the exchange of information on teaching programmes, conferences, jobs etc.

The main language of the group is English, but postings in other languages are also encouraged.

sci.psychology
sci.psychology was one of the original net.* groups.
Newsgroup-based Mailing List: No.
Charter: Psychology.

sci.psychology.digest (Moderated)
Moderated by: Stevan Harnad (psyc-request@phoenix.princeton.edu)
Submissions go to: psyc@phoenix.princeton.edu
Newsgroup-based Mailing List: Yes (psyc@pucc.princeton.edu).
Charter: Psycoloquy, an American Psychological Association-sponsored refereed e-journal.

sci.psychology.research (Moderated)
Moderated by: John Grohol, George Briggs, and Al Black (psy-research-request@psy.psych.nova.edu)
Submissions go to: psy-research@psy.psych.nova.edu
Newsgroup-based Mailing List: No.
Charter: Newsgroup dedicated to experimental issues.

Frequently Asked Questions

Artificial Intelligence
An FAQ in six parts:
Questions & Answers 1/6
AI Newsgroups and Discussion Lists 2/6
AI Associations and Journals 3/6
Artificial Intelligence Bibliography 4/6
Artificial Intelligence FTP Resources 5/6
Artificial Intelligence FTP Resources 6/6
Maintainer: mkant+@cs.cmu.edu (Mark Kantrowitz)
Where on Usenet: comp.ai
Where it's archived:
rtfm.mit.edu:pub/usenet/news.answers/comp.ai
What it's for: Commonly asked questions and answers on issues pertaining to artificial intelligence.

Expert System Shells
Maintainer: mkant+@cs.cmu.edu (Mark Kantrowitz)
Where on Usenet: comp.ai
Where it's archived:
rtfm.mit.edu:pub/usenet/news.answers/comp.ai
What it's for: Analysis of expert system shells.

comp.ai.neural-nets FAQ
Maintainer: prechelt@ira.uka.de (Lutz Prechelt)
Where on Usenet: comp.ai.neural-nets
Where it's archived:
rtfm.mit.edu:pub/usenet/news.answers/comp.ai.neural-nets
What it's for: A great deal of information on neural networks.

Discussion Lists

agen-ks
agen-ks@rutvm1
ASAE Knowledge Systems

apasd-l
apasd-l@vtvm1
APA Research Psychology Network

auditory
auditory@mcgill1
Research in auditory perception

brunswik
brunswik@albnyvm1
Brunswikian psychology and Social Judgment

comms-l
comms-l@vtvm1
Ergonomics-related communications
issues

compsy-l
compsy-l@uiucvmd
Midwest Forum for community/ecological

hfs-l
hfs-l@vtvm1
Human Factors and Ergonomics Society
Va Tech

iapsy-l
iapsy-l@albnyvm1
Interamerican Psychologists List (SIPNET)

ioob-l
ioob-l@uga
Industrial Psychology

ioobf-l
ioobf-l@uga
Industrial Psychology Forum

learn-l
learn-l@mizzou1
Discussions of cognitive psychology

live-eye
live-eye@yorkvm1
Color and Vision Discussion Forum

mentor
mentor@indycms
Psychology B104 Computer Communications

mpsych-l
mpsych-l@brownvm
Society for Mathematical Psychology

neuron
neuron-request@cattell.psych.upenn.edu
(Peter Marvit)
Neural networks.

virtpsy
virtpsy@sjuvm
SJU Virtual Psychology List

viscom
viscom@templevm
Visual Communications Discussion

visual-l
visual-l@vtvm1
VISUAL-L DISCUSSION LIST

Artificial Intelligence Resources

Gopher Resources

McGill Research Centre for Intelligent
  Machines, Montreal, Canada
  lightning.mcrcim.mcgill.edu

WWW Resources

ACIA—Cataloan Association for Artificial
  Intelligence
  http://www.iiia.csic.es/ACIA/ACIA.html

ACM SIG on Artificial Intelligence
  http://sigart.acm.org/

Adaptive Behavior
  http://www-mitpress.mit.edu/jrnls-catalog/
  adaptive.html

Agent Info
  http://www.cs.bham.ac.uk/~amw/agents/
  index.html

Agents and Mediators
  http://www-ksl.stanford.edu/knowledge-
  sharing/agents.html

AI Applications in Knowledge Navigation
  CFP
  http://cs-www.uchicago.edu/~burke/
  aiakn.html

AI Resources on the Internet
  http://ai.iit.nrc.ca/ai_point.html

AI, Cognitive Science and Robotics WWW
  Resources
  http://www.cs.ucl.ac.uk/misc/ai/

AI-related FAQs
  http://www.cs.cmu.edu/afs/cs/project/ai-
  repository/ai/html/faqs/top.html

AI-related Job Posting Archives
  http://www.cs.cmu.edu/Web/Groups/AI/html/
  other/jobs.html

American Association for Artificial
  Intelligence
  http://www.aaai.org/

Annotated Blackboard-Systems Bibliography
  http://www.bbtech.com/bibli.html

Applied Logic Lab - Univ. of Idaho
  http://www.cs.uidaho.edu/lal/homepage.html

ARPA Knowledge Sharing Effort public
library
http://www-ksl.stanford.edu/knowledge-
sharing/README.html

Artificial Intelligence Applications
Institute
http://www.spie.org/

Artificial Intelligence at TNT
http://www.tnt.uni-hannover.de/data/info/www/
tnt/subj/sci/ai/overview.html

Artificial Intelligence Resources
http://ai.iit.nrc.ca/ai_point.html

Artificial Intelligence Subject Index
http://ai.iit.nrc.ca/misc.html

Association for Computing Machinery
http://info.acm.org/

ASTAP
http://www.demon.co.uk/ar/ASTAP/

Austrian Research Institute for Artificial
Intelligence (OFAI) and Dept. of Medical
Cybernetics and Artificial Intelligence at
the Univ. of Vienna
http://www.ai.univie.ac.at/

Bibliography of Research in Natural
Language Generation
http://liinwww.ira.uka.de/bibliography/Ai/
nlg.html

Boston Univ.
http://web.bu.edu/CNS/CNS.html

Center for the Neural Basis of Cognition
http://www.cs.cmu.edu/afs/cs/project/cnbc/
CNBC.html

Clarkson AI Lab Pages
http://jupiter.ece.clarkson.edu:5050/

CMU Artificial Intelligence Repository
http://www.cs.cmu.edu/Web/Groups/AI/html/
repository.html

CMU SCS OZ Project
http://www.cs.cmu.edu/afs/cs.cmu.edu/
project/oz/web/oz.html

Cogent Prolog and Amzi! Things
http://world.std.com/~amzi/

Cognition and Affect Project
http://www.cs.bham.ac.uk/~axs/cogaff.html

Computational Intelligence Research Lab.
http://cirl.uoregon.edu/cirl.html

Computational Intelligence Research
Laboratory
http://cirl.uoregon.edu

Computer Based Learning Unit: Univ. of
Leeds
http://cbl.leeds.ac.uk/~www/home.html

Computer Generated Writing
http://www.uio.no/~mwatz/c-g.writing/

Computer Science Technical Reports
Archive Sites
http://www.rdt.monash.edu.au/tr/siteslist.html

Computer Vision
http://www.cs.cmu.edu/afs/cs/project/cil/ftp/
html/txtvision.html

Computing as Compression
http://www.sees.bangor.ac.uk/~gerry/
sp_summary.html

Computing Research Association
http://cra.org/

Connectionist Natural Language Processing
http://www.cs.bham.ac.uk/~jah/CNLP/
cnlp.html

CSCW Research Group
http://orgwis.gmd.de

Ctr. for Artificial Intelligence Research,
Korea
http://cair-archive.kaist.ac.kr/

Ctr. for Biological and Computational
Learning at MIT
http://www.ai.mit.edu/projects/cbcl/web-
homepage/web-homepage.html

Dave Brown's AI Page
http://cs.wpi.edu/~dcb/

Decision/Risk Analysis Page
http://www.lumina.com/lumina/DA.html

DFKI
http://www.dfki.uni-sb.de/

Distributed Artificial Intelligence and
Multi-Agent Systems
http://www-lgis.univ-savoie.fr/~stinckwi/
sma.html

Distributed Artificial Intelligence Lab
http://dis.cs.umass.edu/

Distributed Object Computing
http://info.gte.com/ftp/doc/doc.html

DSI Neural Networks group home page
http://www-dsi.ing.unifi.it/neural/home.html

Ecole Polytechnique, la bibliotheque
http://www.polytechnique.fr/htbin/bcx.pl

EEB
http://www.eeb.ele.tue.nl/index.htm

ELIS Speech Lab
http://www.elis.rug.ac.be/ELISgroups/speech/

Eliza
http://www.cl.cam.ac.uk/users/mh10006/
eliza.html

EPFL-MANTRA
http://didecs1-e.epfl.ch:80/w3mantra/

ESSIR
http://www.dcs.gla.ac.uk/essir/

European Neural Network Society
http://www.neuronet.ph.kcl.ac.uk/neuronet/
organisations/enns.html

First Australian Workshop on
Commonsense Reasoning
http://frey.newcastle.edu.au/~is/
ai95wshop.html

First International Conference on
Multiagent Systems
http://centaurus.cs.umass.edu:80/ICMAS/

FLAIRS
http://www.cis.ufl.edu/~ddd/FLAIRS/

Forschungsgruppe Neuronale Netzwerke
http://www.hrz.uni-kassel.de/fb17/neuro/

GA Visualisation Questionnaire
http://kmi.open.ac.uk/~trevor/Quest1.html

Genetic Programming
http://www.salford.ac.uk/docs/depts/eee/
genetic.html

Genetically Programmed Music
http://nmt.edu/~jefu/notes/notes.html

Georgia Tech Artificial Intelligence
http://www.gatech.edu/ai/ai.html

Gerry Wolff's WWW Pages
http://www.sees.bangor.ac.uk/~gerry/

Goddard AI/IT Conference
http://defiant.gsfc.nasa.gov/aiconf/AI-conf-
General.html

Graduate Students Who's Who in Robotics
http://www.sm.luth.se/csee/ra/sm-roa/
Robotics/WhoSWho.html

Graphic Presentation of Subjects
http://ACS.TAMU.EDU/~jpf6745/subjects.html

Gunnar Blix's AI Page
http://www-ilg.cs.uiuc.edu/~blix/

Handwriting Recognition
http://hcslx1.essex.ac.uk/

Human Cognition Research Lab. at The
Open Univ., UK
http://hcrl.open.ac.uk/

Human-Languages Page
http://www.willamette.edu/~tjones/Language-
Page.html

IEEE Neural Networks Council
http://www.ieee.org/nnc/index.html

IJCAI
http://ijcai.org/

IlliGAL
http://gal4.ge.uiuc.edu/illigal.home.html

IMKAI/OFAI Homepage
http://www.ai.univie.ac.at/

Indiana Univ. - Knowledge Base of
Computing Information
http://scwww.ucs.indiana.edu/kb/search.html

Inductive Inference at Monash
http://www.cs.monash.edu.au/research/
inference.html

Information and Computation
http://theory.lcs.mit.edu/~iandc/

Information Extraction
http://ciir.cs.umass.edu/info/ie.html

Institut Dalle Molle d'Intelligence
Artificelle Perceptive (IDIAP)
http://www.idiap.ch/

Intelligent Software Agents
http://www.cl.cam.ac.uk/users/rwab1/
agents.html

International Journal of Applied Expert
Systems
http://www.abdn.ac.uk/~acc025/ijaes.html

IRCS
http://www.cis.upenn.edu/~ircs/
homepage.html

ISSCO, Univ. of Geneva
http://issco_www.unige.ch/

JNNS
http://jnns-www.okabe.rcast.u-tokyo.ac.jp/
jnns/home.html

Joel's Hierarchical Subject Index
http://www.cen.uiuc.edu/~jj9544/index.html

Jon Iles' AI Page
http://www.cs.bham.ac.uk/~jpi/

Jrnl. of Artificial Intelligence Research
http://www.cs.washington.edu/research/jair/
home.html

Juan Carlos Santamaria Information Page
http://www.cc.gatech.edu/ai/students/Ai-
students/carlos/home.html

Julia's AI Page
http://fuzine.mt.cs.cmu.edu/mlm/julia.html

Knowledge Sharing
http://logic.stanford.edu/knowledge.html

Knowledge Sharing Effort
http://www.cs.umbc.edu/kse/

Knowledge Systems Lab. (Canada)
http://ai.iit.nrc.ca/home_page.html

KQML - Knowledge Query and Manipulation Language
http://www.cs.umbc.edu/kqml/

KQML Mailing Lists
http://www.cs.umbc.edu/kqml/mail/

KRUST
http://www.scms.rgu.ac.uk/research/kbs/
krust/

Linguistic Geometry
http://ucdacm.cudenver.edu/cse/boris.html

Lockheed Artificial Intelligence
http://hitchhiker.space.lockheed.com/aic/
README.html

Logic Group
http://Logic.Stanford.edu

London Parallel Applications Centre Web
Server
http://www.lpac.ac.uk

Mathematics For Computer Generated
Spoken Documents
http://www.cs.cornell.edu/Info/People/raman/
aster/aster-toplevel.html

Medical Cybernetics and Artificial
Intelligence at the Univ. of Vienna and
the Austrian Research Institute for
Artificial Intelligence
http://www.ai.univie.ac.at/

MIT Artificial Intelligence Lab
http://www.ai.mit.edu/

Morgan Kaufmann, Publishers
http://market.net/literary/mkp/index.html

NASA
http://www.gsfc.nasa.gov/
NASA_homepage.html

Neural and Multimedia Center
http://synap.neuro.sfc.keio.ac.jp/

Neural Networks at UT Austin
http://www.cs.utexas.edu/~sirosh/nn.html

Neural Web
http://www.erg.abdn.ac.uk/projects/
neuralweb/

NEuroNet
http://www.neuronet.ph.kcl.ac.uk/

Nicole English's AI Page
http://cctr.umkc.edu/user/nenglish/index.html

NIPS: Neural Information Processing
Systems
http://www.cs.cmu.edu/afs/cs/project/cnbc/
nips/NIPS.html

Northwestern Univ. - Learning Through
Collaborative Visualization Project
http://www.covis.nwu.edu/

NSF Strategic Planning Workshop for
Design Engineering
http://cs.wpi.edu/~dcb/NSF/NSF-wkshp.html

OFAI Library Information System Biblio
http://www.ai.univie.ac.at/biblio.html

Outsider's Guide to Artificial Intelligence
http://www.mcs.net/~jorn/html/ai.html

Parallel Computing and Imaging Laboratory
http://teal.ece.jhu.edu

Parsing Techniques - A Practical Guide
http://www.cs.vu.nl/~dick/PTAPG.html

Prehistory of AI
http://www.mcs.net/~jorn/html/ai/
prehistory.html

QRNET
http://www.dcs.aber.ac.uk:80/QRNET/

Qualitative Reasoning at U Texas
http://www.cs.utexas.edu/~qr/

Qualitative Reasoning Group at North-western Univ.
ftp://multivac.ils.nwu.edu/pub/MOSAIC/qrg.html

Ralph Becket's AI Page
http://www.cl.cam.ac.uk:80/users/rwab1/

Research Group Autonomous Mobile Robots
http://ag-vp-www.informatik.uni-kl.de/

Robin Burke - Univ. of Chicago
http://cs-www.uchicago.edu/~burke/

Robot Web - Robotics resources on the WWW
http://www.sm.luth.se/csee/ra/sm-roa/RoboticsJump.html

Robot Wisdom
http://www.mcs.net/~jorn/home.html

Sandip Sen's AI Page
http://euler.mcs.utulsa.edu/~sandip/sandip.html

SEL-HPC Article Archive
http://www.lpac.qmw.ac.uk/SEL-HPC/Articles/index.html

SGAICO
http://expasy.hcuge.ch/sgaico/

SIGART Electronic Information Service
http://sigart.acm.org/

Speech
http://mambo.ucsc.edu/psl/speech.html

Spot's Sandoz Home
http://www.cs.cmu.edu:80/afs/cs.cmu.edu/Web/People/spot/

SRI Artificial Intelligence Ctr.
http://www.ai.sri.com/aic/

Stanford Concurrency Group
http://boole.stanford.edu

Stanford Knowledge Systems Laboratory
http://www-ksl.stanford.edu/

Steven Woods' AI Page
http://logos.uwaterloo.ca/sgwoods/

Supercomputing & Parallel Computing: Conferences & Journals
http://www.cs.cmu.edu/Web/Groups/scandal/www/conferences.html

UCI Machine Learning Group
http://www.ics.uci.edu/AI/ML/Machine-Learning.html

UCL-DICE Neural Net Group
http://www.dice.ucl.ac.be/neural-nets/NNgroup.html

UCSD Neuroscience
http://salk.edu/NeuroWeb/

Univ. of Edinburgh Artificial Intelligence
http://www.dai.ed.ac.uk

Univ. of Essex
http://www.essex.ac.uk

Univ. of Leeds
http://lethe.leeds.ac.uk/

Univ. of New Hampshire Cooperative Distributed Problem Solving Research
http://cdps.cs.unh.edu/

Univ. of Sussex at Brighton - School of Cognitive and Computing Sciences
http://www.cogs.susx.ac.uk/

Univ. of Washington
http://www.cs.washington.edu/research/projects/ai/www/

Univ. Video Communications
http://www.uvc.com/

VLSI Vision Chips
http://www.eleceng.adelaide.edu.au/Groups/GAAS/Bugeye/visionchips/

William Ward Armstrong's AI Page
http://web.cs.ualberta.ca/~arms/

WPI AIDG — AI in Design Webliography
http://cs.wpi.edu/Research/aidg/AlinD-hotlist.html

WWWVirtual Library: Artificial Intelligence
http://www.comlab.ox.ac.uk/archive/comp/ai.html

YODA at Temple Univ.
http://yoda.cis.temple.edu

Astronomy & Astrophysics

See also Aeronautics & Aerospace, Optics, Physics

Usenet Newsgroups

sci.astro
Newsgroup-based Mailing List: No
Charter: Generic discussion-group concentrating on topics that aren't covered in any of the four specialized sub-groups. More "talky" than the sub-groups.

sci.astro.amateur
Created by: Ken Kirksey
<kkirksey@world.std.com>
Call for Votes Date: August 12, 1994
Newsgroup-based Mailing List: No.
Charter (from Call for Votes):
sci.astro.amateur is a forum dedicated to the discussion of topics relating to the hobby of amateur astronomy.

sci.astro.fits
Created by: dwells@fits.cx.nrao.edu (Don Wells)
Call for Votes date: February 11, 1992
Newsgroup-based Mailing List: Yes.
Charter (from Call for Votes):
This newsgroup will provide a forum for the discussion of all topics concerning the FITS [Flexible Image Transport System] data format. The newsgroup will be interfaced to the Email exploder fits-bits@fits.cx.nrao.edu so that traffic originating on either the newsgroup or the exploder will be automatically transmitted to the other. This new newsgroup will replace existing newsgroup alt.sci.astro.fits.

sci.astro.hubble (Moderated)
Created by: uk1@spacsun.rice.edu (Paul A. Scowen)
Moderated by: Paul A. Scowen
Submissions go to: sah@wfpc3.la.asu.edu

Call for Votes date: January 13, 1992
Newsgroup-based Mailing List: No.
Charter (from Call for Votes):
The group's primary goal is to serve as a discussion forum for the processing and reduction of data taken with the Hubble Space Telescope. Emphasis will be given to the extraction of useful scientific information, instead of the emphasis on producing cosmetically pleasing imagery that has prevailed in the mission history so far.

sci.astro.planetarium
Created by: Davin C. Flateau
<davin@telerama.pgh.pa.us>
Call for Votes date: August 1, 1993
Newsgroup-based Mailing List: No.
Charter (from Call for Votes):
sci.astro.planetarium will be a newsgroup that provides a common forum for patrons of planetaria, planetarium professionals, planetarium audio-visual developers, and anyone interested in astronomy education to come and exchange their ideas, news, and calendar events.

sci.astro.research (Moderated)
Created by:
sulkanen@pecos.msfc.nasa.gov
(Martin E. Sulkanen)
Moderated by: Martin E. Sulkanen
Submissions go to: astres-request@pecos.msfc.nasa.gov
Call for Votes date: April 22, 1994
Newsgroup-based Mailing List: No.
Charter (from Call for Votes):
The purpose of this newsgroup is the discussion of astronomy & astrophysics research, and the dissemination of information related to astronomy & astrophysics research.

Frequently Asked Questions

Astro/Space Frequently Seen Acronyms

Maintainer: mark@ncar.ucar.edu (Mark Bradford)
Where on Usenet: sci.answers
Where it's archived:
rtfm.mit.edu:pub/usenet/sci.astro
What it's for: A quick-reference list of many of the acronyms commonly seen on the astronomy and space technology newsgroups on Usenet.

Astronomical Image Processing System (AIPS)

Maintainer: pmurphy@nrao.edu (Patrick P. Murphy)
Where on Usenet: news.answers
Where it's archived:
rtfm.mit.edu:pub/usenet/sci.astro
http://info.cv.nrao.edu/aips
What it's for: Information on AIPS, a software package used to deal with two- and three-dimensional radio images from the NRAO's Very Large Array.

Electronic Jrnl. of the ASA (EJASA)

Maintainer: klaes@mtwain.enet.dec.com (Larry Klaes)
Where on Usenet: sci.astro
Where it's archived:
rtfm.mit.edu:pub/usenet/sci.astro
What it's for: Electronic Jrnl. of the Astronomical Society of the Atlantic.

Purchasing Amateur Telescopes FAQ

Maintainer: ronnie@cisco.com (Ronnie B. Kon)
Where on Usenet: sci.astro
Where it's archived:
rtfm.mit.edu:pub/usenet/sci.astro
What it's for: Tips on how to buy a telescope, aimed at amateur astronomers.

Sky & Telescope News Bulletins

Maintainer: mrastro@aol.com (Stuart Goldman)
Where on Usenet: sci.astro
Where it's archived:
rtfm.mit.edu:pub/usenet/sci.astro

What it's for: Sky & Telescope magazine's summary of events of immediate interest.

Discussion Lists

astro
astro@gitvm1
Astronomy
earthandsky
majordomo@lists.utexas.edu
Earth & Sky radio series from the McDonald Observatory.

Astronomy Resources

FTP Resources

Primary Astronomy Archive List
    seds.lpl.arizona.edu/pub/faq/astroftp.html
AASTeX
    blackhole.aas.org/pubs/aastex.v30
Ames SPACE Archive
    explorer.arc.nasa.gov/pub/SPACE/
Analyz
    naic.edu/pub/Analyz
CADC Tools
    cadcwww.dao.nrc.ca/pub/cadc/
Canada France Hawaii Telescope
    ftp.cfht.hawaii.edu/pub/
Centre de Données astronomiques de Strasbourg
    cdsarc.u-strasbg.fr/
Cerro Tololo Interamerican Observatory - Schedules
    ctios1.ctio.noao.edu/pub/schedule/
CNAM (National Conservatory of Arts & Works)
    ftp.cnam.fr/pub/Astro
Colloquium
    fs1.mpifr-bonn.mpg.de/pub/kolloq/kolloquium/
Compton/GRO FTP Directories
    grossc.gsfc.nasa.gov/
CTIO
    ctios1.ctio.noao.edu/ctio/
EDI (Electronic Document Interchange) Newsletter (ESA)
    mesis.esrin.esa.it/pub/edi

Einstein Observatory
    sao-ftp.harvard.edu/pub/einstein

EVN anonFTP directory at JB
    jbss0.jb.man.ac.uk/pub/evn/

FITS Information Archive
    fits.cv.nrao.edu/

Five College Radio Astronomy Observatory - Schedules
    fcrao1.phast.umass.edu/pub/fcrao/

High Altitude Observatory
    hao.ucar.edu/pub/

HST PR-images
    ecf.hq.eso.org/pub/testimages/pubrel-HST-images

IDL Astronomy Library
    idlastro.gsfc.nasa.gov/

Infra-Red Telescope Facility - Schedules
    irtf.ifa.hawaii.edu/pub/Schedule/

Infrared Space Observatory - Schedules
    hp.ifsi.fra.cnr.it/pub/iso_open_time

Intl. Earth Rotation Service
    maia.usno.navy.mil/ser7/ser7.dat

IRAF (Image Reduction and Analysis Facility)
    iraf.tuc.noao.edu/iraf

James Clark Maxwell Telescope - Schedules
    ftp.jach.hawaii.edu/pub/vaxdir/mtsched

Johns Hopkins Univ. - FOS
    jhufos.pha.jhu.edu/pub/

KHOROS Software
    ftp.khoros.unm.edu/pub/

Kitt Peak National Observatory
    orion.tuc.noao.edu/kpno/

La Palma - Isaac Newton Group - Schedules
    cast0.ast.cam.ac.uk/pub/service/ing_schedules/

LISP-STAT code library
    ftp.stat.ucla.edu/pub/lisp/xlisp/xlisp-stat/

Lowell Observatory
    lowell.edu/

Meteosat images of Europe, Africa, Atlantic and World
    liasun3.epfl.ch/pub/weather

Munich Image Data Analysis System
    ftphost.hq.eso.org/midaspub/

NASA space images and information
    ames.arc.nasa.gov/pub/SPACE

NETLIB Software
    research.att.com/

Network Resources for Astronomers
    blackhole.aas.org/info/net/
    net_resources.mem

NOAO preprints
    pandora.tuc.noao.edu/preprints

NOD
    fs1.mpifr-bonn.mpg.de/pub/nod

Observatoire de Lyon
    image.univ-lyon1.fr/pub/

Princeton Univ. - Pulsar Group
    pulsar.princeton.edu/pub/

PROS Software
    sao-ftp.harvard.edu/

Smithsonian Astrophysical Observatory (SAO)
    sao-ftp.harvard.edu/pub/

Solar, Auroral, Ionospheric Information
    ftp.uleth.ca/pub/solar/

SPIE-The Intl. Society for Optical Engineering
    ftp.spie.org

ST-ECF Archives
    ns3.hq.eso.org/pub/

ST-ECF Astronomical Software Library
    ecf.hq.eso.org/pub/swlib/

Steward Observatory
    as.arizona.edu/pub/

TAI-UTC
    maia.usno.navy.mil/ser7/tai-utc.dat

TCL Archives
    harbor.ecn.purdue.edu/pub/tcl/

TeX Archive
    ftp.shsu.edu/tex-archive

Univ. of Alabama - Dept. of Physics and Astronomy: Preprints
    crux.astr.ua.edu/preprints/

Univ. of Hawaii IfA: 2.2m Telescope - Schedule
    hubble.ifa.hawaii.edu/pub/88inch/schedule/current.dvi

Very Large Array - Schedules
info.aoc.nrao.edu/doc/vla/schedules/this_dir.html

Very Long Baseline Array / Global Network - Schedules
info.aoc.nrao.edu/doc/vlba/schedules/this_dir.html

Whipple Observatory / Multiple Mirror Telescope - Schedules
cfa0.harvard.edu/pub/sched/

Wilcox Solar Observatory (Stanford Univ.)
solar.stanford.edu/

Gopher Resources

3-Hour Solar and Geophysical Report
xi.uleth.ca:79

Astronomical Information from the Net
ucogo.ucsc.edu

Astronomy Resources
halcon.dpi.udec.cl

Astronomy_and_Astrophysics
cwis.usc.edu

Big Bear Solar Observatory
stsci.edu

Daily Solar and Geophysical Report
xi.uleth.ca:79

Global Change Data and Information System
esdim2.esdim.noaa.gov

Harvard-Smithsonian Ctr. for Astrophysics Theory Group
cfata4.harvard.edu

Institute of Astronomy & Royal Greenwich Observatory
cast0.ast.cam.ac.uk

Instituto de Astrofísica de Canarias
gopher.ll.iac.es

Johnson Space Ctr.
krakatoa.jsc.nasa.gov

Los Alamos National Lab. (LANL)
mentor.lanl.gov

NASA Research Announcements
stsci.edu

NOAO-Gopher
gemini.tuc.noao.edu

Numerical Recipes Software
cfata4.harvard.edu

PASP abstracts archive, STScI
stsci.edu

Sci.image.processing Newsgroup Archive
skyking.oce.orst.edu

Search and Retrieve Graphics Software and Data
merlot.welch.jhu.edu

SISSA received astrophysical preprints
babbage.sissa.it

Sky and Telescope Weekly News Bulletin
gopher.cic.net

Space Telescope Electronic Information System (STScI)
stsci.edu

SPIE-The Intl. Society for Optical Engineering
gopher.spie.org

STScI Newsletter
gopher.cic.net

TIM (Telescope Imaging Model)
stsci.edu

UCO/Lick: Keck Telescope
doulos.ucsc.edu

UCO/Lick: Mount Hamilton
doulos.ucsc.edu

Univ. of California, Berkeley
worms.berkeley.edu:1234

Univ. of California, Santa Cruz - UCO/Lick
ucogo.ucsc.edu

Univ. of Chicago
granta.uchicago.edu

Univ. of Colorado
gopher.colorado.edu

Univ. of N. Carolina - images
stsci.edu

US National Weather Service Forecasts
ashpool.micro.umn.edu

WWW Resources

A.A.O Telescope Information
http://aaoepp.aao.gov.au/telescope.html

Abstracts of Astronomical Publications
http://fits.cv.nrao.edu/www/
yp_library.html#abstracts

ADS Einstein Archive Service
http://adswww.harvard.edu/
einstein_service.html

Advanced Computing Research Institute
http://www.tc.cornell.edu/InBriefs/ACRI.html

Albert-Ludwigs-Univ.Freiburg - Fakultät
für Physik
http://hpfrs6.physik.uni-freiburg.de/

American Astronomical Society
http://blackhole.aas.org/AAS-homepage.html

Anglo-Australian Observatory
http://aaoepp.aao.gov.au/aaohomepage.html

Anne's CyberJunk Drawer
http://as.arizona.edu/~aturner/home.html

Anti-matter Research Through the Earth
Moon Ion Spectrometer
http://polhp5.in2p3.fr:8000/u1/data/www/
artemis.html

Apache Point Observatory
http://www.apo.nmsu.edu/

APS Catalog of POSS I
http://isis.spa.umn.edu/homepage.aps.html

Archive of Starlink Newsgroups
http://cast0.ast.cam.ac.uk/starnews/

Arizona State Univ.
http://info.asu.edu/asu-cwis/las/phys-astro/

Armagh Observatory
http://star.arm.ac.uk/

ASA Goddard Space Flight Center's Solar
Data Analysis Ctr. (SDAC)
http://umbra.gsfc.nasa.gov/sdac.html

Aspen Ctr. for Physics
http://www-aspen.het.brown.edu/aspen/

Astronet - Navigation in Astronet
http://www.pd.astro.it/Astronet/Home-
Page.html

Astronomer's Bazaar
http://cdsweb.u-strasbg.fr/Cats.html

Astronomer's Guide to On-line Bibliographic Databases and Information
Services
http://fits.cv.nrao.edu/www/temp-cd.ps

Astronomical Anonymous FTP Sites
http://seds.lpl.arizona.edu/pub/faq/
astroftp.html

Astronomical Data Analysis Software and
Systems
http://ra.stsci.edu/ADASS.html

Astronomical Image Processing Center
http://www.cv.nrao.edu/aips/

Astronomical information on the Internet
http://ecf.hq.eso.org/astro-resources.html

Astronomical Internet Resources
http://nearnet.gnn.com/wic/astro.08.html

Astronomical Internet Resources (CFHT)
http://www.cfht.hawaii.edu/html/
astro_info.html

Astronomical Journal
http://www.astro.washington.edu/astroj/
index.html

Astronomical League
http://bradley.bradley.edu/~dware/al.html

Astronomical Society of the Pacific
http://maxwell.sfsu.edu/asp/asp.html

Astronomical World Wide Web Resources
http://anarky.stsci.edu/astroweb/net-www.html

Astronomie im Internet
http://aquila.uni-muenster.de/astro-im-net/
astronomy.html

Astronomy & the Web
http://cast0.ast.cam.ac.uk/overview.html

Astronomy and Astrophysics Journals
http://cnidr.org/other_links/astronomy.html

Astronomy and Astrophysics Sites
http://kudzu.cnidr.org/astronomy.html

Astronomy at ADFA
http://www.adfa.oz.au/physics/astro/
astron.htm

Astronomy Cafe
http://www2.ari.net/home/odenwald/cafe.html

Astronomy Index at the USGS
http://info.er.usgs.gov/network/science/
astronomy/index.html

Astronomy Information Systems
http://fits.cv.nrao.edu/www/yp_infosys.html

Astronomy Magazine
http://www.kalmbach.com/astro/
astronomy.html

Astrophysics Data System
http://adswww.colorado.edu/adswww/adshomepg.html

AstroWeb Consortium
http://fits.cv.nrao.edu/www/astroweb.html

AstroWeb: Astronomy / Astrophysics on WWW
http://meteor.anu.edu.au/anton/astronomy.html

Australia Telescope Compact Array
http://www.atnf.csiro.au/ATNF/Narrabri-Site-information.html

Australian National Univ. - Mt. Stromlo & Siding Spring Observatories
http://meteor.anu.edu.au/home.html

Australian Working Group for Antarctic Astronomy
http://newt.phys.unsw.edu.au/~mgb/awgaa.html

AVHRR Land Pathfinder Data Set
http://xtreme.gsfc.nasa.gov/

AXAF [Advanced X-ray Astrophysics Facility] Science Ctr.
http://hea-www.harvard.edu/asc/axaf-welcome.html

Backgrounds Data Ctr.
http://bradbury.nrl.navy.mil/

Be Star Newsletter
http://chara.gsu.edu/BeNews/intro.html

Berkeley Illinois Maryland Association
http://bima.astro.umd.edu/bima/home.html

Bernhard Beck-Winchatz, Astronomy
http://www.astro.washington.edu/bbeck/

Board on Physics and Astronomy
http://www.nas.edu/0/bpa/bpa.html

Bologna 152cm Telescope - Schedules
http://boas3.bo.astro.it/loiano/schedula.html

BONNAREL François
http://cdsweb.u-strasbg.fr/people/fb.html

Boston Univ. Center for Space Physics
http://bu-ast.bu.edu/csp.html

Bradford Robotic Telescope
http://www.eia.brad.ac.uk/

Bradley Observatory
http://www.algorithm.com/~asadun/bradley.html

Brittany Ctr. of Informatical Resources
http://www.univ-rennes1.fr/ASTRO/astro.english.html

Brookhaven National Lab.
http://suntid.bnl.gov:8080/bnl.html

Brown Univ. Astronomy
http://www-astro.physics.brown.edu/astro/

Cagliari Astronomical Observatory
http://caosun.unica.it/welcome.html

Caltech Astronomy
http://astro.caltech.edu/astro.html

CalTech - High Energy Astrophysics Group
http://www.ccsf.caltech.edu/astro/heastro.html

CalTech - Infrared Astrophysics Group
http://www.cco.caltech.edu/~rknop/ira.html

CalTech - Physics, Mathematics and Astronomy
http://www.caltech.edu/caltech/PMandA.html

CalTech - Pulsar Group
http://kaa.caltech.edu/

CalTech - Space Radiation Lab.
http://www.srl.caltech.edu/srl/

CalTech Submillimeter Observatory
http://www.cco.caltech.edu/~hunter/csotext.html

CalTech - Submillimeter Wave Astrophysics Group
http://www.cco.caltech.edu/~hunter/submm.html

CalTech -Theoretical Particle Physics
http://www.theory.caltech.edu/

Cambridge LFST
http://cast0.ast.cam.ac.uk/MRAO/mrao.clfst.html

Cambridge Ryle Telescope
http://cast0.ast.cam.ac.uk/MRAO/mrao.ryle.html

Cambridge Univ. Astronomy
http://cast0.ast.cam.ac.uk/

Campus Universitaire de St Martin d'Hères.
http://www.grenet.fr/campus.html

Canada France Hawaii Telescope
http://www.cfht.hawaii.edu/

Canadian Astronomy Data Centre
http://cadcwww.dao.nrc.ca/

Cardiff Star Formation
http://www.astro.cf.ac.uk/local/groups/
starform/

Catalog of Galactic SNR's
http://cast0.ast.cam.ac.uk/MRAO/
snrs.intro.html

CCD Images of Messier Objects
http://zebu.uoregon.edu/messier.html

CDS
http://cdsweb.u-strasbg.fr/astroweb.html

Centre de Données Astronomiques de
Strasbourg [English]
http://cdsweb.u-strasbg.fr/CDS.html

CERN Preprint Server
http://darssrv1.cern.ch/

Cerro Tololo Interamerican Observatory
http://ctios2.ctio.noao.edu/ctio.html

CfA Optical and Infrared Astronomy
Division
http://oir-www.harvard.edu/oir.html

CfA Radio and Geoastronomy Division
http://cfa-www.harvard.edu/cfa/rg.html

CfA Whipple Observatory
http://cfa-www.harvard.edu/cfa/whipple.html

CFHT at CADC
http://cadcwww.dao.nrc.ca/cfht/cfht.html

CNAM (French National Conservatory of
Arts & Works)
http://www.cnam.fr/astro.english.html

Compton Observatory Science Support
Ctr.
http://enemy.gsfc.nasa.gov/cossc/cossc.html

Conservatoire National des Arts et Métiers
(English text)
http://web.cnam.fr/astro.english.html

Cornell Univ. Theory Ctr.
http://www.tc.cornell.edu/ctc.html

Corporate Research Institute
http://www.tc.cornell.edu/InBriefs/CRI.html

Cracow Observatory - Solar Radio
Emission
http://www.oa.uj.edu.pl/sol/

Ctr. for Advanced Space Studies NASA
Johnson SC
http://cass.jsc.nasa.gov/CASS_home.html

Ctr. for Applied Parallel Processing
http://www.cs.colorado.edu/mcbryan/home/
capp/Home.html

Ctr. for Earth and Planetary Studies
http://ceps.nasm.edu:2020/homepage.html

Ctr. for Extreme Ultraviolet Astrophysics
http://cea-ftp.cea.berkeley.edu/
HomePage.html

Ctr. for Subatomic Research
http://inuit.phys.ualberta.ca/

Daedalus
http://mimas.ethz.ch/Daedalus/
daedalusdoc.html

Daily Planet
http://www.atmos.uiuc.edu/

DAO Virtual Library
http://www.dao.nrc.ca/librarymap.html

Dark Matter
http://www-hpcc.astro.washington.edu/
simulations/DARK_MATTER/

Data Reduction Expert Assistant
http://lor.stsci.edu/draco/draco.html

Defense Meteorological Satellite Program
Data Archive
http://www.ngdc.noaa.gov/dmsp/dmsp.html

Design Research Institute
http://dri.cornell.edu/Info/DRI.html

Deutsches Elektronen-Synchrotron
http://info.desy.de/

Distributed Astronomical Data Archives
http://cnidr.org/cnidr_papers/archives.html

Dominion Astrophysical Observatory
http://www.dao.nrc.ca/DAO-homepage.htm

Dutch Astronomy Services
http://eems.strw.leidenuniv.nl/astroned.html

Earth & Sky
http://www.quadralay.com/EarthSky/
es_home.htm

Earth Satellite Ephemeris Service
http://chara.gsu.edu/sat.html

Edinburgh Royal Observatory
http://www.roe.ac.uk/

Effelsberg Radio Telescope
http://www.mpifr-bonn.mpg.de/effberg.html

EINET Astronomy Listings
http://galaxy.einet.net/galaxy/Science/
Astronomy.html

Einstein Data Archive
http://hea-www.harvard.edu/einstein/
Ein_home/ein_welcome.html

Electronic TextBook
http://bovine.uoregon.edu/text.html

ESIS on-line image (GIF) files
http://ecf.hq.eso.org/ESIS-GIF.html

ESO / ST-ECF Data Archive
http://arch-http.hq.eso.org/ESO-ECF-
Archive.html

ESO Preprints Database
http://arch-http.hq.eso.org/cgi-bin/wdb/eso/
preprints/form

ESRIN - European Space Agency
http://www.esrin.esa.it/htdocs/esrin/esrin.html

ETH
http://www.ethz.ch/

ETH Solar Radio Spectrometer
http://mimas.ethz.ch/catalogs.html

European Incoherent Scatter
http://seldon.eiscat.no/homepage.html

European Southern Observatory
http://www.hq.eso.org/eso-homepage.html

European VLBI Network
http://rzmws10.nfra.nl:8081/jive/header.html

EUVE Guest Observer Ctr.
http://cea-ftp.cea.berkeley.edu/EGO/
EGOProgram.html

Extreme UltraViolet Explorer
http://cea-ftp.cea.berkeley.edu/

Fermilab
http://fnnews.fnal.gov/

FITS
http://fits.cv.nrao.edu:/FITS.html

Five College Radio Astronomy Observatory
http://donald.phast.umass.edu/Docs/
GradProg/fcrao.html

Flexible Image Transport System
http://fits.cv.nrao.edu/

FNAL
http://fndauh.fnal.gov:8000/

Freie Univ.Berlin - Institut für
Meteorologie [English]
http://www.met.fu-berlin.de/english/

Front Range Consortium
http://www.cs.colorado.edu/mcbryan/home/
frc/Home.html

Galactic PNe data base Innsbruck
http://ast2.uibk.ac.at/index.html

Gemini 8m Telescopes Project
http://www.gemini.edu/

George Smoot Astrophysics Research
http://spectrum.lbl.gov

Glasgow Univ.
http://info.astro.gla.ac.uk/

Global Land Information System
http://sun1.cr.usgs.gov/glis/glis.html

Global Oscillation Network Group
http://helios.tuc.noao.edu/gonghome.html

GOES Image Sequences of Solar Eclipse on
May 10, 1994
http://ageninfo.tamu.edu/eclipse/

Gravitational Lensing Conference
http://www.ph.unimelb.edu.au/astro/
glconf.html

Grenoble Image and Line Data Analysis
Software
http://iraux2.iram.fr/www/doc/gildas.html

Hafak Astronomical Society
http://www.csn.net/~emorse/haf/haf.html

Hard Labor Creek Observatory
http://chara.gsu.edu/hlco.html

Harvard Astrophysics Data System
http://adsabs.harvard.edu/

Harvard College Observatory
http://cfa-www.harvard.edu/hco-home.html

Harvard-Radcliffe Student Astronomers
http://hcs.harvard.edu/~stahr/

Harvard-Smithsonian Center for
Astrohysics
http://cfa-www.harvard.edu/cfa-home.html

Hat Creek Radio Observatory
http://bima.astro.umd.edu/bima/hatcreek/

Haystack Observatory
http://hyperion.haystack.edu/haystack/
haystack.html

HEAT (High-Energy, Antimatter Telescope)
http://tigger.physics.lsa.umich.edu/www/heat/
heat.html

High Energy Astrophysics Science Archive
Research Ctr.
http://heasarc.gsfc.nasa.gov/

Hiraiso Solar Terrestrial Research Ctr./
CRL
http://hiraiso.crl.go.jp/

Hubble Space Telescope
http://ucluelet.dao.nrc.ca/hst.html

Hubble Space Telescope Astrometry
Science Team
http://dorrit.as.utexas.edu/

IAU: Minor Planet Center
http://cfa-www.harvard.edu/cfa/ps/mpc.html

Icarus
http://astrosun.tn.cornell.edu/Icarus/
Icarus.html

IDL Astronomy User's Library
http://idlastro.gsfc.nasa.gov/homepage.html

Image Reduction and Analysis Facility
http://iraf.noao.edu/iraf-homepage.html

Imperial College, Univ. of London -
Theory Group: Preprints
http://euclid.tp.ph.ic.ac.uk/Papers/

Indiana Univ.
http://astrowww.astro.indiana.edu/

Infra-Red Telescope Facility
http://irtf.ifa.hawaii.edu/

Infrared Processing & Analysis Ctr.
http://www.ipac.caltech.edu/

Infrared Sky Survey Atlas
http://brando.ipac.caltech.edu:8888/ISSA-PS

Infrared Space Observatory
http://isowww.estec.esa.nl/

Infrared Subnode
http://esther.la.asu.edu/asu_tes/

Innsbruck - Galactic Planetary Nebulae
Database
http://ast2.uibk.ac.at/

Institut d'Astrophysique Spatiale (1)
http://www.ias.fr/

Institut de Radio Astronomie
Millimétrique
http://iraux2.iram.fr/www/iram.html

Institut National de Physique Nucléaire et
de Physique des Particules
http://info.in2p3.fr/

Institut National de Recherche en
Informatique et en Automatique
http://zenon.inria.fr:8003/

Institute for Astronomy Innsbruck
http://ast7.uibk.ac.at/

Institute for Space and Terrestrial Science
http://www.ists.ca/Welcome.html

Instituto de Astrofísica de Canarias
http://www.iac.es/home.html

Inter Univ. Ctr. for Astronomy and
Astrophysics
http://iucaa.iucaa.ernet.in/

Intl. Astronomy Conferences and Meetings
http://cadcwww.dao.nrc.ca/meetings/
meetings.html

Ionia 1 km AVHRR Global Land Data Set
Net-Browser
http://shark1.esrin.esa.it/

IRAF (preliminary)
http://iraf.noao.edu/iraf-homepage.html

Istituto di Astrofisica Spaziale - C.N.R.
http://titan.ias.fra.cnr.it/ias-home/ias-
home.html

Istituto di Fisica Cosmica e Tecnologie
Relative
http://www.ifctr.mi.cnr.it/

Istituto di Radioastronomia, Bologna -
C.N.R.
http://trantor.ira.bo.cnr.it/HomePage.html

Istituto Nazionale di Fisica Nucleare -
Astrofisica
http://hpl33.na.infn.it/Astr/Astr.html

IUE Data Analysis Ctr.
http://iuesn1.gsfc.nasa.gov/iue/
iuedac_homepage.html

James Clark Maxwell Telescope
http://malama.jach.hawaii.edu/
JCMT_intro.html

Joint Astronomy Centre
http://jach.hawaii.edu/

Joint Australian Centre for Astrophysical Research in Antarctica
http://newt.phys.unsw.edu.au/~mgb/jacara.html

Joint Institute for VLBI in Europe / European VLBI Network
http://www.nfra.nl/home_jive.html

JPL Space Very Long Baseline Interferometry Project
http://sgra.jpl.nasa.gov/

Keck Observatory
http://astro.caltech.edu/keck.html

Kernfysisch Versneller Instituut
http://kviexp.kvi.nl/

Kestrel Institute
http://kestrel.edu/pub/mosaic/kestrel.html

Kitt Peak National Observatory
http://www.noao.edu/kpno/kpno.html

Konkoly Observatory
http://ogyalla.konkoly.hu/

La Palma - Isaac Newton Group
http://cast0.ast.cam.ac.uk/~lpinfo/

La Palma - Nordic Optical Telescope
http://nastol.astro.lu.se/Html/not.html

La Palma - Telescopio Nazionale Galileo
http://www.pd.astro.it/TNG/TNG.html

La Silla - All Telescopes
http://lw10.ls.eso.org/lasilla/Telescopes/Telescopes.html

Lab. for Atmospheric and Space Physics
http://laspwww.colorado.edu:7777/lasp_homepage.html

Lab. for Computational Astrophysics
http://zeus.ncsa.uiuc.edu:8080/lca_home_page.html

Laboratoire d'Astrophysique de Grenoble
http://gag.observ-gr.fr/

LAI Olivier
http://www.obspm.fr/~lai/

LaRC
http://mosaic.larc.nasa.gov/nasaonline/nasaonline.html

Large Binocular Telescope (LBT) Project
http://as.arizona.edu/lbtwww/lbt.html

Lawrence Berkeley Lab.
http://www.lbl.gov/LBL.html

Leeds Univ. Astrophysics
http://ast.leeds.ac.uk/

Loiano Telescopes - Bologna
http://boas3.bo.astro.it/loiano/LoianoHome.html

Los Alamos National Lab Preprint Server
http://xxx.lanl.gov/

Low Surface Brightness galaxies
http://zebu.uoregon.edu/paper/lsb.txt

Ludwig Maximilians Univ.München - Institut für Astronomie und Astrophysik
http://www.bl.physik.tu-muenchen.de/sektion/

Lund Observatory
http://nastol.astro.lu.se/Html/home.html

Magellan Image Browser
http://delcano.mit.edu/cgi-bin/midr-query

Malin Space Science Systems, Inc.
http://barsoom.msss.com/

Mars Atlas
http://fi-www.arc.nasa.gov/fia/projects/bayes-group/Atlas/Mars/

Max-Planck-Institut für Astrophysik
http://www.mpa-garching.mpg.de/

Max-Planck-Institut für Extraterrestrische Physik
http://hproe1.mpe-garching.mpg.de/

Max-Planck-Institut für Radioastronomie
http://www.mpifr-bonn.mpg.de/index.html

McGill Univ. - Earth and Planetary Science
http://stoner.eps.mcgill.ca/AboutEPS/abouteps.html

McMaster Univ.'s Dept. of Physics and Astronomy
http://www.physics.mcmaster.ca/

Mees Observatory
http://www.solar.ifa.hawaii.edu/mees.html

Microcomputer Image Processing System
http://fits.cv.nrao.edu/www/news_mips.txt

Millstone Hill Observatory
http://hyperion.haystack.edu/homepage.html

MIT - Massachusetts Institute of Technology
http://hyperion.haystack.edu/mit/mit.html

MIT Lab. for Nuclear Science
http://marie.mit.edu/

MIT Microwave Subnode
http://delcano.mit.edu/

Mopra Antenna
http://www.atnf.csiro.au/ATNF/
Coonabarabran-Site-information.html

Mount Laguna Observatory/San Diego
State Univ.
http://mintaka.sdsu.edu/

Mount Stromlo and Siding Spring Observatories - Schedules
http://meteor.anu.edu.au/dave/schedule/
schedule.html

Mount Wilson Observatory
http://www.mtwilson.edu/

MPA Galaxy Formation Group: Preprints
http://www.mpa-garching.mpg.de/Galaxien/
Prep.html

MPA Gravitational Lensing Group:
Preprints
http://www.mpa-garching.mpg.de/Lenses/
Prep.html

MPA Hydro Gang: Preprints
http://www.mpa-garching.mpg.de/Hydro/
Prep.html

MPIfR - Bonn 100-m Telescope Surveys
http://www.mpifr-bonn.mpg.de/survey.html

MSSS Viking Image Archive
http://barsoom.msss.com/http/vikingdb.html

MSSSO
http://meteor.anu.edu.au/anton/
astronomy.html

Mullard Radio Astronomy Observatory
http://cast0.ast.cam.ac.uk/MRAO/
mrao.home.html

Multi Telescope Telescope
http://chara.gsu.edu/mtt.html

Multiple Mirror Telescope Observatory
http://oir-www.harvard.edu/MMT/mmto.html

Munich Image Data Analysis System
(WWW)
http://http.hq.eso.org/midas-info/midas.html

NASA ADC Online Information System
http://hypatia.gsfc.nasa.gov/about/
adc_online.html

NASA Homepage (with Links to Everywhere Else at NASA)
http://www.nasa.gov/

Nation River Observatory
http://hydra.carleton.ca/nro/nrohome.html

National Climatic Data Ctr.
http://www.ncdc.noaa.gov/ncdc.html

National Consortium for High Performance Computing
http://info.lcs.mit.edu/

National Ctr. for Atmospheric Research
http://http.ucar.edu/metapage.html

National Ctr. for Supercomputing Applications - Publications
http://www.ncsa.uiuc.edu/Pubs/
NCSAPubs.html

National Geophysical Data Ctr.
http://www.ngdc.noaa.gov/ngdc.html

National Information Infrastructure
Testbed
http://www.esi.com/niit/

National Institute of Space Research
http://www.inpe.br/astro/home

National MetaCenter for Computational
Science and Engineering
http://www.ncsa.uiuc.edu/General/
MetaCenter/MetaCenterHome.html

National Optical Astronomy Observatories
http://www.noao.edu/

National Radio Astronomy Observatory
http://info.aoc.nrao.edu/

National Solar Observatory
http://argo.tuc.noao.edu/

Naval Research Lab.
http://www.cmf.nrl.navy.mil/home.html

NEMO Stellar Dynamics Toolbox
http://bima.astro.umd.edu/nemo/

Nerd World Astronomy Links (massive)
http://www.tiac.net/users/dstein/nw37.html

Netherlands Foundation for Research in
Astronomy
http://www.nfra.nl/home_nfra.html

New Mexico State Univ.
http://charon.nmsu.edu/

Nicolaus Copernicus Astronomical Ctr.
http://www.ncac.torun.pl/

Nine Planets
http://seds.lpl.arizona.edu/nineplanets/
nineplanets/nineplanets.html

NOAA - National Oceanographic and
Atmospheric Administration
http://www.ncdc.noaa.gov/noaa.html

North Carolina State Univ. - Mars Mission
Research Ctr.
http://www.mmrc.ncsu.edu/

Northwestern Univ. - Astronomy
http://www.astro.nwu.edu/home.html

Numerical Algorithms Group
http://www.nag.co.uk:70/

Oak Ridge National Lab.
http://jupiter.esd.ornl.gov/home.html

OAT Astronomical Services
http://www.oat.ts.astro.it/astro-services/
overview.html

Observatoire du Mont Mégantic
http://ftp.astro.umontreal.ca/omm/
omm_eng.html

Observatories and Astronomical Institutions on WWW
http://sousun1.phys.soton.ac.uk/
Institutions.html

Optical Astronomy Group at Leeds Univ.
http://ast.leeds.ac.uk/opti-home.html

Optical Gravitational Lensing Experiment
http://www.astrouw.edu.pl/~udalski/ogle.html

OPTICS.ORG - The Photonics Resource
Center
http://optics.org/

Orbiting Very Long Baseline Interferometry
http://info.gb.nrao.edu/ovlbi/OVLBI.html

OSSE
http://enemy.gsfc.nasa.gov/cossc/OSSE-
desc.html

Osservatorio Astrofisico di Arcetri
http://helios.arcetri.astro.it/

Osservatorio Astrofisico di Catania
http://convex.ct.astro.it/

Osservatorio Astronomico Collurania di
Teramo
http://terri1.te.astro.it/oact-home/home.html

Osservatorio Astronomico di Bologna
http://boas3.bo.astro.it/

Osservatorio Astronomico di Padova
http://www.pd.astro.it/

Osservatorio Astronomico di Palermo
http://www.astropa.unipa.it/

Osservatorio Astronomico di Roma
http://oar.rm.astro.it/home.html

Osservatorio Astronomico di Trieste
http://www.oat.ts.astro.it/oat-home.html

Oxford Workshop on Evidence for Tori in
AGN
http://www-astro.physics.ox.ac.uk/torus/

Pacific Northwest Lab.
http://romana.crystal.pnl.gov/

Padova: Ekar 182cm Telescope - Schedules
http://www.pd.astro.it/CurrentSchedule.html

Parallel Tools Consortium
http://www.llnl.gov/ptools/ptools.html

Parkes Radio Telescope
http://www.atnf.csiro.au/ATNF/Parkes-Site-
information.html

PASP Abstract Service at CDS
http://cdsweb.u-strasbg.fr/PASP.html

PDS Planetary Rings Node
http://ringside.arc.nasa.gov/

Pennsylvania State Univ. - Dept. of
Astronomy and Astrophysics
http://www.astro.psu.edu/

Peora Astronomical Society
http://bradley.bradley.edu/~dware/

Physikalisch-Astronomisch-
Technikwissenschaftliche Fakultät
http://www.physik.uni-jena.de/

Pico Veleta
http://iraux2.iram.fr/www/veleta.gif

Pine Mountain Observatory
http://zebu.uoregon.edu/pine.html

Pittsburgh Supercomputing Ctr.
http://pscinfo.psc.edu/

Planetary Astronomy
http://fits.cv.nrao.edu/www/yp_planetary.html

Planetary Society
http://wea.mankato.mn.us/tps/

Pomona College
http://shanti.pomona.claremont.edu/

Princeton Univ. Astrophysics Library
http://astro.princeton.edu/library/

Princeton Univ. Observatory
http://minos.princeton.edu/

Princeton Univ. - Pulsar Group
http://pulsar.princeton.edu/

Radio Astronomy Group (RAG)
http://mimas.ethz.ch/home.html

Rennes' Univ.
http://www.univ-rennes1.fr/

Rensselaer Polytechnic Institute
http://www.rpi.edu/dept/phys/astro.html

Repository Based Software Engineering
http://rbse.jsc.nasa.gov/eichmann/rbse.html

Research Institute for Computing and
Information Systems
http://rbse.jsc.nasa.gov/

RGSC
http://tdc-www.harvard.edu/software/
rgsc.html

Rice Univ.
http://spacsun.rice.edu/

Robert Lentz's Astro Resources
http://www.astro.nwu.edu/lentz/astro/home-
astro.html

Royal Greenwich Observatory
http://cast0.ast.cam.ac.uk/RGO/RGO.html

Royal Observatory, Edinburgh
http://www.roe.ac.uk/

Rutherford Appleton Lab.
http://www.rl.ac.uk/home.html

RVSAO
http://tdc-www.harvard.edu/iraf/rvsao/
rvsao.html

Sac Peak Preprint Library
http://www.sunspot.noao.edu/Library/
preprints/

Sacramento Peak Observatory
http://sunspot.noao.edu/SP-home.html

Saint Mary's Astronomy and Physics
http://mnbsun.stmarys.ca/www/
smu_home.html

Saint-Louis Nicole
http://ftp.astro.umontreal.ca/membres/
stlouis.html

San Diego Supercomputer Ctr.
http://gopher.sdsc.edu/Home.html

Sandia National Labs.
http://www.cs.sandia.gov/pub/WWW/
Sandia_home_page.html

SAO Telescope Data Ctr.
http://tdc-www.harvard.edu/TDC.html

sci.astro.research Archive
http://xanth.msfc.nasa.gov/xray/sar.html

Science on the Edge of Chaos Cosmology
http://arti.vub.ac.be/www/chaos/cosmology/
description.html

Seoul National Univ.
http://astrox.snu.ac.kr/

Set of Identifications, Measurements, and
Bibliography for Astronomical Data
http://cdsweb.u-strasbg.fr/Simbad.html

SETI Institute
http://www.metrolink.com/seti/SETI.html

Sidewalk Astronomers
http://lausd.k12.ca.us/~npatteng/sa.html

SIS junctions lab
http://iraux2.iram.fr/www/sis.html

Sky & Telescope magazine
http://www.skypub.com/

SKYMAP
http://tdc-www.harvard.edu/software/
skymap.html

SkyView
http://skyview.gsfc.nasa.gov/skyview.html

Sloan Digital Sky Survey
http://astro.princeton.edu/

Small Astronomical Image Library
http://donald.phast.umass.edu/gs/
wizimlib.html

Smithsonian Astrophysical Observatory
http://cfa-www.harvard.edu/sao-home.html

Solar and Heliospheric Observatory
http://umbra.gsfc.nasa.gov/soho/anglais/
soho.html

Solar Astronomy
http://fits.cv.nrao.edu/www/
yp_areas.html#solar

Solar Workshops
http://www.oat.ts.astro.it/isps/
sworkshops.html

Southampton Univ. Astronomy Group
http://sousun1.phys.soton.ac.uk/

Southern Columbia Millimeter Telescope
http://ctiot6.ctio.noao.edu/

Space Astrophysics Lab.
http://nereid.sal.ists.ca/Welcome.html

Space Environment Lab.
http://www.sel.bldrdoc.gov/

Space Infrared Telescope Facility
http://kromos.jpl.nasa.gov/sirtf.html

Space Physics Resources on the Internet
http://www.esrin.esa.it/htdocs/esis/
sp_resources.html

Space Telescope - European Coordinating
Facility
http://ecf.hq.eso.org/ST-ECF-homepage.html

Space Telescope Electronic Information
Service
http://stsci.edu/top.html

Space Telescope Science Institute
http://www.stsci.edu/top.html

SPIE-The Intl. Society for Optical Engineering
http://www.spie.org/

Stanford Public Information Retrieval
System
http://www-spires.slac.stanford.edu/FIND/
spires.html

STAR
http://tdc-www.harvard.edu/software/star.html

Star*s Family
http://cdsweb.u-strasbg.fr/~heck/sf.htm

StarBits
http://cdsweb.u-strasbg.fr/~heck/sfbits.htm

Starcat
http://arch-http.hq.eso.org/starcat.html

StarHeads
http://cdsweb.u-strasbg.fr/~heck/sfheads.htm

STARLINK (at UCL)
http://zuaxp6.star.ucl.ac.uk/mainindex.html

StarTrax: an Astrophysics Information
System
http://heasarc.gsfc.nasa.gov/StarTrax.html

StarWorlds
http://cdsweb.u-strasbg.fr/~heck/sfworlds.htm

Statistical Consulting Ctr. for Astronomy
http://www.stat.psu.edu/scca/homepage.html

STECF
http://ecf.hq.eso.org/astro-resources.html

STELAR project
http://hypatia.gsfc.nasa.gov/Welcome.html

Sterrewacht Leiden
http://eems.strw.leidenuniv.nl/

Steward Observatory
http://as.arizona.edu/www/so.html

STScI
http://stsci.edu/net-resources.html

STScI-EPA HST Images
http://ra.stsci.edu/EPAimages.html

Students for the Exploration and Development of Space
http://seds.lpl.arizona.edu/

Study of Electronic Literature for Astronomical Research
http://hypatia.gsfc.nasa.gov/
STELAR_homepage.html

SUNY Stony Brook Astronomy Group
http://sbast3.ess.sunysb.edu/home.html

Superconducting Super Collider Lab.
http://www.ssc.gov/

Sussex Starlink
http://star-www.maps.susx.ac.uk/index.html

Texas Astronomical Society - Dallas
http://fohnix.metronet.com/~cajun/tas.html

THE Star
http://www.oat.ts.astro.it/isps/isps.htm

TIPSY
http://hermes.astro.washington.edu/tools/
TIPSY/

TL Systems - Astronomy & Satellite
Products
http://PoliticsUSA.com/PoliticsUSA/news/

Today's Solar Weather
http://www.sel.bldrdoc.gov/today.html

Two Micron All-Sky Survey
http://scruffy.phast.umass.edu/GradProg/
2mass.html

UK Infra-Red Telescope
http://malama.jach.hawaii.edu/
UKIRT_intro.html

UMASS Astronomy Image Library
http://donald.phast.umass.edu/gs/wizimlib.html

UniPOPS
http://info.cv.nrao.edu/html/unipops/unipops-home.html

Univ. di Bologna - Dipartimento di Astronomia
http://boas3.bo.astro.it/dip/DepHome.html

Univ. di Roma " Tor Vergata" Astrophysics
http://itovf2.roma2.infn.it/

Univ. of Adelaide - Astrophysics Group
http://bragg.physics.adelaide.edu.au/astrophysics/home.html

Univ. of Alabama
http://crux.astr.ua.edu/AlabamaHome.html

Univ. of Amsterdam - Astronomical Institute
http://helios.astro.uva.nl:8888/home.html

Univ. of Birmingham - Space Research
http://www.sr.bham.ac.uk:8080/

Univ. of Bradford - Engineering in Astronomy Group
http://www.eia.brad.ac.uk/eia.html

Univ. of Calgary
http://bear.ras.ucalgary.ca/department.html

Univ. of California, Berkeley
http://astro.berkeley.edu/home.html

Univ. of California, Los Angeles
http://www.igpp.ucla.edu/

Univ. of California, San Diego
http://www.ucsd.edu/

Univ. of California, Santa Cruz - UCO/Lick
http://ucowww.ucsc.edu/

Univ. of Cantabria - Departamento de Física Moderna
http://esanu1.unican.es/

Univ. of Chicago
http://bio-3.bsd.uchicago.edu/htbin/lookup-building?AAC

Univ. of Colorado Astrophysics Data System
http://adswww.colorado.edu/adswww/adshomepg.html

Univ. of Edinburgh
http://www.ph.ed.ac.uk/index.html

Univ. of Groningen - Kapteyn Astronomical Institute
http://kapteyn.astro.rug.nl/

Univ. of Hawaii - Institute for Astronomy
http://www.ifa.hawaii.edu/

Univ. of Hawaii IfA: 2.2m Telescope
http://www.ifa.hawaii.edu/88inch/88inch.html

Univ. of Leicester
http://www.star.le.ac.uk/

Univ. of Manchester
http://axp2.ast.man.ac.uk:8000/

Univ. of Maryland
http://pdssbn.astro.umd.edu/

Univ. of Maryland, College Park
http://www.astro.umd.edu/

Univ. of Massachusetts
http://www-astro.phast.umass.edu/

Univ. of Massachusetts, Amherst
http://donald.phast.umass.edu/umasshome.html

Univ. of Melbourne
http://www.ph.unimelb.edu.au/

Univ. of Minnesota
http://ast1.spa.umn.edu/

Univ. of Montréal
http://ftp.astro.umontreal.ca/index_eng.html

Univ. of Nevada, Las Vegas
http://pauli.lv-physics.nevada.edu/

Univ. of New Mexico
http://wwwifa.unm.edu/

Univ. of New South Wales
http://newt.phys.unsw.edu.au/

Univ. of Oxford - Astrophysics
http://www-astro.physics.ox.ac.uk/

Univ. of Oxford - Atmospheric, Oceanic & Planetary Physics.
http://www-atm.atm.ox.ac.uk/index.html

Univ. of Pennsylvania
http://dept.physics.upenn.edu/

Univ. of Pittsburgh
http://artemis.phyast.pitt.edu/

Univ. of Rochester - Near Infrared Group
http://sherman.pas.rochester.edu/
URNIRHome.html

Univ. of Southampton - Astronomy Group
http://sousun1.phys.soton.ac.uk/

Univ. of Texas, Austin - McDonald
Observatory
http://www.as.utexas.edu/

Univ. of Tokyo - Gravitational Wave
Group
http://www.phys.s.u-tokyo.ac.jp/local/
research/tsubono/res94-e.html

Univ. of Tokyo - Theoretical Astrophysics
Group
http://www.phys.s.u-tokyo.ac.jp/local/
research/astrophys/res94-e.html

Univ. of Tokyo - X-Ray Astronomy Group
http://www.phys.s.u-tokyo.ac.jp/local/
research/maxima/res94-e.html

Univ. of Toronto - Canadian Institute for
Theoretical Astrophysics
http://www.physics.utoronto.ca/department/
groups_partners/cita.html

Univ. of Toronto Astronomy Library Book
and Software Reviews
http://www.astro.utoronto.ca/reviews1.html

Univ. of Tübingen - Theoretische
Astrophysik ünd Computational
Physics
http://aorta.tat.physik.uni-tuebingen.de/

Univ. of Utrecht - Sterrenkundig Instituut
http://stkwww.fys.ruu.nl:8000

Univ. of Victoria
http://info.phys.uvic.ca/uvphys_welcome.html

Univ. of Vienna - Institut für Astronomie
http://charon.ast.univie.ac.at/index.html

Univ. of Virginia
http://www.astro.virginia.edu/

Univ. of Wales at Cardiff
http://www.astro.cf.ac.uk/

Univ. of Washington
http://www.astro.washington.edu/

Univ. of Western Ontario
http://phobos.astro.uwo.ca/

Univ. of Wisconsin-Madison
http://www.astro.wisc.edu/

Uppsala Astronomical Observatory,
Sweden
http://www.astro.uu.se/

UUNA Astronomy Listings
http://sturgeon.mit.edu:8001/uu-nna/meta-
library/index.html?astronomy

Vassar College
http://noether.vassar.edu/

Viking Orbiter
http://www.gsfc.nasa.gov/planetary/
Viking.HTML

Warsaw Univ. - Astronomical Observatory
http://www.astrouw.edu.pl/

Warsaw Univ. - Optical Gravitational
Lensing Experiment
http://www.astrouw.edu.pl/~udalski/ogle.html

Weather World
http://www.atmos.uiuc.edu/wxworld/html/
top.html

Weaving the Astronomy Web
http://cdsweb.u-strasbg.fr/waw.html

WebStars: Astrophysics in Cyberspace
http://guinan.gsfc.nasa.gov/WebStars.html

Westerbork Synthesis Radio Telescope
http://kapteyn.astro.rug.nl/UserDoc.html

Whipple Gamma-Ray Observatory
http://egret.sao.arizona.edu/index.html

Whipple Observatory
http://oir-www.harvard.edu/FLWO/FLWO/
whipple.html

Williams College
http://albert.astro.williams.edu/

Wilson Synchrotron Lab.
http://w4.lns.cornell.edu/

Woodman Astronomical Library
http://uwast.astro.wisc.edu/~astrolib/
WoodmanLibrary.html

World Data Ctr. A for Rockets and
Satellites
http://hypatia.gsfc.nasa.gov/about/
about_wdc-a.html

X-Ray WWW Server
http://xray.uu.se/

Xerox Palo Alto Research Ctr.
http://pubweb.parc.xerox.com/

Biology & Biotechnology

See also Agriculture, Chemistry, Medicine, Optics, Physics

Usenet Newsgroups

bionet

The bionet groups (see list below) were designed by and are intended for researchers active in the biological sciences. The bionet groups are separate and distinct from the regular USENET hierarchy. The project is funded by a variety of US agencies, including the National Science Foundation, the U. S. Dept. of Energy, and the National Institutes of Health in the United States. A British iteration is funded by the Engineering Research Council, Daresbury Lab. in the United Kingdom.

Bionet is free of charge, and is accessible via USENET software or via e-mail. For more information, send e-mail to:

```
biosci-server@net.bio.net
```
and include either line below in the body (depending on whether you want the UK or US versions):

```
info ukinfo
info usinfo
```
For a copy of the FAQ, include

```
info faq
```
in the body of the message.

Current groups in the bionet hierarchy include:

bionet.agroforestry
bionet.biology.computational
bionet.biology.grasses
bionet.biology.tropical
bionet.biophysics
bionet.cellbiol
bionet.cellbiol.cytonet
bionet.chlamydomonas
bionet.drosophila

bionet.general
bionet.genome.arabidopsis
bionet.genome.chrom22
bionet.genome.chromosomes
bionet.immunology
bionet.info-theory
bionet.jobs
bionet.journals
bionet.metabolic-reg
bionet.microbiology
bionet.molbio.ageing
bionet.molbio.bio-matrix
bionet.molbio.embldatabank
bionet.molbio.evolution
bionet.molbio.gdb
bionet.molbio.genbank
bionet.molbio.gene-linkage
bionet.molbio.gene-org
bionet.molbio.genome-program
bionet.molbio.hiv
bionet.molbio.methds-reagnts
bionet.molbio.proteins
bionet.molbio.rapd
bionet.molbio.yeast
bionet.molec-model
bionet.mycology
bionet.n2-fixation
bionet.neuroscience
bionet.parasitology
bionet.photosynthesis
bionet.plants
bionet.population-bio
bionet.prof-society.biophysics
bionet.protista
bionet.sci-resources
bionet.software
bionet.software.acedb
bionet.software.gcg
bionet.software.sources
bionet.structural-nmr
bionet.users.addresses
bionet.virology

bionet.women-in-bio
bionet.xtallography

comp.ai.genetic

Created by: arras@forwiss.uni-erlangen.de
(Mike Arras)
Call for Votes date: November 24, 1992
Newsgroup-based Mailing List: No.
Charter (from Call for Votes):
This group will be devoted to the subject
of genetic algorithms.

sci.bio

sci.bio is one of the original net.* groups.
Newsgroup-based Mailing List: No.
Charter: Oriented around biological
topics. Popular science, job offers, general
chit-chat.

sci.bio.botany

Created by: Una Smith
<una.smith@yale.edu>
Call for Votes Date: May 12, 1995
Newsgroup-based Mailing List: No.
Charter (from Call for Votes):
For discussion of the scientific study of
plants: vascular, nonvascular, and
unicellular photosynthetic, autotrophic
organisms, and other taxa traditionally
considered to be plants.

sci.bio.conservation (Moderated)

Created by: Una Smith
<una.smith@yale.edu>
Call for Votes Date: October 12, 1994
Moderated by: Preston Hardison
<consreq@u.washington.edu>
Submissions go to:
conssub@u.washington.edu
Newsgroup-based Mailing List: No.
Charter (from Call for Votes):
Sci.bio.conservation is a forum for
conservation biologists and others
interested in conservation biology. The
specific goal of this newsgroup is to help
develop the scientific and technical means
for the protection, maintenance, and
restoration of life on this planet.

sci.bio.ecology

Created by: Una Smith
<una.smith@yale.edu>
Call for Votes date: July 8, 1993
Newsgroup-based Mailing List: Yes.
Charter (from Call for Votes):

sci.bio.ecology is an active newsgroup
with a gated mailing list (ECOLOG-L) of
about 900 subscribers.

sci.bio.entomology.lepidoptera

Created by: Christopher Majka
<nextug@ac.dal.ca>
Call for Votes Date: September 21, 1994
Mailing list: leps-l@yalevm.cis.yale.edu
Charter (from Call for Votes):
Sci.bio.entomology.lepidoptera is an
unmoderated newsgroup to provide a
forum for the discussion of all aspects of
lepidoptera (butterflies and moths) and
topics pertaining to them both on an
amateur and professional level.

sci.bio.entomology.misc

Created by: Maarten van Helden
<maarten.vanhelden@medew.ento.wau.nl>
Call for Votes Date: April 19, 1995
Newsgroup-based Mailing List: No.
Charter (from Call for Votes):
Discussion, news, and queries concerning
the study of insects and other (non-
marine) arthropods not covered in more
specialised newsgroups. The newsgroup is
meant to cover a wide variety of entomo-
logical topics, including postings about
arachnology, myriapodology and other
studies with affinities to entomology.

sci.bio.ethology

Created by: Una Smith
<una.smith@yale.edu>
Call for Votes date: December 2, 1993
Newsgroup-based Mailing List: Yes,
ethology@searn.sunet.se.
Charter (from Call for Votes):
For discussion of the scientific study of
animal behavior and behavioral ecology.

sci.bio.evolution (Moderated)

Created by: colby@bio.bu.edu (Chris
Colby)
Moderated by: Josh Hayes
(josh@pogo.cqs.washington.edu)
Submissions go to:
evolution@pogo.cqs.washington.edu
Call for Votes date: December 24, 1993
Newsgroup-based Mailing List: Yes,
evolution@pogo.cqs.washington.edu.
Charter (from RFD/Call for Votes):

sci.bio.evolution will be dedicated to discussions of evolutionary biology.

sci.bio.fisheries
Created by: Lawrence Dorsey <lgdorsey@unity.ncsu.edu>
Call for Votes Date: March 17, 1995
Newsgroup-based Mailing List: No.
Charter (from Call for Votes):
sci.bio.fisheries will be a forum for discussion between fisheries students,professionals, and others with an interest in fisheries science.

sci.bio.food-science
Created by: Rachel Zemser <zemser@uxa.cso.uiuc.edu>
Call for Votes Date: April 24, 1995
Newsgroup-based Mailing List: No.
Charter (from Call for Votes):
[The principal goal of this newsgroup is:]

To discuss topics and issues related to food chemistry, food microbiology, food engineering/processing, food biotechnology, dairy science, agriculture, fermentation, nutrition, toxicology, and food safety.

sci.bio.herp
Created by: Una Smith <una.smith@yale.edu>
Call for Votes date: December 2, 1993
Newsgroup-based Mailing List: Yes, herp-l@xtal200.harvard.edu.
Charter: For discussion of the natural history, biology, conservation, and scientific study of amphibians and reptiles.

sci.bio.microbiology
Created by: Una Smith <una.smith@yale.edu>
Call for Votes Date: October 12, 1994
Newsgroup-based Mailing List: No.
Charter (from Call for Votes):
Sci.bio.microbiology is devoted to broad discussion of microbiology, including organismic studies (ecology, biodiversity, bioremediation, classical genetics, and other types of applied microbiology) and systematics.

sci.bio.misc
Created by: Una Smith <una.smith@yale.edu>
Call for Votes Date: May 12, 1995
Newsgroup-based Mailing List: No.
Charter (from Call for Votes):
One of the oldest, most widely read, and most lively newsgroups in the sci.* hierarchy, sci.bio.misc (formerly sci.bio) welcomes discussion of all topics having to do with biology.

sci.bio.paleontology
Created by: Bob Myers <stssram@st.unocal.com>
Call for Votes Date: December 6, 1994
Newsgroup-based Mailing List: No.
Charter (from Call for Votes):
The newsgroup sci.bio.paleontology is open to discussion on scientific topics concerning paleontology.

sci.bio.phytopathology (Moderated)
Created by: Thorsten Kraska <kraska@mbox.ipp.uni-hannover.de>
Call for Votes Date: August 14, 1995
Moderated by: Thorsten Kraska <phytopathology@mbox.ipp.uni-hannover.de>
Submissions go to:
phytopathology@mbox.ipp.uni-hannover.de
Newsgroup-based Mailing List: No.
Charter (from Call for Votes):
Sci.bio.phytopathology is a moderated discussion forum on all aspects of phytopathology and plant health including pests

sci.bio.systematics
Created by: Una Smith <una.smith@yale.edu>
Call for Votes Date: May 12, 1995
Newsgroup-based Mailing List: No.
Charter (from Call for Votes):
For discussion of the science of taxonomy and systematics, and both practical and theoretical issues pertaining to: hierarchical information systems; biological nomenclature; cladistics; phylogenetics; species concepts; comparative analysis and integration of morphological, ana-

tomical, molecular, and other data; and the documentation and study of large-scale and long-term patterns of evolution and biodiversity.

sci.bio.technology
Newsgroup-based Mailing List: No. **Charter**: Apparently related to bio technology, but really just a version of the parent group, sci.bio.

Frequently Asked Questions

ACEDB Genome Database Software FAQ
Maintainer: acedbfaq@s27w007.pswfs.gov (ACEDB FAQ Pseudouser)
Where on Usenet: bionet.software.acedb
Where it's archived: rtfm.mit.edu:pub/usenet/ bionet.software.acedb
What it's for: Information on acquiring and using ACEDB, a database system for cataloging the genome.

BIOSCI/bionet Frequently Asked Questions
Maintainer: BIOSCI Administrator <biosci-help@net.bio.net>
Where on Usenet: bionet.announce
Where it's archived: rtfm.mit.edu:pub/usenet/ bionet.announce
What it's for: Provides details of the BIOSCI forums.

Biological Information Theory and Chowder Society FAQ
Maintainer: toms@ncifcrf.gov (Tom Schneider)
Where on Usenet: bionet.info-theory
Where it's archived: rtfm.mit.edu:pub/usenet/bionet.info-theory
What it's for: Information theory and ideas in the biological sciences.

Discussion Lists

algae-l
algae-l@irlearn
ALGAE-L : digest information on botany
ar-news
ar-news-request@cygnus.com
News on animal rights.
ar-talk
ar-talk-request@cygnus.com
Discussion of animal rights.
bee-l
bee-l@albnyvm1
Discussion of Bee Biology
biocis-l
biocis-l@sivm
Biology Curriculum Innovation Study
biodidac
biodidac@uottawa
Electronic Discussion Group for Biology teachers
biodiv-l
listserv@bdt.ftpt.ansp.br
Biodiversity topics.
biomat-l
biomat-l@hearn
Biomaterials Mailing List
biomch-l
biomch-l@hearn
Biomechanics and Movement Science listserver
biomet-l
biomet-l@albnydh2
BUREAU OF BIOMETRICS AT ALBNYDH2
biopi-l
biopi-l@ksuvm
Secondary Biology Teacher Enhancement PI
biosafty
biosafty@mitvma
Biosafety
biosph-l
biosph-l@ubvm
Biosphere, ecology
biosym
dibug-request@comp.bioz.unibas.ch (Reinhard Doelz)
User list of Biosym Technologies software products.

biotech
biotech@umdd
Biotechnology
biovote
biovote@irlearn
BIOSCI Ballot Box
cellwall
cellwall@ndsuvm1
Plant Cell Wall Biology
confocal
confocal@ubvm
Confocal Microscopy List
consgis
consgis@uriacc
Biological Conservation and GIS
crust-l
crust-l@sivm
Crustacean systematics, distribution ecology
cturtle
cturtle@nervm
Sea Turtle Biology and Conservation
cyan-tox
cyan-tox@trearn
The Cyanobacterial Toxins
d-oral-l
d-oral-l@nihlist
Oral Microbiology/Immunology Interest Group
diatom-l
diatom-l@iubvm
Research on the diatom algae
embinfo
embinfo@ibacsata
EMBNet (European Molecular Biology Network)
gedcom-l
gedcom-l@ndsuvm1
Genealogical Data Communications Specs
gene-l
gene-l@gitvm1
Genealogy discussion list
gsa
gsa@iubvm
GSA - Genetic Stock Administrators
hep-ph
hep-ph@jpnyitp
Preprint server for Particle Phenomenology
inhib
inhib@mcgill1

Growth inhibitory molecule theme research
lactacid
lactacid@searn
Lactic Acid Bacteria Forum
lines-l
lines-l@ndsuvm1
LifeLines Genealogical System
marmam
marmam@uvvm
Marine Mammals Research and Conservation
molbio-l
molbio-l@mizzou1
Molecular Biology Discussion
morphmet
morphmet@cunyvm
Biological Morphometrics Mailing List
mxdiag-l
mxdiag-l@albnydh2
Molecular Pathology and Diagnostics
ph-bsg
ph-bsg@searn
Biological Sciences Group, STACnet-Philippines
photosyn
photosyn@taunivm
Photosynthesis Researchers' List
NPLC
tout@genesys.cps.msu.edu (Walid Tout)
Plant lipids.
rmbl-l
rmbl-l@umdd
Rocky Mountain Biological Lab's List
roots-l
roots-l@ndsuvm1
ROOTS-L Genealogy List
socinsct
socinsct@albnyvm1
Social Insect Biology Research
taxacom
taxacom@harvarda
Biological Systematics
uvicbio2
uvicbio2@uvvm
UVICBIO2 - UVic Biology Dept. Announcements
vrtpaleo
vrtpaleo@uscvm
The Vertebrate Paleontology Community

Environmental Issues Discussion Lists

aquifer
aquifer@ibacsata
Pollution and groundwater recharge

ecolog-l
ecolog-l@umdd
Ecological Society of America: grants, jobs

ecology
ecology@emuvm1
Politics and the Environment

ecovis-l
ecovis-l@yalevm
Trends in Ecology of Vision

envinf-l
envinf-l@hearn
List for Environmental Information

envst-l
envst-l@brownvm
Environmental Studies

reactive
reactive@mcgill1
List: Short-lived reactive air pollutants.

scanning
SCANNING@UTARLVM1
UTA environmental scanning evaluation group

usiale-l
usiale-l@uriacc
Intn'l Assc. of Landscape Ecology

water-l
water-l@wsuvm1
Water Quality

Biology Resources

Gopher Resources

AIDS
odie.niaid.nih.gov/11/aids

Arnold Arboretum
huh.harvard.edu/11/collections_info/
institution/harvard/aa

Beth Israel Hospital
gopher.bih.harvard.edu/1

Biodiversity Gopher
huh.harvard.edu/1

Biology Internet Resources
genome-gopher.stanford.edu

BIOSCI (Bionet) News Group Archives &
Index to Biologists
net.bio.net/

BIOSCI/bionet - Electronic News
gopher.bio.net/

Caenorhabditis Genetics Ctr.
elegans.cbs.umn.edu

Dana-Farber Cancer Institute
gopher.dfci.harvard.edu

Darwin's "On the Origin of Species by
Means of Natural Selection"
gopher.hs.jhu.edu/1/Scientists.On.Disk/
Darwin/Origin.of.Species

Epidemiology Gopher
cedr.lbl.gov

Harvard Botany/Zoology/Organismic
and Evolutionary Biology Gopher
huh.harvard.edu:75

Harvard School of Public Health
hsph.harvard.edu

Herbarium
huh.harvard.edu

History of Science Gopher
gopher.hs.jhu.edu

Image Library of Biological Macromol-
ecules
gopher.imb-jena.de

Index (BOING)
gopher.gdb.org:3005

Indiana Univ. Biology Gopher
ftp.bio.indiana.edu

Insect Database
bluehen.ags.udel.edu:7

Joe Felsenstein's Bibliography of Theoretical Population Genetics
gopher.gdb.org

Jrnl. Contents
gopher.bio.net

Massachusetts General Hospital
weeds.mgh.harvard.edu

Museum of Comparative Zoology
huh.harvard.edu

National Institute of Allergy and Infectious
Disease Gopher
gopher.niaid.nih.gov

NIGHTINGALE Nursing Server
nightingale.con.utk.edu

NIH Gopher
gopher.nih.gov

Not Just Cows
snymorva.cs.snymor.edu

Plant Images
huh.harvard.edu

Protein Data Bank
pdb.pdb.bnl.gov

Ribosomal Database Project
rdpgopher.life.uiuc.edu

UMICH Sciences Ctr.
una.hh.lib.umich.edu

Univ. Delaware Botanic Gardens
bluehen.ags.udel.edu:71

Virtual Reference Desk
peg.cwis.uci.edu:7000

WWW Resources

3D Image Reconstruction Information
http://biocomp.arc.nasa.gov/3dreconstruction

Aachen Institute of Physiology
http://www.physiology.rwth-aachen.de/

AAnDB
http://keck.tamu.edu/cgi/aandb/anid.html

ABtDB
http://keck.tamu.edu/cgi/bov/bov.html

Addison-Wesley
http://www.germany.eu.net/shop/AW/

Aging Server
http://www.hookup.net/mall/aging/
agesit59.html

AGsDB
http://keck.tamu.edu/cgi/agsdb/
agsdbserver.html

Alces
http://alces.med.umn.edu/start.html

ALSCRIPT and AMPS manuals
http://geoff.biop.ox.ac.uk/manuals.html

American Society of Plant Physiologists
(ASPP)
http://www.aspp.org/

American Type Culture Collection (ATCC)
http://merlot.welch.jhu.edu/11/Database-
local/cultures/atcc

Arabidopsis cDNA Sequence Analysis
Project
http://lenti.med.umn.edu/arabidopsis/
arab_top_page.html

Arabidopsis thaliana Data Base
http://weeds.mgh.harvard.edu/

Argonne National Lab.
http://www.anl.gov/

Artificial Life & Complex Systems
http://www.seas.upenn.edu/~ale/cplxsys.html

Artificial Life Online
http://alife.santafe.edu/

Auburn College of Veterinary Medicine
http://www.vetmed.auburn.edu/

Australian Herpetological Directory
http://www.jcu.edu.au/dept/Zoology/herp/
herp2.html

Australian National Botanic Gardens
http://155.187.10.12/index.html

Australian National Univ.
http://life.anu.edu.au/

Avery Lab Caenorhabditis elegans Server
http://eatworms.swmed.edu/

Bacterial Species Nomenclature
http://www.ftpt.br/cgi-bin/bdtnet/bacterianame

Barton Group
http://geoff.biop.ox.ac.uk/

Base de Dados Tropical
http://www.ftpt.br/

Baylor College of Medicine
http://www.bcm.tmc.edu/

Baylor Molecular Biology Information
Resource
http://mbcr.bcm.tmc.edu:8080/home.html

Beekeeping
http://alfred1.u.washington.edu:8080/~jlks/
bee.html

Berkeley Molecular and Cell Biology
http://mendel.berkeley.edu/homepage.html

Berkeley Plant Biology
http://mendel.berkeley.edu/pb/
pbhomepage.html

Bermuda Biological Station for Research
http://www.bbsr.edu/

BEST North America
http://best.gdb.org/best.html

Bio-wURLd
http://www.ebi.ac.uk/htbin/bwurld.pl

BioBanco
http://fiss.org.ec/

Biobox
http://shamrock.csc.fi/brochure.html

BioCatalog
http://www.ebi.ac.uk/biocat/biocat.html

BioCatalogue
http://www.genethon.fr/exterieur/
bio_catal_resume.html

Biochemical Metabolism Pathway
Database
http://www.mcs.anl.gov/home/towell/
metabhome.html

Biocomputing and Modeling
http://www-bio.unizh.ch/xmosaic.home

Biocomputing Survival Guide
http://www.ch.embnet.org/jam/jam.html

BioData
http://www.biodata.com/

Biodiversity and Biological Collections
Web Server
http://muse.bio.cornell.edu/

Biodiversity and Ecosystems Network
(BENE)
http://straylight.tamu.edu/bene/bene.html

Biodiversity around the World
http://www.igc.apc.org/igc/ian.html

Biodiversity at Australia National Univ.
http://life.anu.edu.au/biodiversity.html

Biodiversity Consortium
http://www.bio.bris.ac.uk/sbsbd.htm

Bioinformatics at Australia National Univ.
http://life.anu.edu.au/

Bioline
http://www.ftpt.br/cgi-bin/bioline/bioline

Bioline Publications
http://golgi.harvard.edu/biopages/
all.html#Brazil

Biological Databases Online
http://www.abc.hu/bio/part2.html

Biological Evolution
http://perpmc1.vub.ac.be/BIOEVOL.html

Biological Journals
http://golgi.harvard.edu/journals.html

Biological Molecules
http://golgi.harvard.edu/sequences.html

Biological Resources
http://biomaster.uio.no/biological.html

Biological Software and Data FTP Archives
http://www.gdb.org/Dan/softsearch/
softsearch.html

Biologist's Control Panel
http://gc.bcm.tmc.edu:8088/bio/
bio_home.html

Biology Indexes
http://gulib.lausun.georgetown.edu/blommer/
biology/

Biology WWW Sites
http://calvin.stemnet.nf.ca/subjects/
biology.html

BioMedNet
http://www.cursci.co.uk/BioMedNet/
biomed.html

BioMolecular Engineering Research Ctr.
http://bmerc-www.bu.edu/

Biomolecules Virtual Library
http://golgi.harvard.edu/sequences.html

BIONET Software Archives
http://www.ch.embnet.org/bio-www/info.html

BiOS - The Biomedical Optics Society
http://www.spie.org/web/working_groups/
biomedical_optics/bios_desc.html

BIOSCAN Sequence Similarity Search
http://www.cs.unc.edu/bioscan/bioscan.html

BIOSCI/bionet Electronic Newsgroup
Network for Biology
http://www.bio.net/

BioSciences (en Espaniol)
http://fiss.org.ec/BioBanco/BioCuentas/
BioSciences.html

Biosequence comparison
http://twod.med.harvard.edu/seqanal/

BioSpace Biotechnology Center
http://www.biospace.com/

Biotechnology Ctr. of Oslo, Norway
http://biomaster.uio.no/

Biotechnology Information Ctr.
http://www.inform.umd.edu/EdRes/Topic/
AgrEnv/Biotech

Biotechnology Lab, Univ. of British
Columbia
http://bc-education.botany.ubc.ca/
biotech_lab/biotech.htm

Biotechnology Resources
http://biotech.chem.indiana.edu/

BioViz
http://bioviz.biol.trinity.edu/

Birding on the Web
http://
compstat.wharton.upenn.edu:8001?~siler/
birding.html

BITMed
http://bitmed.ucsd.edu/

BLITZ protein database searches
http://www.embl-heidelberg.de/searches/
blitz.html

BLOCKS Server
http://www.blocks.fhcrc.org/

Boston College
http://darkstar.bc.edu/

Boston College Bio-Inorganic Chemistry
Server
http://chemserv.bc.edu/Bioinorganic/
BioInorganic.html

Boston Univ. Biophysics
http://med-biophd.bu.edu/

Boston Univ. School of Public Health
http://www-busph.bu.edu/

Boston University
http://bio.bu.edu/

Brain Mapping Database Conference
http://biad38.uthscsa.edu/brainmap/
brainmap94.html

BRASS
http://mbisg2.sbc.man.ac.uk/brassp.html

Breast Cancer Information Clearinghouse
http://nysernet.org/bcic/

Brigham and Women's Hospital
http://golgi.harvard.edu/biopages/
all.html#HMS

Brock U. Biology Department
http://aqueous.labs.brocku.ca/

Brookhaven National Lab.
http://suntid.bnl.gov:8080/bnl.html

Brown University
http://biomedcs.biomed.brown.edu/

Caenorhabditis elegans Data Base
http://moulon.inra.fr/acedb/acedb.html

Caenorhabditis elegans WWW Server at
UTSW
http://eatworms.swmed.edu/

California Academy of Sciences Museum
http://www.calacademy.org/

Caltech Molecular Neuroscience
http://www.cns.caltech.edu/molecula/

Cambridge Dept.of Biochemistry
http://www.bio.cam.ac.uk/

Cambridge Scientific
http://www.camsci.com/

Canadian Genome & Analysis Technology
Bioinformatics
http://cgat.bch.umontreal.ca

Canadian Medical Research Council
http://hpb1.hwc.ca:8100/

CancerNet
http://biomed.nus.sg/Cancer/welcome.html

Candida Biology
http://alces.med.umn.edu/Candida.html

CAOS
http://www.caos.kun.nl/

Carleton Biology/Ecology Jrnl.
http://journal.biology.carleton.ca/

Carthew Drosophila Lab
http://flies3.bio.pitt.edu/

Catalogue of Molecular Biology Programs
http://www.genethon.fr/exterieur/
bio_catal_resume.html

CEPH-Genethon Human Genome Physical
Map
http://gc.bcm.tmc.edu:8088/bio/
ceph_genethon_interface.html

CGSC: E.coli Genetic Stock Ctr.
http://cgsc.biology.yale.edu/top.html

Cold Spring Harbor Lab
http://www.cshl.org

Collaborative BioMolecular Tools
http://www.dl.ac.uk/CBMT/HOME.html

Collaborative Clickable Biology
http://s-crim1.dl.ac.uk:8000/HOME.html

Colorado State Univ. Entomology
http://www.colostate.edu/Depts/Entomology/
ent.html

Colorado Univ. Institute for Behavioral
Genetics
http://ibgwww.colorado.edu/

Columbia Univ. Biochemistry and
Molecular Biophysics
http://cuhhca.hhmi.columbia.edu/

Columbia-Presbyterian Medical Ctr.
http://www.cpmc.columbia.edu/

Computational Biochemistry Research
Group
http://cbrg.inf.ethz.ch/

Cooperative Human Linkage Ctr.
http://www.chlc.org/

Cornell Cooperative Extension
http://empire.cce.cornell.edu/

CSUBIOWEB
http://arnica.csustan.edu/

CSUBIOWEB - Biotechnology
http://arnica.csustan.edu/biotech.html

CSUBIOWEB - Cell Biology
http://arnica.csustan.edu/ce.html

CSUBIOWEB - Microbiology
http://arnica.csustan.edu/mi.html

CTI Centre for Biology
http://www.liv.ac.uk/ctibiol.html

Dana-Farber Cancer Institute
http://golgi.harvard.edu/biopages/
all.html#HMS

Daniel Hartl Lab
http://golgi.harvard.edu/hartl/

DELTA Project - Biological Sciences
http://www.calpoly.edu/delta.html

Dendrome, A Genome Database for Forest
Trees
http://s27w007.pswfs.gov/

DENTalTRAUMA
http://www.unige.ch/smd/orthotr.html

Developmental Biology (Biosciences)
Virtual Library
http://golgi.harvard.edu/biopages/
develop.html

Developmental Studies Hybridoma Bank
http://www.gdb.org/Dan/DSHB/dshb.intro.html

Dialog Information Services, Inc
http://www.dialog.com/

Dinosaur Exhibit
http://www.hcc.hawaii.edu/dinos/dinos.1.html

Division of Refuges
http://bluegoose.arw.r9.fws.gov/

Dog Genome Project
http://mendel.berkeley.edu/dog.html

Domestic Animal Endocrinology
http://www.ag.auburn.edu/dae/dae.html

Drosophila Server
http://flies3.bio.pitt.edu/

Duke Univ. Center for In Vivo Microscopy
http://wwwcivm.mc.duke.edu

Duke Univ. Medical Ctr.
http://www.mc.duke.edu/

Duke Univ. Medical Informatics
http://dmi-www.mc.duke.edu/

E. coli Genetic Stock Ctr.
http://cgsc.biology.yale.edu/top.html

Eccles Institute of Human Genetics
http://www-genetics.med.utah.edu/

EcoNet
http://www.igc.apc.org/

EcoWeb
http://ecosys.drdr.virginia.edu/EcoWeb.html

Edinburgh Univ. Chemical Engineering
Dept.
http://www.chemeng.ed.ac.uk/

Educational Technology Branch
http://wwwetb.nlm.nih.gov/

EGCG manuals
http://biomaster.uio.no/gcgman/
egcgmain.html

Eli Lilly and Company
http://www.lilly.com/

EMBL Data Library & European
Biocomputing Institute
http://www.embl-heidelberg.de/

EMBL Nucleotide Sequence Database
http://www.ebi.ac.uk/ebi_docs/embl_db/
embl_db.html

EMF-Link
http://archive.xrt.upenn.edu:1000/emf/top/
emf-link.html

Encyclopedia Radiologica
http://www.xray.hmc.psu.edu/
EncyclopediaRadiologica.html

EnviroLink Network
http://envirolink.org/about.html

Environmental Information Services
http://www.esdim.noaa.gov/

Environmental Protection Agency
http://www.epa.gov/

Environmental Resources Information
Network
http://kaos.erin.gov.au/erin.html

EnviroWeb
http://envirolink.org/

Enzyme Nomenclature Database
http://www.gdb.org/Dan/proteins/ec-
enzyme.html

European Biocomputing Institute
http://www.ebi.ac.uk/

European Bioinformatics Institute
http://www.embl-heidelberg.de/ebi_home.html

European Molecular Biology Network
http://beta.embnet.unibas.ch/embnet/info.html

European Synchrotron Radiation Facility
http://fox.esrf.fr:3600/

ExPASy Molecular Biology Server
http://expasy.hcuge.ch/

Experimental Searchable Index for the
WWW VL Biosciences
http://golgi.harvard.edu/htbin/biopages

EXtension TOXicology NETwork
http://sulaco.oes.orst.edu:70/1/ext/extoxnet

Finnish Forest Research Institute
http://www.metla.fi/

FINS
http://www.actwin.com/fish/index.html

FireNet - Landscape Fire Information
http://life.anu.edu.au/firenet/firenet.html

Fish, and other Aquatic Animals
http://www.actwin.com/WWWVL-Fish.html

Flea News!
http://www.public.iastate.edu/~entomology/
FleaNews/AboutFleaNews.html

Florida Agricultural Information
http://hammock.ifas.ufl.edu/

Forestry College
http://www.environment.sfasu.edu:1080/

Fred Hutchinson Cancer Research Ctr.
http://www.fhcrc.org/

French Genomics Server, Moulon
http://moulon.inra.fr/

Frog Dissection Server
http://george.lbl.gov/ITG.hm.pg.docs/dissect/
info.html

FROGGY Page
http://www.cs.yale.edu/HTML/YALE/CS/
HyPlans/loosemore-sandra/froggy.html

Fujita Health Univ.
http://pathy.fujita-hu.ac.jp/pathy.html

Fungal Genetics Stock Ctr.
http://kufacts.cc.ukans.edu/cwis/units/fgsc/
main.html

G protein-Coupled Receptor Database
(GCRDb)
http://receptor.mgh.harvard.edu/
GCRDBHOME.html

G.M. Church Lab
http://twod.med.harvard.edu/

Ganglion - Medical Ctr.
http://ganglion.anes.med.umich.edu/

GasNet Anaesthesiology Server
http://gasnet.med.nyu.edu/HomePage.html

GENETHON - Human Genome Centre
http://www.genethon.fr/genethon_en.html

Genetics at Univ. Naples, Italy
http://biol.dgbm.unina.it:8080/

Genetics Biopages
http://golgi.harvard.edu/biopages/
genetics.html

GenoBase Server
http://specter.dcrt.nih.gov:8004/

Genome Machine
http://www.pathology.washington.edu/
GDB_select_chromosome.html

Genome Therapeutics Corporation
http://www.cric.com/

GenomeNet
http://www.genome.ad.jp/

Genosys Biotechnologies, Inc.
http://www.genosys.com/

Geographic Information Systems Lab.
http://ice.gis.uiuc.edu/

Georgia Tech Medical Informatics
http://www.cc.gatech.edu/gvu/
medical_informatics/
medinfo_home_page.html

Globewide Network Academy
http://uu-gna.mit.edu:8001/uu-gna/

Globin gene server
http://globin.cse.psu.edu/

Glucoamylase
http://www.public.iastate.edu/~pedro/glase/
glase.html

Good Medicine Magazine
http://none.coolware.com/health/good_med/
ThisIssue.html

Gordon Conference Information
http://hackberry.chem.niu.edu:70/1/
ConferenceListings/GordonConferences

Guide to Public Health
http://128.196.106.42/ph-hp.html

GUIs in Bioinformatics Workshop
http://nimsn41.nimr.mrc.ac.uk/mathbio/t-
flores/GUI-Bioinform/meeting.html

Habitat Ecology
http://biome.bio.ns.ca/

Harvard Biochemistry, Molecular Biology,
and Biophysics
http://golgi.harvard.edu/biopages/

Harvard Bioinformatics
http://golgi.harvard.edu/gilbert-bi.html

Harvard Biolabs
http://golgi.harvard.edu/biopages/all.html

Harvard Biological Labs.
http://golgi.harvard.edu/homepage.genome

Harvard Biostatistics
http://biosun1.harvard.edu/

Harvard College of Pharmacy
http://golgi.harvard.edu/biopages/
kerouac.pharm.uky.edu/Default.html

Harvard Ctr. for Imaging and Pharmaceutical Research
http://cipr-diva.mgh.harvard.edu/

Harvard Dept. of Radiology
http://count51.med.harvard.edu/BWH/
BWHRad.html

Harvard Evolution
http://golgi.harvard.edu/biopages/
evolution.html

Harvard Medical Ctr.
http://golgi.harvard.edu/www-
med.stanford.edu/MedCenter/welcome.html

Harvard Microbiology & Virology
http://golgi.harvard.edu/biopages/micro.html

Harvard Neurobiology
http://golgi.harvard.edu/biopages/neuro.html

Harvard Plant Biology
http://golgi.harvard.edu/biopages/botany.html

Hawkes Nest
http://www.ucalgary.ca/~rhawkes/

HBPLUS - Hydrogen Bond Calculator
http://128.40.46.10/pub/hbplus/home.html

Health & Medicine
http://nearnet.gnn.com/wic/med.toc.html

Health Resources
http://alpha.acast.nova.edu/medicine.html

HealthNet
http://debra.dgbt.doc.ca/~mike/home.html

Herpetology Resources
http://xtal200.harvard.edu:8000/herp/

Historical Ctr. for the Health Sciences
http://http2.sils.umich.edu/HCHS/

History of Medicine Exhibits
http://www.nlm.nih.gov/hmd.dir/hmd.html

History of Science, Technology and
Medicine
http://coombs.anu.edu/SpecialProj/ASAP/
WWWVL-HSTM.html

HIV/AIDS information
http://vector.casti.com/QRD/.html/AIDS.html

Hopkins Bio-Informatics Home Page
http://www.gdb.org/hopkins.html

Human Genome Ctr. at LBL
http://www-hgc.lbl.gov/GenomeHome.html

Human Genome Ctr. at the Univ. of
Michigan
http://mendel.hgp.med.umich.edu/Home.html

Human Genome Map Search
http://www.cis.upenn.edu/~khart/form1.html

Human Genome Mapping Project
http://www.hgmp.mrc.ac.uk/

Human Genome Project Resources and
Meetings
http://gdbwww.gdb.org/gdbdoc/
genomic_links.html

Human Life
http://www.cen.uiuc.edu/~jj9544/4.html

ICGEB
http://base.icgeb.trieste.it/

Idaho State Univ. College of Pharmacy
http://pharmacy.isu.edu/welcome.html

IEHS Lab. of Molecular Biophysics
http://epr0.niehs.nih.gov/

Illinois Natural History Survey
http://www.inhs.uiuc.edu:70/

Image Processing and Analysis Group
http://noodle.med.yale.edu/

Information Ctr. for the Environment
http://ice.ucdavis.edu/

Insect Collection
http://iris.biosci.ohio-state.edu/inscoll.html

Institut fuer Molekulare Biotechnologie
http://www.imb-jena.de/

Institut fuer Pharmazeutische Technologie
http://www.tu-bs.de/pharmtech/pht.html

Institute for Health Informatics
http://www.ihi.aber.ac.uk/index.html

Institute of Biodiversity
http://www.inbio.ac.cr/

Integrated Botanical Information System
http://155.187.10.12/ibis/ibis-home.html

Integrated Genome Database
http://moulon.inra.fr:8001/acedb/igd.html

Interactive Frog Dissection
http://curry.edschool.virginia.edu/~insttech/
frog/

Internet/Bitnet Health Science Resources
http://kufacts.cc.ukans.edu/cwis/units/
medcntr/menu.html

Intl. Centre for Genetic Engineering and
Biotechnology
http://www.icgeb.trieste.it/

Intl. Institute of Genetics and Biophysics
http://sun01.iigb.na.cnr.it/

Intl. Organisation of Palaeobotany
http://sunrae.uel.ac.uk/palaeo/index.html

Intl. Organization for Plant Information
http://life.anu.edu.au/biodiversity/iopi/iopi.html

Introduction to ACEDB
http://www.caos.kun.nl/genomics/ACeDB.tut/
TOC.html

Iowa Entomology Server
http://www.public.iastate.edu/~entomology/

Iowa State College of Veterinary Medicine
http://www.iastate.edu/colleges/vetmed/
index.html

Jackson Lab.
http://www.jax.org/

Japan Animal Genome Database
http://ws4.niai.affrc.go.jp/jgbase2.html

Japanese Dairy Cattle Improvement
Program
http://ws4.niai.affrc.go.jp/dairy/dairy.html

JASON Project
http://seawifs.gsfc.nasa.gov/JASON/
JASON.html

Joel's Hierarchical Subject Index
http://www.cen.uiuc.edu/~jj9544/index.html

Johns Hopkins Univ. Bioinformatics
http://www.gdb.org/hopkins.html

Journal of Biomedical Optics
http://www.spie.org/web/journals/
webbiomed.html

La Jolla Cancer Research Foundation
http://192.231.106.66/

Lab. for Biological Informatics and
Theoretical Medicine
http://bitmed.ucsd.edu/

Landscape Ecology & Biogeography
http://life.anu.edu.au/landscape_ecology/
landscape.html

LANL Medical Data Analysis Projects
http://www.c3.lanl.gov/cic3/projects/Medical/main.html

Larg*net
http://johns.largnet.uwo.ca/

Lateiner Dataspace
http://www.dataspace.com/

Lawrence Berkeley Lab.
http://www.lbl.gov/LBL.html

Leeds Dept. of Biochemistry and Molecular Biology
http://gps.leeds.ac.uk/bmb.html

Life Science Computing
http://ftp.cognet.ucla.edu/

LLNL Biology and Biotechnology Research Program
http://www-bio.llnl.gov/bbrp/bbrp.homepage.html

Los Alamos National Lab.
http://www.lanl.gov/welcome.html

Lynn Cooley Lab
http://info.med.yale.edu/cooley/index.html

Macquarie Univ.
http://www.bio.mq.edu.au/

Magnetic Resonance Imaging Group
http://www-mri.uta.edu/

Magnetic Resonance Technology for Basic Biological Research
http://bmrl.med.uiuc.edu:8080/

Maize Genome Project
http://teosinte.agron.missouri.edu/top.html

Major Histocompatibility Complex page
http://histo.cryst.bbk.ac.uk/

Manatee Information
http://www.satelnet.org/manatee/

Marine Biological Lab.
http://www.mbl.edu/

Markus Meister Lab
http://rhino.harvard.edu/

Mass Extinction Simulation
http://www.lassp.cornell.edu/newmme/extinction.html

Massachusetts General Hospital
http://golgi.harvard.edu/biopages/all.html#HMS

Master Gardener Information
http://leviathan.tamu.edu:70/1s/mg

Mathematical Biology Lab
http://www.ncifcrf.gov:2001/

Mayo Foundation Biomedical Imaging Resource
http://autobahn.mayo.edu/BIR_Welcome.html

McNally Lab at Washington University
http://tyrone.wustl.edu/~keith/intro.html

Meat Animal Research Ctr.
http://sol.marc.usda.gov/

Mechanistic Biology and Biotechnology Ctr.
http://www.anl.gov/CMB/cmb_welcome-revs.html

Medical Physics
http://info.biomed.abdn.ac.uk/

MedLink
http://www.ls.se/medlink/

MedSearch America
http://www.medsearch.com:9001/

MEERC - Multiscale Experimental Ecosystem Research Ctr.
http://kabir.umd.edu/Welcome.html

Mendelian Inheritance in Man
http://gdbwww.gdb.org/omimdoc/omimtop.html

Metabolic Pathways Charts
http://www.mcs.anl.gov/home/towell/metabhome.html

Michigan State Entomology
http://esalsun10.ent.msu.edu/dept/main.html

Midwifery
http://www.csv.warwick.ac.uk:8000/midwifery.html

MILLIPORE Corporation
http://www.millipore.com/

Millipore On-line Catalog
http://www.gdb.org/Dan/catal/milli-intro.html

Miscellaneous Biomedical Information Archives
http://www.nlm.nih.gov/current_news.dir/biomed.html

Mississippi State Univ. College of Veterinary Medicine
http://pegasus.cvm.msstate.edu/

Missouri Botanical Garden
http://straylight.tamu.edu/MoBot/
welcome.html

MIT Ctr. for Biological and Computational
Learning
http://www.ai.mit.edu/projects/cbcl/web-
homepage/web-homepage.html

MIT Ctr. for Genome Research at the
Whitehead Institute
http://www-genome.wi.mit.edu/

Molecular Biophysics Lab
http://biop.ox.ac.uk/

Molecular Simulations
http://www.msi.com/

Molecular Virology
http://www.bocklabs.wisc.edu/

Molybdoenzyme Research Lab
http://www.nick.med.usf.edu/

Monash Medical Informatics
http://adrian.med.monash.edu.au/

Mouse Genome Database
http://www.informatics.jax.org/mgd.html

Mouse Locus Catalog
http://www.gdb.org/Dan/mouse/mlc.html

MultiMedia Medical Biochemistry Server
http://ubu.hahnemann.edu/

Multimedia Medical Textbooks
http://indy.radiology.uiowa.edu/
MultimediaTextbooks.html

Museum of Paleontology, Berkeley
http://ucmp1.berkeley.edu/

MycDB
http://kiev.physchem.kth.se/MycDB.html

Mycoplasma capricolum Genome Project
http://uranus.nchgr.nih.gov/myc.html

Nagoshi Lab
http://fly2.biology.uiowa.edu/

Nagoya Univ. School of Medicine
http://www.med.nagoya-u.ac.jp/

NASA Ames Biocomputation Ctr.
http://biocomp.arc.nasa.gov/

National Cancer Ctr.
http://www.ncc.go.jp/

National Ctr. for Biotechnology Information

http://www.ncbi.nlm.nih.gov/

National Ctr. for Genome Resources
http://www.ncgr.org/

National Environmental Information
Service
http://www.cais.com/tne/neis/default.html

National Institute for Basic Biology
http://nibb1.nibb.ac.jp/

National Institute of Animal Industry
http://ws4.niai.affrc.go.jp/niai/NIAI.html

National Institute of Biodiversity
http://www.inbio.ac.cr/

National Institute of Environmental
Health Sciences
http://www.niehs.nih.gov/Home.html

National Institute of Standards and
Technology
http://www.nist.gov/

National Institutes of Health
http://www.nih.gov/

National Integrated Pest Mgmt. Information System
http://ipm_www.ncsu.edu/

National Library of Medicine (NLM)
http://www.nlm.nih.gov/

National Marine Fisheries Service
http://kingfish.ssp.nmfs.gov/home-page.html

National Science Foundation
http://www.nsf.gov/

National Toxicology Program
http://www.niehs.nih.gov/ntp/ntp.html

National Univ. of Singapore Biocomputing
http://biomed.nus.sg/

Natural History Museum
http://www.nhm.ac.uk/

NCSA Digital Gallery - Science
http://www.ncsa.uiuc.edu/SDG/DigitalGallery/
DG_science_theater.html

NCSU College of Veterinary Medicine
http://www2.ncsu.edu/ncsu/cvm/
cvmhome.html

NCSU Entomology
http://ent2.ent.ncsu.edu/

NetBiochem
http://www.hahnemann.edu/Heme-Iron/
NetWelcome.html

NetVet — Veterinary Medicine
http://netvet.wustl.edu/

Neural Networks
http://www.cs.utexas.edu/~sirosh/nn.html

Neuro-Implant Program
http://he1.uns.tju.edu/~doctorb/bppp.html

Neuroscience Internet Resource Guide
http://http2.sils.umich.edu/Public/nirg/
nirg1.html

NeuroWeb
http://salk.edu/

New England Biolabs
http://www.neb.com/

NIH Biomedical Resources
http://www.nlm.nih.gov/current_news.dir/
biomed.html

NIH GenoBase Server
http://specter.dcrt.nih.gov:8004/

NIH Guide to Grants and Contracts
http://www.med.nyu.edu/nih-guide.html

NIH Health and Clinical Topics
http://www.nih.gov/health

NIH Molecular Biology Databases
http://www.nih.gov/molbio

NIH Molecular Modeling
http://www.nih.gov/molecular_modeling/
mmhome.html

Northwest Fisheries Science Ctr.
http://listeria.nwfsc.noaa.gov/

Nottingham Arabidopsis Stock Centre
http://nasc.nott.ac.uk/

Nova Scotia Agricultural College
http://www.nsac.ns.ca/

Nova-Links
http://alpha.acast.nova.edu/start.html

NRL-3D
http://www.gdb.org/Dan/proteins/nrl3d.html

NYU Anesthesiology
http://gasnet.med.nyu.edu/index.html

NYU Biochemistry
http://www.med.nyu.edu/Biochem/
HomePage.html

NYU Medical Ctr.
http://www.med.nyu.edu/HomePage.html

NYU Neurological Surgery
http://www.med.nyu.edu/NeuroSurgery/
HomePage.html

Oak Ridge National Labs., Environmental
Science
http://jupiter.esd.ornl.gov/

Ohio State College of Biological Sciences
http://hagar.biosci.ohio-state.edu/

Oklahoma State Univ. College of Veterinary Medicine
http://www.cvm.okstate.edu/

Oncogene Database
http://mbcr.bcm.tmc.edu:8080/oncogene.html

OncoLink
http://cancer.med.upenn.edu/

Organelle Genome Megasequencing
Project
http://megasun.bch.umontreal.ca/
welcome.html

OWL non-redundant protein sequence
database
http://www.gdb.org/Dan/proteins/owl.html

Oxford Univ. Centre for Molecular
Sciences
http://nmra.ocms.ox.ac.uk/

Oxford Univ. Lab. of Molecular Biology
http://biop.ox.ac.uk/

Oxford Univ. Plant Sciences
http://ifs.plants.ox.ac.uk/

P450 Containing Systems
http://www.icgeb.trieste.it/p450/

Pacific Northwest Lab. Medical Technology and Systems
http://www.emsl.pnl.gov:2080/docs/cie/
MTS.html

Pacific Rim Biodiversity Catalog
http://ucmp1.berkeley.edu/pacrim.html

Palaeontology
http://nearnet.gnn.com/wic/palaeon.toc.html

Palo Alto Medical Foundation
http://www.service.com/PAMF/home.html

Palynology & palaeoclimatology
http://life.anu.edu.au/landscape_ecology/
pollen.html

Pathology WWW Server
http://www.pathology.washington.edu/

Pathy for medical information
http://www.med.nagoya-u.ac.jp/pathy/
pathy.html

PCR Guide
http://bioinformatics.weizmann.ac.il:70/1s/
bioguide

Periodic Table of the Elements
http://143.167.43.25/chemistry/web-elements/
periodic-table.html

Periodical references to journals in the area
of molecular biology
http://nxoc01.cern.ch:8001/net.bio.net/
biology-journal-contents?

Pharmacy Server
http://157.142.72.77/

PHYLIP Documentation
http://www2.pasteur.fr/~tekaia/phylip.doc.html

Phylogenetic Tree Construction
http://www.mcs.anl.gov/summaries/
overbeek93/overbeek93.html

Physical Map of the Human Genome
http://ceph-genethon-map.genethon.fr/ceph-
genethon-map.html

Plant Disease Handbook
http://cygnus.tamu.edu/Texlab/tpdh.html

Plant Genome
http://probe.nalusda.gov:8000/plant/
index.html

Plant Genome WWW Server
http://probe.nalusda.gov:8000/index.html

Plant Pathology
http://resc9.res.bbsrc.ac.uk/plantpath/molbio/

Plant Pathology Dept. at Rothamsted
Experimental Station
http://resc9.res.bbsrc.ac.uk/plantpath/

Poisons Information Database
http://biomed.nus.sg/PID/PID.html

Polio and Post-Polio Resources
http://www.eskimo.com/~dempt/polio.html

Pollen Data
http://www.unlv.edu/CCHD/pollen/

Polyfiltronics - Microplate News
http://www.polyfiltronics.com/

Portable Dictionary of the Mouse Genome
http://mickey.utmem.edu/front.html

Positron Emission Tomography
http://pss023.psi.ch/

Primer on Molecular Genetics
http://www.gdb.org/Dan/DOE/intro.html

Principia Cybernetica
http://pespmc1.vub.ac.be/

Principles of Protein Structure
http://seqnet.dl.ac.uk:8000/vsns-pps/

PRODOM Protein Domain Server
http://www.sanger.ac.uk/~esr/prodom.html

Programs for Comparison and Recognition of Protein Structures
http://www-lmmb.ncifcrf.gov/~nicka/info.html

PROSITE protein pattern searches
http://www.embl-heidelberg.de/searches/
prosite.html

Protein Identification Resource
http://www.gdb.org/Dan/proteins/pir.html

Protein Science (peer-reviewed journal)
and the Proteins Society
http://www.prosci.uci.edu/

Protein Structure Group
http://www.yorvic.york.ac.uk/

Protist Image and Data Collection
http://megasun.bch.umontreal.ca/protists/
protists.html

Purdue Univ. Indianapolis Biology
http://www.biology.iupui.edu/

Queen's Univ.
http://biology.queensu.ca/

Quest 2D Protein Database
http://siva.cshl.org/index.html

Radiology Imaging Ctr.
http://visual-ra.swmed.edu/

Radiology Webserver
http://www.rad.washington.edu/

REBASE - restriction enzymes
http://nxoc01.cern.ch:8001/bio.vu.nl:9000/
rebase

Recherche en Sciences de la Vie et de la
Santé
http://www.rsvs.ulaval.ca/

Reference Library DataBase
http://gea.lif.icnet.uk/

Representation Models in Molecular Graphics
http://scsg9.unige.ch/eng/toc.html

Rethinking AIDS
http://enuxsa.eas.asu.edu/~jvagner/

Rice Univ. Biochemistry and Cell Biology
http://helix.rice.edu/Bioch_info/

Rice Univ. Institute of Biosciences and Bioengineering
http://helix.rice.edu/Institute/

Rothamsted Experimental Station
http://resc9.res.bbsrc.ac.uk/

Royal (Dick) School of Veterinary Studies
http://www.vet.ed.ac.uk/

Royal Botanic Gardens
http://www.rbgkew.org.uk/

Royal Free Hospital of Medicine
http://www.rfhsm.ac.uk/

Royal Postgraduate Medical School
http://mpcc3.rpms.ac.uk/rpms_home.html

Saccharomyces (Yeast) Genome
http://genome-gopher.stanford.edu/

Salk Institute
http://salk.edu/

San Diego State Computational Biology
http://www.sdsc.edu/1/SDSC/Research/Comp_Bio

Sanger Centre
http://www.sanger.ac.uk/

Sci. Bio.Evolution Home Page
http://www.cqs.washington.edu/~evolution/

Science & Math Resources for Education
http://life.anu.edu.au/education.html

Scripps Research Institute
http://www.scripps.edu/

Selected Topics in General Virology
http://www.bocklabs.wisc.edu/Tutorial.html

SeqAnalRef
http://expasy.hcuge.ch/

SEQNET
http://www.dl.ac.uk/SEQNET/home.html

Sequence Annotation Server
http://dot.imgen.bcm.tmc.edu:9331/seq-annot/home.html

Smoky Mountain Field Station
http://www.ce.utk.edu/smokey.html

Society for Applied Spectroscopy
http://esther.la.asu.edu/sas/

Soil Science Web Server
http://saturn.soils.umn.edu/

South Florida Environmental Reader
http://envirolink.org/florida/

Southeastern Biological Science Ctr.
http://www.nfrcg.gov/

Stanford Medical Media and Information Technologies
summit.stanford.edu/welcome.html

Stanford Univ. Ctr. for Advanced Medical Informatics
http://camis.Stanford.EDU/

Sumeria
http://werple.apana.org.au/sumeria/

Swiss-2DPAGE
http://expasy.hcuge.ch/ch2d/ch2d-top.html

Swiss-3DIMAGE
http://expasy.hcuge.ch/pub/Graphics

SWISS-PROT Protein Sequence Database
http://www.ebi.ac.uk/ebi_docs/swissprot_db/swissprot.html

SwissProt
http://expasy.hcuge.ch/sprot/sprot-top.html

Symposium on Computer Aided Chemistry and Bioinformatics
http://www.caos.kun.nl/symposium/

TALARIA: Clinical Practice Guidelines for Cancer Pain
http://www.stat.washington.edu/

Tasmanian Parks & Wildlife Service
http://www.parks.tas.gov.au/tpws.html

Temple Univ.
http://astro.ocis.temple.edu/~myers

Temple Univ. Dept. of Physiology
http://astro.ocis.temple.edu/~roy/physio.html

Texas A&M Univ. Biology Herbarium
http://straylight.tamu.edu/tamu/biology/biology_herbarium.html

Texas A&M University - Biology Department
http://bio-www.tamu.edu/

Texas Extension Plant Pathologists
http://cygnus.tamu.edu/Texlab/people.html

Theoretical Biophysics Group
http://www.ks.uiuc.edu:1250/

Thomas Jefferson Univ.
http://www.tju.edu/

Timelines and Scales of Measurement List
http://cast0.ast.cam.ac.uk/Xray_www/niel/
scales.html

TraumAID
http://www.cis.upenn.edu/~traumaid/
home.html

Tree Physiology
http://sol.uvic.ca/treephys/

Tulane Medical Ctr.
http://www.mcl.tulane.edu/

Type Specimen and Other Catalogs
http://ucmp1.berkeley.edu/catalogs.html

U.S. Dept. of Health and Human Services
http://www.os.dhhs.gov/

U.S. National Science Foundation
http://stis.nsf.gov/

UC Davis College of Veterinary Medicine
http://vmgopher.ucdavis.edu/

UCLA Anesthesiology
http://hypnos.anes.ucla.edu/index.html

UCLA Biology
http://www.lifesci.ucla.edu/bio/

UCLA Biology Repository
http://lifesci.ucla.edu/repository/biology/

UCLA Chemistry and Biochemistry
http://www.chem.ucla.edu/dept/
Chemistry.html

UCLA Life Sciences
http://lifesci.ucla.edu/

UCSD Chemistry and Biochemistry
http://checfs1.ucsd.edu/

UFL Dept. of Anesthesiology
http://www.anest.ufl.edu/

UIUC School of Life Sciences
http://www.life.uiuc.edu/

UMDS
http://www.umds.ac.uk/

UMDS Medical Image Processing Group
http://nothung.umds.ac.uk/

UMich Genome Ctr.
http://www.hgp.med.umich.edu/Home.html

United States Geological Survey
http://info.er.usgs.gov/network/science/
biology/index.html

Univ. Berlin, Institut fuer Biochemie
http://www.chemie.fu-berlin.de/fb_chemie/ibc/
ibc_ag.html

Univ. of Bonn Medical Ctr.
http://imsdd.meb.uni-bonn.de/

Univ. of Cambridge School of Biological
Sciences
http://www.bio.cam.ac.uk/

Univ. of Colorado, Institute for Behavioral
Genetics
http://ibgwww.colorado.edu/

Univ. of Delaware
http://www.udel.edu/

Univ. of Florida Ctr. for Structural Biology
and Ctr. for Mammalian Genetics
http://ufthm.health.ufl.edu/

Univ of Florida Center for Structural
Biology
http://csbnmr.health.ufl.edu/

Univ. of Florida Microbiology and Cell
Science
http://micro.ifas.ufl.edu/

Univ. of Geneva (ExPASy)
http://expasy.hcuge.ch/

Univ. of Genoa, Ctr. for Biomedical and
Biophysical Technologies
http://citbb.unige.it/

Univ. of Georgia Dept. of Botany
http://dogwood.botany.uga.edu/

Univ. of Huston Gene-Server
http://www.bchs.uh.edu/

Univ. of Illinois College of Medicine
http://www.med.uiuc.edu/

Univ. of Indiana Ctr. for Innovative
Computer Applications
http://www.cica.indiana.edu/projects/Biology/
index.html

Univ. of Iowa
http://indy.radiology.uiowa.edu/

Univ. of Iowa, Radiation and Free Radical Biology
http://everest.radiology.uiowa.edu/~rad/radhome.html

Univ. of Kansas Medical Ctr.
http://kufacts.cc.ukans.edu/cwis/units/medcntr/library.html

Univ. of Minnesota Biomedical Engineering
http://pro.med.umn.edu/bmec/bmec.html

Univ. of Minnesota Medical School
http://lenti.med.umn.edu/

Univ. of Montreal
http://merck.bch.umontreal.ca/homepages/bchnet.html

Univ. of Nijmegen Laboratory for Biomaterials
http://www.kun.nl/biomat

Univ. of Oregon Biology Resources
http://darkwing.uoregon.edu/~tklassen/biohome/bio.html

Univ. of Pennsylvania
http://www.upenn.edu/

Univ. of Pennsylvania Bioengineering
http://www.seas.upenne.edu/be/behome.html

Univ. of Rochester Biophysics
http://www.urmc.rochester.edu/smd/biophys/index.htm

Univ. of Sheffield
http://143.167.43.25/

Univ. of Southampton Biomedical server
http://medstats.soton.ac.uk/

Univ. of Tennessee Biomedical Engineering
http://www.mecca.org/BME/bme-home.html

Univ. of Texas Southwestern Medical Ctr.
http://www.swmed.edu/

Univ. of Texas/Houston Dept. of Pathology
http://hyrax.med.uth.tmc.edu/

Univ. of Texas/Houston School of Public Health
http://utsph.sph.uth.tmc.edu/

Univ. of Vermont
http://www.uvm.edu/

Univ. of Washington Pathology
http://www.pathology.washington.edu/

Univ. of Washington Physiology/Biophysics
http://www.physiol.washington.edu/pbio/homepage.htm

Univ. of Wisconsin Computational Biology
http://www.cs.wisc.edu/~shavlik/uwcompbio.html

Univ. of Zürich Biocomputing and Modeling
http://www-bio.unizh.ch/xmosaic.home

Univ. Salzburg, Molekular Biology
http://www.gen.sbg.ac.at/info/internet/start.html

UPENN Chr22DB
http://www.cis.upenn.edu/~cbil/chr22db/chr22dbhome.html

UPENN Computational Biology and Informatics Lab.
http://www.cis.upenn.edu/~cbil/home.html

UPenn Medical Image Processing Group
http://mipgsun.mipg.upenn.edu/

USGS Biology
http://info.er.usgs.gov/network/science/biology/index.html

Utah State Dept. of Biology
http://www.biology.usu.edu/index.html

Vermont Entomology
http://nut.ento.vt.edu/

Victoria State Emergency Service
http://www.citri.edu.au/~jck/vicses/vicses.html

Victorian (Australia) Institute of Forensic Pathology
http://www.vifp.monash.edu.au/

Virginia Tech/Univ. of Maryland College of Veterinary Medicine
http://www.vetmed.vt.edu/

Virology
http://www.bocklabs.wisc.edu/Welcome.html

Virtual Genome Ctr.
http://alces.med.umn.edu/VGC.html

Virtual School of Natural Sciences
http://uu-gna.mit.edu:8001/uu-gna/schools/vsns/index.html

Viruses
http://life.anu.edu.au/./viruses/virus.html

VISBL Laboratory, University of Chicago
http://http.bsd.uchicago.edu/visbl/

Vision & Robotics Group
http://www.cs.yale.edu/HTML/YALE/VISION/
GroupPR.html

Vrije Universiteit Brussel
http://dinf.vub.ac.be/sciences/dbio/
dbiohome.html

W.J. Freeman Lab
http://sulcus.berkeley.edu/

W.M. Keck Ctr. for Genome Informatics
http://keck.tamu.edu/ibt.html

Wageningen Agricultural Univ.
http://www.wau.nl/welcome.html

Walter Gilbert Lab
http://golgi.harvard.edu/gilbert.html

Warwick Dept. of Nursing
http://www.csv.warwick.ac.uk:8000/
default.html/

Washington U (St. Louis) Biomedical
Engineering
http://ibc.wustl.edu/

Washington Univ.
http://biogopher.wustl.edu/

Washington Univ. Institute for Biomedical
Computing
http://ibc.wustl.edu/

Webb Miller Lab Globin Server
http://globin.cse.psu.edu/

Weizmann Institute Bioinformatics
http://bioinformatics.weizmann.ac.il:70/

Welch Medical Library
http://www.welch.jhu.edu/

West Virginia School of Medicine
http://musom.mu.wvnet.edu/

Whitehead Institute for Biomedical
Research and MIT Ctr. for Genome
Research
http://www-genome.wi.mit.edu/

Whole Internet Catalog
http://nearnet.gnn.com/wic/
newrescat.toc.html

Wildlife & Fisheries Biology Dept.
http://www-wfb.ucdavis.edu/

Wisconsin Regional Primate Ctr. Research
Ctr.
http://www.primate.wisc.edu/

Worcester Foundation for Experimental
Biology
http://sci.wfeb.edu/

World Health Organization (WHO)
http://www.who.ch/

World Wide Web Journal of Biology
http://epress.com/w3jbio/

WWW in Biology
http://www.ch.embnet.org/bio-www/info.html

WWW Virtual Library of Biosciences
http://golgi.harvard.edu/biopages.html

Xenopus laevis page
http://timpwrmac.clh.icnet.uk/
xenopusintro.html

Yale Univ.
http://www.yale.edu/

Yale Univ. Ctr. for Medical Informatics
http://paella.med.yale.edu/

Yale Univ. Ctr. for Theoretical and Applied
Neuroscience
http://www.cs.yale.edu/HTML/YALE/CTAN/
FrontDoor.html

Young Scholars Page
http://davinci.vancouver.wsu.edu/omsi/
OMSIYS.html

Zebrafish Information Server
http://zebra.scarolina.edu/

Zebrafish Server
http://zfish.uoregon.edu/

Zimmer-Faust Lab
http://tbone.biol.scarolina.edu/

Molecular Biology

ALSBYTE Biotech Products
http://www.alsbyte.com/bio/

Australian National University - Molecular Biology
http://life.anu.edu.au/molbio.html

Biochemistry, Biophysics, and Molecular
Biology Virtual Library
http://golgi.harvard.edu/biopages/
biochem.html

BioMolecular Engineering Research Center
http://bmerc-www.bu.edu/

Biomolecular Engineering and Structural Biology
http://www.cryst.bbk.ac.uk/CEC/eupage.html

Cell Mechanics and Cellular Engineering
http://msrbsgi1.mc.duke.edu/~farsh/cv/cellmech.html

European Molecular Biology Laboratory (EMBL)
http://www.embl-heidelberg.de/

Göteborg Univ.
http://www.lundberg.gu.se/mol/mol-top.html

GTF-LAB
http://www.algonet.se/~gtflab/

Hopkins Bio-Informatics Home Page
http://www.gdb.org/hopkins.html

Macromolecular Biology Project at CRS4
http://www.crs4.it/~enzo/group_mbp.html

Mass General Hospital Molecular Biology
http://xanadu.mgh.harvard.edu/DMB_Home_Page.html

Meeting on Interconnection of Molecular Biology Databases
http://www.ai.sri.com/people/pkarp/mimbd.html

Molecular Biology Core Facilities / Dana-Farber Cancer Institute
http://mbcf.dfci.harvard.edu/

Molecular Biology Software Guide
http://www.public.iastate.edu/~pedro/research_tools.html

Molecular Biology Vector Sequence Database
http://biology.queensu.ca/~miseners/vector.html

Molecular Biology WWW Servers
http://www.genome.ad.jp/other_servers/other_servers.html

MWG-Biotech
http://www.mwgdna.com/biotech/

NIH Molecular Modeling
http://www.nih.gov/molecular_modeling/mmhome.html

Standards and definitions for molecular biology software
http://ibc.wustl.edu/standards/

Starting Points for Molecular Biology Scientists
http://www.gen.sbg.ac.at/info/internet/start.html

Univ. of Oregon Institute of Molecular Biology
http://darkwing.uoregon.edu/~jhaack/

Biochemistry

Aberdeen Univ, Biochemistry Graphics Room
http://www.biochem.abdn.ac.uk/

Biochemistry Bits
http://biop.ox.ac.uk/www/biochem.html

Biochemistry Lab. at KAIST
http://biochem.kaist.ac.kr/

Computational Biochemistry Research Group
http://cbrg.inf.ethz.ch/

Molecular Biophysics and Biochemistry
http://bmb.wustl.edu/

Purdue University department of Biochemistry
http://www.biochem.purdue.edu/

Royal Institute of Technology, Sweden
http://kiev.physchem.kth.se/

Synthetic Genetics
http://inetsol.com/syngen/

UCHC Molecular Biology and Biochemistry
http://panda.uchc.edu/~mbb/mbb.html

Univ. of Leeds
http://gps.leeds.ac.uk/bmb.html

Univ. of Toronto Biochemistry
http://bioinfo.med.utoronto.ca/biochemistry.html

Biology Publications Online

Gopher Publications

AIDS
  gopher.cic.net

American Society of Plant Taxonomists
Newsletter
  nmnhgoph.si.edu

Bean Bag: Leguminosae Research Newsletter
  huh.harvard.ed

Biology
  gopher.cic.net

CICNet Electronic Jrnl. Indices
  gopher.cic.net

Discover; The World of Science
  gopher.internet.com:2100

Environment
  gopher.cic.net

Flora Online: Jrnl. for Collections-Oriented
Botanical Research
  huh.harvard.edu

GenTools
  gopher.gdb.org

History of Science Gopher
  gopher.hs.jhu.edu

Library of Congress Electronic Journals
Index
  gopher.cic.net

Medicine
  gopher.cic.net

On the Origin of Species by Means of
Natural Selection
  gopher.hs.jhu.edu

Protein Science
  ftp.uci.edu:1071

Science
  gopher.cic.net

SeqAnalRef
  gopher.gdb.org

Springer Journals: Table of Contents
Service
  morris.lib.udel.edu

TOCSSearch
  gopher.genethon.fr

WWW Publications

Annual Reviews Inc. Index
  http://www.ncifcrf.gov:2001/annRev.html

BINARY: Computing in Microbiology
  http://www.ftpt.br/cgi-bin/bioline/bi/

Biocomputing News
  http://beta.embnet.unibas.ch/basel/bcnews/
  default.html

Bioline Publications
  http://www.ftpt.br/cgi-bin/bioline/bioline

Biology & Medicine
  http://golgi.harvard.edu/biopages.html

Bionic
  http://nearnet.gnn.com/wic/molbio.05.html

Cold Spring Harbor Lab. Press
  http://www.cshl.org/about_cshl_press.html

Complexity Intl.
  http://life.anu.edu.au/ci/ci.html

Conservation Ecology
  http://journal.biology.carleton.ca/Jrnl./
  Overview.html

Drosophila Information Newsletter
  http://gopher.cic.net/11/e-serials/alphabetic/d/
  drosophila

Human Genome Newsletter (U.S. DOE)
  http://gopher.gdb.org/11/Genome/hgnews

More information on electronic journals
  http://journal.biology.carleton.ca/Jrnl./
  background/HotArticles.html

National Animal Genome Research
Program Newsletter
  http://probe.nalusda.gov:8000/animal/
  NAGRPnews/index.html

Technology Review
  http://www.mit.edu:8001/afs/athena/org/t/
  techreview/www/tr.html

The Scientist
  http://ds.internic.net/11/pub/the-scientist

Tree Physiology
  http://sol.uvic.ca/treephys/Tree

World Health Organization Library Digest
  http://gopher.who.ch/11/.hlt/.digest

Chemistry

See also Biology & Biotechnology, Electronics & Electrical
Engineering, Engineering, Energy, Medicine, Physics

Usenet Newsgroups

sci.chem
Newsgroup-based Mailing List: No.
Charter: All topics relating to chemistry.

sci.chem.analytical
Created by: Cato Brede
<catob@kjemi.uio.no>
Call for Votes Date: May 8, 1995
Newsgroup-based Mailing List: No.
Charter (from Call for Votes):
Sci.chem.analytical is an unmoderated
newsgroup for the discussion of organic
and inorganic analytical chemistry. This
newsgroup will provide a place for
professional analytical chemists to meet
and exchange ideas.

sci.chem.electrochem
Created by: nagy@cmt.anl.gov (Zoltan
Nagy)
Call for Votes date: March 9, 1994
Newsgroup-based Mailing List: No.
Charter (from Call for Votes):
The aim of sci.chem.electrochem is to
provide an open discussion forum for the
electrochemistry community on the
internet. This newsgroup would allow
rapid, timely and focussed discussions of
opinions and information that would take
months or years (or not at all) on conventional paper journals.

sci.chem.electrochem.battery
Created by: Russell Bramley
<russellb@dmp.csiro.au>
Call for Votes Date: September 5, 1995
Newsgroup-based Mailing List: No.
Charter (from Call for Votes):
The newsgroup
sci.chem.electrochem.battery will be an
open discussion forum for the interna-
tional battery technology community on
the internet/usenet.

sci.chem.labware
Created by: Rafael Ibanez Puchades
<ibanez@mac.uv.es>
Call for Votes Date: June 27, 1994
Newsgroup-based Mailing List: No.
Charter (from Call for Votes):
The purpose of sci.chem.labware is to
provide an open discussion forum for the
scientific community on the internet on
chemical laboratory equipment. The
newsgroups allow the rapid and easy
discussion of opinions and information
that would not normally be possible.

sci.chem.organomet
Created by: cabku01@mailserv.zdv.uni-
tuebingen.de (Hartwig Kuehbauch)
Call for Votes date: November 1, 1992
Newsgroup-based Mailing List: No.
Charter (from Call for Votes):
The main purpose of this newsgroup
would be to give organometallic chemists
all over the world the chance to communicate with each other about everything related to organometallic chemistry,
postdoc positions.

sci.polymers
Created by: ig25@rz.uni-karlsruhe.de
Call for Votes date: July 26, 1993
Newsgroup-based Mailing List: No.
Charter (from Call for Votes):
This newsgroup should be a forum for dis-
cussing different aspects of polymers,
including, but not limited to chemical,
physical and engineering aspects of pure
polymers, polymer blends and solutions.

sci.techniques.mass-spec (Moderated)
Created by: David Bostwick <david.bostwick@chemistry.gatech.edu>
Call for Votes Date: May 8, 1995
Moderated by: David Bostwick <mass.spec-request@chemistry.gatech.edu>
Submissions go to: mass.spec@gatech.edu
Newsgroup-based Mailing List: No.
Charter (from Call for Votes):
Sci.techniques.mass-spec will be open to discussion of all areas of mass spectrometry. Topics may include, but are not limited to: ionization, mass analysis, mechanisms, hyphenated techniques, and troubleshooting.

Frequently Asked Questions

sci.chem.electrochem
Maintainer: Zoltan Nagy, Argonne National Lab. <NAGY@cmt.anl.gov>
Where on Usenet: sci.chem.electrochem
Where it's archived:
rtfm.mit.edu:pub/usenet/sci/chem/electrochem/
What it's for: The aim of the newsgroup sci.chem.electrochem is to provide an open discussion forum for the electrochemistry community on the Internet (Usenet). This newsgroup allows rapid, timely and focused discussions of opinions and information that would take months or years (or not at all) on conventional paper journals.

Discussion Lists

applspec
applspec@uga
Society for Applied Spectroscopy

chem
chemclub@umslvma
Chemistry Club

chemdisc
chemdisc@umdd
ChemConf Discussion

cheme-l
cheme-l@psuvm
Chemical Engineering List

chemic-l
chemic-l@taunivm
Chemistry in Israel List

chiral-l
chiral-l@dearn
CHIRAL & BI(an)ISOTROPIC microwave materials

cimtlk-l
cimtlk-l@qucdn
Metallurgy Club

hep-lat
hep-lat@jpnyitp
Preprint server for Computational and Lattice Matrices

hiris-l
hiris-l@icineca
High Resolution Infrared Spectroscopy

ics-l
ics-l@umdd
Intl. Chemometrics Society

meddchem
meddchem@waynest1
Macromolecular Engineering, Drug Design

mossba
mossba@usachvm1
Mossbauer Spectroscopy, Software & Forum

polymer
polymer@technion
Polymer - Polymer-related discussions

share-l
share-l@frmop11
Spectroscopic Happenings on Actinides

Chemistry Resources

FTP Resources

AMSOL/MOPAC6
   crocus.medicine.rochester.edu/jones

Brookhaven Protein Data Bank
   irisc2.chm.bnl.gov/

Buckminsterfullerene bibliography
   physics.arizona.edu/afc

Chemistry Manual
cscihp.ecst.csuchico.edu/pub/chemistry

Chemistry Software via IQ UNICAMP,
Brazil
ftp.iqm.unicamp.br/pub/chemistry

Computational Chemistry Archive
infomeister.osc.edu/pub/chemistry

EMILY (Electronic Membrane-Information
Library)
aqua.ccwr.ac.za/pub/emily/emily.html

FUNET Chemistry Archives
nic.funet.fi/pub/sci/chem/

Mopac6.0,CHELPG, Oakland
ouchem.chem.oakland.edu/pub

TeX Archive
ftp.shsu.edu/tex-archive

Gopher Resources

American Chemical Society Gopher
acsinfo.acs.org

American Chemical Society Publications
infx.infor.com:4500

Australian Defence Academy, Chemistry
Listings
ccadfa.cc.adfa.oz.au

Computational Chemistry Newsletter
blanca.tc.cornell.edu/11/Forefronts/
Computational.Chemistry.News

CSC Chemistry Gopher in Finland
gopher.csc.fi

Duke Univ.
gopher.chem.duke.edu

Imperial College
gopher.ch.ic.ac.uk

Journal of Chemical Physics Express
Service
jcp.uchicago.edu/

Macquarie Univ.
gopher.chem.mq.edu.au

Material Safety Data Sheets
atlas.chem.utah.edu/11/MSDS

Michigan State Univ
gopher.cem.msu.edu

North Carolina State Univ., Chemistry
Software
dewey.lib.ncsu.edu

Northern Illinois Univ.
hackberry.chem.niu.edu

Northwestern Univ.
nuinfo.nwu.edu

Regensburg Theoretical Chemistry
rchs1.chemie.uni-regensburg.de/11/

Rice Univ., Chemistry Information
chico.rice.edu

Standard Reference Data Program (SRD)
gopher-server.nist.gov:75

UNICAMP, IQ Resources
gopher.iqm.unicamp.br

Univ. of California Davis
gopher-chem.ucdavis.edu

Univ. of California Santa Barbara
ucsbuxa.ucsb.edu:3001

Univ. of Houston, Analytical Chemistry
Ctr.
oac.hsc.uth.tmc.edu

Univ. of Illinois
gopher.uiuc.edu

Univ. of Missouri-St. Louis
slvaxa.umsl.edu

Washington and Lee Univ.
liberty.uc.wlu.edu:1020

Wisconsin Univ.
gopher.chem.wisc.edu

Yale Univ.
yaleinfo.yale.edu:7000

WWW Resources

Aberdeen Univ.
http://www.abdn.ac.uk/~che210/

Academia Sinica, Inst. of Chemistry
http://www.ch.sinica.edu.tw/

Akron Univ.
http://atlas.chemistry.uakron.edu:8080/

Alchemist's Den - Internet Resources for
Organic Chemist
http://gpu.srv.ualberta.ca/~psgarbi/
psgarbi.html

Americal Chemical Society
http://www.acs.org/

Applied Molecular Science (SOUKAN),
IMS
http://solaris.ims.ac.jp/soukan.html

Aquapal
http://www.i-way.co.uk/~janthony/
aquapal.html

ARSoftware's Online Internet Catalog
http://arsoftware.arclch.com/

ASD
http://pluto.njcc.com/~bpapp/chempoin.html

Auburn Univ.
http://www.duc.auburn.edu/chemistry/
faculty_interests.html

Beckman Instruments, Inc.
http://www.beckman.com/

Beilstein Info. System
http://www.beilstein.com/

BioInorganic Chemistry Server
http://chemserv.bc.edu/Bioinorganic/
BioInorganic.html

Bioinorganic Chemistry Server
http://sbchm1.sunysb.edu/koch/biic.html

Biomolecular and Biosequence Databases
http://golgi.harvard.edu/sequences.html

BioSupplyNet
http://www.biosupplynet.com/bsn/

Biosym Technologies
http://www.biosym.com/

Birkbeck College, Univ. of London
http://www.bbk.ac.uk/

Birmingham Univ. School of Chemistry
http://chemwww.bham.ac.uk/
Chemistry_home.html

Boston College, Merkert Chemistry Center
http://chemserv.bc.edu/

Boston Univ.
http://chem.bu.edu/

Brazilian Chemical Society
http://www.sbq.org.br/

Brigham Young Univ.
http://nmra.byu.edu/welcome.html

Bristol Univ.
http://www.bristol.ac.uk/

Brookhaven National Lab
http://www.chemistry.bnl.gov/chemistry.html

Brown Univ.
http://www.chem.brown.edu/index.html

Bruker Analytische Messtechnik GmbH
http://www.bruker.de/Bruker.html

Budapest Univ. of Technology
http://www.fsz.bme.hu/bme/chemical/

Bullfrog
http://www-leland.stanford.edu/~lefig/
index.html

Butler Univ.
http://www.butler.edu/www/chemistry

California State Univ. Fresno
http://129.8.104.30:8080/

California State Univ. Stanislaus
http://wwwchem.csustan.edu/

Caltech
http://www.caltech.edu/caltech/
Chemistry.html

Calvin College Biochemistry
http://www.calvin.edu/~grayt/
Chemistry_at_Calvin.html

Cambridge Crystallographic Data Centre
http://csdvx2.ccdc.cam.ac.uk/

Cambridge Scientific Computing, Inc.
http://www.camsci.com/

Cambridge Univ.
http://www.ch.cam.ac.uk/

CambridgeSoft Corp.
http://www.camsci.com/

Campinas State Univ.
http://www.iqm.unicamp.br/iqm.html

Canadian Society for Chemistry Organic
Chemistry
http://www.chemistry.mcmaster.ca/csc/orgdiv/
orgdiv.html

Canadian Society for Chemistry Surface
Science Division
http://www.inrs-ener.uquebec.ca/surfsci/
index.html

Carnegie Mellon Univ.
http://www.chem.cmu.edu/

Case Western Reserve Univ.
http://chemwww.cwru.edu/

Center for Molecular Design
http://wucmd.wustl.edu/

Center for Scientific Computing
http://www.csc.fi/lul/csc_chem.html

Chalmers Univ.
http://www.che.chalmers.se/

ChemFinder Searching
http://chemfinder.camsoft.com/

Chemical Abstracts Service
http://info.cas.org/welcome.html

Chemical Education Resources
http://www.cerlabs.com/chemlabs

Chemical Engineering Index
http://www.che.ufl.edu/WWW-CHE/index.html

Chemical Heritage Foundation
http://beckman1.sas.upenn.edu/index.htm

Chemical Industry Inst. of Toxicology
http://www.ciit.org/HOMEP/ciit.html

Chemical Marketing Online
http://www.chemon.com/

Chemical MIME Pro
http://chem.leeds.ac.uk/Project/MIME.html

Chemical On-line Presentations, Talks, and Workshops
http://www.ch.ic.ac.uk/talks/

Chemical Physics Preprint Database
http://www.chem.brown.edu/chem-ph.html

Chemical Reactions, Kinetics, and Dynamics Group
http://www-cst6.lanl.gov/

Chemical Resources in Italy
http://chpc06.ch.unito.it/chempointers_it.html

Chemical Society of Japan
http://www.syp.toppan.co.jp:8082/bcsjstart.html

Chemist's Art Gallery
http://www.csc.fi/lul/chem/graphics.html

Chemistry Associates
http://www.vicnet.net.au/~chemas/education.htm

Chemistry Hypermedia Project
http://www.chem.vt.edu/chem-ed/vt-chem-ed.html

Chemistry Principles
http://www.unm.edu/~dmclaugh/Principles.html

Chemistry Textbook Archive
http://www.umsl.edu/divisions/artscience/chemistry/books/welcome.html

Chemistry UK Internet resource Index from U-NET Limited
http://www.u-net.com/ukchem/

Chemists Address/Phone Book
http://hackberry.chem.niu.edu:70/0/ChemDir/index.html

ChemSearch Corp.
http://www.sonic.net/chemsearch

ChemSource
http://www.chemsource.com/

CNRS, Departement deSciences Chimiques
http://www.cpma.u-psud.fr/

Coatings Industry Alliance
http://www.coatings.org/cia/

Columbia Univ.
http://www.cc.columbia.edu/~chempub/

Computational Chemistry Center
http://derioc1.organik.uni-erlangen.de/

Computational Medicinal Chemistry Group
http://cmcind.far.ruu.nl/

Computer Ctr. Institute for Molecular Science (CCIMS)
http://ccinfo.ims.ac.jp/

Cornell Univ.
http://www.chem.cornell.edu/

Crystallography
http://www.unige.ch/crystal/crystal_index.html

Ctr. for Scientific Computing, Chemistry Server
http://www.csc.fi/lul/csc_chem.html

Czech Academy of Sciences, Inst. of Chemical Process Fundamentals
http://www.icpf.cas.cz/

Danish Chemical Society
http://www.ruc.dk/dis/chem/kemfor/kemfor.htm

Database of Conjugated Polymers
http://www.imc.uni-hannover.de/elektro/database-engl.html

Diamond Growth Research Group
http://www.hw.ac.uk/cheWWW/DIAMOND/group.html

Electrochemical Society, Inc.
http://www.electrochem.org/

Electronic Publishing and Chemical MIME
http://kaupp.chemie.uni-oldenburg.de/~haak/
hyper/hypermoleculs.html

Enke Research Laboratory, Mass Spectrometry
http://enke.unm.edu/

European Chemical Society
http://ecs.tu-bs.de/ecs

Fisher Scientific, Internet Catalog
http://www.fisher1.com/

German Virtual Library - Chemie
http://www.rz.uni-karlsruhe.de/Outerspace/
VirtualLibrary/54.html

Global Instructional Chemistry Forum
http://www.ch.ic.ac.uk/GIC/

Hyperactive Molecules (Chemical MIME in action)
http://www.ch.ic.ac.uk/chemical_mime.html

Imperial College
http://www.ch.ic.ac.uk/

Indiana Univ. Purdue Univ. Indianapolis
http://chem.iupui.edu/homepage.html

Institute of Physical and Theoretical Chemistry
http://pctc.chemie.uni-erlangen.de/

International Society of Heterocyclic Chemistry
http://euch6f.chem.emory.edu/ishc.html

Iowa General Chemistry Network: A FIPSE Project
http://www.public.iastate.edu/~fipse-chem/
homepage.html

Journal of Chemical Education:Software
http://jchemed.chem.wisc.edu/cheds.html

Katholieke Universiteit Leuven, Center for Surface Chemistry and Catalysis
http://134.58.73.250/ifc/interph.htm

Laboratory Equipment Exchange
http://www.magic.mb.ca/~econolab/

Laboratory for Magnetic Resonance
http://hawserv80.tamu.edu/hawhomepage/
Haw1.html

LANL Inorganic Elemental Analysis Group
http://mwanal.lanl.gov/Group_Homepages/
CST-8

Louisiana State Univ.
http://chrs1.chem.lsu.edu/

M A G N E T: Magnetic Resonance
http://atlas.chemistry.uakron.edu:8080/
cdept.docs/nmrsites.html

Macquarie Univ
http://www.chem.mq.edu.au/

MacroModel Home Page
http://www.cc.columbia.edu/~chempub/
mmod/mmod.html

Mass Spectrometry Laboratories
http://www.nd.edu/~dgriffit/MassSpec/
masspec.html

Millipore On-Line Catalog
http://www.millipore.com/

MOLGEN
http://btm2xd.mat.uni-bayreuth.de/molgen/
mghome.html

Multimedia Journal of Chemical Education
http://chemistry.uca.edu/mjce/

Nanotechnology on the WWW
http://www.arc.ab.ca/~morgan/Nano.html

Nanotechnology Page from Xerox PARC
http://nano.xerox.com/nano/

National Center for Supercomputing Applications, NCSA ChemViz Group
http://eads.ncsa.uiuc.edu/~datkins/

National Inst. of Chemistry in Ljubljana
http://www.ki.si/

National Inst. of Materials and Chemical Research
http://www.aist.go.jp/NIMC/

National Institute of Health, Molecular Modeling Page
http://www.nih.gov/molecular_modeling/
mmhome.html

North American Catalysis Society
http://www.dupont.com/nacs/

Ohio Supercomputer Ctr., Computational Chemistry List
http://www.osc.edu/chemistry.html

Oxford Molecular Group
http://www.oxmol.co.uk/

Pacific Northwest Laboratories, Environmental and Molecular Sciences Lab
http://www.emsl.pnl.gov:2080/

Polish Chemical Society
http://python.chem.uw.edu.pl/

Poly-Links
http://www.polymers.com/

PolyNet
http://www.cilea.it/polynet/

Radiation Research Journal
http://www.whitlock.com/kcj/science/radres/default.htm

Rensselaer Polytechnic Institute
http://www.rpi.edu/dept/chem/cheminfo/chemres.html

Representation of Molecular Models and Rendering Techniques
http://scsg9.unige.ch/eng/toc.html

Research Organics
http://resorg.com/

Rockefeller Univ. Physical Biochemistry
http://mriris.rockefeller.edu/

Stanford Univ. Journal of Biological Chemistry
http://www-jbc.stanford.edu/jbc/

Technical Ceramics References
http://www.ikts.fhg.de/ceramics.html

Technical Research Centre of Finland
http://www.vtt.fi/ket/kethome.html

Technical Univ. Dresden, Germany,
http://ctch03.chm.tu-dresden.de/

Tel Aviv Univ.
http://www.tau.ac.il/chemistry/

Theoretical Chemistry Postdoctoral Clearinghouse
http://www.chem.emory.edu/1/cheminfo

U. S. Occupational Safety and Health Administration
http://www.osha.gov/

Univ. College (UNSW) in Canberra
http://apamac.ch.adfa.oz.au/

Univ. of California Berkeley
http://www.cchem.berkeley.edu/index.html

Univ. of California Davis
http://www-chem.ucdavis.edu/

Univ. of California San Diego
http://checfs1.ucsd.edu/

Univ. of Durham
http://www.dur.ac.uk/~dch0www/index.html

Univ. of Groningen
http://www.chem.rug.nl/

Univ. of Korea
http://jschem.korea.ac.kr/

Univ. of Liverpool, Computers in Teaching Initiative (CTI) Centre for Chemistry
http://www.liv.ac.uk/ctichem.html

Univ. of Rhode Island
http://www.chm.uri.edu/index.html

Univ. of Sheffield
http://www2.shef.ac.uk/chemistry/chemistry-home.html

Univ. of Southern Mississippi, Polymer Science Research Ctr.
http://www.usm.edu/psrc/dps-menu.html

Univ. of Sussex
http://tcibm.mols.sussex.ac.uk/

Univ. of Zürich, Biocomputing and Molecular Modeling
http://www-bio.unizh.ch/xmosaic.html

Vienna Univ. of Technology, Institute of Analytical Chemistry
http://www.iac.tuwien.ac.at/

Virginia Tech
http://www.chem.vt.edu/

Web Chemistry Index
http://www.latrobe.edu.au/chejs/chem.html

WebElements Home Page
http://www.shef.ac.uk/uni/academic/A-C/chem/web-elements/web-elements-home.html

World Association of Theoretical Organic Chemists
http://www.ch.ic.ac.uk/watoc.html

World Wide Chemnet, Inc.
http://www.galstar.com/~chemnet/index.html

WWW Chemicals
http://soho.ios.com/~ilyak

X-ray and Mass Spectrometry
http://laue.chem.ncsu.edu/web/xray.welcome.html

Computer Science

See also Artificial Intelligence, Electronics & Electrical Engineering, Engineering, Imaging Technologies, Mathematics, Optics, Physics, Security, and Virtual Reality

Not surprisingly, computer science has a *huge* presence on the Internet—far too large for any one book to cover. Therefore I have compiled this resource chapter to best cope with the scale of the task.

A few considerations to keep in mind: First, I have included only those sources that are academic in nature, as opposed to recreational, commercial, or very narrowly applied resources. For example, I have not included any information on the hundreds of Usenet newsgroups covering topics such as binaries (except sources), word processors, e-mail software, multimedia, social implications, and user-level discussions of operating system workings.

Second, the formatting for the Usenet section is different that it is for the other topics. In an effort to provide the most important information here, I have divided the Usenet section into 30 subtopics within the **comp.sys** newsgroup hierarchy. Therefore, instead of a separate FAQ listing, the FAQs are listed as part of each newsgroup listing, along with information such as a moderator's name and discussion list address, when these elements exist. There are, however, additional discussion lists noted in a separate section, since many discussion lists are not tied to a Usenet newsgroup.

Finally, I have attempted to not let the number of gopher, FTP, and WWW resources get out of control, which they very easily could do. These resources are designed to be starting points for exploration.

Usenet Newsgroups

ARCHITECTURES

Newsgroups focusing on design and engineering issues related to computer systems architectures, including the following subgroups and their specific topics.

comp.arch
    comp.arch.arithmetic
    comp.arch.bus.misc
    comp.arch.bus.vme
    comp.arch.fpga
    comp.arch.mips
    comp.arch.storage
    • FAQ available:
        ftp://rtfm.mit.edu/pub/usenet-by-group/
        comp.arch.storage/

COMPILERS

Discussions addressing the topics of compilers in particular and programming language design and implementation in general. Recent topics have included optimization techniques, language design issues, announcements of new compiler tools, and book reviews.

comp.compilers
- Moderator:
  John Levine <compilers-request@iecc.com>
- Discussion List:
  compil-l@auvm.american.edu
- FAQ available:
  ftp://rtfm.mit.edu/pub/usenet-by-group/comp.compilers.tools.pccts

COMPRESSION

Discussions about data compression, both lossless (for text or data) and lossy (for images, sound, etc.). comp.compression.research was created later to provide a forum for current research on data compression and data compression algorithms; this group is now moderated. If you are not experienced in data compression, please post in comp.compression only.

comp.compression
- FAQ available:
  ftp://rtfm.mit.edu/pub/usenet-by-group/comp.compression.research

comp.compression.research
- Moderator:
  Peter Gutmann <compression-request@cs.aukuni.ac.nz>

DATABASES

Discussions about a wide variety of database applications and techniques.

comp.databases
comp.databases.informix
comp.databases.ingres
- Discussion List:
  info-ingres@math.ams.com

comp.databases.ms-access
comp.databases.object
- FAQ available:
  ftp://rtfm.mit.edu/pub/usenet-by-group/comp.databases.object/

comp.databases.olap
comp.databases.oracle

comp.databases.paradox
- FAQ available:
  ftp://rtfm.mit.edu/pub/usenet-by-group/comp.databases.paradox/

comp.databases.pick
comp.databases.rdb
comp.databases.sybase
- FAQ available:
  ftp://rtfm.mit.edu/pub/usenet-by-group/comp.databases.sybase/

comp.databases.theory
comp.databases.xbase.foxapp
- FAQ available:
  ftp://rtfm.mit.edu/pub/usenet-by-group/comp.databases.xbase/

comp.databases.xbase.misc
- FAQ available:
  ftp://rtfm.mit.edu/pub/usenet-by-group/comp.databases.xbase

DATA COMMUNICATIONS

Discussions on networking and telecommunications hardware, software, systems, protocols, and architectures.

comp.dcom
comp.dcom.cabling
comp.dcom.cell-relay
- FAQ available:
  ftp://rtfm.mit.edu/pub/usenet-by-group/comp.dcom.cell-relay/

comp.dcom.fax
- FAQ available:
  ftp://rtfm.mit.edu/pub/usenet-by-group/comp.dcom.fax/

comp.dcom.frame-relay
- Discussion list:
  frame-relay@indiana.edu

comp.dcom.isdn
- FAQ available:
  ftp://rtfm.mit.edu/pub/usenet-by-group/comp.dcom.isdn/

comp.dcom.lans
- FAQ available:
  ftp://rtfm.mit.edu/pub/usenet-by-group/comp.dcom.lans/

comp.dcom.lans.ethernet
- FAQ available:
  ftp://rtfm.mit.edu/pub/usenet-by-group/comp.dcoms.lan.ethernet/

comp.dcom.lans.fddi
comp.dcom.lans.hyperchannel

comp.dcom.lans.misc
comp.dcom.lans.novell
comp.dcom.lans.token-ring
comp.dcom.lans.v2lni
comp.dcom.modem
comp.dcom.modems
- Discussion List:
  modems-l@vm.its.rpi.edu
- FAQ available:
  ftp://rtfm.mit.edu/pub/usenet-by-group/
  comp.dcom.modems/

comp.dcom.net-management
comp.dcom.servers
- FAQ available:
  ftp://rtfm.mit.edu/pub/usenet-by-group/
  comp.dcom.servers/

comp.dcom.sys.cisco
- Discussion List:
  cisco@spot.colorado.edu
- FAQ available:
  ftp://rtfm.mit.edu/pub/usenet-by-group/
  comp.dcom.sys.cisco/

comp.dcom.sys.wellfleet
comp.dcom.telecom
- Moderator:
  Patrick Townson <telecom-
  request@eecs.nwu.edu>
- Discussion List:
  telecom@eecs.nwu.edu

comp.dcom.telecom.tech

DOCUMENTATION

Discussions on and information
dissemination for technical reports
distributed and archived on the Internet.

comp.doc
- Moderator:
  Brian Kantor <comp-doc@ucsd.edu>

comp.doc.techreports
- Moderator:
  Richard Golding <compdoc-techreports-
  request@ftp.cse.ucsc.edu>
- FAQ available:
  ftp://rtfm.mit.edu/pub/usenet-by-group/
  comp.doc.techreports/

EDUCATION

Discussion on education in the computer
sciences.

comp.edu
comp.edu.composition
comp.edu.computer-law
comp.edu.languages.natural

EMULATORS

Discussions pertaining to programs
running on one platform to simulate the
feature-set of a different machine architecture.

comp.emulators
comp.emulators.announce
- Moderator:
  Ron Dippold <emulators-
  request@qualcomm.com>
- FAQ available:
  ftp://rtfm.mit.edu/pub/usenet-by-group/
  comp.emulators.announce/

comp.emulators.apple2
comp.emulators.cbm
comp.emulators.misc
comp.emulators.ms-windows.wine
- FAQ available:
  ftp://rtfm.mit.edu/pub/usenet-by-group/
  comp.emulators.ms-windows.wine/

HUMAN FACTORS

Discussion on human factors engineering,
man-machine interfaces, systems designs,
and related topics.

comp.human-factors
- FAQ available:
  ftp://rtfm.mit.edu/pub/usenet-by-group/
  comp.human-factors/

INFORMATION SYSTEMS

Wide variety of newsgroups covering
information systems design, protocols,
implementation, maintenance, and related
topics.

comp.infosystems
comp.infosystems.announce
- Moderator:
  Richard W Wiggins <infosys-
  request@msu.edu>

comp.infosystems.gis
- Discussion List:
  gis-l@ubvm.cc.buffalo.edu

- FAQ available:

  ftp://rtfm.mit.edu/pub/usenet-by-group/
  comp.infosystems.gis/

comp.infosystems.gopher

- FAQ available:

  ftp://rtfm.mit.edu/pub/usenet-by-group/
  comp.infosystems.gopher/

comp.infosystems.interpedia

- FAQ available:

  ftp://rtfm.mit.edu/pub/usenet-by-group/
  comp.infosystems.interpedia/

comp.infosystems.kiosks

- Moderator:

  Arthur Lee Wilson <kiosks-
  request@lanl.gov>

- Discussion List:

  kiosks-l@lanl.gov

comp.infosystems.wais

- FAQ available:

  ftp://rtfm.mit.edu/pub/usenet-by-group/
  comp.infosystems.wais/

comp.infosystems.www

- FAQ available:

  ftp://rtfm.mit.edu/pub/usenet-by-group/
  comp.infosystems.www/

comp.infosystems.www.kiosks
comp.infosystems.www.misc

- FAQ available:

  ftp://rtfm.mit.edu/pub/usenet-by-group/
  comp.infosystems.www.misc/

comp.infosystems.www.providers

- FAQ available:

  ftp://rtfm.mit.edu/pub/usenet-by-group/
  comp.infosystems.www.providers/

comp.infosystems.www.users

- FAQ available:

  ftp://rtfm.mit.edu/pub/usenet-by-group/
  comp.infosystems.www.users/

comp.internet.library

- Moderator:

  Yoshiyasu Takefuji
  <takefuji@axon.cwru.edu>

comp.internet.net-happenings

- Moderator:

  Gleason Sackman <net-happenings-
  owner@is.internic.net>

LANGUAGES

Nothing but programming languages.

comp.lang
comp.lang.ada

- Discussion List:

  info-ada@vm1.nodak.edu

- FAQ available:

  ftp://rtfm.mit.edu/pub/usenet-by-group/
  comp.lang.ada/

comp.lang.apl

- Discussion List:

  apl-l@unb.ca

- FAQ available:

  ftp://rtfm.mit.edu/pub/usenet-by-group/
  comp.lang.apl/

comp.lang.asm.x86
comp.lang.asm370
comp.lang.awk
comp.lang.basic.misc
comp.lang.basic.visual

- FAQ available:

  ftp://rtfm.mit.edu/pub/usenet-by-group/
  comp.lang.basic.visual/

comp.lang.basic.visual.3rdparty

- Moderator:

  Matthew W. Heinrichs

- Discussion List:

  vbasic-submit@cc.umanitoba.ca

comp.lang.basic.visual.announce

- Moderator:

  Matthew W. Heinrichs

- Discussion List:

  vbasic-submit@cc.umanitoba.ca

comp.lang.basic.visual.database
comp.lang.basic.visual.misc
comp.lang.beta

- FAQ available:

  ftp://rtfm.mit.edu/pub/usenet-by-group/
  comp.lang.beta/

comp.lang.c.moderated

- Moderator:

  Peter Seebach <clc-
  request@solutions.solon.com>

- Discussion List:

  info-c@arl.army.mil

- FAQ available:

  ftp://rtfm.mit.edu/pub/usenet-by-group/
  comp.lang.c/

comp.lang.c++

- Discussion List:

  help-c++@prep.ai.mit.edu

- FAQ available:

  ftp://rtfm.mit.edu/pub/usenet-by-group/
  comp.lang.c++/

comp.lang.c++.leda
comp.lang.clos

- FAQ available:

  ftp://rtfm.mit.edu/pub/usenet-by-group/
  comp.lang.clos/

comp.lang.clu
comp.lang.cobol

- FAQ available:

  ftp://rtfm.mit.edu/pub/usenet-by-group/
  comp.lang.cobol/

comp.lang.clipper
comp.lang.dylan
comp.lang.eiffel

- FAQ available:

  ftp://rtfm.mit.edu/pub/usenet-by-group/
  comp.lang.eiffel/

comp.lang.forth

- Discussion List:

  umforth@weizmann.bitnet

- FAQ available:

  ftp://rtfm.mit.edu/pub/usenet-by-group/
  comp.lang.forth/

comp.lang.forth.mac
comp.lang.fortran

- FAQ available:

  ftp://rtfm.mit.edu/pub/usenet-by-group/
  comp.lang.fortran/

comp.lang.functional

- FAQ available:

  ftp://rtfm.mit.edu/pub/usenet-by-group/
  comp.lang.functional/

comp.lang.hermes
comp.lang.icon

- FAQ available:

  ftp://rtfm.mit.edu/pub/usenet-by-group/
  comp.lang.icon/

comp.lang.idl
comp.lang.idl-pvwave

- FAQ available:

  ftp://rtfm.mit.edu/pub/usenet-by-group/
  comp.lang.pvwave/

comp.lang.java
comp.lang.lisp

- FAQ available:

  ftp://rtfm.mit.edu/pub/usenet-by-group/
  comp.lang.lisp/

comp.lang.lisp.franz
comp.lang.lisp.mcl
comp.lang.lisp.x

comp.lang.logo
comp.lang.misc
comp.lang.ml

- Moderator:

  Greg Morrisett <comp-lang-ml-
  request@cs.cmu.edu>

- FAQ available:

  ftp://rtfm.mit.edu/pub/usenet-by-group/
  comp.lang.ml/

comp.lang.modula2

- Discussion List:

  info-m2@ucf1vm.bitnet

- FAQ available:

  ftp://rtfm.mit.edu/pub/usenet-by-group/
  comp.lang.modula2/

comp.lang.modula3

- FAQ available:

  ftp://rtfm.mit.edu/pub/usenet-by-group/
  comp.lang.modula3/

comp.lang.mumps

- Discussion List:

  mumps-l@uga.cc.uga.edu

comp.lang.oberon

- FAQ available:

  ftp://rtfm.mit.edu/pub/usenet-by-group/
  comp.lang.oberon/

comp.lang.objective-c

- FAQ available:

  ftp://rtfm.mit.edu/pub/usenet-by-group/
  comp.lang.objective-c/

comp.lang.pascal

- Discussion List:

  info-pascal@arl.army.mil

comp.lang.perl

- FAQ available:

  ftp://rtfm.mit.edu/pub/usenet-by-group/
  comp.lang.perl/

comp.lang.perl.announce

- Moderator:

  Randal Schwartz
  <merlyn@stonehenge.com>

comp.lang.perl.misc

- Moderator:

  Robert Haas
  <rhaas@cygnus.arc.nasa.gov>

comp.lang.perl.tk
comp.lang.pop
comp.lang.postscript

- FAQ available:

  ftp://rtfm.mit.edu/pub/usenet-by-group/
  comp.lang.postscript/

comp.lang.prograph
- Discussion List:
  info-prograph@grove.iup.edu

comp.lang.prolog
- Discussion List:
  prolog@score.stanford.edu
- FAQ available:
  ftp://rtfm.mit.edu/pub/usenet-by-group/
  comp.lang.prolog/

comp.lang.python
- FAQ available:
  ftp://rtfm.mit.edu/pub/usenet-by-group/
  comp.lang.python/

comp.lang.rexx
- Discussion List:
  rexxlist@uga.cc.uga.edu

comp.lang.sather
- FAQ available:
  ftp://rtfm.mit.edu/pub/usenet-by-group/
  comp.lang.sather/

comp.lang.scheme
- FAQ available:
  ftp://rtfm.mit.edu/pub/usenet-by-group/
  comp.lang.scheme/

comp.lang.scheme.c
comp.lang.sigplan
- Moderator:
  Barbara Ryder <sigplan-
  request@cs.rutgers.edu>

comp.lang.smalltalk
- Discussion List:
  info-cls@vm.gmd.de
- FAQ available:
  ftp://rtfm.mit.edu/pub/usenet-by-group/
  comp.lang.smalltalk/

comp.lang.tcl
- FAQ available:
  ftp://rtfm.mit.edu/pub/usenet-by-group/
  comp.lang.tcl/

comp.lang.verilog
- FAQ available:
  ftp://rtfm.mit.edu/pub/usenet-by-group/
  comp.lang.verilog/

comp.lang.vhdl
- FAQ available:
  ftp://rtfm.mit.edu/pub/usenet-by-group/
  comp.lang.vhdl/

comp.lang.visual
- Moderator:
  David McIntyre <visual-
  request@morgan.com>

- FAQ available:
  ftp://rtfm.mit.edu/pub/usenet-by-group/
  comp.lang.visual/

MISCELLANEOUS
General discussions and topics that don't
fit into other categories.

comp.misc
- FAQ available:
  ftp://rtfm.mit.edu/pub/usenet-by-group/
  comp.misc/

ORGANIZATIONS
Organizations heavily involved with
supporting the computer science community.

comp.org
  comp.org.acm
  - Discussion List:
    acm-l@kentvm.kent.edu

  comp.org.cpsr.announce
  - Moderator:
    Unknown <cpsr-announce-
    owner@cpsr.org>

  comp.org.cpsr.talk
  comp.org.decus
  - FAQ available:
    ftp://rtfm.mit.edu/pub/usenet-by-group/
    comp.org.decus/

  comp.org.eff.news
  - Moderators:
    Christopher Davis & Helen Rose
    <eff@eff.org>
  - Discussion List:
    eff-news@eff.org
  - FAQ available:
    ftp://rtfm.mit.edu/pub/usenet-by-group/
    comp.org.eff/

  comp.org.eff.talk
  - Discussion List:
    eff-talk@eff.org

  comp.org.fidonet
  - Moderator:
    Tim Pozar <pozar@hop.toad.com>

  comp.org.ieee
  comp.org.isoc.interest
  comp.org.issnnet
  comp.org.lisp-users
  comp.org.sug

comp.org.uniforum
comp.org.usenix
comp.org.usenix.roomshare

PARALLEL PROCESSORS

Discussions of massively parallel hardware and software systems.

comp.parallel
comp.parallel.mpi
- Moderators:

  Harry Berryman, et al.<comp-parallel-request@cs.yale.edu>
- FAQ available:

  ftp://rtfm.mit.edu/pub/usenet-by-group/comp.parallel.mpi/

  comp.parallel.pvm

PATENTS

Patents, patents pending, patent laws, and related issues.

comp.patents
- Moderator:

  Peter John Treloar <pjt@cs.su.oz.au>

PROGRAMMING

Discussions of programming issues which are not limited to a specific machine, operating system, or language: in particular, algorithms of all types.

comp.programming
- FAQ available:

  ftp://rtfm.mit.edu/pub/usenet-by-group/comp.programming/

comp.programming.literate
- Discussion List:

  litprog@shsu.edu
- FAQ available:

  ftp://rtfm.mit.edu/pub/usenet-by-group/comp.programming.literate/

  comp.programming.threads

PROTOCOLS

Newsgroups discussing specific networking transport protocols and their applications.

comp.protocols.*
comp.protocols.appletalk

comp.protocols.dicom
- FAQ available:

  ftp://rtfm.mit.edu/pub/usenet-by-group/comp.protocols.dicom/

comp.protocols.ibm
comp.protocols.iso
- FAQ available:

  ftp://rtfm.mit.edu/pub/usenet-by-group/comp.protocols.iso/

comp.protocols.iso.dev-environ
comp.protocols.iso.x400
comp.protocols.iso.x400.gateway
comp.protocols.kerberos
- Discussion List:

  kerberos@athena.mit.edu
- FAQ available:

  ftp://rtfm.mit.edu/pub/usenet-by-group/comp.protocols.kerberos/

comp.protocols.kermit
comp.protocols.kermit.announce
- Moderator:

  Frank da Cruz <info-kermit-request@watsun.cc.columbia.edu>

comp.protocols.kermit.misc
comp.protocols.misc
comp.protocols.nfs
comp.protocols.pcnet
comp.protocols.ppp
- FAQ available:

  ftp://rtfm.mit.edu/pub/usenet-by-group/comp.protocols.ppp/

comp.protocols.pup
comp.protocols.smb
comp.protocols.snmp
- FAQ available:

  ftp://rtfm.mit.edu/pub/usenet-by-group/comp.protocols.snmp/

comp.protocols.tcp-ip
- Discussion List:

  tcp-ip@nic.ddn.mil
- FAQ available:

  ftp://rtfm.mit.edu/pub/usenet-by-group/comp.protocols.tcp-ip/

comp.protocols.tcp-ip.domains
comp.protocols.tcp-ip.ibmpc
- Discussion List:

  pcip@list.nih.gov

comp.protocols.time.ntp

REAL-TIME PROCESSING

Discussion of both the theory and practice of real-time computer systems.

comp.realtime

- FAQ available:
  ftp://rtfm.mit.edu/pub/usenet-by-group/
  comp.realtime/

RESEARCH IN JAPAN

Discussions of current computer science research in Japan.

comp.research.japan

- Moderator:
  Rick Schlichting <rick@cs.arizona.edu>
- Discussion List:
  res-japan-group@cs.arizona.edu

RISKS

Discussions of computer-related risks and risk management theory.

comp.risks

- Moderator:
  Peter G. Neumann <risks-
  request@csl.sri.com>
- Discussion List:
  risks@csl.sri.com

ROBOTICS

Discussions of computers and robotic systems, machine vision, and artificial intelligence.

comp.robotics

- FAQ available:
  ftp://rtfm.mit.edu/pub/usenet-by-group/
  comp.robotics/

SIMULATION

Computer simulation.

comp.simulation

- Moderator:
  Patrick W. Dowd <simulation-
  request@eng.buffalo.edu>

SOFTWARE ENGINEERING

Software engineering and related topics, including CASE tools.

comp.software-eng

- FAQ available:
  ftp://rtfm.mit.edu/pub/usenet-by-group/
  comp.software-eng/

SOURCES

Source code (programs) posted to the net; classified by destination architecture.

comp.sources

comp.sources.3b1
- Moderator:
  David H. Brierley
  <dave@galaxia.network23.com>

comp.sources.acorn
- Moderators:
  Peter Gutmann & Edouard Poor
  <moderators@cs.aukuni.ac.nz>

comp.sources.amiga
- Moderator:
  Michael 'Moose' Dinn <amiga-
  request@uunet.uu.net>

comp.sources.apple2
- Moderator:
  Jonathan Chandross
  <jac@paul.rutgers.edu>

comp.sources.atari.st
- Moderator:
  Annius Groenink <avg@cwi.nl>
- FAQ available:
  ftp://rtfm.mit.edu/pub/usenet-by-group/
  comp.sources/

comp.sources.bugs
comp.sources.d
- FAQ available:
  ftp://rtfm.mit.edu/pub/usenet-by-group/
  comp.sources.d/

comp.sources.games
- Moderator:
  Bill Randle <games-
  request@saab.cna.tek.com>

comp.sources.games.bugs
comp.sources.hp48
- Moderator:
  Chris Spell <spell@seq.uncwil.edu>

comp.sources.mac
- Moderator:
  Roger Long <bytebug@uunet.uu.net>

comp.sources.misc
- Moderators:
  Kent Landfield & Alec David Muffett
  <sources-misc-request@uunet.uu.net>

- Discussion List:
  unix-sources@arl.army.mil
- FAQ available:
  ftp://rtfm.mit.edu/pub/usenet-by-group/
  comp.sources.misc/

comp.sources.postscript
- Moderator:
  Jonathan Monsarrat <postscript-
  request@cs.brown.edu>
- FAQ available:
  ftp://rtfm.mit.edu/pub/usenet-by-group/
  comp.sources.postscript/

comp.sources.reviewed
- Moderator:
  Kevin Braunsdorf <csr-
  request@cc.purdue.edu>

comp.sources.sun
- Moderator:
  Charles McGrew
  <mcgrew@aramis.rutgers.edu>

comp.sources.testers
- FAQ available:
  ftp://rtfm.mit.edu/pub/usenet-by-group/
  comp.sources.testers/

comp.sources.unix
- Moderators:
  Paul Vixie, et al. <unix-sources-
  moderator@vix.com>
- Discussion List:
  unix-sources@pa.dec.com

comp.sources.wanted
- FAQ available:
  ftp://rtfm.mit.edu/pub/usenet-by-group/
  comp.sources.wanted/

comp.sources.x
- Moderator:
  Chris Olson <chris@sterling.com>

SPECIFICATIONS

Techniques on how to draft specifications
for subsequent development work.

comp.specification
- FAQ available:
  ftp://rtfm.mit.edu/pub/usenet-by-group/
  comp.specification/

comp.specification.misc
comp.specification.z
- Discussion List:
  zforum@comlab.ox.ac.uk

- FAQ available:
  ftp://rtfm.mit.edu/pub/usenet-by-group/
  comp.specification.z/

STANDARDS

Computational standards development
and discussion.

comp.std
comp.std.announce
- Moderator:
  John C. Klensin
  <klensin@infoods.mit.edu>

comp.std.c
- FAQ available:
  ftp://rtfm.mit.edu/pub/usenet-by-group/
  comp.std.c/

comp.std.c++
- Moderator:
  Matt Austern <std-c++-
  request@ncar.ucar.edu>

comp.std.internat
- FAQ available:
  ftp://rtfm.mit.edu/pub/usenet-by-group/
  comp.std.internat/

comp.std.lisp
- Moderator:
  Brad Miller <miller@cs.rochester.edu>

comp.std.misc
- FAQ available:
  ftp://rtfm.mit.edu/pub/usenet-by-group/
  comp.std.misc/

comp.std.mumps
- Moderator:
  Hokey <std-mumps-request@pfcs.com>

comp.std.unix
- Moderator:
  Sean Eric Fagan <std-unix-
  request@uunet.uu.net>

comp.std.wireless
- Moderator:
  W. Stuart Jones <jonesw@wes.mot.com>

comp.sw.components

SYSTEMS

Discussions on a wide variety of computer
systems software and hardware.

comp.sys.3b1
- FAQ available:
  ftp://rtfm.mit.edu/pub/usenet-by-group/
  comp.sys.3b1/

comp.sys.acorn

comp.sys.acorn.advocacy
- FAQ available:
  ftp://rtfm.mit.edu/pub/usenet-by-group/
  comp.sys.acorn/

comp.sys.acorn.announce
- Moderator:
  Alan Glover <announce-
  request@acorn.co.uk>
- FAQ available:
  ftp://rtfm.mit.edu/pub/usenet-by-group/
  comp.sys.acorn.announce/

comp.sys.acorn.games
comp.sys.acorn.tech
- FAQ available:
  ftp://rtfm.mit.edu/pub/usenet-by-group/
  comp.sys.acorn/

comp.sys.alliant

comp.sys.amiga
- Discussion List:
  csys-ami%mainecs@cunyvm.cuny.edu
- FAQ available:
  ftp://rtfm.mit.edu/pub/usenet-by-group/
  comp.sys.amiga/

comp.sys.amiga.advocacy
comp.sys.amiga.announce
- Moderator:
  Dan Zerkle <zerkle@cs.ucdavis.edu>

comp.sys.amiga.applications
comp.sys.amiga.audio
comp.sys.amiga.cd32
comp.sys.amiga.datacomm
comp.sys.amiga.emulations
comp.sys.amiga.games
comp.sys.amiga.graphics
comp.sys.amiga.hardware
- Discussion List:
  ami-hard%mainecs@cunyvm.cuny.edu

comp.sys.amiga.introduction
comp.sys.amiga.marketplace
comp.sys.amiga.misc
comp.sys.amiga.multimedia
comp.sys.amiga.networking
comp.sys.amiga.programmer
comp.sys.amiga.reviews
- Moderator:
  Daniel J. Barrett <amiga-
  reviews@math.uh.edu>

comp.sys.amiga.tech
- Discussion List:
  ami-tech%mainecs@cunyvm.cuny.edu

comp.sys.amiga.telecomm
comp.sys.amiga.unix
comp.sys.amiga.uucp

comp.sys.amstrad.8bit

comp.sys.apollo
- Discussion List:
  apollo@umix.cc.umich.edu
- FAQ available:
  ftp://rtfm.mit.edu/pub/usenet-by-group/
  comp.sys.apollo/

comp.sys.apple2
- Discussion List:
  info-apple@apple.com
- FAQ available:
  ftp://rtfm.mit.edu/pub/usenet-by-group/
  comp.sys.apple2/

comp.sys.apple2.comm
comp.sys.apple2.gno
comp.sys.apple2.marketplace
comp.sys.apple2.programmer
comp.sys.apple2.usergroups

comp.sys.arm

comp.sys.atari.8bit
- Discussion List:
  info-atari8-request@pine.cse.nau.edu
- FAQ available:
  ftp://rtfm.mit.edu/pub/usenet-by-group/
  comp.sys.atari.8bit/

comp.sys.atari.advocacy
comp.sys.atari.announce
- Moderator:
  Yat Siu <atari-request@lexicor.com>

comp.sys.atari.st
- Discussion List:
  info-atari16-request@pine.cse.nau.edu
- FAQ available:
  ftp://rtfm.mit.edu/pub/usenet-by-group/
  comp.sys.atari.st/

comp.sys.atari.st.tech

comp.sys.att
- FAQ available:
  ftp://rtfm.mit.edu/pub/usenet-by-group/
  comp.sys.att/

comp.sys.cbm
- FAQ available:
  ftp://rtfm.mit.edu/pub/usenet-by-group/
  comp.sys.cbm/

comp.sys.cdc

comp.sys.concurrent
- Moderator:
  Brian Carlton <concurrent-request@bdcsys.suvl.ca.us>

comp.sys.convex

comp.sys.dec
- FAQ available:
  ftp://rtfm.mit.edu/pub/usenet-by-group/comp.sys.dec/

comp.sys.dec.micro

comp.sys.encore

comp.sys.handhelds

comp.sys.harris

comp.sys.hp
- FAQ available:
  ftp://rtfm.mit.edu/pub/usenet-by-group/comp.sys.hp/

comp.sys.hp.apps
comp.sys.hp.hardware
comp.sys.hp.hpux
comp.sys.hp.misc
comp.sys.hp.mpe
- Discussion List:
  hp3000-l@utcvm.utc.edu

comp.sys.hp28
comp.sys.hp48
- FAQ available:
  ftp://rtfm.mit.edu/pub/usenet-by-group/comp.sys.hp48/

comp.sys.hp48.d

comp.sys.ibm.pc
comp.sys.ibm.pc.demos
comp.sys.ibm.pc.digest
- Moderator:
  Gregory Hicks <info-ibmpc-request@arl.army.mil>

comp.sys.ibm.pc.games
- FAQ available:
  ftp://rtfm.mit.edu/pub/usenet-by-group/comp.sys.ibm.pc.games/

comp.sys.ibm.pc.games.action
comp.sys.ibm.pc.games.adventure

comp.sys.ibm.pc.games.announce
- Moderator:
  Joseph Cochran <jsciv@vt.edu>

comp.sys.ibm.pc.games.flight-sim
comp.sys.ibm.pc.games.marketplace
comp.sys.ibm.pc.games.misc
- FAQ available:
  ftp://rtfm.mit.edu/pub/usenet-by-group/comp.sys.ibm.pc.misc/

comp.sys.ibm.pc.games.rpg
comp.sys.ibm.pc.games.strategic
comp.sys.ibm.pc.hardware
- FAQ available:
  ftp://rtfm.mit.edu/pub/usenet-by-group/comp.sys.ibm.hardware/

comp.sys.ibm.pc.hardware.cd-rom
comp.sys.ibm.pc.hardware.chips
comp.sys.ibm.pc.hardware.comm
comp.sys.ibm.pc.hardware.misc
comp.sys.ibm.pc.hardware.networking
comp.sys.ibm.pc.hardware.storage
comp.sys.ibm.pc.hardware.systems
comp.sys.ibm.pc.hardware.video
comp.sys.ibm.pc.misc
comp.sys.ibm.pc.programmer
comp.sys.ibm.pc.rt
comp.sys.ibm.pc.soundcard
- FAQ available:
  ftp://rtfm.mit.edu/pub/usenet-by-group/comp.sys.ibm.pc.soundcard/

comp.sys.ibm.pc.soundcard.advocacy
comp.sys.ibm.pc.soundcard.games
comp.sys.ibm.pc.soundcard.gus
comp.sys.ibm.pc.soundcard.misc
comp.sys.ibm.pc.soundcard.music
comp.sys.ibm.pc.soundcard.tech
comp.sys.ibm.ps2
comp.sys.ibm.ps2.hardware

comp.sys.intel
- FAQ available:
  ftp://rtfm.mit.edu/pub/usenet-by-group/comp.sys.intel/

comp.sys.intel.ipsc310

comp.sys.isis

comp.sys.laptops

comp.sys.m6809

comp.sys.m68k
- FAQ available:
  ftp://rtfm.mit.edu/pub/usenet-by-group/comp.sys.m68k/

comp.sys.m68k.pc
- Moderator:

    Mike Meyer <info-68k-request@ucbvax.berkeley.edu>

comp.sys.m88k

comp.sys.mac
- FAQ available:

    ftp://rtfm.mit.edu/pub/usenet-by-group/comp.sys.mac/

comp.sys.mac.advocacy
comp.sys.mac.announce
- Moderator:

    Werner Uhrig
    <werner@rascal.ics.utexas.edu>

comp.sys.mac.app
comp.sys.mac.apps
- FAQ available:

    ftp://rtfm.mit.edu/pub/usenet-by-group/comp.sys.mac.apps/

comp.sys.mac.comm
- FAQ available:

    ftp://rtfm.mit.edu/pub/usenet-by-group/comp.sys.mac.comm/

comp.sys.mac.databases
comp.sys.mac.digest
- Moderator:

    Bill Lipa <info-mac-request@sumex-aim.stanford.edu>

comp.sys.mac.games
- FAQ available:

    ftp://rtfm.mit.edu/pub/usenet-by-group/comp.sys.mac.games/

comp.sys.mac.graphics
comp.sys.mac.hardware
- FAQ available:

    ftp://rtfm.mit.edu/pub/usenet-by-group/comp.sys.mac.hardware/

comp.sys.mac.hypercard
comp.sys.mac.misc
- FAQ available:

    ftp://rtfm.mit.edu/pub/usenet-by-group/comp.sys.mac.misc/

comp.sys.mac.oop.macapp3
comp.sys.mac.oop.misc
comp.sys.mac.oop.tcl
comp.sys.mac.portables
comp.sys.mac.programmer
- FAQ available:

    ftp://rtfm.mit.edu/pub/usenet-by-group/comp.sys.mac.programmer/

comp.sys.mac.programmer.codewarrior
comp.sys.mac.programmer.help
comp.sys.mac.programmer.info
comp.sys.mac.programmer.misc
comp.sys.mac.programmer.tools
comp.sys.mac.scitech
- FAQ available:

    ftp://rtfm.mit.edu/pub/usenet-by-group/comp.sys.mac.scitech/

comp.sys.mac.system
- FAQ available:

    ftp://rtfm.mit.edu/pub/usenet-by-group/comp.sys.mac.system/

comp.sys.mac.wanted
- FAQ available:

    ftp://rtfm.mit.edu/pub/usenet-by-group/comp.sys.mac.wanted/

comp.sys.mentor

comp.sys.mips

comp.sys.misc
- Discussion List:

    micro-l@vm.its.rpi.edu

comp.sys.ncr

comp.sys.newton

comp.sys.newton.announce
- Moderator:

    Michael Nowak <mnowak@umich.edu>

comp.sys.newton.misc
- FAQ available:

    ftp://rtfm.mit.edu/pub/usenet-by-group/comp.sys.newton.misc/

comp.sys.newton.programmer

comp.sys.next
comp.sys.next.advocacy
- Discussion List:

    next-advocacy-d@antigone.com

comp.sys.next.announce
- Moderator:

    Scott Anguish <next-announce-request@digifix.com>
- Discussion List:

    next-announce-d@antigone.com

comp.sys.next.bugs
- Discussion List:

    next-bugs-d@antigone.com

comp.sys.next.hardware
- Discussion List:
  next-hardware-d@antigone.com
- FAQ available:
  ftp://rtfm.mit.edu/pub/usenet-by-group/
  comp.sys.next.hardware/

comp.sys.next.marketplace
- Discussion List:
  next-marketplace-d@antigone.com

comp.sys.next.misc
- Discussion List:
  next-misc-d@antigone.com

comp.sys.next.programmer
- Discussion List:
  next-programmer-d@antigone.com
- FAQ available:
  ftp://rtfm.mit.edu/pub/usenet-by-group/
  comp.sys.next.programmer/

comp.sys.next.software
- Discussion List:
  next-software-d@antigone.com

comp.sys.next.sysadmin
- Discussion List:
  next-sysadmin-d@antigone.com

comp.sys.northstar

comp.sys.novell

comp.sys.nsc.32k

comp.sys.palmtops
- FAQ available:
  ftp://rtfm.mit.edu/pub/usenet-by-group/
  comp.sys.palmtops/

comp.sys.pen

comp.sys.powerpc
- FAQ available:
  ftp://rtfm.mit.edu/pub/usenet-by-group/
  comp.sys.powerpc/

comp.sys.prime
- Discussion List:
  info-prime@blx-a.prime.com

comp.sys.proteon

comp.sys.psion

comp.sys.pyramid

comp.sys.ridge

comp.sys.sequent

comp.sys.sgi
comp.sys.sgi.admin
- FAQ available:
  ftp://rtfm.mit.edu/pub/usenet-by-group/
  comp.sys.sgi.admin/

comp.sys.sgi.announce
- Moderator:
  Matthew Wicks <sgi-announce-
  request@dcdmjw.fnal.gov>

comp.sys.sgi.apps
- FAQ available:
  ftp://rtfm.mit.edu/pub/usenet-by-group/
  comp.sys.sgi.apps/

comp.sys.sgi.audio
- FAQ available:
  ftp://rtfm.mit.edu/pub/usenet-by-group/
  comp.sys.sgi.audio/

comp.sys.sgi.bugs
- FAQ available:
  ftp://rtfm.mit.edu/pub/usenet-by-group/
  comp.sys.sgi.bugs/

comp.sys.sgi.graphics
- FAQ available:
  ftp://rtfm.mit.edu/pub/usenet-by-group/
  comp.sys.sgi.graphics/

comp.sys.sgi.hardware
- FAQ available:
  ftp://rtfm.mit.edu/pub/usenet-by-group/
  comp.sys.sgi.hardware/

comp.sys.sgi.misc
- FAQ available:
  ftp://rtfm.mit.edu/pub/usenet-by-group/
  comp.sys.sgi.misc/

comp.sys.sinclair

comp.sys.stratus

comp.sys.sun
comp.sys.sun.admin
- FAQ available:
  ftp://rtfm.mit.edu/pub/usenet-by-group/
  comp.sys.sun.admin/

comp.sys.sun.announce
- Moderator:
  Scott Hazen Mueller <css-announce-
  request@uunet.uu.net>
- FAQ available:
  ftp://rtfm.mit.edu/pub/usenet-by-group/
  comp.sys.sun.announce/

comp.sys.sun.apps

comp.sys.sun.hardware
- FAQ available:
  ftp://rtfm.mit.edu/pub/usenet-by-group/
  comp.sys.sun.hardware/

comp.sys.sun.misc
- FAQ available:
  ftp://rtfm.mit.edu/pub/usenet-by-group/
  comp.sys.sun.misc/

comp.sys.sun.wanted

comp.sys.super

comp.sys.tahoe
- Discussion List:
  info-tahoe@csd1.milw.wisc.edu

comp.sys.tandy

comp.sys.ti
  comp.sys.ti.explorer

comp.sys.transputer

comp.sys.unisys

comp.sys.vms

comp.sys.xerox
- Discussion List:
  info-1100@tut.cis.ohio-state.edu

comp.sys.zenith
  comp.sys.zenith.z100

THEORY

Theoretical computer science.

comp.theory
  comp.theory.cell-automata
  comp.theory.dynamic-sys
  comp.theory.info-retrieval
- Moderator:
  Unknown <engle@cmsa.berkeley.edu>
  comp.theory.self-org-sys

UNIX

Unix gets its own newsgroup hierarchy.

comp.unix
- FAQ available:
  ftp://rtfm.mit.edu/pub/usenet-by-group/
  comp.unix/

comp.unix.admin
comp.unix.advocacy
comp.unix.aix
comp.unix.amiga

comp.unix.aux
comp.unix.bsd
comp.unix.cray
comp.unix.dos-under-unix
comp.unix.i386
comp.unix.internals
comp.unix.large
comp.unix.misc
comp.unix.msdos
comp.unix.osf.misc
comp.unix.osf.osf1
comp.unix.pc-clone.16bit
comp.unix.pc-clone.32bit
comp.unix.programmer
comp.unix.questions
comp.unix.shell
comp.unix.solaris
- Discussion List:
  solaris@vma.cc.nd.edu

comp.unix.sys3
comp.unix.sys5.misc
comp.unix.sys5.r3
comp.unix.sys5.r4
comp.unix.sysv286
comp.unix.sysv386
comp.unix.ultrix
comp.unix.unixware
comp.unix.user-friendly
comp.unix.wizards
- Moderator:
  David Barr <wizmod-
  request@pop.psu.edu>

comp.unix.xenix.misc
comp.unix.xenix.sco

VIRUSES

Discussions of all types of computer
viruses.

comp.virus
- Moderator:
  Kenneth van Wyk <virus-l@lehigh.edu>
- Discussion List:
  virus-l@lehigh.edu
- FAQ available:
  ftp://rtfm.mit.edu/pub/usenet-by-group/
  comp.virus/

Discussion Lists

Note that these discussion lists are the actual addresses for the lists, not the subscription addresses. For complete instructions on subscribing, see Chapter 6, Discussion Lists.

See also the previous section for discussion lists associated with specific Usenet newsgroups.

ACC-L
ACC-L@GITVM1.BITNET
ACC-L: Advanced Computer Controls

ADP-L
ADP-L@RPITSVM.BITNET
Advanced Device Processing

ADV-PAS
ADV-PAS@BRUFPB.BITNET
List for Advanced Pascal Users

AICS-L
AICS-L@UBVM.BITNET
Architectures for Intelligent Control Systems Discussion List

ASMICRO-L
ASMICRO-L@VME131.LSI.USP.ANSP.BR
Design and use of application-specific microprocessors.

CASE-L
CASE-L@UCCVMA.UCOP.EDU
Computer-aided systems analysis.

CMPHENGL
CMPHENGL@TECHNION.BITNET
CMPHENGL - Inter-Faculty Seminar on Scientific Computing

CNSF-L
CNSF-L@UBVM.BITNET
Cornell National Supercomputer Facility Announcements List

COHERENT
COHERENT@IRISHVMA.BITNET
Coherent operating system

COMP-CEN
COMP-CEN@UCCVMA.UCOP.EDU
Operation of mid- to large-sized computer facilities (CWIS, etc.)

COMP-SCI
COMP-SCI@TAUNIVM.BITNET
Comp-Sci Distribution List

COMP-GAS
COMP-GAS@JPNYITP.BITNET
Preprint server for Computational methods/Time series analysis.

COMPIL-L
COMPIL-L@AMERICAN.EDU
Compilers, interpreters, and other language processors; assemblers, debuggers, and language design.

COMSOC-L
COMSOC-L@AUVM.BITNET
Computers and Society ARPA Digest

COMTEN-L
COMTEN-L%UCSBVM@CUNYVM.CUNY.EDU
Networking hardware and software.

CPSR
CPSR@GWUVM.BITNET
Computer Professionals for Social Responsibility

DOAC-HSC
DOAC-HSC@UMAB.BITNET
Academic Computing at Health Science Centers

ETHICS-L
ETHICS-L@DEARN.BITNET (Peered)
Discussion of Ethics in Computing

FUZZY-MAIL
FUZZY-MAIL@VEXPERT.DBAI.TUWIEN.AC.AT
Fuzzy logic, AI, and computer science.

GENCMP-L
GENCMP-L@GITVM1.BITNET
Genealogy Computing

HEP-LAT
HEP-LAT@JPNYITP.BITNET
Preprint server for Computational and
Lattice Physics

INFO-C@RESEARCH.ATT.COM
INFO-C@RESEARCH.ATT.COM
Forum on C programming.

INFO-FRAME
INFO-FRAME2AEROSPACE.AERO.ORG
System frameworks.

INFO-GCG
INFO-GCG@NET.BIO.NET
Experiences, ideas, problems, and solutions relating to GCG software and/or
research utilizing GCG software.

INFO-MODEMS
INFO-MODEMS@WSMR-
SIMTEL20.ARMY.MIL
Modems and telecommunications.

INFO-TEX
INFO-TEX@SHSU.EDU
Forum on the TeX document processing
system.

INFO-VLSI
INFO-VLSI@THINK.COM
Design and production of integrated
circuitry.

LEPICSP3
LEPICSP3@LEPICS.BITNET
LEPICS Parallel Processing Project Group

NEW-SUPERCOM
S-COMPUT@UGA.BITNET (Peered)
SuperComputers List (UGA)

ORCS-L
ORCS-L@OSUVM1.BITNET
Operations Research/Computer Science
Interface

OPT-PROC
OPT-PROC@TAUNIVM.BITNET
Optical Computing and Holography

PARA94-L
PARA94-L@NEUVM1.BITNET
parallel computing workshop info

PARA-DAP
PARA-DAP@IRLEARN.BITNET
Parallel Computing / AMT DAP

PDPPL
PDPPL@PLEARN.BITNET
Parallel and distributed processing list.

PFUG-L
PFUG-L@JHUVM.BITNET
Parallel FORTRAN Users' Group newslet-
ter

PROTOCOL
PROTOCOL@UIUCVMD.BITNET
Computer Protocol Discussion

PSUPER-L
PSUPER-L@RPITSVM.BITNET
Posix Supercomputing (P1003.10)

RES-COMP
RES-COMP@NKI.BITNET
Research Computing Forum

SBSUPER
SBSUPER@SBCCVM.BITNET
Stony Brook Supercomputer

SCCIM
SCCIM@SIVM.BITNET
Scientific Computing & Collections
Information Management

SCE-LIST
SCE-LIST@HASARA11.BITNET
List of the Society of Computational
Economics

SHOTHC-L
SHOTHC-L@SIVM.BITNET
History of Computing Issues

SOFT-ENG
SOFT-ENG@MWUNIX.MITRE.ORG
Software engineering and related topics.

SOFTWARE-MEASUREMENT
SOFTWARE-
MEASUREMENT@MAILBASE.AC.UK
Software metrics.

SOFTWARE-TESTING
SOFTWARE-
TESTING@MAILBASE.AC.UK
Testing of software.

SOLV-INT
SOLV-INT@JPNYITP.BITNET
Preprint server for Exactly solvable
systems/Integrable PDEs

SUPERIBM
SUPERIBM@UKCC.BITNET
Super Computing Issues Forum

THEORYNT
THEORYNT@NDSUVM1.BITNET
TheoryNet List

TIP
TIP@PLEARN.BITNET
List of the Theoretical Computer Science
TIP list.

VIZGRP-L
VIZGRP-L@UGA.BITNET
Visual Computing Users Group

Computer Science Resources

FTP Resources

Apple Computer
  ftp.apple.com

Argonne National Laboratory
  info.mcs.anl.gov

Australian National Univ.
  csc2.anu.edu.au

Bond Univ.
  bond.edu.au

Boston Univ.
  cs-ftp.bu.edu

California Institute of Technology
  hobiecat.cs.caltech.edu

California State Univ. - Sacramento
  csus.edu

Carnegie-Mellon Univ.
  cs.cmu.edu

Centre Commun d'Etude de Telecommu-
  nication et de Telediffusion
  161.105.2.22

Colorado State Univ.
  beethoven.cs.colostate.edu

Colorado Supernet Inc
  csn.org

Curtin Univ.
  cs.curtin.edu.au

Dartmouth College
  dartcms1.dartmouth.edu

Digital Equipment Corp
  crl.dec.com

ELF Communications Inc.
  asylum.sf.ca.us

Georgia Tech
  aql.gatech.edu

Harvard Univ.
  das.harvard.edu

Indiana Univ. Computer Science
  cs.indiana.edu

Info-Mac Archive
  sumex-aim.stanford.edu

Johns Hopkins Univ.
  blaze.cs.jhu.edu

KAIST Computer Underground Digest
  (CuD) archives (in doc/eff/cud)
  cair.kaist.ac.kr

Katholieke Universiteit Leuven
  cc1.kuleuven.ac.be

Lawrence Berkeley Labs
  csam.lbl.gov

Lawrence Livermore National Lab
  ciac.llnl.gov

Massachusetts Institute of Technology
  cecelia.media.mit.edu

MIT Laboratory of Computer Sciences
  allspice.lcs.mit.edu

Monash Univ.
  broncho.ct.monash.edu.au

Murdoch Univ.
csuvax1.csu.murdoch.edu.au

NASA - Jet Propulsion Laboratory
csi.jpl.nasa.gov

NASA - Langley Advanced Research Ctr.
csab.larc.nasa.gov

National Institute for Standards and
Technology
csrc.ncsl.nist.gov

New Mexico State Univ. Computer
Research Lab (CRL)
clr.nmsu.edu

New York Univ.
cs.nyu.edu

North Carolina State Univ.
csl36h.csl.ncsu.edu

Oklahoma State Univ.
datacomm.ucc.okstate.edu

Oregon Graduate Institute of Science and
Technology
cse.ogi.edu

Oregon State Univ.
cs.orst.edu

Pittsburgh Supercomputing Ctr.
a.psc.edu

Purdue Univ.
coast.cs.purdue.edu

Rice Univ.
cs.rice.edu

Rutgers Univ.
crab.rutgers.edu

Saint Mary's College
cs.stmarys.ca

Software Engineering Institute (SEI),
Computer Emergency Response Team
(CERT)
cert.org

SRI International
csl.sri.com

Stanford Univ.
csli.stanford.edu

TidBITs Macintosh Archive
ftp://ftp.tidbits.com/pub/tidbits/tisk/

Univ. Bern
amftp.unibe.ch

Univ. of Arkansas
csegbbs1.uark.edu

Univ. of Britsh Columbia
cs.ubc.ca

Univ. of California - Irvine
cad.ics.uci.edu

Univ. of California - Riverside
corsa.ucr.edu

Univ. of California - San Diego
cs.ucsd.edu

Univ. of California- Berkeley
allspice.berkeley.edu

Univ. of Georgia AI library
aisun1.ai.uga.edu

Univ. of Hawaii
cs_dept_server_1.uhh.hawaii.edu

Univ. of Indiana
cell-relay.indiana.edu

Univ. of Leeds, School of Computer
Studies (SCS)
agora.leeds.ac.uk

Univ. of Maryland
hobbes.cs.umd.edu

Univ. of Massachusetts
cicero.cs.umass.edu

Univ. of Nebraska - Lincoln
cse.unl.edu

Univ. of Queensland
brolga.cc.uq.oz.au

Univ. of Technology, Sydney
death.socs.uts.edu.au

Univ. of Texas - Austin
cs.utexas.edu

Univ. of Toronto
csri.toronto.edu

Univ. of Utah
cc.utah.edu

Univ. of Wisconsin - Madison
gjetost.cs.wisc.edu

Univ. of Wisconsin - Milwaukee
csd4.csd.uwm.edu

Univ. Pierre et Marie Curie - MASI Lab
cao-vlsi.ibp.fr

US Navy - NPS
cs.nps.navy.mil

Gopher Resources

Arizona State Univ.
info.asu.edu

ASCII
mundo.eco.utexas.edu

Association for Computing Machinery
(ACM)
acm.org

BUBL Subject Tree on Computing
ukoln.bath.ac.uk:7070

CACTUS (Capital Area Central Texas Unix
Society)
cactus.org

Clarion Database Developer Programs -
Data Transfer Group
gopher.thegroup.net

CNS, Inc.
joeboy.micro.umn.edu

Computer Networks and Internet Resource Guides
riceinfo.rice.edu

Computer Solutions
csbh.com

Computer World Magazine
gopher.enews.com

Computers and Software WAIS Server
pinus.slu.se

Computing Journals from CICNet
gopher.cic.net

CPSR (Computer Professionals for Social
Responsibility)
gopher.cpsr.org

CREN/Educom
info.educom.edu

Curtin Univ.
info.curtin.edu.au

Data General's Common Sense Connection
gopher.dg.com

DECUS
gopher.decus.org

Electronic Book Stores
ora.com

Engineering and Computer Science (USC)
cwis.usc.edu

IBM
bcsc02.gov.bc.ca:71

IBM ACIS
isaac.engr.washington.edu

IBM Almaden Research Center
index.almaden.ibm.com

IBM Computer Virus Information Center
index.almaden.ibm.com

IBM, AS/400
as400.rochester.ibm.com

IBMLink Gopher
gopher.ibmlink.ibm.com

IEEE
info.computer.org

Imperial College, Dictionary
wombat.doc.ic.ac.uk

International Federation for Information
Processing (IFIP)
ietf.cnri.reston.va.us

Internet Wiretap (Computer)
wiretap.spies.com

Michigan Clearinghouse on Computer-
Mediated Communication
una.hh.lib.umich.edu

MIT Computer Science
gopher.mit.edu:71

Murdoch Univ. Australia Computer
Science Gopher
infolib.murdoch.edu.au

National Coordination Office for HPCC
(NCO/HPCC)
gopher.hpcc.gov

Naval Ocean System Center
trout.nosc.mil

NCSU Study Carrel on Computer Science
dewey.lib.ncsu.edu

NIST Computer Systems Laboratory
zserve.nist.gov

North Carolina State
gopher.ncsu.edu

Numerical Recipes Software
cfata4.harvard.edu

Oak Ridge National Lab
gopher.ccs.ornl.gov

PSU Computer Science Shelf
psulias.psu.edu

Purdue Math/Computer Sciences
thorplus.lib.purdue.edu

Rice Univ.
riceinfo.rice.edu

Roswell Electronic Computer Bookstore -
owl.nstn.ns.ca

SUN Microsystems News Groups and
Archives - SUNSite
calypso-2.oit.unc.edu

Supercomputing and Parallel Computing
unix.hensa.ac.uk

Texas A&M (Computer Science)
gopher.tamu.edu/11/.dir/compsci.dir

Univ. of California - Santa Barbara
summit.ece.ucsb.edu

Univ. of California - Santa Barbara Library
ucsbuxa.ucsb.edu:3001

Univ. of California - Santa Cruz, InfoSlug
System
darkstar.ucsc.edu

Univ. of Chicago Press
press-gopher.uchicago.edu

Univ. of Michigan
una.hh.lib.umich.edu

Univ. of Nevada Computing
gopher.unr.edu

Univ. of South Carolina
theusc.csd.scarolina.edu

Univ. of Texas - Dallas
gopher.utdallas.edu

USAF Software Technology Support
stsc.hill.af.mil

USCS Media Center
scilibx.ucsc.edu

UT Dallas Computing
gopher.utdallas.edu

UTK
gopher.lib.utk.edu

The WELL's Gopherspace
gopher.well.sf.ca.us

Windows Tech Journal Source Code - Data
gopher.thegroup.net

WWW Resources

ACM SIGGRAPH Online Bibliography
Project
http://www.tu-graz.ac.at:2900/Csiggraphbib

ACM SIGMOD Information Server
http://bunny.cs.uiuc.edu/README.html

Advanced Research Corp
http://info.arc.com/

AHPCRC
http://www.arc.umn.edu/html/ahpcrc.html

Alpha 7
http://www.ife.ee.ethz.ch/music/alpha/
alpha.html

Aminet Amiga Archive
http://ftp.wustl.edu/~aminet/

Apple Computers
http://www.apple.com/

Apple Network
http://www.hsas.washington.edu/ANMA/
ANMA.html

ARPA - Advanced Research Projects
Agency
http://ftp.arpa.mil/

Association for Computational Linguistics
(ACL)
http://www.cs.columbia.edu/~acl/
HOME.HTML

Association for Computing Machinery -
ACM
http://www.acm.org/

Australian Computer Science Academics
Database (ACSADB)
http://coral.cs.jcu.edu.au/acsadb/

Bar Ilan Univ.
http://www.cs.biu.ac.il8080/

Berkeley Systems Design, INC (BSD).
http://www.bsdi.com/

Berlin and Brandenburg CS Depts.
http://www.cs.tu-berlin.de/inf-bb/index.html

Bibliographies in BibTeX Format
http://www.ira.uka.de/ftp/ira/bibliography/
index.html

Bilkent Univ.
http://www.cs.bilkent.edu.tr/

Boston Univ. Center
http://conx.bu.edu/CCS/ccs-home-page.html

Brigham Young Univ.
http://www.cs.byu.edu/homepage.html

Brown Univ.
http://www.cs.brown.edu:8001/home-page.html

BSDI Europe
http://www.hillside.co.uk/

C++ Tutorial Textbook
http://info.desy.de/gna/html/cc/text/index.html

CalPoly
http://www.calpoly.edu/~acs/

CalTech College of Computing
http://www.ccsf.caltech.edu/ccsf.html

CalTech Computation and Neural Systems
http://www.cns.caltech.edu/

Carleton Univ.
http://www.sce.carleton.ca/

Carnegie-Mellon Software
http://www.sei.cmu.edu/FrontDoor.html

CCAE-Lisbon
http://www.inesc.pt/inesc/centros/ccae.html

CCD-Brookhaven
http://docserver.bnl.gov/com/www/default.html

CCRC-Washington Univ.
http://dworkin.wustl.edu/

CCSR-Beckman
http://www.ccsr.uiuc.edu/CCSRHome.html

Center for Innovative Computer Applications
http://www.cica.indiana.edu/news/campus/index.html

Center for Scientific Computing, Finland
http://www.csc.fi/

Center for Software Development
http://www.center.org/csd/home.html

Centre Universitaire d'Informatique
http://cui_www.unige.ch/

CERN
http://www1.cern.ch/

CERN Software Technology Interest Group
http://dxsting.cern.ch/sting/sting.html

Clemson Univ.
http://diogenes.cs.clemson.edu/CSE/.html

Colorado Center for Applied Parallel Processing
http://www.cs.colorado.edu/home/capp/demo.html

Colorado Internet Cooperative Association
http://plaza.xor.com/coop/index.html

Colorado State Univ.
http://www.cs.colostate.edu/

Columbia Univ.
http://www.cs.columbia.edu/

Commodore 64 and 128
http://www.warwick.ac.uk/~stuce/c64.html

Computer Networks and Distributed Systems Research Lab
http://netweb.usc.edu/

Computer Software Management and Information Ctr.
http://www.cosmic.uga.edu/

Computer Wave Newspaper E-Zine
http://computerwave.com/

Computer-Mediated Communications Archive
http://www.rpi.edu/~decemj/cmc/center.html

Concurrent Systems Lab
http://www.comlab.ox.ac.uk/archive/concurrent.html

Cornell Univ.
http://www.cs.cornell.edu/

COSMIC Information
http://www.cosmic.uga.edu/

CPSR
http://www.cpsr.org/home

CPU Info Center
http://www.ncsa.uiuc.edu/General/MetaCenter/MetaCenterHome.html

Cray Research
http://www.cray.com/

CREMISI
http://cremisi.rob.csata.it/

CRL-Japan
http://www.crl.go.jp/

CSHC-U of MD
http://wais.isr.umd.edu/CCDS/homepage.html

CSIRO / Flinders Joint Research Centre in Information
http://www.jrc.flinders.edu.au/

CSL-SRI
http://www.csl.sri.com/

CSP, Italy
http://services.csp.it/welcome.html

CWI
http://www.cwi.nl/default.html

Dartmouth College
http://www.cs.dartmouth.edu/

De Montfort Univ., Leicester, UK
http://www.cms.dmu.ac.uk/Research/

DoD HPC User's Group
http://www.fim.wpafb.af.mil/hpcug/hpcug.html

Duke Univ.
http://www.cs.duke.edu/home-page.html

ECRC GmbH, Germany.
http://www.ecrc.de/

ERCIM
http://www-ercim.inria.fr/

ERG-Aberdeen
http://www.erg.abdn.ac.uk/misc/personnel.html

Ethernet Homepage at U. Texas
http://mojo.ots.utexas.edu/ethernet/ethernet-home.html

European Computer-Industry Research
http://www.ecrc.de/

EWB: The Environment WorkBench
http://satori2.lerc.nasa.gov/DOC/EWB/ewbhome.html

Exeter Univ.
http://www.dcs.exeter.ac.uk/

EXUG
http://www.informatik.uni-dortmund.de/EXUG/EXUG.html

FIZ Karlsruhe
http://www.zblmath.fiz-karlsruhe.de/

Florida State Univ.
http://www.cs.fsu.edu/

Formal Methods Lab
http://www.comlab.ox.ac.uk/archive/formal-methods.html

Fortran 90 Repository
http://www.nag.co.uk/1/nagware/Examples

Fortran 90 Tutorials
http://asis01.cern.ch/CN/CNTUT/f90/Overview.html

Free On-line Dictionary of Computing
http://wombat.doc.ic.ac.uk/

Front Range UNIX Users' Group
http://plaza.xor.com/fruug/index.html

Georgia Tech Graphics, Visualization, and Usability Center
http://www.gatech.edu/gvu/gvutop.html

German National Research Center for Computer Science (GMD)
http://www.gmd.de/

"Grex" Open Computer Conference System.
http://pubweb.parc.xerox.com/

Harvard Univ.
http://das-www.harvard.edu/

HCRC-Edinburgh
http://www.cogsci.ed.ac.uk/hcrc/home.html

Helsinki Univ.
http://www.hut.fi/d_cs.html

High Performance Computing Sites and Resources Worldwide
http://www.nas.nasa.gov/RNR/Parallel/HPC-sites.html

ICBL-Edinburgh
http://www.icbl.hw.ac.uk/

IEE - Institution of Electrical Engineers
http://www.iee.org.uk/

IEEE - Institute of Electrical and Electronics Engineers
http://www.ieee.org/

IEEE Electromagnetic Compatibility Society
http://www.emclab.umr.edu/ieee_emc/

IHNS-Japan
http://www.glocom.ac.jp/IHNS/intro.html

IIASA-Austria
http://www.iiasa.ac.at/welcome.html

Index to Multimedia Information Sources
http://cui_www.unige.ch/OSG/MultimediaInfo/
index.html

Indiana Univ.
http://www.cs.indiana.edu/

Info-Mac Hyperarchive
http://hyperarchive.lcs.mit.edu/
HyperArchive.html

Information and Computation
http://theory.lcs.mit.edu/~iandc/

Information Science Research Inst.
http://www.isri.unlv.edu/

Institute for Advanced Computer Studies.
http://www.umiacs.umd.edu/

Integrated Computer Solutions
http://www.ics.com/

Intergraph Online
http://www.intergraph.com/

Internet Computer Index (ICI)
http://ici.proper.com/

Internet DTP Jumplist
http://www.cs.purdue.edu/homes/gwp/dtp/
dtp.html

Iowa State Univ.
http://www.cs.iastate.edu/

IRIS-Brown
http://www.iris.brown.edu/iris

ISI-USC
http://www.isi.edu/

ISR
http://www.isr.umd.edu/

ISRI-UNLV
http://www.isri.unlv.edu/

ISS-Singapore
http://www.iss.nus.sg/

Johns Hopkins Univ.
http://www.cs.jhu.edu/

Kaman Sciences Data and Analysis Center
http://www.utica.kaman.com:8001/

Khoral Research Home
http://www.khoros.unm.edu/

Khoros Informatics
http://www.infc.ulst.ac.uk/local/khoros/

Khoros Model
http://cornea.mbvlab.wpafb.af.mil/khoros.html

Khoros Toolbox Development
http://www.c3.lanl.gov:1331/c3/projects/
Khoros/main.html

KSL NRC, Canada.
http://ai.iit.nrc.ca/home_page.html

Lateiner Dataspace, USA.
http://www.dataspace.com/

Leiden Univ. - CS Department
http://www.wi.leidenuniv.nl/

Linux Documentation Project
http://sunsite.unc.edu/mdw/linux.html

LIT-Switzerland
http://litsun.epfl.ch/

LLNL
http://www-atp.llnl.gov/

Logic Programming
http://www.comlab.ox.ac.uk/archive/logic-
prog.html

Lund Institute of Technology, Sweden
http://www.dna.lth.se/

Macintosh FAQs
http://www.astro.nwu.edu/lentz/mac/faqs/
home-faqs.html

Mathematica World
http://www.vut.edu.au/MW/

MathSource - Resource for Mathematica
http://mathsource.wri.com/

Mathworks Home Page
http://www.mathworks.com/

Maui High Performance Computing
Center
http://www.mhpcc.edu/mhpcc.html

McDonnell Douglas Aerospace
http://pat.mdc.com/

Microsoft Advanced Technology Div.
http://www.research.microsoft.com/

Mississippi State Univ.
http://www.cs.msstate.edu/dist_computing/
mpi.html

Mississippi Univ.
http://www.mcsr.olemiss.edu/

MIT Laboratory for Computer Science
http://www.lcs.mit.edu/

MIT Telemedia, Networks and Systems
Group
http://www.tns.lcs.mit.edu/tns-www-
home.html

Mobile and Wireless Computing
http://snapple.cs.washington.edu:600/mobile/
mobile_www.html

Monash Univ.
http://www.cs.monash.edu.au/

Multimedia Communications Research
Lab
http://mango.genie.uottawa.ca/

NASA Ctr. for Computational Sciences
http://farside.gsfc.nasa.gov:80/NCCS/

NASA Digital Library Technology
http://farside.gsfc.nasa.gov:80/ISTO/DLT/

National Energy Research Supercomputer
Center
http://www.nersc.gov/

National Institute for Management
Technology (NIMT), Ireland.
http://www.nimt.rtc-cork.ie/nimt.htm

NCSA - National Center for
Supercomputing Applications
http://www.ncsa.uiuc.edu/General/
NCSAHome.html

NECTEC-Thailand
http://www.nectec.or.th/nectec.html

Net Guru Technologies Inc.
http://www.internet-is.com/netguru/

Netlib
http://www.netlib.org/

Network Computing Devices, Inc. (NCD)
http://www.ncd.com/

Newton Info Page
http://www.uth.tmc.edu/newton_info/

NeXT news and information
http://www1.cern.ch/CENeXT/Overview.html

North Carolina State Univ. ACS
http://www.acs.ncsu.edu/Sybase/Archive.html

Northeast Parallel Architectures Center
(NPAC)
http://www.npac.syr.edu/

Novell European Support Center
http://ftp.novell.de/default.html

Novell Online Services
http://www.novell.com/

NPAC-Syracuse
http://minerva.npac.syr.edu/home.html

NRL-AITB
http://www.ait.nrl.navy.mil/home.html

Numerical Algorithms Group Ltd (NAG),
UK
http://www.nag.co.uk/

Object-oriented Programming
http://www.clark.net/pub/howie/OO/
oo_home.html

Ohio Supercomputer Center
http://www.osc.edu/welcome.html

Old Dominion Univ.
http://www.cs.odu.edu/index.html

OPTICS.ORG - The Photonics Resource
Center
http://www.optics.org/

Oregon Graduate Institute
http://www.cse.ogi.edu/

Oxford Univ.
http://www.comlab.ox.ac.uk/

Paradigm Software
http://192.246.168.15/Paradigm.html

Paragon Manuals
http://www.ccsf.caltech.edu/paragon/
man.html

Parallel Computing Meta FAQ
http://ivory.nosc.mil/~trancv/ppdir/PP-
mFAQ.new.html

Parallel Tools Consortium
http://www.llnl.gov/ptools/ptools.html

Partnership in Advanced Computing
Technologies (PACT), Bristol, UK.
http://www.pact.srf.ac.uk/

PERL - Practical Extraction and Report
Language
http://www.cs.cmu.edu:8001/htbin/perl-man

Pitt SCC
http://pscinfo.psc.edu/

PowerPC News
http://power.globalnews.com:8000/

Princeton Univ.
http://www.cs.princeton.edu/

Programming Languages
http://src.doc.ic.ac.uk/bySubject/Computing/
Languages.html

Programming Technology Lab
http://progwww.vub.ac.be/prog/home.html

Purdue Univ.
http://www.cs.purdue.edu/

QMS, Inc.
http://www.qms.com/

Quadralay
http://www.quadralay.com/home.html

RAND
http://www.rand.org/

RENATER-Paris
http://www.urec.fr/Renater/

Research Institute for Computing and
Information Systems
http://ricis.cl.uh.edu/

RICIS-Houston
http://rbse.jsc.nasa.gov/

Robert Lentz's Macintosh Resources
http://www.astro.nwu.edu/lentz/mac/home-
mac.html

Rochester Institute of Technology
http://www.cs.rochester.edu/

Rocky Mountain Internet Users' Group
http://plaza.xor.com/rmiug/index.html

Royal Institute of Technology, Stockholm
http://www.nada.kth.se/index-en.html

Rutherford Appleton Laboratory
http://web.inf.rl.ac.uk/

Safety-Critical Systems
http://www.comlab.ox.ac.uk/archive/
safety.html

San Diego Supercomputer Center
http://www.sdsc.edu/

Sandia National Lab
http://www.sandia.gov/

Scandal Supercomputing Project
http://parallel.scandal.cs.cmu.edu/www/

SCO Open Systems Software
http://www.uniforum.org/

Silicon Graphics (SGI).
http://www.sgi.com/

Society for Information Display
http://www.display.org/sid/

Software for MIMD Parallel Computers
http://www.ccsf.caltech.edu/software.html

SRC-Digital
http://www.research.digital.com/SRC/
home.html

SRI
http://www.csl.sri.com/

Stanford Center for Design Research
(CDR).
http://gummo.stanford.edu/

Stanford Center for Information
http://logic.stanford.edu/cit/cit.html

Stanford Univ. Knowledge Systems
http://www-ksl.stanford.edu/

SUN Microsystems
http://www.sun.com/

Sunergy
http://www.sun.com/sunergy/

Sunsite Northern Europe
http://src.doc.ic.ac.uk/public/aminet/info/www/
home-src.doc.html

Supercomputer Computations Research
Institute (SCRI), Florida, USA.
http://www.scri.fsu.edu/

Swarthmore College Computer Society
http://sccs.swarthmore.edu/

SymbolicNet
http://symbolicnet.mcs.kent.edu/

SYNERGY Project
http://argo.cis.temple.edu:4000/

Tandem Computers
http://www.tandem.com/

Technical Reports Master archive site
http://www.cs.indiana.edu/ucstri/sitelist.html

Technology Board of Trade (reusable
software)
http://www.service.com/tbot/

Technology Review
http://www.mit.edu:8001/afs/athena/org/t/
techreview/www/tr.html

TeX documentation
http://noa.huji.ac.il/tex/www/top.html

UMTK
http://www.cs.usm.my/utmk/utmkhome.htm

Unified Computer Science TR Index
http://cs.indiana.edu/cstr/search

United Technologies Research Center
http://utrcwww.utc.com/UTRC/General/
UTRCGen.html

Univ. of British Columbia
http://www.cs.ubc.ca/home

Univ. of California - Berkeley
http://http.cs.berkeley.edu/

Univ. of California - Santa Barbara
http://www.ece.ucsb.edu/

Univ. of Chile
http://www.dcc.uchile.cl/

Univ. of Colorado
http://www.cs.colorado.edu/

Univ. of Florida
http://www.cis.ufl.edu/

Univ. of Helsinki
http://www.cs.helsinki.fi/

Univ. of Illinois at Chicago
http://www.eecs.uic.edu/

Univ. of Illinois at Urbana-Champaign
http://www.cs.uiuc.edu/

Univ. of Iowa
http://www.cs.uiowa.edu/

Univ. of Iowa COMPS Lab
http://caesar.cs.uiowa.edu/

Univ. of Limerick
http://itdsrv1.ul.ie/CSIS/computer-science-info.html

Univ. of Manchester
http://www.cs.man.ac.uk/

Univ. of Manitoba
http://ftp.cs.umanitoba.ca/

Univ. of Maryland
http://gimble.cs.umd.edu/

Univ. of Maryland Baltimore County
http://www.cs.umbc.edu/

Univ. of Massachusetts Dartmouth
http://ciswww.cogsci.umassd.edu/
welcome.html

Univ. of Missouri - Rolla
http://www.cs.umr.edu/

Univ. de Montréal (DIRO)
http://www.iro.umontreal.ca/

Univ. of Newcastle
http://catless.ncl.ac.uk/

Univ. of Nottingham
http://web.cs.nott.ac.uk/Papers/index.html

Univ. of Pisa
http://www.di.unipi.it/welcome.html

Univ. of S. Louisiana CACS
http://www.cacs.usl.edu/Departments/CACS/

Univ. of Salzburg
http://www.cosy.sbg.ac.at/welcome.html

Univ. of Saskatoon
http://alf.usask.ca/Home.html

Univ. of Southern California, Information
Sciences Institute
http://www.isi.edu/

Univ. of Sydney, Basser
http://www.cs.su.oz.au/

Univ. of Tennessee
http://www.utcc.utk.edu/

Univ. of Texas - Austin
http://www.cs.utexas.edu/

Univ. of Texas - Neural Nets
http://www.cs.utexas.edu/~nn/

Univ. of Toronto
http://www.cdf.utoronto.ca/

Univ. of Tromso, Norway
http://www.cs.uit.no/en/

Univ. of Washington
http://www.cs.washington.edu/

Unix HENSA Archive (U. of Kent)
http://www.hensa.ac.uk/

Uppsala Univ., Sweden
http://www.csd.uu.se/

USENIX Association
http://www.usenix.org/

Women and Computer Science
http://www.ai.mit.edu/people/ellens/
gender.html

Worcester Polytechnic
http://cs.wpi.edu/

X Consortium.
http://www.x.org/

Xerox PARC

http://pubweb.parc.xerox.com/

Electronics & Electrical Engineering

See also Chemistry, Computer Science, Energy, Engineering, Imaging Technologies, Physics

Usenet Newsgroups

comp.lsi
Newsgroup-based Mailing List: No.
Charter: Large-scale integrated circuits.

rec.audio.tubes
Created by: Reid Kneeland
<reid@tti.com>
Call for Votes Date: July 19, 1995
Newsgroup-based Mailing List: No.
Charter (from Call for Votes):
Rec.audio.tubes is dedicated to the discussion of vacuum tube audio equipment.

sci.electronics
Newsgroup-based Mailing List: No.
Charter: Discussion group on electronics.

sci.electronics.basics
Created by: Mark Zenier
<mzenier@netcom.com> or
<mzenier@eskimo.com>
Call for Votes Date: October 2, 1995
Newsgroup-based Mailing List: No.
Charter (from Call for Votes):
A forum for discussion of electronics where there is no such thing as a stupid question. Beginners' questions. Discussion of electronics education. Requests for other sources of information.

sci.electronics.cad
Newsgroup-based Mailing List: No.
Charter: Discussion group on CAD.

sci.electronics.components
Created by: Mark Zenier

<mzenier@netcom.com> or
<mzenier@eskimo.com>
Call for Votes Date: October 2, 1995
Newsgroup-based Mailing List: No.
Charter (from Call for Votes):
Discussions of electronics at the component level. The use, limitations, and identification of resistors, capacitors, integrated circuits, connectors, enclosures, ... and so on. Locations and contact information for Manufacturers, Distributors, and other sources for supply and technical information.

sci.electronics.design
Created by: Mark Zenier
<mzenier@netcom.com> or
<mzenier@eskimo.com>
Call for Votes Date: October 2, 1995
Newsgroup-based Mailing List: No.
Charter (from Call for Votes):
Discussions relevant to the design of electronics circuits.

sci.electronics.equipment
Created by: Mark Zenier
<mzenier@netcom.com> or
<mzenier@eskimo.com>
Call for Votes Date: October 2, 1995
Newsgroup-based Mailing List: No.
Charter (from Call for Votes):
Discussion of the application and internal operation and relative merits of test equipment, laboratory equipment, and industrial equipment. This is not a forsale group. Buying/selling is supposed to occur in the relocated misc.industry.electronics.forsale group. (Discussions on the relative merits of various consumer electronics equipment

are better held in the groups in the rec hierarchy devoted to those topics.)

sci.electronics.misc

Created by: Mark Zenier <mzenier@netcom.com> or <mzenier@eskimo.com>
Call for Votes Date: October 2, 1995
Newsgroup-based Mailing List: No.
Charter (from Call for Votes):
General discussions on the topic of electronics. (Discussions on the relative merits of various consumer electronics equipment are better held in the groups in the rec hierarchy devoted to those topics.)

sci.electronics.repair

Newsgroup-based Mailing List: No.
Charter: Discussion group on electronics repair.

sci.engr.television.advanced

Created by: Rob Chambers <robgc@freenet.edmonton.ab.ca>
Call for Votes Date: April 24, 1995
Newsgroup-based Mailing List: No.
Charter (from Call for Votes):
This is the renaming of the current group sci.engr.advanced-tv to sci.engr.television.advanced. The current charter of this group will remain the same.

sci.engr.television.broadcast

Created by: Rob Chambers <robgc@freenet.edmonton.ab.ca>
Call for Votes Date: April 24, 1995
Newsgroup-based Mailing List: No.
Charter (from Call for Votes):
This newsgroup will be used for the technical discussions of equipment relating to the operation of a broadcast television facility. This scope will include equipment that is used to transmit, store, manipulate, or generate broadcast quality signals. Engineering standards, practices and troubleshooting will also be discussed.

Recognized groups (such as NAB, SMPTE, etc) will also be encouraged to discuss upcoming conferences and information relating to the broadcast industry.

Frequently Asked Questions

68hc11 microcontroller FAQ

Maintainer: sibit@datasrv.co.il (Russ Hersch)
Where on Usenet: comp.robotics
Where it's archived:
rtfm.mit.edu:pub/usenet/sci.electronics/68hc11_microcontroller_FAQ
What it's for: Reference sources ftp sites, etc. pertaining to the Motorola 68hc11 microcontroller.

8051 microcontroller FAQ

Maintainer: sibit@datasrv.co.il (Russ Hersch)
Where on Usenet: comp.sys.intel
Where it's archived:
rtfm.mit.edu:pub/usenet/comp.sys.intel
What it's for: A collection of information sources on the Intel 8051 family of microcontrollers (and variants).

Electrical Wiring FAQ

Maintainer: clewis@ferret.ocunix.on.ca (Chris Lewis)
Where on Usenet: sci.electronics
Where it's archived:
rtfm.mit.edu:pub/usenet/sci.electronics/Electrical_Wiring_FAQ_[Part_1_2]
rtfm.mit.edu:pub/usenet/sci.electronics/Electrical_Wiring_FAQ_[Part_2_2]
What it's for: A great deal of information on house wiring.

Mail Order Electronics Companies

Maintainer: jfw@ksr.com (John F. Woods)
Where on Usenet: sci.electronics
Where it's archived:
rtfm.mit.edu:pub/usenet/sci.electronics
What it's for: A reference list for mail-order electronics companies.

Microcontroller primer and FAQ

Maintainer: sibit@datasrv.co.il (Russ Hersch)
Where on Usenet: comp.robotics
Where it's archived:
rtfm.mit.edu:pub/usenet/comp.robotics
What it's for: A primer and general FAQ about microcontrollers.

Sci.Engr.Semiconductors FAQ
Maintainer: fbertsch@msc.cornell.edu
Where on Usenet: sci.engr.semiconductors
Where it's archived:
rtfm.mit.edu:pub/usenet/sci.astro
What it's for: Information on how to effectively use the various topical newsgroups and where to go for more information.

Electronics and Electrical Engineering Resources

FTP Resources

Numerical Electromagnetics Code Archive
ftp.netcom.com/pub/rander/NEC

Rome Lab. Electronics Reliability Div. Status Report
erda.rl.af.mil:80/pub/status/

TeX Archive
ftp.shsu.edu/tex-archive

Gopher Resources

Electric Power Research Institute
burrow.cl.msu.edu

EE (ADFA)
ccadfa.cc.adfa.oz.au

Electrical Wiring FAQ
biome.bio.ns.ca

Electromagnetic Resources (UC Santa Barbara/Auburn)
summit.ece.ucsb.edu

Eletter on Systems, Control, & Signal Processing
gopher.cic.net

IEEE Computer Society
info.computer.org

Improving Electric Power Utility Efficiency: Issues
ftp.worldbank.org

Univ. Texas
ftp.cc.utexas.edu:3003

UWM EE
alpha1.csd.uwm.edu

Wisconsin Electric
calvin.biotech.wisc.edu

WWW Resources

Aalborg Univ.
http://www-i8.auc.dk

Aberdeen Univ.
http://www.erg.abdn.ac.uk/

American Electronics Association
http://www.aeanet.org/

American Institute of Physics
http://aip.org/

American Physical Society
http://aps.org/

American Solar Energy Society
http://www.engr.wisc.edu/centers/sel/ases/ases2.html

American Vacuum Society
http://www.vacuum.org/

Argonne National Lab.
http://epics.aps.anl.gov/argonne.html

Arizona State Univ.
http://www.eas.asu.edu:7001/

ARPA STARS Program
http://www.stars.ballston.paramax.com/index.html

Association for Computing Machinery
http://info.acm.org/

Association for Computing Machinery at UIUC
http://www.acm.uiuc.edu/

Aston Univ.
http://www.eeap.aston.ac.uk/home.html

AT&T Bell Labs. Research
http://www.research.att.com/

Audio Engineering Society
http://www.cudenver.edu/aes/index.html

BCS - British Computer Society
http://www.gold.net/bcs/

Bel Canto
http://math-www.uio.no/bel-canto/

Bilkent Univ. - EEE
http://manisa.ee.bilkent.edu.tr:2222/

Biofuels Information Network
http://www.esd.ornl.gov/BFDP/BFDPMOSAIC/binmenu.html

Bogazici Univ.
http://dec002.cmpe.boun.edu.tr/

Bottom Line Archive
http://www.oulu.fi/tbl.html

Bradley Univ.
http://cegt201.bradley.edu/

British Electrophoresis Society
http://sunspot.bioc.cam.ac.uk/BES.html

Broker at USC/ISI
http://drax.isi.edu:70/

Brookhaven National Lab.
http://suntid.bnl.gov:8080/bnl.html

BYU
http://www.ee.byu.edu/

California Polytechnic State Univ.
http://www.elee.calpoly.edu/

Caltech
http://www.micro.caltech.edu

Canadian Association of Physics
http://www.inrs-ener.uquebec.ca/surfsci/
index.html

Carleton Univ.
http://www.sce.carleton.ca/

Carnagie Mellon Univ.
http://www.ece.cmu.edu/

Catania Systems and Control Group
http://imdes02.dees.unict.it

CCDs for Material Scientists
http://zebu.uoregon.edu/ccd.html

Centro de Pesquisa e Desenvolvimento em
Engenharia Eletrica
http://www.cpdee.ufmg.br/

Chalmers Univ.
http://www.ce.chalmers.se/

Clemson Univ.
http://www.eng.clemson.edu/~ECE/

Colorado State Univ.
http://www.lance.colostate.edu/ee/

Columbia CTR WWW
http://www.ctr.columbia.edu/
CUCTR_Home.html

Common LISP Hypermedia Server
http://www.ai.mit.edu/projects/iiip/doc/cl-http/
server.html

Community Computer Network Surveys
http://www.cs.washington.edu/research/
community-networks/

Computer and Communication Companies
http://www-atp.llnl.gov/atp/companies.html

Computer and Network Security Index
http://www.tansu.com.au/Info/security.html

Computer Integrated Manufacturing at
Maryland
http://gimble.cs.umd.edu/cim/cim.html

Computer Sciences Tech Report Index (U.
Indiana)
http://cs.indiana.edu/cstr/search

Computer Security FAQ
http://www.cis.ohio-state.edu/hypertext/faq/
usenet/security-faq/faq.html

Computer Systems Lab, NTU, Taiwan
http://earth.csie.ntu.edu.tw/

Concordia Univ.
http://www.ece.concordia.ca/

Continuous Electron Beam Accelerator
Facility
http://www.cebaf.gov:3000/cebaf.html

Ctr. for Display Technology & Manufacturing
http://dtm.eecs.umich.edu/

Ctr. for Information Technology
http://logic.stanford.edu/cit/cit.html

Delft Univ. of Technology
http://www.twi.tudelft.nl/welcome.html

Distributed ELectronic Telecommunications Archive (DELTA)
http://gozer.idbsu.edu/business/nethome.html

Distributed Multimedia Survey: Standards
http://cui_www.unige.ch/OSG/MultimediaInfo/
mmsurvey/standards.html

Duisburg Univ., Optoelectronics
http://optorisc.uni-duisburg.de/

Duke
http://www.ee.duke.edu/

ECCI
http://sass577.endo.sandia.gov/ecci/
white_paper.html

Edinburgh Univ.
http://www.ee.ed.ac.uk/

Edupage Newsletter
http://www.ee.surrey.ac.uk/edupage/

EE/CS Mother Site
http://www-soe.stanford.edu/soe/ieee/eesites.html

EEB Home Page
http://www.eeb.ele.tue.nl/index.html

Electric Power Research Institute
http://www.epri.com/

Electric Press, Inc. Vol. 1, No. 1
http://www.elpress.com/homepage.html

Electrical Engineering Circuits Archive
http://weber.u.washington.edu/~pfloyd/ee/index.html

Electrical Engineering Virtual Library
http://arioch.gsfc.nasa.gov/wwwvl/ee.html

Electricity Association
http://www.cityscape.co.uk/users/bm27/index.htm

Electrochemical Society
http://www.electrochem.org/

Electronic Circuit Design Group (EEB)
http://www.eeb.ele.tue.nl/

Electronic Materials Research
http://weber.u.washington.edu/~pearsall/

Electronic Resources Index
http://pasture.ecn.purdue.edu/~laird/Electronics/index.html

ElectroScience Lab.
http://hertz.eng.ohio-state.edu/

Electrotechnik
http://www.rz.uni-karlsruhe.de/Outerspace/VirtualLibrary/621.3.html

EMC Gateway at SETH Corp.
http://www.sethcorp.com/

Employment in Engineering
http://www.wpi.edu/Academics/IMS/Library/jobguide/engin.html

EMS Technologies, Inc.
http://www.elmg.com/

Energy Sciences Network
http://www.es.net/

Fermi National Accelerator Ctr.
http://fnnews.fnal.gov/

Finnish WWW servers
http://www.cs.hut.fi/finland.html

Fintronic Linux Systems Catalog
http://www.fintronic.com/linux/catalog.html

Florida State Univ.
http://ealpha1.eng.fsu.edu/ee.html

Formal Methods
http://www.comlab.ox.ac.uk/archive/formal-methods.html

Free Compilers List
http://cui_www.unige.ch/OSG/Langlist/Free/free-toc.html

Free Univ. of Brussels
http://pespmc1.vub.ac.be/VUBULB.html

George Mason Univ.
http://bass.gmu.edu/

Georgia Tech
http://www.ee.gatech.edu/

HCI Resources Page
http://www.ida.liu.se/labs/aslab/groups/um/hci/

Helsinki Univ. of Technology
http://www.hut.fi/d_ee.html

Helsinki Univ. of Technology Circuit Theory Lab
http://picea.hut.fi/

Heriot-Watt Univ.
http://www.cee.hw.ac.uk/

HobokenX
http://www.stevens-tech.edu/hobokenx/

HUT Circuit Theory Lab.
http://picea.hut.fi/

IEE - Institution of Electrical Engineers
http://www.iee.org.uk/

IEEE - Institute of Electrical and Electronics Engineers
http://www.ieee.org/

IKEDA lab.Chiba
http://www.hike.te.chiba-u.ac.jp/

Illinois Institute of Technology
http://www.ece.iit.edu/

Imperial College
http://www.ee.ic.ac.uk/

Information Processing Science
http://rieska.oulu.fi/

Information Systems in Austria
http://www.cosy.sbg.ac.at/directories/austria.html

Innovatronix Inc. Home Page
http://www.globe.com.ph/~tronix/

Institute for Technology Development
http://www.aue.com/ITD_info.html

Institute of Physics
http://www.iop.org/

Institute of Technology, Lund, Sweden.
http://www.elmat.lth.se/

Instituto de Engenharia de Sistemas
http://albertina.inesc.pt/

Intl. Commission on Illumination
http://www.hike.te.chiba-u.ac.jp/ikeda/CIE/home.html

Intl. Computer Science Institute
http://http.icsi.berkeley.edu/

Intl. Electrotechnical Commission,IEC
http://www.hike.te.chiba-u.ac.jp/ikeda/IEC/home.html

Intl. Teletimes — Biographies
http://www.wimsey.com/teletimes.root/biography.html

IRC in Polymer Science and Technology (Leeds)
http://irc.leeds.ac.uk/

ISDN Page
http://alumni.caltech.edu/~dank/isdn/

ISU Computing and information Services
http://www.ilstu.edu/

ITEA Southern Cross Chapter Home Page
http://130.220.64.152/iteahome.htm

Johns Hopkins Univ. Sensory Communications and Analog VLSI Laboratories
http://olympus.ece.jhu.edu/

JVC Service & Engineering
http://www.jvc-us.com/

KAIST
http://ee.kaist.ac.kr/

Kansas State Univ.
http://www.eece.ksu.edu/

King's College London
http://www.eee.kcl.ac.uk/

KTH Sweden
http://www.e.kth.se/home/elektro-home-eng.html

KU Leuven
http://www.esat.kuleuven.ac.be/

Kuhnke GmbH
http://www.cls.de/kuhnke/Welcome.html

Kuwait Univ.
http://burgan.eng.kuniv.edu.kw:8080/

Kyoto Univ. Info Science Lab
http://www.lab1.kuis.kyoto-u.ac.jp/

Kyushu Univ., Japan
http://www.ee.kyushu-u.ac.jp/index.html

Laboratory for EM Fields and Microwave
http://www.ifh.ee.ethz.ch/

Lamont-Doherty Earth Observatory Mosaic
http://www.ldeo.columbia.edu/

LANL Advanced Computing Lab.
http://www.acl.lanl.gov/Home.html

Laser WWW Information Server
http://www.law.indiana.edu/misc/laser.html

Launch Pad for UK Electronic Engineers
http://www.ibmpcug.co.uk/~sunrise/index.htm

Lawrence Berkeley Lab.
http://www.lbl.gov/LBL.html

Lawrence Livermore National Lab.
http://www.llnl.gov/

LESO-PB: Laboratoire d'Énergie Solaire et de Physique du Bâtiment
http://lesowww.epfl.ch/index.html

Lexicon of Semiconductor Terms
http://rel.semi.harris.com/docs/lexicon/

LLNL High Energy Physics Group
http://gem1.llnl.gov/

Lober & Walsh Engineering
http://www.lober-and-walsh.com/

Lockheed
http://hitchhiker.space.lockheed.com/aic/README.html

Los Alamos National Lab.
http://www.lanl.gov/

Lublin Technical Univ., Poland
http://volt.pol.lublin.pl/

Massana Ltd., Dublin, Ireland - ASIC design for DSP applications
http://www.massana.ie/

MBONE - an overview
http://www.cs.ucl.ac.uk/mice/mbone_review.html

MCC
http://epims1.gsfc.nasa.gov/MCC/MCC.html

McCann Electronics
http://www.mccann1.com/

McDonald Distributors
http://www.mcdonald.com/mcdonald/

MCNC Transfers Technolgy to Interpath
http://www.interpath.net/INTERPATH/
Interpath.html

MDA - Houston
http://pat.mdc.com/

Measurement Science & Technology,
NASA Langley Research
http://ndb1.larc.nasa.gov/

Michigan Technological Univ.
http://www.ee.mtu.edu/

Microelectronics Research Ctr.
http://www.mrc.uidaho.edu/

Microsensor & Actuator Technology
(MAT) Berlin
http://www-mat.ee.tu-berlin.de/

Mississippi State Univ.
http://www.ee.msstate.edu/

MIT - Research Laboratory of Electronics
http://rleweb.mit.edu/

Monash Univ.
http://www.cs.monash.edu.au/

MTL Instruments Group plc
http://www.mtl-inst.com/

Multimedia Information Sources Index
http://cui_www.unige.ch/OSG/MultimediaInfo/
index.html

N.R.C. Canada Autonomous Systems Lab
http://autsrv.iitsg.nrc.ca/choice.html

Nagoya Univ. - Bio-Electronics Lab
http://www.bioele.nuee.nagoya-u.ac.jp/

Nanoelectronics Lab, Univ. of Cincinnati
http://www.eng.uc.edu/nano/nanohome.html

NASA/Goddard Space Flight Ctr.
http://hypatia.gsfc.nasa.gov/
GSFC_homepage.html

National Microelectronics Research Centre
http://nmrc.ucc.ie/

National Technical Univ. of Athens
http://www.ntua.gr/

NAVE Navigating and Acting in Virtual
Environments (virtual reality, spatial

sound, CU Boulder)
http://www.cs.colorado.edu/homes/cboyd/
public_html/Home.html

Network Nation Revisited
http://www.stevens-tech.edu/~dbelson/thesis/
thesis.html

Neurosciences Internet Resource Guide
http://http2.sils.umich.edu/Public/nirg/
nirg1.html

New Mexico State Univ.
http://pslwww.nmsu.edu/Welcome.html

New Mexico Tech - EE/Physics
http://www.ee.nmt.edu/

North Carolina State Univ.
http://www.ece.ncsu.edu/

Northwestern Univ.
http://www.eecs.nwu.edu/

NSF SUCCEED Engineering Visual
Database
http://succeed.edtech.vt.edu/

NTUA WWW Server - SoftLab
http://www.ntua.gr/

Numerix - DSP Solutions
http://www.compulink.co.uk/~numerix/

Oak Ridge National Lab.
http://jupiter.esd.ornl.gov/

OCEAN Users Manual
http://olt.et.tudelft.nl/usr1/patrick/public_html/
docs/wwman/wwman.html

Ocean Sea-of-Gates Design System
http://olt.et.tudelft.nl/ocean/ocean.html

Ohio State ElectroScience Laboratory
http://hertz.eng.ohio-state.edu/

OPTICS.ORG - The Photonics Resource
Center
http://www.optics.org/

Oregon State Univ.
http://www.ece.orst.edu/

Pacific Northwest Lab.
http://romana.crystal.pnl.gov/pnl.html

Parallel Computing Archive at HENSA/
Unix
http://www.hensa.ac.uk/parallel/

Philadelphia IEEE Consultants' Network
http://www.ece.vill.edu:80/conet/

Pioneer Global Home Page
http://www.pn.com/

PNL Medical Technology and Systems Initiative
http://www.emsl.pnl.gov:2080/docs/cie/MTS.html

Politechnika Gdanska - Electronics
http://www.gumbeers.elka.pg.gda.pl/

Project Mgmt Software Reviews
http://www.wst.com/projplan/proj-plan.reviews.html

Purdue Univ.
http://dynamo.ecn.purdue.edu/

Quadralay Cryptography Archive
http://www.quadralay.com/www/Crypt/Crypt.html

Radiated Immunity Software by Spectrasoft
http://www.wolfenet.com/~jmason/spectrasoft.html

Radiology Imaging Research Ctr., UT Southwestern
http://visual-ra.swmed.edu/

Raven Systems Home Page
http://eskinews.eskimo.com/~ravensys/

Reliability Engineering
http://rel.semi.harris.com/

Rensselaer Polytechnic Univ.
http://ecse.rpi.edu/

Risk-Related research at LBL
http://www.lbl.gov/LBL-Programs/Risk-Research.html

Robotech HazHandler
http://www.arc.ab.ca/robotech/

Rockwell Network Systems
http://www.rns.com/rockwell/about.html

Royal Institute of Technology, Kista, Sweden, Teleinformatics
http://www.it.kth.se/

Ruhr-Universitaet Bochum Elektrische Steuerung und Regelung
http://www.esr.ruhr-uni-bochum.de/

Russian and East European Studies Resources
http://www.pitt.edu/~cjp/rstech.html

Safety-Critical Systems
http://www.comlab.ox.ac.uk/archive/safety.html

Sandia National Lab.
http://www.cs.sandia.gov/pub/WWW/Sandia_home_page.html

Santa Clara Univ.
http://pcsel10.scu.edu/coen

SEAS
http://www.cc.saga-u.ac.jp/saga-u/riko/ee/ee.html

Sendai Univ. Information Engineering
http://infodm.info.sendai-ct.ac.jp/

Seoul National Univ.
http://ce11.snu.ac.kr/

Seoul National Univ.
http://soeemotp.snu.ac.kr/

Shoreham Nuclear Plant Equipment
http://users.aol.com/tim3456/shoreham.htm

Signal Processing Information Base (SPIB)
http://spib.rice.edu/spib.html

Society for Information Display
http://www.display.org/sid/

SonicPRO Home Page
http://www.human.com/sonic/sonic.html

Southern Methodist Univ.
http://www.seas.smu.edu/ee.html

Space Electronics Research Group
http://www.vuse.vanderbilt.edu/~pagey/serg/serg.html

Space Environment Effects Branch
http://satori2.lerc.nasa.gov/

Space Shuttle News Reference Manual
http://www.ksc.nasa.gov/shuttle/technology/sts-newsref/stsref-toc.html

SPIE-The Intl. Society for Optical Engineering
http://www.spie.org/

SRI-CSL-FM
http://www.csl.sri.com/sri-csl-fm.html

SSC Home Page
http://pdsppi.igpp.ucla.edu/ssc/Welcome.html

St.Cloud State Univ.
http://condor.stcloud.msus.edu/ee/index.html

Stanford Linear Accelerator Ctr.
http://slacvm.slac.stanford.edu/FIND/

SLAC.HTML

Stanford Univ.
http://www.stanford.edu/

Stanford Univ. Information Systems
Laboratory
http://www-isl.stanford.edu/

STO's Internet Patent Search System
http://sunsite.unc.edu/patents/intropat.html

Stony Brook
http://www.sunysb.edu/

Subjective Electronic Information Repository
http://cbl.leeds.ac.uk/nikos/doc/
repository.html

Superconducting Super Collider
http://www.ssc.gov/

Swansea
http://faith.swan.ac.uk/chris.html/DeptEEE/
eeehome.html

Swiss Federal Institute of Technology,
Zurich - Electrical Engineering
http://www.ee.ethz.ch/

TCAD
http://www-ee.stanford.edu/tcad.html

Technical Reports, Preprints and Abstracts
- NASA LaRC Technical Library
http://www.larc.nasa.gov/org/library/abs-
tr.html

Technical Univ. of Berlin - High Voltage
and Power Engineering
http://IHS.ee.TU-Berlin.DE/

Technical Univ. of Budapest
http://www.fsz.bme.hu/bme/bme.html

Technical Univ. of Delft, Netherlands
http://muresh.et.tudelft.nl/

Technical Univ. of Dresden
http://eietu2.et.tu-dresden.de/ET-en.html

Technical Univ. of Szczecin, Poland
http://www.tuniv.szczecin.pl/electric.html

Telecommunications Library
http://www.wiltel.com/library/library.html

Telemedia, Networks, and Systems
http://tns-www.lcs.mit.edu/tns-www-
home.html

Temple Univ.
http://opus.eng.temple.edu/

Texas A&M Energy Systems Lab
http://www-esl.tamu.edu/

Texas A&M Univ.
http://eesun1.tamu.edu/

Thant's Animations Index
http://mambo.ucsc.edu/psl/thant/thant.html

Therma-Wave, Inc.
http://www.thermawave.com/

Trinity College Dublin
http://www.tcd.ie/

Tufts Univ.
http://www.cs.tufts.edu/

UC Berkeley
http://www.ece.ucsb.edu/

UC Davis
http://www.ece.ucdavis.edu/

UC Los Angeles
http://www.ee.ucla.edu/

UC San Diego
http://ece.ucsd.edu/

UC Santa Barbara
http://www.ece.ucsb.edu/

UCL - Microelectronics Laboratory
http://www.dice.ucl.ac.be/lab.html

UIUC EE
http://www.ece.uiuc.edu/

UIUC Photonic Systems Group
http://www.phs.uiuc.edu/

UK Solar Energy Society
http://sun1.bham.ac.uk/thorntme/

UMR
http://www.ee.umr.edu/

Union College
http://dragon.union.edu/

United Technologies Research Ctr.
http://utrcwww.utc.com/UTRC/General/
UTRCGen.html

Univ. Berlin Meteorology
http://www.met.fu-berlin.de/DataSources/
MetIndex.html

Univ. College Cork
http://www.ucc.ie/ucc/depts/elec/elec-
home.html

Univ. College Salford
http://www.ucsalf.ac.uk/~bens/eleclink.htm

Univ. de Nantes - IRESTE
http://ireste.ireste.fr/

Univ. del Valle
http://maxwell.univalle.edu.co/

Univ. Kaiserslautern
http://www.uni-kl.de/

Univ. of Adelaide
http://www.eleceng.adelaide.edu.au/

Univ. of Alabama at Huntsville
http://eb-p5.eb.uah.edu/ece/ecehome.html

Univ. of Alberta
http://nyquist.ee.ualberta.ca/

Univ. of Calgary
http://www.enel.ucalgary.ca/Welcome.html

Univ. of Cape Town
http://www.ee.uct.ac.za/

Univ. of Cincinnati
http://www.cas.uc.edu/

Univ. of Cincinnati Nanolab
http://uceng.uc.edu/ece/Nano/
Nanohome.html

Univ. of Connecticut
http://www.eng2.uconn.edu/ese/

Univ. of Evansville
http://uenics.evansville.edu/eecs.html

Univ. of Florida
http://www.eel.ufl.edu/

Univ. of Ghent
http://www.elis.rug.ac.be/

Univ. of Hawaii
http://www.eng.hawaii.edu/UHCOEhome.html

Univ. of Hawaii at Manoa
http://spectra.eng.hawaii.edu/

Univ. of Iowa Virtual Hospital
http://indy.radiology.uiowa.edu/
VirtualHospital.html

Univ. of Kansas
http://www.tisl.ukans.edu/EECS/EECS.html

Univ. of Kansas TISL
http://www.tisl.ukans.edu/TISL-Home.html

Univ. of Karlsruhe Institute of Computer
Design and Fault Tolerance Univ. of

Karlsruhe
http://goethe.ira.uka.de/

Univ. of Laval
http://www.gel.ulaval.ca/

Univ. of Manitoba
http://www.ee.umanitoba.ca/

Univ. of Manitoba - High Voltage Power
Transmission Research Laboratory
http://www.ee.umanitoba.ca/Groups/
highvolt.html

Univ. of Maribor, Slovenia
http://www.uni-mb.si/

Univ. of Maryland at College Park
http://www.ee.umd.edu/

Univ. of Maryland Baltimore County
http://www.engr.umbc.edu/~itl/ee.html

Univ. of Maryland Baltimore County
http://www.engr.umbc.edu/~itl/ee.html

Univ. of Massachusetts - Lowell
http://www.uml.edu/Dept/EE/

Univ. of Massachusetts Lab. for Perceptual Robotics
http://piglet.cs.umass.edu:4321/lpr.html

Univ. of Memphis
http://lear.csp.ee.memphis.edu/

Univ. of Michigan
http://www.eecs.umich.edu/

Univ. of Nebraska
http://engr-www.unl.edu/ee/

Univ. of Nebraska-Lincoln
http://www.engr.unl.edu/ee/

Univ. of Neuchatel Institute of
Microtechnology
http://www-imt.unine.ch/

Univ. of New Hampshire
http://www.ece.unh.edu/

Univ. of Nottingham
http://www.nott.ac.uk/

Univ. of Oulu, Finland
http://ee.oulu.fi/EE/
Electrical.Engineering.html

Univ. of Padova
http://www.dei.unipd.it/

Univ. of Reading
http://www.elec.rdg.ac.uk/

Univ. of Rhode Island
http://www.ele.uri.edu/

Univ. of South Carolina
http://www.ece.sc.edu/

Univ. of Southern California
http://www.engr.scarolina.edu/

Univ. of Surrey
http://www.ee.surrey.ac.uk/

Univ. of Technology, Sydney
http://www.ee.uts.edu.au/eeo/eeo.html

Univ. of Texas at Arlington
http://www-ee.uta.edu/

Univ. of Texas El Paso
http://cs.utep.edu/csdept/../engg/eeeng.html

Univ. of the Witwatersrand, Johannesburg
http://www-eng.wits.ac.za/elec/elec.html

Univ. of Tokyo
http://www.ee.t.u-tokyo.ac.jp/

Univ. of Toronto
http://www.eecg.toronto.edu/

Univ. of Twente
http://utelicehp4.el.utwente.nl/

Univ. of Victoria
http://www-ece.uvic.ca/

Univ. of Virginia
http://www.ee.virginia.edu/

Univ. of Washington
http://www.ee.washington.edu/

Univ. of Westminster
http://www.wmin.ac.uk/CMSA/welcome.html

Univ. of Wyoming
http://wwweng.uwyo.edu/

Univ.of Arizona
http://www.ece.arizona.edu/

UTS
http://www.uts.edu.au/home.html

UW-Madison ANS Student Chapter
http://trans4.neep.wisc.edu/ANS/

Vanderbilt - Space Electronics Research
Group
http://www.vuse.vanderbilt.edu/~pagey/serg/
serg.html

Vexcel Corporation
http://www.vexcel.com/

W3EAX - Univ. of Maryland
http://w3eax.umd.edu/w3eax.html

Warsaw Univ. of Technology
http://www.iem.pw.edu.pl/

Washington State Univ.
http://www.eecs.wsu.edu/

Weather & global monitoring
http://life.anu.edu.au/weather.html

West Virginia Univ. - Concurrent Engineering Research Ctr.
http://www.cerc.wvu.edu/

Willow Availability & Demos
http://www.cac.washington.edu/willow/
demos.html

WilTel
http://www.wiltel.com/

Yale Univ. Image Processing and Analysis
http://noodle.med.yale.edu/

Z notation
http://www.comlab.ox.ac.uk/archive/z.html

Z39.50 Resources
http://ds.internic.net/z3950/z3950.html

Energy

See also Chemistry, Electronics &
Electrical Engineering, Engineering, Physics

Usenet Newsgroups

sci.energy
Newsgroup-based Mailing List: No.
Charter: Issues pertaining to energy sources.

sci.energy.hydrogen (Moderated)
Created by: Robert Cinq-Mars
<cinqmarr@vader.egr.uri.edu>
Call for Votes date: August 18, 1993
Newsgroup-based Mailing List: Yes,
hydrogen@uriacc.uri.edu.
Charter (from Call for Votes):
The purpose of sci.energy.hydrogen is to promote a better understanding of the concepts, terminology, materials, processes and issues relating to the production, storage, transportation, and use of hydrogen as an alternative fuel.

The goal of this newsgroup is to stimulate growth and interest in the use of hydrogen and to encourage the development of an environmentally sound energy infrastructure.

Subscribers are welcome from universities, government, and industry and are encouraged to post all pertinent news, information, research, references, product and service announcements, conference and seminar notices, government procurements, and the general discussion of topics. It is of particular importance to the group that a strong and serious effort be made on the part of each subscriber to post all important, relevant, public domain information, such as: Masters theses; Ph.D. dissertations; press releases; government R&D announcements, solicitations, procurements and awards; technical abstracts, research reports and memoranda.

A bi-directional gateway will be used to connect this newsgroup with the Internet hydrogen listserver list.

misc.industry.utilities.electric
Created by: Chuck Preecs
<preecs@ix.netcom.com>
Call for Votes Date: March 20, 1995
Newsgroup-based Mailing List: No.
Charter (from Call for Votes):
misc.industry.utilities.electric is an unmoderated newsgroup for the discussion of all issues related to the electric utility industry. Topics will cover a wide spectrum of issues of interest to electricity consumers, engineers, attorneys, financial folk, regulatory agencies, consumer advocacy groups, economists, scientists, and many others. Other interests may develop from the fuel supply industry, especially as related to natural gas, oil and coal contract issues.

misc.transport.trucking
Created by: Garry Ricketson
<garryr@netcom.com>
Call for Votes Date: May 1, 1995
Newsgroup-based Mailing List: No.
Charter (from Call for Votes):
The proposed unmoderated newsgroup misc.transport.trucking will be open to discussions on all topics related to the trucking industry.

misc.transport.urban-transit
Created by: Robert Coe <bob@1776.COM>
Call for Votes Date: 21 June 1994
Mailing list: transit-l@cc.umanitoba.ca

Newsgroup-based Mailing List: No.
Charter (from Call for Votes):
The proposed newsgroup will serve as a forum for the discussion of urban public transportation systems, emphasizing - but not limited to - rail and bus transit systems in metropolitan centers worldwide. Within this charter will be discussion of all aspects of public transit, including planning, financing, selection of routes and equipment, operating procedures, histor- ical factoids, sociological implica- tions, etc. It is NOT intended to supplant any existing newsgroup. And it should not be seen as an extension of rec.railroad, whose charter includes at least three areas (long-distance travel, freight railroads, and recreational fan trips) that are at most tangential to misc.transport.urban-transit. It will be gatewayed with the <Transit@GITVM1.BITNET> mailing list.

Frequently Asked Questions

Conventional Fusion FAQ
Maintainer: Robert F. Heeter
<rfheeter@pppl.gov>
Where on Usenet: sci.physics.fusion
Where it's archived:
rtfm.mit.edu:pub/usenet/sci/energy/
What it's for: Fusion energy represents a promising alternative to fossil fuels and nuclear fission for world energy produc- tion. This FAQ answers Frequently Asked Questions (from the sci.physics.fusion newsgroup) about conventional areas of fusion energy research. It also provides other useful information about the subject. This FAQ does NOT discuss unconven- tional forms of fusion (like Cold Fusion).

Discussion Lists

ae
AE@SJSUVM1
Alternative Energy

alternative energy
cvisser@ucrmath.ucr.edu
Alternative energy sources.

asia-re
ASIA-RE@KSUVM
Asian Renewable Energy

energy-1
ENERGY-L@TAUNIVM
Energy List

et-iufro
ET-IUFRO@SEARN
Workshop on Wood for Energy in the Tropics

hydrogen
HYDROGEN@URIACC
Hydrogen as an alternative fuel

wind energy weekly
tgray@igc.apc.org (Tom Gray)
Wind energy.

Energy Resources

FTP Resources

Energy And Climate Information Ex-
    change (ECIX) Files
    igc.apc.org/pub/ECIX

Home Power Magazine
    sunsite.unc.edu/pub/academic/environment/
    alternative-energy/energy-resources/
    homepower-magazine/archives

SunSite (Univ. Of North Carolina)
    sunsite.unc.edu/pub/academic/environment/
    alternative-energy

TeX Archive
    ftp.shsu.edu/tex-archive

Gopher Resources

4-H Energy Education Resources Database
    k12.ucs.umass.edu:70/11/fourh

Energy Ideas Newsletter
    gopher.cic.net/11/e-serials/alphabetic/e/
    energy-ideas

Idaho National Energy Laboratory's Clean
    Air Act
    dewey.tis.inel.gov:2012/11/.caa

Industrial Reports
    una.hh.lib.umich.edu/11/ebb/industry/

Telnet Resources

Washington State Energy Office Electric Ideas Clearinghouse
eicbbs.wseo.wa.gov/

WWW Resources

Advanced Research Projects Agency - Electric & Hybrid Vehicle Data Center
http://www.ev.hawaii.edu/

AE-Guide
http://solstice.crest.org/online/aeguide/aehome.html

Aerometric Information Retrieval System
http://www.epa.gov/docs/airs/airs.html

Air Infiltration and Ventilation Center
http://www.demon.co.uk/aivc

Air Resources Board
http://www.cahwnet.gov/epa/arb.htm

Alan Glennon's Geyser Page
http://www.wku.edu:80/~glennja/pages/geyser.html

Alternative Fuels Data Center
http://www.afdc.nrel.gov

American Council for an Energy Efficient Economy
http://solstice.crest.org:80/efficiency/aceee/index.html

American Nuclear Society
http://www.ans.org

American Society of Engineering Technology
http://pegasus.cc.ucf.edu/~aset/

American Solar Energy Society
http://www.engr.wisc.edu/centers/sel/ases/ases2.html

Argonne National Laboratory
http://www.anl.gov

ARI's CoolNet — Air-Conditioning and Refrigeration Inst.
http://www.ari.org

Army Profiler Research Facility, White Sands Missile Range
http://aprf.arl.mil/aprf.html

Assocation of Energy Services Professionals
http://www.dnai.com:80/AESP/

Biomass Archive, NCSR, Greece
http://www.ariadne-t.gr/phaethon/biomass/bresource.html

Biomass Energy Alliance
http://www.biomass.org/biomass/

Biomass Resource Information Clearinghouse
http://asd.nrel.gov/projects/rredc/data/biomass

BioTools — Useful sites for Biomass and Biomass Energy compiled by T.R. Miles, Consulting Engineer
http://www.teleport.com/~tmiles/biotools.htm

Bonneville Power Administration
http://www.bpa.gov/

BRIDGE — British Mid Ocean Ridge Initiative
http://www.nwo.ac.uk/iosdl/Rennell/Bridge/

Brookhaven National Laboratory
http://www.bnl.gov/bnl.html

Building Industry Exchange Foundation
http://www.building.com/bix/

CADDET — Centre for the Analysis and Dissemination of Demonstrated Energy Technologies
http://www.ornl.gov/CADDET/caddet.html

California Energy Commission
http://www.energy.ca.gov/energy/homepage.html

California Energy Commission's Agricultural Energy Assistance Program
http://www.sarep.ucdavis.edu/aeap

California Environmental Resources Evaluation System
http://www.ceres.ca.gov/

California Fleet News — Magazine for National and California Fleets
http://www.fleetnews.com/~corbett

California Governor's Office of Emergency Services
http://www.oes.ca.gov:8001/

California Inst. for Energy Efficiency
http://eande.lbl.gov/CIEE/ciee_homepage.html

California's Natural Resources
http://www.ceres.ca.gov/ceres/calweb/Natural_Resources.html

CALSTART — California's Advanced
Transportation Consortium
http://www.dnai.com/~jandro/calstart.html

Canada's Dept. of Natural Resources
Energy Sector
http://es1.es.emr.ca/

Center for Renewable Energy and Sustainable Technology
http://solstice.crest.org/

Centre for Alternative Technology - Wales,
U.K.
http://www.foe.co.uk:80/CAT/

Centre for Alternative Transportation
Fuels — BC Research Inc.
http://www.bcr.bc.ca/catf/default.htm

Chrysler Corporation - Info on Alternative
Fuels
http://www.chryslercorp.com/environment/
alternative_fuels.html

Clean Vehicles and Fuels for British
Columbia
http://www.env.gov.bc.ca/~cvf/

ClimateStudies
http://info.cern.ch/hypertext/DataSources/
bySubject/Overview.html#ove2

Coal Research at Univ. of Texas
http://www.utexas.edu/research/beg/coal.html

Coalition for Safer Cleaner Vehicles
http://www.access.digex.net/~drmemory/
cscv.html

Coso Geothermal Project
http://www1.chinalake.navy.mil/
Geothermal.html

CREST's Intro to Geothermal
http://solstice.crest.org/renewables/geother-
mal/grc/index.html

Directory of Energy-Related Graduate
Programs in U.S. Universities
http://solstice.crest.org/social/grad/index.html

DOE Univ. of California
http://labs.ucop.edu/

DOE's Energy Partnerships for a Strong
Economy
http://www.eren.doe.gov/ee-cgi-bin/ccap.pl

Dual-Mode Electric Vehicle System: the
RUF System
http://weber.u.washington.edu:80/~jbs/PRT/
RUF_Concept.html

Earth Sciences Catalogue and Search
Facility
http://www.einet.net/galaxy/Science/
Geosciences.html

Eco-Motion Electric Cars
http://www.cyberzine.org/html/Electric/
ecomotion.html

EcoElectric Corporation
http://www.primenet.com/~ecoelec/

Electric and Hybrid Vehicles
http://www.csv.warwick.ac.uk/~esrjo/
ev_hp.html

Electric Power Research Inst.
http://www.epri.com/

Energy Efficiency and Renewable Energy
Clearinghouse
http://nrelinfo.nrel.gov/web_info/documents/
erec_fact_sheets/erec.html

Energy Efficiency Office
http://www.bre.co.uk/bre/otherprg/eeobp

Energy Efficient Housing in Canada
http://web.cs.ualberta.ca/~art/house/

Energy Federation Inc.
http://www.efi.org/biz/efi/home.html

Energy Ideas
http://www.rl.ac.uk/Dept.s/tec/erunrg.html

Energy Quest — Energy Education from
the California Energy Commission
http://www.energy.ca.gov/energy/education/
eduhome.html

Energy Yellow Pages
http://www.ccnet.com/~nep/yellow.htm

EnviroLink Network
http://envirolink.org/issues/energy.html

Environment
http://ecosys.drdr.virginia.edu/
Environment.html

Environment Canada's National Pollutant
Release Inventory
http://ellesmere.ccm.emr.ca/npri/clone/
npri_ec.html

Environmental and Engineering Geophysical Society (EEGS)
http://www.esd.ornl.gov:80/EEGS/

Environmental Measurements Laboratory
http://www.eml.doe.gov/

Environmental Network
http://envirolink.org/enviroed/

Federal Emergency Management Agency
http://www.fema.gov/

Ford Motor Company — Exploring the
Alternatives to Gasoline
http://www.ford.com/corporate-info/environ-
ment/GasAlt.html

Fourth International Meeting on Heat
Flow and the Structure of the GeoSphere
(1996)
http://www.eps.mcgill.ca/~hugo/heat.html

Franklin Inst. Science Museum — Future
Energy Exhibit
http://sln.fi.edu/tfi/exhibits/f-energy.html

Franklin Inst. Science Museum — Wind
Study Unit
http://sln.fi.edu/tfi/units/energy/wind.html

Gaining Ground — Sustainable Energy
http://www.nceet.snre.umich.edu/GAIN/
GG.W95.html

Geothermal Energy in Iceland
http://www.os.is/os-eng/geo-div.html

Geothermal Exploration in Korea
http://www.kigam.re.kr/env-geology.html

Geothermal Heat Pump Consortium
http://www.ghpc.org/index.html

Geothermal Heat Pump Initiative in the
U.S.
http://www.eren.doe.gov/ee-cgi-bin/
cc_heatpump.pl

Geothermal Resources Council Library &
Information
http://grclib.html

Green Wheels Electric Car Company
http://northshore.shore.net/~kester/

Greenpeace — Climate Crisis Homepage
http://www.greenpeace.org/~climate/

GREENTIE — Greenhouse Gas Technology Information Exchange
http://www.greentie.org/greentie

Home Energy Magazine On Line
http://www.eren.doe.gov/ee-cgi-bin/hem.pl

Home Systems Network — Home
automation
http://www.ionet.net/mall/hsn/index.htm

HVAC Contract Services Canada
http://www.wchat.on.ca/hvacr/index.htm

Hybrid Electric Vehicle Program
http://info.nrel.gov/research/hev/resources/
hybrid1.html

Idaho National Engineering Laboratory
http://www.inel.gov/

IEA Solar Heating and Cooling
http://www-iea.vuw.ac.nz:90/

Indoor Air '96 — Triennial Conference
Information
http://www.kimura.arch.wwaseda.ac.jp/
indair1st/indoor-air.html

International Association for Solar Energy
Education
http://www.hrz.uni-oldenburg.de/~kblum/
iasee.html

International Geothermal Association
http://www.demon.co.uk/geosci/igahome.html

International Radiation Protection
Association
http://www.tue.nl/sbd/irpa/irpahome.htm

Joint Ctr. for Energy Mgmt.
http://bechtel.colorado.edu/ceae/Centers/
Jcem/jcemmain.html

K-12 Environmental Resources on the
Internet for Teachers
http://www.envirolink.org/enviroed/
envirok12.html

Lawrence Berkeley Laboratories' Energy
and Environment department
http://eande.lbl.gov/EE.html

LBL's Center for Building Science
http://eande.lbl.gov/CBS.html

LPG as an Automotive Fuel
http://wps.com/LPG/index.html

National Center for Vehicle Emissions
Control and Safety
http://www.colostate.edu/Depts/NCVECS/
ncvecs.html

National Energy Foundation
http://www.xmission.com/~nef/

National Energy Information Center
Energy Education Guide
http://solstice.crest.org/social/eerg/index.html

National Renewable Energy Laboratory
http://info.nrel.gov/

New Brunswick Dept. of Environment—
Air Quality Section
http://www.gov.nb.ca/environm/operatin/air/
air_1.html

NOAA's Air Resources Laboratory
http://www.cdc.noaa.gov/PandP/ARL.html

Oak Ridge National laboratory — Energy
Efficiency & Renewable Energy
http://www.ornl.gov/ORNL/Energy_Eff/
Energy_Eff.html

Office of Surface Mining - U.S. Dept. of the
Interior
http://info.er.usgs.gov/doi/office-of-surface-
mining.html

Pacific Northwest National Laboratory
http://www.pnl.gov:2080/

Pantex Nuclear Weapons Plant
http://www.pantex.com/PX/about.htm

Partnership for a New Generation of
Vehicles
http://picard.aero.hq.nasa.gov/index.html

Partnership for a New Generation of
Vehicles
http://www.eren.doe.gov/ee-cgi-bin/ee_news-
PNGV.pl

Physics Overview
http://info.cern.ch/hypertext/DataSources/
bySubject/Physics/Overview.html

Planet Earth's Energy Listings on Web
http://godric.nosc.mil/planet_earth/
energy.html

Renaissance Cars
http://www.qualcomm.com/users/sck/ev/
renaissance.html

Renewable Energy Education Module
http://solstice.crest.org/renewables/re-kiosk/
index.shtml

Retro-Vision Magazine — Residential
Energy Efficiency
http://es1.es.emr.ca/retro/retro.html

Rocky Mountain Inst.
http://solstice.crest.org/efficiency/rmi/
index.html

Rotorua, New Zealand, Geothermal Areas
http://www.akiko.lm.com/NZ/NZTour/Rotorua/
Geothermal.html

Sacramento Electric Vehicle Association
http://www.calweb.com/~tonyc/
sevahome.html

Santa Barbara County Air Pollution
Control District
http://rain.org/~sbcapcd/sbcapcd.html

Solar and Renewable Energy Conferences
Calendar
http://nrelinfo.nrel.gov:70/1m/hot-stuff/
calendar.html

Solar Energy and Building Physics Lab.
http://lesowww.epfl.ch/index.html

Stanford Univ. Geothermal Program
http://ekofisk.stanford.edu/geotherm.html

Texas A&M's Energy Science Lab.
http://www-esl.tamu.edu/

Transportation and the Economy
http://sunsite.unc.edu/darlene/tech/
report9.html

UK Solar Energy Society
http://sun1.bham.ac.uk/thorntme/

Univ. of Oregon Energy and Environment
http://zebu.uoregon.edu/energy.html

Univ. of Strathclyde Energy Systems
Research Unit
http://www.strath.ac.uk/Dept.s/ESRU/
esru.html

US Dept. of Energy
http://www.doe.gov/

U.S. Environmental Protection Agency
http://www.epa.gov/

Utility Biomasss Energy Commercializa-
tion Association
http://www.paltech.com/ttc/ubeca/index.htm

Virtual Library
http://info.cern.ch/hypertext/DataSources/
bySubject/Overview.html

Washington Univ.'s Center for Air
Pollution Impact and Trend Analysis
http://capita.wustl.edu

WWW Virtual Library: Energy
http://solstice.crest.org/online/virtual-library/
VLib-energy.html

Zero Energy Building Project
http://www.ncsa.uiuc.edu/evl/science/zero/
zero.html

Engineering

See also Aeronautics & Aerospace, Chemistry, Computer Science, Electronics & Electrical Engineering, Energy, Imaging Technologies, Optics, Physics

Usenet Newsgroups

comp.cad.cadence
Created by: pas@jupiter.ic.cmc.ca (Peter Stokes)
Call for Votes date: April 24, 1992
Newsgroup-based Mailing List: No.
Charter (from Call for Votes):
Almost any topic related to products from Cadence Design Systems, including:
- CAD/CAE tools installation & usage
- gripes, wishes, product futures
- requests for assistance
- solutions to problems
- exchange of public materials such as application notes, bug reports, PCRs
- Cadence customer service issues
- Cadence tool training issues
- company mergers and purchases
- questions and exchange of SKILL code
- migration to Opus/Amadeus/Valid tools
- documentation issues (CD ROM, HyperMedia...)
- local and intl. User Group news, announcements.

No question is to be considered too elementary. Cadence employees are welcome to participate.

EXCLUSION: Discussion on the Verilog language as this is taking place on comp.lang.verilog.

comp.cad.compass
Created by: lccha@nb.rockwell.com (Lloyd C. Cha)
Call for Votes date: May 10, 1993

Newsgroup-based Mailing List: No.
Charter (from Call for Votes):
The proposed newsgroup comp.cad.compass will serve as a medium for discussing issues and exchanging information with regards to the Compass Design Automation EDA tools.

The following topics would be appropriate for the newsgroup:

- Useful hints on using the Compass Design Automation Software more effectively
- Identification of bugs/shortcomings in the software
- Suggestions for improving the design tools
- Information regarding integration of the Compass Design Automation tools with other design software
- Hardware related issues when using the tools
- Applications notes
- Scripts/programs which can assist in doing a design using the Compass Design Automation software
- Benchmarks
- Information regarding Compass User Group activities.

comp.cad.gnuplot
Created by: d-lewart@uiuc.edu (Daniel S. Lewart)
Call for Votes date: September 1, 1992
Newsgroup-based Mailing List: Yes (info-gnuplot@dartmouth.edu).
Charter (from Call for Votes):
- This group is for the discussion of the GNUPLOT plotting program by developers and users.
- This group will be gatewayed with a

mailing list (if someone volunteers to maintain it).

- An FAQ list will be maintained.

- GNUPLOT is a command-driven interactive function plotting program which:
  - Plots data or functions
  - Has been tested on Unix, VMS, MSDOS, MS-Windows, OS/2, Amiga, and Atari platforms
  - Supports many different graphics devices
  - Is authored by Thomas Williams, Colin Kelley, Russell Lang, Dave Kotz, John Campbell, Gershon Elber, and many others
  - Is not part of the GNU project.

comp.cad.i-deas
Created by: Peter Osterberg <oster@mtl.mit.edu>
Call for Votes Date: March 30, 1995
Newsgroup-based Mailing List: No.
Charter (from Call for Votes):
The comp.cad.i-deas newsgroup will be open to discussion on all aspects of the SDRC I-DEAS Masters Series Software and other software products by SDRC and relevant third parties. This includes discussion of technical issues as they pertain to the use, implementation, programming and hardware and software issues of SDRC I-DEAS Masters Series Software.

comp.cad.microstation
Created by: David Barberi <dbarberi@sunsite.unc.edu>
Call for Votes Date: January 5, 1995
Newsgroup-based Mailing List: No.
Charter (from Call for Votes):
The comp.cad.microstation newsgroup will be open to discussion on all aspects of the MicroStation and other software products by Bentley Systems and relevant third parties. This includes discussion of technical issues as they pertain to the design, implementation, and programming of MicroStation and application programs written in MDL (MicroStation Development Language).

comp.cad.pro-engineer
Created by: boliver@cae.ppd.ti.com (William Oliver)
Call for Votes date: June 21, 1993
Newsgroup-based Mailing List: No.
Charter (from Call for Votes):
This newsgroup is intended as a forum for the exchange of information and experience dealing with Parametric Technology Corporation's Pro/Engineer software package.

comp.cad.synthesis
Created by: div@nad.3com.com (Dinesh Venkatachalam)
Call for Votes date: May 19, 1993
Newsgroup-based Mailing List: No.
Charter (from Call for Votes):
The purpose of the newsgroup "comp.cad.synthesis" would be for exchange of information (and tools) to help designers and software developers (commercial and academic) in the field of logic synthesis.

Discussions could pertain to issues such as:

- Logic Synthesis development
- Exchange ideas about effective ways to use commercial synthesis tools
- Moving from Verilog/VHDL towards synthesis
- Analog HDL and Synthesis

It is anticipated that readers of the group would be Logic and ASIC designers, Software Designers, Students and Professors who are doing research in the field of Logic synthesis and maybe Software Vendors having products in this field.

misc.industry.quality
Created by: David Casti <david@quality.org>
Call for Votes Date: May 1, 1995
Newsgroup-based Mailing List: No.
Charter (from Call for Votes):
The misc.industry.quality newsgroup will be open to discussion of the intent, interpretation, and proper application of quality principles and standards — the most famous of which is ISO 9000.

sci.engr

Newsgroup-based Mailing List: No.
Charter: Discussion-group on general engineering topics.

sci.engr.advanced-tv

Created by: Bob Myers
<myers@fc.hp.com>
Call for Votes date: August 18, 1993
Newsgroup-based Mailing List: No.
Charter (from Call for Votes):
Background: Currently, there are several mailing lists which have been used to exchange comments and proposals relating to HDTV/DATV standards. This proposal is intended to establish a group which will open this discussion to a wide range of interested professionals and users, something which would be impossible within the context of the current mail distributions without flooding the members of those lists with mail.

The establishment of a standard for digital HDTV broadcast, plus the related standards for HDTV or DATV production, compression, non-broadcast transmission, display, and so forth are topics which have generated a good deal of interest, and are of concern to the current television production and broadcast community and a wide range of other industries, such as computer graphics, medical and scientific imaging, and so forth. In establishing this group, we will have created a forum for discussion between all interested users, one which hopefully can have an impact during the standards-making process and later, once the standard has been established, on the implementation of DATV worldwide.

sci.engr.biomed

Created by: Brett Kottmann
<bkottmann@falcon.aamrl.wpafb.af.mil>
Call for Votes date: January 7, 1992
Newsgroup-based Mailing List: No.
Charter (from Call for Votes):
The purpose of the group is to facilitate discussions and the exchange of information pertaining to the field of Biomedical Engineering. Biomedical Engineering being (but not limited to): design and manufacture of artificial limbs and organs; scientific research involving medicine/the body and artificial materials; mature discussions on ethical matters; computer programs/hardware related to Biomed Engineering, data collection, and electronic muscle stimulation; modeling/simulation of Biomed systems; and schools/courses involved with Biomedical Engineering.

sci.engr.chem

Newsgroup-based Mailing List: No.
Charter: Discussion-group on chemical engineering.

sci.engr.civil

Created by: jaykay@orion.oac.uci.edu (R.Jayakrishnan)
Call for Votes date: February 6, 1992
Newsgroup-based Mailing List: No.
Charter (from Call for Votes):
The purpose of this newsgroup is to encourage discussions and the exchange of information pertaining to the field of Civil Engineering. The different areas for discussion in Civil Engineering are (but not limited to):

Structural analysis and design; Structural materials; Structural dynamics; Structural mechanics; Finite element techniques; Structural stability; Earthquake engineering; Construction technology and management; Transportation systems and planning; Traffic engineering; Transportation demand analysis; Highway materials and engineering; Pavement design; Geotechnical engineering; Foundation design; Soil mechanics; Soil-structure interaction; Water Resources engineering; Hydraulics; Hydrology; Fluid dynamics; Environmental engineering; Water and Waste treatment; Air-pollution control; Hazardous wastes; Computer analysis, modelling and simulation in these areas; Numerical methods in civil engineering; Artificial intelligence and expert systems applications in civil engineering; Stochastic processes & reliability analysis in civil engineering; Optimization in design and resource planning; Economic analysis in civil engineering; Social, ethical legal, political, educational, research and industrial issues in civil engineering.

sci.engr.control
Created by: Chris Jobling
<eechris@pyramid.swansea.ac.uk>
Call for Votes date: August 1, 1992
Newsgroup-based Mailing List: No.
Charter (from Call for Votes):
This forum aims to encourage discussion and free exchange of ideas amongst practicing control engineers, researchers and students on any subject related to the practice or theory of control systems and control engineering.

The group aims to cover any subject related to control engineering including theory, research, and practice but particularly the use and future development of computer-based applications for the analysis, design, simulation and implementation of control systems. Examples of suitable topics would be

- data definitions for control systems design packages
- user interfaces for control systems design packages
- system modelling languages
- simulation packages
- environments for the integration of CAD tools for control
- the application of new computer science techniques in control systems design and implementation
- commercial control systems design and analysis packages
- new theories
- applications of control (e.g. process industries, aerospace, transport, manufacturing,)
- real-time software
- social and environmental impact of control systems
- non-engineering applications (e.g. economics, social, ...)
- control systems education

sci.engr.heat-vent-ac
Created by: Lynnette Edrington
<EDRN@DLEP1.itg.ti.com>
Call for Votes Date: April 18, 1995
Newsgroup-based Mailing List: No.

Charter (from Call for Votes):
This unmoderated group is for discussion of Heating, Ventilating, Air Conditioning (HVAC) and Refrigeration issues. Discussion from the viewpoint of researchers, engineers and technicians involved in the research, design, specification, control, construction, operation and maintenance of HVAC topics is encouraged.

sci.engr.lighting
Created by: cbelcher@kuhub.cc.ukans.edu (Clay Belcher)
Call for Votes date: October 25, 1993
Newsgroup-based Mailing List: No.
Charter (from Call for Votes):
The object of sci.engr.lighting is to provide a forum for the discussion of all aspects of the science and art involved in the creation of lighting methods and solutions for safe, productive, and enjoyable use of the built environment, and in theater and film and related fields. The term "built environment" includes not only architecture, but also transportation media such as roadways and aviation-related construction. This statement is intended to be as broad as possible in its inclusion of all topics related to natural and manufactured light. A representative list of some of the broad categories of topics which would be appropriate for discussion in sci.engr.lighting follows. The fact that a topic does not appear on the list does not indicate that that topic could not be discussed.

Eye, vision and visibility • Color • Manufactured light sources • Daylight availability/application • Psychological and nonvisual concerns • Luminaires • Control strategies/technology • Quantity and quality assessment • Light and energy conservation/management • Lighting economics • Light Pollution

It is expected that the list will be gatewayed to the group sometime in the future.

sci.engr.manufacturing
Created by: tjbecker@tinman.mke.ab.com (Thomas Becker)
Call for Votes date: April 30, 1993

Newsgroup-based Mailing List: No.
Charter (from Call for Votes):
A discussion group for "Manufacturing Engineering" is a means for interested parties to learn about current developments, events, and issues in regards to manufacturing. It provides a forum for people with similar needs to make contact and will help establish new news groups specific to special manufacturing topics (i.e. Design for Manufacture, Simulation, Optimization, Holonic Manufacturing, etc.).

sci.engr.mech

Created by: muthu@mecad.uta.edu (S.N. Muthukrishnan)
Call for Votes date: April 13, 1992
Newsgroup-based Mailing List: No.
Charter (from Call for Votes):
This group will be used for the discussion of problems related to work or research in mechanical engineering. The fields that this group would cover may be mechanics,dynamics, control, fluids, heat, manufacturing, computer aided design, and a bunch of other areas that may be discussed in the process of creating this group.

Problems could be related to school (not homeworks!), research, work, software related queries and whatever one can think of as a problem that can be addressed to a Mechanical Engineer.

Posts of the following types are expected though this is not intended to be an exhaustive list.
* Problems related to design of equipments
* Modelling related problems
* Math related to Mechanical Engineering
* Software and programs related to Mechanical Engineering
* Problems related to Standards (although I don't think we can establish standards for practice)
* Research findings

sci.engr.metallurgy

Created by: Doug Swinbourne
<drs@rmit.edu.au>

Call for Votes Date: November 7, 1994
Newsgroup-based Mailing List: No.
Charter (from Call for Votes):
The purpose of sci.engr.metallurgy is to provide an open discussion forum for all members of the metallurgy community, no matter what their area of interest, on the Internet. The newsgroups allow the rapid and timely discussion of opinions and information that would take months or years (or not at all) on conventional paper journals.

sci.engr.safety

Created by: Sethu R Rathinam
<rathinam@netins.net>
Call for Votes Date: February 24, 1995
Newsgroup-based Mailing List: No.
Charter (from Call for Votes):
This newsgroup is being proposed as an open forum to discuss safety issues of systems conceived and/or built by humans. All aspects of safety relating to the risk of, or actual, human injury and/or loss of human life fall within this charter. Safety issues and concerns relating to all phases in a product's life cycle as well as discussions of Regulatory Issues and System Safety Processes and Software issues relating to safety fall within this charter.

sci.engr.semiconductors

Created by: fbertsch@msc.cornell.edu (Fred Bertsch)
Call for Votes date: February 7, 1994
Newsgroup-based Mailing List: No.
Charter (from Call for Votes):
The aim of sci.engr.semiconductors is to provide an open forum for the discussion of semiconductors and related fields on the internet.

Topics for discussion would include the following: semiconductor materials, semiconductor and device physics, diodes, transistors, semiconductor lasers & LEDs, photodetectors, solar cells, microelectromechanical systems, vacuum microelectronics, quantum effect devices, thin film linear devices, thin film displays, other semiconductor devices, thin film superconducting devices, integrated optics, nonlinear optical devices, crystal growth, oxidation, lithography, diffusion, ohmic contacts, ion implantation, etching, deposition, other thin film processing techniques, analytical techniques, process simulation, device simulation, interconnects, reliability/testing, microelectronic and optoelectronic packaging, vacuum technology, equipment - specs/opinions/ etc., clean room technology, economics of IC fabrication, software, databases, announcements/reviews of papers/ conferences, general discussion/opinions/ questions, education, positions vacant, or anything else that is relevant to semiconductors in general.

sci.engr.surveying

Created by: Michael MacInnis <mmacinni@nmsu.edu>
Call for Votes Date: May 12, 1995
Newsgroup-based Mailing List: No.
Charter (from Call for Votes):
This unmoderated newsgroup is being formed for the discussion of scientific and professional issues relating to earth measurement in all its forms. Topics such as; land surveying, marine surveying, hydrographic surveying, geodetic surveying, geodetic GPS positioning, geodesy, gravity models, photogrammetry, coordinate systems, datums, cartography, land information systems, statistical adjustments and analysis, etc., and legal issues relating to all of the above, are encouraged on a local and international level.

sci.materials

Created by: kwg@creare.com (Kent Goeking)
Call for Votes date: January 6, 1992
Newsgroup-based Mailing List: No.
Charter (from Call for Votes):
The group "sci.materials" will provide a forum for the discussion of topics related to the processing, characterization, modeling, application and general understanding of materials of technological importance.

sci.nanotech (Moderated)

Moderated by: . Storrs Hall (josh@aramis.rutgers.edu)
Submissions go to:

nanotech@aramis.rutgers.edu
Newsgroup-based Mailing List: No.
Charter: Nanotechnology. Little machines.

sci.op-research

Created by: msodhi@agsm.ucla.edu (Mohan Sodhi)
Call for Votes date: August 1, 1993
Newsgroup-based Mailing List: No.
Charter (from Call for Votes):
The main purpose of this group is to act as the umbrella group from which different operations research interest groups will branch off in the future, as envisioned by the technology committee of the ORMS board.

In the interim, the newsgroup will support the **research**, **application**, and **teaching** of operations research through the exchange of information through various activities including:

Research and Application
- Posting information about accepted papers
- Asking questions and posting summaries of replies
- Posting Frequently Asked Questions (FAQ) and other lists such as
- Ajay Shah's list of Free C/C++ programs for numerical methods
- Arthur Geoffrion's list of mail reflectors relevant to O.R.
- John Gregory's FAQ on LP

   Those interested in a particular area could bring out regular FAQs answering questions or likely questions from those new to their area.

- Posting information about archives (e.g. those at Rutgers, Bilkent)

Teaching
- Sharing teaching approaches
- Announcement of new textbooks; Discussion on existing textbooks

Application
- New product announcements
- Users' impressions of commercial software (No advertisements.)

Other
- Job announcements in universities and industry

Discussion Lists

acc-l
acc-l@gitvm1
ACC-L: Advanced Computer Controls Discussion

asee-ied
asee-ied@etsuadmn
Industrial Engineering Div. of ASEEWVUVTC-L

asee-l
asee-l@vtvm1
American Society of Engineering Education

autocad
autocad@jhuvm
AUTOCAD Discussion List

bogen-l
bogen-l@ualtavm
Discussion on the Industrial Engineering

biomch-l
listserv@nic.surfnet.nl (Ton van den Bogert)
Biomechanics. Funded by the Intl. Society of Biomechanics.

caeds-l
caeds-l@suvm
Computer Aided Engineering Design (CAEDS) In+

caej-l
caej-l@uottawa
Canadian Association of Electronic Jrnl. Publishers

case-l
case-l@uccvma.ucop.edu
Computer Aided Software Engineering

chem-eng
trayms@cc.curtin.edu.au (Dr. Martyn Ray)
Chemical engineering.

civil-l
civil-l@unbvm1
Civil Engineering Reasearch & Education

ecc-l
ecc-l@mcgill1
Engineering Committee on Computing

ecdm_list

ecdm_lab@ie.uwindsor.ca (andrew j. spicer)
Environmentally Conscious Design, Manufacturing, and Engineering.

ecma-l
ecma-l@ksuvm
Engineering College Magazines Associated

ev
listserv@sjsuvm1.sjsu.edu
Electric vehicles.

emieee-l
emieee-l@psuorvm
EMIEEE Engineering Mgmt. Forum

eng-sub
eng-sub@uhupvm1.uh.edu
IET-Engineering Subcommittee

enginet
enginet@bingvmb
SUNY Engineering Programs

engrnews
engrnews@uicvm
Engineering Undergraduate News

enveng-l
enveng-l@templevm
Environmental Engineering Discussion

eppd-l
eppd-l@unbvm1
Engineering and Public Policy

ethcse-l
ethcse-l@utkvm1
Ethical Issues in Software Engineering

fbus_users
majordomo@theus.rain.com
Futurebus+.

info-optomech
info-optomech@spie.org
Optomechanical and Precision Instrument Design

marnos-l
marnos-l@hearn
MARNOS : Reactor Noise studies

mat-dsgn
mat-dsgn@jpnimrtu
Forum on Materials Design by Computer

matdb-l
matdb-l@jpnimrtu
Forum on Materials Database System

materi-l
materi-l@taunivm
Material List

matls-l
matls-l@psuvm
Materials Synthesis

mech-l
mech-l@utarlvm1
Mechanical Engineering

paces-l
paces-l@unbvm1
Publications Assoc. of Canadian Engineering

Engineering Resources

FTP Resources

Bond University, Gold Coast, Queensland
  bond.edu.au

Mechanical Engineering Software Archive
  ftp://ftp.mecheng.asme.org/pub/

Univ. of Alberta, Edmonton, Alberta, EE Dept.
  bode.ee.ualberta.ca

Univ. Karlsruhe (University of Karlsruhe)
  ftpipr.ira.uka.de

Gopher Resources

C++ Database Applications with the Paradox Engine
  chimchim.xor.com

Home Built Rocket Engines
  wiretap.spies.com

Object-Oriented Software Engineering
  chimchim.xor.com

sci.engr.mech (Mechanical Engineering)
  gopher.sdsc.edu

Software Engineering on Sun Workstations
  chimchim.xor.com

Software Engineering with PERL
  chimchim.xor.com

XOR Network Engineering Inc
  chimchim.xor.com

WWW Resources

Acoustical Society of America
  http://asa.aip.org

Acoustics and Vibration Virtual Library
  http://web.mit.edu/org/a/avlab/www/vl.home.html

Advanced Computational Engineering Lab, Univ. of Texas, Austin
  http://diana.ae.utexas.edu/

Aeronautics and Aeronautical Engineering Virtual Library
  http://macwww.db.erau.edu/www_virtual_lib/aeronautics.html

Aerospace Engineering Virtual Library
  http://macwww.db.erau.edu/www_virtual_lib/aerospace.html

American Ceramic Society
  http://www.smartpages.com/acers/

American Electronics Association
  http://www.aeanet.org/

American Institute of Physics
  http://aip.org/

American Mathematical Society
  http://www.ams.org

American Nuclear Society
  http://www.ans.org

American Society for Engineering Education
  http://www.asee.org/

American Vacuum Society
  http://www.vacuum.org/

American Water Works Association
  http://www.awwa.org

Applied Research Lab at Penn
  http://www.arl.psu.edu/

Archtecture, Land. Archtecture Virtual Library
  http://www.clr.toronto.edu:1080/VIRTUALLIB/archGALAXY.html

Arizona State Univ. MAE Design Automation Lab
  http://asudesign.eas.asu.edu/

Army Construction Engineering Research Labs.
  http://www.cecer.army.mil/

ARPA iMEMS (integrated MicroElectroMechanical Systems) Program
http://nitride.eecs.berkeley.edu:8001/

Association for Computing Machinery
http://info.acm.org/

ASU Design Automation Lab
http://ASUdesign.eas.asu.edu/

Audio Engineering Society
http://www.cudenver.edu/aes/index.html

BMEnet - Biomedical Engineering
http://bme.www.ecn.purdue.edu/bme

Bridge Engineering
http://www.best.com/~solvers/bridge.html

Brigham Young Univ. ADCATS
http://vince.et.byu.edu/

Brown Univ. Fluid Mechanics
http://www.cfm.brown.edu/

Caltech Mechanical Engineering Ctr.
http://avalon.caltech.edu/me/

Cambridge Univ.
http://www.eng.cam.ac.uk

Carleton Systems and Computer Engineering
http://www.sce.carleton.ca/

Carnegie Mellon Software Engineering Institute
http://www.sei.cmu.edu/FrontDoor.html

Carnegie Mellon Univ. E&CE
http://www.ece.cmu.edu/Home-Page.html

Center for Research on Computation and Applications
http://www.cerca.umontreal.ca/

CESR
http://pdsppi.igpp.ucla.edu/cesr/Welcome.html

Chemical Engineering Virtual Library
http://www.che.ufl.edu/WWW-CHE/index.html

CIM Systems Research Ctr. at Arizona State Univ.
http://enws324.eas.asu.edu/

Civil Engineering at Christian Brothers Univ.
http://www.cbu.edu/engineering/ce/cehome.htm

Civil Engineering Virtual Library
http://howe.ce.gatech.edu/WWW-CE/home.html

Clarkson Univ. Materials Engineering
http://m_struct.mie.clarkson.edu/VLmae.html

Clemson Univ. Design
http://www.eng.clemson.edu/dmg/DMG.html

Clemson Univ. Mechanical Engineering
http://macmosaic.eng.clemson.edu/Academic.Depts/ME/ME.html

Colorado School of Mines
http://www.mines.colorado.edu/

Computational Fluid Dynamics Resources at Chalmers
http://www.tfd.chalmers.se/CFD_Online/

Computational Fluid Dynamics, Univ. of Texas at Austin
http://diana.ae.utexas.edu/

Computer and Communication Companies
http://www-atp.llnl.gov/atp/companies.html

Computer and Network Security Reference Index
http://www.tansu.com.au/Info/security.html

Computer Integrated Manufacturing at Maryland
http://gimble.cs.umd.edu/cim/cim.html

Consortium on Green Design and Manufacturing server
http://euler.berkeley.edu/green/cgdm.html

Control Engineering Virtual Library
http://www-control.eng.cam.ac.uk/extras/Virtual_Library/Control_VL.html

Cornell Univ. Chemical Engineering
http://latoso.cheme.cornell.edu/

Cornell Univ. Engineering M&AE
http://www.tc.cornell.edu/~maxfield/mae/

Cranfield Univ.
http://www.cranfield.ac.uk

Ctr. for Case Studies in Engineering
http://www.civeng.carleton.ca/ECL/about.html

Curtin Univ., Perth, Western Australia
http://guri.cage.curtin.edu.au/~fish/home.html

Delft Univ. of Technology
http://www.twi.tudelft.nl/welcome.html

DesignNet Directory of Mechatronic and Engineering Services
http://cdr.stanford.edu/html/SHARE/DesignNet.html

Earthquake Engineering, UC Berkeley
http://nisee.ce.berkeley.edu/

ECSEL Coalition
http://echo.umd.edu/

ECSEL Program (Penn State)
http://albatross.psu.edu/

Edinburgh Chemical Engineering
http://www.chemeng.ed.ac.uk/

Electrical Engineering Virtual Library
http://www.ece.iit.edu/~power/power.html

Electronic & Manufacturing Engineering
http://www.wmin.ac.uk/CMSA/welcome.html

Embry-Riddle Aerospace Engineering
http://macwww.db.erau.edu/www_virtual_lib/aerospace.html

Energy Systems Lab. - Texas A&M Univ.
http://www-esl.tamu.edu/

Engineering & Technology at EINet Galaxy
http://galaxy.einet.net/galaxy/./Engineering-and-Technology.html

Engineering Council
http://www.engc.org.uk/

Engineering Employment EXPO
http://stimpy.cen.uiuc.edu/comm/expo/

Engineering Software Exchange
http://www.engineers.com/ese/ese.html

Engineering Virtual Library
http://arioch.gsfc.nasa.gov/wwwvl/engineering.html

Environmental Engineering
http://www.nmt.edu/~jjenks/engineering.html

ERIM - Environmental Research Institute of Michigan
http://www.erim.org/

FedWorld Beta Home Page
http://www.fedworld.gov/

Fishnet
http://www.cs.washington.edu/homes/pauld/fishnet/issue/

Formal Methods Virtual Library
http://www.comlab.ox.ac.uk/archive/formal-methods.html

Fraunhofer Institute of Ceramic Technologies and Sintered Materials
http://www.ikts.fhg.de/ikts.engl.html

Gas Dynamics Lab, Princeton Univ.
http://ncd1901.cfd.princeton.edu/

Geometry Ctr. at the Univ. of Minnesota
http://freeabel.geom.umn.edu/

Georgia Tech Civil Engineering
http://howe.ce.gatech.edu/WWW-CE/home.html

Geotechnical Engineering Virtual Library
http://geotech.civen.okstate.edu/wwwVL/index.html

HCI Resources
http://www.ida.liu.se/labs/aslab/groups/um/hci/

HCRL Home Page at The Open Univ., UK
http://hcrl.open.ac.uk/

Houston Internet Connection
http://www.jsc.nasa.gov/houston/HoustonInternet.html

Hydromechanics
http://www50.dt.navy.mil/

ICARIS - CIC research network
http://audrey.fagg.uni-lj.si/ICARIS/index.html

IEE - Institution of Electrical Engineers
http://www.iee.org.uk/

IEEE - Institute of Electrical and Electronics Engineers
http://www.ieee.org/

IKEDA lab. Chiba
http://www.hike.te.chiba-u.ac.jp/

Industrial Engineering Virtual Library
http://isye.gatech.edu/www-ie/

IndustryNET
http://www.industry.net/

Institute of Fluid Science
http://hh.ifs.tohoku.ac.jp/

Institute of Physics
http://www.iop.org/

International Centre for Heat and Mass Transfer
http://www.metu.edu.tr:80/~hersoy/index.html

International Council on Systems Engineering
http://usw.interact.net/incose/

International Society for Measurement and Control (ISA)
http://www.isa.org/

International Union of Materials Research Societies
http://mrcemis.ms.nwu.edu/iumrs/index.html

Intl. Centre For Heat and Mass Transfer (ICHMT)
http://www.metu.edu.tr/~hersoy/index.html

ISA - The International Society for Measurement and Control
http://www.isa.org/

ISSI Biography
http://www.issi.com/issi/issi-bio.html

Journal of Fluids Engineering
http://borg.lib.vt.edu/ejournals/JFE/jfe.html

Journal of Mechanical Design
http://www-jmd.engr.ucdavis.edu/jmd/

Kansas State Univ. College of Engineering
http://www.engg.ksu.edu/home.html

Kyushu Univ., Japan
http://www.ee.kyushu-u.ac.jp/index.html

Lulea Univ., Div. of Energy Engineering
http://www.luth.se/depts/mt/ene/

Manhattan College School of Engineering
http://www.mancol.edu/engineer/engrpage.html

Materials Engineering Virtual Library
http://m_struct.mie.clarkson.edu/VLmae.html

Materials Research Society
http://dns.mrs.org/

Mechanical Engineering Software
ftp://ftp.mecheng.asme.org/pub

Mechanical Engineering Virtual Library
http://cdr.stanford.edu/html/WWW-ME/home.html

Mississippi State Univ.
http://www.msstate.edu/

Nanotechnology on the WWW
http://www.arc.ab.ca/~morgan/Nano.html

NASA Johnson Space Flight Ctr. Software Engineering
http://rbse.jsc.nasa.gov/virt-lib/soft-eng.html

NASA Langley Research Ctr.
http://www.larc.nasa.gov/larc.html

NASA Technical Report Server (NTRS)
http://techreports.larc.nasa.gov/cgi-bin/NTRS

Naval Architecture and Ocean Engineering Virtual Library
http://arioch.gsfc.nasa.gov/wwwvl/engineering.html#naval

NCCOSC Home Page
http://www.nosc.mil/NCCOSCMosaicHome.html

NCSU College of Engineering Home Page
http://www.eos.ncsu.edu/coe/coe.html

NIST Manufacturing Engineering Lab.
http://www.nist.gov/mel/melhome.html

Nonlinear Dynamics Lab, Saratov, Russia
http://chaos.ssu.runnet.ru/

Northwestern Univ.
http://voltaire.mech.nwu.edu/

Notre Dame Aerospace and Mechanical Engineering
http://www.nd.edu/Departments/EN/AME/HomePage.html

NSF SUCCEED Engineering Visual Database
http://succeed.edtech.vt.edu/

Nuclear Engineering Virtual Library
http://neutrino.nuc.berkeley.edu/NEadm.html

On-line Catalog at the Technical Univ. of Darmstadt
http://venus.muk.maschinenbau.th-darmstadt.de/rth/rk/rkhome.html

Optical Engineering Virtual Library
http://www.spie.org/wwwvl_optics.html

OPTICS.ORG - The Photonics Resource Center
http://optics.org/

Patent Information
http://sunsite.unc.edu/patents/intropat.html

Penn State
http://www.esm.psu.edu

Pohang Univ. of Science and Technology (Postech), Korea:
http://firefox.postech.ac.kr/

Power Engineering Virtual Library
http://www.analysys.co.uk/commslib.htm

Production and Design Engineering Lab.
http://utwpue.wb.utwente.nl/

Project Mgmt. Software FAQ
http://www.wst.com/projplan/proj-
plan.FAQ.html

PSU College of Earth and Mineral Sciences
http://www.ems.psu.edu/

Queens University Engineering Society
http://engsoc.queensu.ca

Rapid Prototyping Virtual Library
http://arioch.gsfc.nasa.gov/wwwvl/
engineering.html#proto

RBSE Program
http://rbse.jsc.nasa.gov/eichmann/rbse.html

Robotech HazHandler
http://www.arc.ab.ca/robotech/

Robotics Internet Resources Page
http://piglet.cs.umass.edu:4321/robotics.html

RUL Mathematics & Computer Science -
Software Engineering and IS
http://www.wi.leidenuniv.nl/CS/SEIS/
summary.html

Russian and East European Studies Net
Resources
http://www.pitt.edu/~cjp/rstech.html

Russian and East European Studies Virtual
Library
http://www.pitt.edu/~cjp/rees.html

Safety-Critical Systems Virtual Library
http://www.comlab.ox.ac.uk/archive/
safety.html

SHARE DesignNet Page
http://cdr.stanford.edu/html/SHARE/
DesignNet.html

Sheffield Dept of Automatic Control &
Systems Engineering
http://www2.shef.ac.uk/acse/ACSE.html

Shock & Vibration Information Analysis
Ctr. (SAVIAC)
http://saviac.usae.bah.com/

Society for Applied Spectroscopy
http://esther.la.asu.edu:80/sas/

Society of Manufacturing Engineers
http://www.sme.org/

Software Engineering Virtual Library
http://www-control.eng.cam.ac.uk/extras/
Virtual_Library/Control_VL.html

Software Technology for Fluid Mechanics
http://www.ts.go.dlr.de/sm-sk_info/STinfo/
STgroup.html

Solid Mechanics, Chalmers Univ. of
Technology, Sweden
http://www.solid.chalmers.se/

Space Shuttle News Reference Manual
http://www.ksc.nasa.gov/shuttle/technology/
sts-newsref/stsref-toc.html

SPIE-The Intl. Society for Optical Engineering
http://www.spie.org/

Stanford Knowledge Systems Lab.
http://www-ksl.stanford.edu/

Stanford Univ.
http://CDR.stanford.edu/html/WWW-ME/
home.html

Stanford Univ. Ctr. for Design Research
http://gummo.stanford.edu/

STO's Internet Patent Search System
http://sunsite.unc.edu/patents/intropat.html

Structural Engineering Virtual Library
http://touchstone.power.net/seaoc/
sevhmpg1.htm

Subjective Electronic Information Repository
http://cbl.leeds.ac.uk/nikos/doc/
repository.html

Swarthmore College
http://www.engin.swarthmore.edu/

Switzerland - Information servers
http://heiwww.unige.ch/switzerland/

Systems and Control Engineering Virtual
Library
http://src.doc.ic.ac.uk/bySubject/Computing/
Overview.html

Technical Univ. of Budapest
http://www.fsz.bme.hu/bme/bme.html

Technical Univ. of Darmstadt
http://venus.muk.maschinenbau.th-
darmstadt.de/

Technical Univ. of Nova Scotia
http://www.tuns.ca/

Texas A&M Univ.
http://www.tamu.edu/default.html

Thermal Design and Analysis
http://www.kkassoc.com:80/~takinfo/

UALR Biologic Fluid Dynamics
http://giles.ualr.edu/

UC Berkeley
http://www.Berkeley.EDU/

UCSD Science & Engineering Library
http://scilib.ucsd.edu

UIUC Engineering
http://stimpy.cen.uiuc.edu/comm/eoh

UIUC Student Engineering Council
http://stimpy.cen.uiuc.edu/

UMBC Computer Science WWW Server
http://www.cs.umbc.edu/

Univ. of Alabama in Huntsville
http://www.uah.edu/colleges/engineering/
engineering.html

Univ. of Alberta EE
http://nyquist.ee.ualberta.ca/index.html

Univ. of Alberta Water Resources Engineering
http://maligne.civil.ualberta.ca/home.html

Univ. of Bradford - Engineering in Astronomy Group
http://www.eia.brad.ac.uk/eia.html

Univ. of Bristol, UK
http://www.fen.bris.ac.uk/welcome.html

Univ. of Calgary Micronet Multidimensional Signal Processing Research Group
http://www-mddsp.enel.ucalgary.ca/

Univ. of Edinburgh
http://ouse.mech.ed.ac.uk/

Univ. of Evansville
http://www-cecs.evansville.edu/

Univ. of Florida Chemical Engineering
http://www.che.ufl.edu/WWW-CHE/index.html

Univ. of Florida Process Improvement Lab.
http://www.che.ufl.edu/

Univ. of Hawaii
http://www.eng.hawaii.edu/

Univ. of Illinois EE
http://www.ece.uiuc.edu/

Univ. of Ljubljana, FAGG
http://www.fagg.uni-lj.si/index.html

Univ. of Manitoba Civil and Geological Engineering
http://www.ce.umanitoba.ca/homepage.html

Univ. of Maryland Institute for Systems Research
http://gimble.cs.umd.edu/cim/cim.html

Univ. of Michigan
http://www.engin.umich.edu/college/

Univ. of Minnesota Biomedical Engineering
http://pro.med.umn.edu/bmec/bmec.html

Univ. of Minnesota Geometry Ctr.
http://freeabel.geom.umn.edu/

Univ. of New Hampshire Robotics
http://www.ece.unh.edu/robots/rbt_home.htm

Univ. of Portland
http://www.up.edu/

Univ. of Queensland, Computational Fluid Dynamics
http://www.uq.edu.au/~e4ppetri/CFD.html

Univ. of South Carolina Engineering
http://www.engr.scarolina.edu/

Univ. of Tennessee Biomedical Engineering
http://www.mecca.org/BME/bme-home.html

Univ. of Twente Lab. of Production & Design Engineering
http://utwpue.wb.utwente.nl/

Univ. of Virginia Engineering Physics
http://bohr.ms.virginia.edu/ep/

Univ. of Washington Computer Science & Engineering
http://www.cs.washington.edu/

Univ. of Wyoming
http://wwweng.uwyo.edu/

US Army Advanced Simulation and Software Engineering Technology
http://lincoln.cecer.army.mil/asset.html

US Patents Searchable Archive
http://town.hall.org/patent/patent.html

Wastewater Engineering Virtual Library
http://www.halcyon.com/cleanh2o/ww/
welcome.html

Welding Engineering Virtual Library
http://www.bath.ac.uk/Centres/AWJU/
wwwvl3.html

Geology & Geophysics

See also Meteorology, Oceanography

Usenet Newsgroups

comp.infosystems.gis
Created by: bonnett@seismo.css.gov (H. David Bonnett)
Call for Votes date: January 14, 1992
Newsgroup-based Mailing List: Yes, (gis-l@ubvm.cc.buffalo.edu).
Charter (from Call for Votes):
This newsgroup will be for discussion of the developing field in information managment known as GIS (Geographic Information Systems).

This includes, but is not limited to:
* questions about specific GIS/LIS packages in the public and commercial domains (e.g., MOSS, GRASS, ARC/INFO, ERDAS, ER MAPPER, etc...)
* questions on data issues (e.g., availability, sources, types...)
* discussions about GIS analysis and display methodologies (e.g., image processing, cartography, classification, etc.)
* discussions about users use of GIS for attaining research goals

It is expected that discussions relating to both GIS and other newsgroups may be cross-posted.

The group will be gatewayed with the existing GIS-L Listserver and the extant bit.gis-l group will be removed upon creation of this group.

sci.engr.geomechanics
Created by: George S. Kalamaras <GSK1@psu.edu>
Call for Votes Date: January 22, 1995

Newsgroup-based Mailing List: No.
Charter (from Call for Votes):
The main aim of sci.engr.geomechanics is to provide an open forum for the discussion of all aspects of geomechanical engineering (soil & rock mechanics). Relevant topics for this newsgroup should be limited only by what the participants in this proposed newsgroup regard as relevant. Topics for Discussion may include but are not necessarily limited to: Soil Mechanics: exploration, soil properties, foundations, reinforcement, soil slope stability, tunneling in soft ground, earthquake design, ... Rock Mechanics: strata control (mining related topics), rock slope stability, tunneling, microtunneling, underground space design, foundations in rock, reinforcement, ... Soil and Rock related: groundwater flow, probabilistic analysis, decision making in geomechanics engineering, experimental, numerical, empirical, analytical, observational methods.

sci.engr.marine.hydrodynamics
Created by: Haavard Holm <hholm@mari1.marina.unit.no>
Call for Votes Date: January 5, 1995
Newsgroup-based Mailing List: No.
Charter (from Call for Votes):
The proposed unmoderated newsgroup sci.engr.marine.hydrodynamics will be a newsgroup for people interested in marine hydrodynamics.

sci.geo
Newsgroup-based Mailing List: No.
Charter: General geology.

sci.geo.earthquakes

Created by: Ted Smith
<ted.smith@mtnswest.com>
Call for Votes Date: November 22, 1994
Newsgroup-based Mailing List: :No.
Charter (from Call for Votes)
For discussions relating to earthquakes
(worldwide). Appropriate topics include
but are not necessarily limited to:
- seismicity and seismological techniques
- measurement of earthquakes
- recent and significant historical
earthquakes
- causes of earthquakes
- sources of earthquake data
- secondary phenomena associated
with earthquakes
- geological techniques employed in
earthquake hazard identification
- earthquake safety (in general)
- techniques for mitigating earthquake
hazards
- earthquake prediction technology
- seismic parameters for structural
design

sci.geo.eos

Created by:
posinski@nssdca.gsfc.nasa.gov (Cindy
Posinski)
Call for Votes date: February 6, 1993
Newsgroup-based Mailing List: No.
Charter (from Call for Votes):
The sci.geo.eos newgroup will be used by
the Earth Observing System Data and
Information System (EOSDIS) community
for the sharing of EOSDIS related information. It will include postings of "The
Processor" and "The Earth Observer,"
newsletters containing timely EOS news
events and information on up-coming
meetings. The newsgroup will also contain
information regarding the availability of
new data sets, and other important EOS
related material. There are currently
hundreds of researchers and scientists
around the world involved with EOS, and
this would be a great forum for the
sharing of ideas.

sci.geo.fluids

Created by: Jerry Miller
<miller@rsmas.miami.edu>

Call for Votes date: April 1990
Newsgroup-based Mailing List: No.
Charter: (from Call for Votes):
The discussion and exchange of informa-
tion on problems in geophysical fluid
dynamics and closely related fields.

sci.geo.geology

Created by: Tom Williams
(williams@pangea.stanford.edu)
Call for Votes date: December 1990
Newsgroup-based Mailing List: No.
Charter: (from Call for Votes):
Possible subjects for discussion would
include all aspects of solid earth geology
and geophysics. (Including, but NOT
limited to) plate tectonics tectonophysics,
petrology, mineralogy, volcanology,
structural geology, paleontology, sedimentary processes, basin analysis, seismic
exploration, seismic stratigraphy, petroleum geology, seismology, geochemistry,
glaciation, groundwater hydrology,
geochronology, paleomagnetism, paleoclimatology.

sci.geo.hydrology

Created by: Upmanu Lall
<ulall@pub.uwrl.usu.edu>
Call for Votes date: March 9, 1994
Newsgroup-based Mailing List: No.
Charter (from Call for Votes):
The objective of this newsgroup is to
provide a forum for discussion on issues
pertaining to surface and groundwater
hydrology, their relation to climate, water
quality issues and water resource management and policy issues. It is hoped that
this will lead to frank and open discussion
and identification of key issues and
directions in the field, easier identification
of and access to data sources, a critical
evaluation of modeling and data analysis
methodologies, electronic newsletters, and
provide a consulting role, and stimulate
cooperative research. Announcements of
meetings, special sessions and work in
progress could be facilitated. We also
intend to set up and manage an electronic
archive accessible through ftp, gopher,
www, and mosaic, that will be used as a
repository for contributed manuscripts
(and comments), software and data source
identifiers, and will operate in conjunction

with this news group.

sci.geo.petroleum
Created by: James Huang
<jhu@scandpower.no, james@oslonett.no>
Call for Votes Date: August 1, 1994
Newsgroup-based Mailing List: No.
Charter (from Call for Votes):
The aim of sci.geo.petroleum would be to
provide an informal electronic conference
venue for specialists of varying backgrounds involved in petroleum energy
research and development, recovery and
use. It is hoped that this initiative will lead
to a cross-fertilisation of ideas between
technical experts, managerial staff,
government and environmental
organisations and the general public.
Much of this planet's intellectual man-
power resources remain underutilised,
and this newsgroup would for the first
time encourage global communications
between individuals of widely variable
professional backgrounds and with
different expertise.

sci.geo.satellite-nav
Created by: arkusinski_andy@si.com
(Andy Arkusinski)
Call for Votes date: February 15, 1994
Newsgroup-based Mailing List: No.
Charter: SCI.GEO.SATELLITE-NAV was
chosen because the focus of this group is
on navigation. The SCI.SPACE hierarchy
deals with various aspects of space
exploration and use, but this newsgroup
deals mostly with terrestrial applications.
The fact that the space segment is in space
is almost incidental to the focus of the
newsgroup.

SCI.GEO.SATELLITE-NAV will allow a
centralized location for discussion of
global navigation satellite systems (GNSS).
The charter specifically includes the US
Global Positioning System (GPS) and
Russian GLONASS, but is also open to
discussion of other existing and future
satellite positioning systems.

sci.techniques.xtallography
Created by: Lachlan Cranswick
<lachlan@dmp.csiro.au>

Call for Votes date: September 20, 1993
Newsgroup-based Mailing List: No.
Charter (from Call for Votes):
The purpose of
sci.techniques.xtallography is to provide a
forum for anyone interested in using the
"power" of the internet newsgroups to
discuss (in "near real time"!) issues, results,
problems and applications in crystallography that would take months and years in
conventional paper journals. It would also
allow non-crystallographers to find out
how this field could assist their work.

Frequently Asked Questions

Sci.geo.geology FAQ
Maintainer: R. Spencer Ramshaw
<rsr@amthyst.dweomer.org>
Where on Usenet: sci.geo.geology
Where it's archived:
rtfm.mit.edu:pub/usenet/
sci.geo.meteorology
What it's for: Discussions of interest to
readers of sci.geo.geology, i.e., of a more
academic nature.

Discussion Lists

canspace
canspace@unbvm1
Canadian Space Geodesy Forum

cpgis-l
cpgis-l@ubvm
Chinese Professionals Geographic
Information Society

geoged
geoged@ukcc
Geography Education List

geogfem
geogfem@ukcc
Discussion list for Feminism in Geography

geograph
geograph@searn
Geography

geology
geology@ptearn
Geology

geonet-l
geonet-l@iubvm
Geoscience Librarians

geopol
geopol@ukcc
Discussion list for Political Geography

gis-l
gis-l@ubvm
Geographic Information Systems

gisbus-l
gisbus-l@ecuvm1
Geographic Information Systems for
Business

gist-l
gist-l@ukacrl
GIS Transport Discussion Group

glomod-l
glomod-l@uhccvm
The Global Modeling Forum

kyugis-l
kyugis-l@ukcc
Kentucky Universities Geographic
Information

maps-l
maps-l@uga.cc.uga.edu
Maps and Air Photo Systems Forum

nyjm-top
nyjm-top@albnyvm1
Abstracts of Geometry/Topology papers

palclime
palclime@sivm
Paleoclimate, Paleoecology for late
Mesozoic periods

paleolim
paleolim@nervm
Paleolimnology Forum

rpifdm-l
rpifdm-l@wuvmd
Regional Planetary Image Facility Data
Mgmt.

seism-l
seism-l@bingvmb
Seismological Data Distribution

seismd-l
seismd-l@bingvmb
Seismological Discussion

stat-geo
stat-geo@ufrj
Forum of Quantitative Methods in
Geosciences

volcano
volcano@asuacad
VOLCANO

Geology & Geophysics Resources

Gopher Resources

Atlantic Geoscience Centre
  agcgopher.bio.ns.ca

CIESIN Global Change Information
  Gateway
  gopher.ciesin.org

Davis - Geology Gophers
  geogopher.ucdavis.edu

Fault-mapping data
  alum.wr.usgs.gov/pub/map

IGWR - Inst. for Ground Water Research
  igwmc.mines.colorado.edu:3851/1

National Coal Resources Data System
  ncrds.er.usgs.gov

National Information Service for Earthquake Engineering
  nisee.ce.berkeley.edu:71/1

Oklahoma Geological Survey Observatory
  wealaka.okgeosurvey1.gov/

Pacific Marine Geology
  walrus.wr.usgs.gov

Paleontological Soc.
  gopher.uic.edu/11/research/paleon/palsoc

Public Seismic Network
  gopher.ceri.memphis.edu:70/

Santa Barbara Geological Sciences
  gopher.geol.ucsb.edu/

Seismology and Tectonophysics Info
  garlock.wr.usgs.gov/pub

Smithsonian Global Volcanism Program
  nmnhgoph.si.edu/11/.gvp

Smithsonian Institution Natural History
  nmnhgoph.si.edu/

Southern California Seismicity Reports
  and Maps
  scec.gps.caltech.edu/pub/ca.earthquakes

UC Davis
geogopher.ucdavis.edu:70/1

United Nations
nywork1.undp.org/1

Univ of Illinois Weather Machine
wx.atmos.uiuc.edu

Univ. of Minnesota - Soil Science
gopher.soils.umn.edu:70/1

Univ. of Texas at El Paso
dillon.geo.ep.utexas.edu

WWW Resources

Aberdeen Univ.
http://hutton.geol.abdn.ac.uk/

ADEPT - Aquifer Data Evaluation
http://www.us.net/adept/welcome.html

Agency for Toxic Substances and Disease
Registry
http://atsdr1.atsdr.cdc.gov:8080/
atsdrhome.html

AGSO - Australian Geological Survey
Organisation
http://garnet.bmr.gov.au/

Alaska Volcano Observatory
http://www.avo.alaska.edu

American Crystallographic Association
http://nexus.mfb.buffalo.edu/ACA/

American Geological Inst.
http://agi.umd.edu/agi/agi.html

American Geophysical Union
http://earth.agu.org/kosmos/homepage.html

American Rescue Team
http://www.Acosta.com/AmerRescue.html

American Rock Mechanics Association
http://sair019.energylan.sandia.gov:70/0/
RockNet/rocknet.html

Analytical Spectral Devices, Inc.
http://www.asdi.com/asd/

Arizona Geographic Information Council
http://www.state.az.us/gis3/agic/
agichome.html

Atlantic Marine Geology
http://bramble.er.usgs.gov

Australian Environmental Resources
Information Network
http://kaos.erin.gov.au/erin.html

Bay Area Digital Geo-Resource
http://www.svi.org/badger.html

British Crystallographic Association
http://www.cryst.bbk.ac.uk/BCA/index.html

Brown Univ.
http://www-geo.het.brown.edu/geo/

Bureau of Indian Affairs - Div. of Energy
and Mineral Resources
http://snake2.cr.usgs.gov/

Bureau of Land Management Geospatial
http://www.blm.gov/gis/gishome.html

California Cooperative Snow Surveys
http://snow.water.ca.gov/

California State Univ., Chico
http://rigel.csuchico.edu/

Caltech Division of Geological and
Planetary Science
http://www.gps.caltech.edu/

Cambridge Earth Sciences
http://rock.esc.cam.ac.uk/main.html

Canada Centre for Mapping
http://www.geocan.nrcan.gc.ca/

Canadian National Net Combined U.S.
Catalog
http://www.geophys.washington.edu/
cnss.cat.html

Carolina Geological Soc.
http://www.geo.duke.edu/cgsinfo.htm

Cascades Volcano Observatory
http://vulcan.wr.usgs.gov

Center for Clean Technology
http://cct.seas.ucla.edu

Center for Remote Sensing and Spatial
Analysis
http://deathstar.rutgers.edu/welcome.html

Center of Excellence for Science
http://192.239.146.18

Centre for Technical Geoscience in Delft,
the Netherlands
http://wwwak.tn.tudelft.nl/CTG/Overview.html

CIESIN Information for a Changing World
http://www.ciesin.org

Coastal Ocean Modeling
http://crusty.er.usgs.gov

Colorado School of Mines
http://gn.mines.colorado.edu/

CREWES Project (Consortium for Research in Elastic Wave Exploration Seismology)
http://www-crewes.geo.ucalgary.ca/

Ctr. for Earth Observation
http://stormy.geology.yale.edu/ceo.html

CWP - Ctr. for Wave Phenomena
http://cwp.mines.colorado.edu:3852/

Dalhousie Univ.
http://www.dal.ca/www_root_es/es-home.html

DeLORME Mapping
http://www.delorme.com/

Desert Research Inst.
http://www.dri.edu

Digital Relief Map of USA
http://ageninfo.tamu.edu/apl-us/

Duke Univ.
http://www.geo.duke.edu/

Earth Observing System Information Server
http://eos.nasa.gov/

Earth Sciences and Resources Inst. - Univ. of Utah
http://www.esri.utah.edu/

Earthquake and Landslide Hazards
http://gldage.cr.usgs.gov

EcoNet - League of Conservation Voters
http://www.econet.org/lcv/

Edinburgh Dept. of Geology and Geophysics
http://www.glg.ed.ac.uk/

EE-LINK - Environmental Education on the Internet
http://www.nceet.snre.umich.edu/index.html

Energy Research Clearing House
http://www.main.com:80/~ERCH/

Energy Resource Surveys Program
http://sedwww.cr.usgs.gov:8080

EnviroLink Network
http://envirolink.org/about.html

Environment Canada's Green Lane in Atlantic Canada
http://www.ns.doe.ca/how.html

Environmental Design College at the Univ.

of California, Berkeley
http://www.ced.berkeley.edu/

Environmental Industry Web Site
http://www.enviroindustry.com/

Environmental Information Services
http://www.esdim.noaa.gov/

Environmental Professional's Homepage
http://www.clay.net

EnviroSense
http://wastenot.inel.gov/envirosense

EnviroWeb
http://envirolink.org/

EROS Data Center
http://sun1.cr.usgs.gov/eros-home.html

Explorer from the Univ. of Kansas
http://unite.tisl.ukans.edu/xmintro.html

Federal Emergency Management Agency
http://www.fema.gov/

Federal Geographic Data Committee
http://fgdc.er.usgs.gov

Flagstaff Field Center
http://wwwflag.wr.usgs.gov

Fossil Fuels & Environmental Geochemistry
http://borg.ncl.ac.uk/

Geneva Univ. - Crystallography
http://www.unige.ch/

GEOBYTE—sponsored by the American Association of Petroleum Geology
http://www.NeoSoft.com:80/aapg/

Geochemical Institute of Goettingen, Germany
http://www.uni-geochem.gwdg.de/docs/home.htm

Geodetic Survey of Canada
http://www.geod.emr.ca/

GeoForschungsZentrum Potsdam
http://www.gfz-potsdam.de/

Geographic Information Systems - GIS
http://www.usgs.gov/research/gis/title.html

Geographic Resources Analysis Support System
http://www.cecer.army.mil/grass/GRASS.main.html

Geological Survey of Canada
http://agcwww.bio.ns.ca/

Geological Survey of Finland
http://www.gsf.fi/

Geological Survey of Japan
http://www.aist.go.jp/GSJ/

Geomagnetism Group
http://ub.nmh.ac.uk/

Geoscience Dept.s Erlangen/Germany
http://www.rrze.uni-erlangen.de/docs/FAU/
fakultaet/natlll/geo_min/

GeoWeb
http://www.pacificnet.net/~gimills/main.html

GIS FAQ
http://www.census.gov/geo/gis/faq-index.html

GIS Planning Council for the State of Texas
http://www.texas.gov/DIR/gis.html

GIS User Guide to Internet Tools
http://jupiter.qub.ac.uk/GIS/GIS.html

Global Change Research Program
http://geochange.er.usgs.gov

Global Environmental Network for
Information Exchange
http://www-genie.mrrl.lut.ac.uk/

Global Land Cover Test Sites Project
http://dia.maxey.dri.edu:80/glcts/

Global Land Information System
http://sun1.cr.usgs.gov/glis/glis.html

Great Lakes Information Network
http://www.great-lakes.net:2200/0/
glinhome.html

Great Lakes Regional Environmental
Information System
http://epawww.ciesin.org

Groundwater Remediation Project
http://gwrp.cciw.ca/

HPCC Earth and Space Science Applications Project
http://nccsinfo.gsfc.nasa.gov:80/ESS/

Hydrologic Information Center
http://www.nohrsc.nws.gov/~hic

Illinois State Geological Survey
http://www.isgs.uiuc.edu/isgshome.html

Incorporated Research Institutions for
Seismology
http://www.iris.washington.edu/

INFO-MINE - Mining Information Online
http://www.info-mine.com/

Initiatives in Environmental Technology
Investment
http://web.wpi.org/uetc/

Inst. for Geology and Palaeontology,
Technical Univ. of Clausthal, Germany
http://www.inggeo.tu-clausthal.de/english/
Welcome-e.html

Inst. for Mineralogy, Technical Univ. of
Clausthal, Germany
http://www.immr.tu-clausthal.de/

Inst. for Technology Development/Space
Remote Sensing Center
http://ma.itd.com/welcome.html

Inst. of Mineralogy at the Freiberg Univ. of
Mining and Technology
http://www.mineral.ba-freiberg.de/
index_en.html

Inst. of Seismology, Univ. of Helsinki
http://smo1.helsinki.fi:2001/HOME/1.html

Inst. of Soil Science
http://134.76.143.27/soil-hmp.htm

Institute of Geology and Palaeontology of
the Technical Univ. of Clausthal
http://www.inggeo.tu-clausthal.de/

Institute of Geophysics and Planetary
Physics at Scripps
http://igpp.ucsd.edu/

International Association for Environmental Hydrology
http://www.hydroweb.com

International Union of Crystallography
http://www.iucr.ac.uk/welcome.html

International Union of Geodesy and
Geophysics
http://earth.agu.org/iugg/internat.html

Ionospheric Physics Group
http://ion.le.ac.uk/index.html

Iowa Geological Survey Bureau
http://www.igsb.uiowa.edu

Istituto Internazionale di Vulcanologia
http://www.iiv.ct.cnr.it/index.html

JASON Project Voyages I-VII
http://seawifs.gsfc.nasa.gov/JASON/
JASON.html

Joint Education Initiative at the Univ. of
Maryland at College Park
http://jei.umd.edu/jei/jei.html

La Trobe Univ. School of Earth Sciences,
Australia
http://www.latrobe.edu.au/WWW/Earth/
earth.html

Lamont Doherty Earth Observatory of
Columbia Univ.
http://lamont.ldgo.columbia.edu/

Lawrence Livermore National Laboratory
http://www-ep.es.llnl.gov/www-ep/igpp.html

LSU Geology
http://gbyerly.geol.lsu.edu/geology/
geology.html

Magnetic Field Monitoring & Charting
Program
http://wwwgeomag.cr.usgs.gov/geomag

Manchester Geology Dept.
http://info.mcc.ac.uk/Geology/home-
page.html

Mapping Applications Center
http://www-nmd.usgs.gov/mac

McGill Univ.
http://stoner.eps.mcgill.ca/

MERLIN - Mutlisource Environmental
Data Display for Internet Archives
http://www.ssec.wisc.edu/software/
merlin.html

Michigan Technological Univ.
http://www.geo.mtu.edu/

Michigan Technological Univ. Volcanoes
http://www.geo.mtu.edu/volcanoes/

Minerals, Metals & Materials Society
http://www.tms.org/

Minnesota Geological Survey
http://geolab.geo.umn.edu:80/mgs/

MIT's Earth Resources Lab.
http://www-erl.mit.edu/

MODIS Airborne Simulator
http://ltpwww.gsfc.nasa.gov/MODIS/MAS/
Home.html

Museum of Palentology, Univ. of California - Berkeley
http://ucmp1.berkeley.edu/

NAISMap WWW-GIS
http://ellesmere.ccm.emr.ca/naismap/
naismap.html

NASA EOS IDS Volcanology Team
http://www.geo.mtu.edu:80/eos/

NASA HPCC Earth and Space Science
Applications Project
http://hypatia.gsfc.nasa.gov/
NASA_homepage.html

National Biological Survey - Environmental Management Technical Center
http://www.emtc.nbs.gov/

National Center for Geographic Information and Analysis
http://www.ncgia.ucsb.edu/

National Earthquake Information Center
http://www.usgs.gov/data/geologic/neic/
index.html

National Geophysical Data Center
http://meridian.ngdc.noaa.gov/ngdc.html

National Mapping Information
http://www-nmd.usgs.gov

National Marine and Coastal Geology
Program
http://marine.usgs.gov

National Supercomputing Center for
Energy and the Environment
http://www.nscee.edu/nscee/

Natural Environment Research Council
http://www.nerc.ac.uk/

Natural Resources Canada
http://www.emr.ca/

Netherland Organization for Applied
Scientific Research-TNO
http://www.tno.nl

New Mexico GISAC
http://www.state.nm.us/gisac/
gisac_home.html

New South Polar Times Project
http://xalph.ast.cam.ac.uk/public/niel/
scales.html

Niel's Timelines and Scales of Measurement List
http://cast0.ast.cam.ac.uk/Xray_www/niel/scales.html

NOAA - National Oceanic and Atmospheric Administration
http://www.noaa.gov/

NOHRSC Snow Maps
http://www.nohrsc.nws.gov/

Northeast River Forecast Center
http://mohawk.ll.mit.edu

NSDI MetaData and WWW Mapping Sites
http://www.blm.gov/gis/nsdi.html

NSF Geosciences UNIDATA Integrated Earth Information Server
http://atm.geo.nsf.gov/

Ocean Bottom Seismometer Program
http://obs.er.usgs.gov

Oklahoma Univ.
http://geowww.gcn.uoknor.edu/www/Geol/Geol.html

Online Resources for Earth Scientists
http://www.csn.net/~bthoen/ores

Pacific Forestry Centre
http://www.pfc.forestry.ca/

Pacific Marine Geology
http://walrus.wr.usgs.gov

Pacific Northwest Laboratory
http://terrassa.pnl.gov:2080/

Palaeobotany International Organisation
http://sunrae.uel.ac.uk/palaeo/index.html

Pasadena Field Office of the U.S. Geological Survey
http://aladdin.gps.caltech.edu/usgs-pas.html

Pennsylvania State Univ. — College of Earth & Mineral Sciences
http://www.ems.psu.edu/

Pennsylvania State Univ. — Earth System Science Center
http://www.essc.psu.edu/

Princeton Geological & Geophysical Sciences
http://wombat.princeton.edu/

Quaternary Research Association
http://www2.tcd.ie/~pcoxon/qra.html

Regional Environmental Center for Central and Eastern Europe
http://www.rec.hu/

Research Program in Environmental Planning & Geographic Information Systems
http://www.regis.berkeley.edu/

Rice Univ.
http://zephyr.rice.edu/Dept./dept_intro.html

Rocky Mountain Mapping Center
http://rmmcweb.cr.usgs.gov

RVARES Group, Reston, VA
http://wwwrvares.er.usgs.gov

San Francisco Bay Area Regional Database
http://bard.wr.usgs.gov

Sandia National Labs Geoscience & Geotechnology Center
http://sair019.energylan.sandia.gov:70/0/Sandia_Geosciences/center.html

Seismological Laboratory at Caltech
http://www.gps.caltech.edu/seismo/seismo.page.html

Sevilleta Long-Term Ecological Research Project
http://sevilleta.unm.edu/

Society for Sedimentary Geology
http://dc.smu.edu/semp_sp/home.html

Society of Exploration Geophysicists
http://sepwww.stanford.edu/seg/

Soil and Water Conservation Soc.
http://www.netins.net/showcase/swcs

South Florida Ecosystem Program
http://fl-h2o.usgs.gov/sfei.html

Southeastern Geology Journal
http://geo.duke.edu/seglgy.htm

Southern Arizona Seismological Observatory
http://www.geo.arizona.edu/saso/

Southern California Earthquake Center Data Center
http://scec.gps.caltech.edu/

Speleology Information Server
http://speleology.cs.yale.edu

Stanford Exploration Project
http://sepwww.stanford.edu/

State of California-Teale data center
http://www.gislab.teale.ca.gov

State Univ. of New York (SUNY) at Stony Brook
http://sbast3.ess.sunysb.edu/home.html

Surfing the InterNet for Earthquake Data
http://www.geophys.washington.edu/seismosurfing.html

Texas WaterNet
http://ageninfo.tamu.edu/twri

U.S. Army Corps of Engineers - Construction Engineering Research Laboratories
http://www.cecer.army.mil/welcome.html

UNAVCO, the Univ. NAVSTAR Consortium
http://www.unavco.ucar.edu/

Union College
http://zircon.geology.union.edu/

United States Geological Survey
http://www.usgs.gov/

Univ. at Buffalo
http://www.geog.buffalo.edu/

Univ. of Arizona
http://www.geo.arizona.edu/

Univ. of Bristol
http://www.gly.bris.ac.uk/

Univ. of Calgary, Dept. of Geology and Geophysics
http://www.geo.ucalgary.ca/

Univ. of California - Berkeley Museum of Palentology
http://ucmp1.berkeley.edu/

Univ. of California, Davis, Information Center for the Environment
http://ice.ucdavis.edu/

Univ. of Chicago
http://geosci.uchicago.edu/

Univ. of Erlangen - Geosciences Departments
http://www.rrze.uni-erlangen.de/tree/FAU/fakultaet/natlll/geo_min

Univ. of Hawaii at Manoa
http://www.soest.hawaii.edu/

Univ. of Idaho Library - Electronic Green Journal
http://www.lib.uidaho.edu:70/docs/egj.html

Univ. of Illinois - The Daily Planet
http://www.atmos.uiuc.edu/

Univ. of Kansas - Explorer
http://unite.ukans.edu/xmintro.html

Univ. of Kassel Ecological Modelling
http://dino.wiz.uni-kassel.de/ecobas.html

Univ. of Manchester
http://info.mcc.ac.uk/Geology/home-page.html

Univ. of Oxford - Dept. of Earth Sciences
http://www.earth.ox.ac.uk/

Univ. of Texas
http://www.utexas.edu/cons/geo

Univ. of Virginia, Environment
http://ecosys.drdr.virginia.edu/Environment.html

USDA-ARS National Soil Erosion Laboratory
http://purgatory.ecn.purdue.edu:20002/NSERL/nserl.html

Virtual Geomorphology
http://hum.amu.edu.pl/~sgp/gw/gw.htm

Volcano Images from the Space Shuttle's Radar
http://southport.jpl.nasa.gov/volcanopic.html

Volcano Systems Center, Univ. of Washington
http://vsc.washington.edu/

Washington Univ.
http://www.geophys.washington.edu/

Water Resources of the United States
http://h2o.er.usgs.gov

Western Region Geologic Information Server
http://wrgis.wr.usgs.gov

World Data Center System
http://www.ngdc.noaa.gov/wdcmain.html

WWWVirtual Library: Environment
http://ecosys.drdr.virginia.edu/Environment.html

Xroads Western Region Center
http://xroads.wr.usgs.gov

Imaging Technologies

See also Computer Science, Electronics & Electrical Engineering, Engineering, Medicine, Optics, Physics, Virtual Reality

Usenet Newsgroups

comp.graphics
Newsgroup-based Mailing List: No.
Charter: Computer graphics general discussions.

comp.graphics.animation
Created by: ddebry@dsd.es.com (David DeBry)
Call for Votes date: August 7, 1992
Newsgroup-based Mailing List: No.
Charter (from Call for Votes):
Discussion of the techinical aspects and technique of computer animation will take place. This **does** include (but is not limited to) such topics as:

- Hardware and software used for an end result of a computer animated sequence. These include modellers, renderers, animators, etc. This topic, however, is limited by a mention later in the charter concerning threads that become TOO system specific.

- Application of knowledge of other types of more "standard" or "formal" animation to computer animation.

- Discussion of the technical aspects or techniques used to generate existing computer animations.

- Forums for showing your own work and viewing other's animations. IE: Film & video shows/contests/ competitions. It's often hard to know where to look to see computer animation, or where to get your own work shown to the public. Hopefully this will alleviate some of the problem.

comp.graphics.algorithms
Created by: hollasch@kpc.com (Steve Hollasch)
Call for Votes date: June 21, 1993
Newsgroup-based Mailing List: No.
Charter (from Call for Votes):
comp.graphics.algorithms is an unmoderated newsgroup intended as a forum for the discussion of the algorithms used in the process of generating computer graphics. These algorithms may be recently proposed in published journals or papers, old or previously known algorithms, or hacks used incidental to the process of computer graphics. The scope of these algorithms may range from an efficient way to multiply matrices, all the way to a global illumination method incorporating raytracing, radiosity, infinite spectrum modeling, and perhaps even mirrored balls and lime jello.

It is hoped that this group will serve as a forum for programmers and researchers to exchange ideas and ask questions on recent papers or current research related to computer graphics.

comp.graphics.avs
Newsgroup-based Mailing List: No.
Charter: The Application Visualization System.

comp.graphics.data-explorer
Created by: markw@Arizona.edu (Mark E. Westergaard)
Call for Votes date: July 8, 1993
Newsgroup-based Mailing List: No.
Charter (from Call for Votes):
A forum for the discussion of issues related to the IBM Visualization Data Explorer software product (commonly known as DX).

comp.graphics.explorer

Created by: Gordon Cameron
<gordonc@epcc.edinburgh.ac.uk>
Call for Votes date: May 7, 1992
Newsgroup-based Mailing List: No.
Charter (from Call for Votes):
IRIS Explorer is an application creation
system developed by Silicon Graphics that
provides visualisation and analysis
functionality for computational scientists,
engineers and other scientists. The
Explorer GUI allows users to build custom
applications without having to write any,
or a minimal amount of, traditonal code.
Also, exisiting code can be easily integrated into the Explorer environment.
Explorer currently is available on SGI and
Cray machines, but will become available
on other platforms in time.

Hopefully the group should serve as an
open forum for discussion on all matters
Explorer-related, in much the same way as
comp.graphics.avs and comp.soft-
sys.khoros work for those products. It
would also be good if the group could
help the users of Explorer by giving them
the option to keep in touch with both each
other, and the developers of Explorer
itself. Questions can be answered, and
opinions heard by those working on future
versions of the software.

comp.graphics.opengl

Created by: bglazier@buffalo.asd.sgi.com
(Buffalo Bill Glazier)
Call for Votes date: September 1, 1992
Newsgroup-based Mailing List: No.
Charter (from Call for Votes):
comp.graphics.opengl will allow for
discussion regarding technical and
marketing issues surrounding the OpenGL
3D application programming interface and
its emergence as a multiplatform graphics
standard for distributed three dimensional
graphics.

Currently a great deal of net discussion
takes place about OpenGL, unfortunately
spread out among either newsgroups
which are too general, vendor specific
newsgroups, or newsgroups dedicated to

competing API's or graphics protocols.

A dedicated newsgroup will allow for:
• Technical discussion of the OpenGL
  API, OpenGL Utility Library, and
  GL/X Wire protocol: Comparison
  versus prior releases of the GL. Input
  concerning desired enhancements or
  new features.

Programming issues and techniques.
• Analysis of implementations in
  different environments (Windows NT,
  Macintosh OS, Unix..). Porting to
  OpenGL.
• Marketing and Business Issues
  Analysis: Product plans of OpenGL
  licensees.

Comparison versus other 2D and 3D
graphics API's. Performance benchmarks
and competitive analysis.

comp.graphics.raytracing

Created by: abw@dsbc.icl.co.uk (Andy
Wardley)
Call for Votes date: February 16, 1994
Newsgroup-based Mailing List: No.
Charter (from Call for Votes):
comp.graphics.raytracing is dedicated to
the discussion of ray tracing and the
software tools and methods available for
generating photorealistic 3d graphics.

For example:
• Ray tracing software (POV-Ray, Vivid,
  etc.).
• Implementations and algorithms for
  ray tracing.
• Modelling software *specifically* for
  generating ray tracing scenes (Moray,
  POVcad, etc.). Discussion of general
  modelling software, CAD, etc., is not
  appropriate.
• Miscellaneous utilities, methods and
  issues.
• Converting between formats
• Generating complex scene informa-
  tion
• Designing Textures
• Creating and using fonts
• Tessellating surfaces
The specific focus on ray tracing does not
necessarily exclude the discussion of other

illumination algorithms and rendering techniques (radiosity, etc.).

The group is primarily aimed at the user level, although some technical discussion of algorithms, implementations, etc., is appropriate. Other newsgroups such as comp.graphics.algorithms are more suitable for in-depth discussions of these issues.

Binaries should not be posted to the group. Pictures should be posted to alt.binaries.pictures.misc and executables to the appropriate comp.binaries group. Scene description files ("source") may be posted to the group.

comp.graphics.research (Moderated)
Newsgroup-based Mailing List: No.
Moderated by: John R. Murray
(graphics-request@scri1.scri.fsu.edu)
Submissions go to:
graphics@scri1.scri.fsu.edu
Charter: Computer graphics theory from an academic perspective.

comp.graphics.visualization
Newsgroup-based Mailing List: No.
Charter: Scientific visualization.

rec.photo.digital
Created by: Robert M. Atkins
<rma@clockwise.att.com>
Call for Votes Date: August 21, 1995
Newsgroup-based Mailing List: No.
Charter (from Call for Votes):
This group is for the discussion of all aspects of digital photography, including digital cameras, scanners, image manipulation software, printers, and CD-ROM technology.

rec.photo.equipment.35mm
Created by: Robert M. Atkins
<rma@clockwise.att.com>
Call for Votes Date: August 21, 1995
Newsgroup-based Mailing List: No.
Charter (from Call for Votes):
This group is for the discussion of all aspects of 35mm camera equipment. This includes 35mm SLR camera bodies and lenses, 35mm point-and-shoot cameras,

35mm rangefinder cameras, 35mm scale focus cameras and 35mm half-frame cameras.

rec.photo.equipment.large-format
Created by: Robert M. Atkins
<rma@clockwise.att.com>
Call for Votes Date: August 21, 1995
Newsgroup-based Mailing List: No.
Charter (from Call for Votes):
This group is for the discussion of any issues related to large format equipment. Large format cameras are normally taken to be those which record their images on individual plates, rather than on roll film, and in which the image size is 4" x 5" or larger. Such cameras are often referred to as "view cameras" and focusing is normally achieved by observing the image on a ground glass screen, which is replaced by the photographic plate prior to exposure. "Plate" in this case refers to either glass plates, or individual sheets of photographic film. The 4" x 5" specification above is not intended to exclude cameras using smaller film size, should they possess the other characteristics of "large_format" or "view" cameras.

rec.photo.equipment.medium-format
Created by: Robert M. Atkins
<rma@clockwise.att.com>
Call for Votes Date: August 21, 1995
Newsgroup-based Mailing List: No.
Charter (from Call for Votes):
This group would be for the discussion of issues related to medium format equipment. Medium format cameras are normally taken to be cameras in which 120 or 620 size roll film is used, producing images in the range of 6cm x 4.5cm to 6cm x 9cm. The cameras used are typically either single lens reflex, twin lens reflex or scale (or rangefinder) focusing. The discussion of panoramic cameras using 120 film size would also be appropriate for this group.

rec.photo.equipment.misc
Created by: Robert M. Atkins
<rma@clockwise.att.com>
Call for Votes Date: August 21, 1995
Newsgroup-based Mailing List: No.

Charter (from Call for Votes):
This group is for the discussion of
equipment not covered by any other
equipment group. This would include
tripods, projectors and screens, camera
bags, lighting equipment, batteries, flash
equipment, light meters, filters. Equipment related to digital photography or
home darkroom use should be posted to
either rec.photo.digital or
rec.photo.darkroom respectively, rather
than in this group. Postings about
cameras not covered by the other equipments groups (e.g. subminiature) may be
made in this group. Postings about movie
cameras using film (but not video cameras, which are covered in the rec.video
groups) would also be appropriate.

rec.photo.film+labs

Created by: Robert M. Atkins
<rma@clockwise.att.com>
Call for Votes Date: August 21, 1995
Newsgroup-based Mailing List: No.
Charter (from Call for Votes):
This group is for the discussion of
photographic film of any format and type.
It is anticipated that the discussions will
concern the imaging characteristics of the
film and conditions under which each
type of film will give optimum results.
This group is also for the discussion of
COMMERCIAL photofinishing services,
i.e. recommendations for and comments
on photo labs. It is *NOT* for advertising
by such labs. Postings about film development related to home darkroom use
should be posted to rec.photo.darkroom,
not rec.photo.film+labs.

rec.photo.moderated (Moderated)

Created by: David Jacobson
<jacobson@hpl.hp.com>
Call for Votes Date: April 7, 1995
Moderated by: Pete Bergstrom <rpm-
request@stroberg.com>
Submissions go to: rpm@stroberg.com
Newsgroup-based Mailing List: No.
Charter (from Call for Votes):
Rec.photo.moderated is a moderated
Usenet newsgroup for the discussion of
topics related to the art and science of
photography and that are of interest to the
serious amateur recreational photogra-
pher.

rec.photo.technique.art

Created by: Robert M. Atkins
<rma@clockwise.att.com>
Call for Votes Date: August 21, 1995
Newsgroup-based Mailing List: No.
Charter (from Call for Votes):
This group is for postings related to art
issues in photography. These would
include what "art" really is, discussions of
particular photographs and what makes
them art, mounting and displaying
pictures as art, fine art photography etc.

rec.photo.technique.misc

Created by: Robert M. Atkins
<rma@clockwise.att.com>
Call for Votes Date: August 21, 1995
Newsgroup-based Mailing List: No.
Charter (from Call for Votes):
This group is for the discussion of issues
of technique which are not covered by any
other technique group. Such subjects
might include sports photography, aerial
photography, architectural photography,
scientific photography, photomicroscopy,
copy work etc.

rec.photo.technique.nature

Created by: Robert M. Atkins
<rma@clockwise.att.com>
Call for Votes Date: August 21, 1995
Newsgroup-based Mailing List: No.
Charter (from Call for Votes)
This group is for the discussion of the
techniques involved in nature photography and other peripheral issues. It is not
intended for discussions of equipment
except where a piece of equipment is
directly related to some other technique
issue. Strictly equipment discussions
should take place in the relevant equipment group. Issues appropriate for this
group would be ethics of nature photography, questions about locations for nature
photography, questions about how to
most effectively *USE* equipment,
questions about projected flash techniques, questions about macro techniques,
etc.

rec.photo.technique.people
Created by: Robert M. Atkins
<rma@clockwise.att.com>
Call for Votes Date: August 21, 1995
Newsgroup-based Mailing List: No.
Charter (from Call for Votes):
This group is for postings related to the photography of people. This includes portraits, figure studies, abstracts, nudes etc. It is not intended for the discussion of equipment except as related to other issues of technique. Suitable topics for posting would include lighting, posing, models, releases, wedding photography etc.

sci.image.processing
Created by: newberry@as.arizona.edu
(Mike Newberry)
Call for Votes date: June 4, 1992
Newsgroup-based Mailing List: No.
Charter (from Call for Votes):
sci.image.processing provides a forum for discussion of the scientific uses of image processing and analysis. Discussions of algorithms and application programs are appropriate, with emphasis on solving real world image processing problems. Discussions of computer graphics, visualization, output, window systems, communications, etc. are not appropriate. Posting of images is strongly discouraged. Images should be posted to alt.binaries.pictures.misc, or made available for FTP.

This group will take a broad definition of the term image processing. Most topics related to the formation and analysis of images are appropriate so long as a more focused newsgroup does not exist. This presently excludes topics such as computer vision (comp.ai.vision) and image compression per se (comp.compression), but not topics such as image detectors or calibration of imaging equipment. Obviously, topics such as the impact of lossy image compression on image processing algorithms or the use of AI to analyze scientific images are not excluded.

One purpose is to develop and maintain Frequently Asked Question (FAQ) articles on the subject. Another is to provide a forum where experimentalists learn about image processing algorithms while computer scientists hear about the uses to which generic algorithms are put, or the requirements of a specific application. Both will discuss what can and cannot be done to improve image quality before and during processing.

The "IEEE Transactions on Image Processing" gives a list of topics which they consider appropriate for that journal. Some of those topics are also appropriate here:

Acoustic Imaging
Architectures and Software
Coded-Aperture Imaging
Coding Filtering Enhancement
Computed Imaging
Computer Holography
Confocal Microscopy
Electron Microscopy
Geophysical and Seismic Imaging
Image Analysis
Image Processing
Image Representation
Interpolation and Spatial Transformations
Magnetic Resonance Imaging
Motion Detection and Estimation Image
Sequence Processing
Multiresolution Processing
Multispectral Processing
Noise Modeling
Radar Imaging Tomography
Radio Astronomy
Real-Aperture Arrays
Restoration
Segmentation
Speckle Imaging
Video Signal Processing
X-ray Crystallography

sci.techniques.mag-resonance
Created by:
mark@ginger.biophys.upenn.edu (Mark Elliott)
Call for Votes date: April 8, 1994
Newsgroup-based Mailing List: No.
Charter (from Call for Votes):
sci.techniques.mag-resonance will exist for discussion in the field of magnetic

resonance imaging and spectroscopy. Possible topics include requests for information, scientific observations, and commentary on all aspects of magnetic resonance. The group would place equal emphasis on clinical studies, new techniques, and basic research. It will be an unmoderated newsgroup.
Some of the topics to be discussed are:

- Questions and answers on the use/performance of commercial MR spectrometers (GE, Siemens, Philips, Bruker, etc.)
- Exchange of pulse sequence algorithms as well as actual implementations.
- Discussion of recent journal articles.
- Results of clinical studies.
- Echo relevant postings found in other, possibly overlooked, newsgroups.

sci.techniques.microscopy

Created by: John.F.Mansfield@umich.edu (John F. Mansfield)
Call for Votes date: January 3, 1994
Newsgroup-based Mailing List: No.
Charter (from Call for Votes):
The main aim of sci.techniques.microscopy is to provide an open forum for the discussion of microscopy and related fields on the Internet.

sci.virtual-worlds (Moderated)

Moderated by: Toni Emerson and Aaron Pulkka
(scivw-request@hitl.washington.edu)
Submissions go to:
scivw@hitl.washington.edu
Newsgroup-based Mailing List: No.
Charter: Largely technology-oriented discussions of virtual reality. Lots of hardware issues.

sci.virtual-worlds.apps (Moderated)

Created by: Robert Jacobson
<cyberoid@u.washington.edu>
Moderated by: Bob Jacobson and Mark DeLoura
(scivwa@media.mit.edu)
Submissions go to:
scivwa@media.mit.edu
Call for Votes date: August 19, 1992

Newsgroup-based Mailing List: No.
Charter: Practical real-world applications of virtual reality.

Frequently Asked Questions

3-D Information for the Programmer FAQ

Maintainer: pat@mail.csh.rit.edu
Where on Usenet:
rec.games.programmers
Where it's archived:
rtfm.mit.edu: pub/usenet/
rec.games.programmers
What it's for: Reference source for 3d algorithms.

Color_space_FAQ

Maintainer:
david.bourgin@ufrima.imag.fr (David Bourgin)
Where on Usenet: comp.graphics
Where it's archived:
rtfm.mit.edu: pub/usenet/comp.graphics
What it's for: Frequently Asked Questions (and their answers) about colors and color spaces.

comp.graphics FAQ

Maintainer: grieggs@netcom.com (John T. Grieggs)
Where on Usenet: comp.graphics
Where it's archived:
rtfm.mit.edu: pub/usenet/comp.graphics
What it's for: Answers a number of the most frequently asked questions about graphics on Usenet.

comp.graphics.algorithms FAQ

Maintainer: jd-stone@destin.dazixco.ingr.com (Jon Stone)
Where on Usenet:
comp.graphics.algorithms
Where it's archived:
rtfm.mit.edu: pub/usenet/
comp.graphics.algorithms
What it's for:
Questions (and their answers) about computer graphics algorithms. It should be read by anyone who wishes to post to the comp.graphics.algorithms newsgroup.

comp.graphics.animation FAQ

Maintainer: angus@cgl.citri.edu.au (angus y montgomery)
Where on Usenet: comp.graphics.animation
Where it's archived: rtfm.mit.edu: pub/usenet/ comp.graphics.animation
What it's for: (from summary) Information on computer animation for end-users, hobbyists, career animators, and programmers.

comp.graphics.gnuplot FAQ

Maintainer: ig25@fg70.rz.uni-karlsruhe.de (Thomas Koenig)
Where on Usenet: comp.graphics.gnuplot
Where it's archived: rtfm.mit.edu: pub/usenet/ comp.graphics.gnuplot
What it's for: (from summary) Discusses the gnuplot program for plotting 2D - and 3D - graphs.

comp.graphics.opengl FAQ

Maintainer: woo@kicksave.asd.sgi.com (Mason Woo)
Where on Usenet: comp.graphics.opengl
Where it's archived: rtfm.mit.edu: pub/usenet/ comp.graphics.opengl
What it's for: (from FAQ) OpenGL is the software interface for graphics hardware that allows graphics programmers to produce high-quality color images of 3D objects. This FAQ describes its featureset and addresses common issues.

Computer Graphics Resource Listing

Maintainer: nfotis@theseas.ntua.gr (Nick C. Fotis)
Where on Usenet: comp.graphics
Where it's archived: rtfm.mit.edu: pub/usenet/comp.graphics
What it's for: Places to find graphics resources: images, formats, algorithms, etc.

JPEG image compression FAQ

Maintainer: tgl@netcom.com (Tom Lane)
Where on Usenet: comp.graphics
Where it's archived: rtfm.mit.edu: pub/usenet/comp.graphics

What it's for: Joint Photographic Experts Group compression format: issues, sources, software, etc.

MPEG FAQ: multimedia compression

Maintainer: phade@cs.tu-berlin.de (Frank Gadegast)
Where on Usenet: comp.graphics
Where it's archived: rtfm.mit.edu: pub/usenet/comp.graphics
What it's for: Issues pertaining to the MPEG multimedia format.

Discussion Lists

3d
JHBercovitz@lbl.gov (John Bercovitz)
3D photography.

data-exp
stein@watson.ibm.com
Visualization Data Explorer Package.

photo-cd
listmgr@info.kodak.com (Don Cox)
Kodak PhotoCD.

photoforum
listserv@listserver.isc.rit.edu
Photographing and digitizing images.

vrapp-l
VRAPP-L@UIUCVMD
VR Apps / sci.virtual-worlds.apps

Imaging Technologies Resources

FTP Resources

Colour Space Conversion
  ftp://wmin.ac.uk/pub/itrg

Image file formats
  ftp://ftp.ncsa.uiuc.edu/misc/file.formats/ graphics.formats

Johns Hopkins Univ. CS dept.
  blaze.cs.jhu.edu

Melbourne Univ.
  gondwana.ecr.mu.oz.au

Rensselaer Polytechnical Institute
  iear.arts.rpi.edu

SPIE - The International Society for Optical Engineering
ftp.spie.org

Technischer Univ. Graz (Graz Institute of Technology), Graz
iicm.tu-graz.ac.at

Univ. of Southern Australia, Signal Processing Research Institute
audrey.levels.unisa.edu.au

Vision List Archive
ftp://teleos.com/VISION-LIST-ARCHIVE/

Gopher Resources

Association of Computing Machinery SIGGRAPH
siggraph.org

alt.cad (CAD Newsgroup) - Usenet
aurora.latech.edu

CAD - comp.lsi.cad (FAQs) - Oregon State Univ.
gaia.ucs.orst.edu

CAD - Ejournal - Cadalyst Magazine (CAD/CAM)
gopher.enews.com

CAD - Software MSDOS
server.uga.edu:8001

Columbia CAD software
mcgnext.cc.columbia.edu

Machine Vision Gopher
gopher://161.29.40.7/

VHDL Intl. Users' Forum
vhdl.org/

WWW Resources

Aalborg Univ. Laboratory of Image Analysis
http://www.vision.auc.dk/~hic/auc-head.html

Advanced Liquid Crystalline Optical Materials, Kent State Univ.
http://alcom.kent.edu/ALCOM/ALCOM.html

AIG-Manchester Advanced Interfaces Group
http://www.cs.man.ac.uk/aig/aig.html

Algorithm Image Gallery
http://axpba1.ba.infn.it:8080/

Amerinex Artificial Intelligence, Inc.
http://www.aai.com/

Arizona State Univ., MAE Design Automation Lab
http://asudesign.eas.asu.edu/

ARPA Display Technology Programs
http://esto.sysplan.com/ESTO/Displays//

Asia Technical Information Progam Flat Panel Display Project
http://www.atip.or.jp/fpd.html

Association for Computing Machinery
http://info.acm.org/

AT&T Bell Laboratories
http://www.research.att.com/

Beckman Institute Visualization Facility
http://delphi.beckman.uiuc.edu:80/

CAD Centre, Univ. of Strathclyde, Glasgow, Scotland
http://www.cad.strath.ac.uk/Home.html

Cadence Design Systems
http://www.cadence.com/

Caltech Interactive Volume Browser
http://www.scp.caltech.edu:80/~mep/ivb.html

Cambridge Univ. Rainbow Research Group
http://www.cl.cam.ac.uk/Research/Rainbow/

Cardiff's VR Page
http://www.cm.cf.ac.uk/User/Andrew.Wilson/VR/

Carlson Center for Imaging Science at RIT
http://www.cis.rit.edu

Carnegie Mellon Computer Vision
http://www.cs.cmu.edu:8001/afs/cs/project/cil/ftp/html/vision.html

Carnegie Mellon Univ. 3D-Stereoscopic Video Display
http://www.cs.cmu.edu/afs/cs/project/sensor-9/ftp/www/homepage.html

CERN Computer Aided Detector Design
http://cadd.cern.ch/welcome.html

CGU-Manchester—The Computer Graphics Unit Research
http://info.mcc.ac.uk/CGU/CGU-research.html

CIDTECH
http://www.cidtec.com

CIE - International Commission on
Illumination
http://www.hike.te.chiba-u.ac.jp/ikeda/CIE/
home.html

Colour Technology Forum
http://www.hike.te.chiba-u.ac.jp/ikeda/Color/
home.html

Coreco
http://www.dspnet.com/dspnet/coreco/
coreh.html

Crew Systems Ergonomics Information
Analysis Ctr.
http://www.dtic.dla.mil/iac/cseriac/cseriac.html

Ctr. for Display Manufacturing and
Technology, Univ. of Michigan
http://dtm.eecs.umich.edu

Ctr. for In Vivo Microscopy
http://wwwcivm.mc.duke.edu/

Ctr. for Information Enhanced Medicine
(CIeMed)
http://ciemed.iss.nus.sg/ciemed.html

Ctr. for Microelectronics and Optoelectronics
http://www-phys.llnl.gov/H_Div/CMO/
cmo.html

Ctr. for Scientific Computing Graphics
Group (Finland)
http://www.csc.fi:80/visualization/
graphics_group.html

Curt Deckert Associates
http://www.deltanet.com/cda

Cybernetic Vision Research Group,
Universidade de Sao Paulo
http://scorpions.ifqsc.sc.usp.br/ifsc/ffi/grupos/
instrum/visao/cybervision.htm

Data Translation
http://www.datx.com

DataCube
http://www.cera.com/datawwwx.htm

David Sarnoff Research Ctr.
http://www.sarnoff.com//

Directed Perception Inc.
http://www.DPerception.com

Diversity Univ. MOO
http://pass.wayne.edu/DU.html

DSPNET - DSP Technology On-line
http://dspnet.com/

DVC
dvc.html

Electronic Engineering Times (EE Times)
http://techweb.cmp.com:2090/techweb/eet/
current/

Environmental Research Institute of
Michigan (ERIM)
http://www.erim.org

Frank DeFreitas Holography Studio
http://www.enter.net/~holostudio/

Frederik Philips Magnetic Resonance
Research Ctr.
http://www.emory.edu/RADIOLOGY/MRI/
FPMRRCb.html

Gamma and Color FAQ
http://www.inforamp.net/~poynton/Poynton-
colour.html

General Imaging Corp.
http://www.gicorp.com

Georgia Institute of Technology's Graphics, Visualization, and Usability Ctr.
http://www.gatech.edu/gvu/gvutop.htm

Georgia Tech Multimedia Technology Lab
http://www.oip.gatech.edu/mmtltop.html

Graduate Hospital Imaging Ctr.
http://www.netaxs.com/~gradimag/

Guy's and St. Thomas' Hospitals Medical
Image Processing Group
http://nothung.umds.ac.uk/

Harvard - Ctr. for Imaging and Pharmaceutical Research Home Page
http://cipr-diva.mgh.harvard.edu/

Harvard Univ. Robotics Laboratory
http://hrl.harvard.edu

Hi-Vision Promotion Ctr. (HDTV)
http://www.sfc.keio.ac.jp/~ishitake/KAWA/
hvc1.html

Hughes STX
http://info.stx.com/

Human Factors and Ergonomics Society
http://vered.rose.utoronto.ca/HFESVE_dir/
HFES.html

Illuminating Engineering Society of North
America
http://www.aecnet.com/IES/ieshome.html

Image Processing With Live Video Sources
http://tns-www.lcs.mit.edu/cgi-bin/vs/vvdemo

Image Science Research Group
http://isg-www.mse.kyutech.ac.jp/ISG/home-e.html

ImageNation
http://www.ImageNation.com

Indiana Univ Display Technology
http://www.cs.indiana.edu/csg/display.html

INRIA Sophia Antipolis RobotVis Project
http://www.inria.fr/robotvis/personnel/vthierry/acvis-demo/demo2/main.html

Institute of Computer Science, Computer Vision, Robotics Laboratory in Greece
http://www.ics.forth.gr/proj/cvrl

IPR - Mobile Robotics - Institute for Real Time Computer Systems and Robotics
http://i60s30.ira.ulka.de/areas/mobilerobots.html

IS&T — Society for Imaging Science & Technology
http://www.imaging.org

JHM
http://jhm.ccs.neu.edu:7043/

John Cowie's video engineering information (w/ SCART)
http://www.bbc.co.uk/aberdeen/tech.htm

Joint Research Program on Digital Video Broadcasting
http://www.tele.unit.no:8080/signal/hdtv.html

Key Centre of Design Computing
http://www.arch.su.edu.au/

Khoros and Khoral Research
http://www.khoros.unm.edu:80/

Kodak
http://www.kodak.com

Lab for Scientific Visual Analysis, Virginia Tech
http://gopher.vt.edu:10021/vizlab/index.html

Laser Focus World
http://www.lfw.com

LBL Imaging and Distributed Computing Group
http://george.lbl.gov:80/ITG.html

Leeds Univ. Medical Imaging
http://agora.leeds.ac.uk/comir/resources/links.html

LIFIA-IMAG
http://cosmos.imag.fr/PRIMA/prima.html

Machine Vision Related Research Papers
http://www.mbvlab.wpafb.af.mil/paper.html

Magnetic Resonance Imaging Group
http://www-mri.uta.edu/

Malin Space Science Systems
http://barsoom.msss.com/

Martin Marietta Energy Systems
http://www.ornl.gov/mmes.html

Massachusetts Institute of Technology
http://www.ai.mit.edu/projects/vision-machine/vm.html

MIT Media Lab - Spatial Imaging Group
http://www.media.mit.edu/

Mathematics Experiences Through Image Processing (METIP)
http://www.cs.washington.edu/research/metip/metip.html

McDonnell Douglas Corp.
http://pat.mdc.com/

Medical Image Processing Lab - SUNY at Stony Brook
http://clio.rad.sunysb.edu

Meta Virtual Environments
http://www.gatech.edu/gvu/people/Masters/Rob.Kooper/Meta.VR.html

Microcosm, Inc.
http://www.softaid.net/spark

Mid-Southwest Data Systems
http://www.webcom.com/~msds/

Molecular Optoelectronics Corp.
http://www.automatrix.com/moec/

Montreal Neurological Institute
http://www.mni.mcgill.ca

Movie Samples from the Open Virtual Reality Testbed
http://nemo.ncsl.nist.gov/~sressler/OVRTmovies.html

MPEG FAQ
http://www.crs4.it/HTML/LUIGI/MPEG/mpegfaq.html

NASA Annotated Scientific Visualization URL Bibliography
http://www.nas.nasa.gov/RNR/Visualization/annotatedURLs.html

NASA Colorless Polyimide Thin Film
Technology
http://www.larc.nasa.gov/tops/Exhibits/Ex_W-619/Ex_W-619.html

NASA Helmet Mounted Displays
http://www.larc.nasa.gov/tops/Exhibits/Ex_D-142e.4/Ex_D-142e.4.html

NASA PRISM-3 Johnson Space Ctr.
http://tommy.jsc.nasa.gov/er/er6/mrl/projects/vision/

NASA/JPL Imaging Radar
http://southport.jpl.nasa.gov/

NASA Vision Science
http://vision.arc.nasa.gov/VisionScience

NAVE Navigating and Acting in Virtual
Environments
http://www.cs.colorado.edu/homes/cboyd/public_html/Home.html

Navy Ctr. for Applied Research in
Artificial Intelligence
http://www.aic.nrl.navy.mil

NIH Imaging Software
zippy.nimh.nih.gov

NII Workshop - Advanced Digital Video
http://www.eeel.nist.gov/advnii/

NIST Intelligent Systems Division
http://isd.cme.nist.gov

NIST Visual Image Processing
http://dsys.ncsl.nist.gov/asd/divsum95/hmisumm.html#Visual

Northeastern Univ. Robotics and Vision
Systems Laboratory
http://r2d2.coe.neu.edu

OOPIC Project - George Mason Univ.
http://gui.gmu.edu:80/OOPIC/oopic_home.html

Open Virtual Reality Testbed
http://nemo.ncsl.nist.gov/~sressler/OVRThome.html

Optical Research Associates
http://www.opticalres.com

OPTICS.ORG - The Photonics Resource
Center
http://optics.org/

Oregon Graduate Institute - Flat Panel
Display Research
http://www.eeap.ogi.edu/~barbero/Flat/FPD.html

Osaka Univ. Dept. of Mechanical Engineering for Computer Controlled
Machinery
http://www_cv.ccm.eng.osaka-u.ac.jp/research/panther.html

Pattern Recognition Group
http://galaxy.ph.tn.tudelft.nl:2000/pr-intro.html

Pattern Recognition Information
http://www.ph.tn.tudelft.nl/PRInfo.html

Paul Scherrer Institute, PET Programm
http://pss023.psi.ch/

Penn State Multidimensional Image
Processing Lab
http://cobb.ece.psu.edu/

Perceptics
http://www.perceptics.com/info

PERCH NMR Software
http://www.uku.fi/perch.html

Pilot European Image Processing Archive
http://peipa.essex.ac.uk/

Poynton's Video Engineering Page
http://www.inforamp.net/~poynton/Poynton-video-eng.html

Precision Digital Images
http://www.precisionimages.com/HOME.HTM

Radiology Imaging Ctr.
http://visual-ra.swmed.edu/

Rochester Institute of Technology—
Carlson Center for Imaging Science
http://www.cis.rit.edu

Rochester Institute of Technology, Imaging
and Photographic Technology
http://www.rit.edu/~andpph/ipt.html

Royal Institute of Technology Computational Vision and Active Perception Lab
(CVAP)
http://www.bion.kth.se/whatis.html

Ruhr Univ. Bochum Institute for
Neuroinformatics
http://www.neuroinformatik.ruhr-uni-bochum.de/ini/PROJECTS/NAMOS/NAMOS.html

Rutgers Lab. for Visiometrics and Modelling
http://vizlab.rutgers.edu/

Scientific Visualization of Plasma MHD
Behavior
http://www.ornl.gov:80/fed/mhd/mhd.html

SHARE PROJECT CDR Page
http://gummo.stanford.edu/html/SHARE/
share.html

SIGGRAPH (ACM Graphics)
http://www.siggraph.org

Signal Processing Information Base (SPIB)
http://spib.rice.edu/spib.html

Signal Processing, Josip Juric, Croatia
http://tjev.tel.etf.hr/josip/DSP/sigproc.html

Signal Processing, Lutz Falkenhagen,
Hannover
http://www.tnt.uni-hannover.de/data/info/www/
tnt/subj/sci/sig/overview.html

Sliicon Graphics
http://www.sgi.com/

SMPTE - Society of Motion Picture and
Television Engineers
http://www.smpte.org

Society for Information Display
http://www.display.org/sid/

Software Spectra (optical thin films
design)
http://www.teleport.com/~sspectra/

Sony
http://www.sony.com/~sspectra/

South Bank Univ. - Imaging and Radio-
therapy
http://www.sbu.ac.uk/SAS/dirt/

Space Science and Engineering Ctr.
Visualization Project at Univ. of Wisconsin-Madison
http://www.ssec.wisc.edu/~billh/vis.html

SPIE - The International Organization for
Optical Engineering
http://www.spie.org/

Stanford Univ. Vision and Imaging Science
and Technology
http://white.stanford.edu/

Subtechnique, Inc.
http://www.subtechnique.com

Swales and Associates Optics Group
http://www.swales.com/optics.html

Synopsys
http://www.synopsys.com/

Technical Reports Index
http://www.cs.indiana.edu/cstr/search

Tecnet
http://www.tecnet.com

Teledyne Brown Electro-Optical Products
Group
http://www.tbe.com/tech-pubs/products/
optics/optics.html

Teleos Research
http://www.teleos.com

3D Graphic file formats
http://www.tnt.uni-hannover.de/data/info/www/
tnt/soft/sci/vis/compgraph/fileformats/
overview.html

TrekMUSE
http://grimmy.cnidr.org/trek.html

Triangle Virtual Reality Group (TRIVR)
http://www.trinet.com/trivr.html

UMDS Medical Image Processing Group
http://nothung.umds.ac.uk/

United Medical & Dental Schools Image
Processing Group
http://www-ipg.umds.ac.uk/

Univ. of Bergen - Section for Medical
Image Analysis and Pattern Recognition
http://www.uib.no/med/avd/miapr/
homepage.html

Univ. of British Columbia Laboratory for
Computational Intelligence
http://www.cs.ubc.ca/nest/lci/home

UCLA Computer Aided Design
http://cad.ucla.edu/Welcome

Univ. of California, Los Angeles - Crump
Institute for Biological Imaging
http://www.nuc.ucla.edu/html_docs/crump/
crump.html

Univ. of Coimbra Institute of Systems and
Robotics
http://info-isr.dee.uc.pt/~jorge/varma.html

Univ. of Connecticut - Ctr. for Biomedical
Imaging Technology
http://panda.uchc.edu/htbit/

Univ. of Derby (UK) Colour Research
Group
http://ziggy.derby.ac.uk/colour/

Univ. of Genova Laboratory for Integrated
Advanced Robotics
http://afrodite.lira.dist.unige.it:81/LIRA/
expsetup/binocul.html

Univ. of Illinois Robotics/Computer
Vision Laboratory
http://www.beckman.uiuc.edu/Facilities/
BIRCVLab.html

Univ. of Iowa College of Medicine -
Physiological Imaging
http://everest.radiology.uiowa.edu/

Univ. of Karlsruhe Institute for Real-Time
Computer Systems and Robotics (IPR)
http://wwwipr.ira.uka.de/~priamos/projects/
kastor/

Univ. of Kiel Cognitive Systems Group
http://www.informatik.uni-kiel.de/inf/Sommer

Univ. of Leeds - Centre of Medical
Imaging Research
http://agora.leeds.ac.uk/comir/comir.html

Univ. of Maryland Computer Vision
Laboratory
http://www.cfar.umd.edu/cvl

Univ. of Massachusetts Laboratory for
Perceptual Robotics
http://piglet.cs.umass.edu:4321/
lpr.html#Facilities

Univ. of Minnesota AHPCRC
http://www.arc.umn.edu/html/Ahpcrc.html

Univ. of Oxford Robotics Research Group
http://www.robots.ox.ac.uk:5000/~lav

Univ. of Pennsylvania GRASP Lab
http://www.cis.upenn.edu/~grasp/head/
PennEyes/PennEyes.html

Univ. of Pennsylvania Medical Image
Processing
http://mipgsun.mipg.upenn.edu/

Univ. of Rochester Vision and Robotics
Lab
http://www.cs.rochester.edu/users/faculty/
brown/lab.html

Univ. of Sheffield Artificial Intelligence
and Vision Research Unit
http://www2.shef.ac.uk/uni/academic/A-C/
aivru

Univ. of Strathclyde Anthropomorphic
Robot Head
http://www.strath.ac.uk/Strath.html

Univ. of Surrey Mechatronic Systems and
Robotics Research Group
http://robots.surrey.ac.uk/Activities/
ActiveVision/activevis.html

Univ. of Surrey Vision, Speech and Signal
Processing Group
http://www.ee.surrey.ac.uk/EE/VSSP/intro/
node18.html

Univ. of Tennessee Computer Vision and
Robotics Research Laboratory
http://kiwi.engr.utk.edu

Univ. of Texas at Arlington Magnetic
Resonance Imaging Group
http://www-mri.uta.edu/

Univ. of Tokyo-Fasol Laboratory - Blue
Light Emitters
http://kappa.iis.u-tokyo.ac.jp/~fasol/
blueledslides.html

Univ. of Toronto Artificial Intelligence
Group
http://www.cdf.toronto.edu:80/DCS/Faculty/
AI-Faculty.html

Univ. of Utah Vision/Robotics Research
Group
http://www.cs.utah.edu:80/projects/robot

Univ. of Washington Virtual Retinal
Display
http://www.hitl.washington.edu/projects/vrd/
sid-vrd.html

Univ. of Western Australia Robotics and
Vision Research Group
http://www.cs.uwa.edu.au/robvis/projects/
StereoVerging.html

Univeristy of Waikato Vision
http://www.waikato.ac.nz/

Utah Raster Toolkit
http://www.arc.umn.edu/GVL/Software/
urt.html

Vanderbilt Univ. Intelligent Robotics
Laboratory
http://www.vuse.vanderbilt.edu/~isac/
pantilt.html

Video Webalog
http://figment.fastman.com/vweb/html/
vidmain.html

Virginia Tech Laboratory for Scientific
Visual Analysis
http://www.sv.vt.edu

Virgo Optics, Division of II-VI
http://innet.com/~virgo/vhome2.html

Virtual Medical Imaging Ctr.
http://www-sci.lib.uci.edu/HSG/
MedicalImage.html

Virtual Reality Forum Mailing List
http://galaxy.einet.net/e-periodicals/virtual-
reality-forum.txt

Vision and Imaging Technology Resource
http://www.vision1.com/

Vision Systems International (VSI)
vsi.html

Visioneering Research Lab. - New Mexico
State Univ.
http://vitoria.nmsu.edu/

Visual Systems Lab., Institute for Simulation
http://www.vsl.ist.ucf.edu/about.html

Visualization at the Cornell Theory Ctr.
http://www.tc.cornell.edu/Visualization/

Visualization at TNT
http://www.tnt.uni-hannover.de:80/data/info/
www/tnt/subj/sci/vis/overview.html

Visualization file formats
http://web.msi.umn.edu/WWW/SciVis/
Formats/formats.html

Washington Univ. - MIR Image Processing
Laboratory
http://imacx.wustl.edu/

Waxweb Mosaic MOO
http://bug.village.virginia.edu:7777/

Yale Univ. Image Processing and Analysis
Group
http://noodle.med.yale.edu/

York Univ. Vision, Graphics and Robotics
Lab
http://www.cs.yorku.ca/labs/vgrlab/
Welcome.html

Zentrum fuer Graphische
Datenverarbeitung e.V., Computer
Graphics Ctr.
http://zgdv.igd.fhg.de/

WAIS Resources

WAIS Indexes for Computer-aided Design
and Engineering
wais://wais.com:210/

Linguistics

Usenet Newsgroups

comp.ai.nat-lang
Created by: Daniel Jones
<danny@language-
linguistics.umist.ac.uk>
Call for Votes date: March 3, 1993
Newsgroup-based Mailing List: No.
Charter (from Call for Votes):
To discuss issues relating to natural
language, especially computer-related
issues from an AI viewpoint. The topics
that will be discussed in this group will
concentrate on, but are not limited to, the
following:

- Natural Language Understanding
- Natural Language Generation
- Machine Translation
- Dialogue and Discourse Systems
- Natural Language Interfaces
- Parsing
- Computational Linguistics
- Computer-Aided Language Learning

This newsgroup will avoid discussing
topics such as speech synthesis, non
computer-related linguistic issues, or other
issues that are better addressed in other
newsgroups such as comp.speech and
sci.lang.

However, because natural language
processing is interdisciplinary, some
overlap will be inevitable. The topic list
above should serve as a guide as to the
nature of topics that should be discussed
in this newsgroup.

While linguistics serves as one of the
foundations to natural language processing, this group is not strictly meant for

linguists. This group is meant to attract
people from linguistics, AI, computer
science, philosophy, and psychology,
(among others) who have interest in
natural language processing.

Although this group is meant as a forum
for those people who work in the field of
natural language processing, and therefore
some discussion may be highly technical
in nature, or may refer to work that is
commonly known for those in the field,
we should also be open to those who are
just beginning in the field, or who have an
active interest in the field but work in a
different area. Because this group is
unmoderated, there will be more noise
(i.e., articles that are deemed by some as
unimportant) than were this group
moderated. Please think of this as a
tradeoff that may lead to better discussion.

comp.speech
Created by: andrewh@ee.su.oz.au
(Andrew Hunt)
Call for Votes date: September 1, 1992
Newsgroup-based Mailing List: No.
Charter (from Call for Votes):
This group will be for the discussion of
issues related to speech technology—
relevant research, application issues and
other related matters.

sci.lang
Newsgroup-based Mailing List: No.
Charter: Linguistics.

sci.lang.japan
Newsgroup-based Mailing List: Yes
(nihongo@mitvma.mit.edu).
Charter: Japanese linguistics.

sci.lang.translation
Created by: James Hester, jrh@nirim.go.jp
Call for Votes Date: 23 September 1994
Newsgroup-based Mailing List: No.
Charter (from Call for Votes):
The proposed group would provide a forum for those interested in the problems, issues and concerns of translators/interpreters.

Frequently Asked Questions

comp.speech FAQ
Maintainer: andrewh@speech.su.oz.au (Andrew Hunt)
Where on Usenet: comp.speech
Where it's archived:
rtfm.mit.edu:pub/usenet/news.answers/comp.speech
What it's for: Information on speech synthesis and recognition.

sci.lang FAQ
Maintainer: markrose@spss.com (Mark Rosenfelder)
Where on Usenet: comp.speech
Where it's archived:
rtfm.mit.edu:pub/usenet/news.answers/sci.lang
What it's for: Info on the scientific analysis of human language.

Discussion Lists

abstract
abstract@tamvm1.tamu.edu
LINGUIST-ABSTRACTS

ads-l
ads-l@uga
American Dialect Society

alt
alt@tamvm1.tamu.edu
The Association of Linguistic Typology

lingua
lingua@arizvm1
Linguistics at the Univ. of Arizona

linguist
linguist@tamvm1.tamu.edu
The LINGUIST

ltest-l
ltest-l@psuvm
Language Testing Research and Practice

schiz-l
schiz-l@umab
Clinical & Basic Science Research of Schizophrenia

scholar
scholar@cunyvm
SCHOLAR: Natural Language Processing

semios-l
semios-l@ulkyvm
Visual and Verbal Semiotics

slling-l
slling-l@yalevm
Sign Language Linguistics List

Linguistics Resources

FTP Resources

Papers in Discourse Analysis and Applied Linguistics
ftp.liv.ac.uk/pub/linguistics/

Survey of corpora and corpus-related resources on the Internet
cogsci.berkeley.edu/pub/CorpusSurvey.Z

Univ. of Michigan
linguistics.archive.umich.edu

Gopher Resources

Archives of the Ctr. for Computer Analysis of Texts (CCAT)
ccat.sas.upenn.edu

CICNet Electronic Jrnl. Project
gopher.cic.net

Directory of Electronic Conferences on Linguistics-Political Science
gopher.usask.ca

Pitzer College Dept. of Linguistics
gopher.claremont.edu/00/pitzer/acad/catalog/Linguistics

Stanford Univ.
csli-gopher.stanford.edu/11/Linguistics

Text Files and Computing in the Humanities
datalib.library.ualberta.ca

Univ.of Georgia Linguistic Atlas Project
hyde.park.uga.edu/1

U of MN Ctr for Advanced Research on
Lang. Acquisition
lctl.acad.umn.edu/1

Univ.of Pennsylvania
ling.upenn.edu/1

WWW Resources

Aboriginal Studies Electronic Data
Archive
http://coombs.anu.edu.au/SpecialProj/
ASEDA/ASEDA.html

ACM SIGIR - Information Retrieval
http://info.sigir.acm.org/sigir/

American Dialect Society
http://www.msstate.edu/Archives/ADS

Applied Science and Engineering Laboratories, U. of Delaware
http://www.asel.udel.edu/

Association for Computational Phonology
http://www.cogsci.ed.ac.uk/phonology/
CompPhon.html

Association for the History of Langugage
http://adhocalypse.arts.unimelb.edu.au/Dept/
Linguistics/nsn/Work/ahl.html

Austrian Research Institute for Artificial
Intelligence (OFAI)
http://www.ai.univie.ac.at/

Birkbeck College
http://144.82.22.3/Dept.s/AppliedLinguistics/
home.html

Brown Univ.
http://www.cog.brown.edu/pointers/
cognitive.html

California State Univ. at Northridge
Program in Linguistics and ESL
http://www.csun.edu/~hflin001/linguist.html

Carnegie Mellon Computational Linguistics Program
http://hss.cmu.edu/HTML/Dept.s/philosophy/
computational_linguistics/
research_comp_ling.html

Carnegie Mellon Univ.- Center for
Machine Translation
http://www.mt.cs.cmu.edu/cmt/CMT-
home.html

CMU Human-Computer Interaction Inst.
http://www.cs.cmu.edu/afs/cs.cmu.edu/user/
hcii/www/hcii-home.html

Center for Cognitive Science, SUNY
Buffalo
http://www.c3.lanl.gov/~rutvik/buffalo.html

Center for the Study of Lang. and Information - Stanford Univ.
http://kanpai.stanford.edu/

Centre for Cognitive Science, Univ.of
Edinburgh
http://www.cogsci.ed.ac.uk/ccs/home.html

Computation and Language E-Print
Archive
http://xxx.lanl.gov/cmp-lg/

Computational Epistemology Lab, U. of
Waterloo, Canada
http://beowulf.uwaterloo.ca/

Computational Linguistics and Information Processing Lab, U. of Maryland
http://www.umiacs.umd.edu/labs/CLIP

Computational Linguistics Group, Univ. of
Zurich
http://www.ifi.unizh.ch/groups/hess/
CLpage.html

Computational Linguistics Laboratory,
Nara University
http://cactus.aist-nara.ac.jp/lab-english/home-
e.html

Computational Linguistics, Univ. of
Erlangen
http://uranus.linguistik.uni-erlangen.de/
Welcome.html

Consortium for Lexical Research
http://crl.nmsu.edu/clr/CLR.html

DFKI - Kaiserslautern
http://www.dfki.uni-kl.de/

ELSNET - European Network in Lang. and
Speech
http://www.cogsci.ed.ac.uk/elsnet/home.html

European Association for Logic, Lang.,
and Information
http://www.fwi.uva.nl/fwi/research/vg2/folli/

European Lingua Project
http://www.loria.fr/exterieur/equipe/dialogue/
lingua/lingua.html

European Speech Communication Association
http://ophale.icp.grenet.fr/esca/esca.html

Georgia Tech - Natural Lang. and Reasoning Research
http://www.cc.gatech.edu/cogsci/nlr.html

German Research Center for AI Computational Linguistics
http://cl-www.dfki.uni-sb.de/

GMD-KONTEXT, Darmstadt
http://www.darmstadt.gmd.de/KONTEXT/kontext.html

Haskins Laboratories, Yale University
http://www.haskins.yale.edu/

Head-Driven Phase Structure Grammar
http://ling.ohio-state.edu/HPSG/Hpsg.html

Hitaka Lab., Kyushu Univ.
http://lang.ai.kyushu-u.ac.jp:8080/nlp.html

Hong Kong Univ.of Science and Technology
http://www.cs.ust.hk

Humboldt Universitat Berlin - Computational Linguistics
http://www.compling.hu-berlin.de/

IJCAI - International Joint Conference on AI
http://ijcai.org

Indonesian Multilingual Machine Translation System
http://nataya.aia.bppt.go.id/immts/immts.html

Inst. for Computational Linguistics, Univ. of Koblenz
http://www.uni-koblenz.de/~compling

Inst. for Logic, Lang. and Computation, Univ. of Amsterdam
http://www.fwi.uva.nl/research/illc/

Inst. for Research in Cognitive Science
http://www.cis.upenn.edu/~ircs/homepage.html

Inst. for Semantic Information Processing
http://hal.cl-ki.uni-osnabrueck.de

Inst. for the Learning Sciences, Northwestern University
http://www.ils.nwu.edu/

Institut d'Informatique de l'Universite de Fribourg
http://www.unifr.ch

Institute of Speech Communication - Stendhal Univ.
http://cristal.icp.grenet.fr:8080/ICP/index.uk.html

Interactive Systems Lab, Univ.of Karlsruhe, Germany
http://werner.ira.uka.de/nnspeech_homepage.html

International Quantitative Linguistics Association
http://www.ldv.uni-trier.de:8080/~iqla

Intl. Clinical Linguistics and Phonetics Association (ICPLA)
http://tpowel.comdis.lsumc.edu/icpla/icpla.htm

Istituto di Linguistica Computazionale
http://www.ilc.pi.cnr.it

Johns Hopkins University
http://www.cog.jhu.edu/index.html

Lancaster Univ.
http://eisv01.lancs.ac.uk/

Lang. & Information Lab - IFI Univ.of Basel
http://www.ifi.unibas.ch/grudo/grudo.html

Language Engineering, UMIST, Manchester
http://www.ccl.umist.ac.uk/

Lexical-Functional Grammar
http://clwww.essex.ac.uk/LFG/

Linguistics Association of Great Britain
http://www.essex.ac.uk/linguistics/LAGB.html

Lund Univ.
http://www.ling.lu.se/

Massachusetts Inst. of Technology - Spoken Lang. Systems Group
http://sls-www.lcs.mit.edu/ec-nsf/mit-sls.html

MENELAS PROJECT, Univ.of Rennes
http://www.med.univ-rennes1.fr/menelas.html

Middle East Technical University
http://www.lcsl.metu.edu.tr

MOL - The Association for Mathematics of Language
http://www-cse.ucsd.edu/users/savitch/MOL/intro.html

National Univ.of Singapore Linguistics Program
http://www.nus.sg/NUSinfo/FASS/linguist.html

Natural Lang. Processing at Columbia
Univ.
http://www.cs.columbia.edu:80/~radev/nlp/

Natural Lang. Processing Lab at IRST
http://ecate.itc.it:1024/

New Mexico State Univ.Computing
Research Lab
http://crl.nmsu.edu/Home.html

New York Univ.Linguistics Dept.
http://www.nyu.edu/pages/linguistics

NLP in Ireland
http://itdsrv1.ul.ie/NLP/nlp_directory.html

Northwestern Univ.
http://www.ling.nwu.edu/

Oregon Graduate Inst. - Center for Spoken
Lang. Understanding
http://www.cse.ogi.edu/CSLU/

Parlevink Linguistic Engineering Project -
Univ. of Twente
http://wwwseti.cs.utwente.nl/Docs/parlevink/
parlevink.html

Psycoloquy — Psychology electronic
journal
http://info.cern.ch/hypertext/DataSources/
bySubject/Psychology/Psycoloquy.html

Research in the Lang., Information and
Computation Laboratory
http://www.cis.upenn.edu/~cliff-group/94/
cliffnotes.html

Simon Fraser University Natural Lang.
Laboratory
http://fas.sfu.ca/0/cs/research/groups/NLL/
toc.html

SNePS Research Group, SUNY Buffalo
http://www.cs.buffalo.edu/pub/sneps/WWW/
index.html

Southern Illinois Univ.at Carbondale.
http://www.siu.edu/Dept.s/cola/ling01

Speech Communication and Music
Acoustics, KTH, Sweden
http://www.speech.kth.se/

SRI AI Center Natural Lang. Program
http://www.ai.sri.com/aic/natural-Lang./

SRI International Speech Technology and
Research Laboratory
http://www-speech.sri.com/

Stanford HPSG Project
http://hpsg.stanford.edu/

Stanford Univ.- CSLI
http://www-csli.stanford.edu/

Technical Univ.of Berlin, Project Group
KIT
http://flp.cs.tu-berlin.de/kit.html

Technion-Laboratory for Computational
Linguistics
http://www.cs.technion.ac.il/~lcl

Tilburg Univ. - Inst. for Lang. Technology
and Artifical Intelligence
http://itkwww.kub.nl:2080/itk/

Turkish Natural Lang. Processing Project,
Bilkent Univ.
http://www.cs.bilkent.edu.tr/~ko/Turklang.html

UC Davis Multilingual Lab
http://escher.cs.ucdavis.edu:1024/

UCREL - Unit for Computer Research on
the English Language
http://www.comp.lancs.ac.uk/computing/
research/ucrel/

UFRL - Linguistics, Jussieu, Paris
http://www.linguist.jussieu.fr/

Umea Univ.Inst. of Linguistics Umea
Univ.Phonetics Lab
http://jean.ling.umu.se/

Unit for Computer Research on the
English Language
http://www.comp.lancs.ac.uk/computing/
research/ucrel/

Univ. Cal. Irvine Dept. of Linguistics
http://www.socsci.uci.edu/ling/index.html

Univ. Cal. San Diego Center for Research
in Language
http://crl.ucsd.edu/

Univ. de Lausanne
http://www.unil.ch/ling/Bienvenue.html

Univ. of Geneva Dalle Molle Inst. for
Studies on Semantics and Cognition
http://issco-www.unige.ch/

Univ. of Goteborg
http://www.cling.gu.se/index-eng.html

Univ. of London
http://www.phon.ucl.ac.uk/

Univ. of Munich
http://www.phonetik.uni-muenchen.de/

Univ. of Reading
http://midwich.reading.ac.uk

Univ. Regensburg
http://rsls8.sprachlit.uni-regensburg.de/

Univ. Sains Malaysia
http://www.cs.usm.my/utmk/utmkhome.html

Univ. of Amsterdam - Inst. for Logic, Lang. and Computation
http://www.fwi.uva.nl/fwi/research/vg2/illc/

Univ. of Amsterdam - Inst. of Phonetic Sciences
http://fonsg3.let.uva.nl/

Univ. of Bielefeld
http://peel.lili.uni-bielefeld.de/

Univ. of Birmingham, Corpus Linguistics Group
http://clg1.bham.ac.uk/

Univ. of Bochum
http://www.linguistics.ruhr-uni-bochum.de/

Univ. of Calgary
http://www.ucalgary.ca/~southerl/ling/ling.html

Univ. of California, Santa Cruz
http://ling.ucsc.edu

Univ. of Cambridge - NLP group
http://www.cl.cam.ac.uk/Research/NL/index.html

Univ. of Chicago
http://ap-www.uchicago.edu/AcaPubs/GradAnno/HumDiv/Lingf.html

Univ. of Copenhagen
http://www.cphling.dk/

Univ. of Delaware - Natural Lang. Interface Group
http://www.asel.udel.edu/natlang/nli.html

Univ.of Durham
http://www.dur.ac.uk/~dcs0rjc/lnle/lnlehome.html

Univ. of Edinburgh Human Communication Research Center
http://www.cogsci.ed.ac.uk/hcrc/home.html

Univ .of Essen, Germany
http://www.uni-essen.de/fb3/linse/home.htm

Univ. of Essex CL/MT Research Group
http://www.essex.ac.uk/clmt

Univ. of Frankfurt
http://www.rz.uni-frankfurt.de/home/ftp/pub/titus/public_html

Univ. of Freiburg - Computational Linguistics
http://www.coling.uni-freiburg.de

Univ. of Groningen, BCN Linguistics
http://www.let.rug.nl/Linguistics/www/

Univ. of Hamburg
http://www.informatik.uni-hamburg.de/Arbeitsbereiche/NATS/home.html

Univ. of Illinois Speech Lab
http://hawaii.cogsci.uiuc.edu/Speech.html

Univ. of Leeds, Speech Lab
http://lethe.leeds.ac.uk/research/cogn/speechlab/

Univ. of Liverpool
http://www.liv.ac.uk/~tony1/linguistics.html

Univ. of Manitoba
http://www.umanitoba.ca/linguistics/local.html

Univ. of Maryland Information Filtering Project
http://www.glue.umd.edu/enee/medlab/filter/filter_project.html

Univ. of Massachusetts - Information Extraction
http://ciir.cs.umass.edu/info/ie.html

Univ. of Melbourne
http://adhocalypse.arts.unimelb.edu.au/Dept/Linguistics/home.html

Univ. of New Mexico
http://www.unm.edu/~bvanb/lingdept.html

Univ. of Nijmegen: Affix Grammars over a Finite Lattice
http://www.cs.kun.nl/agfl/

Univ. of Oregon
http://babel.uoregon.edu/ling.html

Univ. of Ottawa Knowledge Acquisition and Machine Learning Group
http://www.csi.uottawa.ca/dept/kaml/KAML.html

Univ. of Passau
http://www.fmi.uni-passau.de/philf/lehrstuehle/felix/uebersicht.html

Univ. of Pittsburgh Intelligent Systems
Program
http://www.isp.pitt.edu

Univ. of Reading Speech Lab
http://midwich.reading.ac.uk/research/
speechlab/index.html

Univ. of Rochester - Speech Lab
http://www.cs.rochester.edu/research/speech/
speechlab.html

Univ. of Sheffield - NLP
http://www.dcs.shef.ac.uk/research/groups/
nlp/nlp.html

Univ. of Stuttgart Inst. for Natural Lang.
Processing
http://www.ims.uni-stuttgart.de/IMS.html

Univ. of Sussex Computational Linguistics
http://www.cogs.susx.ac.uk/lab/nlp/index.html

Univ. of the Saarland
http://coli.uni-sb.de/

Univ. of Uppsala, Sweden
http://www.ling.uu.se/

USC - Information Sciences Inst.
http://www.isi.edu/

UT Arlington Linguistics
http://ling.uta.edu/

Victoria Univ.of Wellington, New Zealand
http://www.vuw.ac.nz/ling

Xerox Lexical Technology
http://www.xerox.com/lexdemo/

Mathematics

See also Computer Science, Physics

Usenet Newsgroups

comp.ai.fuzzy

Created by: arras@forwiss.uni-erlangen.de (Mike Arras)
Call for Votes date: December 1, 1992
Newsgroup-based Mailing List: Yes (fuzzy-mail@vexpert.dbai.tuwien.ac.at).
Charter (from Call for Votes):
The newsgroup will contain discussions of all aspects and applications of fuzzy logic.

comp.object.logic

Created by: vladimir@cs.ualberta.ca (Vladimir Alexiev)
Call for Votes date: March 29, 1993
Newsgroup-based Mailing List: No.
Charter (from Call for Votes):
The proposed newsgroup is intended to serve as a medium for discussing the issues on Integrating the Object-Oriented and Logic Paradigms, with an emphasis on Integrating OOP and LP.

comp.simulation

Moderated by: Patrick W. Dowd (simulation-request@eng.buffalo.edu)
Submissions go to: simulation@eng.buffalo.edu
Newsgroup-based Mailing List: No.
Charter: Simulation methods.

sci.chaos

Newsgroup-based Mailing List: No.
Charter: Chaos theory.

sci.logic

Newsgroup-based Mailing List: No.
Charter: Logic.

sci.math

Newsgroup-based Mailing List: No.
Charter: Mathematics.

sci.math.num-analysis

Newsgroup-based Mailing List: No.
Charter: Numerical analysis.

sci.math.research (Moderated)

Moderated by: Daniel R. Grayson (dan@math.uiuc.edu)
Submissions go to: sci-math-research@uiuc.edu
Newsgroup-based Mailing List: No.
Charter: Research issues.

sci.math.stat

Newsgroup-based Mailing List: No.
Charter: Statistics.

sci.math.symbolic

Newsgroup-based Mailing List: No.
Charter: Logic and symbolic math.

sci.nonlinear

Created by: caddell@csustan.csustan.edu (Joe Caddell)
Call for Votes date: April 30, 1993
Newsgroup-based Mailing List: No.
Charter (from Call for Votes):
The purpose of this group is to provide a forum for the exchange of ideas in the area of nonlinear science, to discuss any research being done in this field, to provide a means for questions to be answered which people may have concerning nonlinear systems, to announce any conferences, seminars or

meetings which may be held concerning nonlinear systems, to exchange ideas,to try out new ones, and to have fun!

Frequently Asked Questions

comp.ai.genetic FAQ
Maintainer: David Beasley <David.Beasley@cm.cf.ac.uk>
Where on Usenet: comp.ai.genetic
Where it's archived: rtfm.mit.edu:pub/usenet/comp.ai.genetic/
What it's for: Basic information on evolutionary computation.

comp.object FAQ
Maintainer: Bob Hathaway <rjh@geodesic.com>
Where on Usenet: comp.object
Where it's archived: rtfm.mit.edu:pub/usenet/comp.object/
What it's for: Information on object-oriented design and methods.

comp.specification.z FAQ
Maintainer: zforum-request@comlab.ox.ac.uk
Where on Usenet: comp.specification.z
Where it's archived: rtfm.mit.edu:pub/usenet/news.answers/
What it's for: Information concerning the Z formal specification notation.

Fractal Questions and Answers
Maintainer: shirriff@sprite.berkeley.edu (Ken Shirriff)
Where on Usenet: sci.fractals
Where it's archived: rtfm.mit.edu:pub/usenet/news.answers/sci.fractals
What it's for: Fractal software, algorithms, definitions, and references.

Free C,C++ for numerical computation
Maintainer: ajayshah@cmie.ernet.in
Where on Usenet: comp.lang.c
Where it's archived: rtfm.mit.edu:pub/usenet/news.answers/comp.lang.c

What it's for: Sources for source code for numerical computation.

Fuzzy Logic and Fuzzy Expert Systems
Maintainer: mkant+@cs.cmu.edu (Mark Kantrowitz)
Where on Usenet: comp.ai.fuzzy/
Where it's archived: rtfm.mit.edu:pub/usenet/news.answers/
What it's for: Information on fuzzy logic.

Multigrid Methods on the WWW
Maintainer: marcus@x4u2.desy.de (Marcus Speh)
Where on Usenet: sci.math.num-analysis
Where it's archived: rtfm.mit.edu:pub/usenet/news.answers/sci.math.num-analysis
What it's for: Information on accessing Documents on Multigrid methods via the WWW, a distributed HyperText system.

Nonlinear Programming FAQ
Maintainer: jwg@cray.com (John Gregory)
Where on Usenet: sci.op-research
Where it's archived: rtfm.mit.edu:pub/usenet/news.answers/sci.op-research
What it's for: A List of Frequently Asked Questions about Nonlinear Programming.

sci.math FAQ
Maintainer: alopez-o@maytag.uwaterloo.ca (Alex Lopez-Ortiz)
Where on Usenet: sci.math
Where it's archived: rtfm.mit.edu:pub/usenet/news.answers/sci.math
What it's for: Math...

sci.math.research
Maintainer: "Daniel R. Grayson" <dan@math.uiuc.edu>
Where on Usenet: sci.math.research
Where it's archived: rtfm.mit.edu:pub/usenet/news.answers/sci.math.research
What it's for: Introduction to the newsgroup, common archive sites, pointers to other faqs.

Discussion Lists

alg-geom
alg-geom@jpnyitp
Preprint server for Algebraic Geometry

amath-il
amath-il@taunivm
Applied Mathematics in Israel List

axiom
axiom@ndsuvm1
AXIOM Computer Algebra System

cmath-l
cmath-l@uottawa
Canadian Mathematical Society

com-alg
com-alg@ndsuvm1
COM-ALG - Commutative Algebra

fam-math
fam-math@uicvm
Family Math

glim-l
glim-l@ukacrl
GLIM and Generalised Linear Modelling
of Data

graphnet
graphnet@ndsuvm1
GRAPHNET - Graph Theory

graph-l
graph-l@brufpb
Mathematical aspects of Computer
Graphics

hec-l
hec-l@uwf
Higher Education Consortium for Mathematics

imse-l
imse-l@uicvm
Institute for Math and Science Education

jcmst-l
jcmst-l@purccvm
Jrnl. of Computers in Mathematics and
Science

math-l
math-l@technion
MATH-L Technion internal Mathematica

matlab
matlab-users-request@mcs.anl.gov (Chris
Bischof)
For users of MATLAB.

mathdep
mathdep@irlearn
UCD Maths Dept. Distribution List

mathedcc
mathedcc@mcgill1
The Technology in Mathematics Education

mimuw-l
mimuw-l@plearn
Affairs of Warsaw U. Fac. of Math.

msire-l
msire-l@uriacc
RI Math & Science Resource

msproj
msproj@msu.edu
Annenberg/CPB Math & Science Project

msupbnd
msupbnd@ubvm
Math Science Upward Bound

nafips-l
NAFIPS-L@GSUVM1
North American Fuzzy Information
Processing

na-net
na.join@na-net.ornl.gov
Numerical analysis.

ndrg-l
ndrg-l@wvnvm
Nonlinear Dynamics Research Group

nenco-l
nenco-l@wvnvm
Network of Northern W. Virginia

nonlin-l
nonlin-l@nihlist
Economic Nonlinear Dynamics

nonlinss
nonlinss@emuvm1
Nonlinear Dynamical Social Systems

nqthm-users
nqthm-users-request@cli.com
Theorem-proving.

numeric-interest
numeric-interest-request@validgh.com
(David Hough)
Floating-point correctness.

nyjm-alg
nyjm-alg@albnyvm1
Abstracts of Algebra papers in the New
York Jrnl. of Mathematics

nyjm-an
nyjm-an@albnyvm1
Abstracts of Analysis papers in the New York Jrnl. of Mathmatics

nyjmth-a
nyjmth-a@albnyvm1
Abstracts from the New York Jrnl. of Mathematics

ocma-l
ocma-l@humber
Ontario Colleges Math Association List

precalc
precalc@ipfwvm
Precalc/Development Math Curriculum Teaching

scimat-l
scimat-l@uafsysb
Arkansas Science and Math Education

snymap-l
snymap-l@snycenvm
SUNY Mathematics Alert Program Discussion list

susig
susig@miamiu
Teaching in the Mathematical Sciences

techmath
techmath@technion
TECHMATH - Technion Mathematics Net

theorist
theorist@utkvm1
Theorist Math Forum

uic-mtht
uic-mtht@uicvm
UIC Math

uicmath
uicmath@uicvm
UIC Mathematics

vorapp-l
vorapp-l@lavalvm1
Voronoi and Computational Geometry Applications

wvms-l
wvms-l@wvnvm
NASA Classroom of the Future: WV Mathematics

zforum
zforum-request@comlab.ox.ac.uk
(Jonathan Bowen)
Specification notation "Z".

Mathematics Resources

FTP Resources

Argonne National Lab
info.mcs.anl.gov

Linear Programming FAQ
ftp.cray.com/pub/FAQs/linear-programming-faq.html

Nonlinear Programming FAQ
ftp.cray.com/pub/FAQs/nonlinear-program-ming-faq.html

Stanford Univ.
boole.stanford.edu

TeX Archive
ftp.shsu.edu/tex-archive

Universitaet Bern
iamftp.unibe.ch

University of Milan
ghost.dsi.unimi.it

University of Minnesota
geom.umn.edu

University of Western Australia
acacia.maths.uwa.oz.au

Gopher Resources

ACM Directories
gopher.acm.org

American Mathematical Monthly
gopher.maa.org:70/11/pubs/Journals/AMM

American Mathematical Society
e-math.ams.org

Cambridge Univ., Pure Mathematics,
owl.pmms.cam.ac.uk

Cambridge Univ., Statistical Lab.
erlang.statslab.cam.ac.uk

Canadian Journal of Mathematics
camel.cecm.sfu.ca/11/English_Switch/CMS/Abstract/journal

Canadian Mathematical Society
camel.cecm.sfu.ca:105

College Mathematics Journal
gopher.maa.org:70/11/pubs/Journals/CMJ

Commutative Algebra
hazlett.math.ndsu.nodak.edu/11/com-alg/

Computer Algebra Netherland (CAN)
gopher.can.nl

Ecole Normale Superieure
snekkar.ens.fr

Euromath
laurel.euromath.dk:70/11/

Focus
gopher.maa.org:70/11/pubs/Journals/Focus

Functional Analysis
babbage.sissa.it/11/funct-an

Geometric Group Theory
mathstat.usouthal.edu/11/geom-gp

Illinois Journal of Mathematics
gopher.uiuc.edu/11/UI/CSF/upress/journals/ijm

International Centre for Theoretical Physics
gopher.ictp.trieste.it/

Isaac Newton Institute
newton.newton.cam.ac.uk

Journal of Graph Theory
brutus.mts.jhu.edu/11/Journal%20of%20Graph%20Theory

Kluwer Journals
gopher.wkap.nl/

Lake Forest College
davinci.lfc.edu

Lake Forest College Mathematics Node
davinci.lfc.edu/11/MathRelItems

Library of Congress Electronic Library, Mathematics
marvel.loc.gov/11/global/math

London Mathematical Society
gopher.qmw.ac.uk

MAA
gopher.maa.org/11/pubs/Journals

Mathematica Journal
gopher.wri.com/11/MathSource/Publications/Periodicals/TheMathematicaJournal

Mathematics Magazine
gopher.maa.org:70/11/pubs/Journals/MM

Mathematics, Virtual Reference Desk
peg.cwis.uci.edu:7000/11/gopher.welcome/peg/math

MathMagic K-12 project
forum.swarthmore.edu

New York Journal of Mathematics
nyjm.albany.edu:70/1

Rice Univ. Mathematics Node
riceinfo.rice.edu/11/Subject/Math

Selected Journals Contents
gopher.cecm.sfu.ca/11/Resources/Epub/Journals/table_of_content

SIAM gopher
gopher.siam.org

SLATEC (Harvard)
cfata9.harvard.edu

Systems and Control Theory
www.utdallas.edu/11/research/scad/preprints

Univ. of Michigan
gopher.math.lsa.umich.edu

Univ. of Tennessee Math Archives
archives.math.utk.edu

Univ. of Texas
henri.ma.utexas.edu

WWW Resources

Acta Mathematica Universitatis Comenianae
http://www.emis.de/journals/AMUC/_amuc.html

Acta Numerica
http://www.cup.cam.ac.uk/Journals/JNLSCAT95/anu.html

Acta Scientiarum Mathematicarum
http://www.math.u-szeged.hu/publikac/acta/acta.htm

Advances in Computational Mathematics
http://www.math.psu.edu/dna/contents/aicm.html

Advances in Systems Science and Applications
http://assa.math.swt.edu

Algebraic Topology
http://hopf.math.purdue.edu/pub/hopf.html

Algebraic-Number-Theory
http://www.math.uiuc.edu/Algebraic-Number-Theory/

American Journal of Mathematics
http://muse.jhu.edu/journals/american_journal_of_mathematics/

American Mathematical Society
http://e-math.ams.org/

Annales Academiae Scientiarum Fennicae
http://geom.helsinki.fi/Annales/Anna.html

Application-oriented Algorithmic Mathematics
http://elib.zib-berlin.de/

Argonne National Lab
http://www.mcs.anl.gov/index.html

Association for Computing Machinery (ACM)
http://info.acm.org/

Association for Women in Mathematics
http://xerxes.nas.edu:70/1/cwse/AWM.html

Australian CSIRO Math/Stat
http://www.dms.csiro.au/

Australian Mathematical Society
http://solution.maths.unsw.edu.au/htdocs.ams/amswelcome.html

Australian National Univ.
http://pell.anu.edu.au/index.html

Banach Spaces and Functional Analysis
http://math.okstate.edu/cgi-bin/wais.pl/banach

Basic Research Institute in the Mathematical Sciences
http://www-uk.hpl.hp.com/brims/

Biomathematics and Statistics Scotland
http://www.bioss.sari.ac.uk

Bulletin Board for Librarians, Mathematics
http://www.bubl.bath.ac.uk/BUBL/Mathematics.html

Bulletin of the London Mathematical Society
http://www.cup.cam.ac.uk/Journals/JNLSCAT95/blm.html

Calculus of Variations and the Geometry of Nature
http://www.sns.it/html/IPS/Main.html

California Institute of Technology
http://www.ama.caltech.edu/

California State Univ., Hayward
http://www.mcs.csuhayward.edu/mcs.html

Canadian Mathematical Electronic Web
http://camel.cecm.sfu.ca/

Canadian Mathematical Society
http://camel.cecm.sfu.ca/home.html

Catalogue of Algebraic Systems
http://www.math.usf.edu/algctlg/INDEX.html

Category Theory Home Page
http://www.mta.ca/~cat-dist/categories.html

Center for Advanced Studies, Sardinia Applied Math Group
http://www.crs4.it/~valde/group_homepage.html

Center for Applied Mathematics and Theoretical Physics
http://www.uni-mb.si/robnik.html

Center for Complex Systems Research
http://www.ccsr.uiuc.edu/

Center for Dynamical Systems and Nonlinear Studies
http://www.math.gatech.edu/CDSNS/info.html

Center for Geometry Analysis Numerics and Graphics at UMass Amherst
http://www.gang.umass.edu/

Center for Gravitational Physics and Geometry
http://vishnu.nirvana.phys.psu.edu/

Center for Statistical and Mathematical Computing
http://www.indiana.edu/~statmath/

Center for Statistical Consultation and Research
http://www.umich.edu:80/~cscar

Centre for Engineering and Industrial Mathematics
http://www.uow.edu.au/public/faculties/informatics/ceim.html#ceim_top

Centre for Experimental & Constructive Mathematics
http://mosaic.cecm.sfu.ca/

Centre for Industrial and Applied Mathematics
http://phoenix.levels.unisa.edu.au/ciam/index.html

Centrum voor Wiskunde en Informatica
http://www.cwi.nl/

Chalmers Tekniska Högskola/Göteborgs Universitet
http://math.chalmers.se/Public/

CHANCE: Probability or Statistics course information
http://www.geom.umn.edu/docs/snell/chance/welcome.html

Chaos at Univ. of Maryland
http://www-chaos.umd.edu/

CIRM library
http://cirm.univ-mrs.fr/

CMU Center for Nonlinear Analysis
http://www.cmu.edu/mcs/math/cna.html

Coalition of Automated Mathematics and Science Education Databases
http://www.enc.org/camsed/

Combinatorial and Geometric Group Theory
http://zebra.sci.ccny.cuny.edu/web/html/magnus.html

Combinatorics
http://www.c3.lanl.gov/laces

Communications in Analysis and Geometry
http://testweb.acs.uci.edu/mathweb/commin.html

Communications in Numerical Methods in Engineering
http://www.ep.cs.nott.ac.uk/wiley/numeng.html

Complex Dynamics and Hyperbolic Geometry
http://www.msri.org/preprints/cd-hg.html

Computational Fluid Dynamics
http://www.tfd.chalmers.se/CFD_Online/

Computer Algebra Information Network
http://cand.can.nl/

Constructive Approximation
http://www.math.usf.edu/CA

Cornell Center for Applied Mathematics
http://cam.cornell.edu/

Courant Institute of NYU
http://www.cims.nyu.edu/

Cryptography Archive
http://www.quadralay.com/www/Crypt/Crypt.html

CTI Centre for Mathematics and Statistics
http://www.bham.ac.uk/ctimath/

Databases on Mathematics (in German)
http://www.zblmath.fiz-karlsruhe.de/

De Montfort Univ.
http://www.cms.dmu.ac.uk/People/maths-people.html

Delft Univ. of Technology
http://www.twi.tudelft.nl/TWI/Overview.html

Deutsche Mathematiker-Vereinigung
http://www_dmv.math.tu-berlin.de

Differential Geometry and Global Analysis
http://www.msri.org/preprints/dg-ga.html

DIMACS
http://dimacs.rutgers.edu/

Documenta Mathematica
http://www.mathematik.uni-bielefeld.de/DMV-J/

Dynamical Systems
http://math.sunysb.edu/preprints.html

Dynamics and Stability of Systems
http://www.amsta.leeds.ac.uk/Applied/news.dir/dss.dirvol10.html

Dynamics of Continuous, Discrete and Impulsive Systems
http://jeeves.uwaterloo.ca/AM_Dept/dcdis/dcdis.html

École Normale Supérieure - Paris
http://www.ens.fr/

Edinburgh Mathematical Society
http://www.maths.heriot-watt.ac.uk/ems/

Eindhoven Univ. of Technology
http://www.win.tue.nl/

Eisenhower National Clearinghouse
http://www.enc.org/

Electronic Colloquium on Computational Complexity
http://www.eccc.uni-trier.de/eccc/

Electronic Communications in Probability
http://math.washington.edu/~ejpecp/

Electronic Transactions in Numerical Analysis
http://etna.mcs.kent.edu/

EPF Lausanne
http://dmawww.epfl.ch/

Erdos Numbers
http://www.acs.oakland.edu/~grossman/erdoshp.html

Erwin Schrodinger Institute of Mathematical Physics
http://www.esi.ac.at/ESI-home.html

ETH Zürich
http://www.math.ethz.ch/

Euler Institute fot Discrete Mathematics and its Applications
http://www.win.tue.nl/win/math/eidma/index.html

EURHomogenization
http://www.informatik.unibw-muenchen.de/informatik/Institute/inst1/eurohom.html

Euromath Bulletin
http://sophie.helsinki.fi/~emb/

Euromath Center
http://dan-emir.euromath.dk/emc-www/euromath.html

European Mathematical Society
http://www.emis.de/

European Research Consortium for Informatics and Mathematics
http://www-ercim.inria.fr/

Exp(Pi*Sqrt(n)) Page
http://www.ccsf.caltech.edu/~roy/episqrtn.html

Experimental Mathematics
http://www.geom.umn.edu/locate/expmath

Fibonacci Numbers
http://math.holycross.edu/~davids/fibonacci/fibonacci.html

Flanders Mathematics Olympiad
http://www.kulak.ac.be/vwo/vwowww.html

Florida State Univ. Numerical Analysis
http://euclid.math.fsu.edu/Science/num.html

FORTWIHR
http://hpzenger2.informatik.tu-muenchen.de/forschung/fortwihr/fortwihr_e.html

Fractals
http://spanky.triumf.ca/

Freie Univ.Berlin
http://www.math.fu-berlin.de/

Functional Analysis
http://mentor.lanl.gov/eprints/mkheader/funct-an

Furman Univ. Electronic Journal of Undergraduate Mathematics
http://math.furman.edu/~mwoodard/fuejum/welcome.html

Fuzzy Logic Lab. Linz
http://www.flll.uni-linz.ac.at

Center for Geometry, Analysis, Numerics and Graphics

http://www.gang.umass.edu/

Geometry Ctr.
http://www.geom.umn.edu/

Geometry Forum
http://forum.swarthmore.edu/

Geometry in Action-Applications of Discrete and Computational Geometry
http://www.ics.uci.edu/~eppstein/geom.html

Georgia Tech's Applied Chaos Lab.
http://nextworld.cc.gatech.edu:8001/Matt/acl/aclhome.html

Graphics and Analysis Software
http://www-ocean.tamu.edu/~baum/ocean_graphics.html

Groupe Fractales
http://www-syntim.inria.fr/fractales/

Harmonic Maps Bibliography
http://www.bath.ac.uk/~masfeb/harmonic.html

Homogenization and Optimal Design
http://www.informatik.unibw-muenchen.de/informatik/Institute/inst1/preprints.html

Hong Kong Mathematical Society
http://euler.math.cuhk.hk/hkms/hkms.html

Hub Resources for Mathematics Education
http://hub.terc.edu:70/hub/math/

Hypermedia Lab.
http://matwww.ee.tut.fi/hmlab/homepage.html

IMA Journal of Numerical Analysis
http://www.math.psu.edu/dna/contents/imajna.html

Indiana Univ. Ctr. for Statistical and Mathematical Computing
http://www.statmath.indiana.edu/

Industrial Mathematics Institute
http://www.indmath.uni-linz.ac.at/

INFORMS Online
http://www.informs.org/

Institut de Recherche Mathematique de Rennes
http://www.univ-rennes1.fr/labos/IRMAR/IRMAR.html

Institute for Advanced Study
http://www.math.ias.edu/

Institute for Applied Mathematics
http://www.num.uni-sb.de/

Institute for Computer Applications in Science and Engineering
http://www.icase.edu/

Institute for Mathematics and its Applications
http://www.ima.umn.edu/

Institute of Applied and Computational Mathematics
http://www.iacm.forth.gr/

Institute of Cybernetics, Applied Mathematics
http://www.ioc.ee/matem/maths.html

Institute of Information Theory and Automation
http://www.utia.cas.cz/

Institute of Mathematical Modelling (IMM) at The Technical Univ. of Denmark (DTU)
http://snake1.imsor.dth.dk/homepage.html

Institute of Mathematics and Computer Science in Medicine
http://www.uni-hamburg.de/~medizin/imdm

Institute of Mathematics and its Applications
http://www-chel.anglia.ac.uk/~imacrh/index.html

Institute of Mathematics, Physics and Mechanics
http://www.mat.uni-lj.si/bin/counter/webcount.exe?imfm

Institute of Numerical Mathematics
http://www.ac.msk.su/local.docs/inm/inm.html

Instituto de Matematicas y Estadistica
http://www.fing.edu.uy/imerl.html

Instituto Nacional de Pesquisas Espaciais Brazil
http://www.inpe.br/lac/home

Interesting Places for Numerical Analysists
http://aspin.asu.edu/provider/l.lu/num_anal/index.html

International Centre for Mathematical Sciences, Edinburgh
http://www.ma.hw.ac.uk/icms/

International Clifford Algebra Society
http://century22.martin.org/~clf-alg/

International Congress of Mathematicians Berlin 1998
http://elib.zib-berlin.de/ICM98

International Federation of Nonlinear Analysts
http://www.fit.edu/math/ifna.html

International Journal for Numerical Methods in Engineering
http://www.ep.cs.nott.ac.uk/wiley/numeng.html

International Linear Algebra Society
http://gauss.technion.ac.il/iic

International Mathematical Union
http://elib.zib-berlin.de/IMU

Internet Center for Mathematics Problems
http://www.mathpro.com:80/math/mathCenter.html

Interval Computations Homepage
http://cs.utep.edu/interval-comp/main.html

Inverse Symbolic Calculator
http://www.cecm.sfu.ca/projects/ISC.html

Iowa State Univ.
http://www.public.iastate.edu/~math/homepage.html

Isaac Newton Institute for Mathematical Sciences
http://www.newton.cam.ac.uk/

Jobs in Mathematics
http://www.cs.dartmouth.edu:80/~gdavis/policy/jobmarket.html

Jyväskylä Univ.
http://www.math.jyu.fi/

K-theory
http://www.math.uiuc.edu/K-theory/

Kent State Univ.
http://www.mcs.kent.edu/home.html

Konrad-Zuse-Zentrum
http://www.zib-berlin.de/

Lab. for Computer Aided Mathematics
http://sophie.helsinki.fi/

Lajos Kossuth Univ.
http://www.math.klte.hu/

Lancaster Univ.
http://mathssun5.lancs.ac.uk:2080/

Largest Known Primes
http://www.utm.edu/departments/math/
largest.html

Le Journal de maths
http://www.ens-lyon.fr/JME/JME.html

Linear Algebra and its Applications
http://gauss.technion.ac.il/iic/LAA.INDEX

Logic and Set Theory
http://www.math.ufl.edu:80/~logic/

Logic Eprints
http://www.math.ufl.edu/~logic/

London Mathematical Society
http://www.qmw.ac.uk/~lms/lms.html

Los Alamos Combinatorics E-print Server
http://www.c3.lanl.gov/laces

Louisiana Tech Univ.
http://www.math.latech.edu/math/
mathematics.html

Loyola Univ., Chicago
http://www.math.luc.edu/

Luleå Univ.
http://www.sm.luth.se/math/

Lund Univ. / Lund Institute of Technology
http://www.maths.lth.se/

Manchester Centre for Computational
Mathematics
http://www.ma.man.ac.uk/MCCM/MCCM.html

Massey Univ.
http://smis-www.massey.ac.nz/maths/
Math_htmls/maths.html

MATCH
http://btm2xd.mat.uni-bayreuth.de/match

Math-Net at Konrad-Zuse-Zentrum
http://elib.zib-berlin.de:88/Math-Net/Links/
math.html

Mathematica Militaris
http://euler.math.usma.edu:80/militaris.html

Mathematica Related URLs
http://smc.vnet.net/mathsite.html

Mathematica World
http://www.vut.edu.au/MW/

Mathematical Association of America
http://www.maa.org/

Mathematical BBS Ferrara
http://felix.unife.it/

Mathematical Branch of Russian Academy
of Sciences (RAS)
http://www.ras.ru/

Mathematical Institute of the Hungarian
Academy of Sciences
http://www.math-inst.hu/

Mathematical Logic
http://www.math.ufl.edu:80/~logic/

Mathematical Optimization TU
Braunschweig
http://moa.math.nat.tu-bs.de/welcome.html

Mathematical Physics
http://henri.ma.utexas.edu/mp_arc/mp_arc-
home.html

Mathematical Psychology
http://www.uniovi.es/UniOvi/Apartados/
Departamento/Psicologia/metodos/

Mathematical Quotations
http://math.furman.edu/~mwoodard/
mquot.html

Mathematical Resources
http://www.math.okstate.edu/~wrightd/useful/
index.html

Mathematical Resources on the Web
http://www.math.ufl.edu/math/math-web.html

Mathematical Sciences Education Board
http://xerxes.nas.edu:70/0/mseb/mseb.html

Mathematical Sciences Research Institute
http://www.msri.org/

Mathematics of Control, Signals, and
Systems
http://www.cwi.nl/cwi/departments/BS3/
mcss.html

Mathematics On-Line Bookshelf
http://mathbookshelf.fullerton.edu/

Mathematics-related LISTSERV lists
http://www.clark.net/pub/listserv/lsmath1.html

Mathematische Gesellschaft in Hamburg
http://www.math.uni-hamburg.de/math/
mathges/

Mathematisches Forschungsinstitut
Oberwolfach
http://www.mfo.de/

MathSearch
http://ms.maths.usyd.edu.au:8000/
MathSearch.html

MathWorks Home Page
http://www.mathworks.com/homepage.html

MATLAB Gallery
http://www.mathworks.com/gallery.html

McMaster Univ.
http://www.science.mcmaster.ca/MathStat/Dept.html

MegaMath
http://www.c3.lanl.gov/mega-math/index.html

Michael Trick's Operations Research Page
http://mat.gsia.cmu.edu/

Mittag-Leffler Institute
http://www.ml.kva.se/

Monash Univ.
http://www.maths.monash.edu.au/

Mount Allison Univ.
http://www.mta.ca/faculty/science/math/

MSRI E-Print Archive
http://www.msri.org/preprints/archive.html

Multidimensional Analysis
http://www.ctr.columbia.edu/~hart/multanal.html

NA-Digest
http://www.netlib.org/na-digest/html/index.html

National Academy of Science
http://www.nas.edu/

National Council of Teachers of Mathematics
http://www.pbs.org/learning/mathline/nctmhome.html

Netlib Conferences Database
http://www.netlib.org/confdb/Conferences.html

New Zealand Mathematical Society
http://www.math.auckland.ac.nz/~conder/NZMS/

NIST's Guide to Available Mathematics Software
http://gams.nist.gov/

Nonlinear Dynamics and Topological Time Series Analysis Archive
http://t13.lanl.gov/~nxt/intro.html

Nonlinear Dynamics and Topological Time Series Analysis Archive
http://cnls-www.lanl.gov/nbt/intro.html

Nonlinear Programming FAQ
http://www.skypoint.com/subscribers/ashbury/nonlinear-programming-faq.html

Nonlinear Science
http://xyz.lanl.gov/

Nonlinear Science Today
http://www.springer-ny.com/nst

Nonlinearity and Complexity
http://www.cc.duth.gr/~mboudour/nonlin.html

North Carolina State Univ.
http://www2.ncsu.edu/ncsu/pams/math/

Northwestern Univ.
http://www.math.nwu.edu/

NSF Science and Technology Information System
http://stis.nsf.gov/

Number Theory Web
http://www.maths.uq.oz.au/~krm/web.html

Numerical Algorithms
http://www.math.psu.edu/dna/contents/na.html

Numerical Algorithms Group Limited
http://www.nag.co.uk:70/

Numerical Analysis
http://www.na.ms.osakafu-u.ac.jp/

Numerical Harmonic Analysis Group
http://tyche.mat.univie.ac.at/

Oak Ridge National Lab. Mathematical Sciences
http://www.epm.ornl.gov/msr

Odense Univ. preprint archive
http://www.imada.ou.dk/Research/preprints.html

Operations Research and Management Science
http://www.maths.mu.oz.au/~worms/

Operator Algebra Resources
http://darkwing.uoregon.edu/~ncp/opalg.html

Paradoxes
http://neptune.corp.harris.com/paradox.html

pLab Project
http://random.mat.sbg.ac.at/home.html

Planet Earth Mathematics Node
http://white.nosc.mil/math.html

Probability Abstract Service
http://math.washington.edu/~prob

Probability Web
http://www.maths.uq.oz.au/~pkp/probweb/probweb.html

Pure Mathematics Preprints
http://www.mth.uea.ac.uk/maths/maths-preprints-pure.html

Quantum Algebra and Knot Theory
http://www.msri.org/preprints/q-alg.html

Queen's Univ. of Belfast
http://www.am.qub.ac.uk/

Random Number Generation and Stochastic Simulation
http://random.mat.sbg.ac.at/others/

REDUCE Computer Algebra system
http://www.rrz.uni-koeln.de/REDUCE/

Representations and Cohomology of Groups
http://www.math.uga.edu/~djb/archive.html

Research Centre of Applied Mathematics CIRAM
http://eulero.cineca.it/

Results in Mathematics/Resultate der Mathematik
http://www.uni-duisburg.de/FB11/PUBL/RiM/ResMath.html

Revista Colombiana de Matematicas
http://157.253.147.9/~olezama/

Royal Institute of Technology
http://www.nada.kth.se/

Russian Academy of Sciences
http://www.ras.ru/RAS/om.html

Russian Mathematicians Directory
http://www.ac.msk.su/cgi-bin/wld

SAD
http://www.sad.uci.edu

SASIAM
http://fourier.csata.it/

Science Television
http://www.service.com/stv/

Semigroup Forum
http://bach.math.tulane.edu/SF.html

Semigroup Theory
http://www.maths.soton.ac.uk/semigroups/homepage.html

Shell Centre for Mathematical Education
http://acorn.educ.nottingham.ac.uk/ShellCent/

Society for Industrial and Applied Mathematics
http://www.siam.org/

Southwest Journal of Pure and Applied Mathematics
http://rattler.cameron.edu/swjpam.html

Spanky Fractal Database
http://spanky.triumf.ca/

SPIE-The Intl. Society for Optical Engineering
http://www.spie.org/

Statistical Lab., Univ. of Cambridge
http://www.statslab.cam.ac.uk/

Steklov Mathematical Institute
http://www.ac.msk.su/local.docs/mian/mian.html

Stevens Institute of Technology
http://www.stevens-tech.edu/stevens/math/math.html

Stochastic Finite Elements: A Spectral Approach
http://venus.ce.jhu.edu/book/book.html

Stockholm Univ.
http://www.matematik.su.se/

Student Mathematical Societies in the UK
http://info.ox.ac.uk:80/~invar/home.html

SunSITE Mathematical Art Gallery
http://sunsite.unc.edu/pics/mathgif.html

Surveys on Mathematics for Industry
http://www.indmath.uni-linz.ac.at/

Swarthmore Geometry Forum
http://forum.swarthmore.edu/index.html

Systems and Control Archive at Dallas
http://www.utdallas.edu/research/scad/

TANGENTS - The Harvard Mathematics Bulletin
http://www.digitas.org/tangents

Technical Univ. of Budapest, Hungary
http://www.vma.bme.hu/0h/html/home_eng.html

Technical Univ. of Chemnitz-Zwickau
http://www.tu-chemnitz.de/2/mathe/Mathe_E.html

Technische Univ.at München
http://www.mathematik.tu-muenchen.de/

Technische Univ.Berlin
http://www.math.tu-berlin.de/

TeX Archive Network
http://jasper.ora.com

TeX Information
http://www.dante.de

Texas A&M Univ.
http://mosaic.math.tamu.edu/math-home-page.html

Theory and Applications of Categories
http://www.tac.mta.ca/tac/

Transactions of Operations Research and Management Science
http://catt.bus.okstate.edu/itorms/

Transactions on Mathematical Software
http://gams.nist.gov/toms/Overview.html

Transitional Mathematics Project
http://othello.ma.ic.ac.uk/

Trinity College Dublin
http://www.maths.tcd.ie/

Tulane Univ.
http://bach.math.tulane.edu/

Turkish Mathematical Society
http://gopher.bilkent.edu.tr:7001/1s/inet-hotel/tmd/

UK Nonlinear News
http://www.amsta.leeds.ac.uk/Applied/news.dir/index.html

Union Matematica de America Latina y el Caribe
http://umalca.fing.edu.uy/

Unione Matematica Italiana
http://www.dm.unibo.it/~umi

United States Military Academy
http://euler.math.usma.edu/MathSci.html

Univ. de Coimbra
http://www.mat.uc.pt/

Univ. de Sao Paulo
http://www.ime.usp.br/

Univ. do Minho
http://alfa.di.uminho.pt/~mesamr/mosaic/mat/index.html

Univ. of Alaska
http://saturn.uaamath.alaska.edu/home.html

Univ. of Bath
http://www.bath.ac.uk/Departments/maths.html

Univ. Bayreuth
http://btm2xd.mat.uni-bayreuth.de/

Univ. Bern
http://iamwww.unibe.ch/index.html

Univ. of Birmingham
http://sun1.bham.ac.uk/ctimath/home_page.html

Univ. Bonn
http://rhein.iam.uni-bonn.de:1025/

Univ. of California Davis
http://math.ucdavis.edu/

Univ. of California Los Angeles
http://www.math.ucla.edu/

Univ. of Delaware
http://www.math.udel.edu/

Univ. of Durham
http://fourier.dur.ac.uk:8000/

Univ. of East Anglia
http://www.mth.uea.ac.uk/welcome.html

Univ. of Edinburgh
http://www.maths.ed.ac.uk/

Univ. of Florida
http://www.math.ufl.edu/

Univ. Frankfurt
http://www.math.uni-frankfurt.de/

Univ. of Glasgow Preprints archive
http://www.maths.gla.ac.uk/pre-prints.html

Univ. Göttingen
http://namu19.gwdg.de/

Univ. Halle
http://www.mathematik.uni-halle.de/

Univ. Hamburg
http://www.math.uni-hamburg.de/

Univ. of Helsinki
http://sophie.helsinki.fi/

Univ. of Illinois Urbana-Champaign
http://www.math.uiuc.edu/

Univ. Jena
http://www.uni-jena.de/fsu/math.html

Univ. Karlsruhe
http://www.rz.uni-karlsruhe.de/Uni/
Fakultaeten/Mathematik/

Univ. Kiel
http://www.informatik.uni-kiel.de/

Univ. Mainz
http://www.Uni-Mainz.DE/UniInfo/
Fachbereiche/mathematik.html

Univ. Marburg
http://www.mathematik.uni-marburg.de/

Univ. of Maryland Baltimore County
http://math.umbc.edu/

Univ. of Massachusetts Ctr. for Geometry
Analysis Numerics and Graphics
http://www.gang.umass.edu/

Univ. of Massachusetts, Amherst
http://www.math.umass.edu/

Univ. of Melbourne
http://www.maths.mu.oz.au/

Univ. of Michigan, Ann Arbor
http://www.math.lsa.umich.edu/

Univ. of Minnesota Geometry Center
http://www.geom.umn.edu/

Univ. München
http://www.informatik.uni-muenchen.de/lmu/
info/fakultaet.html

Univ. Münster
http://www.uni-muenster.de/

Univ. of Nevada, Reno Mathematics
Center
http://www.scs.unr.edu:80/unr/arts-n-science/
math-center/mathctr.html

Univ. of New England
http://fermat.une.edu.au/

Univ. of Nottingham
http://www.maths.nott.ac.uk/

Univ. of Oslo
http://math-www.uio.no/

Univ. Osnabrück
http://esther.mathematik.uni-osnabrueck.de/

Univ. Paderborn GH
http://math-www.uni-paderborn.de/

Univ. Passau
http://www.fmi.uni-passau.de/fmi/
uebersicht.html

Univ. Salzburg
http://www.mat.sbg.ac.at/home.html

Univ. of Sheffield
http://www2.shef.ac.uk/maths/maths.html

Univ. of Sydney
http://www.maths.usyd.edu.au:8000/

Univ. of Tennessee, Knoxville
http://mathsun1.math.utk.edu/

Univ. of Texas, Austin
http://henri.ma.utexas.edu/

Univ. of Toronto
http://www.cdf.utoronto.ca/math/math-
OverView.html

Univ. of Trondheim
http://www.imf.unit.no/

Univ. of Tsukuba
http://newton.math.tsukuba.ac.jp/

Univ. of Wales College of Cardiff COMMA
http://www.cm.cf.ac.uk/

Univ. of Warwick
http://www.maths.warwick.ac.uk/

Univ. Wuppertal
http://wmwap1.math.uni-wuppertal.de/pub/
Mosaic/Mathematics_WWW.html

Univ. of Zagreb
http://www.math.hr/index.html

Univ. Politecnica de Catalunya - Barcelona
http://maite120.upc.es/

Unsolved Mathematics Problems
http://www.mathsoft.com/asolve/index.html

UTK Mathematical Life Sciences Archives
http://archives.math.utk.edu/mathbio

Victoria Univ. of Wellington
http://www.vuw.ac.nz/directories/depart-
ments/maths/

Visual Math Institute
http://hypatia.ucsc.edu/

Visual Software Support Lab
http://sslab.colorado.edu:2222/sw_list.html

Vrije Universiteit
http://www.cs.vu.nl/welcome.html

Wake Forest Univ.
http://www.wfu.edu/
Academic%20departments/

Warsaw Univ.
http://hydra.mimuw.edu.pl/

Wavelet Digest
http://www.math.scarolina.edu/~wavelet/
index.html

Wavelets
http://www.mat.sbg.ac.at/~uhl/wav.html

Week's Finds in Mathematical Physics
http://math.ucr.edu/home/baez/
README.html#TWF

Weizmann Institute of Science
http://eris.wisdom.weizmann.ac.il/

Wesleyan Univ.
http://www.cs.wesleyan.edu/

World Mathematical Year 2000 Newsletter
http://www.mathp6.jussieu.fr/~jarraud/
ma200.html

WWW Virtual Library Mathematics Node
http://euclid.math.fsu.edu/Science/math.html

Yale Univ.
http://www.yale.edu/HTML/YaleMath-Info.html

Mathematics Journals

FTP Archives

New York Jrnl. of Mathematics
nyjm.albany.edu/

Ulam Quarterly
ftp.math.ufl.edu/pub/ulam/

Gopher Archives

Chronicle of Higher Education
chronicle.merit.edu

Electronic Jrnl. of Differential Equations
ejde.math.unt.edu

Electronic Transactions in Numerical
Analysis
etna.mcs.kent.edu

New York Jrnl. of Mathematics
nyjm.albany.edu

WWW Resources

Electronic Journal of Combinatorics
http://ejc.math.gatech.edu:8080/Journal/
journalhome.html

Electronic Journal of Differential Equations
http://ejde.math.swt.edu/

Electronic Journal of Linear Algebra
http://gauss.technion.ac.il/iic/ela

Electronic Journal of Probability
http://math.washington.edu/~ejpecp/

Journal of Approximation Theory
http://www.math.ohio-state.edu/Groups/JAT/
index.html

Journal of Combinatorial Mathematics and
Combinatorial Computing
http://www.math.mtu.edu/home/math/
JCMCC/JCMCC.html

Journal of Lie Theory
http://www.EMIS.de/

Journal of Mathematics of Kyoto Univ.
http://neptune.kusm.kyoto-u.ac.jp:8080/
journal_e.html

Journal of Number Theory
http://www.math.ohio-state.edu/Groups/JNT/
index.html

Journal of the London Mathematical
Society
http://www.cup.cam.ac.uk/Journals/
JNLSCAT95/jlm.html

Mathematica Militaris
http://euler.math.usma.edu/militaris.html

Mathematical Physics Electronic Journal
http://www.ma.utexas.edu/mpej/MPEJ.html

Mathematical Proceedings of the Cambridge Philosophical Society
http://www.cup.cam.ac.uk/Journals/
JNLSCAT95/psp.html

Missouri Journal of Mathematical Sciences
http://www.mathpro.com/math/mjmsJournal/
mjms.html

New York Journal of Mathematics
http://nyjm.albany.edu:8000/

Medicine

See also Aeronautics & Aerospace, Biology & Biotechnology, Chemistry, Engineering, Imaging Technologies, Optics, Physics

Usenet Newsgroups

misc.emerg-services
Newsgroup-based Mailing List: Yes. emerg-l@vm.marist.edu.
Charter: For EMTs, paramedics.

misc.handicap (Moderated)
Moderated by: Bill McGarry (wtm@bunker.shel.isc-br.com)
Submissions go to: handicap@bunker.shel.isc-br.com
Newsgroup-based Mailing List: No.
Charter: For individuals with disabilities.

misc.health.aids
Created by: James M. Scutero <jscutero@panix.com>
Call for Votes Date: August 30, 1994
Newsgroup-based Mailing List: No.
Charter (from Call for Votes):
The unmoderated newsgroup misc.health.aids will be open to discussing all aspects of AIDS.

misc.health.arthritis
Created by: Taneli Huuskonen <huuskone@cc.helsinki.fi>
Call for Votes Date: November 21, 1994
Newsgroup-based Mailing List: No.
Charter (from Call for Votes):
The proposed group would be intended for discussions about different aspects of arthritis and related autoimmune disorders, such as lupus and scleroderma, mainly from the patient's point of view. Medical discussions are supposed to be informational only, not intended for a substitute of consulting a properly trained medical practitioner.

misc.health.alternative
Created by: kaminski@netcom.com (Peter Kaminski)
Call for Votes date: November 13, 1992
Newsgroup-based Mailing List: No.
Charter (from Call for Votes):
misc.health.alternative is a newsgroup for general non-technical discussion (pro *and* con) of health care and therapies which are alternative, complementary, or not commonly accepted by Western scientific medicine.

Appropriate topics include (but are not limited to): acupuncture, Alexander technique, alternative cancer therapies, aromatherapy, ayurveda, chiropractic, color therapy, healing, herbalism, holistic dentistry, holistic medicine, homeopathy, hypnosis, iridology, macrobiotics, meditation, megavitamin therapy, midwifery, naturopathy, natural vision improvement (Bates method, etc.), osteopathy, radiesthesia, reflexology, shiatsu and do-in, traditional medicine (Arab, Chinese, Native American, etc.), and yoga.

misc.health.diabetes
Created by: kolar@spot.Colorado.EDU (Jennifer Lynn Kolar)
Call for Votes date: March 30, 1993
Newsgroup-based Mailing List: No.
Charter (from Call for Votes):
The purpose of misc.health.diabetes is to provide a forum for the discussion of issues pertaining to diabetes management, i.e.: diet, activities, medicine schedules, blood glucose control, exercise, medical breakthroughs, etc. This group addresses the issues of management of both Type I (insulin dependent) and Type II (non-insulin dependent) diabetes. Both techni-

cal discussions and general support discussions relevant to diabetes are welcome.

misc.health.therapy.occupational
Created by: Susan Burwash <sburwash@unixg.ubc.ca>
Call for Votes Date: September 5, 1995
Newsgroup-based Mailing List: No.
Charter (from Call for Votes):
The scope of the proposed group misc.health.therapy.occupational will include: occupational therapy practice in all areas of specialization; occupational therapy education - including OT and OTA programmes; social, cultural and economic trends affecting occupational therapy practice; continuing education listings and employment opportunities.

sci.med
Newsgroup-based Mailing List: No.
Charter: Medicine.

sci.med.aids (Moderated)
Moderated by: Dan Greening, Phil Miller, Jack Hamilton, and Michelle Murrain (aids-request@cs.ucla.edu)
Submissions go to: aids@cs.ucla.edu
Newsgroup-based Mailing List: Yes (aids@rutvm1.rutgers.edu).
Charter :
Discussion-group on AIDS.

sci.med.diseases.cancer
Created by: Arthur Flatau <flatau@cli.com>
Call for Votes Date: Oct 5, 1994
Newsgroup-based Mailing List: No.
Charter (from Call for Votes)
The purpose of sci.med.diseases.cancer is discussions of the treatment and diagnosis of all forms of cancer.
Sci.med.diseases.cancer is a forum for cancer patients, their families and loved ones, medical professionals and cancer researchers. Discussions of unconventional therapies are explicitly allowed, however claims made of unconventional therapy should substantiated with references to at least the popular press if not scientific literature. Unconventional therapy should be held to the same

scientific standard as conventional therapy. The group will not be moderated.

sci.med.diseases.hepatitis
Created by: Abdul W Abdul <alwahabi.albanna@nildram.co.uk>
Call for Votes Date: Jul 20, 1995
Newsgroup-based Mailing List: No.
Charter (from Call for Votes):
The proposed newsgroup would be devoted to all aspects and kinds of hepatitis diseases. This newsgroup would be a good place where all people interested in the disease (doctors and experts in this field) can communicate with each other and share views and opinions.

sci.med.dentistry
Created by:
ellswort@studsys.mscs.mu.edu (Alec Ellsworth)
Call for Votes date: November 10, 1992
Newsgroup-based Mailing List: No.
Charter (from Call for Votes):
The main objective of sci.med.dentistry is to allow internet users (dentists, dental students, researchers, and patients) the opportunity to discuss dentistry and any dental related issues. Included in this forum would be the issues of dental research, patient/dentist interaction, new technology in dentistry, infection control discussion/answers, legislation issues in dentistry, question and answers, medico-legal issues, and any other related dentistry discussion.

sci.med.emergency (Moderated)
Created by: Josh Heller <sme-admin@emed.gwumc.edu>
Moderated by: Josh Heller <sme-admin@emed.gwumc.edu>
Call for Votes Date: September 21, 1994
Newsgroup-based Mailing List: No.
Charter (from Call for Votes):
A forum for professionals working in the field of emergency medicine. A place to discuss all topics of interest to those in the field of emergency medicine. This newsgroup will not provide medical advice for lay persons

sci.med.immunology
Created by: Camilla Cracchiolo
<camilla@netcom.com>
Call for Votes Date: August 4, 1994
Newsgroup-based Mailing List: No.
Charter (from Call for Votes):
The purpose of this group is to discuss all aspects of immunology and immune-related diseases, with a special emphasis on the diagnosis and treatment of immune related illnesses; and on new research findings in these areas. This group will not be moderated.

sci.med.informatics
Created by: Dean Sittig
<dean.sittig@mcmail.vanderbilt.edu>
Call for Votes Date: September 21, 1994
Newsgroup-based Mailing List: No.
Charter (from Call for Votes):
Biomedical Informatics is an emerging discipline that has been defined as the study, invention, and implementation of structures and algorithms to improve communication, understanding and management of medical information.

sci.med.laboratory
Created by: Glenn D. Schultz
<MedTek2000@aol.com>
Call for Votes Date: September 12, 1995
Newsgroup-based Mailing List: No.
Charter (from Call for Votes):
Discussions to obtaining information about new medical laboratory products, laboratory equipment or instrumentation that others may presently be using or have tried, before considering for purchase.

sci.med.midwifery (Moderated)
Created by: Patrick Hublou
<phublou@innet.be>
Call for Votes Date: September 12, 1995
Newsgroup-based Mailing List: No.
Charter (from Call for Votes)
sci.med.midwifery will be a moderated discussion group on all aspects of the practice of obstetrics by midwives. This can include, but is not limited to case consultation, distribution of new information in the specialty, discussion of the

practice environment and conditions and on the education and training in diversity of midwives.

sci.med.nursing
Created by: cudma@csv.warwick.ac.uk (Denis Anthony)
Call for Votes date: October 20, 1993
Newsgroup-based Mailing List: No.
Charter (from Call for Votes):
Just as sci.med caters to general postings about things medical, this new group would address specifically nursing questions and discussions, and act as a forum.

sci.med.nutrition
Created by: coleman@pop.CS.UCLA.EDU (Mike Coleman)
Call for Votes date: July 17, 1992
Newsgroup-based Mailing List: No.
Charter (from Call for Votes):
The purpose of this newsgroup will be to discuss food, food preparation, eating habits, etc., (including medical, psychological, and social aspects) as it relates to the quality and longevity of human life.

sci.med.occupational
Created by: dwallach@nas.nasa.gov (Dan Wallach)
Call for Votes date: July 16, 1992
Newsgroup-based Mailing List: No.
Charter (from Call for Votes):
sci.med.occupational is for the discussion of occupational injuries, their prevention, detection, and treatment. It is also for the discussion of adapting: both the work environment to the user, and the user to the work environment.

sci.med.orthopedics (Moderated)
Created by: Iain D. Dickey
<idd@unixg.ubc.ca>
Call for Votes Date: March 17, 1995
Moderated by: Iain Dickey <bones-request@unixg.ubc.ca>
Submissions go to: bones@unixg.ubc.ca
Newsgroup-based Mailing List: No.
Charter (from Call for Votes):
This moderated newsgroup will be used for the discussion of Orthopedic Surgery and related issues.

sci.med.pathology

Created by: Leo S. Aish
<lsa@world.std.com>
Call for Votes Date: January 22, 1995
Newsgroup-based Mailing List: No.
Charter (from Call for Votes):
Topics for discussion could include: case studies; new methods and technologies; currently available/upcoming hardware and software; research; seminars and conferences; any other problems, questions and comments.

sci.med.pharmacy

Created by: Paul Hodgkinson <phh@de-montfort.ac.uk>
Call for Votes date: June 11, 1993
Newsgroup-based Mailing List: No.
Charter (from Call for Votes):
To provide pharmacists with a forum for the discussion of issues related to the teaching and practice of the profession. It is expected that sci.med.pharmacy would attract contributions from all the major disciplines including pharmacology and pharmaceutical chemistry as well as areas with more direct professional implications such as pharmacy practice and legislation.

sci.med.physics

Newsgroup-based Mailing List: No.
Charter (from Call for Votes):
Physics of medicine.

sci.med.prostate.bph

Created by: Brad Hennenfent
<chicago@ix.netcom.com>
Call for Votes Date: September 12, 1995
Newsgroup-based Mailing List: No.
Charter (from Call for Votes):
Sci.med.prostate.bph will be an unmoderated discussion about all aspects of benign prostatic hypertrophy.

sci.med.prostate.cancer

Created by: Brad Hennenfent
<chicago@ix.netcom.com>
Call for Votes Date: September 12, 1995
Newsgroup-based Mailing List: No.
Charter (from Call for Votes):
Sci.med.prostate.cancer will be an unmoderated discussion of all aspects of prostate cancer.

sci.med.prostate.prostatitis

Created by: Brad Hennenfent
<chicago@ix.netcom.com>
Call for Votes Date: September 12, 1995
Charter: Sci.med.prostate.prostatitis will be an unmoderated discussion of all aspects of prostatitis.

sci.med.psychobiology

Created by:
lamontg@stein.u.washington.edu (Lamont Granquist)
Call for Votes date: November 28, 1993
Newsgroup-based Mailing List: No.
Charter (from Call for Votes):
sci.med.psychobiology will be an unmoderated common forum for discussions and announcements among those interested in scientific aspects of psychiatry.

sci.med.radiology

Created by: dsc@xray.hmc.psu.edu (David S. Channin)
Call for Votes date: February 24, 1994
Newsgroup-based Mailing List: No.
Charter (from Call for Votes):
There seems to be a need for a place to discuss the clinical, technological, and operational, and political aspects of radiology.

sci.med.telemedicine

Created by: dfp10@csc.albany.edu (D Parsons)
Call for Votes date: February 23, 1993
Newsgroup-based Mailing List: Yes (hspnet-l%albnydh2@cunyvm.cuny.edu).
Charter (from Call for Votes):
Discussion of computer networks that connect between hospitals and/or physician's offices, including international linkages between medical facilities in different countries.

The group will be linked to the bitnet list hspnet-l@albnydh2

sci.med.vision

Created by: Johnnie Cox (jrufus@aol.com)
Call for Votes Date: September 21, 1994
Newsgroup-based Mailing List: No.
Charter (from Call for Votes):

The purpose of this group is to provide an electronic forum to discuss the human visual system, problems that may occur with vision (eg disease processes that affect vision) and the options for correcting visual problems.

Frequently Asked Questions

bit.listserv.transplant FAQ
Maintainer: mhollowa@epo.som.sunysb.edu (Michael Holloway)
Where on Usenet: bit.listserv.transplant
Where it's archived: rtfm.mit.edu:pub/usenet/news.answers/
What it's for: Issues pertaining to organ transplants.

Cancer - Online Information Sources FAQ
Maintainer: ed@titipu.resun.com (Edward Reid)
Where on Usenet: alt.support.cancer
Where it's archived: rtfm.mit.edu:pub/usenet/news.answers/alt.support.cancer
What it's for: A guide to online sources of information on cancer.

Crib and Cradle Safety Regulations
Maintainer: clewis@ferret.ocunix.on.ca (Chris Lewis)
Where on Usenet: misc.consumers.house
Where it's archived: rtfm.mit.edu:pub/usenet/misc.consumers.house
What it's for: Issues of interest in the selection and utilization of cribs for infants.

Medical Image Format FAQ
Maintainer: dclunie@flash.us.com (David A. Clunie)
Where on Usenet: alt.image.medical
Where it's archived: rtfm.mit.edu:pub/usenet/news.answers/
What it's for: Commonly asked questions on medical imaging formats.

misc.health.diabetes FAQ
Maintainer: ed@titipu.resun.com (Edward Reid)
Where on Usenet: misc.health.diabetes
Where it's archived: rtfm.mit.edu:pub/usenet/news.answers/
What it's for: Commonly asked questions on diabetes.

misc.health.diabetes insulin pump discussion
Maintainer: ed@titipu.resun.com (Edward Reid)
Where on Usenet: misc.health.diabetes
Where it's archived: rtfm.mit.edu:pub/usenet/news.answers/misc.health.diabetes
What it's for: An extended discussion of insulin pump usage, models, and features.

misc.health.diabetes software
Maintainer: "Michael D. Wolfe" <MWOLFE@WVNVAXA.WVNET.EDU>
Where on Usenet: misc.health.diabetes
Where it's archived: rtfm.mit.edu:pub/usenet/news.answers/misc.health.diabetes
What it's for: Software packages that may be of help in understanding and managing diabetes.

Powerlines & Cancer FAQs
Maintainer: jmoulder@its.mcw.edu (John Moulder)
Where on Usenet: sci.med.physics
Where it's archived: rtfm.mit.edu:pub/usenet/news.answers/powerlines-cancer FAQ
http://archive.xrt.upenn.edu/0h/faq/powerline_faq
http://www.cis.ohio-state.edu/hypertext/faq/usenet/powerlines-cancer FAQ
What it's for: Topics on the relationship between high-voltage powerlines and forms of cancer.

Psychology & Support Groups Newsgroup Pointer
Maintainer: John M. Grohol <grohol@alpha.acast.nova.edu>
Where on Usenet: alt.support

Where it's archived:
rtfm.mit.edu:pub/usenet/news.answers/
alt.support
What it's for: Newsgroup subject pointer
to psychology & support newsgroups.

Sci.med.AIDS FAQ

Maintainer: Dan Wallach
<dwallach@cs.princeton.edu>
Where on Usenet: sci.med.aids
Where it's archived:
rtfm.mit.edu:pub/usenet/news.answers/
sci.med.aids
What it's for: AIDS: causes, treatments,
etc.

Typing Injuries FAQ

Maintainer: Dan Wallach
<dwallach@cs.princeton.edu>
Where on Usenet: sci.med
Where it's archived:
rtfm.mit.edu:pub/usenet/news.answers/
sci.med
What it's for: Repetitive motion injuries,
specifically typing injuries. Treatments,
issues, etc.

Discussion Lists

4acure-l
4acure-l@albnydh2
Aids Cure

accri-l
accri-l@uabdpo
Anesthesia and Critical Care Resources

admin-l
admin-l@albnydh2
NYS Dept. of Health Admin.

aids
aids@ebcesca1
(Peered) Sci.Med.AIDS Newsgroup

aids@rutvm1
sci.med.aids
Newsgroup

aidsbkrv
aidsbkrv@uicvm
AIDS Book Review Jrnl.

aids_intl
iceca@rutvm1
Intl Committee for Elec Comm on AIDS

alife
alife-request@cognet.ucla.edu
Artificial life.

amied-l
amied-l@mcgill1
American Medical Informatics Association

anest-l
anest-l@ubvm
Anesthesiology

anneal
anneal-request@cs.ucla.edu (Daniel R.
Greening)
Annealing techniques.

aobull-l
aobull-l@albnydh2
NYS Dept. of Health

aphamh-l
aphamh-l@brownvm
American Mental Health APH List

bboplist
bboplist@ubvm
Bulletin Board of Oral Pathology

bhrd-l
bhrd-l@albnydh2
BHRD-L
Bureau of Health Resources Development

biomed-l
biomed-l@ndsuvm1
BIOMED-L Biomedical Ethics

BiOS
info-bios@spie.org
The Biomedical Optics Society

c+health
c+health@iubvm
Health effects of computer use

cancer-l
cancer-l@wvnvm
WVNET CANCER discussion list

canchid
canchid@yorkvm1
Canadian Network on Health

cffc-hhs
cffc-hhs@akronvm
CFFC Health and Human Services List

cfids-l
cfids-l@auvm
Chronic Fatigue Syndrome activist talk
CFS/ME

cfs-d
cfs-d@albnydh2
Chronic Fatigue Syndrome File Storage

cfs-file
cfs-file@sjuvm
Chronic Fatigue Syndrome files CFIDS/
ME

cfs-l
cfs-l@nihlist
Chronic Fatigue Syndrome discussion
CFIDS/ME

cfs-news
cfs-news@nihlist
Chronic Fatigue Syndrome Newsletter
CFIDS/ME

cfs-med
cfs-med@nihlist
Chronic Fatigue Syndrome/CFIDS
medical list

cfs-wire
cfs-wire@sjuvm
Chronic Fatigue Syndrome NEWSWIRE
CFIDS/ME

clan
clan@frmop11
Cancer Liaison and Action Network

clinalrt
clinalrt@umab
Clinical Alerts from NIH

cocamed
cocamed@utoronto
Computers in Canadian Medical Education

compmed
compmed@wuvmd
Comparative Medicine List

conflist
conflist@ucsfvm
School of Medicine Conference List

cromed-l
cromed-l@aearn
CROatian MEDical List

cshcs-l
cshcs-l@emuvm1
Ctr. for Study of Health, Culture and
Society

d-perio
d-perio@nihlist
NIDR, Periodontal Diseases Program
Discussion

dblist
dblist@umab
Databases for Dentistry

deaf-l
deaf-l@siucvmb
Deaf List

deafblnd
deafblnd@ukcc
DEAFBLND--Deaf-Blind Mailing List

dental
members@umab
DENTAL TEST LIST

dental-l
dental-l@irlearn
Cosine Project - Dental Research unit,
UCC

dentalma
dentalma@bitnic
For dentistry-related articles reports

derm-l
derm-l@yalevm
Dermatology (DERM-L)

diet
diet@ubvm
Support and Discussion of Weight Loss

dohmem-l
dohmem-l@albnydh2
New York Dept. of Health Memoranda

ds-4edit
ds-4edit@nihlist
Instructions for editors of Disability Stats.

ds-c-cp1
ds-c-cp1@nihlist
Cerebral Palsy ICIDH Issue #1

ds-c-sb1
ds-c-sb1@nihlist
Spina Bifida ICIDH Issue #1

ds-h
ds-h@nihlist
Major Handicap Issues in the ICIDH

ds-h-mo
ds-h-mo@nihlist
Mobility Handicap Issues in ICIDH

ds-h-oc
ds-h-oc@nihlist
Occupation Handicap Issues in ICIDH

ds-h-or
ds-h-or@nihlist
Orientation Handicap Issues in ICIDH

ds-h-pi
ds-h-pi@nihlist
Physical Independence Handicap Issues in ICIDH

ds-mh-00
ds-mh-00@nihlist
Major Mental Health Issues in ICIDH (many sublists available)

ds-overv
ds-overv@nihlist
Overview of all listservs in disability stats.

egret-l
egret-l@dartcms1
Discussion of EGRET epidemiological software

ehs-l
ehs-l@albnydh2
EHS-L Environmental Health System

emflds-l
emflds-l@ubvm
Electromagnetics in Medicine & Science

family-l
family-l@mizzou1
Academic Family Medicine Discussion.

fibrom-l
listserv@vmd.cso.uiuc.edu
Fibromyalgia.

finan-hc
finan-hc@wuvmd
Health Care Financial Matters

forpsy-l
forpsy-l@mizzou1
Discussion of Issues in Forensic Psychiatry

gerinet
gerinet@ubvm
Geriatric Health Care Discussion Group

hc-l
hc-l@albnydh2
HC-L HEALTHCOM/VM Discussion

heafault
heafault@irlearn
HEAnet Faults database

healr-l
healr-l@gsuvm1
collaborative research in the health sciences

health-l
health-l@irlearn
Intl. Discussion on Health Research

healthco
healthco@rpitsvm
Communication in health/medical context

healthre
healthre@ukcc
Health Care Reform

herb
herb@trearn
Medicinal and Aromatic Plants

hesca
hesca@dartcms1
Health Sciences Communications

hints-l
hints-l@albnydh2
HINTS-L HINTS using the NYS Dept of Health

hspbed-l
hspbed-l@albnydh2
hspbed-l hospital bed availability in NY Health System

hypbar-l
hypbar-l@technion
HyperBaric & Diving Medicine List

hypermed
hypermed@umab
Biomedical Hypermedia Instructional Design

ibdlist
IBDlist-request%mvac23@udel.edu (Thomas Lapp)
Inflammatory Bowel Diseases.

imia-l
imia-l@umab
Intl. Medical Informatics Assn. Board

immnet-l
immnet-l@dartcms1
Medical Immunization Tracking systems

immune
immune-request@weber.ucsd.edu (Cyndi Norman)
Support group for people with immune-system disorders.

info-aids
info-aids@rainbow.UUCP
Info and treatment of AIDS.

inhealth
inhealth@rpitsvm
Intl. Health Communication

injury-l
injury-l@wvnvm
Injury Surveillance Control and Intervention

itd-jnl
itd-jnl@sjuvm
Information and Technology for the Disabled Journal

itd-toc
itd-toc@sjuvm
Information and Technology for the Disabled Journal - Contents

jmedclub
jmedclub@brownvm
Medical Jrnl. Discussion Club

lasmed-l
lasmed-l@taunivm
Laser Medicine

lhu-l
lhu-l@albnydh2
LHU-L Local Health Unit Discussion Forum

ltcare-l
ltcare-l@nihlist
Research on Disability and Long-term care

medimage
medimage@polyvm
Medical Imaging

medinf-l
medinf-l@dearn
MEDINF-L

medlab-l
medlab-l@ualtavm
MEDLAB-L is a discussion group for medical lab technicians

medphy-l
medphy-l@awiimc12
EFOMP Medical Physics Information Services

medphys
medphys-request@radonc.duke.edu
Radiology.

medsea-l
medsea-l@aearn
Marine Biology of the Adriatic Sea

medsup-l
medsup-l@yalevm
Medical Support List

mhcare-l
mhcare-l@mizzou1
Managed Health Care

mis-l
mis-l@albnydh2
NYS Dept. of Health Mgmt. Information

motordev
motordev@umdd
Human Motor Skill Development List

nat-hlth
nat-hlth@tamvm1.tamu.
EDUNAT-HLTH Health Issues of Native Peoples

nce-resp
nce-resp@mcgill1
Respiratory Health Network of Centres of Excellence

nucmed
nucmed-request@uwovax.uwo.ca
Nuclear medicine.

nutepi
nutepi@db0tui11
Nutritional epidemiology

oandm
oandm@msu.edu
Orientation and Mobility

ois-kumc
ois-kumc@ukanvm
KU Medical Ctr. Computing Services

panet-l
panet-l@yalevm
Medical Education and Health Information

parkinsn
parkinsn@utoronto
Parkinson's Disease - Information Exchange

patho-l
patho-l@emuvm1
Pathology discussion group On-Line

physl-tr
physl-tr@tritu
Physiology

prenat-l
prenat-l@albnydh2
Perinatal Outcomes

preteld
preteld@indycms
Learning Disabilities Minors Receiving Grants

qadata-l
qadata-l@albnydh2
New York State Dept. of Health: Data Quality

rceduc-l
rceduc-l@mizzou1
Discussion of issues in Repiratory Therapy

rc_world
rc_world@indycms
Resp. Healthcare profiles World Fourm

smcdcme
smcdcme@waynest1
Continuing Medical Education

smdm-l
smdm-l@dartcms1
Medical Decision Making List

sorehand
sorehand@ucsfvm
Discussion of Carpal Tunnel Syndrome, Tendonitis, and similar

stroke-l
stroke-l@ukcc
Stroke

thphysio
thphysio@frmop11
Thermal Physiology

trnsplnt
trnsplnt@wuvmd
Organ transplant recipients and related.

uvhinf-l
uvhinf-l@uvvm
UVic Health Info Science Bulletins

whca95-l
whca95-l@nihlist
White House Conference on Aging 1995

witsendo
witsendo@dartcms1
Endometriosis Treatment and Support

yeast-l
yeast-l@psuhmc
Yeast-Related Medical

Nursing and EMS Discussion Lists

ajcunurs
ajcunurs@guvm
ajcu conference on nursing programs

cshcn-l
cshcn-l@nervm
Children with Special Health Care Needs

emsny-l
emsny-l@albnydh2
EMS Issues for NYS Providers

gradnrse
gradnrse@kentvm
Questions and Answers About Nursing Practice

nrsinged
nrsinged@ulkyvm
Nursing Educators discussion

nursenet
nursenet@utoronto
NURSENET - A Global Forum for Nursing Issues

nurseres
nurseres@kentvm
Discussion list for nurse researchers

schlrn-l
schlrn-l@ubvm
School Nurse Network

snurse-l
snurse-l@ubvm
SNURSE-L - An Intl. Nursing Students Group

Medicine Resources

FTP Resources

Baylor College of Medicine
bcm.tmc.edu

BiOS—The Biomedical Optics Society
spie.org

Case Western Reserve Univ.
biochemistry.cwru.edu

Lawrence Berkeley Labs
george.lbl.gov

Medical Media and Information Technologies
summit.stanford.edu

sci.med.telemedicine (newsgroup)
babcock.cerc.wvu.edu

Univ. of Texas - Austin
girch1.hsch.utexas.edu

Univ. of Texas - Galveston
atlantis.utmb.edu

Gopher Resources

Agricola bibliographic database
probe.nalusda.gov:7020/77/agricola/agidx

AIDS
odie.niaid.nih.gov

AIDS
gopher.cic.net/11/e-serials/general/science/
medical/aids

Beth Israel Hospital
gopher.bih.harvard.edu

Dana-Farber Cancer Institute
gopher.dfci.harvard.edu

Massachusetts General Hospital
weeds.mgh.harvard.edu

MedSearch America, Inc.
gopher.medsearch.com:9001

National Institute of Allergy and Infectious Disease (NIAID)
gopher.niaid.nih.gov

School of Public Health
hsph.harvard.edu

Univ. of Michigan
una.hh.lib.umich.edu

Virtual Reference Desk
peg.cwis.uci.edu:7000

World Health Organization (WHO)
gopher.who.ch

WWW Resources

Actinomycetes
http://www.bdt.org.br/bioline/bin/ac.cgi

Acute Pain Mgmt.: Operative or Medical Procedures and Trauma
http://text.nlm.nih.gov/ahcpr/apm/www/
apmccvr.html

Alces
http://alces.med.umn.edu/start.html

American Association for the Advancement of Science
http://www.aaas.org/

American Association of Immunologists
http://glamdring.ucsd.edu/others/aai

American Association of Physicists in Medicine
http://www.aapm.org/

American Journal of Nursing
http://www.ajn.org:80/ajn/page1.html

American Medical Association
http://www.ama.org/

American Dental Association
http://www.ada.org/

American Society for Microbiology
http://www.asmusa.org

Amyloid, The International Journal of Clinical and Experimental Investigation
http://med-med1.bu.edu/amyloid/amyloid.html

Annals of Saudi Medicine
http://www.kfshrc.edu.sa/annals/annals.html

Annual Reviews Inc. (series)
http://www.annurev.org/

Antimicrobial Agents and Chemotherapy
http://www.asmusa.org/jnlsrc/aac1.htm

Artificial Life
http://www-mitpress.mit.edu/jrnls-catalog/
artificial.html

Auburn Domestic Animal Endocrinology
http://www.ag.auburn.edu/dae/dae.html

Auburn Univ. College of Veterinary Medicine
http://www.vetmed.auburn.edu/

Australian National University
http://life.anu.edu.au/

Base de Dados Tropical
http://www.ftpt.br/

Baylor College of Medicine
http://www.bcm.tmc.edu/

Biochemistry and Biotechnology
http://kiev.physchem.kth.se/

Biocomputation Ctr., NASA Ames
http://biocomp.arc.nasa.gov/

Biocomputing
http://biomed.nus.sg/

Biocomputing, Biozentrum der Universitaet Basel
http://beta.embnet.unibas.ch

BioInformatics
http://www.gdb.org/hopkins.html

Biomedical Conferences
http://id.wing.net/~chi/upcoming.html

Biomedical Resource List
http://www.nlm.nih.gov/current_news.dir/
biomed.html

Biomedical WWW Sites
http://golgi.harvard.edu/biopages/all.html

bionet.software.www archives
http://www.ch.embnet.org/bio-www/info.html

Biophysical Journal
http://biosci.cbs.umn.edu/biophys/bj/bj.html

Biophysical Society
http://biosci.cbs.umn.edu/biophys/
biophys.html

Bioscene - Journal of College Biology
Teaching
http://papa.indstate.edu/0h/amcbt/
bioscene.html

BIOSCI (Bionet) News Group Archives &
Index to Biologists
gopher://net.bio.net

BioSciences (en Espaniol)
http://fiss.org.ec/BioBanco/BioCuentas/
BioSciences.html

Biospheres
http://biology.uoregon.edu/Biology_WWW/
Biospheres/index.html

BiOS—The Biomedical Optics Society
http://www.spie.org/bios.html

BMES Bulletin
http://www.mecca.org/BME/BMES/
bmeshome.html

Breast Cancer Information Clearinghouse
http://nysernet.org/bcic/

British Medical Journal
http://www.bmj.com/bmj/

CABIOS: Computer Applications in the
Biological Sciences
http://www.oup.co.uk/oup/smj/journals/ed/
titles/cabios/

Cambridge Healthtech Institute
http://id.wing.net/~chi/homepg.html

Canadian Medical Research Council
http://hpb1.hwc.ca:8100/

CancerNet
http://biomed.nus.sg/Cancer/welcome.html

CareerPath
http://www.careerpath.com/

Center for Advanced Medical Informatics
http://camis.Stanford.edu

Centers for Disease Control and Prevention (CDC)
http://158.111.115.15/mosaic/home/
home.htm

Chemistry and Biology Journal
http://www.cursci.co.uk/BioMedNet/cmb/
cmbinf.html

Clinical and Diagnostic Laboratory
Immunology
http://www.asmusa.org/jnlsrc/cdli1.htm

Clinical Microbiology Reviews
http://www.asmusa.org/jnlsrc/cmr1.htm

Cold Spring Harbor Laboratory
http://www.cshl.org

College Nursing
http://indy.radiology.uiowa.edu/Nursing/
Nursing.Renal.html

Columbia-Presbyterian Medical Ctr.
http://www.cpmc.columbia.edu/

Computers in Medicine, Denver Medical
Library,
http://www.csn.net/~dorothys

Ctr. for Biomedical and Biophysical
Technologies
http://citbb.unige.it/

Ctr. for Imaging and Pharmaceutical
Research
http://cipr-diva.mgh.harvard.edu/

Ctr. for Medical Informatics
http://paella.med.yale.edu/

Current Opinion in Biotechnology Journal
http://www.cursci.co.uk/BioMedNet/bio/
bioinf.html

Current Opinion in Cell Biology Journal
http://www.cursci.co.uk/BioMedNet/cel/
celinf.html

Current Opinion in Genetics and Development Journal
http://www.cursci.co.uk/BioMedNet/gen/
geninf.html

Current Opinion in Immunology Journal
http://www.cursci.co.uk/BioMedNet/imm/
imminf.html

Current Opinion in Neurobiology Journal
http://www.cursci.co.uk/BioMedNet/nrb/
nrbinf.html

Current Opinion in Structural Biology
http://www.cursci.co.uk/BioMedNet/stb/
stbinf.html

De Montfort Univ. Pharmacy
http://www.dmu.ac ۱٬۲/0/www/departments/
pharm.html

DELTA Project - Biological Sciences,
CalPoly
http://www.calpoly.edu/delta.html

Den-Tel-Net
http://www.onramp.net:80/Den-Tel-Net/

DENTalTRAUMA
http://www.unige.ch/smd/orthotr.html

Diseases of Aquatic Organisms
http://www.int-res.com/int-res/dao/dao.html

Domestic Animal Endocrinology
http://www.ag.auburn.edu/dae/dae.html

Duke Medical Ctr.
http://www.mc.duke.edu/

Duke Univ. Medical Informatics
http://dmi-www.mc.duke.edu/

EMBO Journal
http://www.informatik.uni-rostock.de/HUM-
MOLGEN/journals/EMBO-J/

Emerging Infectious Diseases
http://www.cdc.gov/ncidod/EID/eid.htm

EMF-Link
http://archive.xrt.upenn.edu:1000/emf/top/
emf-link.html

Encyclopedia Radiologica
http://www.xray.hmc.psu.edu/
EncyclopediaRadiologica.html

Entrez
http://atlas.nlm.nih.gov:5700/Entrez/
index.html

European Biophysics Journal
http://npbsn41.nimr.mrc.ac.uk/ebj1.html

European Molecular Biology Network
http://beta.embnet.unibas.ch/embnet/info.html

Evolutionary Computation
http://www-mitpress.mit.edu/jrnls-catalog/
evolution.html

Experimental Searchable Index for the
WWW VL Biosciences
http://golgi.harvard.edu/htbin/biopages

Fachbereich Biologie
http://www.uni-kl.de/FB-Biologie/AG-Nagl/AG-
Nagl.html

Federation of American Societies for
Experimental Biology (FASEB)
http://www.faseb.org/

Fred Hutchinson Cancer Research Ctr.
http://www.fhcrc.org/

French Genomics Server, Moulon
http://moulon.inra.fr/

Frontiers in Bioscience
http://bayanet.com/bioscience/

Fujita Health Univ.
http://pathy.fujita-hu.ac.jp/pathy.html

Ganglion - Medical Ctr.
http://ganglion.anes.med.umich.edu/

GASNet Anesthesiology Home Page
http://gasnet.med.nyu.edu/HomePage.html

GenBank — National Center for Biotechnology Information
http://www.ncbi.nlm.nih.gov

General Practice On-Line
http://www.cityscape.co.uk/users/ad88/gp.htm

Genes & Development
http://www.cshl.org/journals/gnd/

Genome Data Base
http://gdbwww.gdb.org/

Genome Research
http://www.cshl.org/journals/gr/

Georgia Tech Medical Informatics
http://www.cc.gatech.edu/gvu/
medical_informatics/
medinfo_home_page.html

Good Medicine Magazine
http://none.coolware.com/health/good_med/
ThisIssue.html

Gordon Conference Information
http://hackberry.chem.niu.edu:70/1/
ConferenceListings/GordonConferences

Graduate Programs in the Biological/
Biomedical Sciences
http://www.faseb.org/graduate.html

Guide to Public Health
http://128.196.106.42/ph-hp.html

Guidelines for Cancer Pain
http://www.stat.washington.edu/TALARIA/
TALARIA.html

GUIs in Bioinformatics Workshop
http://nimsn41.nimr.mrc.ac.uk/mathbio/t-
flores/GUI-Bioinform/meeting.html

Guy's and St. Thomas' Hospitals Medical
Image Processing Group
http://nothung.umds.ac.uk/

Harvard Biolabs
http://golgi.harvard.edu/biopages/
medicine.html

Harvard Biological Journals
http://golgi.harvard.edu/journals.html

Harvard Biostatistics
http://biosun1.harvard.edu/

Harvard College of Pharmacy
http://golgi.harvard.edu/biopages/
kerouac.pharm.uky.edu/Default.html

Harvard Medical Ctr.
http://golgi.harvard.edu/www-
med.stanford.edu/MedCenter/welcome.html

Harvard Medical School
http://www.med.harvard.edu/

Health & Medicine
http://nearnet.gnn.com/wic/med.toc.html

Health in Perspective
http://www.perspective.com/health

Health Resources
http://alpha.acast.nova.edu/medicine.html

HealthNet
http://debra.dgbt.doc.ca/~mike/home.html

Henderson Newsletters
http://www.holonet.net/homepage/
samples.htm

Herb, Spice, and Medicinal Plant Digest
http://www-unix.oit.umass.edu/~herbdig/
index.html

Historical Ctr. for the Health Sciences
http://http2.sils.umich.edu/HCHS/

History of Medicine Exhibits
http://www.nlm.nih.gov/hmd.dir/hmd.html

HIV/AIDS information
http://vector.casti.com/QRD/.html/AIDS.html

Hospital News
http://www.gate.net/hospital-news/

HUM-MOLGEN - Internet Communication Forum in Human Molecular
Genetics
http://www.informatik.uni-rostock.de/HUM-
MOLGEN/

Human Genome News
http://www.ornl.gov/TechResources/
Human_Genome/home.html

Human Life
http://www.cen.uiuc.edu/~jj9544/4.html

Human Molecular Genetics
http://www.oup.co.uk/oup/smj/journals/ed/
titles/hmg/

Human Reproduction Update
http://www.oup.co.uk/oup/smj/journals/ed/
titles/hru/

Idaho State Univ. College of Pharmacy
http://pharmacy.isu.edu/welcome.html

Image Processing and Analysis Group
http://noodle.med.yale.edu/

Immunity Journal
http://www.cell.com/immunity

Infection and Immunity
http://www.asmusa.org/jnlsrc/ii1.htm

Institut fuer Pharmazeutische Technologie
http://www.tu-bs.de/pharmtech/pht.html

Institute for Genomic Research
http://www.tigr.org/

Institute for Health Informatics
http://www.ihi.aber.ac.uk/index.html

Inter-Research Science Journal
http://www.int-res.com/int-res/

Interconnection of Molecular Biology
Databases Workshop Summary
http://www.ai.sri.com/people/pkarp/
mimbd.html

InterJournal
http://dynamics.bu.edu/InterJournal

International Antiviral News
http://www.meditech.co.uk/iavn.htm

International Journal of Systematic
Bacteriology
http://www.asmusa.org/jnlsrc/ijsb1.htm

Internet/Bitnet Health Science Resources
http://kufacts.cc.ukans.edu/cwis/units/
medcntr/menu.html

Iowa State College of Veterinary Medicine
http://www.iastate.edu/colleges/vetmed/
index.html

Joel's Hierarchical Subject Index
http://www.cen.uiuc.edu/~jj9544/index.html

Journal of Bacteriology
http://www.asmusa.org/jnlsrc/jb1.htm

Journal of Biological Chemistry
http://www-jbc.stanford.edu/jbc/

Journal of Cell Science
http://www.gold.net/users/ag64/jcsindex.htm

Journal of Clinical Microbiology
http://www.asmusa.org/jnlsrc/jcm1.htm

Journal of Cognitive Rehabilitation
http://www.inetdirect.net/nsp/

Journal of Computer-Aided Molecular
Design
http://wucmd.wustl.edu/jcamd/jcamd.html

Journal of Experimental Biology
http://www.gold.net/users/ag64/jebindex.htm

Journal of Image Guided Surgery
http://www.igs.wiley.com/

Journal of Immunology
http://199.170.0.125/JI/

Journal of Medical Imaging
http://jmi.gdb.org/JMI/ejourn.html

Journal of Quantitative Trait Loci
http://probe.nalusda.gov:8000/

Journal of the Biological Inorganic
Chemistry Society
http://risc3.lrm.fi.cnr.it:8001/~jbic/

Journal of Therapeutic Botulinum Neuro-
toxin: Basic and Clinical Sciences
http://med-amsa.bu.edu/pharmacology/
neuropharm/journal.htm

Journal of Virology
http://www.asmusa.org/jnlsrc/jv1.htm

Journal Previews
http://www.informatik.uni-rostock.de/HUM-
MOLGEN/journals/

Journals of the Biomedical Engineering
Society
http://isdl.ee.washington.edu/ABME/
annals.html

JTCA Reference database
http://www.wdcm.riken.go.jp/htbin/
JTCA_ref.pl

Korean Journal of Parasitology
http://sun.hallym.ac.kr/~shuh/kjp.html

La Jolla Cancer Research Foundation
http://192.231.106.66/

Lab. for Biological Informatics and
Theoretical Medicine
http://bitmed.ucsd.edu/

Lab. of Mathematical Biology
http://www.ncifcrf.gov:2001/

LANL Medical Data Analysis Projects
http://www.c3.lanl.gov/cic3/projects/Medical/
main.html

Larg*net
http://johns.largnet.uwo.ca/

Learning & Memory
http://www.cshl.org/journals/lnm/

Les Sources D'Information En Medecine
Veterinaire
http://brise.ere.umontreal.ca/~jettejp

M.D. Anderson Cancer Center
http://utmdacc.uth.tmc.edu/

M.D. Anderson ONcolog
http://utmdacc.mda.uth.tmc.edu:5009/
homepage.html

Macromolecular Structures
http://www.cursci.co.uk/BioMedNet/mms/
mmsinf.htm

Magnetic Resonance Imaging Group
http://www-mri.uta.edu/

Mallinckrodt Institute of Radiology
http://ibc.wustl.edu:70/1/mir

Marine Ecology Progress Series
http://www.int-res.com/int-res/meps/
meps.html

Mayo Foundation Biomedical Imaging
Resource
http://autobahn.mayo.edu/BIR_Welcome.html

Medical Matrix - Guide to Internet
Medical Resources
http://kuhttp.cc.ukans.edu/cwis/units/medcntr/
Lee/HOMEPAGE.HTML

Medical Physics
http://info.biomed.abdn.ac.uk/

Medical Reporter
http://www.dash.com/netro/nwx/tmr/tmr.html

Medicine and Global Survival
http://www.bmj.com/bmj/mgs/index.html

Medline Genetics Subset
http://ncbi.nlm.nih.gov:2555/r_medline.html

MedLink
http://www.ls.se/medlink/

MedScape
http://www.medscape.com/

MedSearch America
http://www.medsearch.com:9001/

Mendelian Inheritance in Man
http://gdbwww.gdb.org/omimdoc/
omimtop.html

Microbiological Reviews
http://www.asmusa.org/jnlsrc/mr1.htm

Mississippi State Univ. College of Veterinary Medicine
http://pegasus.cvm.msstate.edu/

Molecular and Cellular Biology
http://www.asmusa.org/jnlsrc/mcb1.htm

Molecular Medicine
http://www.informatik.uni-rostock.de/HUM-MOLGEN/journals/MM/

Monash Univ. Medical Informatics
http://adrian.med.monash.edu.au/

Morbidity and Mortality Weekly Report (MMWR)
http://www.crawford.com/cdc/mmwr/
mmwr.html

MultiMedia Medical Biochemistry Server
http://ubu.hahnemann.edu/

Multimedia Medical Textbooks
http://indy.radiology.uiowa.edu/
MultimediaTextbooks.html

Murdoch Univ. - Respiratory Images
http://http://134.115.224.48/vetscINTRO.html

MycDB
http://kiev.physchem.kth.se/MycDB.html

Nagoya Univ. School of Medicine
http://www.med.nagoya-u.ac.jp/

NAS Symposium on Biology of Developmental Transcription Control
http://mirsky.caltech.edu/nas_meeting.html

National Academy of Sciences
http://www.nas.edu/

National Cancer Ctr.
http://www.ncc.go.jp/

National Institutes of Health
http://www.nih.gov/

National Library of Medicine
http://www.nlm.nih.gov/

National Science Foundation
http://stis.nsf.gov/

NetVet — Veterinary Medicine
http://netvet.wustl.edu/

Neuro-Implant Program
http://he1.uns.tju.edu/~doctorb/bppp.html

Neurological Surgery
http://www.med.nyu.edu/NeuroSurgery/
HomePage.html

Neurology
http://132.183.145.103/

Neuron Journal
http://www.cell.com/neuron

Neuroscience Internet Resource Guide
http://http2.sils.umich.edu/Public/nirg/
nirg1.html

Neurotrophin
http://mab.physiol.washington.edu/nrotrphn/
nthompag.htm

New York Univ. Medical Ctr.
http://www.med.nyu.edu/HomePage.html

NIH Guide to Grants and Contracts
http://www.med.nyu.edu/nih-guide.html

North Carolina State Univ. College of Veterinary Medicine
http://www2.ncsu.edu/ncsu/cvm/
cvmhome.html

Nova-Links
http://alpha.acast.nova.edu/start.html

Nucleic Acids Research
http://www.oup.co.uk:80/oup/smj/journals/ed/
titles/nar/

NYU Anesthesiology (Medicine)
http://gasnet.med.nyu.edu/index.html

Oak Ridge National Laboratory Review
http://www.ornl.gov/ORNL/EINS_Reports/
Review/text/home.html

Oklahoma State Univ. College of Veterinary Medicine
http://www.cvm.okstate.edu/

On-Line Mendelian Inheritance in Man
http://gdbwww.gdb.org/omimdoc/omimtop.html

OncoLink
http://cancer.med.upenn.edu/

OPTICS.ORG - The Photonics Resource Center
http://optics.org/

Oxford University Press
http://www.oup.co.uk/

Palo Alto Medical Foundation
http://www.service.com/PAMF/home.html

Pathy for medical information
http://www.med.nagoya-u.ac.jp/pathy/pathy.html

PCR Methods and Applications
http://www.cshl.org/journals/pcr/

Penn State Dept. of Radiology
http://www.xray.hmc.psu.edu/home.html

Pharmacy Case Review
http://pharmacy.isu.edu/pcr/pcr.html

Pharmacy Related Conferences
http://www.cpb.uokhsc.edu/pkin/conf.html

Pharmacy Server
http://157.142.72.77/

Physiological Society
http://physiology.cup.cam.ac.uk/

Physiology and Biophysics
http://www.physiol.washington.edu/pbio/homepage.htm

Poisons Information Database
http://biomed.nus.sg/PID/PID.html

Polio and Post-Polio Resources
http://www.eskimo.com/~dempt/polio.html

Pollen Data
http://www.unlv.edu/CCHD/pollen/

Positron Emission Tomography
http://pss023.psi.ch/

Protein Science (peer-reviewed journal)
http://www.prosci.uci.edu/

Proyecto BioBanco
http://fiss.org.ec/

Psychiatry On-Line and the International Journal of Psychiatry
http://www.cityscape.co.uk/users/ad88/psych.htm

Radiation Research
http://www.whitlock.com/kcj/science/radres/default.htm

Radiology Imaging Ctr.
http://visual-ra.swmed.edu/

Radiology Webserver
http://www.rad.washington.edu/

Raven Press, Medical Publishers
http://www.ravenpress.com/raven/

RNA Journal
http://www.cup.cam.ac.uk/Journals/RNA/RNAHomePage.html

Royal (Dick) School of Veterinary Studies
http://www.vet.ed.ac.uk/

Royal Free Hospital of Medicine
http://www.rfhsm.ac.uk/

Royal Postgraduate Medical School
http://mpcc3.rpms.ac.uk/rpms_home.html

SeqAnalRef
http://expasy.hcuge.ch/sprot/seqanalr.html

Simon Fraser University
http://mendel.mbb.sfu.ca/

SPIE-The Intl. Society for Optical Engineering
http://www.spie.org/

St. Francis Journal of Medicine
http://www.pitt.edu/~leff2/journal/journal.html

Swiss-Shop
http://expasy.hcuge.ch/swisshop/SwissShopReq.html

TALARIA: Clinical Practice Guidelines for Cancer Pain
http://www.stat.washington.edu/

Technical Conference on Plant Genetic Resources
http://web.icppgr.fao.org/

The Scientist
http://ds.internic.net/11/pub/the-scientist

Thomas Jefferson Univ.
http://www.tju.edu/

Threatened Fauna in Australia
http://mac-ra26.sci.deakin.edu.au/fauna.html

TraumAID
http://www.cis.upenn.edu/~traumaid/
home.html

Tulane Medical Ctr.
http://www.mcl.tulane.edu/

U.S. Dept. of Health and Human Services
http://www.os.dhhs.gov/

UC Davis College of Veterinary Medicine
http://vmgopher.ucdavis.edu/

UCLA Dept. of Anesthesiology
http://hypnos.anes.ucla.edu/index.html

UniScience News
http://199.44.59.40/unisci/

Univ. of Bonn Medical Ctr.
http://imsdd.meb.uni-bonn.de/

Univ. of Delaware
http://www.udel.edu/

Univ. of Florida College of Veterinary
Medicine
http://www.vetmed.ufl.edu/

Univ. of Florida, Dept. of Anesthesiology
http://www.anest.ufl.edu/

Univ. of Geneva (ExPASy)
http://expasy.hcuge.ch/

Univ. of Illinois College of Medicine
http://www.med.uiuc.edu/

Univ. of Iowa College of Pharmacy
http://indy.radiology.uiowa.edu/Pharmacy.html

Univ. of Iowa Medical Ctr. (The Virtual
Hospital)
http://indy.radiology.uiowa.edu/
VirtualHospital.html

Univ. of Iowa Virtual Hospital
http://vh.radiology.uiowa.edu/

Univ. of Iowa, College of Medicine, Div. of
Physiologic Imaging
http://everest.radiology.uiowa.edu:8080/
home.html

Univ. of Kansas Medical Ctr.
http://kufacts.cc.ukans.edu/cwis/units/
medcntr/library.html

Univ. of Michigan Dept. of Anesthesiology
http://ganglion.anes.med.umich.edu/

Univ. of Michigan Neurosciences Internet
Resource Guide
http://http2.sils.umich.edu/Public/nirg/
nirg1.html

Univ. of Minnesota Dept. of Food Science
and Nutrition
http://fscn1.fsci.umn.edu/

Univ. of Oregon
http://biology.uoregon.edu/

Univ. of Pennsylvania
http://www.penn.edu/

Univ. of Pennsylvania Medical Image
Processing Group
http://mipgsun.mipg.upenn.edu/

Univ. of Pisa Dept. of Radiology
http://www.rad.unipi.it:7080/
IRMosaicHome.html

Univ. of Pittsburgh Dept. of Anesthesiology and Critical Care Medicine
http://www.pitt.edu/~anes

Univ. of Queensland Anaesthesiology
http://www.uq.oz.au/anaesth/home.html

Univ. of Southampton Biomedical server
http://medstats.soton.ac.uk/

Univ. of Texas/Houston Pathology
http://hyrax.med.uth.tmc.edu/

Univ. of Vermont
http://www.uvm.edu/

Univ. of Washington Dept. of Pathology
http://www.pathology.washington.edu/

Victoria State Emergency Service
http://www.citri.edu.au/~jck/vicses/vicses.html

Victorian (Australia) Institute of Forensic
Pathology
http://www.vifp.monash.edu.au/

Virginia Tech/Univ. of Maryland College
of Veterinary Medicine
http://www.vetmed.vt.edu/

Weizmann Institute Bioinformatics
http://bioinformatics.weizmann.ac.il:70

Welch Medical Library
http://www.welch.jhu.edu/

Whitehead Institute for Biomedical
Research
http://www.wi.mit.edu/

World Health Organization (WHO)
http://www.who.ch/

Meteorology

See also Geology & Geophysics, Oceanography

Usenet Newsgroups

comp.infosystems.gis
Created by: bonnett@seismo.CSS.GOV (H. David Bonnett)
Call for Votes date: January 14, 1992
Newsgroup-based Mailing List: Yes, (gis-l@ubvm.cc.buffalo.edu).
Charter (from Call for Votes):
This newsgroup will be for discussion of the developing field in information managment known as GIS (Geographic Information Systems).

This includes, but is not limited to:

- questions about specific GIS/LIS packages in the public and commercial domains (e.g., MOSS, GRASS, ARC/INFO, ERDAS, ER MAPPER, etc...)

- questions on data issues (e.g., availability, sources, types...)

- discussions about GIS analysis and display methodologies (e.g., image processing, cartography, classification, etc.)

- discussions about users use of GIS for attaining research goals

It is expected that discussions relating to both GIS and other
newsgroups may be cross-posted.

The group will be gatewayed with the existing GIS-L Listserver and the extant bit.gis-l group will be removed upon creation of this group.

sci.geo.eos
Created by:
posinski@nssdca.gsfc.nasa.gov (Cindy Posinski)
Call for Votes date: February 6, 1993
Newsgroup-based Mailing List: No.
Charter (from Call for Votes):
The sci.geo.eos newgroup will be used by the Earth Observing System Data and Information System (EOSDIS) community for the sharing of EOSDIS related information. It will include postings of "The Processor" and "The Earth Observer," newsletters containing timely EOS news events and information on up-coming meetings. The newsgroup will also contain information regarding the availability of new data sets, and other important EOS related material. There are currently hundreds of researchers and scientists around the world involved with EOS, and this would be a great forum for the sharing of ideas.

sci.geo.fluids
Created by: Jerry Miller
<miller@rsmas.miami.edu>
Call for Votes date: April 1990
Newsgroup-based Mailing List: No.
Charter: (from Call for Votes)
The discussion and exchange of information on problems in geophysical fluid dynamics and closely related fields.

sci.geo.geology
Created by: Tom Williams
(williams@pangea.stanford.edu)
Call for Votes date: December 1990
Newsgroup-based Mailing List: No.
Charter (from Call for Votes):
Possible subjects for discussion would include all aspects of solid earth geology and geophysics. (Including, but NOT

limited to: plate tectonics tectonophysics, petrology, mineralogy, volcanology, structural geology, paleontology, sedimentary processes, basin analysis, seismic exploration, seismic stratigraphy, petroleum geology, seismology, geochemistry, glaciation, groundwater hydrology, geochronology, paleomagnetism, paleoclimatology.)

sci.geo.hydrology

Created by: Upmanu Lall
<ulall@pub.uwrl.usu.edu>
Call for Votes date: March 9, 1994
Newsgroup-based Mailing List: No.
Charter (from Call for Votes):
The objective of this newsgroup is to provide a forum for discussion on issues pertaining to surface and groundwater hydrology, their relation to climate, water quality issues and water resource management and policy issues. It is hoped that this will lead to frank and open discussion and identification of key issues and directions in the field, easier identification of and access to data sources, a critical evaluation of modeling and data analysis methodologies, electronic newsletters, and provide a consulting role, and stimulate cooperative research. Announcements of meetings, special sessions and work in progress could be facilitated. We also intend to set up and manage an electronic archive accessible through ftp, gopher, www, and mosaic, that will be used as a repository for contributed manuscripts (and comments), software and data source identifiers, and will operate in conjunction with this news group.

sci.geo.meteorology

Created by: Jason J. Levit
<vortex@vpnet.chi.il.us>
Call for Votes date: March 1991
Newsgroup-based Mailing List: No.
Charter (from Call for Votes):
Our lives are affected daily by the weather. However, this is not new news. In the past few years, meteorology has fast become a cutting-edge science. Scientists are now optimizing the way forecasts are made; supercomputers are studying chaos theory and its relation to the atmosphere; fascinating research is taking place on

severe weather and tornados, with research on new types of radar; microbursts and wind shear are being studied heavily; of course global warming, hurricane research, lightning...the list goes on and on.

This newsgroup was created to foster interesting discussions and to be a benefit to professionals in the field, students, and the general public through the exchange of information on the various topics of the atmosphere.

sci.geo.satellite-nav

Created by: arkusinski_andy@si.com
(Andy Arkusinski)
Call for Votes date: February 15, 1994
Newsgroup-based Mailing List: No.
Charter: sci.geo.satellite-nav was chosen because the focus of this group is on navigation. The SCI.SPACE hierarchy deals with various aspects of space exploration and use, but this newsgroup deals mostly with terrestrial applications. The fact that the space segment is in space is almost incidental to the focus of the newsgroup.

sci.geo.satellite-nav will allow a centralized location for discussion of global navigation satellite systems (GNSS). The charter specifically includes the US Global Positioning System (GPS) and Russian GLONASS, but is also open to discussion of other existing and future satellite positioning systems.

sci.nonlinear

Created by: caddell@csustan.csustan.edu
(Joe Caddell)
Call for Votes date: April 30, 1993
Newsgroup-based Mailing List: No.
Charter (from Call for Votes):
The purpose of this group is to provide a forum for the exchange of ideas in the area of nonlinear science, to discuss any research being done in this field, to provide a means for questions to be answered which people may have concerning nonlinear systems, to announce any conferences, seminars or meetings which may be held concerning nonlinear systems, to exchange ideas,to try

out new ones, and to have fun! The topics of discussion will include, but not be limited to, chaotic systems. Any system which is nonlinear in behavior will be considered as being covered under this charter. The expectation, in creating this group, is that people from a wide range of backgrounds that are interested in nonlinear systems will participate in the discussions. Specifically, it is hoped that theory and experiment will both be involved, as well as a wide variety of disciplines.

Frequently Asked Questions

Meteorology Resources FAQ
Maintainer: ilana@kiowa.scd.ucar.edu (Ilana Stern)
Where on Usenet: sci.geo.meteorology
Where it's archived:
rtfm.mit.edu:pub/usenet/
sci.geo.meteorology
What it's for: References to academic and published sources dealing with meteorology.

Ozone Depletion FAQ
Maintainer: rparson@spot.Colorado.EDU (Robert Parson)
Where on Usenet: sci.environment
Where it's archived:
rtfm.mit.edu:pub/usenet/
sci.geo.meteorology
What it's for: Answers to commonly asked questions on ozone depletion.

Sea Level, Ice, and Greenhouse FAQ
Maintainer: rmg3@access.digex.net (Robert Grumbine)
Where on Usenet: sci.environment
Where it's archived:
rtfm.mit.edu:pub/usenet/sci.environment
What it's for: Global climate issues.

Sources of Meteorological Data FAQ
Maintainer: ilana@kiowa.scd.ucar.edu (Ilana Stern)
Where on Usenet: sci.geo.meteorology
Where it's archived:

rtfm.mit.edu/pub/usenet/
sci.geo.meteorology/
What it's for: An index to the weather resources available on the net.

Tropical Cyclone Weekly Summary
Maintainer: beven@hrd-tardis.nhc.noaa.gov (Jack Beven)
Where on Usenet: sci.geo.meteorology
Where it's archived:
rtfm.mit.edu:pub/usenet/
sci.geo.meteorology
What it's for: A summary of recent tropical cyclonic disturbances.

Discussion Lists

climlist
climlist@psuvm
CLIMLIST Climatology Distribution List

pcgeos-list
listserv@pandora.sf.ca.us
For users of PC/GEOS products.

wx-natnl
wx-natnl@uiucvmd
National Wx Summary and Selected City Fcsts

wx-pcpn
wx-pcpn@uiucvmd
WX-PCPN Precipitation WX products

wxsat
wxsat-request@ssg.com (Richard B. Emerson)
Weather info based on GOES and polar weather satellites.

wx-stlt
wx-stlt@uiucvmd
WX-STLT Satellite interpretive messages

wx-sum
wx-sum@uiucvmd
WX-SUM Summary Weather Products

wx-swo
wx-swo@uiucvmd
WX-SWO Severe Weather Outlooks

wx-talk
wx-talk@uiucvmd
WX-TALK General weather discussions.

wx-tor
wx-tor@uiucvmd
Tornado Warning dissemination

wx-tropl

wx-tropl@uiucvmd
WX-TROPL Tropical Storms and Hurricanes

wx-watch

wx-watch@uiucvmd
WX-WATCH WX Watches and cancellations

wx-wstat

wx-wstat@uiucvmd
WX-WSTAT WX Watch status and storm reports

Meteorology Resources

FTP Resources

AARNet Archive Server
  plaza.aarnet.edu.au/

Carbon Dioxide Information Analysis Ctr.
  cdiac.esd.ornl.gov/pub

CENA, Ctr. for Aerial Navigation Studies
  ada.cenaath.cena.dgac.fr

DMSP
  ftp.ncdc.noaa.gov/

EPF Lausanne
  liasun3.epfl.ch/pub/weather/

GMS
  plaza.aarnet.edu.au/Weather/gms

GOES
  westsat.com/pub/images

Intl. AVS Ctr.
  avs.ncsc.org

Meteosat
  cs.nott.ac.uk/pub/sat-images/

NASA
  boa.gsfc.nasa.gov/Weather/gms/

NASA Explorer
  explorer.arc.nasa.gov/pub/Weather/

NERC Satellite Station, Dundee Univ.
  ftp.sat.dundee.ac.uk/

NOAA (Asia)
  hydro.iis.u-tokyo.ac.jp/data/noaa/

NOAA-11/12 (North America)
  rainbow.physics.utoronto.ca/pub/sat_images/

Satellite IR
  cumulus.met.ed.ac.uk/images/jpeg/

Satellite Japan
  hydro.iis.u-tokyo.ac.jp/data/noaa/

Smithsonian Images
  photo1.si.edu//More.Smithsonian.Stuff/
  nasm.planetarium/weather.gif/

Stanford Univ.
  wilbur.stanford.edu/pub/weathergifs

U.S. Geographical Survey, Lakewood County
  info.er.usgs.gov

Univ. of Nottingham
  cs.nott.ac.uk/pub/

Univ. of Tokyo
  hydro.iis.u-tokyo.ac.jp/data

Univ. Studies on Svalbard
  durnik.unis.no/vaerdata/

Gopher Resources

American Meteorological Society
  atm.geo.nsf.gov

Aviation Weather
  geograf1.sbs.ohio-state.edu./1/wxascii/
  aviation/airways

Austrailian National Univ.
  life.anu.edu.au

Bureau of Meteorology, Melbourne
  babel.ho.bom.gov.au

Canada
  owl.nstn.ns.ca

Climate of Chile
  tortel.dcc.uchile.cl

Croatian Academic and Research Network
  madhz.dhz.hr

Ecole Polytechnique Federale de Lausanne
  cognac-f.epfl.ch

Florida State Univ.
  metlab1.met.fsu.edu

Freie Univ.Berlin
  gopher.fu-berlin.de

GMS
  gopher.ncc.go.jp

GOES Satellite
  gopher.ssec.wisc.edu

Intenational weather observations
metlab1.met.fsu.edu

Intenational Weathermaps
unidata.ucar.edu

Intl. City Report
wx.atmos.uiuc.edu

Japan Satellite
gopher.ncc.go.jp

LSU Southern Regional Climate Ctr.
nevado.srcc.lsu.edu

Meteosat (Deutschland)
gopher.rrz.uni-koeln.de

Meteosat (UK)
src.doc.ic.ac.uk

Michigan State Univ.
burrow.cl.msu.edu

NOAA and GMS Satellite
gopher.ncc.go.jp

NSF Maps
atm.geo.nsf.gov

Purdue Univ.
meteor.atms.purdue.edu

Satellite, Reports
life.anu.edu.au

SSEC Satellite
gopher.ssec.wisc.edu

Temperature and Precipitation Maps
atm.geo.nsf.gov

UCAR Unidata Program Ctr.
unidata.ucar.edu

Univ. Bayreuth
gopher.uni-bayreuth.de

Univ. de Chile
tortel.dcc.uchile.cl

Univ. of Colorado Alliance Research Maps
and Images
www.ucar.edu

Univ. of Edinburgh
src.doc.ic.ac.uk

Univ. of Illinois
wx.atmos.uiuc.edu

Univ. Köln
gopher.rrz.uni-koeln.de

Univ. of Melbourne
gopher.austin.unimeld.edu.au

Univ. of Minnesota
ashpool.micro.umn.edu

Univ. of Wisconsin-Madison
gopher.ssec.wisc.edu

US Cities Statistics
unidata.ucar.edu

Weather of US and Canada
wx.atmos.uiuc.edu

Weathermap Japan
unidata.ucar.edu

Western US Infrared Satellite Image
wx.atmos.uiuc.edu/I9/Images/
Satellite%20Images/Satellite%20West%20IR/
00LATEST.GIF

Zagreb, Meteorological and Hydrological
Service
madhz.dhz.hr

WWW Resources

Alfred Wegener Institute
http://www.awi-bremerhaven.de/

Arizona State Univ.
http://aspin.asu.edu/provider/geography/
climate/

Arkansas Basin River Forecast Ctr.
(NOAA/NWS)
http://gopherpc.abrfc.noaa.gov/abrfc.html

Atmospheric and Oceanic Science at
NCSA
http://redrock.ncsa.uiuc.edu/AOS/home.html

Australian National Univ.
http://life.anu.edu.au/weather.html

BLUE-SKIES for Java
http://cirrus.sprl.umich.edu/javaweather/

Boreal Ecosystem-Atmosphere Study
(BOREAS)
http://boreas.gsfc.nasa.gov/

Centre for Atmospheric Science, Cambridge Univ.
http://www.atm.ch.cam.ac.uk/MiscMet.html

Clima, Satellite Images
http://www.dkrz.de/forschung/forschung.html

Climate Diagnostics Ctr. (CDC)
http://noaacdc.colorado.edu/cdc/
cdc_home.html

Climate Modelling Laboratory
http://www.scar.utoronto.ca/homes/envsci/gough/

Climate Prediction Ctr.
http://nic.fb4.noaa.gov/

Climatic Research Unit
http://www.cru.uea.ac.uk/

Cloud Physics Modelling
http://www.op.dlr.de/~pa1u/

Colorado State Univ. - Atmospheric Science
http://www.atmos.colostate.edu/

Creighton Univ. - Atmospheric Sciences
http://sundog.creighton.edu/cuhome.html

Ctr. for Air Sea Technology of Mississippi Univ.
http://www.cast.msstate.edu/

Ctr. for the Study of Terrestrial and Extraterrestrial Atmospheres (CSTEA)
http://www.cstea.howard.edu/

Current Weather Maps/Movies
http://clunix.cl.msu.edu/weather/

Current Weather, Climate and Forecast Maps
http://grads.iges.org/pix/head.html

Daily Planet
http://www.atmos.uiuc.edu/

Defense Meteorological Satellite Program (DMSP)
http://www.ngdc.noaa.gov/dmsp/dmsp.html

Deutsche Meteorologische Gesellschaft
http://www.met.fu-berlin.de/deutsch/DMG/index.html

Deutsches Klimarechenzentrum
http://www.dkrz.de/

DSU Weatherlink
http://www.dsu.edu/projects/weather/weather.html

Earthquake and Weather Station
http://www.geopages.com/RodeoDrive/1091/

Eindhoven Univ. of Technology (NOS Teletext)
http://www.win.tue.nl/teletext/index.en.html

EISCAT Scientific Association
http://seldon.eiscat.no/homepage.html

European Space Agency - ESA/ESRIN
http://shark1.esrin.esa.it/

FAQ - Weather
http://www.cis.ohio-state.edu/hypertext/faq/usenet/weather/top.html

Finnish Meteorological Institute - Geophysics
http://www.geo.fmi.fi/

Florida Institute of Technology
http://sci-ed.fit.edu/wx.html

Florida State Univ. - Meteorology
http://thunder.met.fsu.edu/

Freien Universität Berlin Institut für Meteorologie
http://www.met.fu-berlin.de/

Geophysical Data of Norway
http://www.service.uit.no/geofysisk/geofysisk.html

Georgia Tech
http://www.gatech.edu/eas/eas.html

Global Atmospheric Modeling
http://rossby.larc.nasa.gov/

Global Energy and Water Cycle Experiment (GEWEX)
http://www.cais.com/gewex/gewex.html

Global Warming Update
http://www.ncdc.noaa.gov/gblwrmupd/global.html

Gold Coast Weather Ocean Chart Access
http://www.vcnet.com/goldcoastwx/home.html

Great Lakes Forecasting System
http://glfs.eng.ohio-state.edu/

GSI Hamburg
http://www.gsi.de/misc/misc.html

HAPEX SAHEL Information System
http://www.orstom.fr/hapex/

Idaho's Weather Station
http://www.mrc.uidaho.edu/weather/weather.html

Indiana Univ. Computer Science Web
http://cs.indiana.edu/

INPE
http://www.inpe.br/

Institut für Meteorologie FU-Berlin
http://www.met.fu-berlin.de/index.html

Institut für Meteorologie und
Klimaforschung Karlsruhe
http://imkhp3.physik.uni-karlsruhe.de/
index.html

Institute for Global Change Research and
Education (IGCRE)
http://space.hsv.usra.edu/

Institute for Global Environment and
Society, Inc.
http://grads.iges.org/home.html

Institute for Meteorology and Climate
Research (Germany)
http://imkhp3.physik.uni-karlsruhe.de/

INTELLiCast
http://www.intellicast.com/

Interactive Marine Observations
http://thunder.met.fsu.edu/~nws/buoy/

Interactive Weather Browser
http://rs560.cl.msu.edu/weather/
interactive.html

Interactive Weather Information Ctr.
http://thunder.atms.purdue.edu/interact.html

Intl. HIRLAM Project
http://www.knmi.nl/hirlam/

Intl. Severe Storms Interceptors
http://www.indirect.com/www/storm5/issi.html

Intl. Society of Biometeorology
http://www.acru.uq.oz.au/~isb

Intl. Weather Watchers
http://groundhog.sprl.umich.edu/IWW/

Irregular Reports about German Weather
http://www.meteocon.nl/meteofax/index.html

Jeremy's WX Reference
http://www.teleport.com/~joebaby/
wxmain.htm

Lawrence Livermore National Laboratory
Atmospheric Research
http://www-ep.es.llnl.gov/www-ep/atm.html

LDEO Climate Data Catalog
http://rainbow.ldgo.columbia.edu/
datacatalog.html

Live Access to Climate Data
http://ferret.wrc.noaa.gov/ferret/main-
menu.html

Lyndon State College
http://apollo.lsc.vsc.edu/

Macquarie Univ. - Atmospheric Science
http://atmos.es.mq.edu.au/

Maryland Earthcast
http://www.metolab3.umd.edu/EARTHCAST/
earthcast.html

Maui Weather Today
http://weather.satlab.hawaii.edu/

McGill - Centre for Climate and Global
Change Research
http://www.meteo.mcgill.ca/

Meteo Consult B.V.
http://www.meteocon.nl/index.html

Meteo France
http://www.meteo.fr/

Meteofax Wetterdienste GmbH
http://www.meteocon.nl/meteofax/index.html

Meteorology Students Mailing List
http://www.met.fu-berlin.de/texte/met-
stud.html

Meteorology Virtual Library
http://www.met.fu-berlin.de/DataSources/
MetIndex.html

Meteorology: Mother of all Bulletin Boards
http://www.cs.colorado.edu/homes/mcbryan/
public_html/bb/41/summary.html

Meteosat
http://www.crs4.it/~luigi/METEO/meteo.html

Meteosat 3 (South America)
http://www.inpe.br/grid/meteosat

Michigan State Univ.
http://rs560.cl.msu.edu/weather/
textindex.html

MIT Ctr. for Meteorology and Physical
Oceanography
http://www-cmpo.mit.edu/CMPOhome.html

MIT Lincoln Laboratory Weather Sensing
Group
http://jaquenetta.wx.ll.mit.edu/

MIT Radar Lab
http://graupel.mit.edu/Radar_Lab.html

MIT Weather Gateway
http://www.mit.edu:8001/weather

MITSA - Weather Page
http://acro.harvard.edu/GA/weather.html

Monthly Temperature Anomalies
http://www.ncdc.noaa.gov/onlineprod/
ghcnmcdwmonth/form.html

Nansen Environmental and Remote Sensing Ctr. (NERSC)
http://www.nrsc.no:8001/

NASA Ames Mars Global Circulation Modeling Group
http://www-mgcm.arc.nasa.gov/MGCM.html

National Climatic Data Ctr. (NCDC)
http://www.ncdc.noaa.gov/

National Ctr. for Atmospheric Research
http://www.ucar.edu/

National Institute of Space Research - INPE Environmental Geochemistry
http://www.met.inpe.br/geochem/home

National Institute of Water and Atmosphere - NIWA
http://www.niwa.cri.nz/

National Severe Storms Laboratory
http://www.nssl.uoknor.edu/

National Weather Service Tallahassee
http://thunder.met.fsu.edu/~nws

Nationwide School Weather Network
http://www.aws.com/index.html

Nationwide Weather Links
http://www.icon.net/users/tornado/tornado.html

Naval Environmental Operational Nowcasting System (NEONS)
http://helium.nrlmry.navy.mil/neons_home.html

NCSU Meteorology
http://meawx1.nrrc.ncsu.edu/

NERC Satellite Station, Dundee Univ.
http://www.sat.dundee.ac.uk/

New Jersey Forecast (WOI)
http://woi.com/woi/weather.html

NEXOR
http://web.nexor.co.uk/places/satelite.html

NOAA Weather Page
http://www.esdim.noaa.gov/weather_page.html

NOAA Weather Venues
http://www.nnic.noaa.gov/weather.html

NOAA-11/12 (Europe)
http://www.sat.dundee.ac.uk/

NOS TeleText
http://www.win.tue.nl/cgi/tt2www/nos/gpage/701-1.html

Ohio State Univ. Dept.
http://www.cis.ohio-state.edu/hypertext/faq/usenet/weather/top.html

Perilous Times
http://www.teleport.com/~jstar/

Pine, Colorado Weathercam
http://www.igc.apc.org/mushroom/pine.html

Planteforsk (The Norwegian Crop Research Institute)
http://norpre.nlh.no/weather/

Plymouth State College Meteorology
http://vortex.plymouth.edu/

POLES
http://psc.apl.washington.edu/poles/

Potsdam Institute for Climate Impact Research
http://www.pik-potsdam.de/

Princeton - Department of Hydroclimatology
http://earth.princeton.edu/

Program for Climate Model Diagnosis and Intercomparison
http://www-pcmdi.llnl.gov/

Purdue Weather Processor
http://thunder.atms.purdue.edu/

Royal Meteorological Society (RMS)
http://typhoon.rdg.ac.uk/rms/rms.html

Rutgers Univ. Meteorology
http://snowfall.rutgers.edu/meteorology/

School of Mathematics UEA
http://www.mth.uea.ac.uk/climateinfo.html

SILMU, The Finnish Research Programme on Climate Change
http://www.etla.fi/Silmu/silmu.html

South Carolina Drought Information Ctr.
http://sercc.dnr.state.sc.us/sc/drought.html

SPAM: Schools of the Pacific Atmosperic Monitoring
http://aaron.gcn.uoknor.edu/spam/index.html

Texas A&M Meteorology
http://www.met.tamu.edu/

Todays Space Weather
http://www.sel.bldrdoc.gov/today.html

Todd Gross' (of Ch. 7, Boston) Weather & Astronomy Page
http://www.weatherman.com/

UC Davis, Atmospheric Science Group
http://www-atm.ucdavis.edu/home.html

UCLA Atmospheric Sciences
http://www.atmos.ucla.edu/

UNAVCO, Univ. NAVSTAR Consortium
http://www.unavco.ucar.edu/

Univ. at Albany, SUNY
http://www.atmos.albany.edu/

Univ. Berlin Meteorology
http://www.met.fu-berlin.de/DataSources/MetIndex.html

U of I - Institute of Aviation Wx Page
http://www.aviation.uiuc.edu/institute/weather.html

UIUC Weather Machine
gopher://wx.atmos.uiuc.edu/1

Univ. of Hawaii
http://lumahai.soest.hawaii.edu/

Univ. of Maryland at College Park
http://metolab3.umd.edu/meteorology.html

Univ. of Missouri - Columbia
http://www.phlab.missouri.edu/~wxcat/

Univ. of New Jersey
http://aristarchus.rutgers.edu/

Univ. of North Carolina at Asheville
http://vortex.atms.unca.edu/

Univ. of North Dakota
http://www.aero.und.nodak.edu/

Univ. of Oklahoma - Ctr. for Analysis and Prediction of Storms
http://wwwcaps.uoknor.edu/

Univ. of Oklahoma - Weather Radar Laboratory
http://aaron.gcn.uoknor.edu/index.html

Univ. of Utah
http://www.met.utah.edu/

Univ. of Washington
http://www.atmos.washington.edu/

USGS Global Change and Climate History
http://geochange.er.usgs.gov/gch.html

Utah Climate Ctr. Network Resources
http://tsunami.agsci.usu.edu/

Virginia State Climatology Office
http://faraday.clas.virginia.edu/~climate

Weather & Global Monitoring
http://life.anu.edu.au/weather.html

Weather Channel
http://www.weather.com

Weather Links
http://dana.ucc.nau.edu/~jdd/weather.html

Weather Report
http://www.best.com/~piraeus/cookies/weathrep.shtml

Weather Station IDs
http://rs560.cl.msu.edu/weather/wids.html

Weather Underground of Hong Kong
http://www.underground.org.hk/

Weather Unit
http://faldo.atmos.uiuc.edu/WEATHER/weather.html

Weather World
http://www.atmos.uiuc.edu/wxworld/html/top.html

Weatherboy Online! Weather Information
http://www.cybercom.com/~weather/

WeatherLinks USA
http://ngwwmall.com/frontier/vortex/

Weatherman
http://www.pixi.com/~gattoga/index.html

WeatherNet
http://cirrus.sprl.umich.edu/wxnet/

WeatherNet4
http://wxnet4.nbc4.com/

WebWeather
http://www.princeton.edu/Webweather/ww.html

World Climate Report
http://www.nhes.com/

World Wide Weather on the Internet
http://www.weather.net/fn/submitit.weather.html

Yankee Weather Index
http://www.tiac.net/users/macgyver/wea.html

Oceanography

See also Geology & Geophysics, Meteorology

Usenet Newsgroups

comp.infosystems.gis

Created by: bonnett@seismo.CSS.GOV (H. David Bonnett)
Call for Votes date: January 14, 1992
Newsgroup-based Mailing List: Yes, (gis-l@ubvm.cc.buffalo.edu).
Charter (from Call for Votes):
This newsgroup will be for discussion of the developing field in information managment known as GIS (Geographic Information Systems).

This includes, but is not limited to:

* questions about specific GIS/LIS packages in the public and commercial domains (e.g., MOSS, GRASS, ARC/INFO, ERDAS, ER MAPPER, etc...)
* questions on data issues (e.g., availability, sources, types...)
* discussions about GIS analysis and display methodologies (e.g., image processing, cartography, classification, etc.)
* discussions about users use of GIS for attaining research goals

It is expected that discussions relating to both GIS and other newsgroups may be cross-posted.

The group will be gatewayed with the existing GIS-L Listserver and the extant bit.gis-l group will be removed upon creation of this group.

sci.geo

Newsgroup-based Mailing List: No.
Charter: General geology.

sci.geo.eos

Created by:
posinski@nssdca.gsfc.nasa.gov (Cindy Posinski)
Call for Votes date: February 6, 1993
Newsgroup-based Mailing List: No.
Charter (from Call for Votes):
The sci.geo.eos newgroup will be used by the Earth Observing System Data and Information System (EOSDIS) community for the sharing of EOSDIS related information. It will include postings of "The Processor" and "The Earth Observer," newsletters containing timely EOS news events and information on up-coming meetings. The newsgroup will also contain information regarding the availability of new data sets, and other important EOS related material. There are currently hundreds of researchers and scientists around the world involved with EOS, and this would be a great forum for the sharing of ideas.

sci.geo.fluids

Created by: Jerry Miller <miller@rsmas.miami.edu>
Call for Votes date: April 1990
Newsgroup-based Mailing List: No.
Charter: (from Call for Votes)
The discussion and exchange of information on problems in geophysical fluid dynamics and closely related fields.

sci.geo.geology

Created by: Tom Williams (williams@pangea.stanford.edu)
Call for Votes date: December 1990
Newsgroup-based Mailing List: No.
Charter (from Call for Votes):
Possible subjects for discussion would include all aspects of solid earth geology and geophysics. (Including, but NOT

limited to: plate tectonics tectonophysics, petrology, mineralogy, volcanology, structural geology, paleontology, sedimentary processes, basin analysis, seismic exploration, seismic stratigraphy, petroleum geology, seismology, geochemistry, glaciation, groundwater hydrology, geochronology, paleomagnetism, paleoclimatology.)

sci.geo.hydrology

Created by: Upmanu Lall
<ulall@pub.uwrl.usu.edu>
Call for Votes date: March 9, 1994
Newsgroup-based Mailing List: No.
Charter (from Call for Votes):
The objective of this newsgroup is to provide a forum for discussion on issues pertaining to surface and groundwater hydrology, their relation to climate, water quality issues and water resource management and policy issues. It is hoped that this will lead to frank and open discussion and identification of key issues and directions in the field, easier identification of and access to data sources, a critical evaluation of modeling and data analysis methodologies, electronic newsletters, and provide a consulting role, and stimulate cooperative research. Announcements of meetings, special sessions and work in progress could be facilitated. We also intend to set up and manage an electronic archive accessible through ftp, gopher, www, and mosaic, that will be used as a repository for contributed manuscripts (and comments), software and data source identifiers, and will operate in conjunction with this news group.

sci.geo.meteorology

Created by: Jason J. Levit
<vortex@vpnet.chi.il.us>
Call for Votes date: March 1991
Newsgroup-based Mailing List: No.
Charter (from Call for Votes):
Our lives are affected daily by the weather. However, this is not new news. In the past few years, meteorology has fast become a cutting-edge science. Scientists are now optimizing the way forecasts are made; supercomputers are studying chaos theory and its relation to the atmosphere; fascinating research is taking place on

severe weather and tornados, with research on new types of radar; microbursts and wind shear are being studied heavily; of course global warming, hurricane research, lightning...the list goes on and on.

This newsgroup was created to foster interesting discussions and to be a benefit to professionals in the field, students, and the general public through the exchange of information on the various topics of the atmosphere.

sci.geo.satellite-nav

Created by: arkusinski_andy@si.com
(Andy Arkusinski)
Call for Votes date: February 15, 1994
Newsgroup-based Mailing List: No.
Charter: sci.geo.satellite-nav was chosen because the focus of this group is on navigation. The SCI.SPACE hierarchy deals with various aspects of space exploration and use, but this newsgroup deals mostly with terrestrial applications. The fact that the space segment is in space is almost incidental to the focus of the newsgroup.

sci.geo.satellite-nav will allow a centralized location for discussion of global navigation satellite systems (GNSS). The charter specifically includes the US Global Positioning System (GPS) and Russian GLONASS, but is also open to discussion of other existing and future satellite positioning systems.

sci.nonlinear

Created by: caddell@csustan.csustan.edu
(Joe Caddell)
Call for Votes date: April 30, 1993
Newsgroup-based Mailing List: No.
Charter (from Call for Votes):
The purpose of this group is to provide a forum for the exchange of ideas in the area of nonlinear science, to discuss any research being done in this field, to provide a means for questions to be answered which people may have concerning nonlinear systems, to announce any conferences, seminars or meetings which may be held concerning nonlinear systems, to exchange ideas,to try

out new ones, and to have fun! The topics of discussion will include, but not be limited to, chaotic systems. Any system which is nonlinear in behavior will be considered as being covered under this charter. The expectation, in creating this group, is that people from a wide range of backgrounds that are interested in nonlinear systems will participate in the discussions. Specifically, it is hoped that theory and experiment will both be involved, as well as a wide variety of disciplines.

sci.physics.computational.fluid-dynamics

Newsgroup-based Mailing List: No.
Charter: Computational fluid dynamics.

Discussion Lists

asaonet
asaonet@uicvm
Oceanic Anthropology Discussion Group

deepsea
deepsea@uvvm
Deep Sea and Vent News

scuba
scuba@tritu
Discussion of SCUBA diving

scuba-d
scuba-d@brownvm
Scuba Digest Redistribution

scuba-l
scuba-l@brownvm
Scuba diving discussion list

Oceanography Resources

FTP Resources

Current-Meter Data-Assembly
  shemesh.oce.orst.edu/pub/dac/

Data Information Unit
  diu.cms.udel.edu/pub/

Dynamic Topography Solutions
  ftp.csr.utexas.edu/pub/sst/

Florida State Univ.
  atlantic.ocean.fsu.edu/pub

GFDL MOM Archive
  ftp.gfdl.gov/pub/GFDL_MOM

Hydrographic Program Data
  nemo.ucsd.edu/

Hydrographic Program SAC
  ftp.dkrz.de/pub/woce/

Institute of Oceanographic Sciences
  wocomms.nwo.ac.uk/pub/

Miami ocean model archive
  nutmeg.rsmas.miami.edu/bleck/

Naval Postgraduate School, Monterey
  taurus.cs.nps.navy.mil/pub/mosaic/
  nps_mosaic.html

NCAR
  huron.scd.ucar.edu/catalogs/.html/
  README.html

NERC Research Vessel Services
  ua.nrb.ac.uk/pub/rvshome.html

Ocean data available at NCAR
  huron.scd.ucar.edu/catalogs/.html/odl.html

PODAAC
  shrimp.jpl.nasa.gov/

Rutgers ocean model archive
  ftp://ahab.rutgers.edu/pub/

Sea Level DAC (Hawaii)
  kia.soest.hawaii.edu/

Univ. of Hawaii Satellite Oceanography Lab.
  satftp.soest.hawaii.edu/pub

Gopher Resources

American Meteorological Society
  atm.geo.nsf.gov/

Aquaculture Network Information Ctr. (AquaNIC)
  thorplus.lib.purdue.edu

Ctr. for Coastal Studies (Scripps)
  gopher-ccs.ucsd.edu

Data Zoo (Scripps)
  gopher-ccs.ucsd.edu

Environmental Internet Catalog
  infoserver.ciesin.org

Habitat Ecology Div., Bedford Institute of Oceanography
  biome.bio.dfo.ca

National Oceanographic Data Ctr.
(NODC)
gopher.nodc.noaa.gov

NOAA Environmental Information
esdim1.nodc.noaa.gov

Ocean information Centre
diu.cms.udel.edu

Ontario Climate Gopher (including CAC
ENSO advisories)
cmits02.dow.on.doe.ca

Scripps Institution of Oceanography
Gopher
sio.ucsd.edu

SSTs from the Univ. of Wisconsin-Madison
SSEC
gopher.ssec.wisc.edu

USGS Branch of Atlantic Marine Geology
bramble.er.usgs.gov

Woods Hole Oceangraphic Institution
gopher.whoi.edu

WWW Resources

Acoustic Thermometry of Ocean Climate
http://atoc.ucsd.edu/

Air Project
http://www-rocq.inria.fr/air/

Alfred Wegener Institute
http://www.awi-bremerhaven.de/

Algalita Marine Research Foundation
http://www.vandelay.com/surfrider/algalita

American Geophysical Union
http://earth.agu.org/kosmos/homepage.html

American Society of Limnology and
Oceanography
http://www.ngdc.noaa.gov/paleo/aslo/
aslo.html

AquaNet
http://www.aquanet.com/aquanet/

Atmospheric & Oceanic Science Group,
NCSA
http://redrock.ncsa.uiuc.edu/AOS/home.html

Australian Oceanographic Data Ctr.
http://www.aodc.gov.au/AODC.html

AWI Polar and Marine Research Database
http://www.awi-Bremerhaven.de/Index/

Baltic Sea Resources
http://biomac.io-warnemuende.de/baltic

Bedford Institute of Oceanography
http://biome.bio.ns.ca/

Bermuda Biological Station for Research,
Inc.
http://www.bbsr.edu/

BODC: The British Oceanographic Data
Ctr.
http://biudc.nbi.ac.uk/bodc/bodcmain.html

British Antarctic Survey
http://www.nerc-bas.ac.uk/

Brookhaven National Laboratory
http://bnloc7.das.bnl.gov/ocean/oasd.html

Canadian Coast Guard College
http://www.cgc.ns.ca/

Centre for Climate and Global Change,
McGill Univ.
http://www.meteo.mcgill.ca/

CME
http://www.ucar.edu/oceanmodel.html

Coastal Ocean Modeling at the USGS
http://crusty.er.usgs.gov/

Common Heritage Corp
http://www.aloha.com/~craven/

Coral Reef Alliance
http://www.coral.org/

Coral Reefs and Mangroves: Modelling
and Management
http://ibm590.aims.gov.au/

CSIRO Marine Laboratories
http://www.ml.csiro.au

Ctr. for Climate and Global Change,
McGill Univ.
http://www.meteo.mcgill.ca

Ctr. for Coastal Physical Oceanography
http://www.ccpo.odu.edu/

Ctr. for Coastal Studies
http://www-ccs.ucsd.edu/

Ctr. for Earth and Ocean Research, Univ. of
Victoria
http://wikyonos.seaoar.uvic.ca/

Ctr. for Earth Observation - Coastal Zone
http://acri.cica.fr/Coastal.html

Ctr. for Marine Science Research
http://www.uncwil.edu/sys$disk1/cmsr/
cmsr.html

Ctr. of Biological Research, La Paz
http://www.cibnor.conacyt.mx

Ctr. of Excellence for Research in Ocean
Sciences
http://www.ceros.org

Ctr. of Scientific Research and Superior
Education, Ensenada
http://www.cicese.mx

Dalhousie Univ.
http://www.phys.ocean.dal.ca

Dartmouth Gulf of Maine Project
http://fundy.dartmouth.edu/

Data Zoo
http://www-ccs.ucsd.edu/ccs/
about_datazoo.html

Deep Submergence Laboratory
http://www.dsl.whoi.edu/

Deep-Sea Research, Univ. of Victoria
http://darwin.ceh.uvic.ca/deepsea/
deepsea.html

Delft Univ. of Technology
http://dutlru8.lr.tudelft.nl

Digital Information Analysis Laboratory
http://tone.whoi.edu/

Distributed Ocean Data System
http://lake.mit.edu/dods.html

DOE Survey of CO2 in the Oceans
http://www.oasdpo.bnl.gov/~oasdpo/mosaic/
DOECO2/

DSI: Information processing System
Development
http://www.ifremer.fr:80/ditidsiw3/

Earth Sciences Virtual Library
http://www.geo.ucalgary.ca/VL-
EarthSciences.html

El Nino and climate-related information
http://rainbow.ldeo.columbia.edu/

El Nino Theme Page
http://www.pmel.noaa.gov/toga-tao/el-nino/
home.html

Electronic Journals
http://www.mth.uea.ac.uk/ocean/
oceanography.html#electronicjournals

Electronic preprint archive
http://www.gfdl.gov/~smg/pointers/
announcement.html

Environment Virtual Library
http://ecosys.drdr.virginia.edu/
Environment.html

Environmental and Engineering Geophysical Society (EEGS)
http://www.esd.ornl.gov:80/EEGS/

Environmental Information Services
http://www.esdim.noaa.gov/

Environmental Research Laboratories
http://www.erl.gov/

ESA/ESRIN Ionia Global AVHRR Data Set
Browser
http://shark1.esrin.esa.it/

Estuarine and Coastal Oceanography
Laboratory, Univ. of South Carolina
http://coast.geol.scarolina.edu/office.html

European Geophysical Society (EGS)
http://www.mpae.gwdg.de/EGS/EGS.html

Fachbereich Geowissenschaften der
Universität Bremen
http://www.palmod.uni-bremen.de/

Finnish Institute of Marine Research
http://www.fimr.fi/

Five-College Marine Science WWW Guide
http://geology.smith.edu/marine/marine.html

Flinders Institute for Atmospheric and
Marine Sciences, Adelaide
http://www.es.flinders.edu.au/FIAMS/

Florida State Univ.
http://ocean.fsu.edu/

FRAM
http://www.mth.uea.ac.uk/ocean/fram.html

Geophysical Fluid Dynamics Lab.
http://www.gfdl.gov/gfdl.html

Geophysical Institute, Univ. of Bergen
http://www.gfi.uib.no/

Geophysics Virtual Library
http://www-crewes.geo.ucalgary.ca/VL-
Geophysics.html

German Climate Computer Ctr.
http://www.dkrz.de/

German Virtual Library - Geosciences
  http://www.rz.uni-karlsruhe.de/Outerspace/
  VirtualLibrary/55.html

GFDL Modular Ocean Model
  http://www.gfdl.gov/MOM/MOMWWW.html

GLOBEC Georges Bank Information
  http://lake.mit.edu/globec.html

Great Lakes Forecasting System, Ohio
  State Univ.
  http://glfs.eng.ohio-state.edu

Gulf of Maine Project, Dartmouth
  http://fundy.dartmouth.edu/

Habitat Ecology Div., Bedford Institute of
  Oceanography
  http://biome.bio.ns.ca/

Hadley Ctr.
  http://www.meto.govt.uk/sec5/sec5pg1.html

Helium Isotope Laboratory
  http://kopernik.whoi.edu/

Hopkins Marine Station, Stanford Univ.
  http://www-marine.stanford.edu/

Hydrographic Atlas of the Southern Ocean
  http://www.awi-bremerhaven.de/Atlas/SO/
  Deckblatt.html

Icelandic Fisheries Laboratories
  http://www.rfisk.is/

IFREMER
  http://www.ifremer.fr/

Inland Waters, Coastal and Oceans
  Information Network
  http://192.139.141.30/

Institut Pierre Simon Laplace-Numerical
  Modelling Group
  http://www-ipsl.lodyc.jussieu.fr

Institute for Marine and Atmospheric
  Research Utrecht
  http://ruund3.fys.ruu.nl

Institute of Geophysics and Planetary
  Physics
  http://igpp.ucsd.edu/

Institute of Marine and Coastal Sciences,
  Rutgers Univ.
  http://marine.rutgers.edu

Institute of Marine Research, Bergen
  http://www.imr.no/0N/IMR.html

Institute of Numerical Mathematics,
  Russian Academy of Sciences
  http://www.ac.msk.su/local.docs/inm/inm.html

Institute of Oceanographic Sciences
  http://www.nerc.ac.uk/ios/

Institute of Oceanology PAS, Sopot,
  Poland
  http://www.iopan.gda.pl/

International Arctic Buoy Program
  http://iabp.apl.washington.edu/

International Council for the Exploration
  of the Sea, ICES
  http://www.ices.inst.dk/

InterRidge
  http://www.dur.ac.uk/~dgl0zz1/

James Rennell Centre
  http://www.nso.ac.uk/

JAMSTEC: Japan Marine Science &
  Technology Ctr.
  http://www.jamstec.go.jp/

Joint Research Ctr.
  http://me-www.jrc.it/home.html

KK Tech International, Hong Kong
  http://www.hk.linkage.net/~kkt/

Lamont-Doherty Earth Observatory
  http://www.ldeo.columbia.edu

LDEO Climate Data Catalog
  http://rainbow.ldgo.columbia.edu/
  datacatalog.html

Live DMS Ocean Biological Model
  http://me-www.jrc.it/dms/dms.html

LLNL Climate Model Diagnosis and
  Intercomparison
  http://www-pcmdi.llnl.gov

Marine Biological Laboratory
  http://www.mbl.edu/

Marine Geology and Geophysics Servers
  http://www.ngdc.noaa.gov/mgg/othermarine/
  othermarine.html

Marine Minerals Bibliography and
  Database
  http://www.ngdc.noaa.gov/mgg/geology/
  mmdb.html

Marine Research Institute - Iceland
  http://www.hafro.is/

Marine Sciences Research Ctr., Stony Brook
http://www.msrc.sunysb.edu/

Mediterranean Oceanic Data Base
http://modb.oce.ulg.ac.be

Meteorology Virtual Library
http://www.met.fu-berlin.de/DataSources/MetIndex.html

Miami Isopycnic Coordinate Model
http://www.rsmas.miami.edu/groups/micom.html

Mississippi State Univ. Ctr. for Air Sea Technology
http://www.cast.msstate.edu/

MIT Ctr. for Meteorology and Physical Oceanography
http://www-cmpo.mit.edu/CMPOhome.html

MMarie, Application of High Performance Computing Techniques for the Modeling of Marine Ecosystems
http://www.kuleuven.ac.be/mmarie/

Mother of all Bulletin Boards: Meteorology
http://www.cs.colorado.edu/homes/mcbryan/public_html/bb/41/summary.html

Nansen Environmental and Remote Sensing Ctr., Bergen
http://www.nrsc.no:8001/

NASA Earth Observing System (EOS) Project
http://spso2.gsfc.nasa.gov/spso_homepage.html

NASA Global Change Master Directory
http://gcmd.gsfc.nasa.gov/

NASA Goddard Physical Oceanography Group
http://oraac.gsfc.nasa.gov/~rienecke/phys_o_home_page.html

NASA Goddard Space Flight Ctr.
http://hypatia.gsfc.nasa.gov/NASA_homepage.html

NASA Jet Propulsion Lab
http://podaac-www.jpl.nasa.gov/

NASA SeaWiFS Project
http://seawifs.gsfc.nasa.gov/seawifs.html

NASA TOPEX/POSEIDON
http://topex-www.jpl.nasa.gov/

NASA/NOAA AVHRR Oceans Pathfinder
http://podaac-www.jpl.nasa.gov/sst/

National Estaurine Research Reserve Centralized Data Management
http://inlet.geol.scarolina.edu/nerrscdmo.html

National Marine Fisheries Service
http://kingfish.ssp.nmfs.gov/home-page.html

National Oceanographic Data Ctr. (NODC)
http://www.nodc.noaa.gov/index.html

NATO SACLANT Undersea Research Ctr.
http://www.saclantc.nato.int/

Naval Architecture and Ocean Engineering Virtual Library
http://arioch.gsfc.nasa.gov/wwwvl/engineering.html#naval

Naval Command, Control & Ocean Surveillance Ctr..
http://trout.nosc.mil/NCCOSCMosaicHome.html

Naval Oceanographic Office
http://www.navo.navy.mil/

Naval Research Laboratory
http://www.nrl.navy.mil/

NCAR
http://www.ucar.edu/metapage.html

Near-Earth Navigation & Geodesy Section ESOC
http://nng.esoc.esa.de/

NEMO - Oceanographic Data Server (SIO)
http://nemo.ucsd.edu/

Newcastle Univ.
http://www.ncl.ac.uk/~nmscmweb/mscm/index.html

New Zealand Limnological Society
http://webtwo.rsnz.govt.nz/limsoc/limsoc.html

NOAA Web Servers (many)
http://www.noaa.gov

North Atlantic Fisheries College
http://www.zetnet.co.uk/nafc/

Northeast Fisheries Science Ctr.
http://www.wh.whoi.edu/noaa.html

NRaD
http://trout.nosc.mil/NRaDMosaicHome.html

OCCAM
http://www.mth.uea.ac.uk/ocean/occam.html

Ocean Acoustics Laboratory
http://www.oal.whoi.edu/

Ocean Awareness
http://www.cs.fsu.edu/projects/sp95ug/
group1.7/ocean1.html

Ocean Drilling Program, Texas A&M
http://www-odp.tamu.edu

Ocean Information Center (OCEANIC)
http://diu.cms.udel.edu/

Ocean Information Technology Showcase
http://www.summit.halifax.ns.ca/oceans/

Ocean Research Institute, Univ. of Tokyo,
Japan
http://www.ori.u-tokyo.ac.jp/

Ocean Systems Laboratory, Heriot Watt,
Edinburgh
http://anchovy.cee.hw.ac.uk

Ocean Voice International
http://www.conveyor.com/oceanvoice.html

Ocean-Science Related Acronyms
http://www.pmel.noaa.gov/pubs/
acromain.html

Oceanographic & Earth Science Institutions Directory
http://orpheus.ucsd.edu/sio/dataserv/

Oceanographic USENET News groups
http://www.mth.uea.ac.uk/ocean/
oceanography.html#usenet

Oceanography and Atmospheric Science
Hotlist
http://bnloc7.das.bnl.gov/ocean/

Oceanography Society
http://www.tos.org/

Oceanography Virtual Library
http://www.mth.uea.ac.uk/ocean/
oceanography.html

Oceanography WWW servers
http://www.whoi.edu/html/www-servers/
oceanography.html

Oceanor, Trondheim
http://www.oceanor.no/

Oceans and Ice Branch
http://biggles.gsfc.nasa.gov/~adamec/
971.home_page

Old Dominion Univ.
http://www.ocean.odu.edu/

Oregon Sea Grant Home Page
http://seagrant.orst.edu

Oregon State Univ.
http://www.oce.orst.edu

Our Living Oceans Annual Report
http://kingfish.ssp.nmfs.gov/olo.html

Oxford Univ.
http://www-atm.atm.ox.ac.uk/index.html

Pacific Knowledge Research Foundation
http://pk.org/pkrf

Pacific Marine Environmental Lab.
(PMEL)
http://www.pmel.noaa.gov/pmelhome.html

Pacific Sea Surface Temperature Images
http://satftp.soest.hawaii.edu/avhrr.html

Parallel Ocean Program (POP) Model
http://dubhe.cc.nps.navy.mil/~braccio/

Patagonian Shelf - Falkland Islands
Models
http://biudc.nbi.ac.uk/gslc/glorioso.html

Pathfinder Cafe: AVHRR SST Image
Archive
http://satori.gso.uri.edu/archive/images.html

Physical Oceanography Distributed Active
Archive Ctr.
http://seazar.jpl.nasa.gov/

Physical Oceanography Group
http://oraac.gsfc.nasa.gov/~rienecke/
phys_o_home_page.html

Physical Oceanography Research Div.
http://jedac2.ucsd.edu/

Planetary Coral Reef Foundation
http://pk.org/pcrf

Plymouth Marine Laboratory
http://www.npm.ac.uk/

Princeton Univ. Geophysical Fluid
Dynamics Laboratory
http://www.gfdl.gov/

Proudman Oceanographic Laboratory
http://biudc.nbi.ac.uk/

Radio Expeditions' Ocean of Life
http://www.npr.org/RE/

Reef Ball Development Group Ltd
http://www.america.net/~reefball/

REINAS Project
http://sapphire.cse.ucsc.edu/MosaicMet/top-view.html

Remote Sensing Virtual Library
http://www.vtt.fi/aut/ava/rs/virtual/

RIDGE Multibeam Synthesis Project
http://imager.ldeo.columbia.edu/

Ridge Inter Disciplinary Global Experiment
http://copper.whoi.edu/RIDGE

Rosenstiel School of Marine and Atmospheric Science
http://www.rsmas.miami.edu/

SALMON: Sea Air Land Modeling Operational Network
http://modb.oce.ulg.ac.be/SALMON/Welcome.html/

San Diego's Ocean
http://orpheus.ucsd.edu/sio/ocean/

Satellite and Ocean Dynamics Branch
http://www.grdl.noaa.gov/SAT/SAT.html

Satellite Observing Systems
http://www.satobsys.co.uk

Save Our Seas
http://www.hotspots.hawaii.com/sos.html

School of Ocean and Earth Science Technology
http://www.soest.hawaii.edu/

School of Ocean Sciences
http://www.sos.bangor.ac.uk/

sci.geo.meteorology FAQ
http://www.cis.ohio-state.edu/hypertext/faq/usenet/weather/top.html

Scripps directory of oceanographic servers
http://orpheus.ucsd.edu/sio/inst/

Scripps Institution of Oceanography
http://sio.ucsd.edu/

Sea Surface Temperature Satellite Images
http://dcz.gso.uri.edu/avhrr-archive/archive.html

SeaWiFS Project
http://seawifs.gsfc.nasa.gov/SEAWIFS.html

SISMER: Marine Scientific Information Systems
http://www.ifremer.fr/sismer/

Skidaway Institute of Oceanography
http://minnow.skio.peachnet.edu/

South African Data Ctr. for Oceanography
http://fred.csir.co.za/ematek/sadco/sadco.html

Southampton Oceanography Ctr.
http://www.soc.soton.ac.uk/

Southern California Sea Grant Program
http://www.usc.edu/dept/seagrant/seagrant.html

Space Research and Technology, Delft Univ. of Technology
http://dutlru8.lr.tudelft.nl/

Stable Isotope Laboratory, Univ. of East Anglia, Norwich
http://www2.env.uea.ac.uk/sil/ocean.html

Stellwagen Bank National Marine Sanctuary
http://vineyard.er.usgs.gov/

Stephen Birch Aquarium-Museum
http://aqua.ucsd.edu/

Supplements to Atmospheric & Oceanic Publications
http://www-cmpo.mit.edu/met_links/index.html

Technical Univ. of Denmark
http://www.ish.dtu.dk/

Technology Review
http://www.mit.edu:8001/afs/athena/org/t/techreview/www/tr.html

Texas A&M Univ.
http://www-ocean.tamu.edu/

Tidal Modelling, Applied Mathematics, Univ. of Adelaide
http://michell.maths.adelaide.edu.au/UA_DAM_FLUIDS/TIDAL/tidalhome.html

TOGA COARE International Project Office
http://www.coare.ucar.edu/

Topex/Poseidon - The Ocean Topography Experiment
http://topex-www.jpl.nasa.gov/

U.K. Ocean Drilling Program
http://www.dur.ac.uk/~dgl0zz3/

U.S. Coast Guard Navigation Ctr.
http://www.navcen.uscg.mil

USGS Oceanography Resources
http://www.usgs.gov/network/science/earth/oceanography.html

U.S. JGOFS Information
http://lake.mit.edu/jgofs.html

U.S. Joint Global Ocean Flux Study
(JGOFS)
http://www1.whoi.edu/jgofs.html

US Navy Advanced Arctic Ocean model
with sea ice
http://vislab-www.nps.navy.mil/~braccio/
maslowski/arctic.html

US Navy Fleet Numerical Meteorology
and Oceanography Ctr.
http://www.fnoc.navy.mil/

US Navy Parallel Ocean Climate Model
http://vislab-www.nps.navy.mil/~rtt/

U.S. WOCE
http://www-ocean.tamu.edu/WOCE/
uswoce.htm

UNAVCO
http://www.unavco.ucar.edu/

Under Waterworld, Deep Sea
Submersibles off Oregon
http://www.teleport.com/~samc/seas/
deep1.html

Underwater Technology
http://www.u-net.com/scotweb/rov/home.htm

Univ. of Alaska, Fairbanks
http://www.ims.alaska.edu:8000/

Univ. of British Columbia
http://www.ocgy.ubc.ca/

Univ. of California at Davis
http://www-wfb.ucdavis.edu/

UC Santa Cruz
http://scilibx.ucsc.edu/iamslic/ucsc/ucsc.html

Univ. of Cape Town, South Africa
http://emma.sea.uct.ac.za/

Univ. of Colorado Astrodynamics Research
http://shaman.colorado.edu

Univ. of Colorado, Boulder
http://marigold.colorado.edu/

Univ. of Delaware
http://triton.cms.udel.edu/

Univ. of East Anglia, Norwich
http://www.mth.uea.ac.uk/climateinfo.html

Univ. of Guelph
http://www.uoguelph.ca/zoology/ocean/
indexg.htm

Univ. of Hawaii
http://www.soest.hawaii.edu/

Univ. of Massachusetts/Boston
http://www.es.umb.edu/

Univ. of North Carolina at Wilmington
http://www.uncwil.edu/sys$disk1/cmsr/
welcome.html

Univ. of Rhode Island
http://www.gso.uri.edu/

Univ. of Southern Mississippi/Stennis
Space Ctr.
http://www.coam.usm.edu/

Univ. of Tokyo Underwater Robotics and
Application Lab.
http://manta.iis.u-tokyo.ac.jp/Welcome-e.html

Univ. of Tokyo, Ocean Research Institute
http://www.ori.u-tokyo.ac.jp/

Univ. of Trieste
http://oce715a.ogs.trieste.it/

Univ. of Washington
http://www.ocean.washington.edu/

Univ. of Washington Fisheries
http://www.fish.washington.edu/

UNSW Mathematics Fluid Dynamics
Group, Sydney
http://solution.maths.unsw.edu.au/
WWW.fluids/homepage/

Wave Vectors from APL Processor, John
Hopkins Univ.
ftp://fermi.jhuapl.edu/sirc/sirc.html

WHOI Deep Submergence Lab.
http://www.dsl.whoi.edu/

WHOI Helium Isotope Lab.
http://kopernik.whoi.edu/

WHOI Marine Biology Lab.
http://alopias.mbl.edu/Default.html

WHOI Ocean Acoustics Lab.
http://www.oal.whoi.edu/

WHOI Ridge Inter Disciplinary Global
Experiment
http://copper.whoi.edu/RIDGE

Optics

See also Aeronautics & Aerospace, Astronomy & Astrophysics, Biology & Biotechnology, Computer Science, Engineering, Imaging Technologies, Medicine, Physics, Virtual Reality

Usenet Newsgroups

sci.optics
Created by: ebstokes@maxwell.crd.ge.com
Call for Votes date: December 1990
Newsgroup-based Mailing List: No.
Charter: Optics.

sci.techniques.mag-resonance
Created by:
mark@ginger.biophys.upenn.edu (Mark Elliott)
Call for Votes date: April 8, 1994
Newsgroup-based Mailing List: No.
Charter (from Call for Votes):
Sci.techniques.mag-resonance will exist for discussion in the field of magnetic resonance imaging and spectroscopy. Possible topics include requests for information, scientific observations, and commentary on all aspects of magnetic resonance. The group would place equal emphasis on clinical studies, new techniques, and basic research. It will be an unmoderated newsgroup.

Some of the topics to be discussed are:

*   Questions and answers on the use/ performance of commercial MR spectrometers (GE, SIEMENS, PHILIPS, BRUKER, ...)
*   Exchange of pulse sequence algorithms as well as actual implementations.
*   Discussion of recent journal articles.
*   Results of clinical studies.
*   Echo relevant postings found in other, possibly overlooked, newsgroups.

sci.techniques.microscopy
Created by: John.F.Mansfield@umich.edu (John F. Mansfield)
Call for Votes date: January 3, 1994
Newsgroup-based Mailing List: No.
Charter (from Call for Votes):
The main aim of sci.techniques.microscopy is to provide an open forum for the discussion of microscopy and related fields on the Internet.

sci.techniques.spectroscopy
Created by: David Knapp <knapp@spot.colorado.edu>
Call for Votes date: January 24, 1994
Newsgroup-based Mailing List: No.
Charter (from Call for Votes):
The main aim of sci.techniques.spectroscopy is to provide an open forum for the discussion of spectroscopy and related fields on the Internet and to provide a catalyst for improved dissemination of information between those working with spectroscopy.

Discussion Lists

catia-l
catia-l@suvm
Computer Aided Three-Dimensional Interactive Applications
info-adopt
info-adopt@spie.org
Adaptive Optics
info-bios
info-bios@spie.org
BiOS (Biomedical Optics Society)
info-ei
info-ei@spie.org

info-fibers
info-fibers@spie.org
Fiber Optics

info-holo
info-holo@spie.org
Holography

info-lasersrc
info-lasersrc@spie.org
Laser Sources

info-lasertrans
info-lasertrans@spie.org
Laser Transmission

info-opcom
info-opcom@spie.org
Optical Processing and Computing

info-optomech
info-optomech@spie.org
Optomechanical and Precision Instrument
Design

info-robo
info-robo@spie.org
Robotics and Machine Vision

ingrafx
ingrafx@ubvm
Information graphics

opt-proc
opt-proc@taunivm
Optical Computing and Holography List

photo-l
photo-l@buacca
Photography Forum

povgui-l
povgui-l@trearn

Optics Resources

FTP Resources

Optical Society of America
ftp.osa.org

SPIE—The International Society for
Optical Engineering
ftp.spie.org

Gopher Resources

ACS
acsinfo.acs.org

Ctr. for Advanced Space Studies
cass.jsc.nasa.gov

IEEE Gopher
gopher.ieee.org

Laval Univ.
gopher.ulaval.ca/

National Science Foundation
stis.nsf.gov

U.S. Agency for Intl. Development
(USAID)
gopher.info.usaid.gov

UC/Berkeley Astronomy
worms.berkeley.edu:1234

WWW Resources

Advanced Research Projects Agency
(ARPA)
http://ftp.arpa.mil/

American Astronomical Society
http://blackhole.aas.org/AAS-homepage.html

American Institute of Physics
http://aip.org/

American Mathematical Society
http://www.ams.org

American Physical Society
http://aps.org/

Amerinex Artificial Intelligence, Inc.
http://www.aai.com/

Ansel Adams photographs
http://bookweb.cwis.uci.edu:8042/
SlicedExhibit/oru.html

Association for Computing Machinery
http://www.acm.org

Astronomy and Astrophysics Virtual
Library
http://www10.w3.org/hypertext/DataSources/
bySubject/astro/astro.html

Astronomy Group, Univ. of Manchester
http://axp2.ast.man.ac.uk:8000/

AT&T Bell Laboratories
http://www.research.att.com/

Bell Atlantic
http://www.ba.com/ba.html

Biomedical Optics Society
http://www.spie.org/web/working_groups/
biomedical_optics/bios_desc.html

Boston Univ. Center for Photonics Research
http://eng.bu.edu/Photonics_Center/

California Institute of Technology
http://www.caltech.edu/

Canada-France-Hawaii Telescope
http://www.cfht.hawaii.edu/

Capovani New and Used Optical Equipment
http://www.capovani.com/

Carnegie Mellon Univ. Computer Vision
http://www.cs.cmu.edu:8001/afs/cs/project/cil/ftp/html/vision.html

CASIX
http://www.newsight.com/newsight/casix.htm

Center for Electromagnetic Materials and Optics Systems
http://www.uml.edu/Dept/EE/RCs/CEMOS

Center for Extreme Ultraviolet Astrophysics
http://cea-ftp.cea.berkeley.edu/HomePage.html

Center for Nondestructive Evaluation (Iowa State University)
http://www.cnde.iastate.edu/cnde.html

Center for Particle Astrophysics
http://physics7.berkeley.edu/home.html

Charged Particle Optics Software
http://wwwdo.tn.tudelft.nl/bbs/cposis.htm

CIDTECH (CID cameras)
http://www.cidtec.com/info/cid/index.html

CIE - International Commission on Illumination
http://www.hike.te.chiba-u.ac.jp/ikeda/CIE/home.html

COBRA InterUniv. Research Institute on Communication Technology
http://www.cobra.tue.nl/

Coherent Laser Instrument Div.
http://cid.cohr.com/

Colorado State Univ.
http://www.lance.colostate.edu/optical/index.html

Colorado Video
http://www.colorado-video.com

Conferences, Workshops, etc.
http://www.automatrix.com/conferences/

CONNECT - New England Alliance of Photonics Technology Deployment
http://www.eotc.tufts.edu/CONNECT.html

Consortium for Optical and Optoelectric Technologies in Computing
http://co-op.gmu.edu

COSMIC Information Services
http://www.cosmic.uga.edu/

Curt Deckert Associates
http://www.deltanet.com/cda

Cygnus Support
http://www.cygnus.com

Defense Research and Engineering
http://www.acq.osd.mil/ddre

Defense Technology Information Ctr.
http://www.dtic.dla.mil/defenselink

Delft Univ. of Technology Electronic Instrumentation Laboratory
http://guernsey.et.tudelft.nl/

Delft Univ. of Technology Optics Research Group
http://www.tn.tudelft.nl/optica/optica.html

Delft Univ. of Technology Pattern Recognition Group
http://galaxy.ph.tn.tudelft.nl:2000/pr-intro.html

Department of Energy (U.S.)
http://apollo.osti.gov/home.html

DLR Particle Image Velocimetry course
http://www.dlr.de/dlr_calendar_PIV.html

Duisburg Univ., Optoelectronic Department
http://optorisc.uni-duisburg.de/

DVC Company
http://www.optics.org/dvc/dvc.htm

Early Instruments of the Institute of Physics of Naples: Optics Instruments
http://hpl33.na.infn.it/Museum/Optics.html

Electro-Optics Technology Ctr. (EOTC)
http://www.eotc.tufts.edu/

Electron Microscope Images
http://www.uq.oz.au/nanoworld/images_1.html

EULF
  http://luce.iesl.forth.gr/~ulf/ulfhome.htm

European Optical Society
  http://www-eos.unine.ch

European Physical Society
  http://www.nikhef.nl/www/pub/eps/eps.html

European Southern Observatory
  http://http.hq.eso.org/eso-homepage.html

European Space Agency
  http://www.esrin.esa.it/

European Space Research and Technology
Centre
  http://www.estec.esa.nl/

European Ultraviolet Laser Facility
  http://luce.iesl.forth.gr/~ulf/ulfhome.htm

Federal Laboratory Consortium for
Technology Transfer
  http://ixc.net/zyn/trpa.html

FedWorld Information Network
  http://www.fedworld.gov/

Fiber Optic Marketplace
  http://fiberoptic.com/

Fraunhofer Resource Center for Laser
Technology
  http://www.ilt.fhg.de/

Friedrich-Schiller-Univ. Jena, Physics and
Astronomy
  http://einstein.physik.uni-jena.de/

General Imaging Corporation
  http://www.gicorp.com

German Aerospace Research Establishment (DLR)
  http://www.dlr.de/

Harvard Univ. Experimental and Optical
Physics
  http://em-office.harvard.edu/
  MazurPhysWWW.html

Harvest search software from Univ. of
Colorado
  http://harvest.cs.colorado.edu/

High Energy Physics Automated E-print
Archives
  http://xxx.lanl.gov/

High Energy Physics Information Server
  http://www.hep.net/

High Performance Computing Article
Archive
  http://www.lpac.qmw.ac.uk/SEL-HPC/Articles/
  index.html

Hologramas de Mexico
  www.holomex.com

Hughes STX Corporation
  http://info.stx.com/

Human Computer Interaction Article
Archive
  http://www.lpac.qmw.ac.uk/SEL-HPC/Articles/
  HciArchive.html

Human Computer Interaction Bibliography
  http://www.tu-graz.ac.at/CHCIbib

Human Interface Technology Laboratory
  http://www.hitl.washington.edu/

Icarus — The International Journal of Solar
System Studies
  http://astrosun.tn.cornell.edu/Icarus/
  Icarus.html

IEE
  http://www.iee.org.uk

IEEE
  http://www.ieee.org

Image Processing and Analysis Group
  http://noodle.med.yale.edu/

Institute of Computer Science, Hebrew
Univ. of Jerusalem
  http://www.cs.huji.ac.il/

Institute of Physics
  http://www.iop.org

Institute of Physics Publishing
  http://www.ioppublishing.com/IOPP/
  ioppwelcome.html

Instituto de Astrofisica de Canarias
  http://www.iac.es/

International Commission on Illumination
  http://www.hike.te.chiba-u.ac.jp/ikeda/CIE/
  home.html

Intl. Standards Organization (ISO)
  http://www.hike.te.chiba-u.ac.jp/ikeda/ISO/
  home.html

IRIA Infrared Information Analysis
Center, ERIM
  http://www.erim.org/IRIA/iria.html

IS&T — Society for Imaging Science & Technology
http://www.imaging.org

ISPRS Congress 1996
http://www.ipf.tuwien.ac.at/isprs.html

KAOS Advanced Optoelectronic Systems Research Group
http://drip.colorado.edu/

Laboratory for Materials, Device and Circuit Simulation
http://nida.eng.wayne.edu/

Lambda Research Corporation
http://www.lambdares.com/

Large Binocular Telescope Information System
http://euterpe.arcetri.astro.it/

Laser Focus World
http://www.lfw.com

Laser Stars
http://www.achilles.net/~jtalbot

Laser WWW Information Server
http://www.law.indiana.edu/misc/laser.html

Lasers & Electro-Optics Society (IEEE)
http://msrc.wvu.edu/leos/

Lattice High Energy Physics
http://info.desy.de/user/projects/Lattice.html

Laval Univ. (in English)
http://www.ulaval.ca/texte.anglais.html

Lawrence Berkeley Lab.
http://www.lbl.gov/LBL.html

Lawrence Livermore National Lab.
http://www.llnl.gov/

Lebedev Physical Institute
http://www.lpi.msk.su/

Lightwave Communications Research Laboratory
http://optics.genie.uottawa.ca:8080/LtComResLab.html

Liquid Mirror Telescope, University of British Columbia
http://www.geop.ubc.ca/~cabanac/lmt.html

loQtus: Quotations Resources on the Internet
http://pubweb.ucdavis.edu/Documents/Quotations/homepage.html

Los Alamos National Lab.
http://www.lanl.gov/

Lunar and Planetary Institute
http://cass.jsc.nasa.gov/lpi.html

Martin Marietta Energy Systems
http://www.ornl.gov/mmes.html

Materials Research Society
http://dns.mrs.org/

Matlin Space Science Systems
http://barsoom.msss.com/

Maui High Performance Computing Center
http://www.mhpcc.edu/mhpcc.html

McDonnell Douglas Corporation
http://pat.mdc.com/

McGill Univ. - Physics Servers around the World
http://www.physics.mcgill.ca/deptdocs/physics_services.html

Medical Radiography Home Page
HTTP://users.aol.com/ricter/private/home/med.rad.home.html

Mercury Project: Remote Robotic Tele-excavation via WWW
http://www.usc.edu/dept/raiders/

Micro-Electromechanical Systems Information Clearinghouse
http://esto.sysplan.com/ESTO/MEMS/

Microcosm, Inc.
http://www.softaid.net/spark

MIT Media Lab
http://www.media.mit.edu/

MIT Microsystems Technology Laboratories
http://www-mtl.mit.edu/

Molecular Manufacturing Shortcut Group
http://www.gpl.net/mmsg/mmsg.html

Molecular Optoelectronics Corp.
http://www.automatrix.com/moec/

Mossberg Optical Physics Laboratory
http://opticb.uoregon.edu/~mosswww/Home.html

Motion Analysis FAQ
http://www.redlake.com/imaging/faq.htm

Mount Wilson Observatory
http://www.mtwilson.edu/

NASA
http://hypatia.gsfc.nasa.gov/
NASA_homepage.html

NASA Astrophysics Data System Abstract
Service
http://adswww.harvard.edu/abs_doc/
abstract_service.html

NASA Cool Site of the Week
http://www.jsc.nasa.gov/~mccoy/nasa/
Cool.html

NASA EOS IDS Volcanology Team
http://www.geo.mtu.edu/eos/

NASA Goddard Space Flight Ctr.
http://hypatia.gsfc.nasa.gov/
NASA_homepage.html

NASA, Guide to Online Resources
http://naic.nasa.gov/naic/guide/

NASA/JPL Imaging Radar Home Page
http://southport.jpl.nasa.gov/

NASA/JSC Digital Image Collection
http://images.jsc.nasa.gov/html/home.htm

NASA Langley Research Center
http://mosaic.larc.nasa.gov/larc.html

NASA Solar Data Analysis Center
http://umbra.gsfc.nasa.gov/sdac.html

NASA Technical Report Server
http://techreports.larc.nasa.gov/cgi-bin/NTRS

National Institute of Standards and
Technology (NIST)
http://www.nist.gov/welcome.html

National Optical Astronomy Observatories
http://www.noao.edu/

National Research Council Canada,
Photonic Systems Group
http://alpha.ps.iit.nrc.ca/

NCSA Virtual Reality Lab
http://www.ncsa.uiuc.edu/Viz/VR/
vr_homepage.html

Neural Networks Article Archive
http://www.lpac.qmw.ac.uk/SEL-HPC/Articles/
NeuralArchive.html

New England Fiber Optics Council
http://www.eotc.tufts.edu/nefc.html

New Mexico State University, Applied
Optics Laboratory
http://gauss.nmsu.edu:8000/optics/
optics.html

Nonlinear Optics Resource
http://marv.eng.uiowa.edu/

Northwestern Univ. EE/CS
http://www.eecs.nwu.edu/eecs-home.html

NSF Microelectronics Research Center (U.
of Idaho)
http://www.mrc.uidaho.edu/

NSF Optoelectronic Computing Systems
Ctr. (Colorado State Univ.)
http://www.lance.colostate.edu/optical/
index.html

NSFNET Backbone Statistics
http://www.cc.gatech.edu/gvu/stats/NSF/
merit.html

Oak Ridge National Lab.
http://www.ornl.gov/

Office of Technology Assessment
http://www.ota.gov/

Office of the Secretary of Defense (U.S.)
http://enterprise.osd.mil/

Opkor
http://www.opkor.com

Optical Research Associates
http://www.opticalres.com

Optical Society of America
http://www.osa.org/

OptiComp Corporation
http://www.opticomp.com

Optics and Machine Vision Applications
http://www.iti.org/eoe/index.htm

OPTICS 1
http://www.optics1.com

OPTICS.ORG — The Photonics Resource
Center
http://optics.org/

OptikWerk
http://www.optikwerk.com

Optoelectronics Technology Center
http://www.ece.ucsb.edu/OTC/

OptoSigma Corporation
http://www.optosigma.com

Oregon Univ.
http://opticb.uoregon.edu/

Oriel Instruments
http://www.oriel.com/WWW/adv/oriel.html

Particle Optics Research, Technical Univ. of Delft
http://wwwdo.tn.tudelft.nl/

Patent Search System
http://sunsite.unc.edu/patents/intropat.html

Perceptics
http://www.perceptics.com/info

Phillips Laboratory, Kirtland AFB
http://www.plk.af.mil/

Photek Ltd.
http://www.spie.org/photek/photek.html

Photonics Switching and Integrated Optoelectronics Lab, Univ. of Maryland
http://www.ee.umd.edu/photonics/

Portland State Univ.
http://www.ee.pdx.edu/

Precision Digital Images
http://www.precisionimages.com/gateway.htm

Prentiss Group, Harvard Univ.
http://atomsun.harvard.edu/

Radiology Imaging Ctr.
http://visual-ra.swmed.edu/

Radiology Webserver
http://www.rad.washington.edu/

Redlake Camera
HTTP://www.redlake.com/imaging/

Remote Sensing Virtual Library
http://www.vtt.fi/aut/ava/rs/virtual/

RLE - Research Laboratory of Electronics
http://rleweb.mit.edu

Rochester Institute of Technology, Imaging and Photographic Technology
http://www.rit.edu/~andpph/ipt.html

Rockwell Laser Industries LASERNET
http://iac.net/~rli/

Sandia National Laboratories
http://www.cs.sandia.gov/
Sandia_home_page.html

Satellite TV Page
http://itre.uncecs.edu/misc/sat.html

Semiconductor Corporations
http://mtmis1.mis.semi.harris.com/semi.html

Semiconductor Subway
http://www-mtl.mit.edu/cgi-bin/Mapgen/
subway/

SemiWeb
http://www.semiweb.com

SensorPhysics
http://www.sensorphysics.com

Shoemaker-Levy Comet impact
http://alfred1.u.washington.edu:8080/~roland/
sl/sl.html

Sloan Digital Sky Survey
http://www-sdss.fnal.gov:8000/

Smithsonian Astrophysical Observatory
http://sao-www.harvard.edu/home.html

Society for Applied Spectroscopy
http://esther.la.asu.edu/sas/

Society for Industrial and Applied Mathematics
http://www.siam.org/

Society for Information Display
http://www.display.org/sid/

Society of Manufacturing Engineers
http://www.sme.org

Software Spectra (optical thin films design)
http://www.teleport.com/~sspectra/

Space Activism Home Page
http://muon.qrc.com/space/start.html

Space Telescope Science Institute
http://stsci.edu/top.html

Spacecraft Planetary Imaging Facility (SPIF) at Cornell Univ.
http://astrosun.tn.cornell.edu/SPIF.html

SPIE — The International Society for Optical Engineering
http://www.spie.org/

SRI International's Visual Sciences Program
http://os.sri.com/vision

Stanford Univ.
http://www.stanford.edu/stanford.html

Stanford Univ., Holography and Optical
Data Storage Group
http://www-leland.stanford.edu:80/group/
holography/

Stereoscopic Volume Visualization
http://www.dataspace.com/WWW/documents/
stereoscopic.html

Swales and Associates Optics Group
http://www.swales.com/optics.html

Swedish Optical Society
http://www.optics.kth.se/sos/

Technological Institute of Costa Rica
http://www.cic.itcr.ac.cr/cic.html

Technology Review magazine
http://web.mit.edu/afs/athena/org/t/
techreview/www/tr.html

Tecnet
http://www.tecnet.com

Teledyne Brown Electro-Optical Products
Group
http://www.tbe.com/tech-pubs/products/
optics/optics.html

Tufts Univ. Electro-Optics Technology
Center
http://www.eotc.tufts.edu/

U.S. Dept. of Energy
http://apollo.osti.gov/home.html

U.S. Patent and Trademark Office
http://www.uspto.gov/

UCSD Science & Engineering Library
http://scilib.ucsd.edu

UIUC Photonic Systems Group
http://www.phs.uiuc.edu/

UMASS Astronomy
http://donald.phast.umass.edu/
umasshome.html

UMASS Lowell, Ctr. for Electromagnetic
Materials and Optical Systems (CEMOS)
http://web.uml.edu/Dept/EE/RCs/CEMOS/

Univ. of Arizona Optical Sciences Center
http://www.opt-sci.arizona.edu/

Univ. of Calgary Micronet Multidimensional Signal Processing Research Group
http://www-mddsp.enel.ucalgary.ca/

Univ. of California/San Diego Optoelectronic Computing Group
http://soliton.ucsd.edu/

Univ. of California/Santa Barbara,
Optoelectronics Technology Center
http://www.ece.ucsb.edu/department/centers/
otc.html

Univ. of Colorado, Boulder
http://ocswebhost.colorado.edu/

Univ. of Connecticut Photonics Research
Center
http://www.eng2.uconn.edu/prc/index.html

Univ. of Delaware EE/CIS
http://www.eecis.udel.edu/

Univ. of Edinburgh Applied Optics Group
http://prism.ph.ed.ac.uk/

Univ. of Florida EE
http://www.eel.ufl.edu/

Univ. of Illinois: Center for Compound
Semiconductor Microelectronics
http://www.ccsm.uiuc.edu/micro

Univ. of Iowa College of Medicine Div. of
Physiologic Imaging
http://everest.radiology.uiowa.edu:8080/
home.html

Univ. of Limburg Dept. of Medical
Informatics
http://www.mi.rulimburg.nl/

Univ. of Maryland Baltimore County
(UMBC) Physics Department
http://umbc7.umbc.edu/~dguyke1/dept/
home.html

Univ. of Melbourne Photonics Research
Lab
http://www.ee.mu.oz.au/papers/prl/
PhotonicsPage.html

Univ. of New Hampshire Robotics
http://www.ece.unh.edu/robots/rbt_home.htm

Univ. of Ottawa, Lightwave Communications Research Laboratory
http://optics.genie.uottawa.ca:8080/
LtComResLab.html

Univ. of Pennsylvania Medical Image
Processing Group
http://mipgsun.mipg.upenn.edu/

Univ. of Queensland Centre for Microscopy and Microanalysis
http://www.uq.oz.au/nanoworld/
images_1.html

Univ. of Rochester, Center for Electronic
Imaging Systems
http://www.optics.rochester.edu:8080/CEIS/
ceis.html

Univ. of Southampton (UK), Optolectronic
Research Centre
http://www.orc.soton.ac.uk/

Univ. of Sydney Mathematics and Stat
istics
http://www.maths.usyd.edu.au:8000/

Univ. of Virginia Laboratory for Optics
and Quantum Electronics
http://www.ee.virginia.edu/AEPL/labs/loqe

Univ. of Wales College of Cardiff, Dept. of
Computing Mathematics
http://www.cm.cf.ac.uk/

University of Washington Astronomy
http://www.astro.washington.edu/index.html

Univ. of Washington High Energy Physics
http://squark.phys.washington.edu/

Univ. of Waterloo Electronic Library
http://www.lib.uwaterloo.ca/

Virgo Optics, Division of II-VI
http://innet.com/~virgo/vhome2.html

Virtual Reality Lab, Johnson Space Center
http://www.jsc.nasa.gov/~mle/vr.html

Virtual Reality Society
http://web.dcs.hull.ac.uk/VRS/

Vision and Image Processing Article
Archive
http://www.lpac.qmw.ac.uk/SEL-HPC/Articles/
VisionArchive.html

Visioneering Research Lab.
http://vitoria.nmsu.edu/

Western Washington Univ.
http://www.wwu.edu

Wilkes Univ. School of Science & Engineering
http://www.wilkes.edu/WilkesDocs/
SSEHome.html#101

X-Ray WWW Server
http://xray.uu.se/

Yale Univ. Image Processing and Analysis
Group
http://noodle.med.yale.edu/

Yale Univ. Mathematics
http://www.yale.edu/HTML/YALE/MATH/
FrontDoor.html

Zory Laser Lab, Univ. of Florida
http://nervm.nerdc.ufl.edu/~largent/

Physics

See also Aeronautics & Aerospace, Astronomy & Astrophysics, Biology & Biotechnology, Chemistry, Computer Science, Electronics & Electrical Engineering, Energy, Engineering, Imaging Technologies, Mathematics, Medicine, Optics, Virtual Reality

Usenet Newsgroups

sci.physics
Newsgroup-based Mailing List: Yes (physics@unix.sri.com).
Charter: Physics!

sci.physics.accelerators
Created by: ryne@beta.lanl.gov (Robert Ryne)
Call for Votes date: June 21, 1993
Newsgroup-based Mailing List: No.
Charter (from Call for Votes):
The purpose of the newsgroup sci.physics.accelerators is for discussing issues related to particle accelerators and the physics of beams. Possible topics include, but are not limited to: computer codes and simulation in accelerator physics; experimental methods, instrumentation, diagnostics and measurement; accelerator theory; particle sources; accelerator structures; advanced accelerator concepts; rf power sources; free electron lasers; announcements and news from accelerator laboratories.

sci.physics.computational
Newsgroup-based Mailing List: No.
Charter: Computational methods.

sci.physics.computational.fluid-dynamics
Newsgroup-based Mailing List: No.
Charter: Computational fluid dynamics.

sci.physics.electromag
Created by: thubing@ee.umr.edu (Todd Hubing)
Call for Votes date: February 1, 1994
Newsgroup-based Mailing List: No.

Charter: Sci.physics.electromag will be dedicated to the discussion of topics pertaining to electromagnetics. These include, but are not limited to:

- electromagnetic wave theory
- computational EM modeling
- microwave devices and circuits
- antenna design
- electromagnetic interference
- biological effects
- ELF and VLF fields
- EM measurements
- wave propagation
- shielding electrostatic discharge
- new RF devices and technology.

sci.physics.fusion
Newsgroup-based Mailing List: No.
Charter: Fusion energy.

sci.physics.particle (Moderated)
Created by: rufinus@vxaluw.cern.ch (Jeff Rufinus)
Moderated by: Karl Swartz (kls@ditka.chicago.com)
Submissions go to: airliners@chicago.com
Call for Votes date: November 16, 1993
Newsgroup-based Mailing List: No.
Charter (from Call for Votes):
The sci.physics.particle newsgroup provides a common forum to discuss all aspects of particle physics, theories and experiments.

Topics of discussions are, but not limited to:

- Pre Standard Model
- Standard Model
- Beyond Standard Model

sci.physics.plasma (Moderated)

Created by: eastman@astro.umd.edu (Tim Eastman)
Moderated by: Tim Eastman (plasma-request@glue.umd.edu)
Submissions go to: plasma@glue.umd.edu
Call for Votes date: April 30, 1994
Newsgroup-based Mailing List: No.
Charter (from Call for Votes):
The newsgroup for Plasma Science and Technology is intended as a community forum for sharing new developments and bringing researchers together for potential new collaborations. During 1994, the focus of this NewsGroup will be a community-wide dialogue to formulate a Plasma Science and Technology Initiative which would deliver big-science value with a medium-scale investment. Participation in this dialogue will involve primarily researchers in plasma science and technology although qualified researchers in all related fields are welcome. Executive committees for the Div. of Plasma Physics of the American Physical Society (APS) and the Nuclear and Plasma Sciences Society of IEEE (Institute of Electrical and Electronics Engineers) have given formal approval for this network dialogue.

The Plasma Science and Technology research community seeks an increased dialogue among its multifarious constituencies. Plasmas are as rich as any other state of matter in terms of distinct processes and they encompass distinguishable scales ranging from the atomic to the galactic. Opportunities in plasma science and technology reflect this breadth in phenomena and scales; one recent list contains 135 subject areas and 65 applications areas including thin-film diamond deposition, toxic waste disposal, plasma arcs for steel processing, laser self-focusing, fusion for energy production, gas and arc lamps, cutting and welding, and semiconductor production.

In its initial implementation, Dr. Tim Eastman will be the PLASMA NEWSGROUP moderator. He is a Faculty member of the Institute for Physical Science and Technology at the University of Maryland [ph: 301-405-4829, fax: 301-314-9363, e-mail: eastman@astro.umd.edu]. Dr. Barry Ripin of the Naval Research Lab. will be an alternate moderator. The APS and IEEE Executive Committees will renew or replace the moderator on a yearly basis.

Note: The newsgroup name "sci.physics.fusion" already exists and is appropriate for the subset of Plasma Science and Technology which focuses on plasmas for energy production (i.e., fusion). The proposed newsgroup for plasma is intended to complement the "fusion" group and will primarily orient itself to issues of Plasma Science and Technology other than fusion.

sci.physics.research (Moderated)

Created by: phillies@wpi.WPI.EDU (George D. Phillies)
Moderated by: John Baez, Dale Bass, Bill Johnson, Lee Sawyer. (physics-research-request@ncar.ucar.edu)
Submissions go to: physics-research@ncar.ucar.edu
Call for Votes date: January 14, 1993
Newsgroup-based Mailing List: No.
Charter (from Call for Votes):
Sci.physics.research is a moderated newsgroup for discussions related to current physics research.

Frequently Asked Questions

Particle Physics on the WWW

Maintainer: marcus@x4u2.desy.de (Marcus Speh)
Where on Usenet: sci.physics.particle
Where it's archived: rtfm.mit.edu:pub/usenet/news.answers/sci.physics.particle
What it's for: Information on accessing Documents on Particle Physics and Lattice Field Theory in particular via the WWW.

Sci.Physics FAQ

Maintainer: sichase@csa2.lbl.gov (Scott I. Chase)
Where on Usenet: sci.physics

Where it's archived:
rtfm.mit.edu:pub/usenet/news.answers/
sci.physics
What it's for: Physics. Split into an
introduction, cosmology and astronomy,
general physics, particles/SR/Quantum.

Discussion Lists

aesrg-l
aesrg-l@mizzou1
Applied Expert Systems Research Group
List

ag-exp-l
ag-exp-l@ndsuvm1
AG-EXP-L Ag Expert Systems

alms-nn
alms-nn@ua1vm
AL-MS Neural Network

alpha-l
alpha-l@lepics
L3 Alpha physics block analysis diagram
group

asipp-l
asipp-l@ulkyvm
Chinese Plasma Physics Forum

atp-emtp
atp-emtp@ndsuvm1
ATP-EMTP Electromagnetic Transients
Program

cec
cec@qucdn
Canadian Electro-Acoustics Community
(CEC)

cfd
cfd@ukcc
Computational Fluid Dynamics Group

cond-mat
cond-mat@jpnyitp
Preprint server for Condensed Matter

cuple-l
cuple-l@ubvm
CUPLE (Physics Learning Environment)
Software

dasp-l
dasp-l@csearn
Digital Acoustic Signal Processing

electromagnetics
em-request@decwd.ece.uiuc.edu
Electromagnetism

epp-l
epp-l@buacca
Albert Einstein Papers Project and
Discussion

ese-l
ese-l@sbccvm
Expert Systems Environment mailing list.

fusion
fusion@ndsuvm1
Fusion - Redistribution of
sci.physics.fusion

gr-qc
gr-qc@jpnyitp
Preprint server for General Relativity &
Quantum Physics

hep-ex
hep-ex@jpnyitp
Preprint server for Experimental High
Energy Physics

icrc-l
icrc-l@irlearn
22nd Int'l Cosmic Ray Conference List

inns-l
inns-l@umdd
Intl. Neural Network Society

neural-n
neural-n@andescol
Artificial Neural Networks Discussion

neurl
neurl@uicvm
Neuroscience Strategic Planning

nucl-th
nucl-th@jpnyitp
Preprint server for Nuclear Theory

photreac
photreac@jpntuvm0
Electro- and Photo-Nuclear Reaction

phys-l
phys-l@uwf
Forum for Physics Teachers

phys-ri
phys-ri@uriacc
News and Information on Physics in
Rhode Island

physic-l
physic-l@taunivm
Physics List

physics
physics@marist
(Peered) Physics Discussion

physics
physics-request@qedqcd.rye.ny.us (Mike Miskulin)
Theoretical and experimental physics.

physjob
physjob@waynest1
Physics Jobs

physlrnr
physlrnr@idbsu
PHYSLRNR - Physics Learning Research

polymerp
polymerp@hearn
(Peered) Polymer Physics discussions

relativ1
relativ1@uwf
Group 1 - Special Relativity

ufit-l
ufit-l@trmetu
Applied Physics Group List

wksphys
wksphys@idbsu
WKSPHYS - Workshop Physics

Physics Resources

FTP Resources

ELF Communications Inc
asylum.sf.ca.us

FAQ - FreeHEP
freehep.scri.fsu.edu/freehep/
freehep_documents/freehep.FAQ

FAQ - Physics
ftp.desy.de/pub/faq/physics/physicsFAQ.txt

Macros
ftp.scri.fsu.edu/hep-lat/papers/macros

Pittsburgh Supercomputing Center
a.psc.edu

PostScript files
ftp.desy.de/pub/preprints

Purdue Univ.
bohr.physics.purdue.edu

Reviews
freehep.scri.fsu.edu/freehep/
lattice_field_theory/reviews

Univ. of Bern
iacrs2.unibe.ch

Univ. of Michigan
physics.archive.umich.edu

Univ. of Oregon
bovine.uoregon.edu

Univ. of Southern Australia, Signal Processing Research Institute
audrey.levels.unisa.edu.au

Univ. of Texas - Austin
hagar.ph.utexas.edu

Telnet Resources

CERN library
telnet://alice@vxlib.cern.ch/

NASA Extragalactic Database (NED)
telnet://ned.ipac.caltech.edu/

UCSD Science & Engineering Library
infopath.ucsd.edu

WWW Resources

Advanced Photon Source
http://epics.aps.anl.gov/welcome.html

AMANDA- Antarctic Muon And Neutrino Detector Array
http://dilbert.lbl.gov/www/amanda.html

American Center for Physics
http://acp.org/

American Institute of Physics
http://aip.org/

American Nuclear Society
http://www.ans.org

American Physical Society
http://aps.org/

American Vacuum Society
http://www.vacuum.org/

Argonne National Lab
http://axp1.hep.anl.gov/

Aston Univ. - Electronic Engineering and Applied Physics
http://www.eeap.aston.ac.uk/home.html

Astro, VR, Space, & Infosystems Newsgroups
http://guinan.gsfc.nasa.gov/WebStars/NEWS.html

ATLAS-Japan
http://arkhp1.kek.jp/

Atomic And Molecular Physics Servers
Links {Europe}
http://www.sc.ucl.ac.be:80/~stoop/links/
europe.html

Atomic and Solid State Physics, Cornell
Univ.
http://www.lassp.cornell.edu/

Biophysical Society
http://molbio.cbs.umn.edu/biophys/
biophys.html

Biophysical Society of Hong Kong
http://biosci.cbs.umn.edu/biophys/FBS/HK-
BS.html

BNL
http://suntid.bnl.gov:8080/bnl.html

Bradley Univ.
http://www.bradley.edu/las/phy/

Bristol Univ.
http://gaia.phy.bris.ac.uk/research/pppages/
particle_physics_94.html

Brookhaven National Lab Accelerator
Facility
http://www.tvdg.bnl.gov/~tvdg/tvdg.html

Brown Bag Preprint List - Caltech
http://chaos.fullerton.edu/brownbag.html

Brown Univ. - High Energy Physics
http://www.het.brown.edu/

Brown Univ. Physics
http://www.physics.brown.edu/

Caltech
http://www.theory.caltech.edu/

Caltech GEM Information
http://www.cithep.caltech.edu/gem/gem.html

Caltech High Energy Physics
http://www.cithep.caltech.edu/

Canadian Association of Physics
http://www.inrs-ener.uquebec.ca/surfsci/
index.html

CAP/CIC - Surface Science Index
http://www.inrs-ener.uquebec.ca/surfsci/
index.html

CASS: Univ. of California - San Diego Ctr.
for Astrophysics and Space Sciences
http://cassfos01.ucsd.edu:8080/

CBPF Laboratorio de Cosmologia e Fisica
Experimental de Altas Energias
http://www.lafex.cbpf.br/

Center for Theoretical Studies of Physical
Systems
http://galaxy.cau.auc.edu/

Centre de Physique des Particules de
Marseille
http://marcpl1.in2p3.fr/

CERN
http://www.cern.ch/

CERN Astrophysics
http://www.cern.ch/Space/Overview.html

CERN High Energy Physics
http://www.cern.ch/Physics/HEP.html

CERN Theoretical Physics
http://nxth21.cern.ch/

CfA High Energy Astrophysics Division
http://hea-www.harvard.edu/

Charged Particle Optics Software
http://wwwdo.tn.tudelft.nl/bbs/cposis.htm

Chungbuk National Univ. Theoretical
Physics
http://bohr.chungbuk.ac.kr/welcome.html

CITHEP
http://www.cithep.caltech.edu/

CLEO-II SVX Images
http://charm.physics.ucsb.edu/people/hnn/
svx_images.html

Collisions: When Two Tennis Balls Collide
and a Bowling Ball Flies Out
http://fnnews.fnal.gov/collisions.html

Complex systems
http://life.anu.edu.au/complex_systems/
complex.html

Contemporary Physics Education Project
(CPEP)
http://pdg.lbl.gov/cpep.html

Cornell Univ. Wilson Lab/CLEO
http://w4.lns.cornell.edu/

CPT
http://fourier.dur.ac.uk:8000/

Crystallography Virtual Library
http://www.unige.ch/crystal/crystal_index.html

CSR
http://inuit.phys.ualberta.ca/

DACcess - The Diamond Anvil Cell Forum
http://DACcess.phy.cam.ac.uk/

Daresbury Laboratory home page
http://www.dl.ac.uk/

DESY - Deutsches Electronen-Synchrotron
http://info.desy.de/

DESY Lattice Field Theory
http://info.desy.de/user/projects/Lattice.html

Durham/RAL HEP Databases
http://cpt1.dur.ac.uk/HEPDATA/

E-Print archive at babbage.sissa.it physics
(SISSA - ISAS)
http://babbage.sissa.it/

East Michigan Univ.
http://www.emich.edu/public/art_sci/phy_ast/
p&ahome.htm

Einstein Archive Service
http://adswww.harvard.edu/
einstein_service.html

Electrophysics
http://www.icis.on.ca/homepages/london/
electrophysics/

Elementary Particle Physics, Univ. of
Arizona
http://www.physics.arizona.edu/physics/
research.html#particle

ENSLAPP
http://enslapp.ens-lyon.fr/

ESRS - Synchrotron Radiation Users in
Europe
http://www.fy.chalmers.se/esrs/welcome.html

European Physical Society
http://www.nikhef.nl/www/pub/eps/eps.html

Fermilab
http://fnnews.fnal.gov/

Fermilab Library
http://www-lib.fnal.gov/library/welcome.html

FreeHEP software guide
http://heplibw3.slac.stanford.edu/FIND/
FHMAIN.HTML

Fundamental Physics Section, ETL
http://www.etl.go.jp/Organization/Bussei-kiso/

FZU
http://www-hep.fzu.cs/Welcome.html

GAMS - Guide to Available Mathematical
Software
http://gams.nist.gov/

Gen. Relativity and Quantum Cosmology
http://xxx.lanl.gov/gr-qc

Geomagnetic Index Kp
http://www.gwdg.de/~rhennin/

George Smoot Astrophysics Research
Group
http://spectrum.lbl.gov

Glasgow HEP
http://d1.ph.gla.ac.uk/

GSI
http://www.gsi.de/gsi.html

Harvard Univ. Physics
http://string.harvard.edu/

Health Physics Society
http://www.umich.edu/~bbusby/hps.htm

HEPIC - High Energy Physics Information
Center
http://www.hep.net/

HEP-Phenomenology
http://xxx.lanl.gov/hep-ph

HEP Physics Newsletters
http://www.hep.net/documents/newsletters/
newsletters.html

HEP preprint index
http://slacvm.slac.stanford.edu/find/hep

HEP-Theory
http://xxx.lanl.gov/hep-th

HEP Theory Software
http://heplibw3.slac.stanford.edu/FIND/
FREEHEP/SECTION/heptheory/INDEX

HEPIX
http://info.cern.ch/hepix/Overview.html

High-Energy Physics Virtual Library
http://www.cern.ch/Physics/HEP.html

HEPLIB info
http://heplibw3.slac.stanford.edu/FIND/
HLMAIN.HTML

HEPnet
http://www.hep.net/

HERMES
http://dxhra1.desy.de/

Hi-Tech Commerce
http://guinan.gsfc.nasa.gov/WebStars/
Commerce.html

High Energy Group, Institute of Physics,
Academia Sinica, Taiwan
http://hep3.phys.sinica.edu.tw/

Homeokinetics
http://www.trincoll.edu/psyc/Homeokinetics/

HUT/Materials Physics Lab
http://waist.hut.fi/

I. Physikalisches Institut
http://www.physik.rwth-aachen.de/group/
ibphys/ibphys.html

IAPS Home Page
http://www.tn.tudelft.nl/iaps/iaps.html

ICTP
http://euclid.tp.ph.ic.ac.uk/

IEE - Institution of Electrical Engineers
(UK)
http://www.iee.org.uk/

IEEE - Institute of Electrical and Electronics Engineers
http://www.ieee.org/

IFAE
http://u1.ifae.es/

IFG
http://xwho.cern.ch/WHO/people/01606

IFIC Valencia Univ.
http://evalu0.ific.uv.es/

IHEP
http://www.ihep.ac.cn/ihep.html

IHEP in Heidelberg
http://hp01.ihep.uni-heidelberg.de/

Imperial College - Theoretical Physics
http://euclid.tp.ph.ic.ac.uk/

Imperial College Mathematical Physics
http://telemachus.ma.ic.ac.uk/~psswain/
mathphys.html

Imperial College Theory
http://euclid.tp.ph.ic.ac.uk/

IN2P3 - Institut National de Physique
Nucèaire et de Physiques des Particules
http://info.in2p3.fr

Indiana Univ. - Experimental HEP
http://needmore.physics.indiana.edu/
iuhep.html

Indiana Univ. - High Energy Astrophysics
http://mimosa.astro.indiana.edu/

Institut Laue-Langevin
http://jade.ill.fr/

Institute for Materials Research
http://imr.chem.binghamton.edu/

Institute for Theoretical Atomic and
Molecular Physics (ITAMP)
http://cfa-www.harvard.edu/cfa/itamp.html

Institute of High Energy Physics, Beijing
http://www.ihep.ac.cn:3000/ihep.html

Institute of Physics
http://www.iop.org/

Instituto de Astrofisica de Canarias
http://www.iac.es/home.html

Instituto de Fisica, Uruguay
http://fisica.uy/fisica2/WWW/fisica.html

Instituto Nacional de Pesquisas Espaciais
(INPE) Astrophysics Div. (DAS)
http://www.inpe.br/astro/home/

IPNL
http://lyoinfo.in2p3.fr/

ISA - The International Society for
Measurement and Control
http://www.isa.org/

Kansas State Univ.
http://www.engg.ksu.edu/MEDEPT/

Keith Burnett Group Home Page
http://eve.physics.ox.ac.uk/KBGhome.html

KEK - National Laboratory for High
Energy Physics
http://www.kek.jp/

KEK Theory Physics Group
http://theory.kek.jp/

KVI
http://kviexp.kvi.nl/

Laboratorio de Instrumentacao e Fisica
Experimental de Particulas
http://www.lip.pt/

Laboratory for Materials, Device and
Circuit Simulation
http://nida.eng.wayne.edu/

Laser Stars
http://www.achilles.net/~jtalbot

LASSP
http://www.lassp.cornell.edu/

Lattice Archives
http://info.desy.de/user/projects/Lattice.html

Lawrence Berkeley Lab.
http://www.lbl.gov/LBL.html

Lawrence Livermore National Lab.
http://babar1.llnl.gov/

Los Alamos National Lab.
http://www.strauss.lanl.gov/

LANL Physics e-Print archive
http://xxx.lanl.gov/

LANL Physics Information Service
http://mentor.lanl.gov/Welcome.html

Low Temperature Lab.
http://www.hut.fi/Erill/kylma/

Manchester Univ.
http://h2.ph.man.ac.uk/home.html

Materials Research Society
http://dns.mrs.org/

MAX-lab
http://www.maxlab.lu.se/

Max-Planck-Institut fuer Physik, Munich,
Germany
http://iws132a.mppmu.mpg.de/

McGill Univ.
http://www.physics.mcgill.ca/physics-services/

McMaster Univ.
http://www.physics.mcmaster.ca/

Metaphysics, Metamath
http://www.xnet.com/~raydbias/metamath.htm

Middlesex Univ., Advanced Manufacturing and Mechatronics Centre
http://www.mdx.ac.uk/www/ammc/ammc.html

Mike Wetherley's Home Page
http://www.tcel.com/~mike/

MIT Center for Theoretical Physics
http://ctpa02.mit.edu/

MIT-LNS
http://marie.mit.edu/

Moscow State Univ. - Skobeltsyn Institute
of Nuclear Physics
http://www.npi.msu.su/

Mossberg Optical Physics Laboratory
http://opticb.uoregon.edu/~mosswww/
Home.html

MPI
http://www.mppmu.mpg.de/welcome.html/

MPI-K
http://www.mpi-hd.mpg.de/

Nanotechnology Index
http://erie.csis.gvsu.edu/~vanoflej/NanoTech/

Nanotechnology Resources
http://nano.xerox.com/nano/

NASA - National Aeronautics and Space
Administration
http://hypatia.gsfc.nasa.gov/
NASA_homepage.html

National Hydrogen Association
http://www.paltech.com/ttc/nha/index.htm

National Univ. of Singapore
http://www.physics.nus.sg

ND HEP
http://undhe6.hep.nd.edu/

Niels Bohr Institute
http://www.nbi.dk/

Nijmegen High Energy Physics Institute
http://thef-nym.sci.kun.nl/

NIKHEF
http://www.nikhef.nl/www/pub/default/
NikhefGuide.html

NORDITA - Nordic Institute for Theoretical Physics
http://www.nordita.dk/

Northwestern High Energy Physics Group
http://nuhepz.phys.nwu.edu/welcome.html

Notre Dame HEP
http://undhe6.hep.nd.edu/

Nuclear Physics for Software Resources
http://www.scri.fsu.edu/~drago/srin.html

Nuclear Physics, Netherlands
http://www.nucphys.nl/www/pub/nucphys/
npe.html

Ohio State Univ.
http://www-physics.mps.ohio-state.edu/~cleo/
home.html

OPAL group - Bonn Univ.
http://opalr2.physik.uni-bonn.de/

OPTICS.ORG - The Photonics Resource Center
http://optics.org/

ORNL Physics Division
http://www.phy.ornl.gov/

Oxford Univ. Astrophysics Server
http://www-astro.physics.ox.ac.uk/

Particle Data Group (PDG)
http://www-pdg.lbl.gov/

Particle Optics Research, Technical Univ. of Delft
http://wwwdo.tn.tudelft.nl/

Particle Surface Resources
http://chaos.fullerton.edu/mhslinks.html

PASA - Physics and Astronomy Students Association
http://www.ucalgary.ca/~physastr

Penn State - Gravitational Physics and Geometry
http://vishnu.nirvana.phys.psu.edu/

Physical Societies
http://www.cern.ch/Physics/PhysSoc.html

Physics at the Australian Defence Force Academy
http://www.adfa.oz.au/physics/

Physics Department - Saga Univ., Japan
http://www.cc.saga-u.ac.jp/saga-u/riko/physics/physics.html

Physics Hypertext
http://web.phys.washington.edu/

Physics Servers Around the World - European Server
http://tph.tuwien.ac.at/physics-services/physics_services2.html

Physics Servers Around the World - North American Server
http://www.physics.mcgill.ca/physics-services/physics_services.html

Physics Servers Around the World - Scandinavian Server
http://www.tp.umu.se/physics-services/

Physics World Digest
http://info.desy.de/pub/faq/physics/PhysicsWorld

Physics-Uspekhi On-Line
http://ufn.ioc.ac.ru/

Plasma Gate
http://plasma-gate.weizmann.ac.il/

Plasma Science and Technology
http://www-plasma.umd.edu/

Pohang Univ., Korea
http://sol.postech.ac.kr

Prarie View HEP
http://hp73.pvamu.edu/

PSI
http://www.psi.ch/

PSI F1 Theory Group
http://pss058.psi.ch/

Queen's Univ. of Belfast
http://www.am.qub.ac.uk/

RAL
http://www.rl.ac.uk/home.html

Rechenzentrum der Max-Planck-Gesellschaft in Garching
http://www.ipp-garching.mpg.de/rzg.html

Remote Sensing Virtual Library
http://www.vtt.fi/aut/ava/rs/virtual/

Rensselaer Polytechnic Institute
http://www.rpi.edu/dept/phys/physics.html

Rensselaer Polytechnic Institute - Nuclear and Particle Physics
http://www.rpi.edu/dept/phys/nuclear.html

RIKEN
http://www.riken.go.jp/

Royal Holloway
http://www.ph.rhbnc.ac.uk/research/hep/hep_home.html

RPI - Plasma Dynamics Lab
http://hibp.ecse.rpi.edu/

Saga Univ.
http://www.cc.saga-u.ac.jp/saga-u/riko/physics/physics.html

SCRI at Florida State Univ.
http://dirac.scri.fsu.edu/

Sezione di Trieste
http://www.ts.infn.it/

SHEP
http://wwwhep.phys.soton.ac.uk/

SISSA, Italy
http://babbage.sissa.it/

Society for Applied Spectroscopy
http://esther.la.asu.edu/sas/

Society for Nonlinear Dynamics and Econometrics
http://www.interactive.net:80/~mizrach/SNDE/snde.html

Society of Exploration Geophysicists
http://sepwww.stanford.edu/seg/

Space Research Unit
http://www.puk.ac.za/fskdocs/

Space Science Web Group
http://enemy.gsfc.nasa.gov/sswg/SSWG.html

SPIE - The International Society for Optical Engineering
http://www.spie.org/

SPIRES Databases
http://heplibw3.slac.stanford.edu/FIND/default.html

SRRC : Synchrotron Radiation Reseach Center
http://www.srrc.gov.tw/

SSCL
http://www.ssc.gov/SSC.html

St. Petersburg Nuclear Physics Institute
ftp://rec03.pnpi.spb.ru/web/home.html

Stanford Lattice Field Theory
http://heplibw3.slac.stanford.edu/FIND/FREEHEP/SECTION/lattice_field_theory/INDEX

Stanford Linear Accelerator Center (SLAC)
http://heplibw3.slac.stanford.edu/FIND/SLAC.html

SLAC BaBar Detector Home Page
http://www.slac.stanford.edu/BF/doc/www/bfHome.html

SLAC SPIRES
http://www-spires.slac.stanford.edu/FIND/hep/

SLAC Top-40 Cited Papers
http://www-slac.slac.stanford.edu/find/top40.html

Stanford Univ. Experiments Online
http://slacvm.slac.stanford.edu/find/explist.html

String Theory Group, Queen Mary and Westfield College (Univ. London)
http://stringswww.ph.qmw.ac.uk/

Sudbury Neutrino Observatory (Queens Univ., CA)
http://snodaq.phy.queensu.ca/sno/sno.html

SUNY Stony Brook Xray
http://xray1.physics.sunysb.edu/

Suomen Fyysikkoseura
http://www.physics.helsinki.fi/~sfs/

Super-Kamiokande at UCI
http://www.ps.uci.edu/sk/

Superconducting Super Collider (SSC)
http://www.het.brown.edu/news/ssc/index.html

Swiss Federal Institute of Technology - Institute for Particle Physics
http://wwwphys.ethz.ch/IPP/

Tata Institute of Fundamental Research (TIFR) - Theoretical Physics
http://theory.tifr.res.in/

Tel Aviv Univ. - High Energy Physics
http://proton.tau.ac.il/

Theoretical Physics Group, Tata Insitute of Fundamental Research, Bombay, India
http://theory.tifr.res.in/

Timing, Trigger and Control (TTC) Systems for LHC Experiments
http://www.cern.ch/TTC/intro.html

TRIUMF
http://www.triumf.ca/

TU Vienna - Institute for Theoretical Physics
http://tph.tuwien.ac.at/

UBC Theoretical Physics Web
http://axion.physics.ubc.ca/

UC Berkeley Center for Particle Astrophysics
http://physics7.berkeley.edu/home.html

UC Irvine High Energy Physics
http://www.ps.uci.edu/physics/heexpt.html

UCLA
http://spike.physics.ucla.edu/

UCLA Particle Beam Physics Lab
http://pbpl.physics.ucla.edu/

UCLA Theoretical Elementary Particles Group
http://spike.physics.ucla.edu/

UCSB High Energy Physics
http://charm.physics.ucsb.edu/

UCSD Science & Engineering Library
http://scilib.ucsd.edu

UK Solar Energy Society
http://sun1.bham.ac.uk/thorntme/

Uni Oldenburg - Physics (Theo III)
http://www.physik.uni-oldenburg.de/

UNICAN
http://www.gae.unican.es/

UNIDO
http://www.Physik.Uni-Dortmund.De/

Univ. of Alberta, Ctr. for Subatomic
Research
http://inuit.phys.ualberta.ca/

Univ. of Bayreuth - Theoretical Phsyics
http://btp4x2.phy.uni-bayreuth.de/

Univ. of Boston
http://cbsgi2.bu.edu/cb/cb.html

Univ. of Calgary Geophysics
http://www-crewes.geo.ucalgary.ca/VL-
Geophysics.html

Univ. of Calgary Micronet Multidimensional Signal Processing Research Group
http://www-mddsp.enel.ucalgary.ca/

Univ. of Colorado Condensed Matter Lab
http://bly.colorado.edu/cml/cml.html

Univ. of Colorado Plasma and Accelerator
Physics Group
http://jove.colorado.edu/homepage.html

Universität Erlangen-Nürnberg -
Theoretische Physik II
http://theorie2.physik.uni-erlangen.de/

Univ. of Erlangen-Nürnberg, Institut für
Theoretische Physik III
http://theorie3.physik.uni-erlangen.de/

Univ. of Freiburg
http://hpfrs6.physik.uni-freiburg.de/

Univ. of Illinois - High Energy Physics
http://www.hep.uiuc.edu/

Univ. of Indiana Cyclotron
http://www.iucf.indiana.edu

Univ. of Iowa
http://marv.eng.uiowa.edu/

Univ. of Karlsruhe - Institut für
theoretische Physik
http://itpaxp1.physik.uni-karlsruhe.de/

Univ. of Liverpool
http://www.cern.ch/Liverpool/welcome.html

Univ. of Manitoba - Physics
http://www.umanitoba.ca/physics/

Univ. of Maryland Plasma Science and
Technology
http://www-plasma.umd.edu/

Univ. of Mississippi High Energy Physics
Group
http://beauty1.phy.olemiss.edu/
homepage.html

Univ. Montreal Departement de physique
http://ftp.astro.umontreal.ca/physique/
index.html

Univ. of Napoli, Italy
http://www.na.infn.it/htbin/bib

Univ. of Nevada, Las Vegas
http://pauli.lv-physics.nevada.edu/

Univ. of New Mexico - HEP
http://wwwhep.unm.edu/

Univ. of Newcastle-u-Tyne - Relativity and
Quantum Fields Group
http://matmos.ncl.ac.uk/

Univ. of Oldenburg Physics
http://marvin.physik.uni-oldenburg.de/Docs/
home/phys-links.html

Univ. of Oregon - High Energy Physics
http://zebu.uoregon.edu/~dmason/uohep.html

Univ. of Otago, Dunedin, New Zealand
http://newton.otago.ac.nz:808/homepage.html

Univ. of Oulu - Theoretical Physics
http://jussi.oulu.fi/

Universitaet des Saarlandes - Theoretische
Physik
http://www.uni-sb.de/matfak/fb10/ph10ml/
lusi.html

Univ. of Stockholm - Theoretical Physics
http://vanosf.physto.se/

Univ. at Stony Brook, Institute for Theoretical Physics
http://insti.physics.sunysb.edu/itp/

Univ. of Tasmania - Theoretical Physics Group
http://info.utas.edu.au/docs/njones/TGHome.html

Univ. of Tennessee
http://enigma.phys.utk.edu/

Univ. of Tokyo
http://hep1.c2.u-tokyo.ac.jp/

Univ. of Victoria Physics & Astronomy
http://info.phys.uvic.ca/

Univ. of Virginia Engineering Physics
http://bohr.ms.virginia.edu/ep/

Univ. of Washington Cosmic Ray Lab
http://marge.phys.washington.edu/

Univ. of Washington High Energy Physics
http://squark.phys.washington.edu/

Univ. of Washington Nuclear Physics Lab
http://mist.npl.washington.edu/home_npl.html

Univ. of Winnipeg - Theoretical Physics
http://theory.uwinnipeg.ca/

Universidad Zaragoza - Dept Fisica Teorica (DFTUZ)
http://dftuz.unizar.es/

Vacuum Technology
http://nyquist.ee.ualberta.ca/~schmaus/vac.html

Vector Particle Physics
http://www.best.com/~lockyer/

Visual Techniques Lab.
http://geb.phys.washington.edu/

Warsaw High Energy Physics Group
http://info.fuw.edu.pl/HEP/

Warsaw Univ.
http://info.fuw.edu.pl/

Wayne State High Energy Physics
http://gluon.physics.wayne.edu/

WebStars
http://guinan.gsfc.nasa.gov/WebStars/About.html

Weizmann Institute
http://wissgi.weizmann.ac.il/physics/physics.html

Weizmann Institute - Plasma Laboratory
http://plasma-gate.weizmann.ac.il/

Wilson Lab/CLEO/CESR
http://w4.lns.cornell.edu/hypertext/public/README.html

ZEUS
http://zow00.desy.de:8000/

Security

See also Computer Science

Usenet Newsgroups

alt.privacy.clipper
Charter: Clipper, Capstone, Skipjack, Key Escrow

alt.security
Charter: general security discussions

alt.security.index
Charter: index to alt.security

alt.security.pgp
Charter: discussion of PGP

alt.security.ripem
Charter: discussion of RIPEM

comp.compression
Charter: discussion of compression algorithms and code

comp.org.eff.news
Charter: News reports from EFF

comp.org.eff.talk
Charter: discussion of EFF related issues

comp.patents
Charter: discussion of S/W patents, including RSA

comp.security.announce
Charter: announcements of security holes

comp.security.misc
Created by: Dave Hayes
<dave@elxr.jpl.Nasa.Gov>
Call for Votes date: April 13, 1992
Newsgroup-based Mailing List: No.
Charter (from Call for Votes):
The purpose of this group is to be a
forum for rational discussion on security issues as they apply to computers and networks. This is a wide subject area and as such no attempt will be made to specifically limit the discussion topics as long as the general subject is computer security.

comp.security.unix
Created by: zen@death.corp.sun.com
Call for Votes date: September 8, 1993
Newsgroup-based Mailing List: No.
Charter (from Call for Votes):
Comp.security.unix is an unmoderated newsgroup for the discussion of computer security topics that are directly relevant to the various flavors of Unix. Sample topics of discussion might include (but are not limited to) Unix security tools and packages, differences in security features and relative strengths among the various Unix's, pros and cons of running various network services, etc. Posting security related source code might sometimes be in order, but substantial packages should normally be posted to one of the available source code groups.

misc.legal.computing
Charter: software patents, copyrights, computer laws.

sci.crypt
Newsgroup-based Mailing List: No.
Charter: All aspects of cryptography: algorithms, how to devise them and how to break them.

sci.crypt.research (Moderated)
Created by: Peter Gutmann
<pgut1@cs.aukuni.ac.nz>
Call for Votes Date: 15 August 1994

Moderated by: David Wagner et al <crypt-request@cs.aukuni.ac.nz>
Submissions go to: crypt-submission@cs.aukuni.ac.nz
Newsgroup-based Mailing List: No.
Charter (from Call for Votes):
The discussion of cryptography, cryptanalysis, and related issues, in a more civilised environment than is currently provided by sci.crypt.

Frequently Asked Questions

anonymous-ftp FAQ
Maintainer: cklaus@anshar.shadow.net (Christopher Klaus)
Where on Usenet: alt.security
Where it's archived:
rtfm.mit.edu:/pub/usenet/news.answers/cryptography FAQ
What it's for: A list of archives containing information.

compromise FAQ
Maintainer: cklaus@anshar.shadow.net (Christopher Klaus)
Where on Usenet: alt.security
Where it's archived:
rtfm.mit.edu:/pub/usenet/news.answers/cryptography FAQ
What it's for: This FAQ deals with some suggestions for securing your Unix machine
after it has already been compromised.

cryptography FAQ
Maintainer: crypt-comments@math.ncsu.edu
Where on Usenet: sci.crypt
Where it's archived:
rtfm.mit.edu:/pub/usenet/news.answers/cryptography FAQ
What it's for: Lots and lots of information on cryptography.

RSA Cryptography Today FAQ
Maintainer: faq-editor@rsa.com
Where on Usenet: sci.crypt
Where it's archived:
rtfm.mit.edu:/pub/usenet/news.answers/cryptography FAQ

What it's for: RSA Cryptography

security-patches FAQ
Maintainer: cklaus@anshar.shadow.net (Christopher Klaus)
Where on Usenet: alt.security
Where it's archived:
rtfm.mit.edu:/pub/usenet/news.answers/cryptography FAQ
What it's for: A guide for system administrators who want to secure their systems.

vendor-contacts FAQ
Maintainer: cklaus@anshar.shadow.net (Christopher Klaus)
Where on Usenet: alt.security
Where it's archived:
rtfm.mit.edu:/pub/usenet/news.answers/cryptography FAQ
What it's for: A list of security contacts to reach at various vendors for reporting security vulnerabilities and obtaining new security related patches.

Discussion Lists

crypto-l
crypto-l@jpntuvm0
Forum on Cryptology and Related Mathematics

hack-l
hack@alive.ersys.edmonton.ab.ca (Marc Slemko)
The monthly Hack Report, which warns of hacked, hoax, Trojan Horse, and pirated files that have been seen posted on BBS systems worldwide.

Security Resources

FTP Resources

COAST FTP Security Archive
  coast.cs.purdue.edu/pub

ELF Communications Inc
  asylum.sf.ca.us

NASIRC
  nasirc.nasa.gov/

NIST Computer Security Resource Clearinghouse
  csrc.nist.gov

Security Documents
ftp.dsi.unimi.it/pub/security/docs

Texas A&M
net.tamu.edu/pub/security

TRW Inc.
gumby.dsd.trw.com

US Computer Emergency Response Team
ftp.cert.org/pub

Gopher Resources

DFN-CERT, Univ. Hamburg - Informatik, (DE)
gopher.informatik.uni-hamburg.de/

IBM Computer Virus Information Ctr.
index.almaden.ibm.com

WWW Resources

American Bar Association Guidelines on Digital Signatures
http://www.intermarket.com/ecl/

Ames Research Center
http://ccf.arc.nasa.gov/security

ARL Information Server
http://info.arl.army.mil/

Association for Computing Machinery
http://info.acm.org/

Assorted Security Information Sources
http://galaxy.einet.net/galaxy/Engineering-and-Technology/Computer-Technology/Security/security-links.html

Australian Computer Emergency Response Team
http://www.auscert.org.au/

bsy's Security Related Net-pointers
http://www.cs.cmu.edu:8001/afs/cs.cmu.edu/user/bsy/www/sec.html

CADD Homepage
http://cadd.cern.ch/welcome.html

CERT
http://www.sei.cmu.edu/SEI/programs/cert/CERT.info.html

Christopher L. Menegay's Security page.
http://tamsun.tamu.edu/~clm3840/security.html

CNLS General Information
http://cnls-www.lanl.gov/generalinfo.html

Computer and Network Security Reference Index
http://www.tansu.com.au/Info/security.html

Computer Incident Advisory Capability
http://ciac.llnl.gov/

Computer Security at SAIC
http://mls.saic.com/mls.security.html

CRIMELAB.COM
http://crimelab.com/crimelab.html

Cryptography Archive
http://www.quadralay.com/www/Crypt/Crypt.html

Ctr. for Social Science Computation and Research
http://augustus.csscr.washington.edu/

Dartmouth College
http://www.dartmouth.edu/

ERG
http://www.erg.abdn.ac.uk/

FAQ: Computer Security Frequently Asked Questions
http://www.cis.ohio-state.edu/hypertext/faq/usenet/security-faq/faq.html

FIRST Security Team
http://first.org/

Forum of Incident Response and Security Teams
http://www.first.org/first/

Frank Martin's Hotlist
http://www2.jsc.nasa.gov/security/Computer_Security_Links.html

Georgia Tech Physics
http://www.gatech.edu/physics/PhysicsTech.html

Information about RIPEM
http://cs.indiana.edu/ripem/dir.html

Information Retrieval
http://camis.stanford.edu/people/felciano/informationret.html

Johnson Space Center
http://www2.jsc.nasa.gov/security/JAS_homepage.html

LANL ACL Home Page
http://www.acl.lanl.gov/Home.html

Lewis Research Center
http://gumby.lerc.nasa.gov

MetaCenter Home Page
http://www.ncsa.uiuc.edu/General/
MetaCenter/MetaCenterHome.html

Morning Star Technologies
http://www.morningstar.com/

NASA Information Technology Security
http://www.larc.nasa.gov/org/isd/security

NASIRC
http://nasirc.nasa.gov

National Inst. of Standards and Technologies
http://www.nist.gov/

NIST Computer Security Resource Clearinghouse
http://first.org/

Pretty Good Privacy - PGP
http://www.mantis.co.uk/pgp/pgp.html

Purdue COAST project
http://www.cs.purdue.edu/coast/coast.html

RSA Data Security, Inc.
http://www.rsa.com/

SCRI Home Page
http://www.scri.fsu.edu/

Secure HyperText Transfer Protocol
http://www.commerce.net/information/
standards/drafts/shttp.txt

Secure Sockets Layer Protocol
http://home.netscape.com/info/SSL.html

Security - CSC Security Items.
http://spy.org:70/1s/System/bbs/BBS/SIGS/
SECURITY

Security Issues in Embedded Networking
http://www.mit.edu:8001/people/eichin/
embedded-kerberos.html

Security Reference Index
http://www.tansu.com.au/Info/security.html

Shen: A Security Scheme for the World Wide Web
http://www.w3.org/hypertext/WWW/Shen/ref/
shen.html

SPYBBS Security
http://spy.org:70/1s/System/bbs/BBS/SIGS/
SECURITY

Sunrise project
http://www.acl.lanl.gov/sunrise/sunrise.html

T4 Computer Security Profile
http://www.nuance.com/~fcp/t4.html

Telecom Australia
http://www.telstra.com.au/info/security.html

Telnet URL Problem
http://south.ncsa.uiuc.edu/telnet-details.html

Trusted Information Systems Home Page
http://www.tis.com/

Unix Security
http://www.alw.nih.gov/WWW/security.html

Using the Web to Provide Private Information
http://ursaminor.scs.carleton.ca/Papers/
www94-paper.html

WWW-Security Index
http://www-ns.rutgers.edu/www-security/
index.html

WWW Virtual Library: Cryptography, PGP, and Your Privacy
http://draco.centerline.com:8080/~franl/
crypto.html

Virtual Reality

See also Artificial Intelligence, Computer Science, Imaging Technologies, Optics, Physics

Usenet Newsgroups

comp.graphics.animation
Created by: ddebry@dsd.es.com (David DeBry)
Call for Votes date: August 7, 1992
Newsgroup-based Mailing List: No.
Charter (from Call for Votes):
Discussion of the techinical aspects and technique of computer animation will take place. This *does* include (but is not limited to) such topics as:

- Hardware and software used for an end result of a computer animated sequence. These include modellers, renderers, animators, etc. This topic, however, is limited by a mention later in the charter concerning threads that become TOO system specific.
- Application of knowledge of other types of more "standard" or "formal" animation to computer animation.
- Discussion of the technical aspects or techniques used to generate existing computer animations.
- Forums for showing your own work and viewing other's animations. For example: Film & video shows/ contests/competitions. It's often hard to know where to look to see computer animation, or where to get your own work shown to the public. Hopefully this will alleviate some of the problem.

comp.graphics.explorer
Created by: Gordon Cameron <gordonc@epcc.edinburgh.ac.uk>
Call for Votes date: May 7, 1992

Newsgroup-based Mailing List: No.
Charter (from Call for Votes):
IRIS Explorer is an application creation system developed by Silicon Graphics that provides visualisation and analysis functionality for computational scientists, engineers and other scientists. The Explorer GUI allows users to build custom applications without having to write any, or a minimal amount of, traditonal code. Also, exisiting code can be easily integrated into the Explorer environment. Explorer currently is available on SGI and Cray machines, but will become available on other platforms in time.

Hopefully the group should serve as an open forum for discussion on all matters Explorer-related, in much the same way as comp.graphics.avs and comp.soft-sys.khoros work for those products. It would be also be good if the group could help the users of Explorer by giving them the option to keep in touch with both each other, and the developers of Explorer itself. Questions can be answered, and opinions heard by those working on future versions of the software.

comp.graphics.opengl
Created by: bglazier@buffalo.asd.sgi.com (Buffalo Bill Glazier)
Call for Votes date: September 1, 1992
Newsgroup-based Mailing List: No.
Charter (from Call for Votes):
comp.graphics.opengl will allow for discussion regarding technical and marketing issues surrounding the OpenGL 3D application programming interface and its emergence as a multiplatform graphics

standard for distributed three dimensional graphics.

Currently a great deal of net discussion takes place about OpenGL, unfortunately spread out among either newsgroups which are too general, vendor specific newsgroups, or newsgroups dedicated to competing API's or graphics protocols.

A dedicated newsgroup will allow for:

- Technical discussion of the OpenGL API, OpenGL Utility Library, and GL/X Wire protocol: Comparison versus prior releases of the GL. Input concerning desired enhancements or new features.
- Programming issues and techniques. Analysis of implementations in different environments (Windows NT, Macintosh OS, Unix..). Porting to OpenGL.
- Marketing and Business Issues Analysis: Product plans of OpenGL licensees.
- Comparison versus other 2D and 3D graphics API's. Performance benchmarks and competitive analysis.

sci.virtual-worlds (Moderated)

Moderated by: Toni Emerson and Aaron Pulkka (scivw-request@hitl.washington.edu)
Submissions go to:
scivw@hitl.washington.edu
Newsgroup-based Mailing List: No.
Charter:: Largely technology-oriented discussions of virtual reality. Lots of hardware issues.

sci.virtual-worlds.apps (Moderated)

Created by: Robert Jacobson
<cyberoid@u.washington.edu>
Moderated by: Bob Jacobson and Mark DeLoura (scivwa@media.mit.edu)
Submissions go to:
scivwa@media.mit.edu
Call for Votes date: August 19, 1992
Newsgroup-based Mailing List: No.
Charter:: Practical real-world applications of virtual reality.

Discussion Lists

vrapp-l
VRAPP-L@UIUCVMD
VR Apps / sci.virtual-worlds.apps
virtu-l
virtu-l@vmd.cso.uiuc.edu
Virtual reality—computing, social, and technological issues.

Virtual Reality Resources

FTP Resources

CSCW Bibliography by Saul Greenberg
ftp.cpsc.ucalgary.ca/pub/CSCWbibliography

Guide to Internet Resources
ftp.apple.com /pub/VR/vr_sites

Gossamer 2.0. Real-time 3D walk-through engine for the Macintosh
ftp.apple.compub/VR/graphics.systems

Human Interface Technology Lab (HITL), Univ. of Washington
ftp.u.washington.edu/public/VirtualReality/HITL

MR Toolkit, Univ. of Alberta, Dept. of Computer Science:
menaik.cs.ualberta.ca/pub/graphics/MR.

SIGGCHI, Curricula for Human-Computer Interaction
archive.cis.ohio-state.edu/pub/hci/CDG

Virtual Cities
freedom.nmsu.edu/pub/Virtual_Cities/

Virtual Reality Update
ftp.u.washington.edu/public/VirtualReality/HITL/Bibliographies/VRU/vru-v2n1.txt

VR-386 freeware VR program for the IBM PC (386 and higher) compatibles
psych.toronto.edu/~ftp/pub/vr-386

Univ. of North Carolina at Chapel Hill
ftp.cs.unc.edu/pub/technical-reports

WWW Resources

Chris Hand's VR Page
http://www.cms.dmu.ac.uk:9999/People/cph/vrstuff.html

Cyberspace Report
http://www.ics.uci.edu/~ejw/csr/cyber.html

Delft Univ. of Technology
  http://www.twi.tudelft.nl/welcome.html

DesignSpace
  http://gummo.stanford.edu/html/
  DesignSpace/home.html.

Digital Equipment Corporation
  ftp://gatekeeper.dec.com/pub/DEC/DECinfo/
  html/home.html

Electronic Visualization Lab., Univ. of
Illinois, Urbana Champaign
  http://www.ncsa.uiuc.edu/EVL/docs/
  Welcome.html

Graphics, Visualization and Usability Ctr.,
Georgia Tech
  http://www.gatech.edu/gvu/gvutop.html

HCI Bibliography Project by Gary Perlman
  archive.cis.ohio-state.edu/pub/hcibib

HCI Launching Pad
  http://www.twi.tudelft.nl/Local/HCI/HCI-
  Index.html

Human Interface Technology Lab at Univ.
of Washington (HIT LAB)
  http://www.hitl.washington.edu/

Index to Multimedia Information Resources
  http://cui_www.unige.ch/OSG/MultimediaInfo

Johnson Space Center Virtual Reality Lab
  http://www.jsc.nasa.gov/~mle/vr.html

Lateiner Dataspace
  http://www.dataspace.com/WWW/
  welcome.html

LTRS - Langley Technical Report Server
  http://techreports.larc.nasa.gov/ltrs/ltrs.html

LUTCHI Research Centre
  http://pipkin.lut.ac.uk

McDonnell Douglas Aerospace-Houston
Div.
  http://pat.mdc.com/

NASA Information Services
  http://hypatia.gsfc.nasa.gov/
  NASA_homepage.html

Naval Postgraduate School, Monterey
Calif.
  ftp://taurus.cs.nps.navy.mil/pub/
  NPSNET_MOSAIC/npsnet_mosaic.html

NCSA Virtual Reality Lab
  http://www.ncsa.uiuc.edu/Viz/VR/
  vr_homepage.html

NTT - Nippon Telegraph and Telephone
Corporation.
  http://www.ntt.jp/index.html

Principia Cybernetica Web
  http://pespmc1.vub.ac.be/Default.html

Project GeoSim Information Server
  http://geosim.cs.vt.edu/index.html

Rapid Development Lab (RDL)
  http://ollie.jsc.nasa.gov/~wood/RDL/
  RDL_Home.html

SIGGRAPH On-line Bibliography Project
  http://iicm.tu-graz.ac.at/CSIGGRAPHbib

Silicon Graphics, Inc. - Silicon Surf
  http://www.sgi.com/

Sun Microsystems
  http://sunsite.unc.edu/sun/inform/sun-
  info.html

UK VR-SIG
  http://pipkin.lut.ac.uk/WWWdocs/LUTCHI/
  people/sean/vr-sig/vr-sig.html

Univ. of Maryland
  http://gimble.cs.umd.edu/vrtp/vrtp.html

Univ. of North Carolina at Chapel Hill
  http://www.cs.unc.edu/cs.unc.edu.html

Univ. of Waterloo, Ontario, Canada
  ftp://sunee.uwaterloo.ca/pub/

Virtual Reality Society
  http://web.dcs.hull.ac.uk/VRS/

Virtual Reality Update
  ftp://ftp.u.washington.edu/public/
  VirtualReality/HITL/HITLMosaic/
  onthenet.html.

VR at GVU - animation example
  http://www.twi.tudelft.nl/TWI/IS/
  Afstudeerders/Kooper/Acrophobia.html

VR Resources
  http://www.ncsa.uiuc.edu/Viz/VR/
  vr_other_ftp.html

What is Virtual Reality?
  sunsite.unc.edu/pub/academic/computer-
  science/virtual-reality/papers/

Xerox Palo Alto Research Ctr. (Pub Web)
  http://pubweb.parc.xerox.com/

PERSONAL COMPUTER
BASICS

Introduction to TCP/IP

This section's purpose is to complement the chapters in Part I of this book, where I've demonstrated some of the best Macintosh and Windows freeware and shareware for accessing the Internet. Before you can use any of this great software, your personal computer must have either a direct connection to the Internet (usually from your office or school), or a SLIP/PPP type of modem connection. This appendix describes the basics of setting up your Macintosh or Windows computer for these types of connections to the Internet, with emphasis on SLIP and PPP, since most people who have a direct connection to the Internet also have an in-house network administrator to help get them online. (For more background on the various types of online connections, see Chapter 2: Getting Online.)

As we've discussed throughout this book, the Internet uses a common computer networking language, or *protocol*, called TCP/IP to connect the many different kinds of computers on the net. So, to be *on* the Internet, your computer, or a computer you are connected to, must "speak" TCP/IP. The only other requirement for Internet access is that you have a place to connect to the Internet— that is, a company or organization that either has or provides your computer with a unique Internet address to be identifiable on the Internet, much like your postal address identifies your unique physical location in the world's geography.

Now, we already know that Internet service providers offer access to the Internet through their Unix computers already connected to the Internet. All you have to have is a computer and a modem, with which you make a connection to their Unix computer and log in to your personal *shell* account on it. From there you use that computer's software as your gateway to the Internet. This book's main thread was written with examples for this kind of connection in mind, since it is still a common way to get full Internet connectivity.

However, in the past two years, the technology has surfaced to offer a different and more versatile type of connection to the Internet. This kind of connection, called either SLIP (Serial Inline Internet Protocol) or PPP (Point-to-Point Protocol) requires not only that you have a computer and modem, but also that your computer be capable of operating in the TCP/IP networking environment, just like a service provider's Unix computer. And because a TCP/IP network requires that everyone on it have a unique Internet address, or *IP address*, you would need someone to assign such an address to your computer. This is usually provided by either your in-house network administrator or your Internet service provider.

More and more Internet service providers are offering this kind of service to individuals who wish to run TCP/IP on their computers and connect to the Internet this way. The fundamental difference between this kind of connection and a "traditional" Unix connection is that now you control all the software you use to access the Internet from your own computer. The service provider is only providing you with an IP address; everything else is done by your machine. So you have to have software running on your computer to perform functions such as e-mail, FTP, telnet, gopher, and World Wide Web.

Actually, there is one additional piece of the puzzle an Internet service provider gives you in this situation. While other Internet functions are done in real-time, e-mail is not so simple. Since e-mail sent to you arrives at any time of the day or night, it needs to be stored somewhere so you can download it when you log on. To do this, your network administrator or Internet service provider creates something called a *POP* (Post Office Protocol) *mailbox* that is simply a holding tank for all your incoming mail. Whenever you log on and are ready to read your mail, you use e-mail software on your computer to download all your waiting mail, after which the POP mailbox is empty and waits for new mail. It's a simple and efficient solution.

Finally, I should clarify that although in this appendix we discuss connecting to an Internet service provider via modem, everything I say about the concepts involved and software used also holds true for those of you lucky enough to have a Windows or Macintosh computer connected to the Internet through a direct connection at your work or school. Whether you get your connection via modem or directly, the software you'll use is the same.

SLIP and PPP Connections

This next section describes setting up both SLIP and PPP software on your personal computer. In the case of Windows, I'll describe a typical SLIP setup, which is still very popular and well-supported in that community. For the Macintosh, I'll describe a PPP connection, which is a popular option for that computer type. In either case, while the software interfaces for SLIP and PPP are slightly different, the concepts are the same. This holds true for the commercial products available for SLIP/PPP as well.

Time to explain the difference between SLIP and PPP now. Functionally, there is no difference. Both are terminal emulation software designed to allow TCP/IP packets to be transferred back and forth over a serial (phone) line. The best description I've heard of the difference between the two comes from Adam Engst, who notes that "PPP is SLIP done right." According to the FAQs on the subject, SLIP was developed in a somewhat ad hoc fashion, whereas PPP was designed later by a group of people with standards in mind, and therefore it's more flexible. It supports multiple protocols, so for example you can operate both TCP/IP and AppleTalk or Novell IPX from the same computer at the same time.

But for most users, either SLIP or PPP is fine. If you run into something called CSLIP (compressed SLIP), just make sure your service provider knows what they're talking about before choosing the option. CSLIP is considered an enhanced version of SLIP, but it's not that common.

Getting a SLIP or PPP Account

The resources listed at the end of Chapter 2 are good place to start for finding services in your local area. They often show which providers offer SLIP and PPP connections as part of their account offerings. In some situations you can choose the option to have only a PPP or SLIP account with a POP mailbox; that is, you would not have access to a Unix dial-up "shell" account as well. My suggestion is that if you get a PPP or SLIP account, you should also get a Unix shell account. That way if you ever have problems using the SLIP or PPP account, you can still dial into your shell account and read your e-mail using software on the Unix computer.

Okay, so you've chosen a service provider who offers SLIP and/or PPP (often both). What's next? First, they will probably ask you for information about your personal computer, then send you instructions and information specific to whether you have a Macintosh or Windows computer. In either case, they will give you some numbers and other information that you will need to enter into your TCP/IP software to configure it correctly. We'll go over the specifics for your computer a little later, but for now we'll look at the big picture.

Here is a typical configuration list you might receive from your service provider. In fact, this is taken from an account setup message from CTSNet in San Diego, California:

Your network protocol	PPP
Your machine's host name	spie
Your domain name suffix	cts.com
Your IP address	199.164.191.157
Subnet mask	255.255.255.240
Your gateway IP address	192.188.72.30
Your computer dials into	220-0853, 637-3651
Your computer will login as	pspie
Your computer's password	mrpibbs
Name & Time server address	192.188.72.18 (ns.cts.com)
NNTP news server address	192.188.72.21 (news.cts.com)
POP & SMTP mail server address	192.188.72.17 (crash.cts.com)

So what does all this junk mean? Let's take each item one by one.

Network Protocol
This is either SLIP or PPP (or possibly CSLIP). Just so you and your service provider know how you'll be logging in.

Machine's Host Name and Domain Name Suffix
These two pieces make up your *domain name address*. Some providers won't bother giving you an actual name, and instead you'll only have a number (IP address). In this case, while I'm connected to the Internet, all the other computers on the net see me as both **spie.cts.com** and **199.164.191.157**. For most people it doesn't matter if you have an actual name or not. Functionally there is really no difference. However, most people would prefer having a name because it's easier to remember.

One example where you would want a name (instead of only a number) is if you were running your own WWW, gopher, or FTP *server*. However, if this were the case, you would really need a direct connection to the Internet, not a dial-up, since the only time someone could connect to your server would be when you're actually online, which could get expensive with the hourly rates most Internet providers charge (direct connections are usually priced at a set annual rate).

IP Address
Your real, discrete address on the Internet. Nobody else on the Internet has this number assigned as an address.

Subnet Mask
Just a scary name for further dividing IP addresses to get more mileage out of them. Some Internet providers will give you a subnet mask number, some will not. Just enter the number in as you'll see later on.

Gateway IP Address
Like the subnet mask, some connections will require that you enter a gateway address into the appropriate software settings on your computer. If they give you one, enter it in. If they don't, ignore it.

Computer Dials Into

A roundabout way of telling us what phone number you'll use to dial into your SLIP or PPP account. Don't forget to disable Call Waiting if you have it and don't want incoming calls to cut you off unexpectedly. Most telephone companies have you disable Call Waiting by dialing *70 or 1170 before making your call. Check with your local telephone service provider if you're not sure.

Computer Login and Password

These are usually only logins and passwords to make the SLIP or PPP connection. It may or may not be the same login/password you use if you dial into the service provider's Unix computer and access the Internet that way. Often these are two different sets of logins and passwords.

Name and Time Server Address

The computers on the Internet really refer to other computers by numerical addresses rather than names. However, humans generally like names instead of numbers, since they're easier to remember, and so the domain name system is a big part of the Internet (for more background, see the section on Addressing and Sending E-mail in Chapter 4).

A crucial element of the domain name system are computers called *domain name servers* (DNS), or sometimes just *name servers*. As part of your computer's TCP/IP setup, you'll need to enter the address of one or more computers offered by your Internet provider that functions as a name server.

A **Time Server** is a solution to a simple problem. Computers all have internal clocks set by the computer's operator. The time server help synchronize all the computers. This feature is still relatively new.

NNTP News Server Address

If your Internet Service Provider offers connections to the Usenet bulletin board systems (aka newsgroups), you'll need the IP address of the computer that houses the *newsfeed* so that you can access it. This is a good time to point out that some service providers do *not* offer Usenet access, so if you want to read news, make sure you ask before signing up.

By the way, NNTP stands for Network News Transport Protocol, the Internet protocol used to move Usenet news around. It works very closely with e-mail's SMTP (Simple Mail Transport Protocol—see below).

POP and SMTP Mail Server Address

This is a very important address, as it's the computer where your e-mail POP account is located. As I mentioned, the POP account is where your mail collects until you log in and retrieve it. It may require a separate password from the one you use during your SLIP/PPP login procedure.

Note that all three of the last addresses (name server, news server, and POP server) all included name addresses as well as numerical addresses. Enter them both into your setup software, if provided.

The Black Art of SLIP/PPP

I cannot in good conscience leave off at this point without mentioning a few cautionary things about TCP/IP connections over modem lines, because the odds are that some readers—despite following all instructions they've received either here or from their service provider—will run into problems making this type of connection work—or work reliably.

The truth is that SLIP and PPP connections are still relatively new, and while in most cases they work acceptably, in others they can be problematic, at least until some adjustments are made to fine-tune the setup. The key to success, as with any kind of Internet connection, lies in the service provider, whether it be your network administrator at work or school, or your Internet account provider. To be blunt, if they know what they're doing on the server side, and if they can tell you how to set up your particular computer type for their particular server system, then you're in good hands. However, if they are not well-experienced with SLIP/PPP connections, or provide little or no information about how to configure your computer's TCP/IP software, then chances are good you'll have problems with this kind of connection. It is *not*, as some would have us believe, a "plug and play" system.

My purpose in saying this is not to steer you away from a SLIP or PPP type of connection, but rather the opposite. My advice is, if at all possible, find a service provider that is knowledgeable and experienced with SLIP/PPP, and be prepared for some adjustment period to get your system working correctly. More and more this type of connection works almost "out of the box," but there are still enough variables to keep things interesting for the next couple of years.

Connecting Your Macintosh to the Internet

Required reading: If you didn't read the Introduction to this appendix, do so now.

Getting and Setting Up MacTCP

MacTCP is a control panel from Apple sold separately for Systems 6 and 7, and integrated into System 7.5, although there's no functional difference.

MacTCP is sometimes called a *TCP/IP Manager,* and is comparable to Trumpet TCP Manager for computers running Windows software.

You can get MacTCP directly from Apple (or an Apple dealer) for about $60, or you can obtain it at a lower price through purchase of another product such as a book or software package that bundles a legal copy with it. You can also upgrade to System 7.5 if you haven't already, but you should have at least 4 MB of RAM before considering System 7.5.

Do not use any version of MacTCP earlier than 2.0.4 (2.0.6 is current as I write this). You'll find legally posted copies of older versions of MacTCP on the Internet, and they have Trouble written all over them.

If you are still running System 6 on your Macintosh, I can't guarantee any of this will work, and you're on your own. I highly recommend upgrading to at least 7.1 for any work on the Internet, since much of the software you'll use was designed to work with System 7. If you are running Open Transport, see the instructions that came with your computer.

Put the MacTCP control panel in your system's Control Panels folder, then double-click it to open. It should look something like this, without the PPP element showing in the window, unless you've already installed MacPPP, which I describe later.

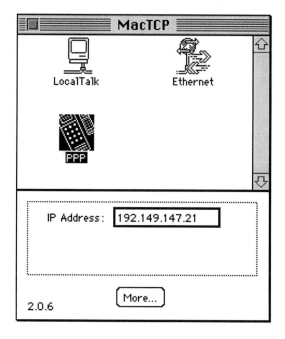

This is where you type in your assigned IP address. If your Internet service provider uses something called dynamic addressing, you won't be assigned an IP address, in which case you'll either leave this blank or type in some null-replacement number that your provider gives you (the default in this box is 0.0.0.0, which doesn't work well for some service providers, so they might give you some nonworking address to replace it).

Now click the More... button and prepare yourself for some really arcane stuff that's looks much worse than it really is:

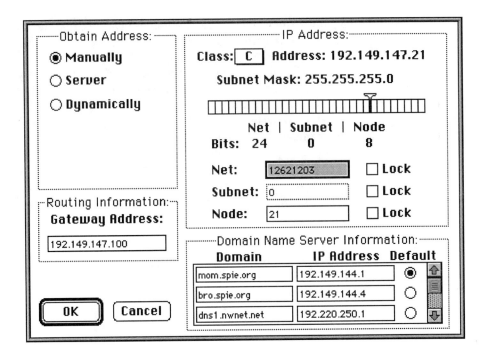

This is the heart of MacTCP—all the good stuff. But we've already talked about most of these things earlier in this appendix, so it's relatively straightforward.

Get out the information your Internet service provider gave you and start plugging in the numbers. First, if they've given you an actual numerical IP address (as shown in this case), then you can assume that you'll be using *manual addressing*. In fact, MacTCP is smart enough to prevent you from adding an IP address in the opening panel if you have the Dynamically button selected above.

Next, if they've given you a *gateway* or *router* address (same thing), enter it into the Gateway Address field.

If they've given you a subnet mask number, just slide the little pointer along the bar below Subnet Mask: until the subnet mask number is the same as the one they've given you. If they didn't give you anything, then ignore the whole IP address section here.

In the Domain Name Server Information section, enter both the domain name and numerical address of the name server they've provided. If they gave you more than one, they will also have told you which one of them was the *primary* or *default* address, so enter them all and click the button next to the primary one. The secondary ones are just backups.

That's it. Close the control panel and restart your Macintosh (any change you make to this panel requires a restart to take place). Also, this is a good time to make sure you have your Network control panel loading at startup, since you'll soon be on a network (the Internet). (Many non-networked-Macintosh owners disable the Network control panel using a utility such as Extensions Manager.)

Getting Started with MacPPP

MacPPP is software for connecting your Macintosh to the Internet with a PPP modem connection to an Internet service provider or other network access point (work, school, etc.). Remember that if your Macintosh is connected *directly* (such as on a local area network) to the Internet through your employer or school, you do not need PPP software. PPP is for modem connections only.

If SLIP is the only connection option your service provider offers, there is also freeware SLIP software available on the Internet. Configuration of this software is similar to setting up PPP. See the next section for information on where to get SLIP and other software.

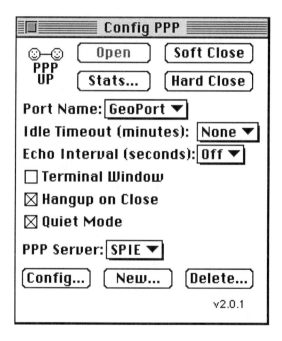

MacPPP is the only Macintosh freeware PPP software available to date. It was developed at, and is copyrighted by, the Merit Network, Inc., and the University of Michigan. You can FTP it from either of these locations, or just about any Info-Mac mirror site:

```
mac.archive.umich.edu/mac/util/comm/
grind.isca.uiowa.edu/3/mac/umich/util/comm/
```

To avoid possible confusion, you should know that the actual filename you'll find MacPPP listed under in FTP archives is usually something like *PPP2.01.hqx*—

not *MacPPP2.01.hqx*, as you might expect. There is also a spin-off version of MacPPP called "FreePPP." It is very similar to MacPPP and works well in most situations.

After you download this software you'll notice that there are actually two pieces: a control panel called Config PPP, and a system extension called PPP. You'll need both of them, so drag them into the proper locations in your System Folder and then restart your Macintosh.

MacPPP also comes with a document called *macppp.txt*, which explains all the configuration procedures and functions. This document is clear and thorough, so there's no point in me rehashing here the instructions given there. Complete the setup instructions using the configuration information provided by your service provider and you should be ready to connect to the Internet over regular phone lines. A high-speed modem is highly recommended for this type of connection.

Where to Get Macintosh Software

In many of the previous chapters I have suggested a few Macintosh software tools for accessing various Internet services, as well as where to find those specific tools. In addition to a specific FTP site mentioned, I've also alluded to something called an *Info-Mac mirror* site.

Info-Mac is the name of the definitive master archive for Macintosh software on the Internet. The archive gets its name from the Info-Mac directory at **sumex-aim.stanford.edu**, where the archive is maintained at Stanford University. However, because the Stanford computer is so inundated with people *uploading* Macintosh software to it all day and night, the standard mechanism for distributing (*downloading*) this software is through one of the hundreds of computers around the world that *mirror* the contents of the Info-Mac directory at Stanford.

So, how do you find a list of these Info-Mac mirror sites? There are several options. You can log into one of the well-known mirror sites and download the *mirror-list.txt* document located in the */help* directory. Here are some well-known info-mac mirrors to get you started:

Info-Mac Mirror	Numerical ID	Directory Tree
archie.au	139.130.4.6	/micros/mac/info-mac
ftp.ucs.ubc.ca	137.82.27.62	/pub/mac/info-mac
ftp.funet.fi	128.214.248.6	/pub/mac/info-mac
ftp.cs.tu-berlin.de	130.14.17.7	/pub/mac/info-mac
ftp.uni-kl.de	131.246.9.95	/pub/info-mac
ftp.iij.ad.jp	192.244.176.50	/pub/info-mac
ftp.fenk.wau.nl	137.224.129.4	/pub/mac/info-mac
king.ncb.gov.sg	160.96.3.121	/sumex
ftp.hawaii.edu	128.171.44.70	/mirrors/info-mac
wuarchive.wustl.edu	128.252.135.4	/systems/mac/info-mac
ftp.tidbits.com	192.135.191.2	/pub/tidbits/tisk

If you're serious about getting lots of Macintosh freeware and shareware, you can order the entire contents collection of Info-Mac files (an incredible archive) on CD-ROM from:

Pacific HiTech, Inc.
4530 Fortuna Way
Salt Lake City, Utah 84124
Tel: (801) 278-2042
Fax: (801) 278-2666
Compuserve: 71175,3152
Orders: 1-800-765-8369

Commercial Macintosh TCP/IP Software Companies

The following companies all offer a variety of Internet software tools, often in full "suites" that offer a single interface to many Internet services such as e-mail, FTP, telnet, gopher, and Usenet. This is by no means a comprehensive list, but it's a starting point.

While it's beyond the scope of this book to discuss their products, you may wish to look into these as alternatives to the free and shareware packages we've already discussed. The advantages of using commercial software can include technical support, upgrade notification, and a more integrated environment.

MacTCP
Apple Computer
10500 N. De Anza Blvd.
Cupertino CA 95014

MacSLIP
Hyde Park Software
800/531-5170
info@hydepark.com

TCP/IP Connect II
Intercon Systems
950 Herndon Parkway
Herndon VA 22070
703/709-5500
info@intercon.com

VersaTerm
Synergy Software
215/779-0522
maxwell@sales.synergy.com

Connecting Your Windows PC to the Internet

Required reading: If you didn't read the Introduction to this appendix, do so now.

Getting and Setting Up Trumpet TCP Manager

One of the most widely used and supported shareware programs available for running TCP/IP protocols and SLIP/PPP connectivity is Trumpet TCP Manager. You can find the latest version of Trumpet at the following FTP site, or at most of the major Windows FTP archives listed later in this section.

```
ftp.utas.edu.au/pub/pc/trumpet/winsock/
```

I should note here that the information in this section does not apply to users of Windows95, Microsoft's replacement for the Windows 3.1x operating environment, since it includes a TCP/IP manager. If you're using Windows95, refer to the instructions that came with the operating system. Also, make sure you are running the current version of that operating system, since early versions had problems with deleting the *winsock.dll* file that stores your Internet configuration.

Once you unzip the Trumpet archive, install the software on your system by running the Setup option from the File menu in the TCP Manager. Here's what it looks like:

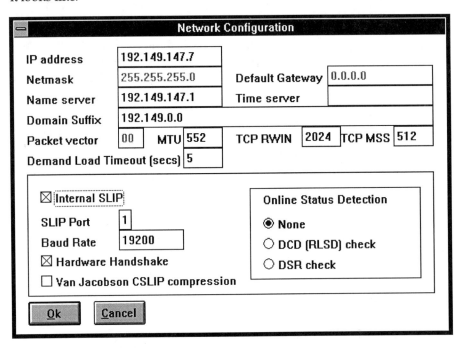

Most of this information was discussed in the Introduction to this appendix, so now we'll just go over what to enter and where.

The Netmask and Default Gateway sections need only be filled in if your service provider or network administrator requires and provides them. Leave them alone if not required.

In the Name Server section, enter the numerical address of the domain name server provided by your administrator.

A Time Server is not yet common on the Internet, but you can fill in the address if you are given one. If you are not given a specific address, you can usually get away with using the address you are given for the name server.

The domain suffix can be thought of as the root address of all the computers on a given system. In the above example, our Internet provider's address is **192.149.147.1**, our machine's address is **192.149.147.7**, and our domain suffix is **192.149.0.0**. In some cases your service provider will want you to enter your entire machine address in the Domain Suffix field.

The Packet Vector section can be ignored if you are using a dial-up SLIP connection and not an existing network connection. If you do have a direct connection over a network then you can set the packet vector field to 00 and it will scan for the correct one.

The MTU, TCP RWIN, and TCP MSS are all interrelated. These numbers regulate the size of the transmission units used (the information you send and receive via modem and the Internet is divided into *packets* for transmission purposes).

If you have a direct connection to the Internet, you should set these values to the highest possible settings. A good set would be:

```
MTU: 1500
TCP RWIN: 4096
TCP MSS: 1470
```

On the other hand, if you are accessing the Internet with a modem over a dial-up SLIP connection then these values should be lower. A good set for this setup would be:

```
MTU: 552
TCP RWIN: 2024
TCP MSS: 512
```

Setting up SLIP

This section describes how to set up SLIP software to connect to your service provider's computer via modem. Remember that if your Macintosh is connected directly to the Internet through (mostly likely) your employer or school), you do not need to use Trumpet's SLIP features. SLIP is for modem connections only.

I should mention here that if you wish to set up a PPP type of connection instead of SLIP, there is also freeware Windows PPP software available on the Internet at any major FTP archive. Configuration of this software is similar to setting up SLIP.

If you have a dial-up SLIP connection, you need to fill in the rest of Trumpet's configuration window based on information unique to your system. First, check the Internal SLIP box (see figure above). After checking it you'll notice that some of the fields will turn gray, meaning that they don't pertain to you now that you've chosen SLIP.

Next, enter the COMM port number your modem is using in the SLIP Port field, and then enter the highest speed your modem is capable of achieving. Check the Hardware Handshake box if you know that your modem and the modem on your service provider's computer support it. You *must* check this box if you are using modem speeds of 14.4 Kbps or higher. Leave the CSLIP box unchecked unless your service provider specifically tells you you'll be using CSLIP.

After the network configuration window is completely filled out, select OK to save the settings. Then exit the Trumpet program and restart it for the settings to take effect.

If you have a direct network connection you can connect just by running the program. You should run it minimized or minimize it after you launch it. If, on the other hand, you're connecting via modem SLIP, you will need to use either Trumpet's built-in dialer or an external telecommunications program to initiate a connection over the modem. If you use Trumpet's internal dialer you have two choices:

1. Manually dial the provider's phone number using AT modem commands (e.g., "atdt7332998"), and then type in the login and password information when prompted. When you finish, you must hit the Escape key and then you are free to minimize the window.

2. Create a *login script* specific to your and your service provider's setup. A login script is a simple command language explained in the documentation that comes with Trumpet. Here is a typical login script:

    ```
    output atz\13
    input 10 OK\n
    output atdt5551234\13
    input 30 CONNECT
    input 30 host:
    output slip\13
    input 30 login:
    output foobar\13
    input 30 password:
    output abc123\13
    ```

    Once you create a script you can simply select Login from the Dial menu. There is also at least one external dialing program available on the Internet. The one I use is very simple and has an easy script creator. The program is called GOSLIP, and among its features is an automatic re-dialer as well as the ability to launch several programs after a connection is made. GOSLIP can also be scripted to do other chores, such as telling Eudora to check your mail right after you log in.

Where to Get Windows Software

In many of the previous chapters I have suggested a few of the many Windows software tools available for accessing various Internet services, as well as where to find those tools. In addition to a specific FTP site mentioned, I've also alluded to Windows FTP archives. This is a generic term I used to describe the many FTP servers on the Internet that accept and distribute Windows freeware, shareware, and even *demoware* (limited-functionality versions of commercial software—lets you try before you buy).

By far the best and most reliable way to get all of this software and much more is at one of the many *mirrors* of the University of Indiana's FTP server, which is one of the largest Windows FTP archives in the world.

What's a mirror site? Mirrors are computers on the Internet that regularly copy many or all of the contents of another computer, usually late at night when activity is low. This process is designed to distribute the load of a major archive so that more people can access the files located there. In this case, the FTP archive at the University of Indiana, better known as **ftp.cica.indiana.edu**, is inundated with people *uploading* Windows software to it all day and night, and therefore many other computer administrators offer a mirror of its contents to anonymous FTP users on the Internet. The idea is to keep the U of I computer free for people who wish to *upload* files to it by directing those who wish to *download* files to an alternate mirror site.

So, how do you find these mirror sites? Here's a list to help you get started. Remember that once you log into one of these sites, you'll still have to seek out the directory where the archives start, since these computers are usually used for other purposes as well. The best place to start is always a */pub* ("public") directory. After navigating to it, look for something indicating what you're looking for. Often sites will use directories such as */mirrors, /cica, /dos,* or */windows.*

Some FTP Mirrors for *ftp.cica.indiana.edu*

```
ftp.uni-paderborn.de
wuarchive.wustl.edu
ftp.cc.monash.edu.au
nctuccca.edu.tw
grind.isca.uiowa.edu
gatekeeper.dec.com
ftp.switch.ch
src.doc.ic.ac.ukftp.technion.ac.il
owl.und.ac.za
ftp.cyf-kr.edu.pl
```

In addition to these mirror sites there are many other FTP archives around the world that accept and distribute Windows freeware and shareware.

Here are some major FTP sites to get you started:

African Sites
ftp.sun.ac.za
owl.und.ac.za
ftp.mpd.co.za
Finnish Sites
garbo.uwasa.fi
ftp.funet.fi
x2ftp.oulu.fi
German Sites
ftp.uni-koeln.de
ftp.uni-paderborn.de
ftp.informatik.rwth-aachen.de
ftp.tu-clausthal.de
ftp.germany.eu.net
Other European Sites
nic.switch.ch
cnuce_arch.cnr.it
ftp.cyf-kr.edu.pl
ftp.sunet.se
ftp.kiae.su
micros.hensa.ac.uk
src.doc.ic.ac.uk
Middle-Eastern Site
ftp.technion.ac.il
Oceanic Sites
archie.au
ftp.cc.monash.edu.au
kirk.bu.oz.au
ftp.psychol.utas.edu.au

North American Sites
oak.oakland.edu
wuarchive.wustl.edu
ftp.uml.edu
ftp.cica.indiana.edu
kermit.columbia.edu
barnacle.erc.clarkson.edu
ftp.cso.uiuc.edu
msdos.archive.umich.edu
info.umd.edu
ftp.shsu.edu
beach.gal.utexas.edu
eugene.gal.utexas.edu
urvax.urich.edu
ftp.hawaii.edu
ftp.uwp.edu
gallifrey.ucs.uoknor.edu
archives.math.utk.edu
archive.orst.edu
Asian Sites
ftp.cs.cuhk.hk
ftp.nectec.or.th
nctuccca.edu.tw
ftp.csie.nctu.edu.tw
iiidns.iii.org.tw

Commercial Windows TCP/IP Software Companies

The following companies all offer a variety of Internet software tools, often in full "suites" that offer a single interface to many Internet services such as e-mail, FTP, telnet, gopher, and Usenet. This is by no means a comprehensive list, but it's a starting point.

While it's beyond the scope of this book to discuss their products, you may wish to look into these as alternatives to the free and shareware packages we've already discussed. The advantages of using commercial software can include technical support, upgrade notification, and a more integrated environment. Note that this is just a starter list; there are new products coming out all the time.

AIR for Windows
Spry, Inc.
1319 Dexter Ave. North
Seattle WA 98109
206/286-1412
sales@spry.com

BW-TCP
Beam & Whiteside, Ltd.
POB 8130
Dundas Ontario
Canada L9H 5E7
416/765-0822
sales@bws.com

Chameleon
NetManage, Inc.
20823 Stevens Creek Blvd.
Cupertino, CA 95014
408/973-7171
support@netmanage.com

Distinct TCP
Distinct Corp.
POB 3410
Saratoga CA 95070
408/741-0781
mktg@distinct.com

MKS
35 King Street North
Waterloo Ontario
Canada N2J 2W9
519/884-2252
inquiry@mks.com

PC/TCP
FTP Software, Inc.
2 High Street
North Andover MA 01845
800/282-4387
sales@FTP.com

Pathway Access
The Wollongong Group
1129 San Antonio Rd.
Palo Alto CA 94303
415/962-7247
sales@twg.com

Piper/IP
Ipswitch, Inc.
580 Main Street
Reading MA 01867
617/942-0621
ub@ipswitch.com

TCP/IP Connect II
Intercon Systems
950 Herndon Parkway
Herndon VA 22070
703/709-5500
info@intercon.com

VersaTerm
Synergy Software
215/779-0522
maxwell@sales.synergy.com

GLOSSARY

access privileges   Permission to access or "log into" another computer, usually requiring an assigned *user ID* and password; or, the ability to open a file or directory on a computer system, usually assigned by an owner or system administrator.

account   A contract with a service provider that gives the account holder the ability to log on and use another computer, as in, "I have accounts on both CompuServe and Netcom." Can include personal services such as e-mail, navigation, and online storage.

address   A specific location on the Internet, such as a person (e-mail address) or computer (e.g., **nasa.gov**), defined by a discrete numerical Internet address.

AIF   A type of digitized audio file (cf. *WAV*).

alias   A software placeholder that allows one thing, such as a file, to be referenced from another location; or, a convenience feature found in many e-mail software interfaces that allows the user to assign a short and easy-to-remember name for a longer one, such as an e-mail address.

anonymous FTP (File Transfer Protocol)   A standard Internet protocol for transferring data from one computer to the other using the TCP/IP transmission protocol. Conceptually, open and public access to a computer archive on the Internet for the purpose of *uploading or downloading* files.

applet   Small *executable* used with *Java*-type client-server interactions. Allows for more efficient use of WWW bandwidth by making the client work more.

application   A software program designed to perform a task or function. Also called an *executable*.

archie   A software searching system accessible on the Internet that allows you to search directories of many anonymous FTP archives at the same time.

ASCII (American Standard Code for Information Interchange)   An important standard for describing computer-readable text, including alphabetic, numeric, and control characters, all coded in hexadecimal notation.

attachment   A document or other digital entity (picture, application, etc.) that is appended to an e-mail message, usually using an "attach" feature of the e-mail software. Since Internet e-mail does not recognize non-ASCII characters, binary files are usually encoded before attaching and sending.

auto-load   Feature supported by most web browsers allowing the user to choose to have all web-page graphics load automatically. If you have a slow or modem-type connection, you should *not* choose auto-load.

bandwidth   Term used to quantify the amount of digital information a circuit or network can carry in a given amount of time. Usually measured in bytes, so "a 56 K line" is a circuit capable of carrying 56 kilobytes per second.

baud   A unit of measurement for describing the number of change states per second in telecommunications processes. The "baud rate" is usually used to describe modem speed. The term is often misused to mean *bits per second* (bps), which is only true in some situations.

BBS (Bulletin Board System)   A computer system that typically provides such services as e-mail, file storage and transfer, and special interest groups that exchange messages by posting them to the BBS's computer for others to read online.

binhex   The de facto standard for encoding non-ASCII Macintosh files and applications for transmission over the Internet.

bit   Unit of measurement used in computer systems, short for "binary element." It's the smallest unit of data—either a 1 or a 0.

BITNET (Because It's Time Network)   An e-mail and file-sharing network used by a large number of academic and research institutions. Origination point for listserv software still used widely for automated management of discussion groups. BITNET now has many gateways to the Internet. See the chapter on Discussion Lists.

body   That portion of an e-mail message where you type your message. See also *header*.

bookmark   A feature of some software interfaces that allows you to "save your place" for future access, usually another computer connected to the Internet.

bounce   Slang for an e-mail message that is returned to the sender as undeliverable, usually for reasons such as incorrect or erroneous addressing. See also *daemon*.

Bourne shell   A type of user interface available on many Unix computers. See also *shell account*.

bps (bits per second)   The number of bits of information transmitted per second through a telecommunications medium.

browser   Software interface for accessing certain services such as the World Wide Web. See also *graphical browser* and *line browser*.

BTW   Common abbreviation in e-mail and news postings meaning "by the way."

bulletin board   See *BBS*.

byte   A unit for measuring data consisting of eight *bits*.

cascade menu   A computer menu that extends more than one level in a hierarchical fashion.

caching   In Internet software, a term used to describe the process of storing in computer memory previously displayed information for quick retrieval. For example, most WWW browsers cache some number of pages you have recently viewed, so that if you return to view those pages, the images are displayed immediately instead of re-downloading them to the browser software. The term "cache" in general denotes any kind of temporary data storage technique used to enhance computer performance.

character-based   See *command-line interface*.

C-shell   A type of interface available on many Unix computers. See also *shell account*.

CLI   See *command line interface*.

client   A computer or process that relies on the resources of another computer (a server) for operations. When you connect to the Internet, in most cases your computer is a client retrieving information from a server computer such as an FTP archive, telnet database, or WWW site.

command-line interface   A non-graphical or non-windowing interface to a computer system. All commands are entered as text from a keyboard, and all information output by the computer is displayed as text.

command prompt   See *prompt*.

commercial online service   Generic term used to describe a handful of large online service providers with multiple transnational or transcontinental access points. Most originated as discrete online environments with no Internet access, but most are now creating gateways to change this.

compression   Software-based algorithms used to reduce the amount of storage or bandwidth that information occupies without permanently altering the content. Much of the information stored in *anonymous FTP* archives is in a compressed format. See also *binhex, uuencode*.

country code   A two-letter extension added to some Internet domain names denoting the country in which that address resides, such as **ulaval.ca** (Canada) or **cosy.sbg.ac.at** (Austria). Not common for U.S.-based addresses but almost universal for non-U.S. addresses.

CSLIP   Compressed SLIP, a variation of *SLIP*.

CWIS (Campus-Wide Information System)   An online service used as a central source of information by the members of a particular community, usually a college or university, but which may also offer partial access to non-members.

daemon   A software program that intercepts information that is unusable due to errors. For example, a *mail daemon* intercepts incoming e-mail messages and sends back any addressed to invalid usernames at that location.

Datapac   See *SprintNet*.

decoding   See *encoding*.

dedicated line   A telephone line directly connecting two Internet domains, providing a continuous connection for Internet access (as opposed to temporary connections, such as over a modem). Many organizations that use the Internet subscribe to this kind of connection for uninterruptable (in theory) and high-bandwidth (fast) connections. Some typical dedicated line bandwidths are 56 Kb (kilobits per second) and T1 (1.54 megabytes per second). See also *ISDN*.

demoware   Software applications released publicly by commercial software companies to demonstrate their products' features.

dial-up   Slang for connecting to another computer using a modem, such as "I have dial-up access to the university's library computer."

direct connection   Internet access through a non-modem connection, such as a computer on a local area network, where that network has a dedicated line to the Internet.

directory   A software structure used for storing data (files, applications, etc.) and listing the contents by executing a command. For example, in a Unix-based computer, you could type "ls -lr" at the command prompt to display all files in the current directory. Most often directory structures are hierarchical in either real or metaphoric terms.

discussion list   Generic term used in this book to describe any type of e-mail-based group communications method, such as listservs and mailing lists, where individuals join or "subscribe" to a group and share a common e-mail address. This address is used as a central forum for posting questions, answers, and commentaries, usually in a particular (and narrow) topical area. Anyone with an Internet e-mail address can participate. See also *lurking*.

DNS   See *domain name system*.

domain name   An Internet convention for constructing an address by using the syntax userID@domain.name, where everything to the right of the @ symbol is the domain name. A domain name is not an actual physical description of a location, but rather a sort of alias for the location's Internet *IP* address, which is numerical. Domain names exist as a convenience, since numerical addresses are more difficult to remember. See also *domain name system*.

domain name system   The online distributed database that translates domain names into numerical IP addresses. DNS *servers* are located throughout the Internet, and no one DNS server contains information for all Internet hosts; rather, they work as a system. Many large Internet sites operate their own domain name servers or *resolvers* (which do the translation work).

dot files   Slang for Unix files that begin with a period (.) or "dot."

download   To move a file from a remote computer to your local computer. When you retrieve a file from another computer, you are downloading it.

dropped   Slang for having a connection terminated, such as when you are connected to another computer via modem and for some reason your connection is severed, as in, "My connection dropped and I lost the whole file!"

e-journal   An electronic journal, usually available online. Sometimes these journals are supplementary to paper journals, but there are also e-journals starting up that are digital-only.

Elm   Popular e-mail software among Unix computers. Precursor to *Pine.*

e-mail   Any electronic mail messaging system.

e-mail address   From the Internet perspective, a user ID + domain name (e.g., **billg@microsoft.com**) that designates a person or service at a particular computer or network host connected to the Internet.

e-mail server   See *mail server.*

emoticon   See *smileys.*

encoding   The process of converting data (usually non-ASCII data) for transmission over the Internet. If not encoded, many types of files will lose attributes during transmission and be unusable by the recipient. Encoding is a common practice on the Internet. See also *binhex, uuencode.*

EPS (Encapsulated PostScript)   A common standard for importing and exporting PostScript language files in all environments. Most commonly used to "describe" an illustration for the purpose of including it with a PostScript data file for printing. See also *PostScript.*

ethernet   A popular local area network system allowing relatively high transmission speeds.

Eudora   A popular Macintosh and Windows e-mail management program with both freeware and commercial versions.

executables   See *applications.*

extension   Technical jargon for a feature built into a web browser that is not actually part of the current HTML standards definition. See also *file extension.*

FAQ (Frequently Asked Questions)   Documents created by Internet users all over the world who are often experts in the particular topic area. FAQs are usually associated with and posted regularly to one or more applicable Usenet *newsgroups.* The term FAQ can also refer to one of the questions that is in fact frequently asked in a newsgroup, as in, "That's an FAQ from the comp.graphics newsgroup."

file server   See *mail server.*

file extension   Usually a two- to four-letter suffix, preceded by a period (.) and appended to the name of a file or other data entity. Sometimes it serves no other purpose than to identify the type of file, such as *.hqx* to indicate that a file is *binhex encoded.*

finger   A program that displays information about one or more users on a particular Internet host.

fixed font   A user-definable setting in most web browsers defining which typeface on the user's computer system is used to display *preformatted* text. "Fixed" means the user should choose a monospace typeface such as Courier. See also *proportional font.*

flame   Virulent and often juvenile response to a message posted to a Usenet newsgroup or discussion list. "Flame wars" are not uncommon in some newsgroups. The term "flame bait" is slang for a message posted by someone designed specifically to incite readers. Flames are best dealt with by just ignoring them.

flavor   Slang term for variation, as in, "Ultrix is one of many flavors of Unix."

follow-up   A response to a message posted to a Usenet newsgroup where the response is posted to the newsgroup, not just to the person who posted the message.

foobar   A nonsense word used as a placeholder, usually for the purpose of example.

forms   A feature supported now by most web browsers that allows the user to type into available fields to send information to a web server.

frames   A web browser feature that allows specially prepared web pages to be divided into multiple "zones" that can function independently of other elements displayed on the web browser. Developed by *Netscape* and expected to be part of the *HTML 3.0* standard.

freeware   Software typically available at FTP archives that is free. There's a lot of this.

FTP (File Transfer Protocol)   An Internet tool that allows you to move a file from one place to another. The word "file" is used to include any type of digital entity—documents, images, artwork, movies, sounds, and software. Anything you can store on a computer can be moved with FTP.

FTPMail   A service that involves sending specific FTP commands in an e-mail message in order to get the FTP site's computer to send you the files you want—via e-mail. See also *mail server.*

gateway   Can mean a number of things, but usually describes a computer or computer system that connects networks that use different communications protocols, such as the Internet and BITNET, often so users on both networks can exchange e-mail, files, and other information.

GIF (Graphics Interchange Format)   An image storage type developed originally by CompuServe and used widely on the Internet.

gopher   An online archiving system that allows information from all over the Internet to be presented to a user in a hierarchically organized interface. You can use gopher to search through archives and retrieve any you find interesting.

gopherspace   Slang for the interconnected burrows of gopher server computers.

graphical browser   A windowing interface with display capabilities beyond that of a *command-line* (character cell) environment, usually including the ability to display color graphics and utilize mouse-driven commands via pull-down menus, icons, and buttons. Graphical browsers are designed to access specific Internet services such as the World Wide Web.

header   Usually refers to that portion of an e-mail message that contains information about the message's origin, destination, and route. Can also refer to the same information attached to Usenet articles and even individual packets of information sent over the Internet.

helper application   An application resident on a user's computer that is designated, via a web browser, to launch whenever a particular file type is encountered that the web browser cannot execute.

hierarchical menu   A computer menu that extends more than one level in a hierarchical fashion.

home page   The first "page" displayed when you access a WWW site. Analogous to the top-level directory of an FTP or gopher site.

host   See *server*.

hotlist   See *bookmark*.

HTML (Hypertext Markup Language)   A text tagging language developed for formatting information available on the World Wide Web.

HTML tags   Simple tags used to mark text to be displayed as formatted text (bold, italic, headline, etc.) in a WWW browser. The "tags" themselves usually surround a given text element. The browser program interprets the tags and converts them to the corresponding formatting for the reader.

HTML 2.0 and 3.0   Refers to a standards definition for HTML features and encoding language. Currently HTML 2.0 is current, with 3.0 due mid-1996.

HTTP (Hypertext Transport Protocol)   Communications protocol used for transmitting information between WWW *servers* and *clients* (*browsers*).

hypertext   A system of "point-and-click" connections between information that allow the user to jump from one information source to another on the Internet.

imagemap   Feature supported by most web browsers that allows the user to click (with a mouse) on various areas of a displayed image in order to be linked to various points on the web server. In other words, areas or zones on the image are hypertext linked to other locations.

IMHO   Common shorthand for "in my humble/honest opinion."

Info-Mac   FTP archive at Stanford University (**sumex-aim.stanford.edu**) housing vast quantities of Macintosh files and applications. Numerous *mirror* sites worldwide.

Internet address   A *domain name* or numerical address identifying a computer location on the Internet. Examples: **spie.org** or **192.149.147.1**

Internet service provider   See *service provider*.

inline viewer   A newer feature of some web browsers that allows another application to be launched and used as part of the web browser, as opposed to being launched separately, as with helper applications.

InterNIC (Internet Network Information Center)   The place where you register domain names, databases, and information services.

IP   The Internet Protocol, an integral protocol used by the Internet for data transfer. See also *TCP/IP*.

ISDN (Integrated Services Digital Network)   Digital (as opposed to analog) telephone service becoming increasingly available and offering relatively high bandwidths for reasonable rates.

Java   Scripting language developed by Sun Microsystems that can be used to write *applets* for creating enhanced or multimedia features on a web browser.

JPEG (Joint Photographic Experts Group)   A standard for image compression and storage.

Kermit   An old but still popular telecommunications protocol and software package. *ZMODEM* is generally considered superior.

line browser   Client interface with only text-based commands and display. You can access the WWW from a line browser (see *Lynx*), but you cannot view any graphics, etc.

link   A connection between two documents or locations on the Internet, usually used to describe a *hypertext* link.

list address   In e-mail discussion lists, the place you send messages you wish to be read by the entire group (cf. *listserv address*).

listserv   Software that originated in the BITNET network of computers and still widely used for managing discussion lists. See also *discussion list*.

listserv address   In listserv-based discussion lists, the place you send command messages (subscribe, signoff, etc.).

login script   A series of text commands designed to automate the process of logging on to a computer. Usually the script waits for a *prompt* from the *host* computer, then inserts the proper information (user ID, password, etc.).

lossy and lossless compression   Defines whether a data compression algorithm, such as JPEG or GIF, causes the item being compressed to lose a portion of its composition during the compression process, usually resulting in a reduction in image quality.

lurking   Slang for someone who joins a discussion list but never sends messages. This is perfectly acceptable behavior.

Lynx   Popular *line browser* for accessing the Internet.

MacTCP   Commercial software from Apple Corp. that allows a Macintosh computer to communicate with *TCP/IP*-based networks such as the Internet.

mail daemon   See *daemon*.

mail server   Generic term for a computer that accepts commands via e-mail and acts according to the commands, such as "send filename_x".

mailing lists   See *discussion lists.*

MIME (Multipurpose Internet Mail Extensions)   Emerging standard for encoding e-mail to allow transmission of non-ASCII data (takes the place of old-style encoding).

mirror   FTP archive that contains an exact replication of files and directories of another FTP archive, usually updated regularly. Designed to distribute the load away from popular FTP servers.

moderated   Usually refers to a newsgroup or discussion list that is monitored for propriety, relevance, length of postings, or for any number of other reasons.

Mosaic   Popular *freeware* WWW browser from the National Center for Supercomputing Applications at the University of Illinois, Urbana/Champaign.

MPEG   Multimedia Photographic Experts Group standard for encoding and compressing video signals.

MUD (Multi-User Dungeon)   Loosely used term to describe a variety of role-playing games. Usage is now expanding into experimental work done in distance education and teleconferencing development.

net   Slang meaning the Internet, as in, "I was on the net last night but didn't check my mail."

netiquette   "Net etiquette," a set of generally agreed-upon rules of conduct for Internet users.

Netscape   Popular web browser software application developed by Netscape Communications. Available for Windows, Macintosh, and XWindows computers. Currently accounts for well over half of all web browsers in use.

newsfeed   A computer that provides another computer with regular updates of Usenet news postings. The entire Usenet system is a large "store and forward" system that relies on many computers handing off postings to other subscribing computers.

newsgroup   Any one of thousands of *Usenet* topical groups.

newsgroup newsreader   Any software interface that allows you to read and post to newsgroups on *Usenet.*

nickname   See *alias.*

nixpub list   A list (uNIX PUBlic access systems) similar to the *PDIAL* that also includes a listing of BBS-type hosts offering some degree of Internet connectivity.

NNTP (Network News Transport Protocol)   The networking protocol used by the Internet to transmit *Usenet* news.

node   Generally used to mean a place (computer) on the Internet with its own address.

numerical address   An Internet address described as a unique set of numerals divided by three periods, such as **149.156.221.2** See also *domain name system*.

online forms   See *forms*.

OPAC (Online Public Access Catalog)   Internet-accessible databases of library holdings, often offering sophisticated and powerful searching tools.

PDIAL (Public Dial-up Internet Access List)   List of Internet service providers maintained by Peter Kaminski.

Pine   Popular *freeware* e-mail management software for Unix, VMS, and other computers available from the University of Washington.

point of presence   Term sometimes used to describe a *service provider's* physical Internet access location, such as "XYZcom has three points of presence on the net."

POP mailbox   E-mail receiving software that uses the Post Office Protocol. Provides user with their own Internet address to receive e-mail even when their computer is not turned on or on the Internet. POP software must reside and run on a computer with a dedicated connection to the Internet.

port   A number assigned (real or actual) to a computer that allows access only when that number is included with the address to that computer. Also, a physical input or output connection on a computer, such as a serial or parallel port for a modem or printer.

post   To add a new message to a *Usenet* newsgroup. See also *follow-up*.

PostScript   Page description language developed by Adobe Systems to describe pages of text and images with ASCII-based coding. Arguably the most versatile and universal language for communicating with printers. Capable of drawing to computer screens and any kind of drawing device.

preformatted text   HTML tagging designation that tells a web browser to display text exactly as it appears in the original document.

PPP (Point to Point Protocol)   Increasingly common method connecting TCP/IP-based computers to each other using modem (serial) connections. Functionally identical to SLIP.

privileges   See *access privileges*.

prompt   A symbol, such as % or $, used in a *command-line interface* to show where the user can type commands.

proportional font   A user-definable setting in most web browsers defining which typeface on the user's computer system is used to display fully *tagged* text. "Proportional" means the user should choose a scalable typeface such as Times Roman or Helvetica. See also *fixed font*.

protocol   A language that computers or networks use to transmit and exchange data.

public-access Internet hosts   See *service provider*.

readme file   Generic term for any document that accompanies any software file or executable for the purpose of documenting it. Often the filename will be something like *readme!, readme.txt,* etc.

relevance feedback   A system of searching used by *WAIS* and other databases that searches for user-provided keywords and reports back the most likely files to be of interest based on the number of "hits" of keywords found in each file. The files are usually listed in descending order in direct relation to the percentage of hits found in each.

remote dial-up   Term used in this book to describe Internet access through a Unix-based (probably) service provider where the user connects to the host computer and uses a Unix shell interface (cf. *direct connection, SLIP, PPP, commercial online services*).

Rich Text Format (RTF)   A common format for saving word processor documents for the purpose of reading them in another word processor while maintaining typesetting elements such as fonts, styles, tables, and similar formatting. Most word processors allow you to save a document in RTF.

root directory   The top-level directory in any hierarchical computer directory structure.

router   See *gateway.*

server   Generically, refers to a computer you log into and either use or retrieve data from (cf. *client*).

service provider   Term used in this book and elsewhere to define any organization that provides access to the Internet for a fee.

SGML (Standard Generalized Markup Language)   The de facto standard for tagging and encoding of complex information (e.g., scientific journals) for redistribution or other uses.

shareware   Publicly archived commercial software released with a "try before you buy" type of licensing agreement, usually described with accompanying documentation.

shell account   A user account on a Unix-based computer.

signature   Several lines of text many Internet users append to their outgoing e-mail messages that provide contact information such as affiliation, address, and telephone number. Often e-mail software can be set to append this information automatically.

site   Generic term for a computer on the Internet, as in, "I found a great site yesterday while looking for some stat software."

SLIP (Serial Inline Internet Protocol)   Probably the original protocol developed for connecting *TCP/IP*-based computers to each other using modem (serial) connections. Functionally identical to *PPP.*

smileys   Use of ASCII characters to create facial expressions that suggest tone of voice and avoid miscommunications. Most common is the :-) smiley.

SMTP (Simple Mail Transport Protocol)   The protocol standard used on the Internet to support transport of e-mail.

snail mail   Slang for regular postal (paper) mail service.

SprintNet   One of a growing number of telephone service companies that offer local phone access in various cities or countries. Usually they sell these services back to commercial online services to give their customers access to the online service in more locations.

streaming   Technology being developed to bring real-time audio and video to web browsers using compression and *Java*-type *applets*. Allows the video or audio clip to be sent to the browser/applet and, after front-loading a small portion, begin streaming the signal continuously to the applet, where it is played for the user.

surfing   Slang for browsing computers on the Internet.

tables   Feature supported by most web browsers that allows properly *tagged* text to be displayed in word processor style tables format. Good for displaying data best viewed in a row-and-column format, such as financial documents.

tagged See *HTML tags*.

TCP/IP (Transmission Control Protocol/Internet Protocol)   The underlying protocol used by the Internet that makes telnet, FTP, electronic mail, and other services possible among the many different computer types on the Internet.

telnet   Standard protocol allowing one computer to access and utilize another computer.

terminal emulation   A software process by which one computer type can emulate another, thus allowing each to communicate. For example, DEC developed the VT series of terminals (VT100, VT200, etc.) for their mainframes, so any terminal emulation software that emulates a VT terminal can operate in that computer's environment. Most telecommunications (modem) software will emulate a variety of terminal types.

text-based   See *command-line interface*.

thread   A topic that is being discussed in a successive series of messages from two or more participants within a newsgroup or discussion lists.

tn3270   A version of telnet software used to emulate and therefore use some IBM mainframe computers.

Trumpet   Popular shareware that allows a DOS/Windows-based personal computer to operate in a TCP/IP networking environment.

Tymnet   See *SprintNet*.

Unix   A multiuser, multitasking operating system that includes many utilities for Internet access. Most FTP sites on the Internet are Unix-based.

unmoderated   Opposite of (and see) *moderated*.

upload   To move a file from your (local) computer to another (remote) computer. See *download*.

URL (Uniform Resource Locator)   An emerging standard syntax for Internet re-source addresses.

Usenet   A global bulletin board service that uses the Internet as an access point. It is composed of thousands of topical groupings that you can read to keep current on the discussions in those groups. Usenet is not a physical entity like the Internet, but rather a software-based structure accessible to Internet hosts.

user ID   The name by which someone can access a computer system. Synony-mous with *username*.

username   See *user ID*.

UUCP (Unix-to-Unix Copy)   (a) A method of sending files and e-mail via mo-dem telecommunications that was originally developed for use between Unix com-puters; or (b) a network that currently uses the UUCP software for transmitting Usenet news and e-mail.

uuencode/uudecode   Unix commands for encoding/decoding binary files for transmission over the Internet via e-mail or UUCP.

veronica   Companion software tool for gopher that allows the user to search for keywords among directories of many gopher locations at the same time.

VT100   Lowest common denominator terminal type on the Internet. See also *ter-minal emulation*.

WAIS (Wide Area Information Server)   Standardized databases with hypertext features and allowing natural language searches, meaning you can type whole sen-tences like "find all papers on polymers and aircraft composite materials" and the software will interpret your query as a Boolean construction. Like the WWW and gopher, WAIS is a client-server arrangement, so you need access to client software, either on your Internet host computer, or via telnet through a public WAIS client. Also emerging recently are web-based public client interfaces.

WAV   A type of digitized audio file (cf. *AIF*).

web   See *World Wide Web*.

World Wide Web   A client-server software interaction that uses *HTTP* and *HTML* (hypertext protocol and tagging conventions) to organize and present information and services throughout the Internet.

WWW   See *World Wide Web*.

Z39.50   An established standard for searching and retrieving information on WAIS databases.

ZMODEM (XMODEM, YMODEM)   Popular data transmission protocols used to transfer (upload/download) files or other information between two computers via a modem connection. ZMODEM is considered the best of the three in terms of speed and functionality.

BIBLIOGRAPHY

In acht Sekunden um die Welt (in German), Gunther Maier/Andreas Wildberger, Addison Wesley (1994). ISBN: 3-89319-701-X.

All About Internet FTP: Learning and Teaching to Transfer Files on the Internet, David Robison, Library Solutions Press (1994). ISBN: 1-882208-04-8 (book alone) or 1-882208-06-4 (book with diskettes).

Canadian Internet Handbook, 1995 Edition, Jim Carroll and Rick Broadhead, Prentice Hall, Canada (1994). ISBN: 0-13-304395-9.

The Complete Internet Companion for Librarians, Allen C. Benson, Neal Schuman Pub. (1995). ISBN: 1555701787.

Connecting to the Internet, Susan Estrada, O'Reilly & Associates (1993). ISBN 1-56592-061-9.

Crossing the Internet Threshold: an Instructional Handbook, Roy Tennant, John Ober, and Anne Lipow, Library Solutions Press (1994). ISBN: 1-882208-07-2.

Directory of Directories on the Internet: A Guide to Information Sources, Gregory B. Newby, Meckler (1994). ISBN: 0-88736-768-2.

Directory of Electronic Journals, Newsletters and Academic Discussion Lists, Lisabeth King and Diane Kovacs, Association of Research Libraries (1994). Contact: ann@cni.org or 202/296-2296.

Doing Business on the Internet, Mary Cronin, Van Nostrand Reinhold (1994). ISBN: 0-442-01770-7.

Electronic Style: A Guide to Citing Electronic Information, Xia Li and Nancy Crane, Meckler (1993). ISBN: 0-88736-909-X.

The Elements of Information Gathering: A Guide for Technical Communicators, Scientists, and Engineers, Donald E. Zimmerman , Michel Lynn Muraski, ORYX PR (1995). ISBN: 089774800X.

The Electronic Traveller—Exploring Alternative Online Systems, Elizabeth Powell Crowe, Windcrest/McGraw-Hill. ISBN: 0-8306-4498-9.

Finding it on the Internet, Paul Gilster, John Wiley & Sons, Inc. (1994). ISBN: 0-471-0387-1.

Hands-On Internet: A Beginning Guide for PC Users, David Sachs & Henry Stair, Prentice Hall (1994). ISBN: 0-13-056392-7.

How the Internet Works, Joshua Eddings, Ziff-Davis Press (1994). ISBN: 1-56276-192-7.

How to Advertise on the Internet, Michael Strangelove, The Internet Business Journal (1994). ISSN: 1201-0758.

Internet Access Providers: An International Resource Directory, Greg Notess, Meckler (1994). ISBN: 0-88736-933-2.

The Internet and Special Librarians: Use, Training and the Future, Sharyn Lander Hope Tillman, Special Libraries Association (1993). ISBN: 0-87111-413-5.

The Internet Business Book, Jill Ellsworth, John Wiley & Sons, Inc. (1994). ISBN: 0-471-05809-2.

The Internet Compendium : Subject Guides to Health and Science Resources (The Internet Compendium, Vol. 2), Louis B. Rosenfeld, et al., Neal Schuman Pub. (1995). ISBN: 1555702198

The Internet Complete Reference, Harley Hahn, Rick Stout, Osborne (1994). ISBN: 0-07-881980-6.

The Internet Directory, Eric Braun, Fawcett Columbine (1994). ISBN: 0-449-90898-4.

Internet Explorer Kit for Macintosh, Adam Engst and William Dickson, Hayden Books (1994). ISBN: 1-56830-0989-1. Includes software.

The Internet for Dummies, John R. Levine, Carol Baroudi, IDG Books Worldwide (1994). ISBN: 1-56884-024-1.

Internet: Getting Started, April Marine, Susan Kirkpatrick, Vivian Neou, Carol Ward, PTR Prentice Hall (1993). ISBN: 0-13-289596-X.

The Internet Guide for New Users, Daniel P. Dern, McGraw-Hill (1993). ISBN 0-07-016511-4.

The Internet Navigator, Paul Glister, John Wiley & Sons (1994). ISBN: 0-471-59782-1.

The Internet Passport: NorthWestNet's Guide to Our World Online, Jonathan Kochmer, NorthWestNet and the Northwest Academic Computing Consortium (1994). ISBN: 0-9635281-0-6.

The Internet Roadmap, Bennet Falk, Sybex, ISBN: 0-7821-1365-6

Internet Starter Kit for the Macintosh With Disk, Adam C. Engst, Hayden Books (1994). ISBN: 1-56830-064-6.

Internet Starter Kit for Windows, Adam Engst, Corwin Low and Michael Simon, Hayden Books (1994). ISBN: 1-56830-094-8.

The Internet Unleashed, Steve Bang, Martin Moore, Rick Gates, et al., Sams Publishing (1994). ISBN: 0-672-30466-X. Includes DOS software.

Life with Unix—A Guide for Everyone, Don Libes and Sandy Ressler, Prentice Hall (1990). ISBN: 0-13-536657-7.

The Mac Internet Tour Guide, Michael Fraase, Ventana Press (1993). ISBN: 1-56604-062-0.

Mastering SunOS, Brent Heslop and David Angell, Sybex (1990). ISBN: 0-89588-683.

MORE Internet for Dummies, John Levine & Carol Baroudi, IDG Books (1994). ISBN: 1-56884-164-7.

The Mosaic Handbook for Microsoft Windows, Dale Dougherty & Richard Koman, O'Reilly & Associates (1994). ISBN: 1-56592-094-5. Includes software.

The Mosaic Handbook for the X Window System, Dale Dougherty, Richard Koman, & Paula Ferguson, O'Reilly & Associates (1994). ISBN: 1-56292-095-3.

Navigating the Internet, Richard J. Smith, Mark Gibbs, SAMS Publishing, ISBN 0-672-30362-0.

Navigating the Internet With Windows '95, Ned Snell, SAMS Publishing (1995). ISBN: 0672307650.

The New Hacker's Dictionary, Eric Raymond and Guy L. Steele (editors), MIT Press (1994). ISBN: 0-262-68079-3.

Online Market Research: Cost-Effective Searching of the Internet and Online Databases, John F. Lescher, Addison-Wesley (1995). ISBN: 0201489295.

OPAC Directory 1994, Mecklermedia (editors), Meckler (1994). ISBN: 0-88736-962-6.

Pocket Guides to the Internet, Mark Veljkov & George Hartnell, Meckler (1994):
> *Volume 1 - Telnetting* (ISBN: 0-88736-943-X)
> *Volume 2 - Transferring Files with File Transfer Protocol (FTP)* (ISBN: 0-88736-944-8)
> *Volume 3 - Using and Navigating Usenet* (ISBN: 0-88736-945-6)
> *Volume 4 - The Internet E-Mail System* (ISBN: 0-88736-946-4)
> *Volume 5 - Basic Internet Utilities* (ISBN: 0-88736-947-2).

A Practical Guide to the Unix System V Release 4, Mark Sobell, Benjamin Cummings (1991). ISBN: 0-8053-7560-0.

A Student's Guide to Unix, Edward T. L. Hardie and Vivian Neo, McGraw-Hill (1993). ISBN: 0-07-025511-3.

TCP/IP Illustrated, Volume 1, The Protocols, W. Richard Stevens, Addison Wesley (1994). ISBN: 0-201-63346-9.

Unix for the Impatient, Paul Abrahams and Bruce Larson, Addison Wesley (1992). ISBN: 0-201-55703-7.

Unix in a Nutshell, Daniel Gilly and O'Reilly staff, O'Reilly (1992). ISBN: 1-56592-001-5.

Unix Power Tools, Jerry Peek, Tim O'Reilly and Mike Loukides, et al., O'Reilly / Bantam (1993). ISBN: 0-553-35402-7.

The Usenet Handbook, Mark Harrison, O'Reilly & Associates (1994). ISBN: 1-56592-101-1.

Welcome to... Internet—From Mystery to Mastery, Tom Badgett, Corey Sandler, MIS:Press (1994). ISBN: 1-55828-308-0.

The Whole Internet User's Guide & Catalog, Ed Krol, O'Reilly & Associates (1994). ISBN 1-56592-063-5.

The Whole Internet for Windows '95 : User's Guide & Catalog, Ed Krol, Paula Ferguson, O'Reilly & Assoc. (1995). ISBN: 1565921550

The World Wide Web Unleashed, John December and Neil Randall, Sams Publishing (1994). ISBN 0-672-30617-4.

Zen & the Art of the Internet: A Beginner's Guide, Brendan P. Kehoe, PTR Prentice Hall, ISBN 0-13-010778-6.

INDEX

About the Author

Brian Thomas graduated from Western Washington University with a degree in English Literature and German. His introduction to online life was as co-founder and technical editor of the first multimedia magazine distributed on the Internet, *Inside Mac Games*. Thomas is currently manager of new media development at SPIE—The International Society for Optical Engineering, where he has developed an online Internet tutorial course (from which this book springs), as well as Internet services, CD-ROM proceedings, and other electronic information products. He also manages SPIE's desktop publishing network and other computer systems. He is a member of the Association for Computing Machinery, for which he has published a paper on CD-ROM development.

In his off-line hours Thomas is a commercial flight instructor and enjoys anything even remotely related to airplanes.

Colophon

This book was typeset by the author in *Microsoft Word* on a Macintosh Quadra 840AV workstation and Macintosh Duo 270c laptop. Figures were taken using Nobu Toge's *Flash-It* screen capture utility, then cropped and reduced in Adobe *Photoshop*. Initial design work for some sections was done in Aldus *Pagemaker*. The cover was created in Aldus *Freehand* and output directly to film negatives.

The text typefaces are Adobe Palatino and Courier; head faces are Adobe Garamond. The cover title text is Adobe Trajan.

Many of the URL and site names were captured online from actual Internet sites using EINet's *MacWeb* browser software. These were then extracted using Richard Siegel's *BBEdit Lite* and manipulated into *Word* tables or *Microsoft Excel* spreadsheets using CE Software's *QuicKeys*.

Final output was done on a Hewlett-Packard *LaserJet 4M* printer. Printing was handled by Edwards Brothers, Inc., Ann Arbor, Michigan.